U.S.
Import
Trade
Regulation

U.S. Import Trade Regulation

Eugene T. Rossides

The Bureau of National Affairs, Inc., Washington, D.C. 20037

Copyright © 1986

The Bureau of National Affairs, Inc.

Library of Congress Cataloging in Publication Data

Rossides, Eugene T.
  U.S. import trade regulation.

  Rev. ed. of: U.S. customs, tariffs, and trade.
c1977.
  Bibliography: p.
  Includes index.
  1. Tariff—Law and legislation—United States.
2. Foreign trade regulation—United States.
I. Rossides, Eugene T. U.S. customs, tariffs,
and trade. II. Title. III. Title: US import
trade regulation.
KF6659.R68   1986   343.73′0877′02636   84-23748
ISBN 0-87179-454-3   347.30387702636

International Standard Book Number: 0-87179-454-3
Printed in the United States of America

To My Children:
Gale, Michael, Alexander, Eleni

Preface

This book fully reflects the many substantial changes in the regulation of imports into the United States since my earlier volume, *U.S. Customs, Tariffs and Trade,* was published in 1977. It comes at a time of great ferment and activity in and debate about international trade, largely occasioned by the continued substantial U.S. trade deficits. In fiscal year 1985 the United States had a $135.6 billion trade deficit.

The 1977 book was the first comprehensive volume on customs and trade law and practice. It stemmed from my four years' experience as Assistant Secretary of the Treasury in charge of customs and trade matters and from the realization that there was no practical handbook available to the business community and legal profession in the United States and abroad dealing with the maze of intricate laws, regulations, and rules regarding the importation of goods into the United States.

U.S. Import Trade Regulation is written for business people concerned with international trade and for their lawyers and other advisors. It provides a thorough analysis of the laws dealing with the regulation of imports, their administration by various agencies, and their interpretation by the courts. Completely up to date with coverage both of the historic Trade Agreements Act of 1979 which internationalized the field and of the Trade and Tariff Act of 1984 and its implementation in 1985, the book explains unfair competition laws such as the antidumping and countervailing duty laws, legislation involving duty preferences and reduction of trade barriers, and injury relief from both unfair and fair competition. The analysis also examines duty classification and valuation, and judicial review of agency rulings. The book contains a table of cases and in the appendices provides the text of the GATT and basic MTN agreements. It is current to mid-October 1985.

If you are planning to import goods, if you are an American manufacturer faced with foreign competition which you believe is unfair or with foreign competition which breaks no law but is substantial in nature and harmful to your business, if you have or are planning assembly or other operations or a joint venture overseas for goods to be imported into the United States, or if you are considering imports from developing countries, this book provides guidance that can save you time and money.

If you are an exporter to the United States, the number one market in the world, this book explains the intricacies of the import process and the laws and policies involved, and provides guidance that can reduce costs and avoid problems.

The continuing ferment in world trade matters requires that the U.S. and foreign business communities be better informed and play a more active role with their governments and in international and regional chambers of commerce if we are to ensure conditions for expanding trade and commerce between nations on a fair basis.

I have organized the format of this book to coincide with that of the loose-leaf Reference File, which I originated, of BNA's *International Trade Reporter* service, of which I am the Chief Import Editor. That service was the first informational service in the field and is still the *only* one which contains (1) a current analysis of import laws and regulations updated six times throughout each year; (2) the text of customs and trade laws, regulations, and principal executive orders; (3) the full text in the Decisions volumes of all import decisions by the courts and administering agencies; and (4) the weekly Current Reports on developments concerning imports and exports.

U.S. Import Trade Regulation is divided into seven parts in order to allow the reader to find information quickly in any particular area of this vast and complex field.

The *Introduction* gives a practical overview of the world trade situation and background information concerning U.S. customs, tariff, and trade laws including their constitutional basis.

Part I, Import Process, sets forth the procedures involved in importing goods—the day-to-day customs operations in getting goods entered and having the entries "liquidated," the use of foreign trade zones, and the steps to be taken to protest, or petition for, customs decisions and to appeal denials to the courts.

Part II, Duties, details the basic rules regarding the classification and valuation of goods, rates of duty, and the preferential duty rates provided for goods from the less-developed countries (GSP), from the Caribbean Basin, and from Israel.

Part III, Import Competition, provides a detailed yet concise analysis of the entire field. It deals with the rules and procedures involved in antidumping and countervailing duty actions, quotas and restraints, Buy American rules, presidential retaliation under Section 301, International Trade Commission protective action under Section 337, other restrictive action, escape clause relief and adjustment assistance from import trade injury for business firms and workers, and in the mechanisms for dealing with market disruption by Communist countries.

Part IV, Negotiations, discusses trade agreement authority and the new U.S. negotiating objectives in the fields of services, foreign investment, and high technology, and also discusses international trade agreements, including the General Agreement on Tariffs and Trade (GATT).

Part V, Regulated Trade, deals with the rules that apply to the goods being imported, including provisions concerning marking; packing; trademark; trade name; copyright, trademark, and patent protection from import infringement for goods produced in the United States; prohibited transactions; and embargoed merchandise.

Part VI, Administration and Enforcement, deals with the administering agencies, sets forth the broad enforcement authority of the Customs Service and its procedures in penalty cases, and discusses judicial review and the requirements of litigation in the Court of International Trade and the Court of Appeals for the Federal Circuit.

Part VII, Appendices, includes the texts of the TSUS General Headnotes and Rules of Interpretation; the General Agreement on Tariffs and Trade; the MTN Subsidies, Antidumping, and Customs Valuation Agreements; the announcement by the International Trade Administration (ITA) of its procedure for protection of proprietary information in import investigations; excerpts from the International Trade Commission (ITC) report on conversion to the harmonized system; ITA lists of antidumping duty findings and orders and countervailing duty orders; and a list of MTN code signatures and acceptances from the office of the United States Trade Representative (USTR). Part VII also includes a chart of federal import standards.

International trade, with its importance to the economic well-being of the United States and the world community, has joined international monetary and financial policy in center stage. Its time has come. It is involved for the first time on a continuing basis in the economic discussions and debates of our time. The removal of barriers to international trade and the development of a doctrine of fairness are now central tasks of the world trading and financial communities.

I gratefully acknowledge the assistance of Charlotte Lloyd Walkup and the encouragement of my partners at the law firm of Rogers & Wells. Completion of this book would not have been possible without the contribution of Mrs. Walkup as editor of the *International Trade Reporter* Reference File. As Charlotte Tuttle Lloyd, she was an Assistant General Counsel of the U.S. Treasury Department. My thanks to Mary Miner, Director of BNA Books, for her faith in this project and to my BNA editor, Tim Darby, for his helpful suggestions. To Mary Picarello, my secretary, a special thanks for her many efforts and good nature throughout the project.

I hope that his book, in stressing the legal and practical aspects of importing goods and the policies and policy processes involved, will assist in the expansion of international trade and the development of mutal interest and understanding in the world community.

Eugene T. Rossides

January 1986
Washington, D.C.

Summary Table of Contents

PART IV. NEGOTIATIONS

PART V. REGULATED TRADE

PART VI. ADMINISTRATION AND ENFORCEMENT

PART VII. APPENDICES

Detailed Table of Contents

PART V. REGULATED TRADE

CHAPTER 24. STANDARDS 431

CHAPTER 25. MARKING 441

PART VI. ADMINISTRATION AND ENFORCEMENT

CHAPTER 28. ADMINISTERING AGENCIES AND INDUSTRY PARTICIPATION

PART VII. APPENDICES

List of Abbreviations

AGP	Agreement on Government Procurement
BDV	Brussels Definition of Value
CAFC	Court of Appeals for the Federal Circuit
CCC	Customs Cooperation Council
CCPA	Court of Customs and Patent Appeals
CFR	Code of Federal Regulations
CIT	Court of International Trade
Cust. Ct.	Customs Court
CSD	Customs Service Decision
EC	European Community
F.2d	Federal Reporter, Second Series
F.Supp.	Federal Supplement
GATT	General Agreement on Tariffs and Trade
GSP	Generalized System of Preferences
ICSA	International Commodity Stabilization Agreement
ITA	International Trade Administration
ITC	International Trade Commission
ITR	International Trade Reporter
ITR Ref. File	International Trade Reporter Reference File
ITRD	International Trade Reporter Decisions
LDC	Less Developed Country
LDDC	Least Developed Developing Country
MFA	Multi-Fiber Arrangement
MTN	Multilateral Trade Negotiations (1979)
Slip Op.	Slip Opinion (CIT)
TD	Treasury Decision
TIAS	Treaties and Other International Acts Series (US)
TSUS	Tariff Schedules of the United States
TSUSA	Tariff Schedules of the United States Annotated
U.S.C.	United States Code
U.S.T.	United States Treaties
USTR	United States Trade Representative
VRA	Voluntary Restraint Agreement

1

Introduction

I. WORLD TRADE SITUATION

Few areas of United States law or policy can match the complexity and importance of international trade. Not only is there a vast and growing body of U.S. laws, regulations, and court decisions, but there is also an important network of international agreements governing U.S. trade relations with foreign countries.

A primary reason for the increased interest in U.S. trade law and international trade policy is the enormous increase in the volume of world trade under a liberalized world trading system. The volume of world trade has increased in all but three years since World War II, according to an annual report of the General Agreement on Tariffs and Trade (GATT). A 2 percent decline in the volume of world trade in 1982 yielded to a 2 percent increase in 1983, although the value of trade actually declined in both years. By 1984, world trade showed an 8 percent increase in volume.

In 1970, the trade volume for the United States was valued at $82.4 billion; imports totaled $39.9 billion and exports were $42.5 billion, leaving a merchandise trade surplus of $2.6 billion. By 1984, total U.S. trade had increased to $559.1 billion in value and the trade deficit of $123.3 billion was the largest in U.S. history. Some estimates for 1985 suggest that the U.S. trade deficit could surpass $150 billion.

The U.S. trade deficit has aggravated trade disputes between the United States and many of its established trading partners. Almost constant trade discussions take place with the European Economic Community and Japan to keep various disputes from erupting. The trade deficits with Mexico and other developing countries reflect changing trade practices on the part of those countries—and nearly doomed the continuation of the U.S. Generalized System of Preferences program prior to its 1984 extension.

As the above figures reflect, the United States has generally been a promoter of free, competitive international trade. Since the enactment of the largely restrictive Tariff Act of 1930, the United States has been a leader in the development of the GATT, and in undertaking several rounds of multilateral trade negotiations resulting in significant reductions in tariffs and nontariff barriers among the world's major trading countries.

In furtherance of its liberal trading policy, the United States has incorporated into its legislation certain basic policies. Perhaps the most significant of these policies is the most-favored-nation principle with regard to tariffs and import taxes. Under this nondiscriminatory principle, a tariff rate reduced in a trade agreement with one country is available to the other trading partners of the United States. The most-favored-nation principle is incorporated in the GATT to which the United States is a signatory.

By trade agreements, the rates established by the Tariff Act of 1930 have, on the average, been reduced to a very low level—a small proportion of the original level. These lower level trade agreement rates are set forth in Column 1 of the Tariff Schedules of the United States (TSUS), and are generally available for imports from most of the countries with which the United States trades.

II. EXCEPTIONS TO LIBERAL TRADE POLICY

A. Preferences and Discrimination

There are important exceptions in U.S. law to the application of the most-favored-nation principle. The tariff laws of the United States grant duty preferences on some articles from certain countries. Territories and possessions of the United States outside the U.S. customs territory (Puerto Rico is within), for example, are able to qualify for duty-free treatment on most of their exports to the United States.

The Trade Act of 1974 incorporated an important new policy into U.S. tariff laws, that is, the authorization to the President to afford duty-free treatment to products of developing countries. This program is known as the Generalized System of Preferences (GSP).[1] The action of the United States in adopting a GSP program followed a policy previously adopted by other member countries of the GATT. This system of preferences can be important for American importers and manufacturers who use materials from developing countries in their operations.

The U.S. GSP program was extended until July 4, 1993, by the Trade and Tariff Act of 1984. The revised law includes greater Presidential flexibility to raise or lower competitive need limitations for certain countries, and, in part, conditions GSP benefits on protection of U.S. intellectual property rights in the developing country.

A more recent U.S. trade preference was contained in the Caribbean Basin Economic Recovery Act enacted in 1983.[2] The Act authorized the President to designate countries eligible to receive duty-free treatment for certain of their articles imported directly into the United States. The Act initially listed 27 countries in Central America, the Caribbean, and

---

[1] For details concerning the Generalized System of Preferences, see Chapter 11.
[2] 19 U.S.C. 2701–2706. For details, see Chapter 10.

northern South America as eligible to be so designated. The 1984 Trade and Tariff Act authorized a free trade agreement with Israel, under which duty preferences have been effected.

In the past there have been special preferences provided in law for the Philippines and Cuba. However, the preferences for the Philippines have now expired, although the Philippines is recognized as a designated beneficiary developing country under the Generalized System of Preferences. The preferences for products of Cuba are at present suspended, and only licensed trade is permitted. Pursuant to the Canadian Automotive Parts Agreement and implementing legislation, certain automobiles, trucks, and automotive parts imported from Canada are admitted duty free.[3]

The United States in general in its tariff laws does not grant most-favored-nation treatment to products of Communist countries. In part, this policy is a holdover from the "Cold War" in the years following World War II. In part, it results from the fact that the USSR has never assumed the obligations of the GATT and trades essentially on a barter basis.

Imports from Communist countries generally receive the rates of duty set forth in Column 2 of the TSUS. These rates are essentially the original Tariff Act of 1930 rates of duty before any reduction by trade agreements.[4] Most Communist countries are thus denied the benefit of the lower rates of duty resulting from trade agreements entered into by the United States.

However, Part IV of the Trade Act of 1974[5] constitutes the beginning of a change in the U.S. policy toward products of Communist countries. It authorizes the President to enter into trade agreements and to provide nondiscriminatory tariff treatment to products of "nonmarket economy" countries upon fulfillment of a number of conditions. One such condition is that these countries shall not deny free emigration to their citizens or maintain tax barriers to such emigration. However, the Act authorizes the President to waive this condition if he determines that this will promote the objective of eventually obtaining freedom of emigration. The waiver is for a short period of time—18 months initially, then 12 months. There are elaborate provisions for reports to the Congress and congressional review of the actions and determinations of the President.

B. Buy American Restrictions

Another important policy embodied in U.S. law is that of preferences for American products in government procurement incorporated in the so-called Buy American laws.[6] The basic requirement is that for civilian government and defense procurement only unmanufactured and manufactured articles, materials, and supplies produced in the United States shall be

---

[3]Details of the preferences mentioned are contained in the General Headnotes at the beginning of the TSUS reproduced in Appendix A, and are presented in Chapters 8, 10, 11, and 22.

[4]For a list of Communist countries to which the Column 2 rates of duty apply, see paragraph 3(d) of the General Headnotes to the tariff schedules.

[5]19 U.S.C. 2431–2441. Part IV is discussed in Chapter 21.

[6]For details concerning the provisions, requirements, and procedures under the Buy American laws, see Chapter 15.

acquired for public use. Contractors and suppliers for public construction also are required to use domestic articles, materials, and supplies.

The Buy American restrictions do not apply to procurement for use outside the United States or to the acquisition of articles, materials, and supplies that are not produced in the United States in sufficient and reasonably available quantities or of a satisfactory quality. The head of a department or agency of the government may waive the requirements of the Buy American restrictions if the cost of domestic articles, materials, and supplies is deemed unreasonable or he determines that a particular acquisition or use of domestic materials would be contrary to the public interest. Regulations of civilian and defense agencies of the government contain formulas for general use in determining when the cost of domestic materials vis-a-vis the cost of foreign materials is unreasonable.

Passage of Title III of the Trade Agreements Act of 1979, which gave approval to the Multilateral Trade Negotiations Agreement on Government Procurement, significantly reduced the applicability of the Buy American provisions. Under the law, the President is authorized to waive, with respect to reciprocating or "least developed" countries, the application of any U.S. law or regulation that treats foreign products less favorably than domestic products.

C. Safeguarding National Security

Another basic policy written into U.S. law is that imports shall not be allowed in such quantities as to threaten impairment of the national security.[7] The Trade Act of 1974 amended the Trade Expansion Act of 1962 to confirm placement of general responsibility for administering this provision of law in the Secretary of the Treasury. This authority has been transferred to the Secretary of Commerce who is charged with conducting investigations, when requested by another department, agency, interested party, or on his own option, to determine the effects on the national security of imports of a particular article, and advising the President of his findings. If the Secretary finds an article is being imported in such quantities or under such circumstances as to threaten to impair the national security, the President is directed to take such action as he deems necessary to adjust the imports of such article and its derivatives so that they will not threaten the national security. The President may disagree with the Secretary's findings, in which case he is not required to act.

Imports from particular countries may be entirely embargoed to protect national security under the authority of the International Emergency Economic Powers Act of 1977 and the continuing authority of the Trading With the Enemy Act, discussed in Chapter 27.

---

[7]Section 232 of the Trade Expansion Act of 1962, 19 U.S.C. 1862.

III. DEVELOPMENT OF U.S. TRADE POLICY

A. Constitutional and Historical Foundations

All tariff and trade requirements and all forms of U.S. government regulation of that trade originate in congressional action and ultimately may be changed only by congressional mandate. The authority of all executive agencies, including that of the President, is derived from the Congress and may be exercised only within the statutory framework provided.

This primary and ultimate power in the Congress proceeds from the U.S. Constitution, which in Article I designates the powers of the Congress. Two clauses in Section 8 of Article I taken separately or together provide the basic national power over tariffs and trade. They read:

> The Congress shall have Power To lay and collect Taxes, Duties, Imposts and Excises, to pay the Debts and provide for the common Defense and general Welfare of the United States; but all Duties, Imposts and Excises shall be uniform throughout the United States; . . .
>
> To regulate Commerce with foreign Nations, and among the several States, and with the Indian Tribes; . . . .

Moreover, in order to make certain that this national power vested in the Congress is exclusive of any power which might be thought to be inherent in the states, Article I, Section 10, provides:

> No State shall, without the Consent of the Congress, lay any Imposts or Duties on Imports or Exports, except what may be absolutely necessary for executing its inspection Laws: and the net Produce of all Duties and Imposts, laid by any State on Imports or Exports, shall be for the Use of the Treasury of the United States; and all such Laws shall be subject to the Revision and Control of the Congress.

The mandate in Article I, Section 8, that all duties be uniform throughout the United States was recently held by the Court of International Trade to require national uniformity in the administration of the tariff laws and to preclude variations in the use classification of a product under differing state laws. *Amorient Petroleum Co.* v. *United States,* 9 CIT ____ , 607 F. Supp. 1484 (1985) 6 ITRD 2307.

The history of tariffs in the United States may be divided into two periods: (1) from 1789 to 1933, and (2) from 1934 to the present.

The first Congress in its first session proceeded to lay duties on "Goods, Wares and Merchandises imported into the United States" in an act of July 4, 1789.[8] On July 31 of that same year the Congress provided for the collection of those duties by designating collection districts and ports of entry in the 11 states that had ratified the Constitution and established the office of collector and other offices to perform in these districts and ports all the basic and now-familiar customs functions of requiring the making of

---

[8] 1 Stat. 25.

entries for imported goods, estimating duties, receiving money for the duties, accepting bonds, reporting collections, investigating frauds, etc.[9] The administration of this new system was completed with the establishment of the Department of the Treasury, with a Secretary of the Treasury at its head who had the responsibilities, among others, to "prepare plans for the improvement and management of the revenue" and to "superintend the collection of the revenue."[10]

In the almost 150 years of the first period, there was a steady rise in the tariffs of the United States and the rest of the world as trading nations jockeyed to obtain a competitive advantage over each other. This period culminated in the enactment of the famous, or infamous, Smoot-Hawley Tariff (the Tariff Act of 1930) that brought U.S. tariff rates to an all-time high level.

The Great Depression brought the realization here and abroad that expanding world trade cannot be achieved through the competitive erection of tariff barriers. It led to the enactment of the Trade Agreements Act of 1934 that signaled the beginning of the second period, a period of mutual reductions of tariff rates. The Trade Agreements Act of 1934 provided authority to the President to negotiate agreements with foreign countries to halt the upward spiral of tariff rates and to establish rules for fair competitive trade. The Trade Expansion Act of 1962 greatly enhanced the tariff-negotiating authority of the President.

In 1947, the United States and eight other major trading nations entered into the General Agreement on Tariffs and Trade (GATT). This agreement froze tariffs at their then-current levels and laid down new internationally agreed upon trading rules, including the "most-favored-nation principle." Today, almost all of the trading nations of the free world have adhered to the GATT. Under the GATT's auspices, seven rounds of multilateral tariff negotiations have been completed, reducing tariffs to comparatively low levels.

As tariffs have been reduced to relatively low levels, their significance as barriers to the free flow of trade has declined. This has led to an increase in the use of other tactics by some of the trading nations to promote their exports and inhibit imports that compete with their domestic industries and agriculture. In recent years, there has been an increase in dumping (sales abroad at less than fair value), export and domestic subsidies, border taxes, administrative restrictions, and other nontariff barriers to trade. To counter these foreign unfair tactics, there has been accelerated activity in the enforcement of the U.S. antidumping law, the U.S. countervailing duty law, and other laws designed to protect against foreign unfair trading practices. Significant amendments of these laws were incorporated in the Trade Act of 1974, the Trade Agreements Act of 1979, and the Trade and Tariff Act of 1984.[11] The 1974 Act also provided expanded opportunities for relief to domestic industries suffering injury from import competition.[12]

---

[9] 1 Stat. 29.
[10] 1 Stat. 65, 31 U.S.C. 301–321.
[11] 19 U.S.C. 1671 et seq.
[12] See Chapters 19, 20, and 21.

B. Tariff Act of 1930 and Amendments Thereof

The Tariff Act of 1930[13] provided the foundation of today's tariff law and customs administration. Its framework still stands although particular provisions have been amended in over 100 subsequent acts, and its tariff schedules were completely revised under the Tariff Classification Act of 1962.[14] The Tariff Act of 1930 provided the basic provisions governing the administration of the customs laws, including basic definitions; the report, entry, and unlading of vessels and vehicles; the ascertainment, collection, and recovery of duties; transportation in bond and warehousing of merchandise; enforcement provisions; and many miscellaneous provisions. Since 1930 the Congress has generally updated the tariff and customs laws in terms of amendments of sections of the Tariff Act of 1930. Consequently, most of the basic statutory provisions in customs administration are still designated by their section number in that Tariff Act, regardless of the number of times the section has been amended.

C. The 1974 Trade Act, the 1979 Trade Agreements Act, and the Trade and Tariff Act of 1984

The Trade Act of 1974,[15] among its various provisions, authorized the President during a five-year period, commencing January 3, 1975, to make further reductions in tariffs. The basic authority permitted the President to enter into trade agreements reducing tariffs a maximum of 40 percent from existing rates; and tariffs which were not more than 5 percent ad valorem as of January 1, 1975, could be reduced to zero.[16] The Act also authorized the President for a period of two years after the five-year negotiating period mentioned above to reduce duties a maximum of 80 percent on products which had not constituted more than 2 percent of the value of total U.S. imports.[17]

For the first time, the President was given, in the Trade Act of 1974, authority to enter into trade agreements providing for the elimination of barriers, including so-called "nontariff barriers" to trade.[18] Thus, the President could give tariff concessions in exchange for foreign countries' elimination of such barriers, or he could agree to the elimination of U.S. barriers in exchange for foreign tariff concessions or elimination of barriers. These agreements were subject to congressional approval.

The outgrowth of this negotiating authority was the Tokyo Round of negotiations, concluded in 1979. Not only did the Tokyo Round result in

---

[13]June 17, 1930, 46 Stat. 590, 19 U.S.C. ch. 4.
[14]May 24, 1962, 76 Stat. 72, 19 U.S.C. 1202.
[15]Pub. L. No. 93-618, 19 U.S.C. ch. 12.
[16]19 U.S.C. 2111.
[17]19 U.S.C. 2134.
[18]19 U.S.C. 2112. The term "barrier" includes American Selling Price valuation and was extended to include "any duty or other import restriction" by Section 401(b) of the Trade and Tariff Act of 1984. The term "nontariff barrier" is used to describe a wide variety of impediments, other than tariffs, to the free competitive flow of trade. It includes absolute quotas, discriminatory taxes, subsidies, and administrative burdens.

agreements reducing many tariffs, but it also produced the elimination or amelioration of many nontariff barriers to trade.

Many of the agreements reached in the Tokyo Round were implemented by the United States in the Trade Agreements Act of 1979.[19] The 1979 Act provided for major changes in U.S. antidumping and countervailing duty laws, significant modifications in U.S. valuation and government procurement laws, and continued reductions of U.S. tariffs. The Act contained no new authority for agreements to reduce tariffs; however, it did continue for eight years the authority in 19 U.S.C. 2112 to enter into trade agreements providing for the harmonization, reduction, or elimination of nontariff barriers to trade.

The Trade and Tariff Act of 1984[20] added extended presidential negotiating authority specifically directed toward the negotiation of trade agreements to reduce nontariff barriers in the areas of trade in services, foreign direct investment, and trade in high technology products and services. The objectives of, the authority for, and the requirements surrounding this negotiating activity, were spelled out in Title III of the 1984 Act, entitled "International Trade and Investment Act."[21] Particularly required was the identification and analysis of policies and practices which constituted significant barriers to trade in the specified areas. Title III also provided new authority for the President to retaliate against foreign discriminatory practices.

The 1984 Act also authorized the negotiation of a free trade agreement with Israel; extended the Generalized System of Preferences for 8½ years; amended the antidumping and countervailing duty laws in ways favorable to the domestic industry; provided enforcement authority for the national policy for the steel industry; and provided for the expansion of the wine trade.

D. Remedies Against Foreign Unfair Trade Practices

Within the framework of the general trade statutes and international agreements, the United States has enacted a number of laws to protect American industry against a variety of foreign unfair trade practices. If a foreign country is selling goods in the United States at below fair value (price discrimination), injuring or threatening injury to an American industry, such products may be subjected to additional antidumping duties.[22] If imports from foreign countries are being subsidized they may be subjected to additional countervailing duties, equal to the amount of the foreign subsidy.[23] For goods from countries which are signatories of the Subsidies Code, it must also be shown that the imports are injuring the U.S. industry. If U.S. trade is being subjected to discrimination or other unjustifiable foreign trade practices, the President is empowered to

---

[19]Pub. L. No. 96-39, 19 U.S.C. ch. 13.
[20]Pub. L. No. 98-573, October 30, 1984.
[21]See Chapter 22.
[22]See Chapter 12.
[23]See Chapter 13.

withdraw trade agreement concessions from the country engaging in such practices or to impose duties or other import restrictions on the products of such foreign country or on any service sector access authorization.[24]

In addition, if imports are injuring or threatening to injure American industry the President can institute tariffs, quotas, or tariff quotas or enter into voluntary export restraint agreements with foreign exporting countries to protect American industry during an adjustment period.[25] Or he can direct that adjustment assistance be provided to industries and workers being injured or threatened with injury by imports.[26] Moreover, if imports from a Communist country are causing market disruption, the President can increase or impose a tariff duty or other import restriction to prevent or remedy such market disruption.[27]

---

[24]See Chapter 16.
[25]See Chapters 14 and 19.
[26]See Chapter 20.
[27]See Chapter 21.

Part I

Import Process

2

Entry

I. ENTRY REQUIREMENTS

A. General Applicability

All imports of goods, whether free or dutiable and regardless of value, are subject to certain procedures to enter the U.S. customs territory.[1] Duties and the liability for their payment accrue upon imported goods on arrival of the importing vessel within a customs port with the intent then and there to unlade. Duties accrue on goods arriving by means other than vessel at the time of their arrival within the customs territory of the United States. The making of entry is then generally required within five working days.

B. Liability of Importer

The liability for duties constitutes a personal debt due from the importer to the United States that can be discharged only by payment in full of all duties legally accruing, unless relieved by law or regulation.[2] The importer is liable for the estimated duties deposited at the time of making entry even though the entries were unliquidated and the government had demanded

---

[1]General Headnote 1 of the Tariff Schedules of the United States (TSUS), 19 U.S.C. 1202, makes all imported articles free or dutiable in accordance with the TSUS, but General Headnote 5 exempts from the TSUS certain articles listed as "intangibles," namely: (a) corpses, together with their coffins and accompanying flowers; (b) currency (metal or paper) in current circulation in any country and imported for monetary purposes; (c) electricity; (d) securities and similar evidences of value; (e) records, diagrams, and other data with regard to any business, engineering, or exploration operation whether on paper, cards, photographs, blueprints, tapes, or other media; (f) articles returned from space within the purview of Section 484a of the Tariff Act of 1930; and (g) vessels which are not "yachts or pleasure boats" within the purview of Subpart D, Part 6, of Schedule 6. General Headnote 2 defines the customs territory of the United States as including the States, the District of Columbia, and Puerto Rico.

In accordance with Sections 484, 484a, and 498 of the Tariff Act of 1930 as amended, 19 U.S.C. 1484, 1484a, and 1498, and the customs regulations, 19 CFR Parts 141 and 142, importations are subject to the process of entry unless they are the exempted intangibles, above listed, or are specifically exempted by law or regulation. Section 484a, added by Section 209 of Pub. L. No. 98-573, effective January 1, 1985, exempts from entry articles returned from space which were launched from U.S. customs territory aboard a spacecraft operated or controlled by U.S. persons and owned wholly or substantially by U.S. persons, and which were solely used and returned by that or a similarly qualified spacecraft, without regard to advance in value or improvement in condition.

[2]See 19 CFR 141.1 for statement of importer's liability and alternative methods of payment.

13

liquidated damages under the importer's bond. *United States* v. *Goodman,* 6 CIT _____ , 572 F. Supp. 1284 (1983) 5 ITRD 1220. Liability for duties may be enforced even though by error the importer was able to pass his goods through customs without such payment. The government's claim for unpaid duties against the estate of a deceased or insolvent importer has priority over obligations to creditors other than prior claims of the United States.

However, the government may not recover from the importer or his surety duties paid by the importer to his broker where the government accepted an uncertified check from the broker when it held only the importer's bond; government regulations must protect importers as well as the United States from defaulting brokers. *United States* v. *Federal Insurance Co.,* 9 CIT _____ , 605 F. Supp. 298 (1985) 6 ITRD 1987.

The liability for duties constitutes a lien upon the imported goods that may be enforced while such goods are in the custody of or subject to the control of the United States. If goods have been consigned to anyone without that person's authority, he is not liable for duties. Such goods are treated as unclaimed.

C. Duties on Reimportations

Dutiable goods imported and subsequently exported, even though duty was paid on the first importation, are liable to duty on every successive importation into the customs territory of the United States. This does not apply to reimported articles for which free entry is specifically provided in the Tariff Schedules of the United States or for certain articles which are specifically exempted by law or regulation. Personal and household effects, professional books, tools of trade taken abroad and brought back to this country, automobiles and other vehicles taken abroad for noncommercial use, outer containers exported filled or empty and returned empty or as the usual containers of merchandise, and articles exported for exhibition or assembly under certain conditions fall into this category. Articles exported from the United States for repairs or alterations may be returned upon payment of duties only on the value of these repairs or alterations at rates applicable to the articles in their repaired or altered conditions.

II. RIGHT TO MAKE ENTRY

A. Entry by Importer of Record

The right to make entry for merchandise was restricted by an amendment of 19 U.S.C. 1484 made by Pub. L. No. 97-446 to the "importer of record." That person was defined to include only the owner or purchaser of the goods, or, when designated by the owner, purchaser, or the consignee, a customs broker.[3] This means that a consignee who is not the owner or the

---

[3] Act of January 12, 1983, Section 201(b), Title II, 96 Stat. 2349.

purchaser may not make entry but may designate a customs broker to make entry on his behalf. Directions as to the application of the entry restrictions to various entry situations are provided in Customs Directive 3530-1 issued January 19, 1984.

Goods may be entered by the person named in the bill of lading under which they are shipped, or by the holder of such bill of lading duly endorsed by the consignee if he is an importer of record. He may also use an extract from a bill of lading or a duplicate copy of the bill of lading, both certified to be genuine by the carrier bringing the goods to the port of entry.[4]

In most instances, however, a "carrier's certificate" with a release order is used as evidence of the right to make entry. In effect, this is a certified statement by the importing carrier that the named person or firm is the owner or consignee of the articles for customs purposes. The articles must be described in the certificate or in an attached document. When goods are not imported by a common carrier, possession of the goods at the time of arrival is considered to be sufficient evidence of the right to make entry.

If the person desiring to make entry of goods imported by common carrier is unable at that time to present a bill of lading or other evidence of right to make entry, the district director may accept a bond for the production of the bill of lading. The bond will be for the production of a bill of lading, even if the person making entry intends to produce a carrier's certificate or a duplicate bill of lading. Upon production of a bill of lading, the bond will be considered as canceled; it may be considered as satisfied but not canceled upon the production of a carrier's certificate or duplicate bill of lading.

Merchandise arriving in the United States must be entered by the importer of record in his own name. Customs employees are not permitted to act as an importer's agent, but they may give advice and assistance upon request. Persons authorized by customs laws to act as agents for importers are customs brokers, who are private individuals and firms licensed by the Customs Service. Customs brokers file the necessary entry papers, pay the duties due, unless paid directly by the importer, effect the release of the merchandise from customs custody, and otherwise represent the importer in customs matters. See Chapter 6.

A nonresident individual, partnership, or corporation has the right to make entry but any bond taken in connection with the entry must have a resident corporate surety. In addition, a foreign corporation must have a resident agent in the state where the port of entry is located who is authorized to accept service of process against such corporation.

B. Importer of Record's Declaration

Every importer of record in whose name an entry is made must execute on the entry form a declaration confirming to the best of his knowledge and belief the truth and accuracy of the facts in the invoice, as discussed in

---

[4]See 19 CFR 141.11 for evidence of the right to make entry for importations by common carrier.

Chapter 3, and in the entry and other entry documents. If the facts prove to be false, the penalty of forfeiture of the domestic value of the merchandise may be asserted against the consignee under 19 U.S.C. 1592. The importer of record has the statutory right to make additions to, or deductions from, the value given in the invoice at the time entry is made. 19 U.S.C. 1487.

C. Actual Owner's Declaration

An importer of record in whose name an entry is made and who wishes to be relieved from statutory liability for the payment of increased and additional duties must declare at the time of entry that he is not the actual owner of the merchandise. He must also furnish the name and address of the owner and file with the district director within 90 days from the date of entry a declaration from the actual owner of the merchandise acknowledging that he will pay all increased and additional duties. The importer of record must also file with the district director within 90 days from the date of entry a bond of the actual owner if he wishes to be relieved of liability under the bond against which the entry was charged.

D. Powers of Attorney

1. Requirement

When entry is made by a customs broker, a customs power of attorney given by the person or firm for whom he is acting is required. The customs power of attorney is normally used to establish the right of an employee to make entry for his employer.

A nonresident individual, partnership, or corporation may issue a power of attorney to a regular employee, customs broker, partner, or corporation officer to transact customs business in the United States. Any person named in the power of attorney must be a resident of the United States who has been authorized to accept service of process on behalf of the person or organization issuing the power of attorney.

2. Form and Contents

Customs Form 5291 may be used to give a power of attorney to transact customs business. If a customs power of attorney is not on Customs Form 5291, it must be either a general power of attorney with unlimited authority or a limited power of attorney as explicit in its terms and executed in the same manner as Customs Form 5291.

If a power of attorney limits the customs districts in which the agent may act, the names of such districts must be stated. This power of attorney may be filed with any district director in a sufficient number of copies for distribution to each district in which the agent is to act.

If a power of attorney has been filed which is not limited to transactions in a specific customs district and it is desired to use it in another district, the district director with whom it is filed, upon the request of the district director of the other district or upon the request of the person or firm which executed the power, will forward a certified copy of the power of attorney to the director of the other district. Any expense in connection with the preparation of such documents will be borne by the interested parties.

A power of attorney executed in favor of a licensed customs broker may specify that the power of attorney is granted to the broker to act through any of his licensed officers or authorized employees. Customs brokers are not required to file powers of attorney with a district director. However, they must retain powers of attorney with their books and records, and make them available to Treasury Department representatives as prescribed by regulations.

Powers of attorney issued by a partnership are limited to a period not to exceed two years from their date of receipt by the district director. All other powers of attorney may be granted for an unlimited period. Any power of attorney is subject to revocation at any time by written notice given to and received by the district director.

III. ENTRY FORMALITIES

A. The Entry Process

The process of entry of merchandise normally proceeds in two steps. First, the importer of record makes entry for imported merchandise by filing an entry form with documents which will be sufficient to enable the appropriate customs officer to determine whether the merchandise may be released from Customs custody. At the same time or within a maximum period of 10 working days, the importer of record must file the entry summary needed for the customs officer to assess properly the duties on the merchandise, collect accurate statistics, and determine the conformity of the merchandise with any applicable requirement of law (such as marking and certification requirements).

Estimated duties are to be deposited at the time of filing the entry documentation or the entry summary documentation when it serves as both the entry and the entry summary, but if the merchandise is released under the entry documentation alone, the deposit of estimated duties must be made at the time of filing the entry summary. However, if the merchandise is entered for warehouse, estimated duties are to be deposited at the time the withdrawal for consumption is presented.

If excess estimated duties are deposited due to clerical error, the excess may be refunded prior to liquidation under an amendment of 19 U.S.C. 1520(a) made by Section 212(b)(7) of the Trade and Tariff Act of 1984. See 19 CFR 173.4a, added July 23, 1985, 50 FR 29957.

The present entry procedure results from the amendment of Section 484 of the Tariff Act of 1930, Entry of Merchandise, and related statutes by the Customs Procedural Reform and Simplification Act of 1978, Public Law 95-410, and the consequently revised Customs Regulations.[5] These regulations are Part 141 Entry of Merchandise, Part 142 Entry Process, and Parts 143 and 144, covering different types of entries, of Title 19 of the Code of Federal Regulations.

B. Notable 1978 Reforms

Among the principal changes from the pre-1978 procedures[6] were (1) the transformation of the prior special permission for immediate release under bond of various kinds of merchandise into the standard first step of entry filing which permits immediate release of merchandise, and (2) the enabling of the Customs Service to send importers periodic consolidated statements for all entries made during the billing period instead of settling the amount of duties due on an entry-by-entry basis.

C. The Entry Documents

1. Generally

The entry papers consist of: (a) a document similar to the former immediate delivery release, generally Customs Form 3461, (b) a commercial invoice, (c) a packing list where appropriate, (d) a bill of lading or other evidence of right to make entry, and (e) other documents required for a particular shipment. This entry documentation will be accepted at a customhouse or other customs location in the district where the merchandise is released. The entry summary is made on Customs Form 7501,[7] and may be filed at time of entry, with estimated duties attached. If it is filed later within the 10-day period allowed, the importer may use the entry documents, returned by Customs, in preparing the summary. The documentation must include the entry record and any documents required for the particular shipment.

Under TD 84-192 importers of merchandise subject to an antidumping or countervailing duty order must include with the entry summary a unique identifying number assigned by the International Trade Administration. Moreover, all entry preparers must show on the appropriate entry forms the applicable two-digit entry type code from the list promulgated by TD 85-5, 50 FR 1499, January 11, 1985, effective February 1, 1985, designed to facilitate Customs' integrated Automated Commercial System (ACS). Further, to facilitate the ACS, Customs issued TD 85-112, 50 FR 27816, July 8, 1985, requiring a new 11-digit number system on entry documentation as of October 1, 1985.

---

[5]TD 79-221, 44 FR 46816, August 9, 1979.
[6]See S. Rep. No. 95-778 on H.R. 8149 (Pub. L. No. 95-410).
[7]Under TD 84-129, 49 FR 23161, June 5, 1984, a revised Customs Form 7501 replaced most other entry forms January 1, 1985.

By statute, 19 U.S.C. 1315, articles are subject to the rate of duty in effect at the time of entry even if the duty is later deposited. Under the regulations "the time of entry" is determined by the type of documentation filed and the time of arrival or release of the merchandise.[8]

2. Export Authorizations

Under the tariff laws, regulatory laws, or international agreements the entry of certain types of merchandise must be accompanied by documents from the exporting country or exporter demonstrating entitlement of the merchandise to entry into the United States or providing required information. Thus, for example, exporting country visas are required under various bilateral textile agreements for entry of certain textiles and textile products (see Chapter 14, section IV); foreign meat inspection certificates are required for certain meat products (see Appendix G); foreign manufacturing information for certain merchandise, including steel shipments over $10,000 in value, is required in invoices pursuant to 19 CFR 141.89; and export certificates are required for certain steel shipments from a member of the European Community proving compliance with the Arrangement of October 21, 1982, between the EC and the United States which terminated the major carbon steel antidumping and countervailing duty complaints filed in January 1982.

D. Importers' Recordkeeping

Current procedures allowing for more informal and regular release of imported goods before submission of all entry-related documents and for consolidation of entry accounts into monthly statements place increased reliance on accurate recordkeeping by importers and their agents. Consequently the Customs Procedural Reform and Simplification Act of 1978 added a new provision, Section 508 of the Tariff Act of 1930 (19 U.S.C. 1508), requiring every "owner, importer, consignee, or agent thereof who imports, or knowingly causes to be imported, any merchandise" to make and keep and render for examination and inspection the records pertaining to the entry of the merchandise which are normally kept in the ordinary course of business. These records are to be kept for the period prescribed by the Secretary of the Treasury, not to exceed five years.

To clarify the application of this requirement the statute provides that a person who orders merchandise from an importer does not "knowingly cause merchandise to be imported" unless he controls the terms and conditions of the order or furnishes technical data, equipment, and production assistance or components with knowledge that they will be used in the manufacture or production of the import.

With the first formal entry or request for services involving the payment of money, a notification of the importer's number and of the ultimate

---

[8]19 CFR 141.68.

consignee's number must be filed on Form 5106. This 9-digit number is the notifier's IRS employer identification number, or his social security number, or if he has neither, a number to be assigned by the customs office. This identifying number is to be used in all future customs transactions requiring an importer number. Two-digit suffixes may be used to identify branch offices.

E. Packages Designated for Examination

Section 499 of the Tariff Act[9] provides that merchandise may not be released from customs custody, except under bond, until it has been inspected, examined, or appraised. The customs officer is required to designate "not less than one package of every invoice and not less than one package of every ten packages of merchandise" for delivery to public stores for examination. However, when the revenue will be amply protected, discretion to examine a lesser number of packages is permitted under a published special regulation or instruction.

19 CFR 151.2(a), first published in September 1981, permits (1) examination of only one package of every invoice in the case of certain uniform or identical imports, and (2) at designated ports the release of merchandise without examination in the discretion of the district director. Nevertheless, the authority remains to follow the law precisely when necessary and it is in fact possible for the Customs Service to examine every package if necessary. However, no appraisement can now be treated as invalid merely because the required number of packages was not designated or examined unless it can be established that the appraisement was incorrect because of that fact.

When an entry for goods has been filed, representative packages are designated for examination by customs officers under conditions properly safeguarding the goods.[10] Examination is necessary to determine (1) the value and dutiable status of the goods, (2) whether the prescribed country of origin markings appear,[11] (3) whether the goods have been truly and correctly invoiced,[12] (4) whether the shipment contains prohibited articles,[13] and (5) whether the invoiced quantities are present. Certain goods must be examined to ascertain their compliance with Agriculture Department, Health and Human Services Department, Federal Trade Commission, and other agency requirements.[14]

Customs officers will weigh, gauge, or measure certain kinds of goods. If the invoice or entry does not state the weight, quantity, or measure of the goods, the expense of ascertaining such facts may be collected from the importer before release of the goods from customs custody.

---

[9] 19 U.S.C. 1499.
[10] 19 CFR Part 151.
[11] See Chapter 25.
[12] See Chapter 3.
[13] See Chapter 27.
[14] See Chapter 24.

F. Failure to Make Entry

If entry is not made within the required period, the goods will be placed in a general order warehouse at the importer's risk and expense, in accordance with the regulations in 19 CFR Part 127. If the goods are not exported or entered within one year from the date of their importation they will be sold at public auction. Perishable goods, goods subject to depreciation, and explosive substances may be sold at once.

Storage charges, expenses of sales, internal revenue taxes, duties, and amounts for the satisfaction of liens must be taken out of the money obtained from the sale of unentered goods. Any surplus remaining after these deductions is ordinarily payable to the holder of a duly endorsed bill of lading covering the goods. If the goods will not bring enough on sale at public auction to pay internal revenue taxes imposed upon or by reason of importation, they are subject to destruction.

G. Goods From Canada or Mexico

Baggage or goods carried on a vehicle or on a vessel of less than five net tons arriving otherwise than by sea from Canada or Mexico must be listed on a manifest, known as an inward foreign manifest. When baggage arrives in the actual possession of a traveler, his declaration will be accepted in lieu of a manifest. In general, the rules and regulations for entry of imported goods are applicable to importations from Canada or Mexico. Special rules on shipments from or through Canada or Mexico are set forth in 19 CFR Part 123.

IV. KINDS OF ENTRY

A. Entry for Consumption

Entry of merchandise can be accomplished in various ways. The most common type of entry is for consumption, which requires compliance with the procedures for the release of imported merchandise described in section III *supra*. Merchandise not held for examination is released under bond. Certain packages are designated for examination by Customs and are released under the same bond after examination has been completed to determine whether the merchandise has been truly and correctly invoiced, and is entitled to admission into the commerce of the United States, and whether its release is not precluded by any law or regulation.

B. Entry for Warehouse

Merchandise which is subject to duty may be entered for warehousing and put in a bonded warehouse at the expense and risk of the importer.[15]

---

[15]19 U.S.C. 1557. Customs regulations covering warehouse entries are found in 19 CFR Part 144.

The principal documentation required is the filing of a warehouse entry summary, after January 1, 1985, on revised Customs Form 7501. No deposit of estimated duties is required until the merchandise is withdrawn for consumption. Perishable merchandise, explosive substances (other than firecrackers), and unconditionally free merchandise may not be entered for warehousing.

If merchandise has been entered under other than a warehouse entry and the merchandise has remained in continuous customs custody, a warehouse entry may be substituted for the previous entry. If estimated duties were deposited with the previous superseded entry, that entry will be liquidated for refund of the estimated duties without awaiting liquidation of the warehouse entry.

The importer designates on the entry the bonded warehouse in which he desires his merchandise to be deposited and the bonded cartman or lighterman he wishes to have transfer the merchandise. Packages designated for examination by Customs elsewhere than at the warehouse will be sent to the warehouse after examination. Merchandise may not remain in warehouse beyond five years from the date of importation. The right to withdraw all or part of the merchandise may be transferred by appropriate endorsement on the withdrawal form, provided that the transferee files an appropriate bond.

Withdrawals from bonded warehouse may be made only by the person primarily responsible for the payment of duties on the merchandise being withdrawn. This can be the importer of record on the warehouse entry, the actual owner if an actual owner's declaration and superseding bond have been filed, or the transferee if the right to withdraw the merchandise has been transferred.

Merchandise may be withdrawn from warehouse for transportation to another port of entry, provided that withdrawal for consumption or exportation can be accomplished at the port of destination before expiration of the warehousing period or any extension thereof. The merchandise may be entered for rewarehousing at the port of destination by the consignee named in the withdrawal.

Merchandise entered for warehousing is dutiable at the rates in effect when withdrawal from warehouse for consumption is made. The time of filing withdrawal documentation is the "time of entry" for determining the rate of duty applicable. Merchandise that is not subject to a quantitative or tariff rate quota and that is covered by an entry for immediate transportation at the port of original transportation is subject to the rates in effect when the immediate transportation entry was accepted at the port of original transportation. Under the 1978 amendment of 19 U.S.C. 1557, merchandise may be withdrawn from warehouse for consumption without payment of the duty thereon at that time if regulations of the Secretary of the Treasury so permit. No subsequent regulations have been issued.

C. Entry for Transportation in Bond

Any merchandise, except explosives and prohibited merchandise, arriving at a port of entry in the United States may be entered for transportation in bond without appraisement to any other port of entry designated by the importer, and by such bonded carrier as he designates.[16] Merchandise received under an immediate transportation without appraisement entry may be entered for transportation and exportation or for immediate transportation, or under any other form of entry. If more than one year has elapsed from the date of original importation, however, only an entry for consumption will be accepted.

Other entries which may be made for merchandise to be transported under bond are (1) warehouse or rewarehouse withdrawal for transportation, (2) warehouse or rewarehouse withdrawal for exportation or for transportation and exportation, (3) entry for transportation and exportation, and (4) entry for exportation. Baggage may be forwarded in bond to another port of entry at the request of the passenger, the transportation company, or the agent of either without examination or assessment of duty at the port of first arrival.

D. Appraisement Entry

Certain goods are eligible for entry by appraisement.[17] These include merchandise damaged during transport; salvaged merchandise; household and personal effects not intended for sale; gifts sent from abroad to U.S. residents; personal effects of U.S. citizens who have died abroad; and certain articles that are deemed to be articles the value of which cannot be declared.

An appraisement entry is made on Customs Form 7501. With it the importer must present any bills or statement of costs relating to the merchandise which may be in his possession. He must also present a declaration that he has no other information as to the value of the merchandise and is unable to obtain such information for the purpose of making entry. Estimated duties must be deposited after notification by Customs of the amount due and before the merchandise is released from customs custody.

E. Informal Entry

Customs may allow the following types of merchandise to be entered under informal entry: (1) shipments of merchandise not exceeding $1,250 in value; (2) any installment, not exceeding $1,250 in value, of a shipment arriving at different times; (3) a portion of one consignment, when such portion does not exceed $1,250 in value and may be entered separately pursuant to regulations; (4) certain household and personal effects and tools

---

[16]19 U.S.C. 1552; 19 CFR Part 18.

[17]Customs regulations covering appraisement and informal entries are found in 19 CFR Part 143.

of trade; (5) books and other articles imported by a library or other public or nonprofit educational, scientific, or religious institution. The foregoing $1,250 value limit, increased from $250 by Section 206 of Public Law 98-573, does not apply to goods classified in Schedule 3 of the TSUS, or in certain parts of Schedule 7, and Parts 2 and 3 of the TSUS Appendix. The district director may require formal entry or appraisement entry for any merchandise if he deems it necessary for the protection of the revenue. Although the 1984 law permits Customs to raise the informal entry limit to $1,250 in value, Customs raised the limit to $1,000 in value by Customs Directive 3550-05, December 10, 1984, effective January 1, 1985, incorporated in 19 CFR Part 143 by TD 85-123, July 23, 1985, 50 FR 29955.

In the case of merchandise imported pursuant to a purchase or intended for sale, the importer must produce the commercial invoices covering the transaction or, in the absence thereof, an itemized statement of value.

Estimated duties must be deposited at the time the informal entry is presented and accepted by a customs officer, whether at the customhouse or elsewhere. If upon examination of the merchandise further duties are found due, they must be deposited before release of the merchandise by customs.

F. Mail Entry

Merchandise may be imported into the United States by mail. All such merchandise is, of course, subject to examination by the Customs Service. Sealed letter class mail which appears to contain matter other than correspondence may be opened by customs officers and employees for examination if they have reasonable cause to suspect the presence of merchandise or contraband. *United States* v. *Ramsey,* 431 U.S. 606 (1977); 19 CFR 145.3. The merchandise may be entered under formal entry or informal entry depending on whether or not the value of the shipment exceeds $1,000, with exceptions noted in section E *supra.*

Joint customs and postal regulations[18] require that all parcel post packages have securely attached a customs declaration on a form provided by the foreign post office giving an accurate description and the value of the contents. Commercial shipments must also be accompanied by an invoice or a statement of fair retail value, securely attached to the outside or enclosed in the parcels bearing the declaration.

Separate shipments not exceeding $1,000 in value, under the 1985 regulations, if mailed abroad at different times, will not be combined for the purpose of requiring formal entry, even though they reach Customs at the same time and are covered by a single order or contract exceeding $1,000. If the mail importation does not exceed $1,000, the customs entry is prepared by a customs officer, and the post office at destination delivers the parcels to the addressee upon payment of duty. The post office also collects a nominal charge for delivering dutiable parcels. If the value of a mail importation

---

[18] 19 CFR Part 145, amended TD 85-123, July 23, 1985, 50 FR 29955.

exceeds $1,000, the addressee is notified to file a formal entry at the customs port nearest him.

Some of the advantages to using the mails for importation of merchandise are: (1) The duties on parcels under $1,000 are collected by the postman delivering the parcel. (2) Small, low-valued packages can usually be sent through the mails less expensively than by other means of shipment. (3) No entry is required for duty-free merchandise not exceeding $1,000 in value. (4) There is no need to clear shipments personally if under $1,000 in value.

V. MANIPULATION PRIOR TO DUTY PAYMENT

A. Customs Bonded Warehouses; Supervision

A customs bonded warehouse is a building or other secured area in which merchandise may be stored or manipulated, or may undergo manufacturing operations, without payment of duty. Bonded warehouses, which numbered about 1,450 in 1985, are divided into eight "classes," depending on the type of operations authorized to take place within them and on whether the merchandise stored therein belongs exclusively to the proprietor of the warehouse or to other owners. The eight classes are described in 19 CFR 19.1.

The Customs Service is responsible for controlling bonded warehouses and the entry and withdrawal of the merchandise therein. Until December 1, 1982, that supervision was exercised generally by customs warehouse officers assigned to each bonded warehouse. Effective on that date, Customs extensively amended its control regulations, principally 19 CFR Parts 19 and 144 to eliminate physical supervision of warehouse transactions by customs warehouse officers and recordkeeping by them which tended to duplicate the recordkeeping of the warehouse proprietors. The proprietors are made responsible and accountable for the proper management of their warehouses. Customs supervision is exercised through audits and spot checks and the general supervision of the district directors.

B. Manipulation Warehouses

Under the customs supervision described above, and at the expense of the proprietor, merchandise may be cleaned, sorted, repacked, or otherwise changed in condition, but not manufactured, in a bonded manipulation warehouse established for that purpose.[19] The merchandise may then be withdrawn for exportation to foreign countries or certain U.S. insular possessions without payment of duties. Also, the merchandise may be withdrawn for consumption upon the payment of duties accruing thereon, in its condition and quantity and at its weight, at the time of withdrawal from warehouse, with such additions or deductions from its final appraised value as may be necessary by reason of change in condition.

---

[19]See 19 U.S.C. 1555–1556, 1562; 19 CFR Part 19.11.

C. Manufacturing Warehouses

Buildings or parts of buildings and other enclosures may be designated as bonded manufacturing warehouses if customs is satisfied that their location, construction, and arrangement afford adequate protection to the revenue. Such warehouses must be used solely and exclusively for the manufacture of articles, in whole or in part of imported merchandise, or of materials subject to internal revenue tax, and intended for exportation without being charged with duty, and without having an internal revenue stamp affixed thereto.[20]

D. Smelting and Refining Warehouses

Metal-bearing materials (ores and crude metals) may be entered into a bonded smelting or refining warehouse without the payment of duties thereon and there smelted or refined, or both, together with metal-bearing materials of domestic origin. Upon arrival at the warehouse of imported metal-bearing materials they will be sampled according to commercial methods and assayed, both under customs supervision. The bond will be charged with an amount equal to the duties which would be payable upon such metal-bearing materials in their condition as imported if entered for consumption, with subsequent adjustments.[21]

---

[20]See 19 U.S.C. 1311 and 19 CFR 19.13, 19.14.
[21]See 19 U.S.C. 1312 and 19 CFR 19.17–19.25.

3

Invoices

I. IMPORTANCE AND FUNCTION

The invoice is one of the most important documents in the import process as it provides the information as to the kind, quantity, composition, price and value, and other facts concerning the merchandise upon which the applicable duty is determined. Various provisions of the Tariff Act of 1930 and of the customs regulations[1] require the presentation of an invoice and prescribe its contents. It is vital, therefore, that the invoice be prepared with the utmost accuracy and care. Failure to do so can lead to difficulties, delays, and possible penal sanctions.

A fundamental rule is that the importer and the exporter must furnish all the information necessary for the Customs Service to determine the tariff status of the goods. It is incumbent on the importer to furnish to Customs at the time of entry information or knowledge of the transaction in his possession which is not contained in the invoice. Each invoice must contain all the information required by law and regulation, and every statement of fact must be true and accurate. Any inaccurate or misleading statement in an invoice presented at the time of entry, or the omission from the invoice of required information, could result in the detention of the goods or a claim against the importer for monetary penalties under 19 U.S.C. 1592. Even though inaccuracies or omissions may have been unintentional, the importer may be required to prove that he exercised due diligence and was not negligent in order to avoid being penalized.

The invoice, with any supplemental documentation, has become the primary basis for the application of the transaction value method of valuation established by the valuation law enacted by the Trade Agreements Act of 1979. See Chapter 9. In anticipation of the coming into effect of this law on July 1, 1980, Customs advised that greater reliance and emphasis would be placed on the invoice and other import documentation and that

---

[1]19 U.S.C. 1481–1485; 19 CFR Part 141, Subpart F.

the invoice must be an actual one covering the transaction and not one created to fulfill the requirements of the new law.[2]

The required type of invoice must be presented for each shipment of merchandise at the time the entry summary is filed.

II. TYPES OF INVOICES

A. Former Special Customs Invoice

A special customs invoice (Customs Form 5515) prepared by the exporter was long required for clearance of each shipment of imported goods subject to duty on value, with a purchase price or value exceeding $500, including all expenses incident to readying the goods for shipment to the United States, unless the merchandise was exempted under 19 CFR 141.83(d). This type of invoice was also required for each shipment of merchandise subject to such duty which is entered under a conditionally free provision when all free entry documents and evidence required to establish the exemption from duty are not produced at the time of filing the entry summary.

However, the Commissioner of Customs' policy decision effective March 1, 1982, not published in the *Federal Register*, permitted alternative use of a commercial invoice, signed by the seller, shipper, or their agent, which contained the information required by 19 CFR 141.86.[3]

The Special Customs Invoice has been eliminated from the customs regulations under amended regulations[4] which require a commercial invoice for most shipments of imported merchandise.

B. Commercial Invoice

A commercial invoice must be presented for each shipment of imported goods that is not excepted from the requirements of a commercial invoice. Although no format is specified, commercial invoices shall be prepared in the manner customary to the trade, contain the information concerning the merchandise and the transaction specified in the invoice regulations (see section III *infra*), and substantiate the statistical information required to be supplied with the entry, entry summary, or withdrawal documentation by the Entry of Merchandise regulations at 19 CFR 141.61(e).

The commercial invoice is used for two kinds of goods—goods acquired by purchase or agreement to purchase, known as "purchased merchandise," and goods acquired by other means, known as "not purchased merchandise." The distinction is critical in proof of value, as the value of purchased merchandise may be evidenced by its purchase price. Other evidence is needed in the case of not purchased merchandise.

[2]Question and Answer No. 30 in Regional Information Bulletin No. 80-12, 24 March 1980.
[3]See New York Region Informational Pipeline No. 644, February 18, 1982.
[4]TD 85-39, 50 FR 9610, March 11, 1985.

Merchandise is considered to be purchased if it is shipped to the United States as a result of a purchase or agreement to purchase made at or before the time the goods were exported from the foreign country and if the price paid by the U.S. purchaser to the foreign seller has been fixed or a definite procedure by which the price is to be determined has been agreed upon at or before exportation. The foregoing pertains regardless of who ships the goods. The goods may be shipped directly to the purchaser, through his agent or branch house in the foreign country, to an agent of the seller, or to the seller's branch house in the United States. Merchandise other than "purchased merchandise" as defined above is considered "not purchased merchandise" and is often designated as consigned merchandise.

Either the seller or the shipper, or his duly authorized agent, must sign the purchase declaration for merchandise shipped in pursuance of a sale or an agreement to sell. The shipper or duly authorized agent must sign the nonpurchase declaration in the case of merchandise shipped otherwise than by purchase or agreement to purchase.

C. Other Invoices

A commercial invoice is not required for the entry of the 15 types of merchandise listed in 19 CFR 141.83(d), but the importer must present an invoice or a memorandum invoice or bill, available to him, or a pro forma invoice. Among the types of merchandise listed in this connection are merchandise valued at $500 or less, merchandise not intended for sale or any commercial use, and merchandise for which an appraisement entry is accepted.

D. Pro Forma Invoice

If the required invoice is not available at the time the goods are entered, the importer may file a pro forma invoice containing all the information necessary for customs purposes. The form to be substantially followed is set forth in 19 CFR 141.85. The importer must also give a bond for the production of the required invoice within six months from the date of the goods' entry. If the required invoice is not filed before the expiration of the six-month period, the importer will incur a liability under his bond.

E. Special Summary Steel Invoice (SSSI)

A special summary steel invoice, Customs Form 5520, is required to be filed for each shipment of certain articles of steel having an aggregate purchase price of $10,000 or over, or, if from a contiguous country, of $5,000 or over.[5] The articles of steel affected are the 32 listed in 19 CFR

---

[5] 19 CFR 141.89(b)(1). Supplies of Customs Form 5520, Special Summary Steel Invoice, may be secured from consular offices of the United States, district directors, port directors, and from Region II, Publications and Reproduction Section, U.S. Customs Service, 6 World Trade Center, New York, N.Y. 10048. Privately printed forms must conform in all respects, including size, color, and wording, to the official forms, except that repetitive data such as the importer's name, etc., may be printed.

141.89(b)(2), and the information required in addition to that required for all customs invoices is set forth in 19 CFR 141.89(b)(1). The purpose of the SSSI is to provide information in the administration of the trigger price mechanism established to monitor the application of the antidumping law to steel imports.

F. Separate Invoices for Shipments

A separate invoice is required for each distinct shipment from one consignor to one consignee by one vessel or conveyance. Goods which are assembled for shipment to the same consignee by one vessel or conveyance may be included in one invoice. The original bills or invoices covering the goods, or extracts therefrom, showing the actual price paid or agreed to be paid, should be attached to the invoice.

G. Installment Shipments

Installments of a shipment covered by a single order or contract and shipped from one consignor to one consignee may be included in one invoice if the installments arrive at the port of entry within a period not to exceed 10 consecutive days. The invoice should be prepared in the same manner as invoices for single shipments; when practicable, it should show the quantities, value, and other invoice data with respect to each installment and the date of shipment of each installment and should identify in which importing conveyance the installment was shipped.

III. CONTENTS OF INVOICES

A. General Requirements

All invoices for goods to be imported into the United States must, under 19 CFR 141.86, as amended by TD 85-39, show:
- The port of entry in the United States to which the merchandise is destined.
- The time when, the place where, and the person by whom and the person to whom the merchandise is sold or agreed to be sold in the case of purchased merchandise. The time when, the place from which shipped, and the person to whom it is shipped in the case of not purchased merchandise.
- A detailed description of the merchandise, including the name by which each item is known, the grade or quality, and the marks, numbers, or symbols under which sold by the seller or manufacturer in the country of exportation. The marks and numbers of the packages in which the merchandise is packed should also be shown.
- The quantities expressed in the weights and measures of the country from which the merchandise is shipped, or in the weights and measures of the United States.

- In the case of purchased merchandise, the purchase price of each item in the currency of the purchase.
- In the case of not purchased merchandise, the value for each item, in the currency in which the transactions are usually made, or, in the absence of such value, the price in such currency that the manufacturer, seller, shipper, or owner would have received or was willing to receive for such goods if sold in the ordinary course of trade and in the usual wholesale quantities in the country of exportation.
- The kind of currency, whether gold, silver, or paper.
- All charges upon the merchandise, itemized by name and amount, including freight, insurance, commission, cases, containers, coverings, and cost of packing; and if not included above, all charges, costs, and expenses incurred in bringing the merchandise from alongside the carrier at the port of exportation in the country of exportation and placing it alongside the carrier at the first U.S. port of entry. The cost of packing, cases, containers, and inland freight to the port of exportation need not be itemized by amount if included in the invoice price, and so identified. Where the required information does not appear on the invoice as originally prepared, it shall be shown on an attachment to the invoice.
- All rebates, drawbacks, and bounties, separately itemized, allowed upon the exportation of the merchandise.
- The country of origin of the merchandise.
- All goods or services furnished for the production of the merchandise (*e.g.,* assists such as dies, molds, tools, engineering work) not included in the invoice price. Goods or services furnished in the United States are excluded.
- The name of a responsible individual who has knowledge of the facts of the transaction.[6]

To satisfy the requirement of a "detailed description of the merchandise," a general description, such as "electrical machinery" is not acceptable. The description must be detailed enough to enable an import specialist to classify the merchandise properly. Any information bearing directly on the classification, such as ornamentation on wearing apparel, or a spring mechanism in a toy, must be indicated.[7]

B. Additional Information

Certain classes of goods require that additional information be shown on the customs invoice. The classes of goods and the information required can be found in 19 CFR 141.89 of the customs regulations.

---

[6]19 CFR 141.86(j).
[7]See New York Region Informational Pipeline No. 996, October 23, 1984.

IV. PREPARATION

A. Mechanics of Preparation

The commercial invoice must be prepared by the exporter of the goods. The original must be forwarded to the importer for use at the time the goods are entered, together with as many copies as the importer may require for his own purposes. The exporter may retain as many copies as needed for his records.

Invoices should, if possible, be typewritten but forms filled out by hand with black ink are also acceptable. In no case, however, should red ink be used since it might lead to confusion with the red ink used by Customs for its notations. Customs requires the invoice and all attachments to be in English or have an accurate English translation attached to them.

B. Declaration by Importer of Record

The obligation to furnish true and relevant information is formalized by the declaration that the importer of record must execute when making entry.[8] He must declare whether the merchandise is purchased or not purchased, that the price or value shown in the invoice is true to the best of his knowledge and belief, that all other invoice statements are true, and that he will furnish any required additional documents and any documentary evidence to the contrary.

V. COMMON ERRORS AND OMISSIONS

Some of the errors or omissions most commonly made in invoicing are:
• Failure to list commissions, royalties, or other charges against the goods in the belief that they are nondutiable.
• Failure to indicate or to correctly indicate whether a commission is a buying commission (nondutiable) or a selling commission (dutiable).
• Failure to include engineering, design, and research and development costs as a part of value, except where those costs are incurred in the United States and relate to exports to the United States since July 1, 1980. See Chapter 9, section II.B.2.
• Goods sold at a list price less a discount but invoiced at the net price without showing the discount.
• Goods sold at a delivered price but invoiced at a price f.o.b. the place of shipment without showing the subsequent charges.
• Goods manufactured partly with materials supplied by the importer but invoiced at the actual cost to the manufacturer without including the materials supplied by the importer.

---

[8] 19 U.S.C. 1485; 19 CFR 141.19.

- Failure to show "assists" (*i.e.,* tools, dies, molds, patterns, materials, and parts, etc.) furnished outside the United States by the importer free of charge or at reduced cost.[9]
- Goods invoiced as purchased when they are, in fact, not purchased, *i.e.,* consigned.

VI. RELATION OF PACKING TO INVOICING

Proper packing of imported goods will help to speed up the clearance of goods through customs. The goods should be invoiced in a manner to show the exact quantity of each item in each box, bale, case, or other package. Each package should have marks and numbers that correspond to the marks and numbers shown on the invoice for the itemization of the contents of the particular package. If possible, packages should contain goods of one kind only or should be packed in such a manner that the contents and values are uniform. This will facilitate the designation of packages for examination and their subsequent examination for customs purposes, and will prevent the delay and confusion that result from unsystematic packing. Normally, when the packing is uniform, a smaller number of packages will be designated for examination.

Goods should be invoiced and packed in such a manner as to make rapid examination possible. This will enable Customs to decide which packages need to be examined, what weighing, counting, or measuring must be done, and whether the goods are properly marked. It will reduce the number of samples to be taken for identification purposes or for laboratory analysis. It will facilitate the verification of the contents of the packages and the determination of missing or excess goods. Most importantly, it will lessen the chance of the importer's being asked to redeliver for examination some or all the packages previously released to him. This can be a very costly procedure to the importer.

VII. AVOIDANCE OF COMMINGLING

General Headnote 7 of the Tariff Schedules of the United States provides that whenever articles subject to different rates of duty are so packed together or mingled that the quantity or value of each class of articles cannot be readily ascertained by customs officers (without physical segregation of the shipment or the contents of any entire package thereof), the commingled articles shall be subject to the highest rate of duty applicable to any part of the commingled goods unless the importer or his agent segregates the goods under Customs supervision. The methods of ready ascertainment specified in General Headnote 7 are (1) by sampling, (2) by verification of packing lists or other documents filed at the time of entry, or (3) by evidence showing performance of commercial settlement

---

[9]See discussion of assists in Chapter 9, section II.B.2.

tests generally accepted in the trade. Any such segregation must be done, at the risk and expense of the importer, within 30 days after notice by Customs that the goods are commingled. The compensation of the customs officers must be paid by the importer.

The "highest applicable rate of duty" rule does not apply to any part of a shipment if the importer furnishes satisfactory proof (1) that such part is commercially negligible, is not capable of segregation without excessive costs, and will not otherwise be segregated prior to its use in a manufacturing process; or (2) that the commingling was not intended to avoid the payment of lawful duties. Any article for which such proof has been furnished shall be considered for all customs purposes as a part of the article subject to the next lower rate of duty with which it is commingled.

4

Bonds and Carnets

I. THE LAW AND REGULATIONS ON CUSTOMS BONDS

A. Importance of and Authority for Customs Bonds

The U.S. Customs Service relies extensively upon customs bonds to insure payment of customs duties and import taxes and compliance with legal requirements concerning the entry, movement, and disposition of imported merchandise.

The authority for requiring bonds for customs purposes which is given to the Secretary of the Treasury by the Congress[1] is very broad. It provides that, on all importations, the Secretary may by regulation or specific instruction require or authorize customs officers to require such bonds or other security as may be deemed necessary to protect the revenue or to insure compliance with any provision of law, regulation, or instruction administered by the Treasury or the Customs Service.

The authority of the Secretary of the Treasury was delegated to the Commissioner of Customs in Treasury Department Order No. 165, Revised, dating from 1954. The Commissioner, in turn, has delegated areas of authority to the district directors in the regulations covering customs bonds, primarily contained in 19 CFR Part 113. Bond provisions also occur in 31 other parts of the customs regulations.

B. Customs Regulations: 1984 Revision

1. Revision Background

The customs bonds regulations were extensively revised in TD 84-213, October 19, 1984, 49 FR 41152, which was effective February 18, 1985. This revision was initiated in an advance notice of proposed rulemaking published May 26, 1981 (46 FR 28172), which proposed to consolidate the

---

[1] 19 U.S.C. 1623.

50 different types of customs bonds and 16 different types of riders attached to bonds, to modify the archaic bond language, to simplify transactions between Customs and the importing community, and to facilitate a computerized bond control system. A formal notice of proposed rulemaking, taking into account the response to the advance notice, was published March 15, 1983 (48 FR 11032). TD 84-213 revised not only 19 CFR Part 113 but the 31 other parts of the customs regulations containing bond requirements. The revision was preceded by 11 pages of explanation and comment. Corrections were issued (49 FR 44867, 50 FR 739).

2. Single Customs Bond Form

The principal change in the regulations was the establishment of a single customs bond form, Customs Form 301, attached to the regulations as Appendix B. This form permits a selection between two types of bonds: a single transaction bond and a continuous bond. Each person required by law, regulation, or specific instruction to post a bond to secure a customs transaction must, under 19 CFR 113.11, submit a bond on Form 301.

3. Regulations Incorporated as Bond Conditions

In order to make the new form a universal one, Form 301 sets up for designation by the signatory 12 alternative types of activity coverage, each of which is coded to the provision in the regulations which provides the conditions applicable to that coverage. These conditions, which are set forth in Subpart G of Part 113, in 19 CFR 113.62–113.73, and are incorporated by reference into the bond, are titled as follows:
- 113.62—Basic importation and entry bond conditions
- 113.63—Basic custodial bond conditions
- 113.64—International carrier bond conditions
- 113.65—Repayment of erroneous drawback payment bond conditions
- 113.66—Control of containers and instruments of international traffic bond conditions
- 113.67—Licensed public gauger bond conditions
- 113.68—Wool and fur products labeling acts and fiber products identification act bond conditions
- 113.69—Production of bills of lading bond conditions
- 113.70—Bond condition to indemnify United States for detention of copyrighted material
- 113.71—Bond condition to observe neutrality
- 113.72—Bond condition to pay court costs (condemned goods)
- 113.73—Foreign trade zone operator bond conditions

These conditions are applicable to either a single transaction bond or a continuous bond, except that a custodian of bonded merchandise must carry a continuous bond, and the person carrying on an activity covered by one of the conditions in 19 CFR 113.68–113.72 may carry only a single transaction bond. Also, if the importation and entry relates to merchandise subject to an exclusion order under 19 U.S.C. 1337 (see Chapter 17), the bond must be a single entry one.

The conditions in the regulations applicable to each type of activity consist of the agreements to which the obligors on the bond subscribe in executing the bond. For example, the conditions for the basic importation and entry bond specify nine agreements, including agreements to pay duties, taxes, and charges; to make or complete entry; to produce documents and evidence; to redeliver merchandise; and to rectify any noncompliance with provisions of admission. Consequently, the regulations are an integral part of the customs bond. If the district director believes that none of the conditions contained in Subpart G is applicable to a transaction to be secured, he is required by 19 CFR 113.14 to draft conditions which will cover the transaction and to submit them to Customs Headquarters for approval.

The integration of the regulations into the form made the form a part of the notices of proposed rulemaking, in contrast to an earlier customs position in CSD 79-217 that rulemaking provisions did not apply to the format of a customs bond since a bond is a contract and not a rule.

4. Bond Approval

The regulations in 19 CFR 113.11 delegate authority to the district director to approve every bond filed with him for transactions in his district. If the transactions will occur in more than one district, the bond may be filed with, and approved by, any district director. The district director determines whether the bond is in proper form and provides adequate security for the transactions. However, a bond covering repayment of an erroneous drawback payment is to be filed with the appropriate regional commissioner for approval.

19 CFR 113.12 provides that the district director may require the filing of an application in the form of a letter for approval of a bond covering a single transaction. The application will identify the value and nature of the merchandise involved. An application is not required when the proper bond in a sufficient amount is filed with the entry summary or with the entry when the entry summary is filed at the time of entry. A bond application, which may be in the form of a letter, must be submitted to the district director by a person wanting to secure multiple transactions through a continuous bond. The application is to contain information on the general character of the merchandise entered, the total amount of ordinary customs duties accruing on merchandise imported by the principal during the preceding calendar year, including any taxes, or if no imports were made during the preceding year, a statement of the duties and taxes estimated to accrue during the current year.

5. Amount of Bond

The minimum amount of a customs bond is $100, except when the law or a regulation expressly provides for a lesser amount. In determining whether the amount of a bond is sufficient, the district director or, in the case of erroneous drawback payments, the regional director, is advised to consider the guidelines set forth in 19 CFR 113.13(b). These guidelines direct consideration of the prior record of the principal in timely payment of charges and in complying with the customs demands for redelivery and other obligations, the value and nature of the merchandise involved in the transaction to be secured, and the degree and type of supervision that Customs will exercise over the transaction. The Customs Service stated that it intended to formulate specific guidelines to be used in conjunction with the foregoing considerations, 49 FR at 41154. Such specific guidelines for determining the amount of a bond were issued in a telex to the Field Service on January 4, 1985, establishing minimum normal bond amounts for the various bondable activities, with authority to the district director to increase the amounts in situations of greater risk.

The district directors and regional commissioners are required by 19 CFR 113.13(c) to review periodically each bond filed to determine whether the bond is adequate to protect the revenue and insure compliance with the law and regulations. If the bond is found inadequate, the principal is notified in writing and has 30 days thereafter to remedy the deficiency.

6. Bond Formalities

The bond must contain the names of the principal and sureties and their places of residence or, in the case of corporations, the principal place of business. The principal may list on the bond trade names and the names of unincorporated divisions of a corporate principal which do not have distinct legal status but which are authorized to use the bond in their own name. The bond also shall show the date it was actually executed, the amount of the bond stated in figures, and the signature of two witnesses in the case of a noncorporate principal or surety.

7. Riders

The regulations permit district directors to accept for filing bond riders which change the name (but not the identity) of a principal, change the address of a principal, or add or delete trade names and names of unincorporated divisions of a corporate principal (19 CFR 113.24).

II. PRINCIPALS AND SURETIES

Subpart D of 19 CFR Part 113 specifies the technical requirements concerning principals and sureties on bonds. Subpart D of the 1984 revision incorporates the body of the provisions with few changes of Subpart D of the prior regulations covering the same subject matter.

A common first provision, now in 19 CFR 113.31, is that individuals, partnerships, and corporations can be principals and sureties on bonds. However, the same person, partnership, or corporation cannot be both principal and surety on a bond. A person may be attorney in fact for both principal and surety, surety and attorney in fact for the principal, or principal and attorney in fact for the surety.

A. Principals

Where the principal of a bond is a partnership, the bond shall give the full names of all members of the partnership as well as the firm name of the partnership and shall be executed in the firm name, with the name of the member or attorney of the firm executing it appearing immediately below the name of the firm. By law, where one member of a partnership executes a bond, the bond is binding on all members of the partnership.

Where the principal of a bond is a corporation, the bond may be executed by an authorized officer of the corporation or by an attorney in fact. The corporate seal must be affixed immediately opposite the signature of the person executing the bond. If the bond is executed by an officer of the corporation, a power of attorney shall not be required if the person signing on behalf of the corporation is known to the district director or regional commissioner to be the president, vice-president, treasurer, or secretary of the corporation. The officer's signature shall be *prima facie* evidence of that officer's authority to bind the corporation. These provisions in 19 CFR 113.33 change the prior provisions which required a corporate power of attorney for the officer signing or a Certificate as to Corporate Principal. When a power of attorney is required, it is to conform to the requirements of Subpart C of 19 CFR Part 141, the Entry of Merchandise regulations.

Where a bond is executed by an attorney in fact, on behalf of a corporate principal, a power of attorney shall be attached (if one is not already on file), executed under the corporate seal by an officer of the corporation whose authority to execute such a power of attorney is documented or known.

The revised regulations in 19 CFR 113.34 permit a bond with a co-principal to be used by a person having a distinct legal status joining another person with the same distinct legal status (*i.e.,* individual, partnership, corporation).

B. Sureties

A surety may be an individual, partnership, or corporation. Any surety may grant a power of attorney to sign as surety on customs bonds.

1. Individual Sureties

If the sureties are individuals, 19 CFR 113.25 provides that there shall be two on each bond unless the district director is satisfied that approval of one surety will be sufficient for the protection of the government. Each individual surety must have unencumbered property in the customs district equal to the amount of any bond executed by him. If a single surety is accepted, he must qualify in an amount equal to twice the amount of the bond. To be accepted as a surety, an individual shall (1) take an oath on Customs Form 3579, setting forth (a) the amount of his assets over and above all his debts and liabilities and such exemptions as may be allowed by law, and (b) a general description and location of one or more pieces of real property owned by him within the customs district and the value thereof over and above all encumbrances; and (2) produce such evidence of solvency and financial responsibility as the district director may require.

An individual surety will be required to prove his continued solvency and financial responsibility as often as the district director deems it advisable, and at least once every six months. The district director may refer the question of the financial responsibility of an individual surety to the special agent-in-charge for investigation.

2. Partners as Sureties

A member of a partnership may not be accepted as a surety on a bond executed by the partnership as principal. However, a partner may be an individual surety for a fellow partner on a bond covering the latter's individual transaction, if the ensuring partner is qualified to be an individual surety (19 CFR 113.36).

3. Corporate Sureties

Corporations authorized to act as sureties on federal bonds are listed annually, on or about June 30, in Treasury Department Circular 570, prepared by the Fiscal Service of that Department. This list, showing the maximum amount for which each corporation may be accepted as surety, is provided by the Secretary of the Treasury to all district directors and published in the *Federal Register*. Unless otherwise directed by the Commissioner of Customs, no corporation shall be accepted as surety on a bond if not named in the current Circular, and no bond shall be for a greater amount than the respective limit stated in the Circular, unless the excess is protected as prescribed in the Fiscal Service regulations, 31 CFR 223.11.

However, the revised regulations on corporate sureties, 19 CFR 113.37–113.39, state definitively for the first time that a district director may reject a corporate surety included in Circular 570 if that surety without just cause is significantly delinquent, and he may seek internal advice on the question of rejection. Likewise, a regional commissioner, when he deems it warranted, may instruct district directors not to accept bonds from a corporate surety which is significantly delinquent without just cause. The Customs Service provides the legal arguments supporting the authority to reject as corporate sureties companies listed in Circular 570 in its explanation of the revised regulations, 49 FR at 41156, October 19, 1984.

A bond executed by a corporate surety shall be signed by an authorized officer or attorney of the corporation and a corporate seal shall be placed opposite the signature of the person executing the bond. Two or more corporations may act as surety on the same obligation providing the obligation does not exceed in amount the limitations of their aggregate qualifying power as fixed and determined by the Secretary of the Treasury. 19 CFR 113.37(f) sets forth the text of the joint agreement that must be made when two or more corporations jointly act as sureties on the same obligation.

4. Attorneys in Fact

Corporations may authorize attorneys in fact to act in their stead in executing bonds as surety. The power of attorney shall be executed on Customs Form 5297 and contain the following information:

(1) Corporate surety name and number;

(2) Name and address of agent or attorney, and his social security number;

(3) District(s) in which the agent or attorney is authorized to act;

(4) Date of execution of the power of attorney;

(5) Seal of the corporate surety; and

(6) Attestation of any two principal officers of the corporation.

The corporate surety power of attorney on Customs Form 5297 is to be filed at the district office unless the district director permits its filing at a port office within the district, in which case it is to be submitted in duplicate. The port director then sends the original to the district office. The district office periodically issues to all ports within the district computer printouts reflecting all valid corporate powers of attorney for use in the district.

C. Acceptance of Deposit in Lieu of Sureties

In any case where a bond is required, the district director is authorized to accept, in lieu of sureties on any bond, deposits of U.S. money, U.S. bonds (except savings bonds), U.S. certificates of indebtedness, Treasury notes, or Treasury bills in an amount equal to the amount of the bond. If cash is deposited in lieu of sureties on the bond, the district director is authorized to apply the cash in whole or in part to the satisfaction of any damages, demands, or deficiencies arising by reason of a default under the bond. Where U.S. Government obligations are deposited in lieu of a surety on the bond, the obligor of the bond must simultaneously deliver to the district director an executed power of attorney and agreement authorizing the district director in case of any default in the performance of any of the conditions of the bond to sell the government obligations and apply the proceeds in whole or in part to the satisfaction of any demands, damages, or deficiencies arising by reason of such default. The form of the power of attorney and agreement when the obligor is a corporation is set forth in 19 CFR 113.40(b). Where the obligor is an individual or partnership, this form can be used with appropriate modifications.

III. BOND PROCEDURES AND ENFORCEMENT

A. Bonds or Stipulations to Produce Required Documents

If an entry of merchandise is made prior to the production of a required document, the importer must indicate in the "Missing Documents" box (Box 16) on Customs Form 7501 the missing document, whether he gives a bond or stipulates to produce the document (19 CFR 113.41). Except when another period is fixed by law or regulations, when a bond is given for the production of any document, that document must, under TD 85-167, October 3, 1985, 50 FR 40361, be delivered to the district director within 120 days, unless an extension of time is granted. Upon written application of the importer, an extension may be given for a further period of up to two months. Any such extension shall not be allowed by the district director for a period of more than two months from the date of expiration of the 120-day period. The district director may not consider any application for an extension of the bond period if the application is received later than two months after the expiration of the period of the bond.

The requirements are not quite so rigid in the case of a required free-entry or reduced-duty document. If such a document is produced prior to liquidation of the entry, or within the period during which a valid reliquidation may be completed, it will be accepted and the bond charge for the production of the document canceled, provided the failure to file was not due to willful negligence or fraudulent intent. When a charge for the production of a missing document is made against a continuous bond, the charge shall be in the amount that would have been taken had the transaction been covered by a single entry bond.

B. Alternative Actions for Breach of Conditions

Where the conditions of a bond are not met, 19 CFR Part 172 provides that the importer may be served with a written notice of liquidated damages incurred under the provisions of the bond, together with a demand for payment. The surety on the bond is also notified in writing at the same time. Except in the case of a bond given for the production of free-entry or reduced-duty documents, unless liability under a bond is satisfied by the principal or the surety within 90 days, the matter is referred to the U.S. attorney for prosecution, except when a timely application for relief has been made by the importer or the surety.

A variety of other options are available to Customs under Subpart F of the bond regulations. The Commissioner of Customs may authorize the cancellation of any bond or any charge against such a bond in the event of a breach of any conditions, upon payment of such lesser amount or penalty, or upon such other terms and conditions as he may deem sufficient. The commissioner or the district director may waive a customs requirement supported by a bond, or relief may be granted upon petition by the principal or the surety.

C. Waiver of Customs Requirements

Three forms of waiver of a customs requirement supported by a bond may be made by the Commissioner of Customs under 19 CFR 113.53:

(1) Unconditional, in which case the importer is relieved from the payment of liquidated damages;

(2) Conditioned upon prior settlement of the bond obligation by payment of liquidated damages; or

(3) Conditioned upon such other terms and conditions as the commissioner may deem sufficient.

In cases where authorized, the district director may also waive a customs requirement supported by a bond but in those cases the waiver shall be unconditional.

D. Petition for Relief From Liquidated Damages

An importer or surety may file a petition for relief from liquidated damages which have been incurred. The requirements for the petition procedure are set forth in 19 CFR Part 172. A petition for relief is filed with the district director for the district in which the liability for liquidated damages was incurred. It is filed in triplicate within 60 days from the date of the notice of liability for liquidated damages. A district director may in his discretion grant an extension of time for the filing of a petition. When the claim for liquidated damages is $100,000 or less, a district director may cancel the claim on such terms and conditions as he deems appropriate. If it is determined that the act or omission forming the basis for a claim for liquidated damages did not in fact occur, the claim is canceled by the district director. In this situation if the liquidated damages have already been paid they shall be refunded by the regional commissioner. Approval by the commissioner is required in all doubtful cases. The regulations contain special authorizations to district directors to act on such petitions in specified types of cases.

If a petition for relief is not timely filed or if a mitigated amount is not promptly paid as required, the matter may be referred, after required collection action, to the U.S. Attorney. Once that happens, the district director no longer has authority to consider the matter further.

If a claim for liquidated damages has been mitigated to a specified amount or canceled on condition that a stated amount shall be paid, any such amount must be remitted within 60 days to the district director. However, if a supplemental petition is filed within the 60-day period, or if arrangements satisfactory to the district director for delayed payment or payment by installments are made, the time may be extended.

A supplemental petition may be filed if the importer or surety is not satisfied with a decision of the district director or the Commissioner of Customs. Such a supplemental petition must be filed within 60 days from the date of notice to the petitioner of the decision on the original petition, or within such other time as is prescribed in the decision. In cases where he has authority, the district director may grant additional relief if he believes it is warranted. The district director shall transmit the supplemental petition to the regional commissioner (or to the Commissioner of Customs if the amount of liability is $50,000 to $100,000) for consideration if the petitioner specifically requests that he do so, if the district director believes no relief is warranted, or if the petitioner is not satisfied with the additional relief granted by the district director. A supplemental petition appealing a decision to the Commissioner of Customs should be filed with the district director who initiated the case for transmittal to the commissioner.

E. Cancellation of Export Bonds

There are special provisions in 19 CFR 113.55 covering the cancellation of bonds to assure the exportation of merchandise. Exportation from the United States has been defined as "a severance of goods from the mass of things belonging to this country with the intention of uniting them to the mass of things belonging to some foreign country."[2] Thus, if merchandise is shipped abroad with the intention of returning it to the United States with a design to circumvent the tariff laws or otherwise secure a benefit accruing to imported merchandise, it is not an exportation.

A bond to assure the exportation of merchandise may be canceled upon exportation. Exportation must be documented by the listing of the merchandise on the outward manifest or the outward bill of lading and on the inspector's certificate of lading, plus there must be a record of clearance of the vessel or departure of the vehicle, and a foreign landing certificate must be produced if required by the district director. A bond may also be canceled upon payment of liquidated damages, if exportation or destruction of articles admitted temporarily free of duty under bond pursuant to Schedule 8, Part 5C, Tariff Schedules of the United States, is not timely. Bonds to insure the exportation of a vessel, vehicle, or aircraft are considered to have been complied with upon the production of the documents listed above.

F. Foreign Landing Certificate

When a foreign landing certificate is required, it must be produced within six months of the date of exportation. It should be signed by a revenue officer of the foreign country to which the merchandise is exported unless that country has no customs administration, in which case it must be signed by the consignee or the vessel's agent at the place of landing (19 CFR 113.55(c)).

A landing certificate is required in every case to establish the exportation of narcotic drugs or, with certain exceptions, of stores or machinery for

---

[2]19 CFR 113.55(a), 101.1(k).

vessels. A district director may require a landing certificate in any case involving the exportation of merchandise when he deems it necessary for the protection of the revenue. An application may be made to the commissioner through the district director for a waiver of the requirement of the landing certificate. The application must be accompanied by such proof of exportation and landing abroad as is available. In the case of articles for which ordinary customs duty estimated at the time of entry did not exceed $10 and which are exported within the period of the bond, the bond may be cancelled upon production of evidence of exportation satisfactory to the district director.

In order to protect U.S. revenue and assist Mexico in the enforcement of its customs laws, a foreign landing certificate was required for each exportation to Mexico of certain commodities exceeding $250 in value specified in TD 79-1.

IV. CARNETS IN PLACE OF CUSTOMS ENTRY DOCUMENTS AND AS CUSTOMS BONDS

A. Carnet Issuance and Guarantee

Pursuant to international conventions to which the United States is a party, the use of carnets is authorized under customs regulations.[3] A carnet is an international customs document, backed by an internationally valid guarantee, that serves simultaneously as a customs entry document and as a customs bond.

Issuing associations and guaranteeing associations must be approved by the commissioner. An issuing association is one that issues the documents for use in the customs territory of the United States, and a guaranteeing association is one that guarantees the payment of obligations under carnets covering merchandise entering the customs territory of the United States. The Commissioner of Customs publishes in the *Federal Register* notices of the approval of issuing and guaranteeing associations.

The authority to issue or guarantee carnets may be suspended or revoked for cause by the commissioner. An approved guaranteeing association may be relieved of future obligations by notifying the commissioner in writing not less than six months in advance of a specified termination date.

B. Types of Carnets and Purposes to Which They Can be Put

The following are the types of carnets and the uses for which they are acceptable:[4]

---

[3] 19 CFR Part 114.

[4] Details as to the scope of coverage of the various types of carnets are in the applicable conventions published in Vol. 20 of the *United States Treaties and Other International Agreements* (TIAS): the Customs Convention on the ATA Carnet for the Temporary Admission of Goods (TIAS 6631); the Customs Convention on the ECS Carnet for Commercial Samples (TIAS 6632), now discontinued; and the 1959 Customs Convention on the International Transport of Goods Under Cover of TIR Carnets (TIAS 6633). The ECS carnet was eliminated in favor of the ATA carnet which has broader coverage. In a General Notice published August 25, 1977, 43 FR 42851, the Customs Service announced the

1. ATA Carnets[5]

The ATA ("Admission Temporaire-Temporary Admission") carnet is used for the temporary duty-free entry of professional equipment, commercial samples, and advertising material. The use of the ATA carnet allows the traveler or businessman to make customs arrangements in advance and to use a single document for goods which will pass through several different countries. ATA carnets are valid for a period of one year. In the United States the U.S. Council of the International Chamber of Commerce has been designated by the Customs Service as the United States issuing and guaranteeing organization for ATA carnets.

2. TIR Carnets[6]

TIR ("Transport International Routier-International Road Transport") carnets authorize road vehicles, containers, and their contents to transit one or more frontiers without customs inspection at intermediate points and with a minimum of other formalities. Road vehicles and containers transit the country or move from port of entry to final destination with their contents under customs seal. Inspection is accomplished at the final destination. TIR carnets are valid until the end of the transit operation. The Equipment Interchange Association has been designated by the Customs Service as the issuing and guaranteeing association for TIR carnets in the United States.

A guaranteeing association is not liable under a TIR carnet until the carnet is "taken on charge" by Customs, i.e., when it is accepted as a transportation entry and the shipment covered thereby is receipted for by the bonded carrier.

The Customs Service proposed on January 11, 1985, 50 FR 1546, to amend its regulations pertaining to the limits of liability of guaranteeing associations under the 1975 TIR Convention, to which the United States acceded in 1981,[7] in conformity with the limitations provided in that Convention. Specifically, the proposal would amend 19 CFR 18.8 on the liability of bonded carriers to limit the liability of a domestic guaranteeing association to $50,000 per TIR carnet for duties, taxes, and sums collected in lieu thereof. The proposal would also amend 19 CFR 114.23(a) of the regulations on carnets to prohibit extension of an ATA carnet beyond one year, and to make editorial changes in 19 CFR Part 114.

---

withdrawal May 11, 1977, of the United States, in accordance with the recommendation of the Customs Cooperation Council in Brussels, from the ECS Convention and the nonacceptance of ECS carnets issued after August 10, 1977.

The 1959 Customs Convention on TIR Carnets has been superseded by the Customs Convention on the International Transport of Goods under Cover of TIR Carnets done at Geneva November 14, 1975 (TIAS). The text of this Convention, with eight Annexes, is published in 16 Cust. Bull. 130–208 (1982), under TD 82-50 announcing the accession of the United States on September 18, 1981, effective March 18, 1982.

[5]TD 82-116, 47 FR 27260, June 24, 1982, defining carnets and amending the carnets regulations.

[6]Ibid.

[7]See supra note 4, last paragraph.

The Customs Service further proposed a new Part 115 to its regulations on certification of cargo containers and road vehicles pursuant to international conventions, 50 FR 20227, May 15, 1985.

C. Special Requirements

The ATA carnets may have a period of validity not exceeding one year from the date of issue. However, a TIR carnet may be accepted without limitation as to time, provided that it is "taken on charge" within the period of validity shown on its front cover. The coverage of an ATA carnet is limited to the list of goods initially enumerated thereon and on any continuation sheet. Items may not be added.

An ATA carnet is discharged unconditionally by the district director when he is satisfied that all merchandise covered by it has been reexported or destroyed. A TIR carnet is discharged unconditionally when all merchandise covered by it has been properly entered, placed in general order, or exported under customs supervision. When a district director has discharged a carnet unconditionally, no claim may be brought against the guaranteeing association for payment unless it can be established that the discharge was obtained fraudulently or improperly or, in the case of an ATA carnet, that there has been a breach of the conditions of temporary importation.

Carnets are not acceptable for importations by mail. Merchandise not entitled to temporary importation under bond shall not be imported under an ATA carnet. Moreover, merchandise not entitled to transportation in bond shall not be transported under a TIR carnet. Liquidated damages assessed against carnets may be canceled by the district director in the same manner as cancellation of liquidated damages assessed under customs bond where it appears that the liability did not in fact accrue.

5

Liquidation, Protests, and Petitions

I. LIQUIDATION

Liquidation is the culmination of a series of actions that began with the entry of the imported goods. At this point, Customs, having determined the proper dutiable value of the goods and the applicable rate of duty, ascertains the amount of duty due. If this amount is the same as the amount deposited at the time of entry, the entry is endorsed "liquidated as entered." In most cases, this closes the transaction. The customs regulations governing liquidation are in 19 CFR Part 159.

A. Difference Between Liquidated Duties and Estimated Duties

If the liquidated duty is greater than that which was deposited at the time of entry, the importer is billed for the difference. If it is less, the importer is given a refund in the amount of the difference. If, however, the net difference is less than $10.00[1] on any entry (other than an informal, mail, or baggage entry), the difference will be disregarded and the entry endorsed "as entered." In the case of an informal, mail, or baggage entry, the amount of duties computed by a customs officer when the entry is prepared by or filed with him will be considered the liquidated assessment.

When reliquidation of an entry is made at the importer's request, such as reliquidation following the allowance of a protest under Section 514 of the Tariff Act of 1930 as amended[2] or a request for correction under Section 520 of the Tariff Act of 1930 as amended,[3] any refund determined to be due will be refunded even if less than $10.00. Any refund or increase determined to be due as the result of the reliquidation of an entry in accordance with a court decision and judgment order will be refunded or collected even if the amount is less than $10.00.

---

[1] 19 U.S.C. 1321(a).
[2] 19 U.S.C. 1514.
[3] 19 U.S.C. 1520.

B. Notice and Date of Liquidation; Duty Payment

The bulletin notice of liquidation constitutes the official notice to the importer of liquidation of formal entries. The bulletin notice is posted in a conspicuous place in the customhouse in the port of entry where the entry was filed. The placing of a bulletin notice on a table, and subsequently on an open shelf, in a public room in the customhouse was held to be posting in a conspicuous place and proper notice in *Frederick Wholesale Corp.* v. *United States,* 754 F.2d 349 (Fed. Cir. 1985) 6 ITRD 1801. The date of the bulletin notice of liquidation is the date of liquidation of the entry. This date is shown on the entry together with the notation "liquidated."

It is incumbent upon the importer or his agent to check the bulletin notice to determine if his entry has been liquidated. Liquidated entries are available for review upon request. Customs seeks to provide importers or their agents with a "Courtesy Notice" for dutiable consumption entries, and various other entries for which a bulletin notice of liquidation is required, which are scheduled to be liquidated or deemed liquidated by operation of law. This is an informal notice and not decisive. (See 19 CFR 159.9(d).)

The imposition of duties on liquidation additional to the estimated duties paid on entry must necessarily be retroactive and is not violative of due process because of the statutory notice of the possibility of further duties. *Peugeot Motors of America, Inc.* v. *United States,* 8 CIT ____ , 595 F. Supp. 1154 (1984) 6 ITRD 1277.

The due date for the payment of the duties determined to be due upon liquidation or reliquidation was specifically prescribed by statute for the first time by Section 210(a) of the Trade and Tariff Act of 1984, Public Law 98-573. Section 210(a) amended 19 U.S.C. 1505 to add the provision that the determined duties are due 15 days after the date of liquidation or reliquidation, and that unless payment is received by Customs within 30 days after that date the duties shall be considered delinquent and bear interest from the 15th day after liquidation or reliquidation at a rate determined by the Secretary of the Treasury. Prior to the provision in Section 210(a), which was effective 30 days after enactment, liquidated duties were not due, under court decisions discussed in section II.A *infra,* until expiration of the statute of limitations on the filing of a civil action contesting the denial of a liquidation protest, or until the filing of the action.

Normally, the effective date of liquidation for informal, mail, and baggage entries is:

(1) The date of payment by the importer of duties due on the entry;

(2) The date of release by Customs or the postmaster when the merchandise is released under such an entry free of duty; or

(3) The date a free entry is accepted for articles released under a special permit for immediate delivery.

Where duties are paid in accordance with (1) above, notice of liquidation is furnished by a suitable printed statement appearing on the receipt issued for duties collected. No other notice of liquidation will be given, but notice of reliquidation will be given on a bulletin notice of liquidation. Notice of liquidation is furnished by release of the merchandise under a free entry in accordance with (2) above or by acceptance of the free entry in accordance with (3) above after release under a special permit for immediate delivery. No further notice will be given.

C. Time Limitation on Liquidations

For entries or withdrawals for consumption made on or after April 1, 1979, the Customs Procedural Reform and Simplification Act of 1978 placed a time limit of one year on customs liquidations generally.[4] The one year runs (1) from the date of entry of the merchandise, or (2) from the date of final withdrawal of all unliquidated merchandise covered by a warehouse entry. If liquidation has not occurred within this year the entry shall be deemed liquidated at the rate of duty, value, quantity, and amount of duties asserted by the importer at the time of filing an entry summary for consumption in proper form, with estimated duties attached, or a withdrawal for consumption in proper form, with estimated duties attached. Notice of liquidation shall be given on the bulletin notice of liquidation. Customs will endeavor to provide a courtesy notice of liquidation.

The district director may, however, extend the one-year period for another year, by giving notice of the suspension of the time limit to the importer, in the following three situations: (1) information needed for proper appraisement or classification is not available to the appropriate Customs officer, (2) suspension is required by statute or court order, or (3) the importer requests such extension and shows good cause therefor. Good cause may be the need for more time to present pertinent information or to await the pendency of a similar question before Customs. Additional one-year extensions may be granted at the instance of the district director or of the importer for a total maximum period of three years. If liquidation has not occurred within four years from the initial dates of the one-year period, an entry shall be deemed liquidated at the rate of duty, value, quantity, and amount of duty asserted by the importer at the time of filing the appropriate entry summary, with estimated duties attached, unless liquidation continues to be suspended by statute or court order. When such a suspension is removed the entry must be liquidated within 90 days.

The time restrictions in 19 U.S.C. 1504 were held not to prevent the suspension of liquidation required under the countervailing duty law, 19 U.S.C. 1303, under consideration by the court. *Ambassador Division of Florsheim Shoe Co.* v. *United States,* 748 F.2d 1560 (Fed. Cir. 1984) 6 ITRD 1422.

D. Net Weights and Tares

In the liquidation of an entry of goods dutiable on the basis of net weight, or upon a value dependent upon net weight, an allowance is made for actual

---

[4] 19 U.S.C. 1504. Implementing regulations are in 19 CFR 159.11 and 159.12. The time limit does not apply to entries made prior to the Act. *F. W. Myers & Co., Inc.* v. *United States,* 9 CIT _____ , 607 F. Supp. 1470 (1985) 6 ITRD 1979.

or schedule tare. 19 CFR 159.22 contains a list of schedule tares that, from experience, have proved to be the average for certain classes of goods. For instance, the tare for apple boxes is eight pounds a box with no additional allowance for paper wrappers. However, for fresh tomatoes, a tare of four ounces per 100 paper wrappers is allowed. Actual tare may be determined on the basis of tests when the tares of the package in a shipment are reasonably uniform. When the actual net weight or tare cannot be reasonably determined and no schedule tare is applicable, liquidation may be made on the basis of the invoice net weight or tare.

The actual tare will be determined in the following circumstances:

(1) If the importer is not satisfied with the invoice tare or with the schedule tare;

(2) If the district director believes that the invoice or schedule tare does not correctly represent the tare of the merchandise; or

(3) If the weigher has reason to believe that the invoice or schedule tare is greater than the real tare.

E. Conversion of Currency

In many instances imported goods are bought and paid for in foreign currency. This means that in liquidating an entry of a transaction in foreign currency, the currency must be converted to U.S. dollars. The conversion is made on the basis of the rate in effect on the date of the exportation of the goods, not the date of entry or the date of liquidation. This takes on added importance in periods of fluctuating exchange rates. The conversion is based on a rate (if any) proclaimed by the Secretary, the certified quarterly rate, or the certified daily rate.[5] These latter rates are certified to the Treasury by the Federal Reserve Bank of New York and are regularly published in the *Customs Bulletin.*

Quarterly rates are certified for the major trading foreign countries (listed at 19 CFR 159.34). These rates are published in the *Customs Bulletin* for the quarter beginning January 1, and for each quarter thereafter. The rates used for quarterly certification are those first certified by the Federal Reserve Bank of New York for such foreign currency for a day in that quarter.

A proclaimed rate, if any, or the certified quarterly rate is used for customs purposes for any day within the quarter except in the following cases:

(1) If a rate has been proclaimed by the Secretary of the Treasury that does not vary by 5 percent or more from the appropriate certified daily rate, notice of such variance will be published in the *Customs Bulletin* and the proclaimed rate will be used in connection with goods exported on that date.

(2) If the certified daily rate for the date of exportation varies by 5 percent or more from the certified quarterly rate, notice of such variance

---

[5] The use of these rates for duty purposes is mandated by 31 U.S.C. 5151, formerly 31 U.S.C. 372. The Secretary of the Treasury has not proclaimed a rate based on the value of foreign coins since January 1, 1957.

and the rate or rates certified for such day will be published in the *Customs Bulletin.* Such certified daily rate will be used in connection with goods exported on that date. The daily buying rate of foreign currency determined by the Federal Reserve Bank of New York and certified to the Secretary of the Treasury will be used for the conversion of foreign currency whenever a proclaimed rate or certified quarterly rate is not applicable.

The daily rate may be ascertained by calling the Customs Information Exchange public recording on (212) 466-5992.

II. PROTESTS AND PETITIONS

A. Protests

The importer may file a protest (Customs Form 19; revised 1984) under Section 514 of the Tariff Act of 1930 if he does not agree with the liquidation of his entry.[6] The protest must be in writing and must be filed within 90 days after the date of notice of liquidation at the port where the entry was made.[7] The importer may request further review of the protest, other than that provided by the district director at the port of entry, by filing a request at the time of filing the protest on the same Customs Form 19 used for filing the protest or on a separate Customs Form 19.

If the district director is satisfied that the claim is valid, he will allow the protest. If he decides that the protest should be denied in whole or in part, and a request for further review has been filed, he must forward the protest for further review to either the regional commissioner of customs in which the district lies or to the Commissioner of Customs, depending upon the issues involved.

The protest must be allowed or denied in whole or in part within two years from the date it was filed, unless a request for accelerated disposition of the protest is filed by the importer. Such a request may be filed at any time after 90 days from the filing of the protest. The district director must then review the protest within 30 days of the filing of the request. If he fails to do so, the protest is deemed denied. If the protest is allowed, a refund of excess duties is given to the importer, with interest allowed by Section 210 of Public Law 98-573. If it is denied, notice of such action is provided to the importer, except in cases in which accelerated disposition has been requested and action has not been taken within 30 days.

Any person whose protest has been denied, in whole or in part, may contest the denial by filing a civil action in the Court of International Trade within 180 days after (a) the date of mailing of notice of denial or (b) the

---

[6]19 CFR Part 174 Protests.

[7]The Customs Court asserted and the CCPA agreed that a valid protest may take the informal character of a letter to Customs sufficiently presenting the objection of the protesting party so that Customs may act on it. *American Export Lines, Inc.* v. *United States,* 85 Cust. Ct. 20, CD 4864, 496 F. Supp. 1320 (1980) 2 ITRD 1421; *rev'd on other grounds, Farrell Lines, Inc.* v. *United States,* 69 CCPA 1, 657 F.2d 1214 (1981) 2 ITRD 1705. However, the CCPA in that opinion and on rehearing treated the letter in question as tolling the 90-day statute of limitations on filing a protest after liquidation in view of the administrative history and the statutory purpose in 19 U.S.C. 1466 to allow petitions for remission of duties on repair abroad of American vessels. *Farrell Lines, Inc.* v. *United States,* 69 CCPA 7, 667 F.2d 1017 (1982) 3 ITRD 1569, Markey and Rich dissenting.

date a protest, for which accelerated disposition was requested, is deemed to have been denied. The presumption of the mailing and delivery of a notice may be rebutted by proof of nonreceipt. *F. W. Myers & Co.* v. *United States*, 6 CIT ____ , 574 F. Supp. 1064 (1983) 5 ITRD 1465. The court will hear the case and render a decision. If adverse to the importer, he may appeal to the Court of Appeals for the Federal Circuit. The CIT will not take jurisdiction of a protest against reliquidation based on a claim not asserted in the protest of the original liquidation. *Audiovox Corp.* v. *United States*, 8 CIT ____ , 598 F. Supp. 387 (1984) 6 ITRD 1399. See also *Computime, Inc.* v. *United States*, CAFC No. 85-1050, September 11, 1985, 7 ITRD 1129.

Prior to Section 210 of Public Law 98-573 the increased duties determined to be due upon the denial of a protest were not required by law to be paid until the filing with the Court of International Trade of a civil action contesting the denial under 28 U.S.C. 1581(a) or until the expiration of the 180-day statute of limitations on the filing of such a civil action under 28 U.S.C. 2636. This was the holding of the Court of Customs and Patent Appeals in *United States* v. *Heraeus-Amersil, Inc.*, 69 CCPA 86, 671 F.2d 1356 (1982) 3 ITRD 1465, *aff'g Heraeus-Amersil* v. *United States*, 1 CIT 249, 515 F. Supp. 770 (1981) 2 ITRD 1503. In view of this holding both courts determined that the Customs Service could not penalize the protesting importer as delinquent under 19 CFR 142.13(b) for failure to pay the increased duties on receipt of the bill.

As a result of the *Heraeus-Amersil* decision the Customs Service in 1983 amended its regulations on financial and accounting procedures, 19 CFR Part 24, Section 24.3(e), to provide that supplemental duties shall be due "upon the expiration of the protest period when no protest is filed, or 180 days after the denial of the protest."[8] These regulations are superseded by Section 210 of Public Law 98-573.

B. Petitions

A "domestic interested party," as defined in Section 516 of the Tariff Act of 1930, as amended, may file a petition under that Section if he believes that the appraised value is too low, the classification is not correct, or the proper rate of duty is not being assessed upon any imported article of a class or kind manufactured, produced, or sold by him.[9] The petition is to be submitted to the Commissioner of Customs. Notice is then published in the *Federal Register* setting forth the filing of the petition, identifying the merchandise and its present and claimed appraised value or classification or rate of duty, and inviting written comment within a stated time.

If it is found that the appraised value is too low, or that the classification of the article or rate of duty assessed thereon is not correct, the commissioner will determine the proper appraised value or classification or rate of duty, notify the petitioner of his determination, and publish the proper value, classification, or rate of duty in the *Federal Register* and the

---

[8] 48 FR 1186, January 11, 1983. See Chapter 31 for court jurisdiction and procedure.
[9] 19 U.S.C. 1516; 19 CFR Part 175.

Customs Bulletin. All such merchandise entered or withdrawn from warehouse more than 30 days after the date such notice to the petitioner is published in the *Customs Bulletin* will be appraised or classified in accordance with the published decision. If the appraised value, classification, or rate of duty is found to be correct, the commissioner will so notify the petitioner, but the decision will not be published. The petitioner, if dissatisfied with the decision, may file with the commissioner not later than 30 days after the date of the decision a notice that he desires to contest in the Court of International Trade the appraised value of, classification of, or rate of duty assessed upon the imported article.

This notice of contest and the decision of the Commissioner of Customs are then published in the *Federal Register* and the *Customs Bulletin.* Thereafter the Commissioner furnishes the petitioner with information as to entries and consignees of the merchandise at the ports designated by the petitioner in his notice of contest.

An American manufacturer's petition under Section 516 can reach only merchandise which is entered for consumption or withdrawn from warehouse after the judgment of the court on the petition. *Timken Company* v. *Regan,* 4 CIT 174, 552 F. Supp. 47 (1982) 4 ITRD 1241.

A petition under Section 516 is not the exclusive means by which American manufacturers may seek a change in a customs position. A trade association of such manufacturers may informally seek an interpretative ruling on the classification of merchandise which results in a change of classification. *Way Distributors, Inc.* v. *United States,* 68 CCPA 57, 653 F.2d 467 (1981) 2 ITRD 1689. See Chapter 8, section III.

C. Administrative Review

The government also has several avenues of recourse to reliquidate an entry. Customs, under Section 501 of the Tariff Act,[10] may reliquidate on its own initiative a liquidation or reliquidation to correct errors in appraisement, classification, or any other element entering into the liquidation or reliquidation, including errors based on misconstruction of applicable law. The action must be taken within 90 days from the date notice of the original liquidation is given to the importer. A voluntary reliquidation may be made even though a protest has been filed, and whether the error is discovered by Customs or is brought to its attention by an interested party. Notice of a voluntary reliquidation must be given to the importer in the same manner as the notice of the original liquidation.

Under Section 520(c)(1) of the Tariff Act of 1930,[11] Customs, upon timely application, may correct a clerical error, mistake of fact, or other inadvertence, in a customs transaction. The action can be taken despite the fact that a valid protest was not filed. The correction may be made only if the clerical error, mistake of fact, or other inadvertence (1) does not amount to an error in the law; (2) is adverse to the importer; and (3) is manifest

---

[10] 19 U.S.C. 1501.
[11] 19 U.S.C. 1520(c)(1); 19 CFR Part 173.

from the record or established by documentary evidence. A clerical error, mistake of fact, or other inadvertence must be brought to the attention of Customs within one year after the date of liquidation or exaction.

Section 520(c)(1) provides a remedy only for mistake or inadvertence occurring *in* an entry, liquidation, or other customs transaction. Thus the error made by the importer in failing to make an entry for imported sugar before its duty-free status ended was held not remedial under Section 520(c)(1), since there was no error in the dutiable entry actually made. *Godchaux-Henderson Sugar Co., Inc.* v. *United States,* 85 Cust. Ct. 68, CD 4874, 496 F. Supp. 1326 (1980) 2 ITRD 1461.

Finally, under Section 521 of the Tariff Act of 1930[12] Customs may review any entry in which fraud is suspected. If there is probable cause to believe there is fraud, Customs may reliquidate the entry within two years, exclusive of the time during which a protest is pending, after the date of liquidation or last liquidation. Otherwise the decision is final and conclusive upon all persons, including the United States and any officer thereof.

Section 521 provides the authority to reliquidate entries upon a finding of probable cause to believe the entries fraudulent in order to assess the correct duties. The statute is independent of the authority of the Customs Service to assess a monetary penalty claim under Section 592 of the Tariff Act of 1930, as amended. In litigation on a denied protest against a Section 521 reliquidation, no presumption of correctness attaches to the decision of the customs official, and the burden of proving fraud is on the government. *A.N. Deringer, Inc.* v. *United States,* 59 Cust. Ct. 148, CD 3101, 272 F. Supp. 987 (1967). In holding that the inadvertent reference by Customs to Section 520(c)(1) in place of Section 521 in a reliquidation was harmless error, the CIT noted that estoppel may not be invoked against the government in cases involving the collection or refund of duties. *American Motorists Insurance Co.* v. *United States,* 5 CIT 33 (1983) 4 ITRD 1711.

An importer must protest an adverse administrative ruling, given in response to a request for internal advice, on the validity of notices of redelivery in order to obtain review of the redelivery notices in the Court of International Trade. *United States* v. *Uniroyal, Inc.,* 69 CCPA 179, 687 F.2d 467 (1982) 3 ITRD 2265. The CCPA held that the CIT had no general jurisdiction to review completed transactions which could have been protested under 19 U.S.C. 1514(a) and reviewed under 28 U.S.C. 1581(a).

It should be noted here that the United States is one of the few countries that provides a broad spectrum of administrative and judicial reviews of customs decisions. In many countries it is costly and often futile to protest customs decisions, although this is not to imply that it is always the reverse in the United States.

---

[12] 19 U.S.C. 1521.

6

Customs Brokers

I. THE LICENSING OF CUSTOMS BROKERS

A. The Governing Law

Since the Act of June 10, 1910, the conduct of customs brokerage has required a license from the Secretary of the Treasury. Section 641 of the Tariff Act of 1930 (19 U.S.C. 1641), as then enacted, authorized the Secretary of the Treasury to prescribe regulations for the licensing of "customhouse brokers" and provided formal procedures for the revocation or suspension of their licenses, with judicial review of any revocation or suspension.

The Trade and Tariff Act of 1984,[1] by Section 212(a), substantially revised Section 641, changing the title to "Customs Brokers," providing new requirements and procedures for obtaining and retaining customs brokers licenses and permits, allowing for monetary penalties, and, for the first time, defining a customs broker and his business. Section 212(a), hereafter referred to as the 1984 Amendment, prohibited the conduct of customs business, except on one's own behalf, without a license granted in accordance with the licensing procedure (Section 641(a)(6)). It also confined the regulatory authority of the Secretary of the Treasury to the customs business of customs brokers (Section 641(f)). These provisions were made generally effective 180 days after the enactment of the Trade and Tariff Act, by Section 214(d) of that Act; *i.e.,* April 29, 1985.

B. Definitions

A "customs broker" is defined by Section 641(a)(1) to mean "any person granted a customs brokers license by the Secretary" under the provisions of Section 641. "Customs business" is defined by Subsection (a)(2) to mean "those activities involving transactions with the Customs Service concern-

---

[1]Pub. L. No. 98-573, October 30, 1984, 98 Stat. 2948.

ing the entry and admissibility of merchandise, its classification and valuation, the payment of duties, taxes, or other charges assessed or collected by the Customs Service upon merchandise by reason of its importation, or the refund, rebate, or drawback thereof."

C. Continuation of Existing Licenses

A license in effect on the date of enactment of the 1984 Act, October 30, 1984, under Section 641 (as in effect before that date) continues in force as a license to transact customs business as a customs broker, subject to the 1984 amendments to the law, and existing licenses are to be accepted as permits for the district or districts covered by the licenses. These provisions are contained in Section 214(d)(2) of the 1984 Act.

D. Transactions Not Requiring a License

The April 1985 Customs Service regulations governing customhouse brokers, 19 CFR Part 111, list in 19 CFR 111.3 the transactions for which a license is not required. This listing, as follows, appears not to be invalidated by Section 641(a)(6) of the 1984 Amendment prohibiting the conduct of customs business for others without a license under Section 641. No change in this section is made in the proposed regulations, discussed in section E.2 *infra*.

(1) an importer or exporter transacting customs business solely on his own account and in no sense on behalf of another and his authorized employees or officers who act only for him in the transaction of such business;

(2) a broker's employee who has been authorized by a power of attorney to sign customs documents or has been authorized to transact other business and for whom the broker has filed with the district director a statement identifying the employee as authorized to transact business on his behalf;

(3) a person transacting business in connection with entry or clearance of vessels or other regulation of vessels under the navigation laws;

(4) any carrier bringing merchandise to the port of arrival or any bonded carrier transporting merchandise for another.

E. Regulations, Fees, and Charges

1. Regulatory Authority

Section 641(f) gives the Secretary of the Treasury authority to prescribe regulations "relating to the customs business of customs brokers" as he deems necessary to protect importers and the revenue of the United States. The phrase quoted is inserted by the 1984 Amendment in the regulatory authority otherwise the same in Section 641(d) prior to amendment. The authority continues to extend to regulations requiring the keeping of books, accounts, and records, the inspection thereof, and the furnishing of information to any accredited officer or employee of the Customs Service (previously to any accredited agent of the United States).

The obligation of the Secretary of the Treasury to make and apply the regulations for the protection of importers as well as for the protection of the revenue from possible fraud by brokers was emphasized by the court in *United States* v. *Federal Insurance Co.,* 9 CIT ___ , 605 F. Supp. 298 (1985) 6 ITRD 1987.

2. Proposed Regulations

The Customs Service issued proposed regulations August 7, 1985, 50 FR 31871, to incorporate into 19 CFR Part III both the revisions made by the 1984 Amendment and certain recommendations of the Customs Headquarters Task Force on broker licensing and regulation. The major revisions provide procedures for: (1) the merger of a broker's licenses into one national license; (2) the conversion of district licenses into permits; (3) the suspension and revocation of licenses and permits and monetary penalties in lieu thereof; and (4) the imposition of other monetary penalties. New provisions are proposed respecting recordkeeping and accounting to clients, and defining "responsible supervision and control" by brokers of their various business operations.

3. Fees and Charges

Section 641(h) authorizes the Secretary to prescribe fees and charges to defray the costs of the Customs Service in carrying out Section 641, including a fee for licenses and tests, but no separate fee may be imposed to defray the cost of an individual audit or of an individual disciplinary proceeding. Subsection (h) is a new provision. However, fees had previously been charged for license examinations.

II. LICENSE REQUIREMENTS

A. Basic Requirements

Under the original and amended Section 641, in order to obtain a customs broker's license, an individual must be a citizen of the United States, but not an officer or employee of the United States; must be at least 21 years of age; must be of good moral character; and must establish through an examination that he has sufficient knowledge of customs and related laws, regulations, and procedures to render valuable service to importers and exporters. Under the 1985 regulations satisfactory knowledge is established in part by attaining a grade of at least 75 percent on the examination.

In order to obtain a broker's license, a partnership must have one member of the partnership who is a licensed broker, and must under the regulations establish that it will have an office in which its customs transactions will be performed by a licensed member of the partnership or a qualified employee under the responsible supervision and control of the licensed members.

An association or corporation, to obtain a customs broker's license, must be empowered under its articles of association or articles of incorporation to transact customs brokerage business; must have at least one officer who is a licensed broker; and must establish that it will have an office in which its customs transactions will be performed by a licensed officer or a qualified employee under the responsible supervision and control of the licensed officer.

The failure of a customs broker licensed as a corporation, association, or partnership to have for a continuous period of 120 days at least one officer or member licensed under Section 641 shall result in the revocation of its license by operation of law, in addition to any other penalties under the section. This provision appears in Section 641(b)(5), as amended in 1984.

B. Application for License

The 1985 customs regulations provide that an application for a broker's license must be submitted in duplicate to the district director of the district in which the applicant intends to do business. The application must be under oath and executed on Customs Form 3124. An application for an individual license must be submitted 30 days before the scheduled examination which the applicant must take. The fee which must accompany any application was raised by TD 84-231 to $230 to cover a 15 percent administrative overhead charge. The fee was increased on or after April 29, 1985, to $300 since the application for a license is treated as including an application for a permit. If an applicant advises before the date of the examination that he wishes to withdraw his application, the district director will refund the application fee.

Under revised procedures reported in Los Angeles District Public Bulletin 85-51, April 19, 1985, and New York Region Informational Pipeline No. 1063, April 29, 1985, an application for a license received on or after April 29, 1985, is treated as an application also for a permit to transact customs business in the district where the application is filed. Applications will be processed in accordance with the existing regulations. Provision is made for the merger of existing multiple licenses into a national license as provided in Section 214(d) of the 1984 Act.

A notice that the application has been filed is posted for at least two weeks in a conspicuous place in the customhouse at the headquarters port and at the subports where the applicant proposes to maintain an office. The notice gives the name and address of the applicant, and if the applicant is a partnership, association, or corporation, the names of the members or officers thereof who are licensed as brokers. The notice invites written comments or information regarding the issuance of the license.

C. Examination for Individual License

The written examination is designed to determine the applicant's knowledge of customs and related laws, regulations, and procedures. The examination is prepared and graded at the headquarters of the U.S. Customs Service.

Examinations are given at each district office on the first Monday in April and October. The district director will give the applicant notice of the exact time and place where the examination will be given.

Under 19 CFR 111.13(c) the Commissioner of Customs may authorize a special examination for an applicant when a partnership, association, or corporation has fewer than two licensed members or officers. Since the 1984 Amendment requires only one licensed member or officer, this provision is proposed to be amended. He may also authorize a special examination for one who will be authorized to continue the business of an individual broker. The application and a statement of the reasons for applying for a special examination must be filed with the district director.

An applicant's failure to appear for a scheduled examination without advance notification or adequate explanation will result in denial of the application by the district director.

D. Investigation of the Applicant

A customs officer is assigned to investigate and report on license applications from candidates who have successfully passed the examination, and from partnerships, associations, or corporations requesting operating licenses. The investigation is designed to establish certain facts relevant to the applicant's qualifications. It covers but is not limited to: (1) the accuracy of the statements made in the application; (2) the business integrity of the applicant; and (3) the character and reputation of the applicant when the applicant is an individual (including a member of a partnership or an officer of an association or corporation).

The special agent in charge gives his report and recommendation to the district director who requested the investigation. The district director then forwards the application and the report to the Commissioner of Customs, together with his recommendation for action on the application.

The commissioner may require further investigation if he feels additional facts are needed to pass upon the application. He may also require the applicant (or in the case of a partnership, association, or corporation, one or more of its members or officers) to appear before him or his designee for the purpose of undergoing additional written or oral examination into the applicant's qualifications for a license.

Where the investigation of an applicant continued four years after he had passed his examination the Court of International Trade directed the Commissioner to complete the investigation and determination within 120 days. The court took jurisdiction under its authority to review the administration of the customs laws under 28 U.S.C. 1581(i)(4). *Allen* v. *Regan,* 9 CIT _____ , 607 F. Supp. 133 (1985) 6 ITRD 2120.

III. LICENSES AND PERMITS

The considerations governing the issuance or denial of a license set out in sections A through C *infra* are those given in the 1985 customs regulations. The considerations governing permits set out in section D *infra* are based on Section 641(c), as amended in 1984.

A. Issuance of License

If the commissioner finds that the applicant is qualified, he issues a license. A license for an individual who is a member of a partnership or an officer of an association or corporation is issued in the name of the individual licensee and not in his capacity as a member or officer of the organization with which he is connected. The license is forwarded to the district director who delivers it to the licensee. Prior to April 29, 1985, the license authorized the transaction of customs business only in the district for which it was issued.

B. Denial of License

If the commissioner determines that the application for a license should be denied for any reason, notice of denial is given by him to the applicant and to the district director of the district in which the application was filed. The notice states the reasons why the license was not issued.

The causes sufficient to justify denial of a license include but are not limited to:

(1) any cause that would justify suspension or revocation of the license of a broker;
(2) failure to meet the prescribed basic requirements;
(3) failure to establish the business integrity and good character of the applicant;
(4) any willful misstatement of pertinent facts in the application;
(5) any conduct that would be deemed unfair in commercial transactions by accepted standards; and
(6) a reputation imputing to the applicant criminal, dishonest, or unethical conduct, or a record of such conduct.

C. Customs Review of the Denial of License

Upon the denial of an application for a license, the applicant may file with the commissioner, in writing, a request that further opportunity be given for the presentation of information or arguments in support of the application by personal appearance, or in writing, or both. The request must be received by the commissioner within 60 days of the denial.

If the commissioner affirms the denial of an application for a license, the applicant may file with the Secretary of the Treasury, in writing, a request for such additional review as the Secretary may deem appropriate. The request must be received by the Secretary within 60 days of the commissioner's affirmation of denial. An applicant who has been denied a license may reapply at any time by complying with the prescribed requirements.

D. Issuance of Permit

The 1984 Amendment provides for the issuance of a permit, in accordance with regulations, for each customs district in which the licensee conducts customs business. The licensee is required to employ regularly in each customs district for which a permit is issued at least one individual who has a customs broker's license and who is employed to exercise responsible supervision and control over the customs business conducted by a licensee in that district. However, the statute permits the Secretary to waive the requirement of an employed licensee in each district if the customs broker can demonstrate that he regularly employs in the customs region in which the district is located at least one individual who is licensed and that sufficient procedures exist within the company for the regional employee to exercise responsible supervision and control over the customs business conducted in the district.

The failure of a customs broker granted a permit to employ for any continuous period of 180 days one individual who is licensed within the district or region (if a waiver has been granted) shall result, under Section 641(c)(3), in the revocation by operation of law of the permit, in addition to any other sanction under Section 641.

The requirements for an employed licensed supervisor in the district (or region) of the broker's business are effective three years after the date of enactment of the Trade and Tariff Act of 1984, under Section 214(d) of that Act.

IV. DUTIES AND RESPONSIBILITIES OF CUSTOMS BROKERS

There follows a survey of the principal duties and responsibilities of licensed brokers, as set forth in Subpart C of the 1985 customs regulations.

A. Record of Transactions

Each broker must keep current in a correct, orderly, and itemized manner records of account reflecting all his financial transactions as a broker. He must keep and maintain on file a copy of each entry made by him with all supporting papers (except those documents he is required to file with Customs) and copies of all his correspondence and other papers relating to his customs business.

In addition to these regular records of accounts each customs broker is required to keep a record of his transactions in the format set forth in 19 CFR 111.22(d), unless an exemption is granted by the district director, upon written request of the broker describing his recordkeeping and agreeing not to change it without approval. The proposed regulations would permit authorization of centralized records.

The books and papers required to be kept by a broker, other than powers of attorney, must be retained within the customs district to which they relate for at least five years after the date of entry. Powers of attorney must be retained until revoked, and revoked powers of attorney and letters of revocation must be retained for five years after the date of revocation. Copies of papers relating to the withdrawal of merchandise from a bonded warehouse must be retained for five years from the date of withdrawal. A broker, with the approval of the district director, may record on microfilm any books or papers, other than books of account or powers of attorney, required to be retained under certain prescribed conditions. A broker may also, with the approval of the district director, utilize other methods of reproduction, including microfiche, for the reproduction of books and records permitted to be microfilmed.

During the period of retention, the broker must maintain his books and papers in such manner that they may be readily examined. They must be made available for inspection, copying, reproduction, or other official use by customs regulatory auditors or special agents on demand within the period of retention or any longer period of time during which they remain in the possession of the broker.

A broker may not refuse access to, conceal, remove, or destroy any books or papers relating to his transactions as a broker that are being sought or may be sought by the Treasury Department, nor may he otherwise interfere with any lawful efforts to procure or reproduce information contained in such books or papers.

Customs through the Regional Director, Regulatory Audit, will make such audit or inspection of the books and papers required to be kept and maintained by a broker as may be necessary for the district director and other officials of the Treasury Department to determine whether or not the broker is complying with the requirements prescribed by regulation. Furthermore, the books and papers may be inspected to obtain information regarding specific customs transactions for the purpose of protecting importers or the revenue of the United States.

B. Responsible Supervision

Every licensed broker must exercise responsible supervision and control over the customs business transacted by his organization. He must submit within 30 days of receipt of a written demand by the district director a list of the names, addresses, social security numbers, and dates and places of birth of persons currently employed. The list must be kept up to date.

C. Diligence in Correspondence and Paying Monies

The regulations, 19 CFR 111.29, require that each broker must exercise due diligence in making financial settlements, in answering correspondence, and in preparing and filing documents relating to any matters handled by him as a broker. Funds received by a broker from a client for payment of duty, tax, or other obligation to the government must be paid to the government within 30 days from date of receipt or date due, whichever is later. Each broker within 60 days must account to clients for funds received for them from the government or received from a client in excess of charges properly payable in response to the client's business. He must account to all other persons within 30 days of receipt for all funds advanced by a client for payment of any charges or obligations due such persons.

Under 1982 amendments to 19 CFR 111.29, a broker is required to notify his active clients annually that an importer of record is not relieved of liability for customs charges if the charges are not paid by the broker and that, consequently, the importer may pay the charges by a check made payable to the U.S. Customs Service, which shall be delivered to Customs by the broker. An active client is defined as a client from whom a broker has obtained a power of attorney, and for whom the broker has transacted customs business on at least two occasions in the preceding 12-month period. The separate check payment provided an alternative method of payment to the usual method of payment by the importer by one check to the broker covering both brokerage fees and expenses and customs duties.

D. Triennial Reports

Customhouse brokers were required under an amendment to 19 U.S.C. 1641 made by Section 113 of the Customs Procedural Reform and Simplification Act of 1978 to make a report of their continuing activity as of February 1, 1979, and each third year thereafter. The report is to state whether the broker is actively engaged in business as such, and the name under, and address at, which the business is transacted. Regulatory requirements are set forth at 19 CFR 111.30(d).

The 1984 Amendment continued this requirement by providing in Section 641(g) for triennial reports, beginning February 1, 1985, and for suspension of the broker's license if the report is not filed by March 1 of the reporting year. The license may thereafter be revoked under the procedures outlined in that subsection. The proposed regulations would require notice of license and business changes.

E. Improper Conduct

A customs broker may not knowingly provide false information, improperly obtain information from government records, accept excessive fees from attorneys, permit his license to be misused by unauthorized persons, make false representations to obtain employment, willfully withhold information from a client or advise him to do something illegal, act on a protest without proper authorization, limit his liability as a customs broker to a client, or engage in business relations with disreputable individuals.

F. Relations With Unlicensed Persons

When a broker is employed by an unlicensed person who is not the actual importer, he must transmit to the actual importer a copy of his bill for services rendered unless the merchandise was purchased on an all-free basis (duty and brokerage charges paid by the unlicensed person).

Freight forwarders are often, but not always, licensed as customs brokers. When acting in their freight-forwarding capacity, they are "unlicensed persons" for the purposes of the subject matter covered in this section. However, under certain prescribed conditions, a broker may compensate an independent freight forwarder for services rendered in obtaining the brokerage business from the actual importer.

V. DISCIPLINARY ACTION

A. Monetary Penalty

A major feature of the 1984 amendment of the customs broker law was the addition of authority to impose monetary penalties to the disciplinary authority of the Secretary of the Treasury, previously limited to the revocation or suspension of a customs broker's license. This addition resulted from extended consideration of revision of the law between the Customs Service and the National Customs Brokers and Forwarders Association of America (1 ITR 507, October 24, 1984).

Section 641(d) authorizes the Secretary to impose a monetary penalty up to $30,000 in all cases listed in Subsection (d)(1), except where the broker has been convicted of a felony or misdemeanor which the Secretary finds involved larceny, theft, robbery, extortion, forgery, counterfeiting, fraudulent concealment, embezzlement, fraudulent conversion, or misappropriation of funds.

A penalty up to $10,000 is authorized by Section 641(b)(6), to be assessed in the same manner as other monetary penalties, for the intentional transaction of customs business for others, without holding a valid broker's license.

B. Grounds for Disciplinary Action

A monetary penalty or the revocation or suspension of a license or permit may occur if it is shown that the broker has committed any of the infractions listed in six subparagraphs of Section 641(d)(1). These are, in brief:

(A) The making of a false or misleading statement with respect to material facts in any application for a customs license or permit;

(B) The conviction after the filing of an application for a license of any felony or misdemeanor which the Secretary finds involved the importation or exportation of merchandise, or arose out of the conduct of customs business, or involved the fraudulent or criminal conduct listed in section A *supra;*

(C) The violation of any law enforced by the Customs Service or the rules or regulations issued under any such law;

(D) The counseling, inducing, procuring, or aiding or abetting of the violation by any other person of any customs law or regulations;

(E) The knowing employment of any person who has been convicted of a felony, without written approval of such employment by the Secretary; or

(F) The willful or knowing deception, misleading, or threatening of any client or prospective client in the course of customs business with intent to defraud.

C. Investigation of Complaints

Under the 1985 customs regulations every complaint or charge against a broker that may be the basis for disciplinary action is forwarded for investigation to the responsible customs officer in the area in which the broker is located. That officer submits a report on the investigation to the director of the appropriate district, with a copy to the commissioner.

The district director reviews the report of investigation to determine if there is sufficient basis to recommend that charges be preferred against the broker. He then submits his recommendation with supporting reasons to the commissioner for final determination, together with a proposed statement of charges when recommending that charges be preferred.

If the commissioner determines that charges will not be preferred, he notifies the district director of his decision. Should he determine that charges will be preferred, the district director will proceed under the formal procedures provided for in Section 641(d)(2).

D. Notice to Show Cause

Formal disciplinary action to impose a monetary penalty or to revoke or suspend a license or permit is initiated by the service by the appropriate customs officer of a notice in writing upon the customs broker concerned to show cause why he should not be subjected to the monetary penalty or to the revocation or suspension of his license or permit. The notice must advise the customs broker of the allegations or complaints against him and shall advise him that he has 30 days within which to respond after the date of the notice.

E. Determination of Monetary Penalties

The customs officer proceeds to consider the allegations or complaints and any timely response made by the customs broker and issues a written decision. The customs broker subjected to a monetary penalty has then an opportunity under Section 618 of the Tariff Act of 1930 (19 U.S.C. 1618) to seek remission or mitigation of the penalty. After decision has been rendered under Section 618, the customs officer provides to the broker a written statement setting forth the final decision and the findings of fact and conclusions of law on which the determination is based.

F. Suspension or Revocation of Licenses or Permits

If the customs broker has not filed a response to the notice to show cause or the appropriate customs officer determines after the response that the revocation or suspension is still warranted, he must notify the customs broker in writing of a hearing to be held within 15 days or at a later date, if the broker so requests and shows good cause therefor, before an administrative law judge appointed pursuant to 5 U.S.C. 3105, who will serve as the hearing officer. The requirement of a hearing before an administrative law judge supersedes the previous procedure under the customs regulations of the appointment of a customs officer as a hearing officer.

If the customs broker fails to appear at the hearing, the hearing officer makes findings and recommendations based upon the record. At a hearing the customs broker may be represented by counsel and all proceedings shall be taken under oath with the right of cross-examination accorded to both parties. Transcripts of the hearing are to be provided to the appropriate customs officer and the customs broker, with reasonable opportunity provided to file a posthearing brief. After the hearing, the hearing officer transmits the record with his findings of fact and recommendations to the Secretary for a decision. The Secretary then issues a written decision based solely on the record setting forth his findings of fact and the reasons for his decision. The decision may provide for the penalty contained in the notice to show cause or any lesser penalty, including a monetary penalty not to exceed $30,000.

In a case involving the Secretary's decision following a hearing officer's report under the disciplinary proceedings prior to the 1984 Amendment the Court of International Trade stayed an order of the Secretary revoking a customs broker's license, and remanded the case to the Treasury, where the revocation had been ordered after exceptions to the favorable hearing officer's report were filed by the Customs Service with the Secretary without notice of the exceptions to the customs broker. *Barnhart* v. *U.S. Treasury Department,* 7 CIT _____ , 588 F. Supp. 1432 (1984) 5 ITRD 2453.

G. Settlement or Compromise

Any disciplinary proceeding may be settled and compromised by the Secretary according to the terms and conditions agreed to by the parties including the reduction of any proposed suspension or revocation to a monetary penalty.

H. Limitation of Actions

Under Section 641(d)(4) no penalty proceedings may be commenced unless the proceeding is instituted by the service of written notice to show cause within five years from the date the alleged violation was committed, with the exception that if the alleged violation consists of fraud, the five-year period of limitation will run from the time the alleged violation was discovered. These limitations apply to the imposition of a monetary penalty for the transaction of customs business for others without a license, prohibited by Section 641(b)(6) as well as to the imposition of a penalty for the improper conduct listed in Section 641(d)(1), set forth in section B *supra*.

I. Cancellation of License Upon Application

Under the 1985 customs regulations, apparently still appropriate under the 1984 Amendment, the Commissioner of Customs may cancel a broker's license "without prejudice" upon written application by the broker if the commissioner determines that the application was not made to avoid proceedings for the suspension or revocation of the license. If he determines that the application was made to avoid such proceedings, he may cancel the license "without prejudice" if authorized by the Secretary of the Treasury.

The commissioner may cancel a broker's license "with prejudice" when specifically requested to do so by the broker. A broker might so request if he wishes to avoid proceedings for the suspension or revocation of his license. When a license is revoked or canceled with prejudice, the ex-broker may not thereafter be relicensed and he may not be employed by or assist a licensed broker, unless he is authorized to do so. Such authorization may be granted by the commissioner upon petition filed five years or more after such cancellation or revocation.

VI. JUDICIAL REVIEW

A. Grounds

Section 641(e) provides that the customs broker or applicant concerned or other person directly affected may appeal to the Court of International Trade any decision of the Secretary denying a license or permit, or revoking a license or permit by reason of failure to have or continue a licensed officer or a licensed person in employment as provided in Section 641(b)(5) or (c)(3), or revoking or suspending a license or permit or imposing a monetary penalty in lieu thereof under the procedures outlined above.

No judicial appeal is provided for the direct imposition of a monetary penalty for which a petition may be made for remission or mitigation under 19 U.S.C. 1618. Court consideration of the merits of the imposition of a penalty in that circumstance is provided through any action by the United States to recover the penalty. Jurisdiction of the Court of International Trade over an action by the United States to recover such a penalty is provided by the amendment made by Section 212(b)(2) of the Trade and Tariff Act of 1984 in 28 U.S.C. 1582(1).

B. Standing and Timing

Section 212(b)(3) of the Trade and Tariff Act amends the jurisdictional provisions in 28 U.S.C. 2631(g) to provide (1) for a civil action in the CIT by the person whose license or permit was denied or was revoked by operation of law under Subsections (b)(5) or (c)(3), and (2) for a civil action by the person against whom the decision was issued for review of any decision to revoke or suspend a customs broker's license or permit or to impose a monetary penalty in lieu thereof under the penalty procedures above described. Under Section 641(e) a written petition requesting modification or setting aside of a decision or order must be filed within 60 days after the decision or order complained of. If no action is brought within the period permitted, the decision of the Secretary becomes final, and any failure to pay a penalty imposed within 60 days thereafter results in the revocation of the broker's license.

C. Court Consideration

In any action to review the suspension or revocation proceedings before the Secretary, the court is confined to a consideration of the record. The Secretary's findings of fact are to be considered conclusive if supported by substantial evidence. If additional evidence is presented which could not be considered in the original proceeding, the court may refer it to the Secretary for consideration and report.

In any proceeding involving the assessment or collection of a monetary penalty the court may not render judgment in a greater amount than sought by the United States but may render judgment in a lesser amount as the court deems just (28 U.S.C. 2643(e), as added by Section 212(b)(6) of the 1984 Act).

D. Effect of Proceedings

The commencement of court proceedings, unless otherwise specifically ordered by the court, will operate as a stay of the decision of the Secretary except in the case of a denial of license or permit.

7

Foreign Trade Zones

I. PURPOSE AND FUNCTION

A. Definition

Foreign trade zones are areas in or adjacent to ports of entry that, under statutory authority, are treated as outside the customs territory of the United States in order to expedite and encourage foreign trade. They are isolated, enclosed, and policed areas furnished with facilities for lading, unlading, handling, storing, manipulating, manufacturing, and exhibiting goods, and for reshipping them by land, water, or air. They are operated as public utilities under the supervision of the Foreign-Trade Zones Board, which is authorized to grant the privilege of establishing a zone in accordance with statutory and regulatory provisions.

The governing statute is the Foreign Trade Zones Act of June 18, 1934,[1] which was amended June 17, 1950, to authorize the manufacture and exhibition of merchandise within a zone, as well as its storage, packaging, grading, cleaning, mixing, or other manipulation. The governing regulations are those issued by the Foreign-Trade Zones Board, covering the establishment and operation of zones, and those issued by the U.S. Customs Service, covering the customs requirements applicable to the entry, handling, and removal of merchandise into, within, and from zones.[2]

B. Economic Advantages

The outstanding fact about a foreign trade zone is that the merchandise admitted, either foreign or domestic, is not subject to the customs laws of the United States (other than those providing for supervision and accountability) until the merchandise is ready to be imported into the United States or exported. A further significant fact is that there is no limit on the length of time in which merchandise may be held and handled within

---

[1] 19 U.S.C. 81a–u.
[2] 15 CFR Part 400, Foreign-Trade Zones Board, and 19 CFR Part 146, U.S. Customs Service.

a zone. These characteristics provide opportunity for gaining economic advantages which are deemed to benefit U.S. trade and American industry participating in zone operations, although they may cause some loss to competing American manufacturers.

Thus importers, intending to develop an American market for foreign merchandise, may hold it in a zone for display to wholesalers or until the market is favorable; or they may hold over-quota merchandise in a zone until a new quota period. More importantly, importers may take advantage of duty differentials between products by bringing into a zone articles subject to one rate of duty and manipulating or manufacturing them into a product carrying a lower rate of duty when brought into customs territory.

On the other hand, an importer has the option of establishing the dutiability of foreign merchandise as of the time he brings it into a zone by applying for a "privileged status" for it, as described later. Only the rate of duty thus established is thereafter paid on such of that foreign merchandise as later enters customs territory, even though the privileged merchandise has been fabricated into articles carrying a higher rate of duty. This option, for example, may make it more advantageous for an American businessman to send domestic merchandise into a zone for assembly with foreign components (given privileged status) than to send it abroad for assembly with foreign components and return, paying duty upon the resulting article at its full value less the value of the domestic component. Further, any unusable waste resulting from the processes of shipment or manipulation may be disposed of or subtracted from total quantities in a zone prior to entry of the foreign merchandise, thus reducing the dutiable amount.

An American exporter may also find economic advantages in using a zone. Domestic goods moved into a zone for export are treated by Customs as exported as of the date of entry into the zone, thus entitling the exporter to any applicable excise tax rebate or drawback, although the goods may be held in the zone awaiting a favorable export opportunity or awaiting manipulation prior to export. Moreover, zone status exempts a manufacturer in a zone from paying duties on foreign components used for its exports.

It is in the substitution of domestic manufacturing operations for overseas operations that the Foreign-Trade Zones Board finds that zones make "their greatest economic contribution."[3] According to the International Trade Commission, manufacturing in zones accounted for approximately two-thirds of shipments from all zones in recent years. More than 90 percent of this manufacturing took place in subzones.[4]

To enhance the benefits to the American economy of zone use, the Customs Service has excluded the cost of American labor, overhead and facilities, and the profits, from the dutiable value of articles produced in a zone entirely or in part from nonprivileged merchandise, foreign or domestic (19 CFR 146.48).

---

[3] *36th Annual Report of the Foreign-Trade Zones Board.*
[4] "The Implications of Foreign-Trade Zones for U.S. Industries and for Competitive Conditions Between U.S. and Foreign Firms," USITC Publication 1496, February 1984.

C. The Board as Economic Arbiter

Obviously, the taking advantage of duty differentials permitted by the usage of trade zones gives rise to economic conflicts between American enterprises. In one such dispute, the Armco Steel Corporation tried unsuccessfully to prevent, as contrary to the statutory authority, the importation of Japanese dutiable steel into a specially created subzone where the steel was manufactured into barges of a special design by an American shipbuilding company. These barges were vessels not subject to any duty upon entry into customs territory. In adjudicating this dispute, the U.S. Court of Appeals for the Second Circuit upheld the authority of the Foreign-Trade Zones Board to use wide discretion in determining what activities may be pursued in a foreign trade zone in conformity with the statutory purpose that a zone "serve this country's interests in foreign trade, both export and import."[5]

D. Statutory Removal From Zone Benefit

The economic advantages of foreign trade zone status were temporarily removed from bicycle component parts by the amendment to Section 3 of the Foreign Trade Zones Act made by Section 231(a)(2) of the Trade and Tariff Act of 1984, Public Law 98-573. The amendment removed until June 30, 1986, the exemption from the customs laws provided by the FTZ Act to bicycle component parts, unless the parts are reexported from the United States. The reason for this action is recited in Section 231(a)(1) of the 1984 Act as a threefold finding by the Congress that (1) a delicate balance of the interests of the bicycle industry and the bicycle components part industry had been achieved through revisions of the Tariff Schedules to allow duty-free import of bicycle component parts not manufactured domestically; (2) this balance would be destroyed by exempting dutiable bicycle component parts from the customs laws by granting foreign trade zone status to bicycle manufacturing and assembly plants in the United States; and (3) the preservation of the delicate balance was in the public interest.

The precipitation of this particular exemption appears in the 1983 Report of the House Ways and Means Committee.[6] The Report states that the Huffy Corporation was currently seeking subzone status for its Celina, Ohio, bicycle manufacturing plant, a status which would allow it to bring into the U.S. marketplace assembled bicycles at a duty less than the weighted average of the current duty on foreign parts and domestic parts which comprise the bicycle. The Report explores the economic effects of the Huffy application and of the proposed legislation.

The amendment made by Section 231(a)(2) of the 1984 Act was effective November 14, 1984. The Customs Service subsequently directed that after that date dutiable bicycle component parts may not be admitted to or

---

[5] *Armco Steel Corporation* v. *Stans,* 431 F.2d 779, 785 (CA 2 1970) 1 ITRD 1302.
[6] H.R. Rep. No. 98-267 on H.R. 3398 at 32–35.

remain in a zone except as zone-restricted merchandise and may be manufactured or manipulated only for exportation.[7] The Huffy subzone application was withdrawn.[8]

E. Law Applicable in Zone

The provision in the Foreign Trade Zones Act that foreign and domestic merchandise may be brought into a zone, without being subject to the customs laws, for various enumerated purposes, 19 U.S.C. 81c, does not mean that such merchandise consumed in the processes of zone manufacture is subject to customs duties because consumption is not an enumerated purpose, as contended by the United States in *Hawaiian Independent Refinery* v. *United States,* 81 Cust. Ct. 117, 460 F. Supp. 1249 (1978) 1 ITRD 1823. The Customs Court, in sustaining a protest to the assessment of duties on oil used as fuel in producing in a zone commercial petroleum products, said that a foreign trade zone is outside customs territory and therefore merchandise therein is not subject to U.S. duties until it enters customs territory.

However, a zone is not outside the reach of the Commerce Clause of the U.S. Constitution, and consequently the Lanham Act provisions for action against trademark infringement apply to infringing acts within a zone. *A. T. Cross Co.* v. *Sunil Trading Corp.,* 467 F. Supp. 47 (DC SNY 1979) 1 ITRD 1875. Nor is a zone outside the jurisdiction of a state court for a wrongful death action, since federal court jurisdiction had not been provided. *Fountain* v. *New Orleans Public Service Inc.,* 387 F.2d 343 (CA 5 1967).

Tangible personal property imported from outside the United States and held in a zone "for the purpose of storage, sale, exhibition, repackaging, assembly, distribution, sorting, grading, cleaning, mixing, display, manufacturing, or processing," and tangible personal property produced in the United States and held in a zone for exportation are exempt from State and local *ad valorem* taxation. The foregoing statement of tax exemption is the provision enacted as an amendment to Section 15 of the Foreign Trade Zones Act by Section 231(b)(1) of the Trade and Tariff Act of 1984, and made retroactive by Subsection (b)(2) to January 1, 1983.

The purpose of this legislation was given in the House Ways and Means Committee Report.[9] The report states that Congress confirmed its intent not to permit the imposition of such taxes and to insure that there would be uniform treatment by nonfederal taxing authorities. In particular, the local taxing jurisdictions in the State of Texas were reported not to have authority under the state constitution to exempt tangible personal property in a zone from taxation. The federal law was intended to preempt the state constitution in this respect.

The House Report makes clear that the legislation would provide tax exemption only to goods in a zone for a *bona fide* customs purpose and that

---

[7] See New York Region Informational Pipelines No. 1002 and Supplement 1, November 26 and December 14, 1984.

[8] 50 FR 6034, February 13, 1985.

[9] *Supra* note 6, 35–36.

it would not apply to machinery and equipment within a zone for use therein.

II. THE BOARD AND ITS OPERATIONS

A. Composition of the Board

The board is composed of the Secretary of Commerce, who is chairman and executive officer, the Secretary of the Treasury, and the Secretary of the Army. The committee of alternates is composed of the Assistant Secretary of Commerce for Trade Administration, the Assistant Secretary of the Treasury (Enforcement and Operations), and the Resident member, Board of Engineers for Rivers and Harbors, Army Civil Works Program. The board's operations are conducted by the executive secretary, and annual reports are required to be submitted to the Congress.

B. Zone Creation

The board creates a foreign trade zone by granting an application made by a public or private corporation for the privilege of establishing, operating, and maintaining a zone in or adjacent to a port of entry. Preference is required to be given to the application of a public corporation, meaning a state or its political subdivision, a municipality, or a public agency. To be eligible for a grant a private corporation must be organized for the purpose of running a zone and be chartered under a special act of the state within which it is to operate.

Every port of entry is entitled to at least one foreign trade zone. As of June 30, 1985, there were 117 zones and 70 subzones authorized to operate. A subzone is an area separate from an existing zone established for one or more of the specialized purposes of storing, manipulating, manufacturing, or exhibiting goods, and is authorized if the board finds that existing zones will not serve the convenience of commerce with respect to the proposed purposes.[10] A subzone is discontinued when its purposes have been accomplished. A zone or subzone may be discontinued by voluntary relinquishment or by revocation of the grant by the board.

C. Application for a Zone

To enable the board to determine whether the establishment of a zone will expedite and encourage commerce, an applicant for a grant is required by the board's regulations to furnish an extensive economic survey and analysis of potential commerce and revenue and of the present trade of the port area in specific detail, and statements of the impact of the zone on the U.S. balance of payments and on the environment. The applicant is also required to describe the proposed facilities it is obligated by statute and

---

[10]15 CFR 400.304.

regulations to provide (see section III.A *infra*) and submit proof of its ability to finance and conduct zone operations. The Customs Service assists in the analysis necessary to determine feasibility of a zone.

D. Public Notice and Hearing

The board provides public notice in the *Federal Register* and by news release of applications to establish a zone, with all relevant information, and the board makes provision for a public hearing or for an opportunity for interested persons to submit views in person or in writing. Information in the application will be available to the public unless the board agrees to the confidentiality of information, which must be requested by the applicant in a separate communication to the board.

III. OPERATION OF ZONES

A successful grantee is required to operate a foreign trade zone as a public utility. This means that the services and facilities are open on a uniform basis to all who apply, subject to U.S. treaties and conventions, and that all rates and charges are fair and reasonable. All operations are carried on under the supervision and inspection of the board. The district director of customs in whose district the zone is located is in local charge of the zone as the board's representative.

Historically, customs administration has been carried on by the physical presence of customs officers at the zone. Because of the increase in the number and business of the zones, Customs proposed to amend its regulations to substitute an audit-inspection system and to place responsibilities for direct supervision, recordkeeping, and merchandise status, movement and security upon the bonded zone operator.[11]

A. Services and Facilities Provided

A grantee is required by the foreign trade zone statute to provide and maintain (1) adequate loading, unloading, and warehouse facilities, and, where the zone is adjacent to water, adequate slips, docks, and wharves; (2) adequate transportation connections so arranged as to permit guarding and inspection for protection of the revenue; (3) adequate facilities for fuel, light, and power; (4) adequate water and sewer mains; (5) adequate quarters and facilities for federal, state, and local officers and employees; (6) adequate enclosures to segregate the zone from customs territory; and (7) such other facilities as may be required by the board. The regulations of the board add sanitation facilities and spell out the specifics of the statutory requirements.

---

[11] 49 FR 28855, July 17, 1984; comment period extended, 49 FR 35658, September 11, 1984.

B. Financing

The grantee has the financial responsibility for providing and operating the services and facilities in the zone and pays the cost of maintaining customs service in the zone. The grantee has the statutory authority to charge for all the services and facilities provided in the zone, but the charges must be fair and reasonable, published and posted, and are subject to approval of the board. The charges are required to be established in schedules designed to assure uniformity of application and simplicity of use.

IV. HANDLING OF MERCHANDISE

A. Admission

Any merchandise, foreign or domestic, including over-quota merchandise, may be brought into a zone unless it is prohibited merchandise. Merchandise may be admitted into a zone only upon application on Customs Form 214, formerly Zone Form D, and issuance of a permit by the district director, unless the merchandise is brought in solely for manipulation after entry has been made or is simply transiting the zone and a permit for prompt lading or unlading has been granted (in which cases the merchandise is treated as remaining in customs territory). Applications for permission to transfer merchandise into a zone, to do anything involving it in the zone, or to remove it from a zone must show the written concurrence of the grantee, except where customs regulations allow the making of applications by the grantee itself or the filing of the grantee's specific or blanket approval.

B. Disposition

Merchandise lawfully in a zone may, in accordance with the board's and customs regulations, be exported, destroyed, or sent into customs territory, in the original package or otherwise; but when foreign merchandise, or domestic merchandise whose identity has been lost, is sent from a zone into customs territory, it becomes subject to the customs laws and regulations governing imported merchandise.

C. Manipulation, Manufacture, and Exhibition

Merchandise lawfully in a zone may, in accordance with the board's and customs regulations, and without limitation of time, be stored, sold, exhibited, broken up, repacked, assembled, distributed, sorted, graded, cleaned, marked as to country of origin, mixed with foreign and domestic merchandise, or otherwise manipulated, or may be manufactured if permission is obtained from the district director. Application for permission to perform any such operation may be made by filing Customs Form 216, formerly Zone Form E, with the district director. The application must provide the descriptive and identifying information designated in 19 CFR 146.32. The district director approves the application unless the proposed operation would be impermissible under the internal revenue or customs law, or the place designated for the operation is not suitable for preventing confusion as to the identity or status of the merchandise and for safeguarding the revenue.

If the application to perform an operation is denied by the district director, the applicant or grantee may appeal the adverse ruling to the board. If revenue protection considerations are involved, the board is to be guided by the determinations of the Secretary of the Treasury.

The statutory authority to store, manipulate, or manufacture merchandise in a zone includes authority to consume the merchandise in the process of manufacture. Thus, foreign crude oil consumed as a secondary source of fuel in a zone refinery is not dutiable as it never entered the customs territory of the United States.[12]

D. Status of Merchandise

All merchandise in a zone, except that considered still in customs territory as described in the Admission discussion above, is given a zone status as either privileged foreign merchandise, privileged domestic merchandise, nonprivileged foreign merchandise, nonprivileged domestic merchandise, or zone-restricted merchandise.

1. Privileged Foreign Merchandise

Merchandise that, at the request of the owner, has had its dutiable status fixed, taxes determined, and duties liquidated in the condition in which it originally came into the zone is privileged foreign merchandise. This dutiable status applies regardless of when or in what changed form it thereafter enters customs territory. Request for this status is made by the owner of the merchandise by application to the district director on Customs Form 214, which combines prior Zone Forms B and D, at the time of filing the admission application or at any time thereafter, provided the merchandise has not then been manipulated or manufactured in a way to alter its tariff classification. An applicant also files a zone customs entry on Customs Form 7501. This initiates the processing of the entry, with appraisement and classification determined as of the date of filing the application forms and the zone customs entry.

The privileged status and the duties and taxes found due remain applicable to the merchandise even if changed in form, except in the case of recoverable wastes. These duties and taxes are paid when the privileged foreign merchandise is sent into customs territory but are not paid if the merchandise is exported or properly withdrawn for supplies, equipment, or repair material for vessels or aircraft.

---

[12]*Hawaiian Independent Refinery* v. *United States,* discussed in section I.D. *supra.*

2. Privileged Domestic Merchandise

The privileged domestic status applies to merchandise of the following kinds upon which all applicable duties and taxes have been paid and for which a privileged status has been requested and granted: (1) the growth, product, or manufacture of the United States on which any applicable internal revenue tax has been paid; (2) previously imported and on which duty and/or tax has been paid; or (3) previously admitted free of duty and tax. Application for privileged domestic status is to be included in the Customs Form 214 admissions application. Privileged domestic merchandise may be returned to customs territory free of quotas, duty, or tax upon compliance with transfer formalities.

3. Nonprivileged Foreign Merchandise

Merchandise that falls into one of the three following types is nonprivileged foreign merchandise: (1) foreign merchandise properly in a zone that does not have privileged status or zone-restricted status; (2) waste recovered from any manipulation or manufacture of privileged foreign merchandise in a zone; or (3) domestic merchandise in a zone that has lost its identity as such. Any domestic merchandise will be deemed to have lost its identity if the district director determines that it cannot be identified positively by customs officers on the basis of examination or submitted proofs.

4. Nonprivileged Domestic Merchandise

All merchandise that could have obtained privileged domestic merchandise status but for which no application for such status was approved is nonprivileged domestic merchandise. This does not include domestic merchandise that has lost its identity and become nonprivileged foreign merchandise, as stated above.

5. Zone-Restricted Merchandise

Merchandise taken into a zone from customs territory for the sole purpose of storage, exportation, or destruction (except destruction of distilled spirits, wines, and fermented malt liquors) is zone-restricted merchandise. This merchandise may not be returned to customs territory for domestic consumption unless the board finds this return to be in the public interest. Application for this status is to be made in the Customs Form 214 admissions application. Under an amendment to the customs regulations published on June 16, 1983,[13] zone-restricted merchandise may be returned from a foreign trade zone without board approval to a customs bonded warehouse for storage pending exportation under procedures prescribed in the amendment.

---

[13]48 FR 27537, amending 19 CFR 146.47.

To destroy merchandise in a zone, application must be made on Customs Form 216, describing the proposed method, designating the place, and identifying the involved merchandise. The district director approves the application if he is satisfied that the destruction will be effective and that the revenue will be protected, but, because of the statutory prohibition, the destruction of distilled spirits, wines, and fermented malt liquors having a zone-restricted status may not be authorized.

Merchandise having zone-restricted status may be considered exported for the purpose of drawback, warehousing, bonding, and other provisions of the Tariff Act of 1930 if all the pertinent customs requirements for actual export are complied with. When foreign merchandise is transferred to the zone from customs bonded warehouses, the bond is canceled and all obligations in regard to duty payment are terminated, since such a transfer may be only for the purpose of exportation or destruction.

V. REMOVAL FROM A ZONE

To remove merchandise from a foreign trade zone it is necessary to comply with the specific requirements tailored by the customs regulations[14] to the status of the merchandise involved and to the purpose of the proposed removal. The purpose may be direct export; withdrawal as supplies, equipment, or repair material for vessels or aircraft, within or without the zone; transfer to another zone; or transfer to customs territory for consumption at the zone port or at another port, for export, for transportation, or for destruction. A removal of merchandise of any status for any one of these purposes generally requires appropriate documentation, which may include full identification of the merchandise; a submission to the district director signed by the zone grantee or, if privileged foreign merchandise is involved, the consignee identified on Customs Form 214; approval by the district director; and release of the merchandise to the grantee. The completion of Customs Form 7512 is required for any removal for transportation, including for delivery to vessels or aircraft; and the completion of Customs Form 7505 is required for removal for consumption purposes. A bond is also required for most operations involving foreign merchandise.

A removal of foreign merchandise, whether or not mixed with domestic merchandise, to customs territory for consumption necessitates the payment of applicable duties and taxes and the appraisement and tariff classification of the foreign merchandise that had not received or retained the status of privileged foreign merchandise. Where such privileged merchandise has not been mixed, combined, or repacked in the zone, the applicant for transfer of the merchandise to customs territory for consumption pays the liquidated duties and determined taxes, as assessed in the liquidation of the zone customs entry, on the quantity of the merchandise to be transferred. Additional documentation is required for the removal of

---

[14] 19 CFR Part 146, Subpart E.

privileged merchandise which has been manipulated or manufactured. Recoverable waste returned to customs territory is dutiable and taxable in accordance with its condition, quantity, and weight at the time of entry.

As part of Customs enforcement of the U.S. Textile Import Program (see Chapter 14, section IV) Section 146.49 was added to the Foreign Trade Zone regulations to prohibit, subject to Foreign-Trade Zones Board authority, the transfer of textiles and textile products from a zone to customs territory for consumption when such items would have been subject to quota, visa, or export license requirements at the time of importation, if during their zone status they were manipulated or manufactured to exempt them from the quota, visa, or export license requirements.[15]

---

[15] TD 84-171, 49 FR 31248, August 3, 1984; TD 85-38, 50 FR 8723, March 5, 1985.

Part II

Duties

8

Classification

I. CLASSIFICATION AND DUTY STATUS

The duty applicable on an import depends upon its valuation and its tariff classification. Classification is the designation of the most appropriate description of the article imported in the enumeration in the tariff law of articles by type, kind, composition, or use. The process of classification may be described as the process of selecting the specific tariff description of imports that most properly applies to the particular import presented for classification.

Classification has been a necessary function of the entry of articles since the first tariff act enumerated "goods, wares and merchandise" and laid specific duties upon each type or kind. The tariff enumeration of imports has grown more comprehensive, complex, specific, and refined over the years. The present Tariff Schedules of the United States (TSUS), prepared in 1960, are comprised of approximately 250 parts and subparts and approximately 5,250 items.[1] Each item shows whether the article is free of duty or, if not, the individual rate or rates of duty applicable.

Where there are alternative rates in the tariff schedules, the selection between the higher, lower, or duty-free rate may depend upon the country of origin of the imported article. But the first step in the determination of the duty applicable is the proper identification of the article under a classification description. This is not always easy in spite of the particularization of classification descriptions. Disputed classification is the source of much litigation, and a body of legal principles governing classification has developed, as will be discussed later in this chapter.

---

[1]Tariff Classification Study, Submitting Report, U.S. Tariff Commission, November 15, 1960, pp. 9 and 22.

II. TARIFF SCHEDULES OF THE UNITED STATES

A. Background and Framework

The present TSUS was formulated by the Tariff Commission in a nine-year study required under the Customs Simplification Act of 1954. In 1960 the Tariff Commission submitted to the Congress a 10-volume study that presented the tariff schedules in the format in which they were later enacted. That format has three main divisions:

(1) The General Headnotes and Rules of Interpretation, which provide the basic statutory provisions and principles;

(2) Schedules 1 through 8, which describe for classification purposes the approximately 5,000 items arranged by schedule, part, and subpart, with each item assigned a five-digit number (three digits, a decimal, and two additional digits in each case) and the rate or rates applicable to each;

(3) The appendix, which contains three parts, namely: Part 1 for temporary legislation, Part 2 for temporary modifications under trade agreements, Part 3 for additional import restrictions under the Agricultural Adjustment Act. Part 4 for temporary duty reductions pursuant to the Educational, Scientific, and Cultural Materials Importation Act of 1982[2] expired August 11, 1985, and was deleted by Proclamation 5365 of August 30, 1985, 50 FR 36220, September 5, 1985.

The Tariff Commission's 1960 Submitting Report analyzed the defects in the 1930 Tariff Act classification system, the influence of international systems of classification and nomenclature, and the benefits to be obtained by the government and industry from a decimal system itemization and tabulation of articles. An analysis of each of the eight schedules was provided in separate report volumes. The Submitting Report was followed by seven supplemental reports improving and refining the schedules. All the revisions were incorporated in the Tariff Schedules of the United States, as published and proclaimed by the President, August 21, 1963, to be effective August 31, 1963, under the authority of the Tariff Classification Act of 1962.[3]

B. Publication of Schedules

The TSUS has been codified at 19 U.S.C. 1202. Since the specific items, and even the more general headnotes, are under constant revision by Congress or by Presidential Proclamations under congressional authority, current versions of the TSUS have not been published in the United States Code commencing with Supplement III of the 1976 Edition. A note to Section 1202 advises that the current edition is the volume published by the U.S. International Trade Commission entitled the "Tariff Schedules of the United States Annotated" (TSUSA).[4] The TSUSA includes statistical

---

[2]Pub. L. No. 97–446.
[3]May 24, 1962, 76 Stat. 72, 19 U.S.C. ch. 4 note.
[4]Each annual volume and its supplements are available from the U.S. Government Printing Office.

identification of articles and other information needed for importations, as discussed further in section E *infra*.

C. Changes in TSUS Effective in 1980 and 1985

1. Changes Effective January 1, 1980

The latter half of 1979 from the enactment of the Trade Agreements Act on July 26, to the final Presidential Proclamations made under that Act in December produced a multitude of changes in the TSUS which became effective January 1, 1980. These changes resulted from the many bilateral and multilateral trade agreements concluded under the authority of Sections 101 and 102 of the Trade Act of 1974, and the approval of the agreements to the extent required, and their implementation by the Trade Agreements Act.

Proclamation 4707 of December 11, 1979,[5] proclaimed and set forth in over 200 pages of annexed schedules the thousands of tariff rate changes and the headnote revisions provided for principally in the U.S. Schedule XX of the Geneva (1979) Protocol to the General Agreement on Tariffs and Trade (negotiated under the President's authority in Section 101 of the 1974 Trade Act), and also in four bilateral agreements negotiated under Section 101, one bilateral agreement negotiated under Section 102, requiring Congressional approval, and in several of the multilateral (MTN) agreements also negotiated under Section 102. The Proclamation brought into effect the several sections of headnote and duty revisions enacted in Title V of the Trade Agreements Act, subject to Presidential determination of appropriate foreign concessions.

Annex III of Proclamation 4707 set forth the staged rate modifications of duties to be made over an eight-year period. The 1980 TSUSA incorporated the immediate full reduction of duties allowed to the Least Developed Developing Countries (LDDCs) permitted under Section 503(a) of the Trade Agreements Act and proclaimed in Annex IV of Proclamation 4707. The 1980 TSUSA also incorporated the new General Headnote 3(d) provided in Annex IV for the identity and products of the LDDCs and the new duty rate column for their fully reduced duties.

The changes in the import limitations on certain cheeses and chocolate crumb, set forth in Appendix Part 3 of the TSUS, which were required by Sections 701 and 703 of the Trade Agreements Act, were proclaimed in Proclamation 4708 of December 11, 1979,[6] and appear in Part 3 of the TSUSA appendix.

Finally, the 1980 TSUSA included the modifications in the Generalized System of Preferences necessitated by the Trade Agreements Act and ordered by Executive Orders 12180 and 12181 of December 11, 1979.[7]

---

[5] 44 FR 72348–72563, December 13, 1979. Annexes III and IV were amended by Proclamation 5365 of August 30, 1985.
[6] 44 FR 72069, December 13, 1979.
[7] 44 FR 72077, 72083, December 13, 1979.

2. Changes Effective July 1, 1980

Important changes in the TSUS became effective July 1, 1980, under Proclamation 4768 of June 28, 1980.[8] This Proclamation brought into effect as of July 1, 1980, the new valuation law contained in Title II of the Trade Agreements Act of 1979, which implemented the MTN Valuation Code. Part of this change in valuation was the elimination of the American Selling Price basis for valuation provided in the TSUS for various articles, particularly benzenoid chemicals. As a consequence, the Subparts of the TSUS classifying and providing rates of duty for these chemicals (Subparts B and C of Part 1 of Schedule 4) were revised by Title II of that Act and by Annex II of Proclamation 4768, which added a Chemical Appendix to the TSUS.

3. Changes Effective September 1, 1985

Proclamation 5365 of August 30, 1985, 50 FR 36220, September 5, 1985, made major changes, generally effective September 1, 1985, in the format of the TSUS and in the tariff treatment of numerous items. The changes in the format were precipitated by the enactment of the United States–Israel Free Trade Area Implementation Act of 1985, Public Law 99-47, June 11, 1985, which approved the U.S.–Israel Free Trade Agreement entered into on April 22, 1985, under the provisions of Title IV of the Trade and Tariff Act of 1984. The Agreement provided for the reciprocal elimination of tariffs on all products traded between the two countries by January 1, 1995, with the elimination or reduction of duties occurring in phases over the ten years. The Free Trade Area Act authorized the President to proclaim modification of duties in accordance with the Agreement. The provisions for such duty modifications were contained in Annexes I, VIII, IX and X attached to the Proclamation.

The provision for duty reductions on Israeli products added to the Tariff Schedules a fourth area of free or reduced duties, the other areas being the Generalized System of Preferences (GSP) program (see Chapter 11), the Caribbean Basin Initiative program, and the preferences for the Least Developed Developing Countries (LDDCs) (see Chapter 10). To accommodate these four areas of preferences the Proclamation provided in Annex I a revision of the format of the Tariff Schedules to provide a separate rate column entitled "Rates of Duty Special," with letter symbols to indicate in the column the applicable program. The Annex eliminated the prior separate columns for the GSP and the LDDCs. The Annex also extensively revised General Headnote 3 of the TSUS which sets forth the rates of duty applicable to various countries and programs. The Headnote directives to cover the four areas of preferences were grouped under a new subdivision (e) entitled "Products Eligible for Special Tariff Treatment."

---

[8] 45 FR 45135.

The enumerations in other Annexes proclaimed by Proclamation 5365 amended the lists of TSUS items eligible for the preference programs and the rates of reduction applicable to various schedules of TSUS items.

The ITC published the revision of the TSUS made by Proclamation 5365 as Supplement 3 to the 1985 TSUSA.

D. Survey of the Contents of the TSUS

There follows an overview of the contents of the TSUS.

1. General Headnotes and Rules of Interpretation

The 12 headnotes and rules which precede the eight schedules set forth the principles governing the classification and duty system. For text current to September 1985 see Appendix A. The substance of these provisions is as follows:

(1) *Tariff Treatment of Imported Articles.* All articles imported into the customs territory of the United States are subject to duty or exempt therefrom as prescribed in General Headnote 3.

(2) *Customs Territory of the United States.* This term includes only the 50 states, the District of Columbia, and Puerto Rico.

(3) *Rates of Duty.* The rates of duty in the columns for Rates of Duty 1, Special, and 2 of the schedules apply to imported articles as follows:

(a) *Products of Insular Possessions.* With stated exceptions all articles imported from insular possessions of the United States are subject to the duty rates in column 1, unless they are the growth or product of the possession, or manufactured or produced in the possession from materials the growth, product, or manufacture of the possession or of the U.S. customs territory, which do not contain foreign materials constituting more than 70 percent of their value, in which case the articles are exempt from duty. Guidelines are added for determining the 70 percent valuation criterion. However, articles in the categories excluded from duty-free treatment under the Caribbean Basin Economic Recovery Act (see Chapter 10, section I.E) may not contain more than 50 percent in value of foreign articles to be exempt from duty.

(b) *Products of Cuba.* These products were entitled to column 1 rates but the entitlement was suspended under the 1962 Tariff Classification Act.

(c) *Products of Canada.* These products are entitled to the column 1 rates of duty. In addition, articles (including any motor vehicle or automobile truck tractor) produced in Canada, other than those produced with the use of materials imported into Canada with an aggregate value of more than 50 percent foreign products (other than U.S. products) if and as specially provided for in the TSUS, are duty free. The TSUS provides duty-free treatment for automotive products as defined and identified in the Automotive Products Trade Act of 1965.

(d) *Products of Communist Countries.* The rates of duty in column 2 (generally higher than those in column 1) apply to products imported directly or indirectly from named Communist-dominated countries and areas. General exceptions to this rule apply in the cases of Hungary, Romania, Yugoslavia, and China. The exception for Poland was suspended by Proclamation 4991 of October 27, 1982, as amended by Proclamation 5048 of April 14, 1983.

(e) *Products Eligible for Special Tariff Treatment.* The "Special" column reflects the rates of duty available under one or more of the reduced or eliminated tariff programs. Subdivision (e) sets out the general principles governing the programs and lists the countries covered. It gives the letter symbols to identify each program in the column and the exceptions to it: For the GSP, A or A*; for the LDDCs, D; for the CBERA, E or E*, and for the Israeli Free Trade Area implementation, I. The asterisks indicate the TSUS items which are not eligible for tariff benefit when imported from the country set opposite the item.

(f) *Products of All Other Countries.* These products are subject to column 1 rates of duty.

(4) *Modification or Amendment of Rates of Duty.* The main principles stated here are that a rate of duty imposed by a separate statute supersedes existing rates in both columns 1 and 2, unless otherwise specified, and that a rate of duty proclaimed pursuant to a trade agreement is reflected in column 1, and if higher than that existing in column 2, also in column 2.

(5) *Intangibles.* This headnote, as amended by Section 201, Public Law 97-446, and Section 309, Public Law 98-573, provides that the following are not considered to be articles subject to the schedules: (a) corpses; (b) current currency; (c) electricity; (d) securities and similar evidences of value; (e) records, diagrams, and other data with regard to any business, engineering, or exploration operation; (f) articles returned from space within the purview of Section 484a of the Tariff Act of 1930; and (g) vessels which are not yachts or pleasure boats within the purview of Schedule 6, Part 6, Subpart D.

(6) *Containers or Holders for Imported Merchandise.* If imported empty or if reusable, containers or holders are subject to duty; but if the containers are the usual or ordinary types, not reusable, or ordinarily sold at retail with their contents and are imported containing articles, they are not separately subject to duty.

(7) *Commingling of Articles.* The principal rule is that when articles subject to different rates of duty are so commingled that the quantity or value of each class cannot be readily ascertained by customs officers, the commingled articles are subject to the highest rate of duty applicable to any part.

(8) *Abbreviations.* The common symbols and abbreviations used in the schedules are listed in this headnote.

(9) *Definitions.* The most important definitions for commercial purposes may be the following ones intended to reduce the litigation, experienced prior to the TSUS, over the meaning of these terms: The terms "of," "wholly of," "almost wholly of," "in part of," and "containing," when used between the description of an article and a material (*e.g.,* "furniture of wood," "woven fabrics, wholly of cotton," etc.), have the following meanings:

- "of" means that the article is wholly or in chief value of the named material;
- "wholly of" means that the article is, except for negligible or insignificant quantities of some other material or materials, composed completely of the named materials;
- "almost wholly of" means that the essential character of the article is imparted by the named material, notwithstanding the fact that significant quantities of some other material or materials may be present; and
- "in part of" or "containing" means that the article contains a significant quantity of the named material.

(10) *General Interpretative Rules.* This section provides a number of principles, including: the application to TSUS provisions of rules of statutory interpretation, developed administratively and judicially; the classification of an article under the provision that most specifically describes it; a classification by use is controlled by use in the United States immediately prior to the date of importation; a classification by actual use of the imported article in the United States is satisfied if the use is intended at the time of importation and proof of the use as intended is made within three years of entry; a tariff description of an article covers the article whether assembled or unassembled; and a provision for parts of an article does not prevail over a specific provision for such part. The content and application of these rules are discussed more fully under the heading Rules of TSUS Construction, section IV *infra*.

(11 and 12) *Issuance of Rules and Regulations.* These sections authorize the Secretary of the Treasury to issue rules and regulations governing the admission of articles under the schedules and to prescribe, as necessary, methods of analyzing, testing, sampling, weighing, gauging, measuring, or other methods to determine properties or characteristics of imported articles.

2. The Schedules

The eight schedules of the TSUS cover a macrocosm of imported articles as follows:

- Schedule 1. Animal and Vegetable Products
- Schedule 2. Wood and Paper; Printed Matter
- Schedule 3. Textile Fibers and Textile Products
- Schedule 4. Chemicals and Related Products
- Schedule 5. Nonmetallic Minerals and Products
- Schedule 6. Metals and Metal Products
- Schedule 7. Specified Products; Miscellaneous and Nonenumerated Products
- Schedule 8. Special Classification Provisions

The first seven schedules classify all imported articles subject to the TSUS by type, kind, or composition, or, in other words, by the article's inherent character. Schedule 8 classifies articles not by what they are but by what has happened or will happen to them or by whom they are imported. Thus, any classifiable article under one of the first seven schedules may in special circumstances be classified, wholly or in part, under a special provision in Schedule 8. That schedule provides special rates of duty, mostly free, for articles that have been exported from the United States and returned after limited processing, for articles covered by the personal exemption for returning travelers; for articles imported by the United States and foreign governments; for articles imported for religious, educational, scientific, and other institutions; and for articles used for samples or exhibition purposes.

The use of the eight schedules is facilitated by the numerical itemization of articles within each schedule and by the alphabetical indexing of all articles itemized. Each schedule is assigned a basic set of numerals corresponding to the schedule number. Thus, Schedule 6, for example, includes items numbered from 601.03 to 696.60. The decimalization within each hundred numbers allows for the refinement of classification into thousands of items. The TSUSA (see *infra*) provides additional decimals for statistical breakdowns under each item.

3. The Appendix

Before a rate of duty shown for an item in the eight schedules is relied upon as the current rate, a check of the appendix to the TSUS is necessary to determine whether the item is subject to a statutory or presidential temporary modification. Moreover, if importation of an agricultural product is contemplated, the appendix should be checked for any quota limitation imposed on the importation of that product. The information in the appendix (informally referred to as Schedule 9) is set forth in the following four parts:

• *Part 1—Temporary Legislation.* Temporary provisions for additional duties and temporary amendments of the schedules are contained in this part. The items are identified by name and by item number in the schedules and given a new decimal number in the series beginning 901.00. For each item there is shown the new rate of duty and the item's effective period.

• *Part 2—Temporary Modifications Proclaimed Pursuant to Trade-Agreements Legislation.* This part contains "escape-clause" actions and the temporary modifications made under the Trade Expansion Act of 1962, under trade agreements, and under Section 125 of the 1974 Trade Act (19 U.S.C. 2135). The items affected by the modifications are listed and described, as in Part 1, with the new rates of duty, or quota quantities, but are numbered in the series beginning 924.20, 1985 TSUSA.

• *Part 3—Additional Import Restrictions Proclaimed Pursuant to Section 22 of the Agricultural Adjustment Act, as Amended.* Here are set forth the additional duties or the quota limitations that the President has proclaimed under authority of Section 22 of the Agricultural Adjustment Act[9] for the purpose of protecting the effectiveness of agricultural programs. The headnotes to this part identify various articles to which the restrictions do not apply. The items subject to the import restrictions are listed, identified as Items 949.80 to 958.18, 1985 TSUSA, and their restrictions described by the quantity limitations applicable to the listed countries of export.

 • *Part 4—Temporary Duty Reductions Pursuant to the Educational, Scientific, and Cultural Materials Importation Act of 1982 (deleted by Proclamation 5365).* This part contained provisions for the duty-free treatment of categories of books, publications, and documents; visual and auditory materials; tools for scientific instruments or apparatus; and articles for the blind or other handicapped persons, as enacted in Subtitle B of Public Law 97-446. This subtitle was enacted to give effect to the Nairobi Protocol to the Florence Agreement on the Importation of Educational, Scientific, and Cultural Materials. The categories set forth in the statute were assigned TSUS numbers 960.10 through 960.80.

The headnotes to the appendix and each of the parts contain important information. The appendix headnotes provide that the general headnotes and rules of interpretation and the respective schedule, part, and subpart headnotes in the eight schedules apply to the provisions of the appendix, unless the context otherwise requires. The headnotes to each part present explanatory material on the application of the legislation and proclamations.

4. Chemical Appendix to the Tariff Schedules

This Appendix, added by Proclamation 4768 as part of the reclassification of benzenoid chemicals and products is described in that Proclamation and in the Chemical Appendix Headnotes as follows:

> This appendix enumerates those chemicals and products which the President has determined were imported into the United States before January 1, 1978, or were produced in the United States before May 1, 1978. For convenience, the listed articles are described (1) by reference to their registry number with the Chemical Abstracts Service (C.A.S.) of the American Chemical Society, where available, or (2) by reference to their common chemical name or trade name where the C.A.S. registry number is not available. For the purposes of these schedules, any reference to a product provided for in this appendix includes such products listed herein, by whatever name known.

E. Additional Import Data in TSUSA

The Tariff Schedules of the United States Annotated sets out the current provisions of the TSUS, certain data required to be included with every customs entry of imported merchandise, and notes on the dates and sources of amendments and modifications of the TSUS. The compilation is

---

[9]7 U.S.C. 624.

published periodically by the ITC and kept current by supplements, under the authority of Section 201 of the Tariff Classification Act of 1962.[10] It fulfills the requirement in Section 484(e) of the Tariff Act of 1930 as amended[11] that the ITC, together with the Secretaries of the Treasury and of Commerce, establish an enumeration of articles in such detail as necessary for statistical purposes, comprehending all merchandise imported into or exported from the United States.

As a consequence of this statistical requirement the TSUSA sets forth general statistical headnotes following the General Headnotes and Rules of Interpretation. These statistical headnotes list the information that persons making entry or withdrawal of imported articles must include in statistical form on the entry or withdrawal forms. Reference is made particularly to the Statistical Annexes A and B following the eight schedules and appendices to the tariff schedules, which list by code number the customs districts and ports and the countries and territories of origin of imported merchandise. Annex C lists the two-letter International Standard Country Codes for the countries of the world.

Of great importance are the additional two-digit suffixes to the decimal number of TSUS items to designate the subdivision of the item into separately reportable items. This subdivision of TSUS items listed in a left-hand column opposite each statistical item, occurs throughout all eight schedules, but is most extensive in Schedule 3 covering Textile Fibers and Textile Products.

F. Harmonized Commodity Description and Coding System

A new international commodity classification system designated as the Harmonized Commodity Description and Coding System, or simply the Harmonized System or Code, is scheduled to be implemented in the United States in 1987. The four-volume ITC report, "Conversion of the Tariff Schedules of the United States Annotated into the Nomenclature Structure of the Harmonized System,"[12] sets forth the submitting report and explanations, the converted tariff schedule, cross-reference from the TSUSA to the converted tariff schedule, and cross-reference from the converted tariff schedule to the TSUSA. Portions of the Executive Summary and of the Description of the System in the report are reproduced in Appendix H.

According to the report, the

> Harmonized System is intended to serve as a single modern product nomenclature for use in classifying products for customs tariff, statistical, and transport documentation purpose. Based on the Customs Cooperation Council Nomenclature (CCCN), the Harmonized System is a detailed classification containing approximately 5,000 headings and subheadings describing articles in trade. These provisions are organized in 96 chapters arranged in 20 sections which, along with the interpretative rules and the legal notes to the chapters and sections, form the legal text of the system.

---

[10] 19 U.S.C. prec. 1202 notes.
[11] 19 U.S.C. 1484(e).
[12] USITC Publication 1400, June 30, 1983.

In November 1983, the U.S. Trade Representative's office held hearings on a proposed international agreement that would result in United States adoption of the international nomenclature of the Harmonized Code. In September 1984, the Trade Policy Staff Committee of the USTR's office published a revised draft conversion of the TSUS and requested public comment.[13] The proposed agreement and Code are under consideration for submission to the Congress in 1986. If the Congress approves, the United States could implement the Harmonized System in 1987.

Because the United States and Canada have maintained since the 18th century a different tariff classification system from the systems followed by major trading partners, the differences in classification and documentation have created persistent confusion and trade disputes. The Harmonized System would revise not only the TSUS but would also result in some changes in the CCCN, the present principal international classification system. The Harmonized System would use a 6-digit itemization and approximately 5,000 classifications, which would accommodate the inventions and new technologies introduced since the organization of the TSUS and the CCCN. Among the changes from the TSUS would be the use of metric terms exclusively, a substitution of weight for value as a basis for classification, a change from the test of "chief use" to "predominant use," a test more easily satisfied, and the combination or division of certain TSUS items. The Harmonized System was designed as a "core" system in order to permit individual countries to make further subdivisions according to their particular tariff or statistical needs. Chapters 98 and 99 of the Harmonized System have been reserved for use by individual nations.

As stated in the ITC Report, international use of a Harmonized Code would provide numerous benefits to the international trading communities in facilitating trade, commercial shipments, and customs administration, and in achieving standardization of documentation and comparability of trade statistics. It would also protect the value of tariff concessions and assist the effectuation of trade agreements.

III. CUSTOMS ADMINISTRATION OF CLASSIFICATION

A. Classification of Entries

The initial classification determination concerning imported merchandise is made by the importer of record making the entry by noting the appropriate TSUSA item number and rate of duty on the entry form next to the article to which they apply.[14] The entered tariff classification is subject to approval by the district director.[15] He is responsible for determining that the merchandise is classified in accordance with the TSUS, as interpreted by administrative and judicial rulings.[16] If the director finds that the classification carries an improper designation or rate, he notifies the importer of a

---

[13]49 FR 35273, September 6, 1984.
[14]19 CFR 141.90(b).
[15]19 CFR 141.90(a).
[16]19 CFR 152.11.

proposed change and normally allows 20 days before liquidating the entry in accordance with his finding.[17] If any discrepancy appears to be the result of a mistake and not of any intent to defraud, no proceedings for forfeiture are taken.[18] If commingling of merchandise is found, the district director notifies the importer who then has 30 days to take the action permitted by TSUS General Headnote 7 and the customs regulations[19] to avoid classification of all the merchandise at the highest rate applicable to any single kind of merchandise included in the commingling, as required by General Headnote 7.

B. Review of Classification

1. Presumption of Administrative Correctness

Importers should bear in mind that the tariff classification made by the Customs Service is accorded by statute and the courts a presumption of correctness.[20] This presumption appears to be based upon the vast reservoir of experience and information available to customs officers and their intended standard of disinterested professionalism. In the past the person protesting a customs classification has had a dual burden. He needed to prove by the weight of evidence not only that the specific classification was wrong but that the alternative TSUS item he proposed was correct.[21] In *Jarvis Clark Co.* v. *United States,* 733 F.2d 873 (Fed. Cir. 1984) 5 ITRD 2137, the CAFC directed the CIT to determine the correct classification, or remand the case to Customs for reclassification, where the plaintiff had proved the government's classification incorrect but not the correctness of his proposal.

The *Jarvis Clark* ruling was restated by the CAFC in *Childcraft Education Corp.* v. *United States,* 742 F.2d 1413 (Fed. Cir. 1984) 6 ITRD 1115. Moreover, the doctrine of *stare decisis* does not prevent the Court of International Trade from reconsidering a classification protest action dismissed prior to the *Jarvis Clark* ruling because the importer had failed to establish its claimed classification. *Eiseman-Ludmar Co.* v. *United States,* 9 CIT ____ , Slip Op. 85-19 (1985) 6 ITRD 1927.

---

[17] 19 CFR 152.2.

[18] 19 CFR 152.3.

[19] 19 CFR 152.13.

[20] 28 U.S.C. 2639 (Pub. L. No. 96-417); *E.R. Hawthorne & Co. Inc.* v. *United States,* 730 F.2d 1490 (Fed. Cir. 1984) 5 ITRD 2009; *Daw Industries, Inc.* v. *United States,* 5 CIT 12, 561 F. Supp. 433 (1983) 4 ITRD 1641; *Esco Manufacturing Co., aka J. Hofert Co.* v. *United States,* CAD 1167, 530 F.2d 949 (CCPA 1976) 1 ITRD 1526. This presumption is not applied when the Customs Service's classification encompasses multiple categories, and no one is implicit in the other, even if the categories come within the same tariff act provision. *United States* v. *Miracle Exclusives, Inc.,* 668 F.2d 498 (CCPA 1981) 3 ITRD 1497.

[21] *Daisy-Heddon* v. *United States,* 600 F.2d 799 (CCPA 1979) 1 ITRD 1741.

2. Classification Protests and Petitions to Customs

a. By Importer

Should the importer wish to dispute the classification made by the district director in the liquidation of the entry, he may request a reliquidation or file a protest.[22] The district director may within 90 days reliquidate an entry to correct an error in classification, even though a protest is filed. He also has a year to correct any clerical error, mistake of fact, or other inadvertence not amounting to an error in the construction of law and clear from the record or established by documentary evidence.[23] If a protest is filed, the question of classification is reviewed by the district director and may be reviewed by the regional commissioner or the Commissioner of Customs if the importer files an application for further review alleging that the classification decision is inconsistent with a prior customs ruling or decision, involves a question of law or fact not previously decided by the commissioner or the courts, involves new facts or legal arguments altering the application of a prior ruling or decision, or involves questions which the headquarters office refused to consider in the form of a request for internal advice.[24] If the protest is denied, the importer may take his issue to the Court of International Trade.[25]

b. By Domestic Interested Parties

American businesses, unions, and trade associations have the right under 19 U.S.C. 1516 to challenge the classification and rate of duty (as well as certain other customs determinations) found by Customs to apply to designated merchandise of a class or kind which is manufactured, produced, or sold by them. The procedure for doing so, set forth in 19 CFR Part 175, is for the concerned businessman to file a petition to the Secretary of the Treasury setting forth the basis for his challenge. The Treasury then publishes his petition and invites written comments. If the Secretary then decides that the challenge is well made, he will determine and publish the proper classification or rate of duty to be thereafter applied. If the Secretary decides that the Customs Service determination was correct, he so notifies the petitioner and the original classification or rate of duty continues to be used. A dissatisfied petitioner may then notify the Secretary that he intends to contest the decision in the Court of International Trade. This notice is published by the Treasury.

A petition under 19 U.S.C. 1516 is not the only means by which American manufacturers may seek a change in import classification. *Way Distributors, Inc.* v. *United States,* 653 F.2d 467 (CCPA 1981) 2 ITRD 1689, *aff'g Way Distributors, Inc.* v. *United States,* 85 Cust. Ct. 54, CD 4870 (1980) 2 ITRD 1215. These decisions recognized that the Customs

---

[22]19 CFR Parts 173 and 174.
[23]19 U.S.C. 1520(c); 19 CFR 173.4.
[24]19 CFR 174.23 and 174.24.
[25]19 U.S.C. 1514; 28 U.S.C. 1581(a) (Pub. L. No. 96-417);19 CFR Part 176.

Service was still authorized to issue an interpretive ruling, in response to inquiry from a domestic manufacturer's association, as to the application of a TSUS item, which affected the merchandise of importers without notice to them or opportunity to them to comment.

C. Prospective Rulings

1. Request for Ruling

To avoid dispute and protest over the classification of merchandise after its importation an importer may request a Customs Service ruling on the classification of a prospective importation. The service has provided comprehensive regulations setting forth the procedures for requesting an advance ruling and the effect of the issuance of a ruling.[26] Under these regulations an importer, or any other person with a direct and demonstrable interest in the question presented, may request a ruling from the Regional Commissioner of Customs, New York Region, on the tariff classification of merchandise the importation of which is contemplated or is undertaken but has not yet resulted in arrival or the filing of an entry or other documents. Hypothetical questions and questions concerning merchandise already in customs processing will not be accepted.

The request for a classification ruling should include a complete description of the article; information as to its chief use in the United States, when relevant; its commercial, common, or technical designation; where composed of two or more materials, the relative value and quantity of each; and also the purchase price and selling price in the United States. Each request should also be accompanied by a drawing, picture, or sample, and copies of all relevant documents. If a particular conclusion is requested, supporting arguments should be provided. In every case the requester should provide as much information as he can as to prior classification decisions by customs or the courts relating to the same or identical merchandise.

2. Ruling Letter Response and Effect

A properly presented request will normally be answered by a ruling letter from the appropriate office.[27] Such a letter is binding on all Customs Service personnel and is therefore to be presented to the customs officials at the time of the transaction to which it relates. However, the service is bound only to the extent that the actual transaction corresponds with the transaction described in the ruling letter. Consequently, a classification ruling applies only to articles that are identical to the sample or description submitted. All ruling letters are available, upon written request, for inspection and copying by any person, with any portions determined to be exempt from disclosure deleted. No portions will be deemed to be exempt

---

[26] 19 CFR Part 177.
[27] 19 CFR 177.8 and 177.9.

unless the ruling request identifies the information claimed to be exempt and sets forth reasons therefor.

D. Published Rulings—Uniform Practice

A ruling which Customs considers will affect a substantial volume of imports or transactions or to be of general interest or importance is published in the *Customs Bulletin*.[28] Customs has ruled that a published ruling regarding a rate of duty will establish a uniform practice for classification purposes.

The establishment of a uniform practice has the important legal consequence that under Section 315(d) of the Tariff Act of 1930[29] no administrative ruling applying a higher rate of duty may be effective prior to 30 days after publication in the *Federal Register* of notice of the new ruling. Section 315(d) is applicable only when the Secretary of the Treasury (in practice, the Commissioner of Customs) finds that "an established and uniform practice" exists. This finding may occur not only by publication of a ruling in the *Customs Bulletin* but, as held in the *Asiatic Petroleum* case,[30] by instructing a district director to liquidate on the basis of a classification, stated to be the established and uniform practice. After that instruction, the Court of Customs and Patent Appeals (CCPA) said the commissioner could not reverse himself and direct a higher rate of duty without giving the required 30 days' notice.

A letter ruling advising an importer on the classification of prospective imports does not constitute a finding of an established or uniform practice, even when followed by liquidation of some 100 of the imports over a two-year period at a single port in conformity with the letter ruling. *Siemens America, Inc.* v. *United States,* 2 CIT 136 (1981) 3 ITRD 1376, *aff'd,* 692 F.2d 1382 (Fed. Cir. 1982) 4 ITRD 1101. However, a letter ruling that acknowledges the existence of an established and uniform practice based upon prior liquidations constitutes a finding of such a practice which applies to a subsequent liquidation even if the importer did not rely on the letter. *Rank Precision Industries, Inc.* v. *United States,* 660 F.2d 476 (CCPA 1981) 3 ITRD 1001.

After a review of the earlier cases the Court of International Trade ruled that an established and uniform practice could be proved by actual uniform liquidations at various ports over a period of time, without showing a formal finding by the Secretary or a published ruling. *Heraeus-Amersil, Inc.* v. *United States,* 8 CIT _____ , 600 F. Supp. 221 (1984) 6 ITRD 1698. Upon proof that over 300 liquidations at two ports had occurred over a 10-year period under the TSUS items claimed by the plaintiff, the court found that an established and uniform practice of such classification existed. *Heraeus-*

---

[28]See 19 CFR 177.10, superseding similar provisions in 19 CFR 152.14(c) and (d), which originated in 19 CFR 16.10a, published in 1950, TD 52588, 15 FR 7358. The Customs Procedural Reform and Simplification Act of 1978, Pub. L. No. 95-410, requires the Customs Service to publish all "precedential" ruling letters.

[29]19 U.S.C. 1315(d), amended by Pub. L. No. 95-410, Section 204, to require publication in the *Federal Register.*

[30]*Asiatic Petroleum Corp.* v. *United States,* CAD 1029, 449 F.2d 1309 (CCPA 1971) 1 ITRD 1343.

Amersil, Inc. v. *United States*, 9 CIT _____ , 612 F. Supp. 396 (1985) 6 ITRD 2448; application clarified in Slip Op. 85-88, Aug. 27, 1985, 7 ITRD 1198.

1. Change of Practice

A published ruling may result in a change of practice or otherwise modify an earlier ruling on classification, but the customs regulations assure the public that no published ruling will have the effect of changing an earlier published ruling or a practice established by other means by imposing a higher rate of duty on an article unless the earlier ruling or practice has been determined to be "clearly wrong."[31] Moreover, not only the required 30-day effective date notice will be given of a change of practice resulting in a higher rate of duty but also an advance *Federal Register* notice that a change of practice is being considered will be given with an opportunity to comment on the proposed change. A change of practice resulting in a higher rate of duty will be applicable only as to merchandise entered for consumption or withdrawn from warehouse for consumption on or after the ninetieth day following publication in the *Federal Register*.[32]

Even where the contemplated change of practice will result in the assessment of a lower rate of duty, an advance *Federal Register* notice with opportunity to make written submissions on the merits will be given if the headquarters office decides that the matter is of sufficient importance to involve the interests of domestic industry.[33] The *Federal Register* procedure incident to a change of practice resulting in a higher rate of duty and the 90-day delayed effective date may be seen in the 1983 change of classification of certain tubular textile braided line.[34]

2. Effective Publication

It is now clear that the Customs Service is bound by a publication only if the publication is of the ruling in full, with a statement indicating intent to establish a practice, over a signature of an authorized officer. This is the result of litigation over the binding effect of the hundreds of abstracts of tariff classification decisions which, up through April 1974, were published in the *Customs Bulletin* and its predecessor weekly publication, the *Treasury Decisions*. A tariff classification abstract described a given commodity and provided its classification under the TSUS and its rate of duty. Occasionally an abstract stated that the classification constituted a change of practice to be effective 30 days after publication.

In 1961, an importer of crown board (hardboard laminated on both sides with a lauan veneer) protested its classification as plywood. The importer buttressed his protest by arguing that a 1958 tariff classification abstract ruled that hardboard, wood veneered, if in chief value of veneer, was

---

[31] 19 CFR 177.10(b).
[32] 19 CFR 177.10(c) and (e).
[33] 19 CFR 177.10(c).
[34] TD 83-102, 48 FR 19508, April 29, 1983.

classifiable as a manufacture in chief value of wood, not specially provided for, which carried a lower duty than plywood. Although sustaining the protest on its merits, the Customs Court rejected the importer's reliance on the 1958 tariff classification abstract on the ground that the abstract, like all the abstracts, was only an abstract of an unpublished decision, and was published unsigned only for the information and guidance of the public.[35]

Despite this opinion an importer in 1970 of gold-covered aluminum chain belts protested their classification as "jewelry and other objects of personal adornment" rather than in accordance with the tariff classification abstract, TD 68-77(3), classifying aluminum chain belts as chains of base metal and carrying a lower rate of duty. The Customs Court in a 1974 opinion and each of the three judges of the Court of Customs and Patent Appeals, writing opinions affirming the Customs Court,[36] denied that publication of an abstract of a classification decision constituted the establishment of a uniform practice or a finding by Treasury that an established or uniform practice existed.

Since this aluminum chain case, there have been no abstracts published. Tariff classification rulings considered by the Customs Service to have precedential importance are published in Customs Bulletins, whether they are ruling letters, internal advice memorandums, or protest review decisions.[37] Moreover, there is published biweekly in the Customs Bulletins a list, describing the issues involved, of unpublished administrative decisions, including classification decisions, made by the Office of Regulations and Rulings. Copies of both published and unpublished classification decisions are available from the Customs Service, and since October 1978, may be obtained in microfiche format.[38]

E. Internal Advice Procedure

In 1975 the Customs Service published for the information and guidance of the public[39] and later partially incorporated into its regulations on administrative rulings[40] its internal advice procedure whereby field officials may obtain advice from headquarters on important unsettled questions arising in the administration of the customs laws. An importer may request a field officer to refer a question concerning his importation to headquarters, even though he may himself present to headquarters only a question concerning prospective importations. If headquarters determines that an importer's question referred to the field officer may better be answered on a protest filed against the field decision in accordance with Part 174 of the regulations,[41] it will refuse to consider the field request.

The field request takes the form of a memorandum to headquarters and must be limited to a specific commodity, manufacturer, seller, or country of

---

[35] *Borneo-Sumatra Trading Co., Inc.* v. *United States,* CD 2624, 56 Cust. Ct. 166 (1966).
[36] *Ditbro Pearl Co., Inc.* v. *United States,* CD 4497, 393 F. Supp. 1398 (1974) 1 ITRD 1393; CAD 1152, 515 F.2d 1157 (1975) 1 ITRD 1398.
[37] 19 CFR 177.10(a) and 177(b)(7).
[38] 43 FR 45931, October 4, 1978.
[39] TD 75-17, 40 FR 2453, January 13, 1975; clarified, TD 75-258, 40 FR 48701, October 17, 1975.
[40] 19 CFR Part 177.
[41] 19 CFR Part 174.

exportation. The memorandum is reviewed by the regional commissioner to determine whether there is already existing an administrative or judicial precedent determining the issue.

F. Role of the Customs Information Exchange

An important part of the internal advice procedure is the requirement that copies of all inquiries sent to headquarters raising questions of classification or value be sent to the Customs Information Exchange (CIE). The CIE, located in the New York regional office, has served as a clearing house for more than 40 years. It assembles, coordinates, and disseminates throughout the Customs Service information on issues and rulings concerning tariff classification and valuation. Its purpose is to assure uniformity and consistency in customs administration. It compiles and circulates a monthly register of headquarters issues, and it receives and coordinates all ruling letters and internal advice memorandums issued under the administrative rulings regulations.

IV. RULES OF TSUS CONSTRUCTION

A. Rules Followed by the Courts

The hundreds of classification protests taken to court annually almost always present the contention of the importer that the import should have been classified under an item in the TSUS which provides for free entry or for a lower rate of duty than that provided for the item under which the Customs Service classified the import. Occasionally, a higher duty rate will be sought to avoid quota or other restrictions. To decide any such contention the Court of International Trade and, on appeal, the Court of Appeals for the Federal Circuit apply the rules of interpretation set forth in General Headnote 10 of the TSUS and "such other rules of statutory interpretation, not inconsistent therewith, as have been or may be developed under administrative or judicial rulings."[42]

In customs classification cases a determination of fact or law with respect to one importation is not *res judicata* as to another importation of the same merchandise by the same parties, and the doctrine of *stare decisis* does not prevent relitigation of a classification decision which was clearly wrong. *Schott Optical Glass, Inc.* v. *United States,* 750 F.2d 62 (Fed. Cir. 1984) 6 ITRD 1529.

B. General Headnote 10—General Interpretative Rules

Eight rules are set forth in Subsections (b) to (ij) of General Headnote 10 that have particular and distinctive application to the classification of

---

[42]General Headnote 10(a), TSUS, 19 U.S.C. 1202.

imported articles under the tariff schedules. Among these rules the following four are most often in issue in classification controversies.

1. Relative Specificity

Of outstanding importance is the rule of "relative specificity" stated in Subsection (c). This rule provides that "an imported article which is described in two or more provisions of the schedules is classifiable in the provision which most specifically describes it." However, there are two limiting considerations. One is that a superior heading in the schedule "cannot be enlarged by inferior headings indented under it but can be limited thereby." The other is that "comparisons are to be made only between provisions of coordinate or equal status." If two or more tariff descriptions are found to be equally applicable to an article, the rule in Subsection (d) requires that the article be subject to duty under the description for which the original statutory rate is highest, and should that rate be applicable to two or more descriptions, the article is to be subject to duty under that description which appears first in the schedules.

2. Use

Subsection (e) makes provision for classification by use.

(a) *Chief use.* A classification controlled by use (other than actual use) is to be determined in accordance with the use in the United States at, or immediately prior to, the date of importation of articles of the class or kind of the imported article, and the controlling use is the chief use.

(b) *Actual use.* A classification controlled by actual use is satisfied only if such use is intended at the time of importation, the imported article is so used, and proof of this is furnished within three years after the article is entered.

3. Chief Value

Subsection (f) governs classification by chief value of a component material. An article is in chief value of a material if that material exceeds in value each other single component material of the article.

4. Parts

A further rule frequently in issue is that governing the classification of parts of an article, stated in Subsection (ij). A provision for "parts" covers a product solely or chiefly used as a part of an article but does not prevail over a specific provision for such part.

C. Rules of Statutory Construction

The foregoing rules peculiarly applicable to classification are only a portion of the governing guidelines drawn upon by the court in determining controversial classifications. The court, complying with General Headnote 10(a), also looks to the general and well-recognized rules of statutory construction applied in determining any question of the application of a statute. The objective is always to find out what the legislative intent was. If the court thinks that the legislative intent is clear on the face of the statute, it makes no further inquiry. But if the intent does not thus appear, the court will seek to find it in the legislative history of the statute, in the administrative or judicial decisions on the issue at or closely following the time the statute was enacted, or in the commercial or common meanings of the terms used in the statute when it was enacted.

D. Judicial Application

The meaning and effect of the various rules of construction applied to the tariff schedules and their interrelation may best be understood by observing the court's use of them in solving particular classification questions. Below is a brief presentation, based upon some representative judicial decisions of the resolution of certain major classification issues through the application of the general headnote rules of interpretation and the general rules of statutory construction.

1. Determining the Relative Specificity

The Great Western Sugar Company protested to the Customs Court the Customs Service's classification of its imported cutting blades for sugar beet slicing machines under Item 649.67, TSUS, covering knives and cutting blades for power or hand machines, other than agricultural or horticultural machines, and carrying a 10 percent *ad valorem* duty rate. The company claimed that the blades should be classified under Item 666.20, TSUS, covering machinery for use in the manufacture of sugar, and parts thereof, entitled to free entry. The company argued that these blades had been classified as parts of sugar manufacturing machinery by judicial decision under the Tariff Act of 1922 and that a Tariff Commission statement indicated that the TSUS intent was to continue the free entry of such parts. However, both the Customs Court and the Court of Customs and Patent Appeals, one judge dissenting, rejected the protest.[43] The CCPA based its decision on the sole headnote to the part embracing Item 666.20, which states that the part does not cover "articles and parts of articles specifically provided for elsewhere," and on the General Headnote 10(ij), which states that a provision for such parts of an article does not prevail over a specific provision for such parts. The court concluded that this headnote and rule applied because the provision in Item 649.67 for knives and cutting blades for power or hand machines was a specific provision and thus removed blades used in the manufacture of sugar from coverage by the item for machinery and parts used in the manufacture of sugar. It further found that

---

[43]*Great Western Sugar Co.* v. *United States,* CAD 1038, 452 F.2d 1394 (1972) 1 ITRD 1351, *aff'g* CD 3971, 64 Cust. Ct. 127 (1970).

the legislative intent was explicit on its face so that the legislative history to the extent shown by the Tariff Commission statement referred to was not controlling.

The CCPA did, however, invoke the legislative history from the Tariff Classification Study underlying the TSUS in determining the relative specificity of two provisions alleged to cover microphones intended for assembly into hearing aids.[44] The importer contended that the microphones should be classified under Item 709.50 as "hearing aids or parts thereof," carrying a 12 percent (later a 9.5 percent) *ad valorem* duty rate. Customs had classified them as "microphones," described by Item 684.70, carrying a 15 percent duty rate. The importer argued that "parts of hearing aids" was a more specific description than "microphones." In rejecting the protest the CCPA noted from the legislative history that the hearing aid item covered nonelectrical hearing aids whereas the term "microphones" pertained only to electrical devices converting acoustical energy into electrical energy and that consequently the description "microphone" was the more specific.

Another test to determine relative specificity is to determine which TSUS item is the more difficult to satisfy. Thus, if one TSUS item describes an article by its specific and only use, *i.e.*, electrical circuit protection in Item 685.90, it is more specific than an item categorizing the article, *i.e.*, electronic tubes in Item 687.60. *United States* v. *Siemens America, Inc.*, 653 F.2d 471 (CCPA 1981) 2 ITRD 1590, *cert. denied*, 102 S.Ct. 1016 (1982) 3 ITRD 1464.

2. Applying the Eo Nomine *Rule*

In the microphone-hearing aid case discussed *supra* the CCPA also applied the *eo nomine* rule in support of the government's classification of the hearing aid microphones as "microphones" rather than as "parts of hearing aids." Under this rule an article is considered to be classified under the item describing that article by name unless there is clear intent by the Congress to exclude it. The CCPA found no intent to exclude a hearing aid microphone from the general term "microphone." It reaffirmed the rule that an *eo nomine* provision for an article includes all forms of that article in the absence of contrary legislative intent.[45]

There are many cases reiterating this rule. The Customs Court held that "Coromandel screens," hand-carved wooden panels, were properly classified, *eo nomine*, under Item 206.67 for wood "screens" and not under "articles of wood not specially provided for," Item 207.00.[46] The Court of International Trade held that electrical sockets specifically designed for use in automobiles were covered by the *eo nomine* provision in TSUS Item 685.90 for electrical lamp sockets rather than the provision in Item 683.65 for electric lighting equipment designed for motor vehicles, and parts thereof. *ITT Thompson Industries, Inc.* v. *United States*, 3 CIT 36, 573 F.

[44]*Knowles Electronics* v. *United States*, CAD 1134, 504 F.2d 1403 (1974), 1 ITRD 1440, *aff'g* CD 4483, 371 F. Supp. 1393 (1973).

[45]*Id.*, at 1405.

[46]*W & J Sloane, Inc.* v. *United States*, CD 4636, 408 F. Supp. 1392 (1976) 1 ITRD 1521.

Supp. 1272 (1982) 3 ITRD 1786, *aff'd*, 703 F.2d 585 (Fed. Cir. 1982) 4 ITRD 1376. Moreover, an *eo nomine* item includes a new item which possesses an "essential resemblance" to the one named in the statute. *FAG Bearings, Ltd.* v. *United States*, 9 CIT ____ , Slip Op. 85-52 (1985) 6 ITRD 2381.

3. The "More Than" Test

It is frequently argued by an importer that an *eo nomine* provision does not apply to an imported article because the article is "more than" the item named. Thus an importer of sealing rings for use in irrigation pipes contended that the sealing rings, which functioned as gaskets, were more than "gaskets," covered by Item 773.25 under which they were classified, because they also operated as valves, releasing water when pressure was cut off. The importer claimed that the rings should be allowed free entry under Item 666.00 for agricultural and horticultural implements not specially provided for. The CCPA found that the additional valve function did not remove the rings from the *eo nomine* gasket classification, since operation as a gasket was the principal function.[47] By the same argument, if the imported article has acquired new functions which diminish or impede the functions of the article described *eo nomine,* the imported article is recognized as being "more than" the article described by name in the disputed item.[48]

4. Ascertaining the Common Meaning

Closely related to the *eo nomine* rule is the common meaning rule by which the court seeks to determine the intent of the TSUS provision by ascertaining what is or was the common meaning of an item description. If the common meaning of an item description covers the imported article, it is not important that the import does not go by the same name. By way of illustration, the CCPA upheld an importer's claim that imported brass candlesticks, candleholders, menorahs, lanterns, and sanctuary lamps came within the common meaning of the term "lamp" and therefore should have been classified under Item 653.35 for "portable lamps for indoor illumination, of brass," at 9 percent *ad valorem* , rather than as "other illuminating articles of brass" under Item 653.37, at 17 percent *ad valorem*.[49] In this case, as in others involving the meaning of words, the court resorted to dictionary definition.

---

[47] *Arthur J. Fritz & Co.* v. *United States,* CAD 1036, 452 F.2d 1399 (1971). To same effect, *Trans-Atlantic Company* v. *United States,* CAD 1088, 471 F.2d 1397 (1973) 1 ITRD 1385, holding that a hinge remains a "hinge" although it is also a door closer, and *Tridon, Inc.* v. *United States,* 5 CIT 166 (1983) 4 ITRD 2078, holding that a motor vehicle signal flasher is not more than an electrical switch because of its audible clicking signal.

[48] *United States* v. *Flex Track Equipment Co.,* CAD 1046, 458 F.2d 148 (1972). Here track tread punched and cut for particular vehicle functions was more than "belting" described in Item 358.10, TSUS.

[49] *United States* v. *Morris Friedman & Co.* and companion cases, CAD 1156, CAD 1157, 524 F.2d 745, 747 (1975). See also *Russ Berrie & Co., Inc.* v. *United States,* CD 4659, 417 F. Supp 1035 (1976) where the Customs Court held that the common meaning of the term "doll" included papier mache souvenir figurines.

Similarly, the dictionary meaning of the word "clasp" as a fastening by which things are held together was sufficient to establish that the common meaning of the term "clasp" in TSUS Item 745.63 made that item applicable to plaintiff's plastic fasteners, "Tach-Its," used to attach identification tags to textile articles. *Bar Zel Expediters, Inc.* v. *United States,* 698 F.2d 1210 (Fed. Cir. 1983) 4 ITRD 1505, *aff'g* 3 CIT 84, 544 F. Supp. 868 (1982) 3 ITRD 1951.

However, since the objective of court construction of the TSUS is to give effect to the congressional intent, a statutory definition of a term is decisive even though it differs from the common meaning of the term. Thus the CCPA held that the definition of metal "alloys" provided in Headnote 2 of Schedule 6, Part 2, although different from the common meaning of "alloys," required sustaining an importer's protest.[50]

In customs cases the court frequently states that the TSUS is drawn in the language of commerce and that the commercial meaning is presumed to be the common meaning,[51] but where there is a difference the commercial meaning governs since it more closely embodies the congressional intent.[52]

5. Use and Actual Use

In deciding whether an imported article should be classified on the basis of its use or its component material in chief value the court, as in other classification questions, seeks to determine the legislative intent by employing the rules of construction discussed above. For example, an importer claimed that small replicas of the Empire State Building and the Statue of Liberty and miniature field cannons, all made of antimony, should not have been classified under Item 654.20 for metal articles not specially provided for of a type used for household use, at a 15 percent and 17 percent duty rate, for the reason that the replicas had no utility and were only decorative. He claimed that the articles were dutiable as in chief value of lead subject to 10 percent and 11.25 percent *ad valorem* duty. The CCPA sustained his protest on the grounds that dictionary definitions of "use" imply active employment and that the relevant Tariff Classification Study of 1960 disclosed a legislative intent confirming the requirement of active utility.[53]

The use of the imported article for making another article does not justify the classification of the import as the other article, finished or unfinished, where the import has not attained individuality as that article. *Terumo-*

---

[50]*United States* v. *C.J. Tower & Sons of Buffalo, Inc.,* CAD 1163, 524 F.2d 1389 (1975).

[51]See *Rohm & Haas Company* v. *United States,* 727 F.2d 1095 (Fed. Cir. 1984) 5 ITRD 1737; *Toyota Motor Sales, U.S.A., Inc.* v. *United States,* 7 CIT __ , 585 F. Supp. 649 (1984) 5 ITRD 2037; *aff'd,* 753 F.2d 1061 (Fed. Cir. 1985) 6 ITRD 1750.

[52]*Ross Products, Inc.* v. *United States,* CAD 994, 433 F.2d 804, 807 (CCPA 1970). See *Stewart-Warner Corp.* v. *United States,* 748 F.2d 663 (Fed. Cir. 1984) 6 ITRD 1417.

[53]*United States* v. *Parksmith Corp.,* CAD 1149, 514 F.2d 1052 (1975) 1 ITRD 1472. See also *Border Brokerage Co.* v. *United States,* 2 CIT 326, 533 F. Supp. 1339 (1981) 3 ITRD 1696, holding that articles used chiefly for rigging in harvesting trees were classifiable as agricultural implements under TSUS Item 666.00. This holding was affirmed by the Court of Appeals for the Federal Circuit in *United States* v. *Border Brokerage Co.,* 706 F.2d 1579 (1983) 4 ITRD 1892.

America, Inc. v. *United States,* 2 CIT 121 (1981) 3 ITRD 1030, concerning 48-inch glass tubes dedicated to use as clinical thermometers.

Proof of use, not any concept of utility, is necessary to sustain a tariff classification which is based on "actual use." As described above, under general interpretative rule 10(e) when the classification depends upon the actual use to which the imported article is put in the United States, the importer must show the intent for such use at the time of importation and that such use occurred, and provide proof of such use within three years. If the proof is not provided within the three years allowed, the classification of actual use is defeated although the importation was in fact used as intended at the time of importation. Thus, in *Czarnikow-Rionda Company* v. *United States,* 468 F.2d 211 (CCPA 1972) the importer of raw Philippine sugar was required to pay the additional duty placed on sugars not to be further refined or otherwise improved in quality, although such further processing occurred, because he had not provided proof of that refining within the three-year period.

6. Chief Value

Imported articles specifically named in a tariff item may nevertheless not be classified under that item if they contain an additional component more valuable than the article named.

The CCPA rejected a protest against the classification under Item 654.20, of imported jewelry boxes with metal musical movements wound by a key.[54] The court refused to accept the importer's claimed classification of these musical jewelry boxes under Item 204.50 for jewelry boxes "of wood." The court applied the definition in General Headnote 9(f)(i) of the word "of" (explained earlier in this chapter), meaning that the article is wholly or in chief value of the named material, and concluded that the chief value of the boxes was the metal musical movement and not the wood. Against the importer's claim that the Congress did not intend in enacting the TSUS definition to change existing definitions or rates of duty, the court pointed to the authority given to the Tariff Commission to suggest incidental changes of rates in proposing the revised TSUS and to the Tariff Classification Study, Submitting Report (1960), by the Tariff Commission explaining the important purposes of the new general and other headnotes in the TSUS.

7. The Doctrine of Entireties

More than 50 years ago the Court of Customs Appeals evolved the doctrine of entireties to allow for classification as a unit of articles having separate identities which are imported together for combined use as a single article of commerce. The Court's original statement of the doctrine was as follows:

---

[54]*Sears Roebuck & Co.* v. *United States,* CAD 1136, 504 F.2d 1400 (1974).

[I]f any importer brings into the country, at the same time, certain parts, which are designed to form, when joined or attached together, a complete article of commerce, and when it is further shown that the importer intends to so use them, these parts will be considered for tariff purposes as entireties, even though they may be unattached or inclosed in separate packages, and even though said parts might have a commercial value and be salable separately.

(*Altman & Co.* v. *United States,* 13 Ct. Cust. App. 315, 318 (1925).)

This formulation of the doctrine was held in *Standard Brands Paint Co., Inc.* v. *United States,* CAD 1148, 511 F.2d 564 (CCPA 1975) to require classification of wooden picture frame moldings, packaged in units of two lengths each prepared for joining to other units of the same or different lengths to make a frame, as picture frames and not as wooden moldings. The court held the doctrine applicable although the parts were separately packaged because only picture frames could be made from the moldings.

However, where a combination of articles imported together in separate packages (namely, a chassis and tape player) are not warehoused or sold together as a "complete article of commerce" but as components of an assembled article (namely, a console or compact) the combination is not an entirety. *Nichimen Co., Inc.* v. *United States,* 5 CIT 140 (1983) 4 ITRD 2056, *aff'd,* 726 F.2d 1580 (Fed. Cir. 1984) 5 ITRD 1811.

In a decision of great importance to the wearing apparel industry the Customs Court allowed classification of suede jackets imported with coordinated wool knit pants and shells as ladies pants suits under the single Item 791.75 for wearing apparel in chief value of leather. *J. C. Penney Purchasing Corporation* v. *United States,* 77 Cust. Ct. 48, CD 4671 (1976). This case confirmed the trend of earlier cases in recognizing particular wearing apparel combinations as entireties when imported as units, and has been followed by the Customs Service. TD 78-93, March 14, 1978, changed the practice of separate tariff classifications of the components of mens and boys cotton suits to a single classification of the suits as entireties.

In a variation of the doctrine of entireties the CIT allowed separate duty treatment of antique tapestry remnants (free of duty) and their fabric frames and backing, dutiable, although imported together as units. *Fisher Galleries* v. *United States,* 8 CIT _____ , 593 F. Supp. 436 (1984) 6 ITRD 1245.

8. The Problems of Parts

On the other side of the coin from the combination of imported units into entireties is the recognition of imported units as parts of an article for classification purposes. There are two major problems of classification. One is to determine whether the merchandise in question, being clearly a part or parts of a TSUS article which carries a specific TSUS listing for its parts, must nevertheless be classified as a separate TSUS article which more specifically describes it. This classification problem arises under General Interpretative Rule 10(ij), above described, which states that a provision for parts of an article "does not prevail over a specific provision for such part."

Another classification problem concerns the determination whether merchandise imported in pieces is to be classified under the provision for parts of the TSUS article into which the pieces fit or as that article itself, unassembled or unfinished, under Rule 10(h).

Judicial solutions to these problems are illustrated by two cases involving the term "furniture." In *Parts Manufacturing Associates* v. *United States*, CD 4552, 377 F. Supp. 1356 (1974), the Customs Court held that imported seats designed exclusively for connection to track in the floor of a certain type of aircraft were properly classified by Customs as furniture and parts thereof not specially provided for, under TSUS Item 727.55, rather than as parts of aircraft under Item 694.60 as the importer claimed. The court found that this result was required by Rule 10(ij) since the headnote of Subpart A of Part 4 of Schedule 7 defined "furniture" as including movable articles designed for aircraft, among other places, and therefore constituted a specific provision for aircraft furniture.

In *Authentic Furniture Products, Inc.* v. *United States*, CAD 1109, 486 F.2d 1062 (CCPA 1973), the court upheld the classification by Customs of unassembled parts of bunk beds as "parts of furniture" under TSUS Item 727.40, rather than as "furniture," as claimed by the importer. The court based its decision not on the fact that the parts were unassembled since assembly was not necessary for classification purposes under Rule 10(h), but on the fact that the import did not include all the parts essential to put together a bunk bed.

The rationale of *Authentic Furniture* was overruled by the Court of Customs and Patent Appeals in *Daisy-Heddon* v. *United States*, 600 F.2d 799 (CCPA 1979) 1 ITRD 1741. The court there said that the test to determine whether articles should be classified as unfinished articles or as parts was not whether a missing part was essential to the use of the imported article by the consumer, but depended on the application of a number of factors, including

(1) comparison of the number of omitted parts with the number of included parts; (2) comparison of the time and effort required to complete the article with the time and effort required to place it in its imported condition; (3) comparison of the cost of the included parts with that of the omitted parts; (4) the significance of the omitted parts to the overall functioning of the completed article; and, (5) trade customs.

The court added that these listed considerations were guidelines and not exhaustive nor necessarily applicable in all cases. The court's specific decision in *Daisy-Heddon* was that imported fishing reel housings were properly classified as unfinished fishing reels and not parts of fishing reels.

The *Daisy-Heddon* decision led the Customs Service to reopen for public comment the question of the correctness of its established practice of classifying imported cab chassis under the provision for bodies (including cabs) and chassis in Item 692.20 TSUS, which carried a duty of 4 percent *ad valorem*, rather than under the provision in Item 692.02 TSUS for automobile trucks valued at $1,000 or more, which carried the proclaimed rate of duty under Item 945.69 TSUS of 25 percent *ad valorem*, among other alternatives.[55] Both the General Accounting Office and the U.S. International Trade Commission had criticized the established classification practice. In TD 80-137[56] the Customs Service found its established practice to be clearly wrong under the guidelines of the *Daisy-Heddon* case and announced that imports of lightweight cab chassis would, effective 90 days after publication, be classified under Item 692.02 TSUS and charged duty under Item 945.69 TSUS.

This Customs Service decision was upheld by the Court of International Trade in *Toyota Motor Sales U.S.A., Inc.* v. *United States,* 7 CIT ____ , 585 F. Supp. 649 (1984) 5 ITRD 2037, *aff'd,* 753 F.2d 1061 (Fed. Cir. 1985) 6 ITRD 1750. Based on the common meaning of the term "chassis" the CIT determined that a cab chassis was not a "chassis"; it then applied the five factors set forth in the *Daisy-Heddon* decision to conclude that a cab chassis was an unfinished truck. A month earlier the court applied the *Daisy-Heddon* factors to decide that the Customs Service was correct in classifying certain electronic components and subassemblies as unfinished organs and not as parts of musical instruments. *Yamaha International Corp.* v. *United States,* 7 CIT ____ (1984) 5 ITRD 2014.

[55] 44 FR 59984.
[56] 45 FR 35057, May 23, 1980.

9

Valuation

I. DEVELOPMENTS IN THE VALUATION PROCESS

A. The Function of Valuation

Rates of duty are generally levied on an *ad valorem* basis; *i.e.,* the rate is stated in terms of a percentage of the value of the import. A system for the determination of the value of imports is necessary to enable the Customs Service to ascertain the amount of duty. When the value determination is final, the merchandise covered is "appraised" and when both the value determination and the determination as to classification (establishing the identity of the product and its rate of duty) have been made, the entry is "liquidated." Further discussion of the meaning and purpose of "classification" and "liquidation" is included in Chapters 8 and 5, respectively.

Liquidation, being the final ascertainment of duties, is necessarily retroactive to the time of the entry and is not thereby a violation of due process; also, each appraisement is necessarily independent of others and cannot create an "established and uniform practice" under 19 U.S.C. 1315(d). *Peugeot Motors of America, Inc. v. United States,* 8 CIT ____ , 595 F. Supp. 1154 (1984) 6 ITRD 1277.

The determination of the value of the import is important even where the rate of duty may be based upon the specific quantity of the import rather than its value, or upon the quantity and value combined, because of the necessity to provide adequate statistics respecting imports for various governmental purposes.

The use of *ad valorem* rates in preference to specific rates was significantly extended in 1979 in order to eliminate the significant erosion in the protective effect of specific rates due to inflation. In the tariff negotiations during the Tokyo Round of the Multilateral Trade negotiations, the United States converted a number of specific rates of duty to *ad valorem* equivalents in column 1 TSUS rates, and Congress followed suit in

110

the Trade Agreements Act of 1979 by converting the specific rates to *ad valorem* equivalents for all the same items in the Column 2 rates of duty.[1]

B. The Varieties of Valuation Systems

The varieties and complexities of the valuation systems used in world trade made an international agreement on Customs Valuation one of the major objectives of the six-year Tokyo Round of the Multilateral Trade Negotiations. The then-current valuation systems were considered major nontariff barriers to world trade. Not only were the systems complex and dissimilar, but they were also administered unpredictably. At the time of the negotiations, the U.S. customs valuation system had nine different methods of determining customs value, including the American Selling Price (ASP) method, which required certain imports to be assessed on the basis of the value of like or similar articles produced in the United States. The U.S. system was criticized by many trade partners who sought to obtain changes in the U.S. law. Similarly, a major U.S. objective in the negotiations was the elimination of arbitrary and protective features from foreign customs valuation systems many of which were based upon the Brussels Definition of Value (BDV). The BDV system was also proving unsatisfactory because of its vagueness and consequent differences in national interpretations and because of its notional concept of valuation.[2]

C. The MTN Customs Valuation Agreement or "Code"

A Customs Valuation Agreement was reached in the Multilateral Trade Negotiations and presented by the President to the Congress on June 19, 1979.[3] The Agreement was designated as the "Agreement on Implementation of Article VII of the General Agreement on Tariffs and Trade" (GATT). It is also known as the Valuation Code. Article VII of the GATT had obligated the contracting parties to give effect to certain valuation principles, including the principle that the value for customs purposes of imported merchandise "should be based on the actual value of the imported merchandise on which duty is assessed, or of like merchandise, and should not be based on the value of merchandise of national origin or on arbitrary or fictitious values." The MTN Customs Valuation Agreement recognized the need to provide rules for the application of the GATT principles and to establish "a fair, uniform and neutral system for the valuation of goods which should, to the greatest extent possible, be based upon the transaction value of the goods being valued."

[1]H.R. Rep. No. 96-317 to accompany H.R. 4537 at 129. Section 514 of Pub. L. No. 96-39, July 26, 1979, 19 U.S.C. 1202, provided the revised column 2 rates. The revised column 1 rates were added to the TSUS by Proclamation 4707 of December 11, 1979, 44 FR 72348.
[2]For a review of the political, historical, and philosophical pressures leading to adoption of the MTN Valuation Code, see Sherman "Customs Valuation," Law and Policy in International Business, Vol. 12, No. 1 at 119.
[3]H.R. Doc. No. 96-153, Part I at 7. For text of the Agreement see Appendix F.

D. U.S. Acceptance and Implementation of the MTN Agreement

In the Trade Agreements Act of 1979, Congress approved "The Agreement on Implementation of Article VII of the General Agreement on Tariffs and Trade (relating to customs valuation)" as the first of 14 MTN agreements approved by that law.[4] The Act implemented this Agreement by providing in Title II a new customs valuation law consistent with the Agreement which was to apply to all imports which were exported on or after the effective date of that Title. The effective date of that Title (except for certain rubber footwear) was designated as January 1, 1981, if the Agreement had entered into force by that date, or such earlier date, not before July 1, 1980, as the President determined that the European Community had accepted the obligations of the Agreement with respect to the United States, and that each of the EC member countries had implemented the Agreement under its laws.[5] The provision for the effective date for the change from ASP valuation of the excepted certain rubber footwear, identified under 700.60 TSUS, was July 1, 1981.

II. THE VALUATION CODE LAW

A. Effective Date and Application

1. Exports On and After July 1, 1980

Proclamation 4768 signed June 28, 1980 determined that the legislative requirements for implementing prior to January 1, 1981, the MTN Valuation Code legislation incorporated in the Trade Agreements Act of 1979 had been met, and accordingly proclaimed that the valuation standards amendments made by Subtitle A of Title II of that Act became effective "with respect to articles exported to the United States on and after July 1, 1980" (Section 2(a)), except for the amendments made by Section 223(b).

The exception from the application of the law for the "amendments made by section 223(b)" of the 1979 Act referred to the amendments made by that section to Schedule 7, Part 1, Subpart A, TSUS, concerning certain footwear. The amendments revised headnote 3 of that subpart and redesignated various footwear items in order to eliminate Item 700.60, for certain rubber or plastic footwear valued on the basis of the American Selling Price. These amendments took effect, under Section 204(c), as of July 1, 1981, for such footwear exported after that date.

Proclamation 4768, implemented by Annexes II and III, also put into effect for articles exported after July 1, 1980, the rate conversions made by Subtitle B of Title II of the 1979 Act pertaining to two articles on the Final List (see section IV *infra*) and all of the articles, particularly chemicals, but

---

[4]Section 2(a) and (c), Pub. L. No. 96-39, 19 U.S.C. 2503(a) and (c).
[5]Section 204, Pub. L. No. 96-39, 19 U.S.C. 1401(a), note.

excepting footwear covered by Item 700.60, TSUS, valued under the American Selling Price System.

2. Exports Prior to July 1, 1980

The effect of Proclamation 4768 was to activate the repeal of the preexisting valuation law (Sections 402 and 402a of the Tariff Act of 1930, 19 U.S.C. 1401a and 1402) as to the valuation of all articles exported on and after July 1, 1980. However, this preexisting law will continue to apply to the valuation of all articles which were exported prior to July 1, 1980. Consequently the preexisting law has indefinite but diminishing application. Prior exports placed in warehouses may remain there up to 5 years, and those previously brought into Foreign Trade Zones may remain there indefinitely. Whenever such prior exports are entered for consumption they must be valued under the preexisting but continuing law. That law is discussed in section IV *infra*.

3. Customs Service Regulations

The regulations issued by the Customs Service TD 81-7, January 12, 1981, recognize the limited continuation of the preexisting law, referred to as the "old value law," by amending the existing appraisement regulations in 19 CFR Part 152, Subpart C, to provide that the value of merchandise exported to the United States prior to July 1, 1980, will be determined under that subpart.

The regulations to cover the new valuation standards were added as Subpart E of Part 152, entitled "Valuation of Merchandise." They restate the provisions of Title II of the 1979 Act in codified form and amplify them with interpretative notes drawn from the Statement of Administrative Action on Customs Valuation and various examples.

These regulations were amended by TD 84-235, November 29, 1984, 49 FR 46886, to bring the treatment of foreign inland freight more in line with the MTN Agreement and the valuation law.

B. Valuation Standards

1. The Five Alternative Bases of Value

The new valuation law takes the form of an amendment to Section 402 of the Tariff Act of 1930 (19 U.S.C. 1401a). It provides for the following five bases for appraising imported merchandise, the first being the primary and preferred basis:

    (a) The transaction value of the imported merchandise;
    (b) The transaction value of identical merchandise;
    (c) The transaction value of similar merchandise;
    (d) The deductive value; and
    (e) The computed value.

Each basis is to be used only if the preceding basis cannot be determined; and, in the case of basis (a), even if the transaction value of the imported merchandise can be determined, that basis may not be used if any of the disqualifications discussed in section 2 *infra* applies. However, the importer may timely elect to have the merchandise appraised on the basis of computed value, rather than deductive value. If none of the five bases can be used, appraisal is to be on the basis of a value derived from one of the bases, with the methods being reasonably adjusted as necessary to arrive at a value.

2. Transaction Value of Imported Merchandise[6]

Several concepts are common to the transaction value of imported merchandise, of identical merchandise, and of similar merchandise. These concepts, concerning the nature of transaction value itself, are discussed in terms of the transaction value of imported merchandise. The next section discusses the unique features applicable to the transaction value of identical merchandise and similar merchandise.

Definition. The transaction value of imported (instant) merchandise is the price actually paid or payable for the merchandise when sold for exportation to the United States, plus amounts equal to:

A. The packing costs incurred by the buyer

B. Any selling commission incurred by the buyer

C. The value of any assist

D. Any royalty or license fee that the buyer is required to pay as a condition of the sale

E. The proceeds, accruing to the seller, of any subsequent resale, disposal, or use of the imported merchandise

These amounts (A through E) are added only to the extent that each (1) is not included in the price, and (2) is based on information establishing the accuracy of the amount. If sufficient information is not available, then the transaction value cannot be determined; and the next basis of value, in order of precedence, must be considered for appraisement.

For example, a royalty is paid on the basis of the price in a sale in the United States of a gallon of a particular product that was imported by the pound and transformed into a solution after importation. Suppose the royalty is based partly on the imported merchandise and partly on other factors having no connection with the imported goods, such as, when the imported goods are mixed with domestic ingredients and no longer separately identifiable. In such a situation, an amount for royalties cannot be accurately added to the price, thus a transaction value for the imported merchandise does not exist. However, if the royalty is based only on the imported goods and is quantifiable, then an amount can accurately be added to the price.

The price actually paid (or payable) for the imported merchandise is the total payment, excluding international freight, insurance, and other C.I.F. charges, that the buyer makes to the seller. This payment may be direct or indirect. Some examples of an indirect payment are when the buyer settles all or part of a debt owed by the seller, or when the seller to settle a debt he owes the buyer reduces the price on current importation. Such indirect payments are part of the transaction value.

---

[6]Reproduced without alteration from the U.S. Customs Service Booklet "Customs Valuation," June 1980, but with outline numbering of the five main headings and with Editor's notes to additional material.

For example, Smith Company in Dayton, Ohio pays $2,000 to Pierre's Toy Factory in Paris, France for a shipment of toys. The $2,000 consists of $1,850 for the toys and $150 for ocean freight and insurance. Pierre's Toy Factory would have charged Smith Company $2,200 for the toys; however, since Pierre's owed Smith Company $350, Pierre's only charged $1,850 for the toys. Assuming the transaction is acceptable, what is the transaction value?

The transaction value of the imported merchandise is $2,200, that is, the sum of the $1,850 plus the $350 indirect payment. Because the transaction value excludes C.I.F. charges, the $150 ocean freight and insurance charge is excluded.

However, if a buyer performs an activity on his own account, other than those listed in the foregoing A through E, then the activity is not considered an indirect payment to the seller, and is not part of the transaction value. This applies even though the buyer's activity might be regarded as benefiting the seller. An example of such activity is advertising.

As can be seen, several items comprise transaction value. Certain others do not. The amounts to be disregarded in determining transaction value are:

A. The cost, charges, or expenses incurred for transportation, insurance, and related services incident to the international shipment of the goods from the country of exportation to the place of importation in the United States.[7]

B. Any decrease in the price actually paid or payable that is made or effected between the buyer and seller after the *date of importation* of the goods into the United States.[8]

As well as, *if identified separately:*

C. Any reasonable cost or charge incurred for:

(1) Constructing, erecting, assembling, maintaining, or providing technical assistance with respect to the goods after importation into the United States, or

(2) Transporting the goods after importation.

D. The customs duties and other Federal taxes, including any Federal excise tax for which sellers in the United States are ordinarily liable.

Limitations. The transaction value of imported merchandise is the appraised value of that merchandise, provided certain limitations do not exist. If any of these limitations are present, then transaction value cannot be used as the appraised value, and the next basis of value will be considered.

The limitations can be divided into four groups: restrictions on the disposition or use of the merchandise, conditions for which a value cannot be determined, proceeds accruing to the seller, and related-party transactions where the transaction value is not acceptable.

Group 1—Restrictions: Generally, if a seller imposes any restrictions on a buyer's disposition or use of the imported merchandise, then transaction value cannot be used. However, exceptions are made to this rule. Thus certain restrictions are acceptable, and their presence will still allow the use of transaction value.

The acceptable restrictions are: (a) those imposed or required by law, (b) those limiting the geographical area in which the goods may be resold, and (c) those not substantially affecting the value of the goods. An example of the last restriction occurs when a seller stipulates that a buyer of new-model cars cannot sell or exhibit the cars until the start of the new sales year.

Group 2—Conditions: If the sale of, or the price actually paid or payable for, the imported merchandise is subject to any condition or consideration for which a value cannot be determined, then transaction value cannot be used. Some examples of this group include when the price of the imported merchandise depends on (a) the buyer's also buying from the seller other merchandise in specified quantities, (b) the price at which the buyer sells other goods to the seller, or (c) a form of payment extraneous to the imported merchandise, such as,

---

[7] *Ed. Note:* See TD 84–235 for exclusion of foreign inland freight.

[8] *Ed. Note:* This provision was added to the Code by the House Ways and Means Committee. Section WMCP: 96-21, May 18, 1979, at 11.

the seller's receiving a specified quantity of the finished product that results after the buyer further processes the imported goods.

Group 3—Proceeds: If part of the proceeds of any subsequent resale, disposal, or use of the imported merchandise by the buyer accrues directly or indirectly to the seller, then transaction value cannot be used. There is an exception however.

The exception is that, if an appropriate adjustment can be made for the partial proceeds the seller receives, then transaction value can still be considered. Whether an adjustment would be made would depend on whether the price actually paid or payable includes such proceeds and, if it does not, the availability of sufficient information to determine the amount of such proceeds.

Group 4—Relationship: This group concerns the relationship between the buyer and seller. The fact that the buyer and seller are related does not automatically negate using their transaction value; however, the transaction value must be acceptable.

What is meant by acceptable? Acceptable means that the relationship between the buyer and seller did not influence the price actually paid or payable. Examining the circumstances of the sale will help make this determination.

Alternatively, acceptable can also mean that the transaction value of the imported merchandise closely approximates any one of the following test values, provided these values relate to merchandise exported to the United States at or about the same time as the imported merchandise:

a. The transaction value of identical merchandise, or of similar merchandise, in sales to unrelated buyers in the United States,

b. The deductive value or computed value for identical merchandise or similar merchandise, or

[c. The transaction value of imported merchandise in sales to unrelated buyers of merchandise, for exportation to the United States, that is identical to the imported merchandise under appraisement, except for having been produced in a different country. No two sales to unrelated buyers can be used for comparison unless the sellers are unrelated.][9]

The test values are used for comparison only. They do not form a substitute basis of valuation.

In determining if the transaction value is close to one of the foregoing test values (a, b, [or c]), an adjustment is made if the sales involved differ in:

• Commercial levels,

• Quantity levels,

• The costs, commissions, values, fees, and proceeds described in A through E of the "Definition" of transaction value, and

• The costs incurred by the seller in sales in which he and the buyer are not related that are not incurred by the seller in sales in which he and the buyer are related.

As stated, the test values are alternatives to the relationship criterion. If one of the test values is met, it is not necessary to examine the question of whether the relationship influenced the price.

Having discussed the "acceptability" of a related-party transaction, the next question that follows is: Who is considered related? For appraisement purposes, any of the following persons are considered related —

• Members of the same family, including brothers and sisters (whether by whole or half blood), spouse, ancestors, and lineal descendants

• Any officer or director of an organization and such organization

• An officer or director of an organization and an officer or director of another organization, if each such individual is also an officer or director in the other organization

• Partners

• Employer and employee

---

[9] *Ed. Note:* This test was eliminated by Pub. L. No. 96-490, Section 2, December 2, 1980, 94 Stat. 2557.

● Any person directly or indirectly owning, controlling, or holding with power to vote, 5 percent or more of the outstanding voting stock or shares of any organization and such organization

● Two or more persons directly or indirectly controlling, controlled by, or under common control with, any person.

As stated previously, if certain limitations exist, the transaction value of the imported merchandise cannot be determined, and the next basis of appraisement will be considered.

So far, this section has discussed the definition of transaction value of imported merchandise and the limitations precluding its use. In defining transaction value, several items were listed which, if not included in the price, require adjusting that price to incorporate the items. It would be appropriate, before ending this section, to discuss each of the items in detail.

Adjustments. As stated previously, the transaction value of imported merchandise is the price actually paid or payable plus, when not included in the price,

A. Packing costs
B. Selling commissions
C. Assists
D. Royalty or license fees as a condition of sale, and
E. Proceeds accruing to the seller.

Item A—Packing. Packing costs consist of the costs incurred by the buyer for all containers and coverings of whatever nature and for the labor and materials used in packing the imported merchandise, ready for export.

Item B—Selling Commissions. Any selling commission incurred by the buyer with respect to the imported merchandise constitutes part of the transaction value. Buying commissions do not. A selling commission means any commission the buyer incurs, other than a buying commission.

Item C—Assists.[10] The apportioned value of any assist constitutes part of the transaction value of the imported merchandise. First the value of the assist is determined; then the value is pro-rated to the imported merchandise.

a. Definition. An "assist" is any of the following items that the buyer of imported merchandise provides directly or indirectly, and free of charge or at reduced cost, for use in the production of or the sale for export to the United States of the imported merchandise:

● Materials, components, parts, and similar items incorporated in the imported merchandise

● Tools, dies, molds, and similar items used in producing the imported merchandise

● Merchandise consumed in producing the imported merchandise

● Engineering, development, artwork, design work, and plans and sketches that are undertaken outside the United States.

The last item listed above "Engineering, development ..." will not be treated as an assist if the service or work is (1) performed by a person domiciled within the United States, (2) performed while that person is acting as an employee or agent of the buyer of the imported merchandise, and (3) incidental to other engineering, development, artwork, design work, or plans or sketches undertaken within the United States.

b. Value. In determining the value of an assist, the following general rules apply:

(1) The value is either (i) the cost of acquiring the assist—if acquired by the importer from an unrelated seller, or (ii) the cost of producing the assist—if produced by the importer or a person related to him.

(2) The value includes the cost of transporting the assist to the place of production.

---

[10]*Ed. Note:* The provision for assists in Section 402 is the first statutory definition and inclusion of assists in determinations of value.

(3) The value of assists used in producing the imported merchandise is adjusted to reflect use, repairs, modifications, or other factors affecting the value of the assists. Assists of this type include such items as tools, dies, and molds. For example, if the importer previously used the assist, regardless of whether he acquired or produced it, the original cost of acquisition or of production must be decreased to reflect the use. Alternatively repairs and modifications may result in the value of the assist having to be adjusted upwards.

(4) In the case of engineering, development, artwork, design work, and plans and sketches undertaken elsewhere than in the United States, the value is

(i) the cost of obtaining copies of the assist, if the assist is available in the public domain

(ii) the cost of the purchase or of the lease, if the assist was bought or leased by the buyer from an unrelated person.

(iii) the value added outside the United States, if the assist was produced in the United States and one or more foreign countries.

So far as possible, the buyer's commercial record system will be used to determine the value of an assist, especially such assists as engineering, development, artwork, design work, and plans and sketches undertaken elsewhere than in the United States.

For example, suppose a company imports a variety of products from several countries. The company has a design center outside the United States. If the company keeps the records of the design center in such a way as to show accurately the cost of the design work attributable to the imported merchandise, then the value of the assist is readily available.

Suppose the company shows the cost of the design center outside the United States as a general overhead expense without allocation to specific products. In this case the total design center cost can be pro-rated over the total production benefiting from the design center. The pro-rated cost on a unit basis can then be added to the price of the imported merchandise.

c. *Apportionment.* Having determined the value of an assist, the next step is to pro-rate that value to the imported merchandise. The apportionment is done reasonably and according to generally accepted accounting principles. By the latter is meant any generally recognized consensus or substantial authoritative support regarding the recording and measuring of assets and liabilities and changes therein, the disclosing of information, and the preparing of financial statements.

The method used to pro-rate the value of the assist depends on the details in the documents the importer provides to substantiate his requested method. For example, suppose the entire anticipated production using the assist is to be exported to the United States. Then the value of the assist could be pro-rated any one of several ways: over the first shipment if the importer wants to pay duty on the entire value at one time, over the number of units produced up to the time of the first shipment, or over the entire anticipated production. If the entire anticipated production is not destined for the United States, some other method of apportionment will be used that is consistent with generally accepted accounting principles.

Item D—Royalty or License Fees. Royalty or license fees that a buyer must pay, directly or indirectly, as a condition of the sale of the imported merchandise for exportation to the United States should be included in the price paid or payable. Ultimately whether a royalty or license fee is dutiable will depend on (a) whether the buyer had to pay them as a condition of the sale and (b) to whom and under what circumstances they were paid. The dutiability status will have to be decided on a case-by-case basis.[11]

---

[11] *Ed. Note:* The necessity for the Customs Service to proceed on a case-by-case basis was recognized during congressional consideration of the valuation law, with continuing application of Custom's existing treatment of royalties. H.R. Rep. No. 96-317 on H.R. 4537 at 80. This treatment was described

Charges for the right to reproduce the imported goods in the United States are not dutiable. This right applies only to the following types of merchandise: (a) originals or copies of artistic or scientific works; (b) originals or copies of models and industrial drawings; (c) model machines and prototypes; and (d) plant and animal species.

Item E—Proceeds. Any proceeds resulting from the subsequent sale, disposal, or use of the imported merchandise that accrue directly, or indirectly to the seller are dutiable. Such proceeds form part of the price actually paid or payable.

This section has discussed the transaction value of imported merchandise—the primary basis of appraisement under the Trade Agreements Act of 1979. The following sections discuss the other or secondary bases of appraisement.

3. Transaction Value of Identical Merchandise or Similar Merchandise[12]

The preceding pages discuss how to determine the transaction value of imported merchandise. If that transaction value cannot be determined, then the customs value of the imported goods being appraised is the transaction value of identical merchandise. If merchandise identical to the imported goods cannot be found or an acceptable transaction value for such merchandise does not exist, then the customs value is the transaction value of similar merchandise.

The same additions, exclusions, and limitations, previously discussed in determining the transaction value of imported merchandise, also apply in determining the transaction value of identical or similar merchandise. Therefore that discussion will not be repeated in this section.

Besides the data common to all three transaction values, certain factors specifically apply to the transaction value of identical merchandise or similar merchandise. These factors concern (a) the exportation date, (b) the level and quantity of sales, (c) the meaning, and (d) the order of precedence of identical merchandise and of similar merchandise.

a. Exportation Date. The identical merchandise, or similar merchandise, for which a transaction value is being determined must have been sold for export to the United States and exported at or about the same time as the merchandise being appraised.

b. Sales Level/Quantity. The transaction value of identical merchandise (or similar merchandise) must be based on sales of identical merchandise (or similar merchandise) at the same commercial level and in substantially the same quantity as the sales of the merchandise being appraised. If no such sale exists, then sales at either a different commercial level or in different quantities, or both, can be used, but must be adjusted to take into account any such difference. Any adjustment must be based on sufficient information, that is, information establishing the reasonableness and accuracy of the adjustment.

For example, a valid price list containing prices for different commercial levels or different quantities provides sufficient information. Suppose the imported goods being valued consists of a shipment of 100 units, the only identical imported goods for which a transaction value exists involves a sale of 500 units, and the seller grants quantity discounts. Adjusting for the difference in quantity can be made by referring to the seller's price list and using the price applicable to 100 units. Note: A sale at 100 units need not have occurred; the important factor is that the price list is established as being *bona fide* through sales at other quantities.

---

in the statement of administrative action on customs valuation, H.R. Doc.No. 96-153, Part II at 443, 444.

[12]Reproduced without alterations from the U.S. Customs Service Booklet "Customs Valuation," June 1980, but with outline numbering.

c. Definition.

(1) Identical Merchandise.

The term "identical merchandise" means merchandise that is

- Identical in all respects to the merchandise being appraised,
- Produced in the same country as the merchandise being appraised, and
- Produced by the same person as the merchandise being appraised.

If merchandise meeting all three criteria cannot be found, then identical merchandise is merchandise satisfying the first two criteria but produced by a different person than the merchandise being appraised. Note: Merchandise can be identical to the merchandise being appraised and still show minor differences in appearance.

i. Exclusion: Identical merchandise does not include merchandise that incorporates or reflects engineering, development, artwork, design work, and plans and sketches provided free or at reduced cost by the buyer and undertaken in the United States.

(2) Similar Merchandise.

The term "similar merchandise" means merchandise that is

- Produced in the same country and by the same person as the merchandise being appraised,
- Like the merchandise being appraised in characteristics and component materials, and
- Commercially interchangeable with the merchandise being appraised.

If merchandise meeting the foregoing criteria cannot be found, then similar merchandise is merchandise having the same country of production, like characteristics and component materials, and commercial interchangeability but produced by a different person.

In determining whether goods are similar; some of the factors to be considered are the quality of the goods, their reputation, and the existence of a trademark.

i. Exclusion: Similar merchandise does not include merchandise that incorporates or reflects engineering, development, artwork, design work, and plans and sketches provided free or at reduced cost by the buyer and undertaken in the United States.

d. *Order of Precedence.* Sometimes more than one transaction value will be present, that is, for identical merchandise produced by the same person, for identical merchandise produced by another person, for similar merchandise produced by the same person, and similar merchandise produced by another person. If this occurs, one value must take precedence.

As stated previously, acceptable sales at the same level and quantity take precedence over sales at different levels and/or quantities. The order of precedence can be summarized as:

(1) Identical merchandise produced by same person

(2) Identical merchandise produced by another person

(3) Similar merchandise produced by the same person

(4) Similar merchandise produced by another person

It is possible that two or more transaction values for identical merchandise (or similar merchandise) will be determined. In such a case, the lowest value will be used as the appraised value of the imported merchandise.

4. Deductive Value[13]

If the transaction value of imported merchandise, of identical merchandise, or of similar merchandise cannot be determined, then deductive value is calculated for the merchandise being appraised. Deductive value is the next basis of appraisement to be used, unless the importer designated, at entry summary,

---

[13]Reproduced without alteration from the U.S. Customs Service Booklet "Customs Valuation," June 1980, but with outline numbering.

computed value as the preferred method of appraisement. If computed value was chosen and subsequently determined not to exist for customs valuation purposes, then the basis of appraisement reverts back to deductive value.

If an assist is involved in a sale, that cannot be used in determining deductive value. So any sale to a person who supplies an assist for use in connection with the production or sale for export of the merchandise concerned is disregarded for deductive value.

Basically deductive value is the resale price in the United States after importation of the goods, with deductions for certain items. In discussing deductive value, the term "merchandise concerned" is used. The term means the merchandise being appraised, identical merchandise, or similar merchandise. Generally, the deductive value is calculated by starting with a unit price and making certain additions to and deductions in that price.

A. Unit Price

One of three prices constitutes the unit price in deductive value. The price used depends on when and in what condition the merchandise concerned is sold in the United States.

1. TIME & CONDITION: The merchandise is sold in the condition as imported at or about the date of importation of the merchandise being appraised.

PRICE: The price used is the unit price at which the greatest aggregate quantity of the merchandise concerned is sold at or about such date.

2. TIME & CONDITION: The merchandise concerned is sold in the condition as imported but not sold at or about the date of importation of the merchandise being appraised.

PRICE: The price used is the unit price at which the greatest aggregate quantity of the merchandise concerned is sold after the date of importation of the merchandise being appraised but before the close of the 90th day after the date of such importation.

3. TIME & CONDITION: The merchandise concerned is not sold in the condition as imported and not sold before the close of the 90th day after the date of importation of the merchandise being appraised.

PRICE: The price used is the unit price at which the greatest aggregate quantity of the merchandise being appraised, after further processing, is sold before the 180th day after the date of such importation.

This third price is also known as the "further processing price" or "superdeductive".[14]

B. Additions.

Packing costs for the merchandise concerned are added to the price used for deductive value, provided such costs have not otherwise been included. These costs are added, regardless of whether the importer or the buyer incurs the cost.

Packing costs means the cost (1) of all containers and coverings of whatever nature and (2) of packing, whether for labor or materials, used in placing the merchandise in condition, packed ready for shipment to the United States.

C. Deductions.

Certain items are not a part of deductive value. These items must be deducted from the unit price. The items are:

1. *Commissions or Profit and General Expenses.* Any commission usually paid or agreed to be paid, or the addition usually made for profit and general expenses, applicable to sales in the United States of imported merchandise that is
   (a) of the same class or kind as the merchandise concerned;
   (b) regardless of the country of exportation;

2. *Transportation/Insurance Costs.* The usual and associated costs of transporting and insuring the merchandise concerned
   (a) From the country of exportation to the place of importation in the United States, and

---

[14]*Ed. Note:* The superdeductive value method is analyzed and applied to defective parts imported to be repaired and resold, in C.S.D. 84-89, 18 Cust. Bull. No. 42 at 38.

(b) From the place of importation to the place of delivery in the United States, provided these costs are not included as a general expense under the preceding paragraph;

3. *Customs Duties/Federal Taxes.* The customs duties and other Federal taxes payable on the merchandise concerned because of its importation, plus any Federal excise tax on, or measured by the value of, such merchandise for which sellers in the United States are ordinarily liable; and

4. *Value of Further Processing.* The value added by the processing of the merchandise after importation, provided sufficient information exists concerning the cost of processing. The price determined for deductive value is reduced by the value of further processing, only if the third unit price (the superdeductive) is used as deductive value. (Under the superdeductive, the merchandise concerned is not sold in the condition as imported and not sold before the close of the 90th day after the date of importation, but is sold before the 180th day after the date of importation.)

In mentioning the unit price and the additions and deductions to it, certain terms are used that need clarification. These terms are "unit price for the greatest aggregate quantity," "profit and general expenses," and "merchandise of the same class or kind".

"Unit Price for the Greatest Aggregate Quantity." The unit price used is the price at which the greatest number of units is sold, in sales to persons who are not related to the persons from whom they buy such goods, at the first commercial level of importation, or after further processing, at which such sales take place. Note: Related-party sales cannot be used in determining the number of units sold.

The unit price must be for a total volume greater than the total volume sold at any other unit price and sufficient to establish the unit price. Whenever all the units of the merchandise concerned have not been resold, then determining what is a sufficient number of units must be made on a case-by-case basis.

Some examples will help illustrate the unit-price principle.

a. The merchandise concerned consists of 800 units. If 500 units are sold at $100 each and 300 are sold at $200 each, then the unit price is $100.

b. Suppose a total shipment of 90 units is sold as follows:

20 units	$10 each
15 units	30 each
30 units	20 each
25 units	40 each

The unit price is $20, the price at which the greatest number of units is sold.

c. If a seller gives lower unit prices for large-volume sales, the unit price used is the unit price for the greatest aggregate quantity sold.

Sale Quantity	Unit Price	Number of Sales	Total Units Sold
1–50	$50	15 sales of 2 units	60
		10 sales of 3 units	
51–100	40	1 sale of 55 units	55

The greatest number of units sold is 60; so, the unit price for the greatest aggregate quantity is $50.

"Profit and General Expenses". The unit price selected for deductive value must be reduced by an amount equal to any commission paid or to be paid or the usual addition for profit and general expenses. In handling the profit and general expenses component, several points must be remembered.

These are:

a. The profit and general expenses are viewed as a whole.

For example, an importer is introducing a new product line and thus is taking little profit ($5). However his general expenses are high ($20) because of introducing the new product.

	Importer	Usual
Profit	$ 5	$15
General Expenses	20	10
Total	25	25

Taken as a whole, the importer's combined profit and general expense figure is consistent with the usual profit and general expense figure and thus is an acceptable figure.

b. The profit and general expenses are based on the importer's profit and general expenses.

If such profits and general expenses are inconsistent with those in sales in the United States of imported merchandise of the same class or kind from all countries, then the deduction will be based on the usual profit and general expenses in such sales.

The information used to determine profit and general expenses must be sufficient to establish the accuracy of the amount and prepared consistent with generally accepted accounting principles in the United States.

c. Any State or local tax imposed on the importer with respect to the sale of imported merchandise is treated as a general expense.

"Merchandise of the Same Class or Kind". The term "merchandise of the same class or kind" means merchandise within a group or range of merchandise produced by a particular industry or industry sector. The narrowest group or range providing the necessary data is used.

Whether goods are of the same class or kind as the merchandise being appraised will be determined on a case-by-case basis. To be considered of the same class or kind, the merchandise need not have been exported from the same country as the merchandise being appraised.

SUPERDEDUCTIVE. The importer has the option to ask that deductive value be based on the further-processing price (the third price shown under the foregoing "A. Unit Price"). If he makes that choice, certain facts concerning valuing the further processing method must be followed. For ease of reference, the further processing method will be called "superdeductive."

Under the superdeductive, an amount equal to the value of the further processing must be deducted from the unit price in determining deductive value. The amount so deducted must be based on objective and quantifiable data concerning the cost of such work as well as any spoilage, waste or scrap derived from that work. Items such as accepted industry formulas, methods of construction, and industry practices could be used as a basis for calculating the amount to be deducted.

Limitations. (a) Generally, the superdeductive method cannot be used if the further processing destroys the identity of the goods. Such situations will be decided on a case-by-case basis for the following reasons:

(1) Sometimes, even though the identity of the goods is lost, the value added by the processing can be determined accurately without unreasonable difficulty for importers or for the Customs Service,

(2) In some cases, the imported goods still keep their identity after processing but form only a minor part of the goods sold in the United States. In such cases, using the superdeductive method to value the imported goods will not be justified.

(b) The superdeductive method cannot be used if the merchandise concerned is sold in the condition as imported before the close of the 90th day after the date of importation of the merchandise being appraised.

5. Computed Value[15]

The last basis of appraisement is computed value. If customs valuation cannot be based on any of the values previously discussed, then computed value is considered. This value is also the one the importer can select at entry summary to precede deductive value as a basis of appraisement.

Computed value consists of the sum of the following items:

a. Materials, fabrication, and other processing used in producing the imported merchandise

b. Profit and general expenses

c. Any assist, if not included in (a) and (b), and

d. Packing costs.

a. *Materials, Fabrication, and Other Processing.* The cost or value of the materials, fabrication, and other processing of any kind used in producing the imported merchandise is based (1) on information provided by or on behalf of the producer and (2) on the commercial accounts of the producer, if the accounts are consistent with generally accepted accounting principles applied in the country of production of the goods.

Note: If the country of exportation imposes an internal tax on the materials or their disposition and refunds the tax when merchandise produced from the materials is exported, then the amount of the internal tax is not included as part of the cost or value of the materials.

b. *Profit and General Expenses.* The producer's profit and general expenses are used, provided they are consistent with the usual profit and general expenses reflected by producers in the country of exportation in sales of merchandise of the same class or kind as the imported merchandise.

Some facts concerning the amount for profit and general expenses should be mentioned:

1. The amount is determined by information the producer supplies and on his commercial accounts, provided such accounts are consistent with generally accepted accounting principles in the country of production.

Note: As a point of contrast, for deductive value the generally accepted principles used are those in the United States, whereas in computed value the generally accepted accounting principles are those in the country of production.

2. The producer's profit and general expenses must be consistent with those usually reflected in sales of goods of the same class or kind as the imported merchandise that are made by producers in the country of exportation for export to the United States. If they are not consistent, then the amount for profit and general expenses is based on the usual profit and general expenses of such producers.

3. The amount for profit and general expenses is taken as a whole. This is the same treatment as occurs, and has been discussed, in deductive value.

---

[15]Reproduced without alteration from the U.S. Customs Service Booklet "Customs Valuation," June 1980, but with outline numbering.

Basically, a producer's profit could be low and his general expenses high, so that the total amount is consistent with that usually reflected in sales of goods of the same class or kind. A producer's actual profit figures even if low, will be used, provided he has valid commercial reasons to justify them and his pricing policy reflects usual pricing policies in the industry concerned.

c. Assists. If the value of an assist used in producing the merchandise is not included as part of the producer's materials, fabrication, other processing or general expenses, then the prorated value of the assist will be included in computed value. It is important that the value of the assist is not included elsewhere because no component of computed value should be counted more than once in determining computed value.

Note: The value of any engineering, development, artwork, design work, and plans and sketches undertaken in the United States is included in computed value only to the extent that such value has been charged to the producer.

d. Packing Costs. The cost of all containers and coverings of whatever nature and of packing, whether for labor or material, used in placing merchandise in condition, packed ready for shipment to the United States is included in computed value.

In discussing computed value, reference was made to "merchandise of the same class or kind." This concept needs further clarification:

"Merchandise of the same class or kind" must be imported from the same country as the merchandise being appraised, and must be within a group or range of goods produced by a particular industry or industry sector. Whether certain merchandise is of the same class or kind as other merchandise will be determined on a case-by-case basis.

In determining usual profit and general expenses, sales for export to the United States of the narrowest group or range of merchandise that includes the merchandise being appraised will be examined, providing the necessary information can be obtained.

NOTE: As a point of contrast, under deductive value "merchandise of the same class or kind" includes merchandise imported from other countries besides the country from which the merchandise being appraised was imported. However, under computed value, "merchandise of the same class or kind" is limited to merchandise imported from the same country as the merchandise being appraised.

As can be seen, computed value relies to a certain extent on information that has to be obtained outside the United States, that is, from the producer of the merchandise. If a foreign producer refuses to or is legally constrained from providing the computed value information, or if the importer cannot provide such information within a reasonable period of time, then computed value cannot be determined.

6. Value If Other Values Cannot be Determined [16]

If none of the previous five values can be used to appraise the imported merchandise, then the customs value must be based on a value derived from one of the five previous methods, reasonably adjusted as necessary. The value so determined should be based, to the greatest extent possible, on previously determined values. Only data available in the United States will be used.

Some examples of how the other methods can be reasonably adjusted are:

---

[16]Reproduced without alteration from the U.S. Customs Service Booklet "Customs Valuation," June 1980, but with outline numbering.

Identical Merchandise (or Similar Merchandise):
(a) The requirement that the identical merchandise (or similar merchandise) should be exported at or about the same time as the merchandise being appraised could be flexibly interpreted.
(b) Identical imported merchandise (or similar imported merchandise) produced in a country other than the country of exportation of the merchandise being appraised could be the basis for customs valuation.
(c) Customs values of identical imported merchandise (or similar imported merchandise) already determined on the basis of deductive value and computed value could be used.
Deductive Method. The 90-day requirement could be administered flexibly.

7. Unacceptable Bases of Value

Following nearly identical provisions in the MTN Valuation Code, Art. 7.2, the statute rules out the use of the following seven bases of valuation which the MTN negotiations considered unfair or arbitrary handicaps to trade:
(i) The selling price in the United States of merchandise produced in the United States;
(ii) A system that provides for the appraisement of imported merchandise at the higher of two alternative values;
(iii) The price of merchandise in the domestic market of the country of exportation;
(iv) A cost of production, other than a value determined under 19 CFR 152.106, Computed Value, for merchandise that is identical merchandise, or similar merchandise, to the merchandise being appraised;
(v) The price of merchandise for export to a country other than the United States;
(vi) Minimum values for appraisement; or
(vii) Arbitrary or fictitious values.

8. Customs Service Decisions

A number of Customs Service Decisions (CSDs) published in the Customs Bulletins interpret and apply the foregoing valuation standards in the 1979 valuation law. CSD 82-121 of March 15, 1982, 16 Cust. Bull. 913, held that escalation payments under a formula agreed to by the foreign manufacturer and the importer prior to the importation should be added to the contract price in determining the transaction value of the merchandise, *i.e.,* the price paid or payable, even though liquidation would need to be postponed until precise determination of the escalation amounts. However, CSD 82-126 of May 19, 1982, in the same volume at 925, holds that a transaction value cannot be adjusted or affected by a retroactive adjustment of the price paid or payable made subsequent to exportation.

Transaction value was held to include a buying commission paid to the exporter for various export services where it was part of the price paid or payable. CSD 82-124 of April 29, 1982, 16 Cust. Bull. 920. Transaction value may not be the basis of valuation where two types of merchandise have been shipped together and, by agreement between the exporter and importer, the price of one type has been artificially raised for free quota purposes, and the price of the other type has been decreased by a like amount. The reason given is that the off-set arrangement has a value which cannot be determined. CSD 82-130 of June 3, 1982, in the same volume at 930.

The cost of tooling paid for by the buyer of the foreign machinery made with the tooling is not an assist where the cost is paid as part of the price paid and payable. CSD 83-3 of July 19, 1982, 17 Cust. Bull. 726. The loan interest expense incurred by an assembler prior to assembly operations in Mexico is to be included in the computed value basis of appraisement as part of the assembler's profit and general expenses. CSD 83-4 of August 6, 1982, also in 17 Cust. Bull. at 727.

Research and development costs of a foreign producer for a model of ship sets may be apportioned over the number of ship sets reasonably anticipated to be produced, although the production contract was terminated prior to full production, because such apportionment would be in accordance with generally accepted accounting principles. This ruling is a departure from prior Customs Service practice which permitted R&D apportionment only over the number of units actually produced or the total to be produced under firm and specific contracts. CSD 83-58 of September 15, 1982, 17 Cust. Bull. 842.

Excess start-up costs may be accounted for under transaction value through the use of a periodically updated excess cost account and the amortization of the excess costs over current and future production in accordance with generally accepted accounting principles. CSD 84-103 of May 1, 1984, in 18 Cust. Bull. No. 46.

C. Administration

1. Customs Notice of Value Determinations

The MTN Valuation Agreement provides for notice by a customs administration of its grounds for rejecting transaction value as the basis of valuation by reason of the relationship of the parties (Art. 1.2.(a)), and, more generally, for the giving of written explanation to any importer, upon written request, as to how the value of his import was determined (Art. 16).[17] According to the House Report on the Trade Agreements Act, Congress expressly implemented the more general requirement and had an understanding that the Customs Service would provide to importers its grounds for rejecting the price as the basis of transaction value.[18]

a. Rejection of Transaction Value

The 1981 Customs Regulations on Valuation, in 19 CFR 152.103(m), require the district director to inform the importer of the grounds for

---

[17]H.R. Doc. No. 96-153, Part I at 9 and 22.
[18]H.R. Rep. No. 96-317 on H.R. 4537 at 86, 87.

rejecting the transaction value declared by the importer, whenever the rejection increases the duty liability, and to afford the importer 20 days to respond in writing if he disagrees. Apparently this requirement applies whether or not the rejection of transaction value is based upon the relationship of the parties. This regulation goes slightly beyond the preexisting and still current appraisement regulation, 19 CFR 152.2, which requires the district director to give notice and a 20-day opportunity to respond if appraisement results in an increase of duty of $15 or more.

b. Basis of Value Determination

The 1981 Valuation Regulations, in 19 CFR 152.101(d), provide a wholly new right to importers. They allow an importer 90 days after the liquidation of his import entry to request in writing an explanation of the basis of the valuation from the district director. The district director is then to provide "a reasonable and concise explanation of how the value was determined." This explanation applies only to the imported merchandise being appraised and is not to serve as authority with respect to the valuation of other merchandise at the same or other ports.

This regulation carries the advice that the explanation given is for information only, does not affect or replace the protest or administrative ruling procedures under 19 CFR Parts 174 or 177, or allow the release of any information not otherwise subject to disclosure under the Freedom of Information Act. Similar advice is appended to 19 CFR 152.103(m), discussed *supra.*

2. Sufficient Information

a. Definition

The statute, Section 402 of the Tariff Act of 1930, as amended, 19 U.S.C. 1401a, specifically requires that certain determinations be made on the basis of "sufficient information." Among these are the additions to the price actually paid or payable to determine transaction value (Section 402(b)(1)), deductions or additions of profit and general expenses (Section 402(d)(3)(B) and (e)(2)(B)), and adjustments made for different commercial levels or quantities in sales of identical or similar merchandise (Section 402(c)(2)). Under the definition, "sufficient information" is "information that establishes the accuracy" of the amount in issue (Section 402(h)(5)).

b. Supplying the Information

No direction is given in the act or regulations as to the responsibility for supplying this information. It appears from the tenor of the regulations that the importer has the initiative to supply the information and Customs has the obligation to judge it on the basis of information available to the Service. The extent to which Customs is responsible to search actively for the information is not clear. If sufficient information is not available to determine the elements of transaction value, Customs may proceed to deductive or computed value as the appraisement basis. However, if neither of these latter bases can be determined from available information, Customs has the responsibility of making a determination under Section 402(f) on the basis of a value derived from the other Section 402 methods of valuation, reasonably adjusted to the extent necessary, as described in section II. B.6 *supra.*

3. Generally Accepted Accounting Principles

a. Definition and Source

The customs regulations (Section 152.102(c)) copy the statute (Section 402(g)(3)) in defining the term "generally accepted accounting principles," often referred to as GAAP, as follows:

(1) Generally accepted accounting principles refers to any generally recognized consensus or substantial authoritative support regarding—
(i) Which economic resources and obligations should be recorded as assets and liabilities;
(ii) Which changes in assets and liabilities should be recorded;
(iii) How the assets and liabilities and changes in them should be measured;
(iv) What information should be disclosed and how it should be disclosed; and
(v) Which financial statements should be prepared.
(2) The applicability of a particular set of generally accepted accounting principles will depend upon the basis on which the value of the imported merchandise is sought to be established, and the relevant country for the point in contention.
(3) Information submitted by an importer, buyer, or producer in regard to the appraisement of merchandise may not be rejected by Customs because of the accounting method by which that information was prepared, if the preparation was in accordance with generally accepted accounting principles.

This definition was, in turn, drawn from the MTN Agreement on Customs Valuation (Interpretative Notes, Annex I).[19]

b. Required Use

Consistent with the purpose in the MTN Agreement, the statute and regulations require the Customs Service to accept appraisement information submitted by the importer if it was prepared in accordance with GAAP. This plainly means that Customs is not to set up requirements that necessitate separate bookkeeping by importers, but is to accept foreign calculations if made in accordance with the GAAP prevailing in the exporting country, even if the accounting methods would not be domestically accepted.[20]

---

[19]H.R. Doc. No. 96-153, Part I at 27.
[20]See Sherman, *supra* note 2 at 147

4. Disclosure of Information

As expressed in the Statement of Administrative Action on Customs Valuation,[21] the Customs Service will continue to be guided by the current U.S. laws relating to confidentiality and disclosure, primarily those contained in the Freedom of Information Act (FOIA), as amended (5 U.S.C. 552), and the Privacy Act of 1974 (5 U.S.C. 552a). See also 18 U.S.C. 1905. Generally speaking, much of the information submitted for purposes of customs valuation is considered to be business confidential and is not subject to disclosure. However, the provisions of the FOIA and the Privacy Act will prevail in any conflict concerning the confidentiality and disclosure of information. In this regard, any information must be disclosed, if requested, where it is administratively determined that the information is not covered by any exemption under the FOIA. Likewise, in accordance with U.S. court decisions, where it is determined that a business confidential exemption has disappeared with the passage of time, the pertinent information will be disclosed despite the fact that it was submitted "on a confidential basis."

5. USTR Supervisory Role

The U.S. Trade Representative has primary responsibility among government agencies, under Reorganization Plan No. 3 of 1979, for policy guidance on all international trade issues arising from the implementation of the MTN Agreements approved by the Congress in the 1979 act. The USTR's office is therefore concerned with supervision of international arrangements for the carrying out of the Valuation Code legislation. This necessarily includes the handling of further acceptances of the Code, relations with the less developed countries, dispute settlements under the GATT, the encouragement of the substitution of the Code standards for the BDV standards, and much more.

6. Reports

Under Section 203 of the 1979 Act (19 U.S.C. 1401a note), the President is required to submit to the Congress a report containing an evaluation of the operation of the MTN Valuation Agreement, both domestically and internationally. This report is due as soon as possible after the close of the two-year period beginning on the effective date of the Valuation legislation. The USTR has responsibility for the making of this report.

The Comptroller General of the United States reviewed the operation of the new valuation system in order to evaluate its impact on the Customs Service, the importers and customs brokers. In a Report to Congress dated July 26, 1982, B-201765, he concluded that the new law had resulted in a "uniform, fair, and greatly simplified system for the valuation of imported

---

[21]H.R. Doc. No. 96-153, Part II at 460.

products" (p. 10). He found that the acceptance by Customs of the price agreed to between the buyer and seller as the basis for valuation had saved time and money and improved the efficiency of entry processes.

III. INTERNATIONAL PROCEDURES UNDER THE MTN VALUATION AGREEMENT

In his Memorandum of January 4, 1979, notifying the Congress of his intention to enter into various international trade agreements being negotiated in the MTN Tokyo Round,[22] the President reported that the Valuation Agreement was "to be administered at the political level by the GATT and at the technical level by the Customs Cooperation Council.[23] He added that a dispute settlement procedure was provided for. Both the technical and political activity on Valuation matters at the international level are of great long-term importance to international traders and to government trade representatives.

A. The GATT Committee on Customs Valuation

The Valuation Agreement provided for the establishment of a Committee on Customs Valuation composed of representatives of the Parties to the Agreement to afford opportunity for consultation on the administration of the agreement. The Committee considers and decides questions on the interpretation and application of the Agreement. For example, on September 24, 1984, it adopted a decision, VAL/8, on the valuation of carrier media bearing software for data processing equipment, finding that it would be consistent with the Agreement for Parties who wish to do so to take into account only the cost or value of the carrier medium and not include the cost or value of the data or instructions, provided that this is distinguished from the cost or value of the carrier medium. The GATT secretariat acts as the secretariat to the Committee.

B. The Technical Committee of the CCC

The Valuation Agreement also establishes a Technical Committee on Customs Valuation under the auspices of the Customs Cooperation Council and assigns to it various specific functions, including:[24]

(1) to examine specific day-to-day technical problems arising in customs valuation systems, and to render advisory opinions;

(2) to study, as requested, valuation laws and practices, and to render reports on the results;

(3) to prepare and circulate annual reports on the technical operation and status of the Agreement;

---

[22]44 FR 1933, January 8, 1979.

[23]See Appendix B for the text of the GATT, and Chapter 23, section II.C for a description of the Customs Cooperation Council (CCC).

[24]Part II of the Agreement, TIAS 10402; Part I at 23 and 55; see Appendix F.

(4) to furnish information, advice, and advisory opinions on valuation matters as requested by parties to the Agreement; and

(5) to facilitate, as requested, technical assistance to the parties in order to further acceptance of the Agreement.

A primary purpose of this technical assistance is to promote uniformity in the application of the Valuation Code by the members accepting the Agreement. In recommending congressional approval of the Agreement the House Ways and Means Committee, in its Report on the legislation, expressed expectation that the CCC would move expeditiously to obtain replacement of the BDV with the Code valuation system.[25] The CCC, for this purpose, is said to offer training assistance to countries lacking the internal resources to effectuate the MTN system.[26] The more successful the CCC can be in providing guidance and uniformity in interpretation, the less likely becomes resort to the political dispute settlement procedure.

C. Dispute Settlement Procedure

The MTN Agreement provides machinery for the settlement of disputes which reach the level of complaint by one government against another. For example, the government of the signatory member whose exports are not receiving the valuation treatment considered appropriate by complaining exporters may invoke the machinery in the Code. First, that government may seek consultations with the importing country and ask the CCC Technical Committee for advice. If no solution is reached, either party may request the full-member Committee on Valuation, established by the Agreement, to meet, investigate the matter, and facilitate a satisfactory solution. The Committee on Valuation may set up a panel to investigate and report to it. The ultimate sanction against the government refusing to accept final recommendation from the Committee is suspension of the government from appropriate obligations of the Agreement.[27] Parties to the Agreement are to utilize the dispute settlement procedures in the Agreement before resorting to any rights they may have under the GATT.[28]

IV. PREEXISTING VALUATION LAWS
APPLICABLE TO PRE-JULY 1, 1980, EXPORTS

The American laws covering valuation, existing prior to the implementation on July 1, 1980, of Title II of the 1979 Trade Agreements Act, and still applicable to pre-July 1, 1980, exports, are complex since they were written to provide for all possible situations. In pre-1980 terms, there is a 1930 "old law,"[29] and a "new law"[30] passed by the Congress in 1956. Which law is used in making determinations of value depends upon the article being

---

[25]H.R. Doc. No. 96-317 at 90.
[26]Sherman, *supra* note 2 at 157.
[27]Part II of the Customs Valuation Agreement, TIAS 10402; see Appendix F.
[28]Article 20.11 of the Agreement.
[29]19 U.S.C. 1402.
[30]19 U.S.C. 1401(a), 1976 Edition.

appraised. The terms "old" and "new" are now confusing. Hereafter reference will be made to the 1930 and 1956 laws.

The 1956 law simplified value by doing away with "foreign value," by substituting "constructed value" for "cost of production," and by making other less important changes. Because most earlier entries require that valuations be made under the 1956 law, the 1930 law is of less consequence. However, the pressures brought by those who feared the possible adverse effect of the 1956 law resulted in retention of the 1930 law for those articles appearing on the so-called "final list."

A. The 1956 Act

1. Valuation Bases

The bases of valuation in the 1956 law are applied in this manner: (1) the export value; (2) if the export value cannot be found, the U.S. value; (3) if neither the export value nor the U.S. value can be found, the constructed value; and (4) the American Selling Price of a domestic article when the article is dutiable on that basis of valuation, as shown in the TSUS. Each of the bases for valuation in the 1956 law is used in the order of preference above to the exclusion of any succeeding item or items, except that if American Selling Price is applicable, it must be used without regard to any other basis for value.

2. Definitions

a. Valuation Bases

1. Export Value. The export value is the usual price of merchandise for exportation to the United States plus the cost of putting the merchandise into condition, ready for shipment. To determine export value, the merchandise, cumulatively, must be (1) such or similar merchandise; (2) freely sold or offered for sale; (3) in the principal market(s) of the country of exportation; (4) in the usual wholesale quantities; (5) in the ordinary course of trade, for exportation to the United States; and (6) at a price which includes the cost of foreign inland transportation, when applicable.

2. U.S. Value. The U.S. value is the price at the time of exportation at which such or similar merchandise is freely sold or offered for sale in the principal market of the United States for domestic consumption, packed ready for delivery, in the usual wholesale quantities, and in the ordinary course of trade, with deductions (1) for any commission usually paid, (2) for any amount usually added for general expenses and profit, (3) for other usual expenses from the place of shipment to the place of delivery, and (4) for the ordinary customs duties and federal excise and other taxes. If no such or similar merchandise was sold or offered for sale at the time of exportation, the U.S. value is calculated from the price at which the merchandise was sold or offered at the earliest date after exportation but before the expiration of 90 days after importation. If no such price is available, then constructed value is used.

3. Constructed Value. The constructed value is the sum of the cost of materials and of the fabrication or other processing employed in producing such or similar merchandise prior to exportation, plus an amount for general expenses and profit equal to that usually reflected in sales of the merchandise and for the cost of containers, coverings, and packing for shipment to the United States.

4. American Selling Price. The American Selling Price (ASP) of an article manufactured or produced in the United States is the price, including the cost of containers, coverings, and packing, at which such article is freely sold or offered for sale for domestic consumption in the United States or the price that the owner would have been willing to receive for such merchandise at the time of exportation of the imported article. This value is only applied to sales in the United States of "such" articles. When there is no such or like article produced in the United States, ASP does not apply and valuation is made on the U.S. value basis.

b. Other Terms

The 1956 law, unlike its predecessor, includes definitions of some of the terms used in the several value provisions:

1. Freely Sold or Offered. This term makes it clear that "offers" are to be considered in determining values only if there are no sales. Sales or offers will not be regarded as "free" if they are not open to acceptance by all purchasers at wholesale. If such sales or offers are to selected wholesale purchasers, they must be in the ordinary course of trade and the price must fairly reflect the market value. Sales or offers may not include restrictions as to the disposition or use of the merchandise by the purchaser, unless imposed or required by law, but restrictions that limit the resale price or the resale territory or that do not substantially affect the value to usual purchasers may be imposed.

2. Ordinary Course of Trade. Merchandise will be regarded as sold in the ordinary course of trade if for a reasonable time prior to exportation the conditions and practices followed in the sale were normal in the trade for merchandise of the same class or kind.

3. Purchasers at Wholesale. This term covers those who buy in wholesale quantity lots for industrial use or for resale to the trade. It does not include those who buy to sell at retail unless there are no others who buy in wholesale quantities. Absent purchasers for retail, the term includes all others who purchase in the usual wholesale quantities.

4. Such or Similar Merchandise. Merchandise is "such or similar" if it is (1) the merchandise under consideration or other identical merchandise produced in the same country by the same person; (2) identical merchandise produced by another person in the same country; (3) merchandise produced in the same country and by the same person which is like the merchandise being appraised in component materials and use, and approximately equal in commercial value to that merchandise; or (4) merchandise produced by another person which otherwise satisfies all the requirements of alternative (3).

In valuing a shipment the appraising officer uses the first available category in the order given above. The overriding criterion in determining similarity is commercial interchangeability, not the ultimate use or cost of production. Merchandise is not disqualified as identical because of minor differences in appearance, such as a difference in color or labeling. Merchandise is not such or similar where finished and unfinished articles are compared. But where identical products are sold under different brand names, one brand commanding a much higher price, the articles may be regarded as not similar. The same is true where labeled articles command a much greater price than unlabeled articles.

5. *Usual Wholesale Quantities.* Where a commodity is sold at varying prices depending upon the quantity purchased, the statute prescribes that the usual wholesale quantity will be that quantity in which more merchandise is sold than in any other quantity.

6. *Transactions Between Related Persons.* The 1956 law permits the appraising officer to disregard direct or indirect transactions between related persons in making a determination of U.S. value or constructed value. Related persons are defined as including members of a family, in a broad sense; officers or directors of an organization or the organization itself; partners; employer and employee; those holding, directly or indirectly, a 5 percent or greater interest in the outstanding voting stock or shares of an organization and the organization itself; and two or more persons directly or indirectly controlling, controlled by, or under common control with any person.

Such transactions may be disregarded if the appraising officer does not believe that the element of value to be considered reflects the amount usually reflected in sales in the market under consideration. If a transaction is disregarded and there are no other transactions available, the determination of the amount required to be considered is made on the best evidence available as to what the amount would have been if the transaction had been between unrelated persons.

B. The 1930 Law—The Final List

The Congress, in enacting the 1956 value law discussed *supra,* decided to retain the 1930 value law for use in the appraisement of articles which would be appraised under the later law at an unfairly low value as compared with the appraised value under the 1930 law. The purpose was to prevent serious dislocations in duty assessments under the later law. The final list, *i.e.,* the list of articles which would have been so appraised, containing such significant items as benzenoid chemicals or coal-tar products, rubber-soled footwear, and automobiles and parts, was published as a *Treasury Decision*[31] on January 20, 1958.

---

[31]TD 54521.

The final list, which remains unchanged, sets forth in specific terms the articles required to be appraised under the 1930 law, because the Secretary of the Treasury found, after following statutory procedures, that they would be reduced in value by 5 percent or more under the valuation provisions of the 1956 law.

The final list is specific in its descriptions. For example, it includes needles, embroidery machines, needles for knitting machines, and other types of needles; airplanes seating six passengers or less but excluding seaplanes, amphibians, or aircraft other than airplanes; and cheddar cheese having a score of 92 or more. If, for instance, the score of cheddar is less than 92, valuation is under the 1956 law; if the score is 92 or more, valuation is under the 1930 law.

The same is true where the final list shows a value criterion as the dividing line. For instance, pleasure boats of fiberglass construction are listed if valued at not more than $15,000 each. Such a pleasure boat whose foreign or export value goes over the specified amount when calculated under the 1930 law would not be on the final list and would be appraised under the later law even though its export value then might be less than $15,000.

1. Valuation Bases

There are several bases of valuation in the 1930 law:

(1) The foreign value or the export value, whichever is higher.

(2) If neither can be found, the U.S. value.

(3) If none of these three values can be found, the cost of production.

(4) The ASP of a domestic article when the article is dutiable on the basis of that valuation.

Each of the bases of valuation mentioned in the first three numbered items is used in the above order of preference to the exclusion of any succeeding item or items. As a matter of practical result, appraisement under this law can be and ordinarily is based upon foreign value or export value. Cost of production requires difficult determinations and calculation. But if ASP is applicable, it must be used without regard to any other basis of value.

2. Definitions

a. Foreign Value and Export Value

The foreign value simply means the price at which the merchandise is sold for home consumption at the time of exportation of the merchandise to the United States, plus the cost of readying the merchandise for shipment. In each foreign value determination, the merchandise cumulatively must be (1) such or similar merchandise, (2) freely offered for sale for home consumption without restrictions as to resale or use, (3) available to all purchasers, (4) in the principal market(s) of the country of exportation, (5) in the usual wholesale quantities, (6) in the ordinary course of trade, (7) at a price which includes the cost of containers, coverings, and packing, and (8) at a price which includes the cost of foreign inland transportation when applicable. Inland transportation is dutiable unless all purchasers are regularly given an allowance for this cost when delivery is made at the factory. Ocean freight, port fees, marine insurance, and similar charges are not included in duty computations, although they are included in c.i.f. (cost, insurance, and freight) computations made for statistical purposes.

The export value is the market value or the price at the time of exportation at which the merchandise is freely offered for sale to the United States. Sales in the domestic market of the exporting country are not considered. The same provisions governing foreign value pertain to export value, *i.e.,* such or similar merchandise, freely offered for sale, to all purchasers, etc.

b. U.S. Value

The U.S. value is the price at which the imported merchandise is freely offered for sale for domestic consumption, with an allowance, in the form of a deduction, for duty, costs of transportation (including foreign inland freight but only when sales are made ex-factory) and insurance, other necessary expenses from the place of shipment to the place of delivery, and a commission not exceeding 6 percent of goods acquired other than by purchase, or, if purchased, profits not to exceed 8 percent and a reasonable allowance for general expenses not to exceed 8 percent.

c. Cost of Production

The cost of production is the total cost of materials and the work done on those materials in manufacturing or producing such or similar merchandise prior to the date of exportation, plus the usual general expenses (not less than 10 percent), the cost of containers, coverings, packing, and other costs for putting the merchandise into condition ready for shipment to the United States, and an addition for ordinary profit of not less than 8 percent of the total amount for the cost of materials and of fabrication and the usual general expenses.

In applying this valuation basis to confectionary products imported during 1978 and 1979 the Court of International Trade held that the sugar-content rebate from the European Community received by the manufacturer after the date of manufacture of the exports may not be deducted from his cost of production, for the reason that the statute fixes the cost of materials at the time when the materials were or could have been purchased for the production of the particular merchandise exported. *M&M/Mars Snackmaster Division of Mars, Inc.* v. *United States,* 7 CIT _____ , 587 F. Supp. 1075 (1984) 5 ITRD 2401.

d. American Selling Price

The ASP of an article manufactured or produced in the United States is computed in substantially the same way as under the definition in the 1956 law.

C. Principal Differences Between the 1930 and 1956 Laws

(1) Under the 1930 law, the usual basis for valuation is foreign value or export value, whichever is higher. The 1956 law omits consideration of the value for sale for home consumption (*i.e.,* foreign value) and provides only for consideration of the value for sale for exportation to the United States (*i.e.,* export value).

(2) The language in the 1930 law results in the possible use of sales to retailers as against sales to wholesalers, which are preferred in the 1956 law.

(3) The definition of "usual wholesale quantities" added in the later law makes the aggregate quantity in which more merchandise is sold than in any other quantity the controlling factor in that law, whereas the number of individual transactions controls under the 1930 law.

(4) The 1956 law gives preference to actual sales over offers for sale in setting values.

(5) There is no maximum allowance limitation in the 1956 law such as the limitation in the 1930 law to 6 percent for commissions and 8 percent each for profit and general expenses in the calculation of U.S. value. Instead, the 1956 law permits deduction of the usual commission paid and the usual profit and general expenses.

(6) The later law permits appraising officers to disregard transactions between related persons in determining U.S. value and constructed value.

(7) Appraisement at U.S. value under the later law may be based on sales or offers made after the date of importation, provided such sales or offers are made within 90 days of that date.

(8) Restrictions on resale price or territory are disqualifying under the old law but not under the later law.

(9) Under the later law, the definition of constructed value permits allowances for sales, turnover, and other internal taxes applicable to the materials used or their disposition, which are remitted or refunded upon exportation.

(10) The 1956 law permits consideration of a transaction between a seller and a selected purchaser at wholesale (even a related purchaser when U.S. value or constructed value applies), provided the transaction fairly reflects the market value.

(11) The later law permits the use of actual general expenses and usual profit in the calculation of constructed value. The 1930 law requires that the general expenses be not less than 10 percent and the profit not less than 8 percent.

D. Special Valuation Problems

1. Absence of Usual Values

If all else fails, the appraising officer is authorized, as to merchandise exported before July 1, 1980, to ascertain or estimate the value of merchandise in the usual quantity in which it is bought and sold "by all reasonable ways and means in his power," any written statement or evidence of cost or cost of production to the contrary notwithstanding.[32]

2. Time of Exportation

The time of exportation, which is critical in finding values in all categories under both value laws, is the time at which merchandise actually leaves the country of exportation for the United States.[33] Since fractions of a day ordinarily are not material in determining the time of exportation, this discussion generally will refer only to the *date* of exportation.

When merchandise is shipped by water directly from the country of export, the date of the sailing of the vessel from that country will be used as the date of exportation for purposes of value. The critical date is the date of leaving the last port of the country of exportation. Thus it was held in *Westway Trading Corp.* v. *United States,* 68 CCPA 1, CAD 1254, 633 F.2d 1388 (1980) 2 ITRD 1543, *aff'g* 83 Cust. Ct. 101, CD 4826, 483 F. Supp. 800 (1979) that sugar laden at one port in Peru prior to a Presidential Proclamation increasing the duty on sugar exported thereafter which was carried to another port in Peru subsequent to the proclamation was covered by the proclaimed increase in duty.

In order to permit appraisement, it is necessary that the date of exportation be established. In the absence of specific evidence of the facts, such as the date of sailing discussed above, Customs will ordinarily assume that the date of the special customs invoice or the commercial invoice relating to the shipment is the date of exportation. However, it seems doubtful whether this assumption would be applied when the circumstances have changed in the interval to the disadvantage of the government, such as following a currency devaluation when the fluctuation in rate of exchange would result in a reduction of duties payable to the United States.

3. Effect of Price Increase or Decrease

Since export value is determined as of the date of exportation, an increase in price occurring after the time of sale of the goods may affect dutiable value adversely. Suppose an agreed price of $10 a unit—the price under a contract negotiated between the parties months previously—has been replaced on the first of a given month with a new price of $12. Shipments exported after the first of the month will be appraised at the higher value,

---

[32] 19 U.S.C. 1500, 1976 Edition. This section was amended by Section 202(a)(4) of the 1979 Act as to exports on or after July 1, 1980.

[33] 19 CFR 152.1(c).

even though the particular shipment may be in completion of the order placed at the lower rate. The export value is thus based upon the conception that at any given date there must be a unit price at which the goods were freely sold to all purchasers at wholesale, or such a price at which the goods were offered in the absence of sales, and that the goods were sold or offered at that price continuously up to the date of exportation. If they are not, the new price will be the export value.

In times of declining prices, it is of course most important that the necessary information be given to customs, which on the same theory would appraise the merchandise at a lower value. If a freely sold or offered price does not exist, the appraiser must turn to the succeeding definitions of value to find dutiable value.

While an increase in price between the purchase contract date and the date of exportation will result in an appraised value at the higher price, the increase must be shown through actual sales or price lists. Customs may not add to the invoice unit values an automatic percentage to represent the percentage amount of the decline of the dollar against the value of the foreign currency in which the purchase was made between the date of the purchase and the date of the exportation. The Customs Court rejected this automatic currency depreciation factor as inconsistent with the statutory definition of export value in 19 U.S.C. 1401a(b). *CBS Imports Corp.* v. *United States,* 80 Cust. Ct. 61, CD 4739, 450 F. Supp. 724 (1978) 1 ITRD 1652. This decision required the Customs Service to review more than two thousand court cases and several thousand protests.

4. Relationship of Sales Terms to Duty Assessment

Importers and exporters to the United States also should keep in mind that the way in which they do business may very well affect the amount of duty that has to be paid. Duty, particularly when value is involved, does not depend entirely on the nature of the product and the exact basic price for that product. Sometimes it is a question of how sales are made and the basis for these sales.[34] An example, a manufacturer in Canada sells dresses at uniform prices including c.i.f. to any destination in the United States. The packages containing the merchandise are shipped through Champlain, N.Y., to points in the United States, sometimes to relatively nearby places, and on other occasions to more distant places. The product is not on the final list and therefore is appraised for customs purposes under the 1956 law. The first basis for value under that law is export value.

The Court of Customs and Patent Appeals held that there was no uniform price for the goods themselves because the c.i.f. prices included transportation to any U.S. point; *i.e.,* the entire package price, not the price of the merchandise at the port of exportation.[35] The court would not allow the appraiser simply to deduct the freight from the point of origin to the New York border. As there was some evidence that the goods were offered

---

[34] 19 CFR 152.1(a) and (b).

[35] *United States* v. *Josef Mfg. Ltd.,* 59 CCPA 146, CAD 1057, 460 F.2d 1079 (1972) 1 ITRD 1366.

at free on board (f.o.b.) prices at the point of origin, the court accepted those prices for valuation.

5. Selected Purchaser

As noted above, merchandise which is the subject of transactions between a seller and a selected purchaser in the ordinary course of trade may be considered under the 1956 law freely sold or offered if the price fairly reflects the market value without restrictions as to disposition or use. Selected purchasers are those chosen, for one reason or another, by the seller.

Some products, for instance, are of such a nature that they are naturally and regularly sold only to selected purchasers. Large ocean-going yachts, not stock models, for example, are products which might not and almost surely would not be sold or offered to all comers. But a sale to a selected purchaser, *i.e.,* a contractor for the building of a yacht, might be regarded as a freely offered and sold transaction if the price fairly reflects the market value. The fact that it might be difficult to determine just what the market value might truly be would not influence this or affect the determination.

6. Price Lists

A published price list may be taken by Customs as *prima facie* evidence of offers to sell freely at wholesale, assuming the price list is directed to wholesalers. If a list is made up for the sole use of the seller and his employees in quoting prices, and if that list is not given out to prospective buyers, it is not a price list which has any significance for customs purposes. Customs must, in that case, turn elsewhere to establish free sales or offers. The prices on a published price list are deemed to be effective as of the effective date shown thereon or as of the date of issuance if no effective date is given. Thereafter, goods shipped even in fulfillment of a previous order are subject to appraisement at the listed price, all other things being equal.

Price lists are regarded as effective only if there are sales made under them. A price list that is intended only to convince a buyer that he is getting a bargain in closing a deal at the price shown is not accepted for appraisement purposes because no knowing buyer would close a deal at such a price and none in fact does so.

7. Varying Prices

If the prices vary within a class of purchaser, *i.e.,* considering wholesalers, jobbers, and retailers separate classes, and the prices to a separate class vary for reasons other than the quantity purchased per order, the Customs Service applies a rule known as the "highest price rule" and appraises on the basis of the highest freely offered prices to that class of purchaser. On the other hand, if the manufacturer has several prices that appear to vary more or less at will with no distinguishable reason for the variances, it may be that the price will be regarded as one for merchandise that is not freely sold or offered to all purchasers at wholesale. In that case, the appraising officer will find the value based on some ground other than export value. If U.S. value is not determinable, constructed value may be used as the basis for the determination. The differences in price cannot be based on such factors as quantities purchased in former years, the potential buying power of the customers, and their status as old customers. Thus, where sales are to wholesalers and to original equipment manufacturers (OEMs), importations will be appraised at the highest price at which the merchandise was sold, unless the difference between the price to wholesalers and OEMs is predicated solely upon the quantity actually purchased.

8. Lowest Price Rule (Prudent Buyer Rule)

The lowest price rule applies only when such or similar merchandise is being compared with the merchandise under appraisement. In this case, when there is more than one product being used for comparison, the lowest freely offered or sold price is used as the value for appraisement. This is on the theory that a prudent buyer of comparable merchandise would, in the normal course, select merchandise at the lowest price available. For this reason, the rule is known as the "prudent buyer rule."

9. Dutiable Commissions

The question of whether commissions are dutiable or not is a very troublesome one. The general rule is that if a commission is paid which is a buying commission, the amount is not dutiable. A buying commission may be paid to a representative of the importer abroad who is concerned in representing that importer in the purchase of goods. He seeks out the best available sources of supply, the most reliable producers, and those who offer the best price. He may also do the actual buying and he may provide other services necessary to purchase the goods and get them to the United States. This can include packing and forwarding as well as, of course, quality control for the benefit of the importer as distinguished from the manufacturer's quality control. These commissions are not part of the dutiable value.

A selling commission, however, paid to a person acting for a foreign manufacturer is dutiable. A selling agency is most frequently found in a case in which the seller himself does not sell directly to importers. In this case, the commission paid becomes part of the dutiable value.

Importers should be careful to establish the exact relationship clearly without equivocation so that additional duties and penalties will not be improperly assessed. This question has been an important aspect of cases where penalties are assessed against the total value of the merchandise because the importer believed that he had a buying commission situation when in fact it was held to be a selling commission.

10. Ex-Factory Sales

Where merchandise is freely offered for sale to all comers at a price that does not include the costs of transportation from the factory to the port of exportation, the charges for inland freight and other expenses such as storage and lighterage are not included in the dutiable value. On the other hand, if the seller regularly sells only at f.o.b. port of exportation, these charges are included in dutiable value. Nevertheless, a court decision has ruled that where sales were made on an f.o.b. basis but offered at an ex-factory price, the inland charges are not dutiable.

Charges incurred after exportation are not dutiable. Even if such charges are paid by the exporter, including the charges for ocean freight and marine insurance, and, particularly in the case of exportations from Canada, for duty assessed, these amounts are not included in dutiable value. In general, charges incurred after the goods are "packed ready for shipment to the United States" are excluded from dutiable value.[36]

V. JUDICIAL REVIEW

A. Review Procedure

The appraised value of merchandise is subject to protest under Sections 514 and 515 of the Tariff Act of 1930 (19 U.S.C. 1514, 1515) in the same manner as is the classification of merchandise. Similarly also, the denial of a protest is subject to judicial review. Appeals of appraised value were reviewed by the Customs Court as Appeals for Reappraisement.

Since the Customs Courts Act of 1980, Public Law 96-417, appeals of denials of protests are made to the Court of International Trade under 28 U.S.C. 1581(a), and appeal from that court since 1982 is to the Court of Appeals for the Federal Circuit. Under 28 U.S.C. 2636 an appeal to the CIT must be made within 180 days from the date of the mailing of the denial of the protest.

B. Possible Remand to Customs

Prior to the Customs Courts Act, a protester of the appraised value had the dual burden, as in classification cases, of establishing that the Customs Service decision was erroneous and that his proposed substitute was correct. *CBS Imports Corp.* v. *United States,* 80 Cust. Ct. 61, CD 4739, 450 F. Supp. 724 (1978) 1 ITRD 1652. However, the CIT has held that under its power to remand a case for further administrative proceedings, given by 28 U.S.C. 2643(b), the court may remand to the Customs Service a protest appeal to allow the Service to determine the correct value where its determination has been proved by the protester to be wrong, but the evidence before the court is insufficient to establish a correct appraisal. *House of Adler, Inc.* v. *United*

---

[36]See 19 CFR 152.1(b).

States, 2 CIT 274 (1981) 3 ITRD 1589, and see note 7 in *United States* v. *Arnold Pickle and Olive Co.,* 68 CCPA 85, CAD 1270, 659 F.2d 1049 (1981) 3 ITRD 1241.

In holding that the Customs Service may not add 20 percent to the entered value of merchandise because of the importer's failure to supply it with requested marketing information, the CIT used its authority under 28 U.S.C. 2643(b) to require further proceedings to determine the proper appraised value. *Ashland Chemical Co.* v. *United States,* 7 CIT ____ (1984) 5 ITRD 2503.

10

Rates of Duty

I. DUTY RATES DETERMINED BY COUNTRY OF ORIGIN

A. Nondiscriminatory (Most-Favored-Nation) Treatment

With certain exceptions, the United States adheres to the most-favored-nation principle insofar as tariffs and import taxes are concerned. Thus a tariff rate reduced in a trade agreement with one country is available to the other trading partners of the United States. By trade agreements the rates established by the Tariff Act of 1930 have, on the average, been reduced to a very low level — a small proportion of the original level. These lower level trade agreement rates are set forth in column 1 of the Tariff Schedules of the United States (TSUS) and are generally available for imports from most of the countries with which the United States trades.

The most-favored-nation principle is incorporated in the GATT[1] to which the United States is a signatory. Article 1 of Part 1 of the GATT provides that except for specific preferences spelled out in the Agreement

> any advantage, favour, privilege or immunity granted by any contracting party to any product originating in or destined for any other country shall be accorded immediately and unconditionally to the like product originating in or destined for the territories of all other contracting parties.

Nondiscriminatory duty treatment of the products of the major trading partners of the United States is embodied in the tariff law by the provision in General Headnote 3(f) of the Tariff Schedules of the United States.[2] That headnote provides that the products of all countries not previously mentioned in Headnote 3, imported into the customs territory of the United States, are subject to the rates of duty set forth in column 1 of the schedules.

The countries previously mentioned in General Headnote 3 are the Communist countries designated in General Headnote 3(d) and Cuba, named in Headnote 3(b),[3] the products of which are subject to the generally

---

[1] A description of the GATT is provided in Chapter 23 and the text in Appendix B.

[2] 19 U.S.C. 1202, TSUSA, Supplement 3, September 1, 1985. See Appendix A.

[3] The entitlement of Cuban products to column 1 rates was suspended by the 1962 Tariff Classification Act, and their importation was prohibited, subject to licensed exceptions, by Proclamation 3447 of February 3, 1962. See Chapter 27, section I.A.

higher rates in column 2 of the schedules, and the insular possessions of the United States referred to in Headnote 3(a); also the beneficiary developing countries designated in Headnote 3(e), certain products of which are entitled to free entry, together with the least developed developing countries, eligible for full tariff reductions, and Israel, added by Proclamation 5365 (see Chapter 8). Although Canada is previously mentioned in Headnote 3(c), this is for the purpose of allowing free entry for certain automotive products; otherwise Canadian articles are subject to column 1 duty rates. Added in 1983 was Headnote 3(g) for beneficiary countries designated under the Caribbean Basin Economic Recovery Act for free trade privileges. The CBERA provisions were incorporated in Headnote 3(e) by Proclamation 5365.

The following paragraphs describe the discrimination or privileges accorded the countries covered by General Headnote 3.

B. Ineligible Communist Countries

The United States in general in its tariff laws does not grant most-favored-nation treatment to products of Communist countries. The column 2 rates applied to imports from Communist countries[4] are essentially the original Tariff Act of 1930 rates of duty before any reduction by trade agreements. Most Communist countries are thus denied the benefit of the lower rates of duty resulting from trade agreements entered into by the United States.

However, Part IV of the Trade Act of 1974[5] instituted a change in the U.S. policy toward products of Communist countries. It authorized the President to enter into trade agreements and to provide nondiscriminatory tariff treatment to products of "nonmarket economy" countries upon fulfillment of a number of conditions, particularly, the allowance, without tax or other barriers, of emigration of their citizens. The conditions, and their possible waiver by the President, are discussed further in Chapters 1 and 21.

C. Preferences to the Insular Possessions and Canada

Territories and possessions of the United States outside the U.S. customs territory (Puerto Rico is within) are able to qualify for duty-free treatment on most of their exports to the United States. Duty-free treatment is accorded to the articles of insular possessions, with specific exceptions, which are the growth or product of the possessions or manufactured or produced therein and do not contain foreign materials to the value of more than 70 percent of their total value, and which come directly to the U.S. customs territory. The governing tariff provisions are in General Headnote 3(a) of the TSUS, and the applicable customs regulations, which list the possessions covered, are in 19 CFR 7.8. A certificate of origin (Customs

---

[4]General Headnote 3(d) designates as of September 1985, 16 countries or geographical areas whose products are subject to column 2 rates.
[5]19 U.S.C. 2431–2441.

Form 3229) signed by the customs officer at the port of shipment must accompany an entry claimed to be duty free.

General Headnote 3(a) was amended in 1983 by Section 214(a) of the Caribbean Basin Economic Recovery Act,[6] to bring the limit of value of foreign materials in articles which are the growth and/or product of the insular possessions, permitted duty-free entry, up to 70 percent from the previous 50 percent limit. Section 214(a) also added a new limitation on the duty-free treatment of articles from the insular possessions, namely, that the articles not contain more than 50 percent in value of foreign articles if the imported articles are excluded under Section 213(b) from the duty-free treatment accorded to eligible articles from designated Caribbean Basin countries. See section I.E. *infra.*

Pursuant to the Canadian Automotive Products Trade Agreement and implementing legislation and the provisions in TSUS General Headnote 3(c), certain automobiles, trucks, and automotive parts imported from Canada are admitted duty free. The Canadian products thus accorded free entry are itemized in Subpart B, Motor Vehicles, of Part 6 of Schedule 6 of the TSUS. The relevant customs regulations are in 19 CFR 10.84.

D. Preferences for Developing Countries

The Trade Act of 1974 incorporated an important policy into the tariff laws, the 10-year authorization to the President to afford duty-free treatment to products of developing countries. This program is known as the Generalized System of Preferences (GSP) and is described in Chapter 11, *infra.* Effective January 1, 1976, the President under this authority designated 140 independent countries, nonindependent countries, and territories as entitled to receive GSP duty-free treatment. He also specified some 2,700 articles that were to receive the duty-free treatment if imported directly from one of the designated beneficiary countries.[7] This action of the United States followed a policy adopted some years ago by the member countries of the GATT. Most of the other major industrial countries of the world had already adopted systems of tariff preferences for products of the developing countries. This system of preferences is particularly important for American importers and manufacturers who use materials from developing countries in their operations. The GSP was extended to July 3, 1993, by Title V of the Trade and Tariff Act of 1984,[8] with modifications and limitations discussed in Chapter 11, *infra.*

In the Trade Agreements Act of 1979 the Congress authorized for the least developed developing countries receiving GSP benefits immediate reduction of duties rather than the staged reduction agreed to in the Multilateral Trade Negotiations. For a discussion of this authorization see section III. C *infra.*

---

[6]Pub. L. No. 98-67.
[7]Executive Order 11888, November 24, 1975, 40 FR 55276, as amended.
[8]Pub. L. No. 98-573.

E. Preferences for Designated Caribbean Basin Countries

1. The CBERA, as Amended

The Caribbean Basin Economic Recovery Act, enacted August 5, 1983, as Title II of Public Law 98-67,[9] authorized the President to designate countries eligible to receive duty-free treatment for their articles, imported directly into the United States, from among 27 listed countries in Central America and the Caribbean. The program is also known as the Caribbean Basin Initiative, or CBI. Section 212 providing for this designation set forth seven restrictions upon any designation, relating largely to respect for private property and prevention of drug traffic, and enumerated 11 criteria to be considered in the determination, including expression of desire to be designated, economic conditions, conformity to the GATT's trading principles, and extent of self-help.

The Act provides in Section 213(c) for duty-free treatment through September 30, 1995, for any directly imported article which is the growth, product, or manufacture of a designated beneficiary country, if the sum of the cost or value of the materials produced in that country, or two or more beneficiary countries, plus the direct costs of processing operations in such country or countries is not less than 35 percent of its appraised value upon entry. Costs incurred in Puerto Rico or the U.S. Virgin Islands may be counted toward the 35 percent criterion, and up to 15 percent of the 35 percent may represent cost or value of materials produced in the United States. However, under Section 213(b), duty-free treatment may not apply to specified textile articles, leather wearing apparel, tuna, petroleum or petroleum products, or watches or watch parts containing material from the Communist countries subject to column 2 duties in the TSUS.

Section 213(c) contains special provisions requiring the import of certain sugars, sirups and molasses and articles of beef and veal to be subject to a stable food production Plan, concerning nutritional levels, land use and ownership, and other concerns, to be submitted by the beneficiary country to the President within 90 days of his designation of that country. Duty-free treatment of these articles is to be suspended if the President does not find the Plan satisfactory or implemented in good faith during the course of his required monitoring of the Plan. Such suspension occurred with respect to sugar and beef products from five CBI countries by Proclamation 5365, which recited that the President had not received stable food production plans from the five countries. Suspension is effected by the use of the symbol E* in the Rate of Duty Special column of the TSUS.

Other provisions of the Act provide for the protection of a price support program for sugar beets and sugar cane established under Section 22 of the Agricultural Adjustment Act, for imposition of duties under the import relief provisions of the Trade Act of 1974, as amended, for reports by the

---

[9]19 U.S.C. 2701-2706.

ITC on the economic impact of the Act upon domestic industry, and by the Secretary of Labor on the impact of the Act upon American workers.

Section 213(a) of the Act setting forth the principles governing the requirement that eligible articles be the growth, product, or manufacture of beneficiary countries was amended by Section 235 of the Trade and Tariff Act of 1984, Public Law 98-573, to add a special provision concerning CBI products entered in Puerto Rico. This provision, added to Section 213(a) as Paragraph (3), provided that "notwithstanding section 311 of the Tariff Act of 1930" (19 U.S.C. 1311, providing for the manufacture and export of merchandise in bonded manufacturing warehouses), products of a beneficiary country imported directly into Puerto Rico may be entered under bond for use in manufacturing in Puerto Rico, and no duty shall be imposed on the withdrawal from warehouse of the product of the manufacture if the product meets the 35 percent value added test. The purpose and application of this provision was explained by the Customs Service in its commentary on the revision of its CBI regulations,[10] discussed in section E.3 *infra*.

2. The Designated Countries

The Caribbean and Central American countries designated in late 1983 as eligible to receive the duty-free benefits of the Caribbean Basin Economic Recovery Act were: Antigua and Barbuda, Barbados, Belize, Costa Rica, Dominica, Dominican Republic, El Salvador, Grenada, Guatemala, Haiti, Honduras, Jamaica, Montserrat, Panama, St. Christopher and Nevis, St. Lucia, St. Vincent and the Grenadines, Trinidad and Tobago, British Virgin Islands, and Netherlands Antilles. See Proclamations 5133, November 30, 1983, and 5142, December 29, 1983. No additional countries were designated in 1984. The Bahamas were added by Proclamation 5308 of March 14, 1985.

3. The Customs Service Regulations

The Customs Service published its Caribbean Basin Initiative regulations as interim but effective regulations, with a request for public comments.[11] These regulations were codified in 19 CFR as Sections 10.191–10.198.

Numerous comments were received in response to the request of the Customs Service which were extensively discussed by the Service.[12] TD 84-237 issued as final regulations, effective January 7, 1985, all sections of the CBI regulations except Section 10.198. This section on the evidence required of the country of origin, covering the necessary documentation of CBI shipments, was issued,[13] effective January 7, 1985, as an interim regulation with request for further public comment.

The principal troublesome topics which were discussed in TD 84-237, with some clarification in the regulations, included the following matters:

---

[10]TD 84-237, 49 FR 47986, December 7, 1984.
[11]TD 84-14, 49 FR 852, January 5, 1984.
[12]TDs 84-237 and 84-238, 49 FR 47986 and 47995, December 7, 1984.
[13]TD 84-238.

(1) Merchandise imported directly from a beneficiary country is not disqualified by passage through a U.S. Foreign Trade Zone prior to entry, and the value of U.S. produced materials used in an FTZ may be counted toward the 15 percent allowable U.S. content if no substantial transformation has occurred. However, the cost or value of materials *produced* in a U.S. FTZ may not be included in the allowable 15 percent U.S. value-added since an FTZ is not part of the customs territory of the United States.

(2) The cost or value of materials produced or added in a Puerto Rican FTZ may be included in computing the 35 percent value-added requirement since Puerto Rico is made a beneficiary country for purposes of the value-added requirement without reference to the customs territory.

(3) The amendment of the CBERA made by Section 235 of the Trade and Tariff Act of 1984 was intended to allow processing or manufacturing in Puerto Rico of products imported directly from a beneficiary country at the tail-end of the manufacturing process, so as to enable the product to meet the 35 percent value-added requirement, and to allow the addition of such value in a customs bonded manufacturing warehouse without the requirement contained in 19 U.S.C. 1311 for exportation of the product manufactured in such a warehouse. Moreover, a product which may be substantially transformed in the warehouse and become a Puerto Rican product would still be entitled to duty-free treatment if (1) the article entering the warehouse was a product of a beneficiary country imported directly into Puerto Rico, and (2) the article withdrawn meets the 35 percent value-content requirement.

(4) The Virgin Islands is not treated under the CBI statute as a beneficiary country for the purpose of the direct importation into the U.S. requirement. Consequently, the Virgin Islands may not engage in tail-end processing operations unless the article is returned to a beneficiary country prior to final exportation to the United States. The Virgin Islands may, however, establish a transshipment industry within the meaning of Section 10.193 defining the direct importation requirement.

(5) Because of the confusion in determining which operations constitute assembly operations insufficient to establish a substantial transformation of a product, the regulations are revised to refer to "complex or meaningful" assembly as distinguished from "simple" assembly and are supplemented by examples of sufficient and insufficient types of operations.

(6) The standards for determining "materials produced in a beneficiary country or countries," set forth in Section 10.196, apply to U.S. materials which may be computed in the 15 percent value-content requirement for U.S. materials.

F. Preferences Authorized for Israel

The President was authorized by Title IV, "Trade with Israel," of the Trade and Tariff Act of 1984, to enter into agreements with Israel for the elimination or reduction of U.S. duties on articles which are the growth, product, or manufacture of Israel and are imported directly from Israel. As in the case of the products of CBERA countries, an eligible product is one in which the sum of the cost or value of materials produced in Israel plus the direct costs of processing operations performed in Israel is not less than 35 percent of the appraised value of the entered article, of which 15 percent may be U.S. content.

Title IV provides safeguards against any conflict between the free trade provisions and relief accorded under any law providing for relief from injury caused by import competition or by unfair import practices. The President may specifically suspend the Israeli duty benefit on any article which is the subject of an import relief proclamation under the Escape Clause provisions of the Trade Act of 1974 (See Chapter 19).

The authority of the President to negotiate a free trade agreement with Israel is added as an amendment to Section 102 of the Trade Act of 1974, but is exempted from the requirements of that Act for advance consultation with the Congressional Committees concerned and the 90-day prior notification procedure of Section 102. However, any trade agreement is to be submitted to Congress for consideration under the special procedures of Sections 151–154 of the 1974 Act (19 U.S.C. 2191–2194).

A free trade agreement was signed for the United States and Israel April 22, 1985, and implementing legislation was enacted June 11, 1985, as Public Law 99-47. Under the agreement tariffs are to be eliminated in reductions over a 10-year period.

Under the authority of Public Law 99-47, 19 U.S.C. 2112 note, the President issued Proclamation 5365 proclaiming duty-free treatment for the products of Israel provided for by the TSUS items in Annex VIII to the Proclamation and staged reductions of duties for the products provided for in Annex IX, effective September 1, 1985, and duty-free treatment, effective January 1, 1995, for the products provided for in Annex X. The Proclamation provided in Annex I a revised format of the TSUS, discussed in Chapter 8, section II, *supra,* to accommodate the Israeli and other special tariff programs.

Eligible imports must be products of Israel under standards similar to those for eligible GSP products and must be accompanied by the GSP Certificate of Origin Form A, appropriately modified.

II. DUTY RATES DETERMINED BY PROCESS, PRODUCT, AND PURPOSE

A. Processing Abroad: Articles Exported and Returned

In recent years, many manufacturers have found that it pays to export products or components for further work and return them to the United States. With relatively high labor rates in the United States, this is particularly true of operations having a high labor content. The tariff treatment of such articles when returned to the United States becomes an important consideration in determining the feasibility of having certain work done abroad. Schedule 8, Part 1, of the TSUS governs articles exported and returned.

The basic rule set forth in Schedule 8 is that articles imported into the United States, whether or not originally produced in the United States, and whether or not previously imported and duty-paid, are dutiable on their full value in accordance with the tariff schedules, unless there is some special provision for a full or partial exemption.

Schedule 8 contains four important exceptions to the basic rule that can be useful to American producers who wish to have certain processes performed abroad. Since these are exceptions, they are strictly construed and administered by the Customs Service. Strict compliance is necessary with the customs regulations requiring the filing of forms incident to these exceptions, 19 CFR 10.1 to 10.24. Failure to file a required form may cause a denial of the benefit of the exception.[14] The four generally applicable exceptions are contained in Items 800.00, 806.20, 806.30, and 807.00, TSUS.

The extent of the use of Items 806.30 and 807.00, TSUS, during 1980 to 1983 was analyzed by the International Trade Commission in a report, Pub. 1688, issued in April 1985. Imports under these items (over 98 percent of which were under Item 807.00) reached a high of $21.6 billion in 1983, accounting for 8.6 percent of all imports. See 2 ITR 649, May 8, 1985.

1. Item 800.00

Item 800.00 provides that products of the United States not advanced in value or improved in condition abroad by any process of manufacture or other means may be entered duty free upon return to the United States. The advantages of this provision for an American producer are limited, but there are a few small operations that can be economically performed abroad and do not, in the view of the Customs Service, operate to advance the value or improve the condition of the merchandise. Also, samples sent abroad for approval, rejected shipments, prototype models for testing or acceptance, and similar shipments could be returned under this item.

A 1974 decision greatly expanded the potential usefulness of Item 800.00.[15] An American producer shipped fishhooks of various sizes in bulk to Hong Kong along with sheets of tin. Hong Kong workers on an assembly line gathered the fishhooks together in predetermined size groups to form variety packages for retail sale, with a total of 40 hooks in each tin can made from the exported sheets of tin. On appeal from a customs decision assessing duty, the courts held that the fishhooks were entitled to duty-free treatment under Item 800.00. The trial court, in the decision[16] that was later affirmed, said that

> absent some alteration or change in the articles themselves, the mere sorting and repacking of goods, even for the purposes of resale to the ultimate consumer, are

---

[14]*F.W. Myers & Co., Inc.* v. *United States*, 72 Cust. Ct. 133, CD 4515, 374 F. Supp. 1395 (1974) 1 ITRD 1415. See *The Aviation Group, Inc.* v. *United States*, 10 CIT _____ , Slip Op. 85-82 (1985) 7 ITRD 1193, for test of item application.

[15]*United States* v. *John V. Carr & Sons, Inc.*, 61 CCPA 52, CAD 1118, 496 F.2d 1225 (1974) 1 ITRD 1410, *aff'g* CD 4377, *infra* note 16.

[16]*John V. Carr & Sons, Inc.*, 69 Cust. Ct. 78, CD 4377, 347 F. Supp. 1390, 1400 (1972) 1 ITRD 1401.

not sufficient to preclude the merchandise from being classified as returned American products under Item 800.00 of the tariff schedules.

In addition to the saving of duty, use of this item where applicable has the advantage that no appraisement or other valuation by Customs is required at the time of reentry of the merchandise. Also, the goods need not be reimported by or for the account of the person or company that exported them. However, only minimal work can be done abroad under this item, and nothing may be done to alter the American article itself. But preparation for retail sale is no longer a disqualification. The exact scope of this exception has yet to be defined by the Customs Service and the courts. The best course to follow, therefore, is to obtain an advance ruling from Customs on the applicability of the exception before finalizing an operation abroad.

2. Item 806.20

Item 806.20 covers articles that are exported in order to be advanced in value or improved in condition by way of repairs or alterations. Duty is payable only on the value of the repairs or alterations based on the cost to the importer as set out in the invoice and entry papers. *Example:* Mushrooms were shipped to Canada in bulk where they were cleaned in a washer, treated in an anti-oxidant solution, rinsed, passed through a freezing tunnel, and packed in boxes or bags. Customs ruled that Item 806.20 applied, unless the mushrooms were cut or packaged in retail containers. *Compare:* Tomatoes were sent to Canada in bulk to be graded and repackaged in 14-oz. cellophane tubes and 20-lb. flats for retail sale. Customs ruled that Item 800.00 did not apply because grading and repackaging for retail sale constituted an advancement in value and improvement in condition; and Item 806.20 did not apply because the operations described were more than repairs or alterations.

Since this provision relates to repairs or alterations, it applies only to the exportation and return of completed articles. Thus, if further manufacturing is to be done abroad or after reimportation, Item 806.20 would not apply. See *Dolliff & Company, Inc.* v. *United States,* 66 CCPA 77, 599 F.2d 1015 (1979), in which the CCPA affirmed the Customs Court's refusal to apply Item 806.20 to the value of chemical and heat operations performed in Canada on U.S. greige goods returned as finished products because the operations were performed on unfinished goods. Also, if the courts find that the work done abroad creates a new article, they will consider Item 806.20 to be inapplicable.[17]

---

[17]*Baylis Bros. Co.* v. *United States,* 64 Cust. Ct. 256, CD 3987 (1970) 1 ITRD 1346, *aff'd,* 59 CCPA 9, CAD 1026, 451 F.2d 643 (1971) 1 ITRD 1349. Note also that the customs rulings on the mushrooms and the tomatoes were promulgated before the decision in the fishhooks case (*see supra* notes 15 and 16) was handed down. Those rulings may be affected in part by the decisions in CD 4377 and CAD 1118 *supra.*

3. Item 806.30

Item 806.30 provides that manufactured articles of metal exported for further processing and returned to the United States for additional processing are dutiable only on the value of the processing outside the United States. To qualify for treatment under this item, the article need not be imported by the same party that exported it for further processing. This item is only applicable if further processing is to be done after reimportation into the United States, and what constitutes further processing can be a tricky question, as can be seen from the following three examples:

(1) A capacitor is finished abroad and is inserted in a piece of electronic equipment in the United States. This constitutes "use," not "further processing," in the United States, and Item 806.30 does not apply.

(2) Following the same facts as above, but the terminal wires are cut after reimportation into the United States. This is "further processing" and Item 806.30 applies.

(3) The stringing of telephone wire in the United States after reimportation is "use" not "processing."

Also, it has always been a basic position of the Customs Service that packaging is not "processing" within the meaning of Item 806.30.

As in Item 806.20, duty is payable only on the value of the work done abroad (but at the rate prescribed for the article in question or the *ad valorem* equivalent), and appraisement of the article is usually not required. In other words, duty is payable only on the value added abroad.[18]

4. Item 807.00

Item 807.00 covers articles assembled abroad in whole or in part of fabricated components, the product of the United States, that (1) were exported in condition ready for assembly without further fabrication; (2) have not lost their physical identity in such articles by change in form, shape, or otherwise; and (3) have not been advanced in value or improved in condition abroad except by being assembled and except by operations incidental to the assembly process, such as cleaning, lubricating, and painting for preservative purposes. Regulations governing the application of Item 807.00 are in 19 CFR 10.11 through 10.24.

a. Exclusions

It is important to note that the first headnote of Schedule 8, Part 1, Subpart B, and the customs regulations specifically exclude from Item 807.00 treatment any component that was exported from the United States (1) from continuous customs custody with remission, abatement, or refund of duty; (2) with benefit of drawback; (3) to comply with any law of the United States or regulation of any federal agency requiring exportation; or

---

[18]One measure of this value is the amount charged by the processor, *Douglas Aircraft Co.* v. *United States,* 72 Cust. Ct. 10, CD 4498, 370 F. Supp. 1404 (1974).

(4) after manufacture or production in the United States under Item 864.05 of the TSUS, which relates to articles admitted temporarily free of duty under bond to be repaired, altered, or processed.

b. Duty Applicable

Duty with respect to articles falling under Item 807.00 is upon the *full value of the imported article less the cost or value of the products of the United States.* This is in marked contrast to Items 806.20 and 806.30, where the duty is applicable only to the cost or value of the work performed abroad. It behooves those making use of Item 807.00 to pay careful attention to accounting and recordkeeping procedures. This method of calculating duty presents other problems, as discussed below. To demonstrate how the item is applied, Customs gives two computation examples in 19 CFR 10.13.

c. Fabricated Components, Products of the United States

In order to qualify for the application of Item 807.00, the components must be products of the United States and must be in condition ready for assembly without further fabrication at the time of their exportation from the United States. However, the fact that certain operations incidental to the assembly are performed on the articles will not disqualify them. Four examples in 19 CFR 10.14 distinguish between articles that are and are not eligible for treatment under Item 807.00.

Foreign materials or articles made abroad may become products of the United States within the meaning of Item 807.00 if they undergo a process of manufacture in the United States that results in their "substantial transformation," *i.e.,* if as a result of the manufacturing process a new and different article emerges. Customs also gives examples to indicate the distinction between foreign articles that have undergone a substantial transformation and those that have not.

d. What Is Assembling?

It is often difficult to determine whether an operation abroad will be considered assembling in the view of the Customs Service or something more that would render the article fully dutiable when it returns to the United States. The regulations state that the assembly operation performed abroad may consist of any method used to join or fit together solid components, such as welding, soldering, riveting, forcefitting, gluing, laminating, sewing, or the use of fasteners. The joining of a component to itself, however, does not constitute an assembly for purposes of Item 807.00, TSUS. CSD 84-106, May 15, 1984, 18 Cust. Bull. No. 46.

The regulations further state that the mixing or combining of liquids, gases, chemicals, food ingredients, and amorphous solids with each other or with solid components is not regarded as an assembly. In order to demonstrate the distinction between activities that are and are not regarded as assembly, Customs gives several examples in its regulations. However, the Court of International Trade did not permit the customs regulation disqualifying as an assembly process the joining of solids and liquids to prevent the application of Item 807.00 to a transfer molding operation in which the molding compound is temporarily in molten form during the joinder of terminal pins into header but solidifies before completion of the joinder process. *Sigma Instruments, Inc.* v. *United States,* 5 CIT 90, 565 F. Supp. 1036 (1983) 4 ITRD 1867; *aff'd,* 724 F.2d 930 (Fed. Cir. 1983) 5 ITRD 1529.

1. Operations Incidental to Assembly. Since Item 807.00 does not apply if the components have been advanced in value or improved in condition abroad in any way, other than by being assembled or by operations incidental thereto, certain operations incidental to the assembly process, whether performed before, during, or after assembly, do not constitute further fabrication and thus do not preclude the application of Item 807.00. See 19 CFR 10.16 for examples of operations that are incidental to the assembly process and those considered not to be incidental to assembly.

Considerable litigation has centered on whether particular operations constituted "further fabrication" or were "incidental to assembly." For example, the Customs Service maintained that cutting operations not integral to assembly but accomplishing a commercial function were further fabrication. But the Court of Customs and Patent Appeals accepted as incidental to assembly the buttonholing and pocket slitting of pants and shirts, since Item 807.00 did not preclude commercially useful processes and those involved were definitely minor in cost and labor time. *United States* v. *Mast Industries, Inc.,* 69 CCPA 47, 668 F.2d 501 (1981) 3 ITRD 1281; *United States* v. *Oxford Industries, Inc.,* 69 CCPA 55, 668 F.2d 507 (1981) 3 ITRD 1285. The CCPA distinguished its decision in *Zwicker Knitting Mills* v. *United States,* 67 CCPA 37, 613 F.2d 295 (1980) 1 ITRD 1907 which had recognized that the finger tipping operation performed abroad on incomplete glove shells constituted a further fabrication because the glove shells were only partially fabricated in the United States.

2. Joining American-Made and Foreign-Made Components. Foreign-made components and materials may be assembled together with American-made components in the assembly process, but only the U.S. components meeting all of the requirements of Item 807.00 are eligible for the exemption. Foreign and U.S. components cannot be assembled interchangeably or commingled in the production process in such a way that a determination cannot be made as to whether a particular component is of foreign origin or of U.S. origin. In order to claim the benefits of Item 807.00, it must be possible to establish and clearly state on the entry documents which components are of U.S. origin.

3. Packaging. The Customs Service has taken a strong and consistent position that Item 807.00 is not applicable to American articles exported merely to be packaged or placed in containers. For example, in one case razor blades were sent to Canada, placed in Canadian dispensers, and blistered to cards. Customs ruled that this was a packaging operation and not an assembly operation; therefore, the full value of the article was found to be dutiable importation into the United States. However, where an article is both assembled and packaged, the packaging does not preclude classification under Item 807.00.

e. Valuation of Assembled Merchandise

As stated under *b supra,* the duty applicable to assembled articles imported under Item 807.00, TSUS, is based upon the "full value of the imported article, less the cost or value of such products of the United States" as are assembled in the imported article. In determining the full value under Section 402 of the present valuation law, as amended by Title II of the Trade Agreements Act of 1979 (19 U.S.C. 1401a), Customs considers first the applicability of transaction value, as set forth in Section 402(b). In the words of CSD 80-124 of May 15, 1980, on this subject, "transfer prices between the parties will serve as a starting point for Item 807 appraisement."[19] The adjustments specified under Section 402(b) and required by the TSUS for an Item 807.00 import are added to or deducted from the transfer price. If the transaction is between related parties, the transaction value will be subjected to the tests for acceptability specified in Section 402(b)(2)(B).

However, a preponderance of the merchandise entitled to Item 807.00 exemption has in the past been appraised on the basis of "constructed value" or "cost of production," as defined under the law applicable prior to July 1, 1980. These terms have been superseded for imports exported after July 1, 1980, by the provisions for "computed value" in Section 402(e). Nevertheless, the detailed instructions in 19 CFR 10.19, for determining constructed value or cost of production and for computing the cost of materials and of fabrication, general expenses and profit, and packing expenses remain pertinent in determining computed value.

f. Valuation of Assists

Among the adjustments to the transfer price used to determine the transaction value under Section 402(b) is "the value, apportioned as appropriate, of any assist," to the extent that such value is not otherwise included within the price actually paid or payable. The term "assist" is defined in Section 402(h)(1)(A) to cover materials, parts, tools and dies used in production, engineering and design services, and similar aids furnished free of charge or at reduced cost by the buyer of the imported merchandise for use in the production or sale for export to the United States of the merchandise. However, the definition excludes engineering and design and similar work undertaken in the United States or any service or work by a U.S. domiciliary or by an agent or employee of the buyer of the imported merchandise.

---

[19]14 Cust. Bull. 921.

In CSD 81-91, October 15, 1980[20] the Customs Service ruled that an assist which would have been dutiable under the former valuation provisions but which is not treated as an assist under the new definition would not be dutiable as a component cost in a "computed value" determination, if the computation was in accordance with the relevant generally accepted accounting principles. Under the same reasoning, an importer of articles assembled in Mexico was advised in CSD 81-174, February 12, 1981[21] that the financial assistance provided by the importer to the assembler by an interest-free loan would not be dutiable as the statutory definition of the term "assist" did not include financial assistance.

g. Marking Required

Articles assembled abroad that are eligible for treatment under Item 807.00 are considered to be products of the country where they are assembled for the purposes of the country of origin marking requirements discussed in Chapter 25. The regulations state that if an imported assembled article is made entirely of American-made materials, the U.S. origin of the material may be disclosed by using a legend, such as "Assembled in ＿＿ from material of U.S. origin."

h. Documentation

As pointed out above, articles assembled abroad may not qualify for treatment under Item 807.00 unless such treatment is claimed. The regulations provide that a declaration by the assembler must be filed with the entry of the assembled articles and it must be endorsed by the importer. The required form of declaration and endorsement is set forth in 19 CFR 10.24. With the approval of the district director at the port of entry, the documentation and procedures may be simplified and streamlined where there are more or less repetitive imports of the same types of assembled articles and where it is deemed practicable.

i. Avoiding Trouble

With so much dependent upon the Customs Service's interpretation of what constitutes manufactured abroad, assembled abroad, further fabrication abroad, losing identity by changing form, shape, or otherwise, what constitutes usual profit for purposes of valuation, etc., how can an American manufacturer determine the feasibility of farming out certain operations to foreign countries? How can such manufacturers determine which, if any, of the items under Schedule 8 of the TSUS are applicable to the proposed operation abroad? The best way is to contact the district director at the port of intended entry, fully inform him on every detail of the

---

[20] 15 Cust. Bull. 920.
[21] 15 Cust. Bull. 1074.

proposed operation, and endeavor to obtain his agreement on the application of Item 807.00.

j. Obtaining a Binding Ruling

On questions of tariff classification of the items in Schedule 8, binding rulings can be obtained from the Regional Commissioner of Customs, Region II, Attn: Classification and Ruling Requests, New York, NY. 10048. Requests for such rulings in valuation and carrier matters should be addressed to the Commissioner of Customs, Washington, D.C. 20229. If the proposed operations to be conducted abroad involve substantial capital investments and/or contractual commitments of substantial amounts of money, then it is important to consider requesting and obtaining a binding ruling before commencing the operation. Otherwise, an investment or commitment may be subjected to a customs determination that renders the operation uneconomical.

5. Miscellaneous Articles Exported and Returned

Part 1 of Schedule 8 contains other provisions dealing with the reimportation of particular items that have been previously exported. These provisions are not treated here because they are not of sufficient general interest. However, in the event of question as to the dutiable status of articles previously exported and now being reimported which are not covered by Items 800.00, 806.20, 806.30, or 807.00, Subparts A and B of Part 1 of Schedule 8 should be examined to see if one of the other provisions may apply.

B. Specific Products and Specific Purposes

Schedule 8 and various specific provisions in other schedules of the TSUS allow entry free of duty or at reduced rates, usually under prescribed conditions, for specific articles or for articles entered for specific purposes. These various specific provisions, like those described above for articles exported and returned, are set forth in 19 CFR Part 10, with the applicable conditions and procedural requirements.

The major types or categories of these special articles are indicated herein, but it is essential to check Part 10 of the regulations for the exact limitations and requirements applicable to the particular imports and for provisions for other articles not covered here. Wherever a duty-free or reduced rate is conditioned upon a prescribed use or purpose of the imported article, the importer must provide a customs bond to cover fulfillment of the condition.

1. Articles Not for Sale Admitted Temporarily

Part 5C of Schedule 8 allows free entry under bond for exportation within one year of a variety of articles imported for purposes of repair or alteration, modeling, examination and testing, participation in contests, and use in theatres, displays, and lectures. Also, professional equipment and trade tools may be so brought into the country by nonresidents.

2. Articles for Educational, Religious, and Similar Institutions and for Governments; Space Articles

Articles imported exclusively for the use of a religious, educational, scientific, or other institution, which are not to be sold or commercially used for five years, are entitled to free entry upon the filing by an executive officer of Customs Form 3321. These include regalia, art objects, drawings and plans, and materials for classroom instruction. However, instruments and apparatus may be admitted free only if no instrument or apparatus of equivalent scientific value is manufactured in the United States. The determination of this condition is made by the Department of Commerce on the basis of information provided on a Commerce Department form submitted to that Department by the Customs Service at the time of entry.[22] The combined Treasury and Commerce Department regulations are in 15 CFR Part 301. The importing institution, and not the Department of Commerce, determines the scientific purpose for which the scientific instrument is obtained, whether the purpose is worthwhile or fruitful, and what functions the instrument needs to perform to fulfill its purpose. *University of North Carolina* v. *Department of Commerce*, 701 F.2d 942 (Fed. Cir. 1983) 4 ITRD 1577.

Moreover, the Court of Appeals for the Federal Circuit further ruled that the Department of Commerce may not limit the duty-free privilege to articles to be used only for formal science-oriented education, such as physics, chemistry, and biology, and may not exclude scientific articles to be used for vocational education in the applied sciences, such as navigation and aviation. *M.M.&P. Maritime Advancement, Training, Education & Safety Program* v. *Department of Commerce*, 729 F.2d 748 (Fed. Cir. 1984) 5 ITRD 1881.

Schedule 8 Part 3 provides for the free entry of enumerated types of articles for various U.S. agencies, and for free entry of supplies and equipment for the use of foreign governments and public international organizations, generally upon the request of the Department of State.

Articles for the National Aeronautics and Space Administration (NASA) to be launched into space and articles imported to be launched into space under agreements with NASA, certified to the Commissioner of Customs to be imported for such purpose, are duty free. Section 116 of Public Law 97-446 added to the TSUS Item 837.00 to this effect and a headnote to Subpart A of Part 3 of Schedule 8 providing that the return of materials from space by NASA "shall not be considered an importation, and an entry of such materials shall not be required."

---

[22] 19 CFR 10.114–10.119.

The status of articles returned from space was defined more explicitly in Section 484a of the Tariff Act of 1930, added by Section 209 of the Trade and Tariff Act of 1984. Section 484a exempts from entry articles returned from space which were launched from U.S. customs territory aboard a spacecraft operated or controlled by U.S. persons and owned wholly or substantially by U.S. persons, and which were solely used and returned by that or a similarly qualified spacecraft, without regard to advance in value or improvement in condition.

The duty-free status of educational, scientific, and cultural articles was expanded by the "Educational, Scientific, and Cultural Materials Importation Act of 1982," which was enacted as Subtitle B of Title I of Public Law 97-446. The Act was intended to implement the Nairobi Protocol to the Florence Agreement on the Importation of Educational, Scientific, and Cultural Materials. The Protocol, opened for signature March 1, 1977, was designed to promote a freer exchange of ideas and knowledge across national boundaries. The Act inserts in various Schedules of the TSUS a number of duty-free items for visual and auditory materials, patterns, and models, of an educational, scientific, or cultural character, architectural and engineering drawings, tools for scientific instruments and apparatus admitted duty free, and articles for handicapped persons. The latter two types of materials are subject to Presidential restrictions to prevent significant adverse impact on a domestic industry.

By Proclamation 5021 the President under authority of the Act proclaimed temporary duty-free status for the articles covered by the Act entered on or before August 11, 1985, and established a Part 4 of the TSUS Appendix for this purpose. In TDs 84-17 and 84-233 the Customs Service issued interim and final regulations as 19 CFR 10.182 covering procedures for entry of duty-free articles for use by handicapped persons other than solely for the blind. Legislation to extend the duty-free status of these articles was pending as of October 1985. Part 4 was deleted by Proclamation 5365.

3. Works of Art and Antiques

Schedule 7 Part 11 defines the kinds of works of art, including paintings, engravings, sculptures, and mosaics, which may be entered duty free; and the regulations, 19 CFR 10.48, specify the evidence, where needed, of the artist's hand work. Antiques made prior to 100 years before their entry are entitled to free entry, except for duty upon the value of any substantial repairs made within the prior three years of entry.

Entry of antique articles must be made at one of the following designated "antique" ports: Boston, Massachusetts; New York, New York; Baltimore, Maryland; Philadelphia, Pennsylvania; Miami, Florida; San Juan, Puerto Rico; New Orleans, Louisiana; Houston, Texas; Los Angeles, California; Honolulu, Hawaii; and O'Hare International Airport, Chicago, Illinois.

4. Specific Products

A number of random articles are given entry free of duty or with reduced rates of duty, subject to various testing or marking requirements specified in the regulations. Included are denatured vegetable oils for mechanical or manufacturing purposes; seed potatoes, seed corn and maize, bolting cloth for milling purposes; camel's wool or hair; copper-bearing fluxing material and ethyl alcohol for nonbeverage purposes.

Visual or auditory materials of an educational, scientific, or cultural character are allowed free entry under Item 870.30, TSUS, if certified as having that character by the International Communications Agency, the successor to the U.S. Information Agency. This certification is to conform with the Agreement for Facilitating the International Circulation of Visual and Auditory Materials of an Educational, Scientific, and Cultural Character.

5. Small Value Imports and Bona Fide Gifts

An importation valued at $5 or less may be imported without duty and without preparation of an entry form unless the district director has reason to believe that the shipment is one of several lots covered by a single contract sent separately to secure free entry.

Further, any article valued in the country of shipment at $50 or less sent as a *bona fide* gift from a person in a foreign country to a person in the United States passes customs free of duty and entry preparation. The limit is $100 for a gift from a person in the Virgin Islands, Guam, and American Samoa.

C. Trade Fairs, Exhibitions, and Expositions

The trade fair program authorized by the Trade Fair Act[23] permits the importation of goods and merchandise free of duties and taxes for use and display in connection with fairs, exhibitions, and expositions. Responsibilities for administering the Act are divided between the Secretary of Commerce and the Secretary of the Treasury.

1. Designation of Fairs

The Secretary of Commerce has the responsibility for designating the "fairs" which should enjoy the privileges of the trade fair program. He is authorized to do so if he is satisfied that the public interest in promoting trade will be served by extending the privileges. The term "fair" means any fair, exhibition, or exposition so designated by the Secretary of Commerce. If he so designates a fair, he notifies the Secretary of the Treasury of the name of the fair, the place where it will be held, the opening and closing

---

[23]19 U.S.C. 1751–1756.

dates, and the name of the operator. From that time on, the responsibilities under the Act are transferred to the Secretary of the Treasury and the responsibilities for compliance with the provisions of the Act and the regulations issued thereunder become those of the designated operator of the fair. The regulations of the Customs Service implementing the Act are found in 19 CFR Part 147.

2. Privileges and Requirements

The basic privilege extended by the Act is that articles may be imported for the purpose of exhibition at a fair, or for use in constructing and maintaining foreign exhibits at a fair without payment of any duty or internal revenue tax. Such articles may be imported directly or may be brought out of a foreign trade zone or otherwise taken out of continuous customs custody. Articles so brought in for exhibition are not subject to any of the marking requirements of the customs laws. Nor are they subject to the packaging, marking, or labeling requirements of the internal revenue laws or the Federal Alcohol Administration Act, except that in lieu of such requirements any article prior to exhibition must be conspicuously marked "not labeled or packaged as required by law—not for sale."

Articles for a fair are entered in the name of the designated fair operator on a special entry form.[24] Articles so entered must be accompanied by an appropriate invoice. Articles may be entered for immediate delivery to the fair, or they may be placed in a bonded warehouse under a "general order permit" at the risk of the fair operator. If unentered after five days, Customs will place the articles in general order. At any time within one year from the date of importation such articles may be entered for a fair, under the general tariff law, or for exportation. After one year, they will be regarded as abandoned to the government. All articles entered for a fair are tentatively appraised before exhibition or use.

3. Disposition of Articles Entered for Fairs

At any time before the closing date of a fair, or within three months after such date, articles entered for the fair free of duty and taxes may be disposed of in any of the following ways:

• Entered for consumption or for warehouse in the United States in the normal way with payment of duty and compliance with all marking, packaging, or labeling requirements;
• Exported;
• Transferred from the fair to other customs custody status or to a foreign trade zone;
• Destroyed, or entered for another fair; or
• Abandoned to the government.

---

[24]19 CFR 147.11.

Such articles may also be transferred in customs custody for use or exhibition in another designated fair.

If an article is still in customs custody under a trade fair entry three months after the closing of the fair for which it was entered, it is deemed to have been abandoned to the government and is subject to sale or destruction in accordance with law. If sold, duties or internal revenue taxes are computed on the basis of its condition and quantity at the time it becomes subject to sale.

4. Responsibilities of Fair Operator

The fair operator is deemed to be the sole consignee and importer of all articles entered under the trade fair program for the fair for which such operator has been designated. Specifically, he is responsible for payment of the actual and necessary customs charges for labor, services, and other expenses in connection with the entry, examination, appraisement, custody, abandonment, destruction, or release of the articles entered under the trade fair program together with the necessary charges for salaries of customs officers and employees in connection with the accounting for, custody of, and supervision over such articles. The designated operator of the fair is required by 19 CFR 147.3 to furnish to the Customs Service a bond on Customs Form 301, containing the provisions set forth in Section 113.62 of the Customs Bonds regulations, 19 CFR Part 113, revised October 19, 1984, 49 FR 41171.

III. DUTY RATES DETERMINED UNDER THE MTN TRADE AGREEMENTS

A. Extent and Methods of Duty Adjustments

As noted in the Ways and Means Committee Report on H.R. 4537, the Trade Agreements Act of 1979, the Multilateral Trade Negotiations (MTN) concluded in Geneva accomplished not only major reductions in nontariff barriers to trade, but major overall reductions in tariffs.[25] The extent of the tariff area covered was in the order of magnitude of the Kennedy Round of multilateral trade negotiations when tariffs were almost the sole focus of the negotiations. The report advised that the tariff negotiations resulted in reductions in duties covering about $126 billion or 90 percent of industrial trade (1976 imports) among the major developing countries and an overall average tariff reduction by the United States, European Communities, Japan, and Canada combined of 29 percent from applied rates.[26] Almost all of the extensive tariff concessions were agreed to under the President's authority in Section 101 of the Trade Act of 1974[27] to enter into trade

---

[25] H.R. Rep. No. 96-317 at 11.
[26] *Ibid.* at 12.
[27] 19 U.S.C. 2111.

agreements with foreign countries and to proclaim modification of existing duties within prescribed limits, and in Section 109 of that Act[28] to stage modifications of duty rates within certain limits over a 10-year period. Other concessions, however, required Congressional approval because they exceeded the limitations placed upon Presidential agreements in the Trade Act of 1974. These are discussed in section C *infra.*

B. Tariff Agreement Changes Proclaimed by the President

The principal changes in tariffs to be accomplished by Presidential action under the MTN were compiled in a protocol designated Schedule XX (Geneva 1979) of the United States to the General Agreement on Tariffs and Trade. This Schedule contained 5,000 to 6,000 revisions in the TSUS duty provisions. The major portion of Schedule XX became effective January 1, 1980, under Proclamation 4707, which set forth the changes to be made in the TSUS. The changes consisted not only in reductions of rates of duty but in some reclassification of TSUS items and revisions of some TSUS headings and nomenclature. The duty reductions were generally to be accomplished in various stages over an eight-year period beginning January 1, 1980. The completion of the implementation of Schedule XX and of other duty changes agreed to in various bilateral agreements was effected by Proclamation 4768. This Proclamation made effective new tariff provisions covering benzenoid chemicals, exported to the United States after July 1, 1980, among other changes authorized by Titles II and V of the Trade Agreements Act.

C. Tariff Agreement Changes Approved by the Congress

1. Presidential Proclamation of Effective Date

Title II of the Trade Agreements Act provided for the inauguration of the new Valuation System under the MTN Code and for the conversion from the ASP basis of valuation (postponed for certain rubber footwear) upon a finding and determination to be made by the President of certain reciprocal acceptances by major trading partners. This finding and determination was made in Proclamation 4768, effective July 1, 1980.

Title V of the Trade Agreements Act provided Congressional approval for various specific tariff reductions involving changes in the rates of duty in excess of the President's authority under the Trade Act of 1974 or changes in headnotes, nomenclature, and classification which should be made by statute. Section 502 of this Title authorized the President to determine the effective date of the amendments made by the Title when he was satisfied that reciprocal concessions had been received from foreign trading partners.

---

[28]19 U.S.C. 2119.

2. Staging of Reductions

Section 503 of the 1979 Act provided authority for staging reduction of certain rates of duty in amounts and over time periods in excess of the statutory limitations on the staging of tariff concessions allowed in Section 109 of the Trade Act of 1974. Among the reductions covered by Section 503 were certain benzenoid chemicals, called "future products," which were defined to be articles which the President determined were not imported into the United States before January 1, 1978, and were not produced in the United States before May 1, 1978.

This section also allowed for advanced staging of full MTN reductions on articles which the President determined were not import sensitive and were the product of a least developed developing country (LDDC). The LDDCs were to have the benefit of the total reduction of duty rates immediately. The LDDCs were defined as those on the United Nations' list of least developed countries which were beneficiaries of the U.S. Generalized System of Preferences.

As set forth in General Headnote 3(e)(vi) of the 1985 TSUSA, Supplement 3, the following countries comprise the LDDC list: Bangladesh, Benin, Bhutan, Botswana, Burkina Faso, Burundi, Cape Verde, Central African Republic, Chad, Comoros, Gambia, Guinea, Haiti, Lesotho, Malawi, Maldives, Mali, Nepal, Niger, Rwanda, Somalia, Sudan, Tanzania, Uganda, Western Samoa, and Yemen Arab Republic (Sanaá).

Advanced staging of duty reductions was also provided in Section 503 for unwrought magnesium and alloys thereof (Item 628.57), for certain agricultural products receiving reciprocal reductions from the European Communities, for certain tobacco items, and for certain wool items.

3. Specific Tariff Changes Approved

The specific TSUS articles for which duty concessions were approved in Title V were those covered by the following sections of the Title:
- Section 505. Goat and Sheep (Except Lamb) Meat;
- Section 506. Certain Fresh, Chilled, or Frozen Beef;
- Section 508. Carrots;
- Section 509. Dinnerware;
- Section 510. Tariff Treatment of Watches;
- Section 511. Brooms;
- Section 512. Agricultural and Horticultural Machinery, Equipment, Implements and Parts; and
- Section 513. Wool

A major tariff change provided for in Title V was the conversion to *ad valorem* equivalents of certain column 2 tariff rates. Several hundred such conversions were listed in Section 514. The column 2 rates converted were those provided for items for which a similar conversion to *ad valorem* rates was made in the column 1 rates of the TSUS under Presidential negotiating authority. The purpose of the conversions both by statute and by

Presidential action was to eliminate the significant erosion in the protective effect of specific rates caused by inflation.

4. Civil Aircraft

The Trade Agreements Act provided significant duty elimination in the approval given by Title VI of the Act of the Agreement on Trade in Civil Aircraft. This Agreement established a framework of rules and duty-free trade in civil aircraft and parts intended to enhance cooperative international development of trade policies respecting civil aircraft. Proclamation 4707 provided that duty-free treatment was to be provided to certain civil aircraft parts specified in the TSUSA, if certified for use in civil aircraft.

The President was given further authority by Section 234 of the Trade and Tariff Act of 1984 to proclaim modifications in the rate of duty and in article descriptions of articles used in civil aviation, designated by specified items in Schedule 6 of the TSUS, in order to provide duty-free coverage comparable to the expanded coverage provided by all other signatories to the Agreement on Trade in Civil Aviation, pursuant to an extension of the Annex on October 6, 1983. Duty modifications were proclaimed under this authority by Proclamation 5291 of December 28, 1984, 50 FR 223, January 3, 1985, to become effective upon determination by the United States Trade Representative. The additional duty-free coverage was made effective by the USTR upon publication of his determination April 26, 1985, 50 FR 16578. Technical errors in certain staged reductions were corrected by Proclamation 5365.

IV. DRAWBACK

A. Definition and Purpose

Drawback means a refund or remission, in whole or in part, of a customs duty, internal revenue tax, or fee lawfully assessed or collected because of a particular use made of the merchandise on which the duty, tax, or fee was assessed or collected.[29] Drawback was authorized in 1789 by the first tariff act of the United States in order to stimulate and encourage American industry and to permit the American manufacturer to compete in foreign markets without the handicap of including in his costs, and, consequently, in his selling price, the duty upon imported merchandise. The duties subject to drawback include all ordinary customs duties, as well as dumping, countervailing, and marking duties.[30]

---

[29]Drawback is authorized under Section 313 of the Tariff Act of 1930 as amended (19 U.S.C. 1313) and administered under the customs regulations in 19 CFR Part 191 (1983) superseding Part 22.

[30]In addition, internal revenue taxes paid on domestic alcohol may also be refunded as drawback where such alcohol is used to manufacture flavoring extracts and medicinal or toilet preparations (including perfumery), which are exported to a foreign country or to certain insular possessions of the United States. Countervailing duties, as well as antidumping duties, were explicitly made subject to drawback by Section 622 of the Trade and Tariff Act of 1984, adding Section 779 to the Tariff Act of 1930.

B. Drawback on Manufactured and Other Articles

1. Requirements

The two principal requirements for articles to qualify for drawback have been that manufacture and exportation must take place. Manufacture occurs when a new and different article emerges from the manufacturing process, having a distinctive name, character, or use. Exportation is defined as the severance of things belonging to this country with the intention of uniting them with the things belonging to some other country. However, no drawback will be allowed unless the completed article is exported within five years after importation of the merchandise supporting the claim.

In the manufacture of the exported articles the imported duty-paid merchandise, or duty-free or domestic merchandise of the "same kind and quality," known as "substitute merchandise," must have been used, and so used within three years of the receipt of the imported duty-paid merchandise.

The drawback statute, 19 U.S.C. 1313, specifies other circumstances not involving manufacture, in which drawback may be obtained. These are principally (1) the exportation of rejected imported merchandise, not conforming to specifications, and (2) under the amendment made by Public Law 96-609, 19 U.S.C. 1313(j), the exportation of imported duty-paid merchandise in the "same condition" as imported, or its destruction under Customs supervision, within three years, provided that it has not been used in the United States other than for incidental operations such as testing, cleaning, and repacking. "Same condition" drawback was extended under certain restrictions by section 202(1)(B) of Public Law 98-573 to domestic or imported merchandise fungible with the duty-paid merchandise and exported or destroyed within three years (19 U.S.C. 1313(j)(3)).

2. 99-Percent Refund

A refund of 99 percent of the duties paid on imported merchandise is allowable as drawback when articles manufactured in the United States with the use of imported merchandise (or "substituted" merchandise of the same kind and quality as the imported merchandise involved) are exported. Also, when imported goods do not conform to the sample or specifications on the basis of which they were ordered, or if they were shipped without the consent of the consignee, a refund of 99 percent of the duties paid may be secured by returning the goods in their unmanufactured condition to customs custody within 90 days (or longer if authorized) after they were released, and exporting them under customs supervision. A 99 percent duty refund is also provided after the exportation of the "same condition" merchandise or its destruction in the circumstances stated in 19 U.S.C. 1313(j).

3. 100-Percent Refund

A refund of the entire amount of duties paid is allowable under the following circumstances:
- When imported goods are found not to be entitled to admission into the commerce of the United States and are exported or destroyed under customs supervision;
- When imported goods are exported from a bonded customs warehouse or from continuous customs custody elsewhere than in a bonded warehouse within the warehousing periods;
- When imported goods are withdrawn for supplies for vessels and aircraft engaged in certain classes of trade or for supplies (including equipment) or maintenance or repair of vessels or aircraft under certain conditions;
- When imported goods entered under bond under any provision of the customs laws are destroyed under customs supervision during the period of the bond; and
- When imported goods in a customs bonded warehouse are voluntarily abandoned to the government by the consignee.

4. Other Drawback Claims

Other conditions under which drawback may be claimed include:
- When imported salt is used for curing fish (the fish need not be exported);
- When imported salt is used for curing meat which is then exported;
- When imported materials are used in the construction and equipment of vessels built for foreign account and ownership, or for the government of any foreign country; and
- When foreign-built jet aircraft engines are overhauled, repaired, rebuilt, or reconditioned with the use of imported materials, including parts, and then exported.

C. Steps for Obtaining Drawback

1. Entry Into a Specific or General Drawback Contract

The manufacturer or producer who proposes to file for drawback must enter into a specific contract with Customs covering his operation in accordance with Subpart B of 19 CFR Part 191 or he must adhere to a general contract published by Customs covering his particular line of manufacture or production in accordance with Subpart D.

a. Specific Drawback Contracts

An applicant seeking a specific drawback contract prepares and submits a drawback proposal to the regional commissioner for the region in which his drawback entries will be liquidated. This proposal must describe his manufacturing operation fully and his method of compliance with all drawback requirements; it must state the records to be kept of identification, manufacture, production, and storage, as required by the regulations, and contain an agreement to follow the methods and keep the records as described in the proposal. A sample proposal may be obtained from the Drawback and Bonds Branch, Office of Regulations and Rulings, Customs Headquarters, upon request. Upon approval, the drawback contract will continue for a period of 15 years with the privilege of renewal for another 15-year period. Synopses of specific contracts are published in the *Customs Bulletin* where each contract is assigned a Treasury Decision (TD) number.

b. General Contracts

Customs Headquarters prepares and publishes in the *Customs Bulletin* offers for general drawback contracts in situations where numerous manufacturers or producers have similar operations and wish to claim drawback. Any manufacturer or producer who can comply with the terms and conditions in the published offer may adhere to it by notifying, with a letter of acceptance, the regional commissioner in the region which will process his drawback claims. In addition to his name and address, he must provide information on the factories which will operate under the contract and, if incorporated, the persons authorized to sign drawback documents. Upon acknowledgement in writing by the regional commissioner, the general drawback contract for that manufacturer or producer will be effective for 15 years from the date of acknowledgement with the option for renewal for another 15-year period.

2. Same Kind and Quality

Where "substituted" merchandise of the same kind and quality is used, the imported merchandise and the merchandise substituted for it do not have to be identical. It is sufficient for "same kind and quality" purposes if the materials are such that they may be used interchangeably in manufacturing the same article, with little or no change in the manufacturing process when switching from imported merchandise to domestic merchandise, or vice versa. Fungible goods are always the same kind and quality merchandise. See Part 191, Subsection C, for the rules governing substituted merchandise.

3. Records Required

The records of the manufacturer must show the quantity, identity, kind, and quality of the duty-paid merchandise or of other articles manufactured under drawback regulations designated as the basis for the allowance of drawback on the exported articles. They must show that the designated merchandise was used in the manufacture of the exported articles within three years after the date on which the merchandise was received by the manufacturer. The records must also show that the exported articles on which drawback is claimed were manufactured either with the use of the designated merchandise or with the use of other imported, duty-free, or domestic merchandise of the same kind and quality as the designated merchandise, or any combination of the foregoing. All records required to be kept by the manufacturer, and records kept by others to complement the records of the manufacturer, must be retained for at least three years after payment of drawback.

4. Proof of Exportation

Proof of exportation of articles covered by a drawback claim must be provided within three years after the exportation. This ordinarily consists of a notice of exportation, Customs Form 7511, a notice of transfer to a foreign trade zone, or of lading, Customs Form 7514. See Part 191, Subpart E.

5. Verification

A drawback claim is subject to verification by customs auditors. Verification will include an examination of not only the manufacturing records but also the sales drawback documents. Other records relating to the transaction may be referred to customs auditors at the discretion of the regional commissioner.

6. Mandatory Compliance

To claim drawback, compliance with the regulations of the Customs Service is mandatory. Citing numerous precedents to that effect the Court of Appeals for the Federal Circuit reversed the allowance of drawback by the Court of International Trade on equitable grounds, where the applicant builder of a vessel for foreign account had failed to submit to Customs the abstract of manufacturing records required by 19 CFR 22.4(g) prior to the departure of the vessel. The CAFC held compliance with the regulation a condition precedent to recovery of the drawback allowed under 19 U.S.C. 1313(g) and noncompliance inexcusable in the face of lack of due care. *United States* v. *Lockheed Petroleum Services, Ltd.*, 709 F.2d 1472 (Fed. Cir. 1983) 4 ITRD 1889.

D. Drawback Payment

1. Liquidation of Drawback Entries

Proper drawback claims may be liquidated (1) after deposit of estimated duties on the imported merchandise and before liquidation of the import entry or (2) after liquidation of the import entry becomes final. Payment of drawback may be based on estimated duties if the import entry has not been liquidated and the drawback claimant and the party responsible for payment of liquidated import duties (if different from the claimant) each file a written request relating to each drawback entry, requesting payment on this basis. A drawback claim once liquidated on the basis of estimated duties is not thereafter adjusted by reason of a subsequent liquidation of an entry. See 19 CFR 191.71.

2. Drawback Payable to Exporter

Drawback is paid to the exporter, unless on the sale or consignment of the articles the manufacturer reserved for himself the right to drawback, with the knowledge and consent of the exporter. A claimant may assign his drawback rights to whomever he wishes simply by so directing on the face of the drawback entry. See 19 CFR 191.73.

3. Accelerated Payment

This is an important procedure that speeds up the payment of drawback claims, which otherwise can often take more than a year to accomplish. A claimant, requesting accelerated payment of his drawback claim, must submit with the claim a computation of the amount due thereon and must file with Customs, either a bond on Customs Form 301, containing the conditions in Section 113.65 of the regulations, or attach a rider to his preexisting General Term Bond for Entry of Merchandise, Customs Form 7595, increasing its amount by the estimated amount of accelerated drawback. If the regional commissioner, after receiving the claim, determines that the claimant is not delinquent or otherwise remiss in his transactions with Customs, and that the claim appears reasonable in amount, he will within three weeks after the claim is filed certify for payment in full the claim as computed by the claimant. After liquidation, the remainder found to be due will be paid, or a demand for refund of any excess payment will be made. The right to receive accelerated payments will be denied claimants repeatedly computing claims erroneously, thereby necessitating demands for refund. See 19 CFR 191.72.

E. Return of Rejected Merchandise

Upon receipt of the drawback entry covering rejected merchandise, the district director will number it, approve the place of deposit, or designate another place that will be suitable, and return the original to the entrant for presentation with the merchandise to the district director at the place of deposit. The merchandise must be delivered into customs custody at such place within 90 days after the date on which it was originally released from customs custody unless, either before or after the return of the merchandise, a longer time is specially authorized by the district director.

The district director, upon written application, may extend the period in those cases where he is satisfied that the importer has been or will be prevented by circumstances beyond his control from returning the merchandise within the 90-day period, and that the importer proposes to return, or has returned, the merchandise within a reasonable time.

Applications for extension of time should be filed with, and will be acted upon by, the district director at the port where the drawback entry will be filed.

A receipt showing the fact and date of delivery to Customs will be furnished to the applicant if he requests it. If the report of the receiving officer shows that the merchandise was not returned to customs custody within the time required, the drawback will be denied.

If the rejected merchandise is to be exported through the mails, it must be deposited with the postmaster with a completed notice of exportation on Customs Form 7511. Further requirements for merchandise exported through the mails are contained in 19 CFR 191.54.

F. Protests

The decision of the district director refusing to pay any drawback claim is final and conclusive upon all persons, unless the person filing the drawback claim or his agent, within 90 days after but not before such decision, files a protest in writing with the district director in the manner required in the case of protests against the liquidation of import entries.

The denial of a protest of the refusal to pay a claim for drawback is, like the denial of other protests covered by 19 U.S.C. 1514, subject to appeal to the Court of International Trade under 28 U.S.C. 1581(a) (see Chapter 31).

11

Generalized System of Preferences

I. DESCRIPTION OF THE GSP PREFERENCES

A. International Origin and Purposes

The phrase "generalized system of preferences" (GSP) refers to a worldwide effort by the industrialized countries to help developing nations grow industrially, agriculturally, and commercially. As a result of negotiations during the mid-1960s in various international organizations under the auspices of the United Nations, industrialized nations such as Japan, the nine Common Market member countries, Canada, the United States, and others agreed to give preferential tariff treatment to goods imported from an agreed-upon list of developing countries. The United States was the last major industrialized country to implement the program, having provided legislative authority for it in the Trade Act of 1974.

The GSP acquired further international legal status as a result of the Tokyo Round of the Multilateral Trade Negotiations and approval by the Trade Agreements Act of 1979 of the resulting Texts Concerning a Framework for the Conduct of World Trade. One of the texts contains a so-called "enabling clause" which provides that contracting parties to the GATT may accord differential and more favorable treatment to developing countries notwithstanding the most-favored-nation principle under the GATT. The GSP is one of the favorable types of treatment specified. However, the text recognized that special treatment should be modified as the development needs of developing countries changed.

B. The GSP Legislation

Title V of the Trade Act of 1974 authorized the President for a 10-year period to grant duty-free treatment to eligible products of eligible developing countries as a means of carrying out the U.S. version of the GSP.[1] The GSP Renewal Act of 1984, Title V of the Trade and Tariff Act of 1984[2] extended this authority eight and one-half years, through July 4, 1993, with amendments restricting further the eligibility of countries and of articles, and specifying further limitations on preferential treatment, effective January 4, 1985.

The value of the GSP to the United States and to international trade was underscored by the Congress in this extension. The legislation cited 10 purposes for the extension, among which were promoting the development of developing countries by trade and not aid; generating the acquisition of foreign exchange by developing countries to promote the increase of U.S. exports to those countries; and encouraging the reduction by developing countries of barriers to both trade and investment. Additional new purposes were encouraging developing countries to provide means for the protection of intellectual property rights and to afford workers internationally recognized worker rights.

In support of this legislation, it was stated that the U.S. economic relationship with developing countries affected every exporting and importing interest in the United States and that 40 percent of U.S. agricultural exports and 45 percent of U.S. manufacturing exports were consumed by developing countries in 1982.[3] However, imports under the GSP represented only a small portion of the total U.S. imports.

C. Designation of Eligible Countries and Articles

1. Eligible Countries

Under the 1974 Act the President under the original 10-year authority designated 140 independent nations and dependencies as entitled to receive GSP tariff preferences. Among the designated beneficiaries are most countries of South and Central America, the Caribbean, Africa, and Southeast Asia, plus island territories of developed countries. Also included as eligible for GSP treatment are Hong Kong, India, Indonesia, Israel, Portugal, Taiwan, Romania, and Yugoslavia.[4]

Section 502(b), as amended by the Trade Agreements Act of 1979, specifically prohibits the President from designating as eligible certain named highly industrialized countries, including members of the European Economic Community and (1) certain Communist countries not receiving most-favored-nation treatment and not belonging to the International Monetary Fund or the GATT; (2) participating members of the Organization of Petroleum Exporting Countries or other arrangement withholding supplies of vital commodities from trade or raising the price of such commodities to unreasonable levels; (3) countries granting reverse preferences to other developed countries with significant adverse effects on U.S.

---

[1]Title V, 19 U.S.C. 2461–2465.
[2]Pub. L. No. 98-573, October 30, 1984, 98 Stat. 2948.
[3]Cong. Rec., September 17, 1984, at S11242.
[4]For complete list of countries, see TSUSA General Headnote (e)(v)(A), Supplement 3, September 1, 1985.

commerce; (4) countries that nationalize property, including patents, trademarks, and copyrights, belonging to U.S. citizens without compensation, negotiation, or arbitration; (5) countries not taking adequate steps to prevent illegal drugs from their countries from entering the United States; (6) countries failing to recognize as binding or to enforce arbitral awards in favor of U.S. citizens or corporations; (7) countries granting sanctuary from prosecution to international terrorists; and (8) countries which have not taken, or are not taking, steps to afford internationally recognized worker rights to workers in their countries.

Disqualification (8) was added by the GSP Renewal Act of 1984, which provided, as an addition to Section 502(a), a definition of the term "internationally recognized worker rights." The definition embraces the right of association; the right to organize and bargain collectively; a prohibition on forced or compulsory labor; a minimum age for child employment; and acceptable conditions of work with respect to wages, hours, and occupational safety and health. The 1984 Act also added to disqualification (4) the inclusion in the term "property" of patents, trademarks, or copyrights. Further, the 1984 Act removed Hungary from the specific listing of disqualified countries in Section 502(b).

The President may, however, designate as eligible a country which is ineligible under prohibition (4), (5), (6), (7), or (8) if he determines that designation will be in the national interest and so reports to the Congress. The President may also exempt from prohibition (2) a country which enters into a bilateral or multilateral agreement which assures the United States of fair and equitable access, at reasonable prices, to supplies of economic importance.

Sections 501 and 502(c) specify the factors which the President is to take into account in determining whether to designate a country as a beneficiary. Section 501 was amended by the 1984 Act to add to the considerations to guide the President's grant of GSP treatment "the extent of the beneficiary developing country's competitiveness with respect to eligible articles." In Section 502(c) the original 1974 factors specified included the willingness of the country, its level of economic development, its designation by other major developed countries, and the extent to which it would provide reasonable access to its markets and basic commodity resources. To these factors the GSP Renewal Act added considerations, several of which were emphasized in other Titles of the Trade and Tariff Act of 1984, namely, assurance by the developing country of restraint from "unreasonable export practices" (added to factor (4)); provision of means for foreign nationals to exercise and enforce "intellectual property rights, including patents, trademarks, and copyrights" (factor 5); action to "reduce distorting investment practices and policies (including export performance requirements)" and to reduce "barriers to trade in services" (factor 6); and steps taken or being taken to afford its workers "internationally recognized worker rights" (factor 7).

2. Eligible Articles

The President was authorized by Section 503 to specify which articles are to receive duty-free treatment if imported directly from one of the designated beneficiary countries. As of October 1985, there were some 3,000 articles on the GSP list, including selected agricultural and fishery products, most wood and paper products, certain organic chemical compounds and primary industrial products, and a broad range of manufactured and semimanufactured products.

Certain groups of products are excluded by Section 503(c) of the Trade Act from qualifying for GSP treatment to avoid causing a negative impact on some domestic industries that are particularly sensitive to competition from imports. Ineligible products include textile and apparel articles which are subject to textile agreements;[5] watches; import sensitive electronic articles and steel articles; footwear articles covered by specified TSUS items; import sensitive semimanufactured and manufactured glass products, and any other articles determined by the President to be import sensitive in the GSP context. An executive order fixing the non-GSP status of an article may be retroactive, but was not respecting solid state electronic digital watches. *North American Foreign Trading Corp.* v. *United States,* 8 CIT _____ , 600 F. Supp. 226 (1984) 6 ITRD 1733.

The GSP Renewal Act expanded the ineligible category of "footwear" to include "footwear, handbags, flat goods, work gloves, and leather wearing apparel which were not eligible articles" for purposes of the GSP on April 1, 1984.

In 1984 GSP was granted to about $13 billion worth of imports from beneficiary countries. This represented about 3.8 percent of the total value of $341.2 billion of 1984 U.S. imports.

D. Implementation

1. Designations

By Executive Order 11888 of November 24, 1975, effective January 1, 1976, the Tariff Schedules of the United States (TSUS) were revised to add a new General Headnote, 3(c) (renumbered as 3(e)(v) as of September 1, 1985), designating 98 eligible independent countries and 39 eligible nonindependent countries and territories, and to add a new column in the left-hand margin of the Schedules entitled "GSP." In this column, now merged into the "Special" rate column, every article eligible for duty-free treatment has either the designation "A" or "A*." The designation "A" means that imports of that article from any beneficiary developing country (BDC) are eligible for duty-free treatment. The designation "A*" means

---

[5]Textile articles which are subject to the Arrangement Regarding International Trade in Textiles, called the Multi-Fiber Arrangement (MFA), but not covered by the bilateral restraint agreements, may not be given GSP treatment. *Luggage and Leather Goods Manufacturers of America, Inc.* v. *United States,* 7 CIT _____ , 588 F. Supp. 1413 (1984) 5 ITRD 2201. This decision was implemented by Executive Order 12483, 49 FR 26185, June 27, 1984, eliminating from the list of articles eligible for GSP the articles provided for in Item 706.39, TSUS.

that imports of that article from the beneficiary developing country set opposite the TSUS item covering that article, as enumerated in General Headnote 3(c)(iii), are not eligible for duty-free treatment. Changes in the designated countries and eligible articles have been made by executive order issued one to four times a year.[6]

Under an amendment of Title V of the 1974 Trade Act made by section 8(b) of the U.S.-Israel Free Trade Act, Public Law 99-47, changes in GSP eligibility may be made by presidential proclamation as well as by executive order. A revised listing of GSP eligible TSUS items was proclaimed in Annexes III and IV to Proclamation 5365, 50 FR 36220, September 5, 1985, as part of the rearrangement, under General Headnote 3(e), of the TSUS provisions for special tariff treatment made by that Proclamation.

2. Removal of Eligibility

Countries and articles may be removed from the eligibility list at any time under Section 504(a) by presidential proclamation if the President determines that continuance of duty-free treatment is contrary to U.S. interests. Articles of a given country must be removed from the list if imports of the article exceed the dollar and percentage limitations discussed *infra*, unless continuation is specifically justified by the President. During the first 10 years the list of eligible articles and countries was revised each year within 90 days after the close of the year and based upon the statistics on imports of the various articles for the preceding year. Revisions under the 1984 Act are described in section II.B.

---

[6]*Federal Register* references for the general Executive orders which have been issued on the GSP as of June 1985, are as follows:

EO 11888: 40 FR 55275, November 26, 1975
EO 11906: 41 FR 8757, February 27, 1976
EO 11934: 41 FR 37084, September 1, 1976
EO 11960: 42 FR 4317, January 24, 1977
EO 11974: 42 FR 11230A, February 28, 1977
EO 12032: 42 FR 64851, December 27, 1977
EO 12041: 43 FR 8099, February 25, 1978
EO 12104: 43 FR 59053, December 19, 1978
EO 12124: 44 FR 11729, March 2, 1979
EO 12180: 44 FR 72077, December 13, 1979
EO 12181: 44 FR 72083, December 13, 1979
EO 12204: 45 FR 20740, March 28, 1980
EO 12222: 45 FR 45233, July 2, 1980
EO 12267: 46 FR 4669, January 19, 1981
EO 12302: 46 FR 19901, April 2, 1981
EO 12311: 46 FR 34305, July 1, 1981
EO 12349: 47 FR 8749, March 2, 1982
EO 12354: 47 FR 13477, March 31, 1982
EO 12371: 47 FR 30449, July 14, 1982
EO 12389: 47 FR 47529, October 27, 1982
EO 12413: 48 FR 13921, April 1, 1983
EO 12459: 49 FR 2089, January 18, 1984
EO 12471: 49 FR 13101, April 3, 1984
EO 12483: 49 FR 26185, June 27, 1984
EO 12519: 50 FR 25037, June 13, 1985
EO 12524: 50 FR 27409, July 3, 1985

3. Reinstatement to Eligibility

Through 1984 once an article was removed from the eligibility list, it would not automatically be reinstated when trade in the article dropped below the applicable dollar or 50-percent limitations. However, as soon after the beginning of each calendar year as relevant trade data were available for the preceding calendar year, the Office of the United States Trade Representative (USTR) considered modifications of the GSP that might be required by the competitive needs provision (the applicable dollar or 50-percent limitations) and also considered any applications by "interested parties" for additions or deletions from the eligibility list. After consideration of the competitive need provision and any applications by interested parties, the USTR recommended to the President any action he deemed required or warranted.

4. Effective Period of Eligibility

The revised list has been effective for one year, commencing on the issuance of an Executive Order not later than 90 days after the close of the preceding calendar year. The 1984 Act allows for changes up to July 1. In many cases orders for foreign goods must be placed many months in advance of shipment. Importers may place orders in late summer or early fall only to find that heavy shipments in the last months of the year have taken the product over the applicable dollar or 50-percent limitations, with resulting loss of duty-free status, for the next calendar year.

E. Reports and Information

1. Presidential Reports to the Congress

The 1984 Renewal Act requires the President to submit to the Congress after five years, namely, on or before January 4, 1990, a full and complete report regarding the operation of the GSP. This parallels the five-year report originally required by the 1974 Trade Act and provided in 1980. See section IV.A *infra*. In addition, the President is required to submit an annual report to the Congress on the status of internationally recognized worker's rights within each BDC. Furthermore, the President is required to advise the Congress as necessary and no later than January 4, 1988, by submitting a report on the application of the sections of the 1984 Act defining the GSP guidelines and the factors determining eligibility of beneficiary developing countries and the extent to which he has taken action to withdraw, suspend, or limit duty-free treatment with respect to any country which has failed to take the actions which are required to be taken into consideration in determining its eligibility.

2. USTR Information Center for the GSP

The USTR established an Information Center for the U.S. Generalized System of Preferences, in accordance with the recommendation made in the President's 1980 Five Year Report on the GSP. The Center is intended to provide information and assistance to all segments of domestic interests. The Executive Director of the Center in the USTR office, as of October 1985, was David Shark at (202) 395-6971.

F. Concern for Agricultural Exports

The 1984 Renewal Act requires the appropriate U.S. agencies to assist beneficiary developing countries to assure that "the agricultural sectors of their economies are not directed to export markets to the detriment of the production of foodstuffs for their citizenry." This provision is added as Section 506 to the Trade Act of 1974.

II. LIMITATIONS ON GSP APPLICABILITY

A. Dollar and Percentage Limitations

The Trade Act of 1974 in Section 504(c) provided for two specific limitations, based on competitive considerations, on the applicability of the duty-free GSP treatment. Under the competitive need provision, the President must suspend GSP eligibility on imports of a specific article from a particular country when that country supplied more than $25 million in value of the article during the previous calendar year or over 50 percent of the value of U.S. imports. The $25 million limitation is adjusted each year by the percentage by which the gross national product of the United States for the preceding calendar year is higher or lower than the gross national product in calendar 1974. That limitation was determined for the calendar year 1984 to stand at $63.8 million.

However, under Section 504(d), as amended, the 50-percent rule does not apply to an article if a like or directly competitive article was not produced in the United States as of January 3, 1985. See B.8 *infra.* The word "article" in this context means an individual article and not the tariff item under which it is classified, where the tariff item encompasses a number of different products, although the word "article" may refer to the tariff item for purposes of applying the 50-percent rule. *West Bend Co.* v. *United States,* 6 CIT ____ , 576 F. Supp. 630 (1983) 5 ITRD 1353. The limitation in Subsection (d) applies only to prevent the mandatory removal by the President of GSP treatment under the 50-percent rule. That subsection does not inhibit his removal of an article from GSP treatment under his broad discretion over the application of the GSP given by Section 504(a). *Florsheim Shoe Company* v. *United States,* 6 CIT ____ , 570 F. Supp. 734 (1983) 4 ITRD 2236, *aff'd,* 744 F.2d 787 (Fed. Cir. 1984) 5 ITRD 2385.

The Trade Agreements Act of 1979 amended Section 504(d) of the Trade Act to allow the President to disregard the 50-percent limitation with respect to any eligible article if the appraised value of the total imports of that article during the preceding calendar year was not in excess of an amount which bears the same ratio to $1 million as the gross national product of the U.S. for that year bears to the gross national product of the U.S. for the year 1979. The limitation for 1984 was $7.5 million.

B. Competitive Need, Cutbacks, Waiver, and Graduation Provisions

1. Basic Provisions

The 1984 Act retained the basic competitive need provisions of the existing law requiring the removal of eligible articles from GSP treatment if the imports of the article from any beneficiary developing country exceed the dollar or percentage limitations stated in Section 504(c) of the 1974 Trade Act, as amended, described *supra*. The removal from GSP treatment is to occur not later than July 1 of the next succeeding calendar year following the determination of the competitive need provisions with respect to any article.

2. Review for Competitiveness

A new cutback process is introduced into Section 504 by the Renewal Act. The President is required, under Section 504(c)(2), not later than January 4, 1987, and periodically thereafter, to conduct a general review of eligible articles based on the considerations described in Sections 501 and 502(c). These considerations are the factors to be regarded in determining the designation of an eligible country, as expanded by the 1984 Act. If the review shows a sufficient degree of competitiveness (relative to other BDCs) with respect to any eligible article, then a more stringent test for removal of GSP treatment shall be applied to such article. The more stringent test is the substitution of 1984 for 1974 as the U.S. GNP comparison year for determining the ratio of the $25 million limitation to the current gross national product, and the substitution of 25 percent for 50 percent as the figure above which the value of the BDC's exports of an eligible article may not exceed the appraised value of the total imports of such article (Section 504(c)(2)(B)).

3. Waiver Authority

The President is authorized, subject to many restrictions set forth in Section 504(c)(3)(A)–(D), to waive the competitive need provisions concerning any eligible article after January 4, 1987 (following the general review period) and before July 1 of the year after the competitive need determination is made with respect to any article. The waiver may be made only after he receives advice from the ITC on whether any industry in the United States is likely to be adversely affected by the waiver and after consideration of the factors for determining GSP eligibility and a determination that the waiver is in the national economic interest of the United States. The President's determination of these considerations is to be published in the *Federal Register*. Further, the President must give great weight to the extent to which the BDC has assured the United States that it will provide equitable and reasonable access to the markets and basic commodity resources of the country and that it provides adequate and effective means for foreign nationals to secure, exercise, and enforce exclusive rights to intellectual property, including patent, trademark, and copyright rights. A waiver may remain in effect until the President determines that it is no longer warranted, due to changed circumstances.

The waiver authority may not be exercised with respect to a quantity of eligible articles entered in any calendar year which exceeds an aggregate value equal to 30 percent of the total value of all articles entered duty free under the GSP during the preceding calendar year. Likewise, the President may not waive more than 15 percent of the total value of all articles entered under the GSP during the preceding calendar year with respect to the more advanced countries, *i.e.,* those that during the preceding calendar year had a per capita gross national product of $5,000 or more, or had exported to the United States, a quantity of articles that was duty free under the GSP which had an appraised value of more than 10 percent of the total imports of all articles that entered duty free under the GSP during that year. In determining the 30 and 15 percent limitations, there is to be counted only that quantity of any eligible article that entered duty free under the GSP during the calendar year and is in excess of the basic dollar and percentage limitations of the competitive need provisions.

The competitive need provisions may be waived by the President with respect to a country with which there has been a historically preferential trade relationship with the United States, and with which a treaty or trade agreement is in force covering economic relations between the country and the United States, and such country does not discriminate against or impose unjustifiable or unreasonable barriers to U.S. commerce. The legislative history shows that this special provision for a waiver in Section 504(c)(4) was meant to apply to the Philippines.

4. The USTR's General Review of Eligible Articles

The USTR initiated a general review of eligible articles based on the considerations described in Sections 501 and 502(c) of the Trade Act of 1974, as amended in 1984, with a notice published in the *Federal Register* of February 14, 1985, 50 FR 6294. The general review, to be completed by January 4, 1987, was stated to have two major purposes. The first was to determine which particular GSP eligible articles from which particular beneficiary countries should be subjected to lower competitive need limitations under the GSP. The second purpose was to consider requests for competitive need limit waivers with respect to specific articles from specific beneficiaries, as well as comments concerning waivers of the 50-percent competitive need limit on the basis of a finding of no U.S. production of like or directly competitive products.

The USTR notice set forth the procedures and timetables in 1985 pertaining to the submission of views by interested parties. Any changes resulting from the general review will be implemented by executive order and announced by January 4, 1987, to take effect on July 1, 1987. The notice also provided the background for the determinations to be made under the general review found in the amendments to the GSP made by the GSP Renewal Act of 1984, consisting generally of the information described *supra* in subsections (2) and (3).

The general review to determine the competitive status of particular eligible articles consists of the consideration of two primary components. The first component is the consideration of the beneficiary country practices under the requirements in Section 502(c)(4)–(7). Written comments respecting this consideration were required by July 15, 1985. The other component of the general review concerns the competitiveness of individual articles and requires consideration by the International Trade Commission, as well as by the USTR. With respect to the USTR's review through the Trade Policy Staff Committee, any written comments on competitiveness of articles must have been provided by November 15, 1985, and any rebuttal respecting such comments must have been submitted by December 15, 1985. A public hearing on the subject of competitiveness in October 1985 was announced, August 7, 1985, 50 FR 31943, corrected 50 FR 34956.

To fulfill the second purpose of the general review, consideration is to be given to requests for a waiver of the competitive need limits with respect to specific articles from specific beneficiaries, in accordance with the President's authority to exercise the waiver authority delineated in Section 504(c)(3) of the 1974 Trade Act as amended in 1984. In such consideration, the USTR takes into account the advice given by the ITC on whether any industry in the United States is likely to be affected adversely by the waiver, as well as the factors concerning beneficiary country practices listed in Sections 501 and 502(c) of the Act. On the basis of the advice from the ITC and the consideration of the country practices, the President then determines whether the waiver would be in the national economic interest of the United States. Requests for competitive need waivers were required to be filed by May 31, 1985. The USTR's notice stated that his office would announce the competitive need waiver requests accepted for formal review by August 1, 1985, and designated a deadline of November 15, 1985, for comments regarding the waiver requests accepted for review.

The requirements, scope, and procedures for general product reviews required under the 1984 Act are set forth in Section 2007.8 of the USTR's 1985 interim regulations in 15 CFR Part 2007. General reviews under Section 504(c)(2) do not preclude or conflict with the ongoing regular reviews under the regulations of the eligibility of articles and BDCs for GSP treatment.

In a notice published May 8, 1985, 50 FR 19513, the USTR announced a public hearing on June 24 and 25 concerning the extent to which BDCs, commensurate with their levels of development, are adhering to the disciplines of the trading system, as delineated in Section 502(c)(4)–(7).

At the request of the USTR, at the direction of the President, the ITC instituted an investigation, 332-218, to provide information and advice relevant to the general review for each article currently designated as a GSP eligible article. 50 FR 36160, September 5, 1985. The ITC's report was requested by February 1, 1986.

5. Redesignation

A country which has been graduated as a BDC with respect to an eligible article may be redesignated as a BDC with respect to such article, subject to consideration of the factors for determining GSP eligibility, if the imports of the article from that country do not exceed the competitive need provisions during the preceding calendar year.

6. Exemption for Least-Developed BDCs

The competitive need provisions do not apply under Section 504(c)(6) to a least-developed BDC, as determined by the President. The President was to make the determination of this status prior to July 4, 1985, and periodically thereafter, with notification to the Congress at least 60 days before any determination becomes final. The President designated 32 countries as exempt LDDCs by Executive Order 12524 of July 1, 1985, 50 FR 27409. They are listed in General Headnote 3(e)(v)(B) of the TSUSA.

7. Exemption of Associations of Countries

The competitive need provisions do not apply to an association of countries which is treated as one country under the eligibility determinations.

8. No Domestic Production

Under Section 504(d)(1) the percent competitive need limitation does not apply with respect to any eligible article if a like or directly competitive article was not produced in the United States on January 3, 1985. The 1984 Act made no change in this provision except with respect to the date, formerly January 3, 1975.

9. De Minimis Waiver

The de minimis waiver introduced in the GSP by the 1979 Trade Agreements Act, above mentioned, was continued by the 1984 Act except that the $1 million figure as the basis for the comparison with the GNP of the United States was raised to $5 million (Section 504(d)(2)).

10. *Mandatory Graduation of a BDC*

Mandatory graduation of a BDC from the GSP is to occur, under new Section 504(f), two years after the President determines that its per capita gross national product for any year after 1984 exceeds an amount which bears the same ratio to $8,500 as 50 percent of the increase of the gross national product for the preceding year bears to the 1984 gross national product. In the intervening two years the competitive need percentage test is reduced from 50 to 25 percent.

C. Administrative Procedures for Additions to or Deletions From the GSP Product Lists

The regulations of the USTR, as revised in 1985, 19 CFR Part 2007, provide procedures for consideration of requests for additions to, deletions from, or other modifications of the GSP product lists. Requests for such review may be filed by a foreign government or other "interested party," *i.e.,* a party which has a significant economic interest in the product or other significant economic interest which would be materially affected by a request. The regulations specify the required content of submissions, and a timetable for receipt, consideration, and determination of requests each calendar year commencing in June.

The timetable for regular product review in Section 2007.3 of the USTR's interim regulations is as follows:

Deadline for acceptance of review petitions	June 1
Announcement of petitions accepted for review	July 15
Public hearings and submission of written briefs	September/October
Announcement of results	by following April
Effective date of changes	July 1

III. CRITERIA FOR PRODUCT ELIGIBILITY

A. General

The listed eligible articles are given duty-free treatment only if
• they are imported directly from the beneficiary developing country into the United States; and
• they are wholly grown, produced, or manufactured in the beneficiary developing country, or not less than 35 percent of the appraised value has been added in the beneficiary developing country. In other words, the sum of the cost or value of the materials produced in the beneficiary developing country and the cost or value of any article incorporated in the eligible article which has resulted from the substantial transformation of any imported material, plus the direct cost of operations performed in the

beneficiary developing country, must be not less than 35 percent of the appraised value.

Developing countries that are members of a free trade area or a customs union or a regional economic integration effort may benefit from the duty-free provisions if not less than 35 percent of the appraised value of an article sent from a member country of such an association represents the cost or value of materials produced in two or more of the member countries plus the direct cost of processing operations performed in such countries. The Trade Agreements Act of 1979 added the regional economic grouping by widening the definitions of a beneficiary developing country to include an association of countries "which is contributing to comprehensive regional economic integration among its members through appropriate means," including the reduction of duties.[7]

The application of the eligibility criteria to particular imports is determined under regulations of the Customs Service.[8] Section 504 of the 1984 Renewal Act requires that these regulations be issued after consultation with the USTR.

B. Definitions

1. Direct Shipment

In order to qualify for preferential tariff treatment, the goods must be shipped directly to the United States:
- without passing through the territory of any other country; or
- in the event of transshipment, without entering into the commerce of any other country while en route to the United States; or
- in the event of shipment from a beneficiary developing country to the United States through a free trade zone in a beneficiary developing country, without entering into the commerce of the country maintaining the free trade zone and without undergoing any operation other than sorting, grading, testing, packing, unpacking, changes of packing, decanting or repacking into other containers, affixing marks, labels, or other like distinguishing signs on articles or their packing, or operations to ensure the preservation of the merchandise. Merchandise may, however, be purchased or resold, other than at retail, for export within the free trade zone.

The definition in the customs regulations of the term "imported directly," 19 CFR 10.175, was amended by TD 83-144 to encompass shipment of an eligible product from a beneficiary developing country to a developed country for auctioning there prior to shipment to the United States. The amendment requires that the eligible article remain under the control of the customs authorities of the intermediate country and not be subjected to any operations other than loading and unloading, and other

---

[7] 19 U.S.C. 2462(a)(3). The Caribbean Common Market (CARICOM), consisting of the 12 member countries named in Executive Order 12354 of March 30, 1982, was designated by that Order as one country for GSP purposes.

[8] Details as to requirements and procedures under the Generalized System of Preferences are contained in the 1985 customs regulations, 19 CFR 10.171–10.178, from which information in section B *infra* is taken.

activities necessary to keep it in good condition. The amendment was developed in order to permit the continuance of the traditional marketing procedure established for Cameroon wrapper tobacco.

2. Cost or Value of Materials

The cost or value of materials produced in the beneficiary developing country includes:
- the manufacturer's actual cost of materials;
- freight, insurance, packing, and all other costs incurred in transporting the materials to the manufacturer's plant, if not already included in the actual cost of the materials;
- the actual cost of waste or spoilage, less the value of recoverable scrap; and
- taxes and/or duties imposed on the materials, provided they are not remitted upon exportation.

3. Direct Costs of Processing Operations

The direct costs of processing operations mean those costs that are either directly incurred in, or can be reasonably allocated to, the growth, production, manufacture, or assembly of the specific merchandise under consideration. Such costs include, but are not limited to:
- all actual labor costs involved in the growth, production, manufacture, or assembly of the specific merchandise, including fringe benefits, on-the-job training, and the cost of engineering, supervisory, quality control, and similar personnel;
- dies, molds, tooling, and depreciation on machinery and equipment which are allocable to the specific merchandise;
- research, development, design, engineering, and blueprint costs insofar as they are allocable to the specific merchandise; and
- cost of inspecting and testing the specific merchandise.

Items not included in the "direct costs of processing" operations are those that are not directly attributable to the merchandise under consideration or are not "costs" of manufacturing the product. These include, but are not limited to:
- profit; and
- general expenses of doing business which are either not allocable to the specific merchandise or are not related to the growth, production, manufacture, or assembly of the merchandise, such as administrative salaries, casualty and liability insurance, advertising and salesmen's salaries, commissions, or expenses.

The principles applied to distinguish between direct and indirect costs of processing operations, with numerous examples for each, are provided by the Customs Service in CSD 80-208 of March 24, 1980, and CSD 80-246 of April 23, 1980, 14 Cust. Bull. 1085 and 1168. See also CSD 84-104, May 7, 1984, 18 Cust. Bull. No. 46, holding that the capitalized interest expense on a loan for the building where processing occurs is not a direct cost of processing.

4. Substantial Transformation

It is important to note that imported materials can be included in the cost or value of materials produced in the beneficiary developing country only if the imported materials have undergone substantial transformation in the beneficiary country, resulting in a new material or article, which is used in producing the eligible article for export to the United States. Such materials or articles which qualify for inclusion in the 35-percent requirement are referred to as "substantially transformed constituent materials."

In TD 76-100 (10 Cust. Bull. 176) Customs gives the following examples of what constitutes substantial transformation:

• Raw skins imported into a beneficiary developing country and tanned into leather could be a substantially transformed constituent material when used in the subsequent manufacture of leather coats.

• Gold bars which are imported into a beneficiary developing country are cast into mountings—rings in which a stone is not yet set. Such mountings are substantially transformed constituent materials of the eligible articles of jewelry when those mountings become constituent elements of rings mounted with precious stones of the beneficiary developing country. (See also CSD 84-102, April 17, 1984, 18 Cust. Bull. No. 46, finding gold wire to be a substantially transformed intermediate product from imported gold bars.)

• Articles produced by the joining and fitting together of components are not considered substantially transformed constituent materials. Articles of this kind may well have been substantially transformed, but they are not produced from substantially transformed constituent materials.

The disqualification of assembly operations in TD 76-100 was criticized and rejected by the CCPA, as described *infra*, and was modified by the Customs Service in CSD 85-25, September 25, 1984, 19 Cust. Bull. No. 14. Customs said in that decision that TD 76-100 should not be read to preclude "complex or meaningful" assembly operations from resulting in substantial transformation, and found that the assembly of a large number of fabricated components into a printed circuit board created a substantially transformed constituent material used in the production of a computer.

The original position of Customs in TD 76-100 had been adopted with approval by the Court of International Trade in *Texas Instruments, Inc.* v. *United States,* 2 CIT 36, 520 F. Supp. 1216 (1981) 2 ITRD 1697. The court there held that the value of the integrated circuits and photodiodes assembled in Taiwan from components fabricated in the United States could not be included in determining whether the cost of materials or direct costs of processing added in Taiwan amounted to 35 percent of the appraised value of the imported cue modules. However, this holding was rejected by the Court of Customs and Patent Appeals in its reversal of the CIT, *Texas Instruments, Inc.* v. *United States,* 69 CCPA 151, 681 F.2d 778 (1982) 3 ITRD 1945. The CCPA examined in detail what was done to the materials imported into Taiwan and concluded that the resulting integrated circuits and photodiodes were substantially transformed material produced in Taiwan and entitled to be included in computing the 35 percent of the appraised value of the imported cue modules of which they were a part.

The two-stage substantial transformation process was held to be required by the GSP statute and regulations in *Torrington Co.* v. *United States,* 8 CIT _____ , 596 F. Supp. 1083 (1984) 6 ITRD 1119, *aff'd,* 764 F.2d 1563 (Fed. Cir. 1985) 6 ITRD 2313. The CIT there held that industrial sewing machine needles imported from Portugal were eligible for GSP treatment since the non-BDC wire from which they were made was first substantially transformed into the constituent material, a separate article of commerce called swaged needle blanks, which was then used in the manufacture of the final article.

5. 35-Percent Criterion

It should be noted that the 35-percent criterion can be satisfied entirely by the cost or value of materials produced in the beneficiary developing country, the direct cost of processing operations, or any combination of the two. See *Texas Instruments supra,* 520 F. Supp. at 1219, 2 ITRD at 1699. The following examples will illustrate the application of the 35-percent criterion: motorcycles are manufactured in a beneficiary developing country and exported to the United States at an ex-factory price of $500. Note that normally the ex-factory price will be the appraised value in that case.

Example 1. The motorcycle is manufactured entirely from local materials. The motorcycle will qualify for preferential treatment as wholly the manufacture of the beneficiary developing country.

Example 2. The motorcycle is manufactured as follows:

(1)	gears imported and incorporated into motorcycle	$100
(2)	chain manufactured from imported steel that has been substantially transformed	$50
(3)	saddle manufactured from imported rawhide that has been substantially transformed	$25
(4)	domestic materials	$50
(5)	direct costs of processing operations	$75
(6)	indirect costs (overhead, profit, etc.)	$200
	Total	$500

In this case, the costs of domestic materials will consist of Items 2, 3, and 4, since the chain and saddle are products of imported materials that have been substantially transformed in the beneficiary country. Thus, the sum of the cost of domestic materials plus the costs of processing is $200, which is 40 percent of the ex-factory price ($500), *i.e.,* not less than 35 percent of the appraised value. Therefore, the motorcycle will qualify for preferential treatment.

Example 3. The motorcycle is manufactured as follows:

(1)	materials imported but not substantially transformed (gears, $100; chain, $50; saddle, $25)	$175
(2)	domestic materials	$75
(3)	direct costs of processing operations	$50
(4)	indirect costs (overhead, profit, etc.)	$200
	Total	$500

In this case, the sum of the cost of domestic materials and the costs of processing is $125, which is 25 percent of the ex-factory price ($500), *i.e.,* less than 35 percent of the appraised value. Therefore, the motorcycle will not qualify for preferential treatment.[9]

C. Proof of Eligibility

The importer is required to submit appropriate shipping papers, invoices, or other documents as evidence that the articles were imported directly. The district director may waive the submission of evidence of direct shipment if he is otherwise satisfied that the merchandise clearly qualifies for GSP treatment. In the case of transit shipments, the invoices, bills of lading, and other documents connected with the shipment must show the United States as the final destination.

A GSP certificate of origin, Form A,[10] filled in and signed by the exporter and certified by the designated governmental authority of the beneficiary developing country, is required for all shipments valued at $250 or more unless waived by the district director under TD 82-165. Customs, however, may require proof of origin regardless of value. If the certificate of origin is not produced at the time of entry, and not waived, the importer may file a bond to produce the certificate within 60 days after such entry or within such additional time as the district director may allow for good cause shown. It is desirable, if at all possible, to produce the certificate of origin at the time of entry, since, by so doing, the clearance of the goods and the processing of the entry will be expedited.

The completion of Form A in accordance with the regulations is sufficient proof of the country of origin of the imported merchandise, including satisfaction of the 35-percent criterion, if further information is not requested by the district director. *House of Ideas, Inc.* v. *United States,* 2 CIT 68 (1981) 3 ITRD 1068.

An importer's failure to file a duty-free consumption entry during the period the imported merchandise was covered by the GSP, due to the importer's ignorance of the GSP eligibility of the merchandise, was not a mistake of fact or other inadvertence justifying reliquidation of the entry

---

[9]Additional examples are given in TD 76-100 (10 Cust. Bull. 176).
[10]This certificate is an international, not a Customs, form. It may be obtained from governments of the beneficiary designated countries.

under 19 U.S.C. 1520(c)(1). *Godchaux-Henderson Sugar Co., Inc.* v. *United States,* 85 Cust. Ct. 68, CD 4874, 469 F. Supp. 1326 (1980) 2 ITRD 1461.

IV. DEVELOPMENT OF GSP GRADUATION

A. Policy Changes Announced in the President's 1980 Five Year Report

The President's Report to the Congress on the first five years' operation of the GSP pointed out that 10 countries supplied 80 percent of the GSP imports in 1979; that in general these countries were the more advanced and the more competitive of the less developed countries and that the least developed and least competitive countries had benefited the least from the operation of the program. In the light of these circumstances, the report announced the introduction of two improvements in the operation of the GSP program in 1980:

> First, a special effort will be made to include on the GSP list products of special export interest to low income beneficiaries, including handicraft items. Second, the President's authority "to withdraw, suspend or limit duty-free treatment" will be used to limit benefits for the more developed beneficiaries where they have demonstrated competitiveness and to provide increased opportunities for less developed, less competitive countries. This authority likewise will be exercised when products are added to the GSP eligible list.[11]

The report stated that this action was

> designed to promote the continued graduation of more advanced developing countries from GSP benefits in products where they have demonstrated competitiveness. In addition, over time such action will help shift the overall share of benefits from the more to the less advanced and less competitive countries.[12]

B. Graduation Process Effected

The process of discretionary graduation was significantly advanced in the issuance of Executive Order 12354 of March 30, 1982. As announced by the USTR in a press release of March 19, 1982, $651 million in imports from seven advanced developing countries were graduated from GSP duty-free treatment for the year beginning March 31, 1982. This amount included $53.9 million in products from Taiwan, Singapore, the Republic of Korea, and Israel removed in response to petitions filed by U.S. producers or labor unions. The remainder represented the value of previously excluded products of the foregoing countries, plus Mexico, Brazil, and Hong Kong, which had become reeligible for GSP treatment and were not redesignated by reason of graduation. A total of $443 million in products was graduated from GSP treatment in 1981.

The process of graduation was continued by Executive Order 12413 of March 30, 1983. The USTR reported in a press release of March 28, 1983,

---

[11]Report to the Congress, April 17, 1980, WMCP 96-58 at 62.
[12]*Ibid.* at 69.

that in response to petitions from U.S. producers and labor unions additional products from Taiwan, Singapore, the Republic of Korea, and Israel were excluded from GSP treatment. The excluded trade was valued at $95 million. The total value of products excluded by graduation in 1982 was approximately $900 million. Taking into account changes in the application of the graduation process since it was first effected in March 1981, over $1 billion in product value was graduated by March 1983, according to advice from the USTR's office.

An additional $215 million worth of goods from South Korea, Hong Kong, Taiwan, and Mexico was graduated under Executive Order 12471 of March 30, 1984, bringing the total import trade excluded under the President's discretionary authority to $1.2 billion.

The House Committee Report on the GSP Renewal Act of 1984, H.R. Rep. No. 98-1090, September 27, 1984, expressed concern that despite the increasing exclusion of their goods through the competitive need limitations and discretionary graduation the three leading BDCs, Taiwan, Korea, and Hong Kong, received 52 percent of total GSP benefits (p. 3).

C. Additional Changes in Coverage

A total of $7.1 billion in imports was determined as of March 1983, to be ineligible under the competitive needs tests specified in the 1974 Trade Act, as amended (see section II *supra*). This total included the value of products determined ineligible in prior years. The total ineligible as of March 1982, was $6.8 billion.

As a result of the March 30, 1984, Executive Order more trade was excluded from duty-free access than was allowed. The total of $1.2 billion excluded by graduation, plus the total of $10.7 billion excluded under the competitive needs limitation surpassed the total trade eligible under the 1984 GSP program of $10.8 billion.

After consideration of the competitive posture of affected U.S. producers 48 new products were made eligible for GSP treatment by Executive Order 12354, March 1982, with an approximate value of $76 million. Over half of the additions were requested by Caribbean countries. Under Executive Order 12413 of March 1983, 29 new items were designated for GSP treatment, representing $10 million in newly eligible trade. Executive Order 12471 of March 1984, added 22 new items not previously eligible, representing $7 million in new trade.

On May 1, 1985, the USTR announced that nearly $3.5 billion in imports were removed from duty-free status since July 1, 1984. This total resulted from the elimination of $1.8 billion under the competitive need limitation and $1.9 billion under discretionary graduation, and the addition of $41 million in new imports and the redesignation of $246 million previously eliminated. The products graduated came from Taiwan, South Korea, Mexico, and Israel (2 ITR 647, May 8, 1985).

Subsequent product reviews will be in accordance with the factors governing review provided in the 1984 Renewal Act and described in section II *supra*.

Part III

Import Competition

12

Dumping Duties

I. THE ANTIDUMPING LAW

A. Current Use

The Antidumping Law provides an increasingly used remedy against below-home-market pricing of imports. After the new Antidumping Law described below took effect in January 1980, the Department of Commerce published a list of 83 then-current antidumping duty findings and orders. By October 1985 there were 107 such findings and orders outstanding, of which nearly one-third applied to Japanese imports. They are listed in Appendix I. These figures do not fully reflect the lively activity in the field, as many dumping investigations have been suspended or terminated, and through 1984 outstanding orders were annually reviewed by the Department of Commerce.

B. The 1979 Antidumping Law, as Amended

Title I, Section 101 of the Trade Agreements Act of 1979, Public Law 96-39, added to the Tariff Act of 1930 a new Title VII, Countervailing and Antidumping Duties.[1] Subtitle B, Imposition of Antidumping Duties, replaces the Antidumping Act of 1921, as amended,[2] which was repealed.[3] The effective date of the new provisions was January 1, 1980, since the Agreements on the implementation of certain articles of the General Agreement on Tariffs and Trade had entered into force with respect to the United States as of that date.[4] The relevant agreements are the Agreement on Interpretation and Application of Articles VI, XVI, and XXIII of the General Agreement on Tariffs and Trade (relating to subsidies and countervailing measures) (see Appendix C), and the Agreement on

---

[1] 19 U.S.C. 1671–1677g.
[2] 19 U.S.C. 160–173 (1976 ed.).
[3] Section 106(a), Trade Agreements Act of 1979. 19 U.S.C. 160 Note.
[4] Section 107, Trade Agreements Act of 1979. 19 U.S.C. 1671 Note.

Implementation of Article VI of the General Agreement on Tariffs and Trade (relating to antidumping measures) (see Appendix D).

The 1979 provisions will hereinafter be referred to as "the Antidumping Law," "the Law," or "the new law." Where it is necessary to make reference to the predecessor statute, it will be cited as "the old law."

The new law has been significantly amended by certain provisions of Title VI of the Trade and Tariff Act of 1984, Public Law 98-573.[5] The effect of these amendments is included in this Chapter. They are hereafter referred to as the 1984 Amendments.

The Trade Agreements Act of 1979 also approved "Statements of Administrative Action" submitted by the Executive Branch along with the proposed new legislation. The statements refer to certain practices in the administration of the old law and to the substance of regulations to be issued in implementation of the new law. They are hereinafter referred to as "Administrative Statement." Information on antidumping administration provided in the Statement on "Title 1—Countervailing and Antidumping Duties" is included in this Chapter. References to the Statement are made to its publication in H.R. Doc. No. 96-153, Part II.

C. Administering Authority

Title VII of the Tariff Act of 1930 placed the authority and responsibility for administration of the law, other than injury determinations, upon the "Administering Authority" which was defined as "the Secretary of the Treasury, or any other officer of the United States to whom the responsibility for carrying out the duties of the Administering Authority under this title are transferred by law.[6]

Pursuant to the President's Reorganization Plan No. 3 of 1979,[7] and Executive Order 12188,[8] authority to administer the Antidumping Law was transferred to the Secretary of Commerce, effective January 2, 1980. The exercise of that authority is under the general supervision of the Under Secretary for International Trade, and the immediate supervision of the Assistant Secretary for Trade Administration who, through the Deputy Assistant Secretary for Import Administration, supervises the import actions of the administering agency, the International Trade Administration (ITA). Hereafter, references to the Secretary or to the ITA, as appropriate, will be made wherever the statutory reference is to the "Administering Authority." The U.S. Customs Service remains in the Treasury Department but assists Commerce in the administration of the Law.

The International Trade Administration issued final regulations in 1980, codified as 19 CFR Part 353, governing antidumping procedures and determinations and access to information. The ITA reserved for later promulgation, on the basis of experience, rules governing certain matters. The ITA invited regulatory proposals in an advance notice of proposed

---

[5]Act of October 30, 1984, 98 Stat. 2948. Effective date rules issued 50 FR 5746, February 12, 1985.
[6]Section 771(1), Tariff Act of 1930 (19 U.S.C. 1677).
[7]44 FR 69273, December 3, 1979. 5 U.S.C. App.
[8]45 FR 989, January 4, 1980.

rulemaking to incorporate in Part 353 the changes made by the 1984 Amendments and to codify existing administrative practices.[9]

The responsibility for making injury determinations is placed upon the International Trade Commission, hereinafter referred to as "the Commission."

D. Summary of Provisions

Simply stated, the Antidumping Law provides that if a foreign manufacturer is selling goods in the United States at less than fair value (LTFV), *i.e.*, less than the amount he charges for the same goods in the home market (dumping), and such sales cause or threaten material injury to a U.S. industry, or materially retard its establishment, then an additional antidumping duty in an amount equal to the amount by which the foreign market value exceeds the U.S. price shall be imposed upon imports of that product from the foreign country in question.

The Secretary is charged with making the determination as to whether merchandise is being sold at a dumping price in the United States, and the Commission is charged with determining the injury question. Consideration of the two issues by the two agencies goes on simultaneously. If the Secretary finds that dumping exists, and the Commission finds material injury (or threat thereof), or material retardation of the establishment of an industry, the Secretary issues an Antidumping Order which orders the assessment and collection of special dumping duties by U.S. customs officers at the ports of entry.

The special dumping duty is an additional duty assessed on top of all regular duties imposed by law. The amount of the special dumping duty is the difference between the home market price and the price at which the goods are sold in the United States. It is calculated on each specific importation. Where the sales in the home market are too small to form a basis for comparison, then the comparison is made between the price to third countries (or a constructed value) and the U.S. price to determine the existence of dumping. In some cases where dumping exists, there may also be foreign subsidization of the exports to the United States. In this case a proceeding under the Countervailing Duty Law may be an alternative or additional remedy.

The major impact of the Antidumping Law comes when the Secretary announces the commencement of an investigation to determine whether a product from a specified foreign country is being dumped. Within 160 days after the petition for the investigation was filed, unless the time is extended, the Secretary must issue a preliminary determination. If it is affirmative as to dumping, the Secretary must issue an order to suspend liquidation of the product in question, *i.e.*, postpone until the conclusion of the proceeding the final determination of all duties collectible on imports of that product. This

---

[9]49 FR 45593, November 19, 1984.

tends to discourage imports since importers do not know what their total liability for duties will be.

Once the proceeding is concluded with an Antidumping Order (sometimes earlier), the foreign manufacturers often adjust their prices to eliminate the dumping margins, either by raising the United States price to the level of the home market (or third country) price, or by lowering the home market (or third country) price to the level of the United States price. Thus, the amount of antidumping duties actually collected, if any, does not fully reflect the effectiveness of the Law. The adjustment of prices accomplishes the purpose of the Law, the elimination of the foreign dumping practice.

E. Standards for Determining the Existence of Dumping

The Antidumping Law specifies in some detail the criteria for determining the existence of sales at less than fair value. To make this determination a comparison of "foreign market value" and the United States price is required.

1. Foreign Market Value

Foreign market value is calculated on the basis of the wholesale price, after certain adjustments to assure comparability, for sales in customary commercial quantities in the home market f.o.b. the factory.[10] If the merchandise is not sold in the home market, or if sales there are so small in relation to the quantity sold for exportation to countries other than the United States as to form an inadequate basis for comparison, usually less than 5 percent, then the foreign market value is determined on the basis of the price at which the merchandise is sold or offered for sale for exportation to third countries or on the basis of "constructed value."[11] Constructed value will generally be used for this comparison where sales to third countries as well as in the home market have been deemed inadequate, or where the Secretary has reason to believe the foreign sales are made at less than the cost of production.[12] For the methodology followed by the ITA in making fair value comparisons in a variety of foreign market circumstances, see *Certain Steel Wire Nails from Korea,* 47 FR 27492, June 24, 1982, 4 ITRD 1171.

Prior to the 1984 Amendments, foreign market value was based upon home market or third country prices existing at the time of exportation of the merchandise to the United States. Under Section 615 of the 1984 Amendments foreign market value now is based, in a related exporter-importer purchase, upon such prices at the time the merchandise is first sold in the United States by the importer to a party unrelated to the importer.

---

[10]Section 773(a)(1)(A), Tariff Act of 1930 (19 U.S.C. 1677b), 19 CFR 353.3.
[11]Section 773(a)(1) and (2), Tariff Act of 1930 (19 U.S.C. 1677b), 19 CFR 353.4, 353.6.
[12]19 CFR 353.7.

Section 615 further responds to the threshold question for purposes of determining foreign market value, as to which country shall be deemed to be the country from which the goods were exported (*i.e.,* the home market) in circumstances where the goods, following manufacture in one country, were transshipped through an intermediate country prior to importation into the United States. The section provides that the intermediate country shall be deemed to be the exporting country if:

(1) the manufacturer sells the goods to a reseller and does not know, at the time of the sale, the country to which the reseller intends to export the goods;

(2) the goods are exported by or on behalf of the reseller to a country other than the United States, enter the commerce of such country, and are not substantially transformed in such country; and

(3) the goods are subsequently exported to the United States.

The foreign market value provisions authorize the use of averaging or generally recognized sampling techniques in determining foreign market value, whenever a significant volume of sales is involved or a significant number of adjustments to prices is required. The 1984 Amendments provide in Section 620 that the Secretary shall have the exclusive authority to select appropriate samples and averages, although the samples and averages are required to be "representative" of the transactions under investigation. Also, the Secretary may decline to take into account adjustments which are insignificant in relation to the price or value of the merchandise. Ordinarily, individual adjustments having an *ad valorem* effect of less than 0.33 percent or any group of adjustments having an *ad valorem* effect of less than 1.0 percent will be disregarded.[13]

2. United States Price

The United States price is defined as the purchase price, or the exporter's sales price.[14]

The purchase price for the purposes of this comparison is the price at which merchandise is purchased prior to the date of importation from a reseller or the manufacturer or producer for exportation to the United States. The provision to permit a reseller's price to serve as the basis for purchase price was added by Section 614 of the 1984 Amendments. Purchase price is normally used where the transaction prior to importation is at arm's length.

Partly because of the 1984 statutory recognition of the reseller's price as a purchase price basis the CIT accepted the ITA's pre-1984 use of the purchase price to U.S. importers set by a Chinese-controlled trading company, this price being also the first price open to market forces in an NME country. *Four "H" Corporation* v. *United States,* 9 CIT ____ , 611 F. Supp. 981 (1985) 6 ITRD 2409.

---

[13]19 CFR 353.23.
[14]Section 772(a), Tariff Act of 1930 (19 U.S.C. 1677a), 19 CFR 353.10.

In certain circumstances, for example, where the U.S. importer and the foreign seller are "related parties," the foreign market value is compared with the "exporter's sales price." Exporter's sales price is the price at which merchandise is sold or agreed to be sold in the United States, by or for the account of the exporter, *i.e.,* the price at which the merchandise is first sold to unrelated purchasers in the United States.[15]

The following are defined by the Law to be "related parties":

(1) Members of a family, including brothers and sisters (whether by the whole or half blood), spouses, ancestors, and lineal descendants.

(2) Any officer or director of an organization and such organization.

(3) Partners.

(4) Employer and employee.

(5) Any person directly or indirectly owning, controlling, or holding with power to vote, 5 percent or more of the outstanding voting stock or shares of any organization and such organization.

(6) Two or more persons directly or indirectly controlling, controlled by, or under common control with, any person.[16]

The types of relationship between the importer and the manufacturer, producer, or exporter (here called simply the "exporter") which will trigger the use of exporter's sales price are set out in Section 771(13) of Title VII (19 U.S.C. 1677(13) and are, briefly, as follows:

(1) The importer is the agent or principal of the exporter.

(2) Either the importer or exporter owns or controls, directly or indirectly, any interest in the business conducted by the other party.

(3) Any person or persons, jointly or severally, directly or indirectly own or control in the aggregate 20 percent or more of the voting power or control in both the importer's business and the exporter's business.

Section 620 of the 1984 Amendments added Section 777A to Title VII (19 U.S.C. 1677f-1), providing for the use of averaging and generally recognized sampling techniques in determining United States price in the same manner as permitted in determining foreign market value.

3. Constructed Value

Constructed value is calculated on the basis of actual costs (materials, processing, labor, etc.) plus the cost of all containers and coverings and other expenses incidental to placing the merchandise in condition for exportation to the United States, and an amount for general expenses and profit. The amount for general expenses and profit is based on amounts reflected by sales of comparable merchandise made in the country of exportation.[17] However, the Law provides that the amount for general expenses shall be not less than 10 percent of the manufacturing costs, and the amount for profit shall be not less than 8 percent of the sum of general expenses and manufacturing costs. For ITA methodology for calculating

---

[15]Section 772(b) and (c), Tariff Act of 1930 (19 U.S.C. 1677a), 19 CFR 353.10, 353.22.
[16]Section 773(e)(3), Tariff Act of 1930 (19 U.S.C. 1677b). ·
[17]Section 773(e)(1), Tariff Act of 1930 (19 U.S.C. 1677b). See *Strontium Nitrate from Italy,* 46 FR 25496, May 7, 1981, 2 ITRD 5526.

the constructed foreign market value and the United States price when the foreign producer uses a U.S. subsidiary as its marketing agent, see *High Power Microwave Amplifiers from Japan,* 47 FR 22134, May 21, 1982, 4 ITRD 1110.

In determining constructed value, any transaction between any of the related parties listed in section 2 *supra* may be disregarded if the amount of the transaction does not fairly reflect the amount usually occurring in such transactions. Where a transaction is disregarded, the Secretary is empowered to use the best evidence available to determine that element of constructed value.

4. Sales at Less than Cost of Production

If the Secretary determines that sales have been made at less than cost of production, such sales shall be disregarded in the determination of foreign market value if the sales at less than cost of production have been made over an extended period of time and in substantial quantities, and are not at prices which permit recovery of all costs within a reasonable period of time in the normal course of trade.[18] If a petitioner in an antidumping investigation brings to the attention of the ITA the need for a cost of production determination, the ITA has a reasonable basis to believe or suspect that home market sales were at less than cost-of-production prices and has a statutory duty to investigate, except for compelling reasons. *Connors Steel Co.* v. *United States,* 2 CIT 242, 527 F. Supp. 350 (1981) 3 ITRD 1355. In an Order and Modification of its opinion the court deleted the requirement in its terms of remand of a cost of production investigation and instead ordered the Secretary of Commerce to submit a statement of the reasons for the conclusion in the original administrative determination that cost of production information, submitted in the final three months period, had been presented "too late to be considered." 3 CIT 79 (1982) 3 ITRD 1857.

5. Imports From State-Controlled-Economy Countries

The Law prescribes special rules for determining foreign market value in cases where the Secretary determines that the economy of the country from which the merchandise is exported is state-controlled to such an extent that sales of merchandise in that country or to third countries do not permit the determination of foreign market value in the usual manner. In such cases foreign market value is to be determined on the basis of the prices at which such or similar merchandise of a non-state-controlled-economy country or countries is sold in the home market of such country or countries, including the United States, or on the basis of the constructed value of such or similar merchandise in a non-state-controlled-economy country.[19]

---

[18]Section 773(b), Tariff Act of 1930 (19 U.S.C. 1677b).
[19]Section 773(c), Tariff Act of 1930 (19 U.S.C. 1677b).

In *Menthol from People's Republic of China,* 46 FR 3258, January 14, 1981, 2 ITRD 5364 (preliminary) and 46 FR 24614, May 1, 1981, 2 ITRD 5661 (final), the ITA analyzed the economy of the People's Republic of China and determined that the state controlled the economy generally, and with respect to its agricultural sector, and exercised such indirect restraints over the relatively free marketing of natural menthol that the foreign market value of natural menthol from the PRC must be determined on the basis of sales of natural menthol from the non-state-controlled economy of Paraguay. Compare the CIT's analysis in the *Four "H" Corporation* decision cited in section E.2 *supra.*

6. Sales by Multinational Corporations

The Law also provides a special rule for determining foreign market value in the cases of certain sales by multinational corporations. In essence, if a corporation owns or controls production facilities in more than one country, if sales in the home market of the exporting country are inadequate as a basis for comparison, and if the foreign market value of the merchandise produced in facilities outside the country of exportation is higher than the foreign market value in the country of exportation, the Secretary may use for comparison purposes the foreign market value at which such or similar merchandise is sold in substantial quantities by one or more facilities outside the country of exportation, with appropriate adjustments for differences in costs of production.[20]

7. Adjustments Necessary to Get Comparable Prices

Adjustments usually are necessary to get comparable prices.[21] Added to the purchase price (or exporter's sales price), for purposes of comparison, are:

(a) when not included in such price, the cost of all containers and coverings and all other costs, charges, and expenses incident to placing the merchandise in condition, packed ready for shipment to the United States;

(b) the amount of any import duties imposed by the country of exportation which have been rebated, or which have not been collected, by reason of the exportation of the merchandise to the United States;

(c) the amount of any taxes imposed in the country of exportation directly upon the exported merchandise or components thereof, which have been rebated, or which have not been collected, by reason of the exportation of the merchandise to the United States, but only to the extent that such taxes are added to or included in the price of such or similar merchandise when sold in the country of exportation; and

(d) the amount of any countervailing duty imposed under U.S. law on the merchandise to offset an export subsidy.

---

[20]Section 773(d), Tariff Act of 1930 (19 U.S.C. 1677b). See *Certain Steel Wire Nails from Korea,* 45 FR 34941, May 23, 1980, 2 ITRD 5563; 4 ITRD 1171, section E.1 *supra.*
[21]Section 772(d), Tariff Act of 1930 (19 U.S.C. 1677a).

Adjustment (d) carries out the provision in Art. VI.5 of the GATT which provides that no product of the territory of one contracting party imported into the territory of another contracting party shall be subject to both antidumping and countervailing duties to compensate for the same situation of dumping or export subsidization. See *Oil Country Tubular Goods from Argentina; Final Determination of Sales at Less Than Fair Value* (50 FR 12595 at 12598, March 29, 1985).

Deducted from the purchase price (or exporter's sales price) are:

(a) the amount, if any, included in such price, attributable to any additional costs, charges, and expenses, and U.S. import duties (other than countervailing duties), incident to bringing the merchandise from the place of shipment in the country of exportation to the place of delivery in the United States; and

(b) the amount, if included in such price, of any export tax, duty, or other charge imposed by the country of exportation on the exportation of the merchandise to the United States other than an export tax, duty, or other charge specifically intended to offset a subsidy received.

The exporter's sales price shall also be adjusted by being reduced by the amount, if any, of:

(a) commissions for selling in the United States the particular merchandise under consideration,

(b) expenses generally incurred by or for the account of the exporter in the United States in selling identical or substantially identical merchandise, and

(c) any increased value, including additional material and labor, resulting from a process of manufacture or assembly performed on the imported merchandise after the importation of the merchandise and before its sale to a person who is not the exporter of the merchandise.[22]

8. Other Adjustments

In addition to the adjustments discussed above, the Law calls for certain other adjustments or allowances to be made for quantity discounts, for differences in circumstances of sale, and for differences in the merchandise.[23] Allowances for differences in quantity are applied if the ITA is satisfied that the amount of any price differential is wholly or partially due to such differences in quantity. Consideration is given to the practice of the industry in respect to affording discounts for quantity sales which are freely available to customers who purchase in the ordinary course of trade. Ordinarily an allowance will not be made for differences in quantity unless (1) during the preceding six-month period the exporter gave comparable discounts on 20 percent or more of such or similar merchandise sold in the home (or third country) market; or (2) the exporter can provide a cost justification for such allowance for differences in quantity.[24]

---

[22]Section 772(e), Tariff Act of 1930 (19 U.S.C. 1677a).
[23]Section 773(a)(4), Tariff Act of 1930 (19 U.S.C. 1677b).
[24]19 CFR 353.14. See use of weighted average price in home market in *Melamine in Crystal Form from Austria*, 45 FR 20151, March 27, 1980, 2 ITRD 5639.

Allowances will be made for differences in circumstances of sale, which are the most controversial adjustments, if the ITA is satisfied that the amount of any price differential is wholly or partly due to such differences.[25] In general, such allowances are limited to circumstances which bear a direct relationship to the sales which are under consideration. Differences in circumstances of sale for which adjustments may be made include: differences in credit terms, guarantees, warranties, technical assistance, servicing, sales commissions, and assumptions by a seller of a purchaser's advertising or other selling costs.

Reasonable allowances for selling expenses generally will be made in cases where a reasonable allowance is made for commissions in one of the markets under consideration, the amount of such allowance being limited to the actual selling expense incurred in that market or the total amount of the commission allowed in the other market, whichever is less. Allowances generally are not made for differences in production costs and other selling costs unless such costs are attributable to a later sale of merchandise by a purchaser.

In determining the amount of allowance to be approved for any difference in circumstances of sale, the ITA will be guided primarily by the cost of such differences to the seller but, where appropriate, may also consider the effect of such differences upon the market value of the merchandise. In making comparisons using the exporter's sale price, reasonable allowance will be made for actual selling expenses incurred in the home market up to the amount of the selling expenses incurred in the U.S. market.

Allowances are also made for differences in physical characteristics of the merchandise in question. Again, in determining such allowances the ITA will be guided primarily by the differences in the cost of manufacture, if it is established to its satisfaction that the amount of any price differential is wholly or partly due to such differences.

9. Portable Electric Typewriter Decisions

An extensive review of the validity of the ITA regulation defining differences in circumstances of sales and prescribing the method for determining allowances, 19 CFR 353.15, was given by the Court of International Trade in the consolidated action *Brother Industries, Ltd. and Brother International Corporation, Plaintiffs* v. *United States, Defendant, Smith-Corona Group, Consumer Products Division, SCM Corporation, Party-in-Interest,* (Action I); *Smith Corona Group, Consumer Products Division, SCM Corporation, Plaintiff* v. *United States, Defendant, Brother Industries, Ltd., and Brother International Corporation; Silver Seiko, Ltd., and Silver Reed America, Inc., Parties-in-Interest* (Action II), 3 CIT 125, 540 F. Supp. 1341 (1982) 3 ITRD 1833; injunction pending appeal, 3 CIT 242, 3 ITRD 2144. In its Opinion the court also closely examined four

---

[25] 19 CFR 353.15. See *Countertop Microwave Ovens from Japan,* 45 FR 80157, December 3, 1980, 2 ITRD 5584.

specific adjustments for differences in circumstances of sale and an adjustment for differences in physical characteristics, under 19 CFR 353.16, made by the ITA in comparing the foreign market value and the United States price in *Portable Electric Typewriters from Japan; Determination of Duties,* on August 13, 1980, 45 FR 53853, as clarified and corrected, 46 FR 14006 (1980). The court noted that it was deciding "a number of highly complex issues which are of novel impression, and undoubtedly are of great significance in the administration of the nation's anti-dumping laws" (3 CIT 126). The correctness of the ITA position was confirmed on each issue.

The Smith-Corona Group, Consumer Products Divison, SCM Corporation ("SCM"), the only domestic manufacturer of portable electric typewriters ("PETs") challenged the adjustments granted by the ITA to the Brother and Silver companies, Japanese manufacturers and importers from Japan, as contrary to law and unsupported by substantial evidence, principally because they were not directly related to the sales under consideration by the ITA or were not based upon actual values but rather upon "estimates, approximations, or averages," contrary to the holding in *F.W. Myers & Co., Inc.* v. *United States,* 72 Cust. Ct. 219, 376 F. Supp. 860 (1974). Its comprehensive challenge to all contested adjustments was the alleged failure of 19 CFR 353.15 to require a causal link between the differences in circumstances of sale and the differential between United States price and the foreign market value, as required by Section 773(a)(4) of the Tariff Act. The Brother companies contested the denial by ITA of an additional adjustment to foreign market value for the cost of a promotional giveaway campaign in Japan. This challenge to the ITA determination of dumping duties was also rejected by the court.

The specific allowances given by the ITA which were attacked by SCM were the adjustment of the foreign market value of each typewriter model:

(1) for differences in packing costs and in inland freight incurred in sales in the home market and to the United States;

(2) by the amount of certain types of rebates in connection with sales in Japan;

(3) pursuant to 19 CFR 353.15(c) for the exporter's sales price (ESP) offset where foreign market value was compared with the exporter's sales price;

(4) by the amount for certain advertising expenses incurred in sales in Japan; and

(5) for differences in physical characteristics by an amount which was equal to the difference in costs of certain accessories and printed materials provided in connection with sales in Japan and to the United States.

The CIT found that the first four adjustments were appropriate differences in the circumstances of sale and related directly to the sales under consideration and, where the amounts were based upon allocations to particular models of actual total costs, they were sufficiently definite. The fifth adjustment for cost differences between the accessories and printed materials sold with the PETs in Japan and those sold to the United States was found to be a legitimate difference in physical characteristics of the PETs being compared pursuant to Section 773(a)(4)(C) and 19 CFR 353.16.

In reaching its conclusions the court drew upon the legislative history of the various provisions in Section 773 of the Tariff Act and the administrative practice in both the Treasury and Commerce Departments.

The Court of Appeals for the Federal Circuit (CAFC) affirmed the CIT on all major issues, in *Smith-Corona Group* v. *United States,* 713 F.2d 1568 (1983) 4 ITRD 2297, *cert. denied,* 104 S.Ct. 1274 (1984) 5 ITRD 1944.

While the validity of the ESP offset was upheld by the appeals court, the CIT ruled in a subsequent case involving PETs that the "cap" on the ESP offset contained in 19 CFR 353.15(c) was invalid. *Silver Reed America, Inc.* v. *United States,* 7 CIT _____ , 581 F. Supp. 1290 (1984) 5 ITRD 1673. The court noted that since Congress stipulated the deduction of all selling expenses from the United States price, undoubtedly the intent was that the same treatment be accorded foreign market value. The CAFC reversed, upholding the ITA regulation, *SCM Corp.* v. *United States,* 753 F.2d 1033 (Fed. Cir. 1985), 6 ITRD 1737. Concerning the level of trade adjustment of 19 CFR 353.19, the court in *Silver Reed* noted that while generally the level of trade will correlate with the quantity involved in the sales, this is not always the case and the ITA must look beyond the quantities to determine if other adjustments are required. Following the CAFC decision the CIT vacated its remand of the case to the ITA on the level of trade adjustment, as well as the ESP offset cap limitation, on the ground that the actual duty assessments were governed by administrative reviews subsequent to the final ITA dumping determination and any CIT decision concerning the ITA's action on remand could be advisory only. *Silver Reed America, Inc. and Silver Seiko, Ltd.* v. *United States,* 9 CIT _____ , Slip Op. 85-51 (1985) 6 ITRD 2330.

10. Required Study of Adjustments

The foregoing review of the litigation over the application of adjustments to find comparable prices suggests the reason for the study of this subject required by Section 624 of the 1984 Amendments. That section requires the Secretary of Commerce to make, and complete in one year, a study of the current practices applied in the making of adjustments to purchase prices, exporters sales prices, foreign market value, and constructed value, including a review of private sector comments at Congressional hearings, and to report to Congress with recommendations for simplifying and modifying current practices.

11. Currency Conversion

For purposes of price comparison, 19 CFR 353.56(a) provides that values expressed in terms of foreign currencies are converted into equivalents in U.S. dollars (1) as of the date of purchase, or agreement to purchase, if purchase price is being used; or (2) as of the date of exportation, if exporter's sales price is being used, in accordance with the conversion of currency statute 31 U.S.C. 5151 (formerly 372). However, Section 353.56(b) of the regulations provides that in fair value investigations where prices are affected by temporary exchange rate fluctuations no differences between prices being compared which result solely from such exchange rate fluctuations will be taken into account. The validity of this Subsection (b) was upheld by the CAFC as a reasonable exercise of the ITA's administrative authority, which reversed the invalidation of this so-called "90 day lag rule" by the CIT.[26]

II. PROCESSING AN ANTIDUMPING PROCEEDING

A. Starting the Proceeding; Assistance Available

An antidumping proceeding can be initiated by the Secretary or by a petition filed by an interested party on behalf of a domestic industry.[27] If the Secretary commences the proceeding, he promptly notifies the Commission. In this case it is also the practice to notify and consult with the authorities of the foreign country concerned.

A petition by an interested party must be filed simultaneously with the Secretary and the Commission, and so certified in submitting the petition to the Secretary. The petition and supporting documents must be in the form prescribed by 19 CFR 353.36. An "interested party" is one described in Section 771(9) as (C) a manufacturer, producer, or wholesaler in the United States of a like product; (D) a certified union or group of workers representative of an industry engaged in the manufacture, production, or sale at wholesale in the United States of a like product; and (E) a trade or business association, the majority of whose members manufacture, produce, or sell at wholesale a like product in the United States.[28] This section was not specifically amended by Section 612(b)(2) of the 1984 Amendments to include the association of interested domestic parties described in new Paragraph (F) of the interested party definition in Section 771(9), although the Conference Report indicates an intent to do so (H.R. Rep. No. 98-1156 at 175).

The Law requires that the petition allege "the elements necessary for the imposition of the [antidumping] duty."[29]

According to the ITA regulations,[30] a petition by an interested party shall contain, or be accompanied by, information, to the extent reasonably available to the petitioner, in substantially the following form:

(1) The name and address of the petitioner and any other person, firm, or association the petitioner represents, if appropriate;

(2) The industry on whose behalf the petition is filed, including the names of other enterprises included in such industry;

(3) A statement indicating whether the applicant has filed, or is filing, for import relief pursuant to Section 201 of the Trade Act of 1974 (19

---

[26]*Melamine Chemicals Inc.* v. *United States,* 732 F.2d 924 (Fed. Cir. 1984) 5 ITRD 2077, *rev'g Melamine Chemicals, Inc.* v. *United States,* 5 CIT 116, 561 F. Supp. 458 (1983) 4 ITRD 1705.
[27]Section 732, Tariff Act of 1930 (19 U.S.C. 1673a).
[28]Section 732(b)(1), Tariff Act of 1930 (19 U.S.C. 1673a).
[29]*Ibid.*
[30]19 CFR 353.36

U.S.C. 2251), or has initiated proceedings pursuant to Section 337 or 702 of the Act (19 U.S.C. 1337, 1671a), Section 232 of the Trade Expansion Act of 1962 (19 U.S.C. 1862), or Section 301 of the Trade Act of 1974 (19 U.S.C. 2411) with respect to the merchandise which is the subject of the proceeding;

(4) A detailed description of the imported merchandise in question, including its technical characteristics and uses, and, where appropriate, its tariff classification under the Tariff Schedules of the United States;

(5) The name of the country or countries from which the merchandise is being, or is likely to be, exported to the United States and, if the merchandise is produced in a country other than that from which it is exported, the name of the country in which it is produced;

(6) The names and addresses of all known foreign enterprises believed to be manufacturing, producing, or exporting the merchandise in question;

(7) All pertinent facts as to the price at which the foreign merchandise is sold or offered for sale in the United States and in the home market in which produced or from which exported, including information concerning transportation and insurance charges, and if appropriate, information regarding sales in third countries or the cost of producing the merchandise. Petitioners unable to furnish information on foreign sales or costs may present information concerning U.S. domestic producers' costs adjusted for differences in the foreign country in question from information publicly available;

(8) If the merchandise is being exported from a country which is considered to be a state-controlled-economy-country, any information pertaining to the price or prices at which such or similar merchandise of a non-state-controlled-economy-country or countries, considered to be comparable in terms of economic development to the state-controlled-economy-country, is sold for consumption in the home market of that country or countries or to other countries (including the United States), or the constructed value of such or similar merchandise in a non-state-controlled-economy-country, determined in accordance with 19 CFR 353.8;

(9) Evidence, if any, that sales in the home market are being made at a price which represents less than the cost of production of the merchandise, and the circumstances under which such sales are made;

(10) The volume and value of imports of the merchandise from the country in question in the most recent two-year period, and also other periods if the petitioner believes such other periods to be more representative, or, if the merchandise is not presently imported into the United States or is not imported in significant quantities, information as to the likelihood of its importation;

(11) The names and addresses of enterprises believed to be importing the merchandise;

(12) The names and addresses of other enterprises in the United States engaged in the production, manufacture, or sale of like merchandise. If numerous, information need not be provided with respect to any enterprises that accounted for less than 2 percent of domestic production, manufacture, or sale of such merchandise during the most recent 12-month period;

(13) Information as to the material injury or threat thereof to, or the material retardation of the establishment of, a U.S. industry by reason of the imported merchandise alleged to be sold at less than fair value, as described in 19 CFR 207.11 and 207.26;

(14) If "critical circumstances" are alleged, information should be presented—(A) as to a history of dumping or (B) that the importer knew or should have known the exporter was selling at less than fair value, and (C) that injury which is difficult to repair is caused by reason of massive imports in a relatively short period; and

(15) Any documentation on which petitioner relies in making its petition.

Forms for the submission of petitions may be adopted from time to time. The use of such forms shall not be mandatory, provided the information required thereby and reasonably available to the petitioner is otherwise included in the petition.

Giving price information on foreign and U.S. sales of the merchandise for different time periods is a frequent error. Caution should be taken to submit data for comparable time periods and to show a dumping margin, *i.e.,* lower prices in the United States than in the home or third country markets.

Technical assistance in the filing of petitions was required by Section 221 of the 1984 Amendments to be provided to eligible small businesses by each agency administering a trade law, specifically including the agencies administering the antidumping and countervailing duty laws. An eligible small business was defined to mean any business concern which in the agency's unreviewable judgment has not the resources or financial ability to obtain qualified outside assistance in preparing and filing petitions. The agency is required to consult with any other agency which has provided this assistance to the business concerned and may consult the Small Business Administration.

The Commission was also specifically required by Section 221 to establish a Trade Remedy Assistance Office to provide information to the public upon request on the remedies and benefits available under the trade laws and on petition and application procedures and filing dates.

B. Steps in the Processing of an Antidumping Proceeding

There are various steps which have to be taken from the time of the initiation of an antidumping proceeding until the issuance of the antidumping duty order. The following is an outline of these steps:

1. Commencement of Proceeding

The proceedings may be commenced either by the Secretary of Commerce or by the filing of a petition by an interested party.

2. Determination of Sufficiency of Petition

Within 20 days of the filing of a petition, the ITA must decide whether the petition contains sufficient information to initiate an investigation.

If the determination is affirmative, the Secretary publishes a notice of commencement of an investigation and notifies the Commission and petitioner. If the determination is negative, the Secretary dismisses the petition, terminates the proceedings, and notifies the Commission and petitioner.

3. Preliminary Commission Determination on Injury

The Commission must make its preliminary determination within 45 days of the filing of the petition or of notification by the Secretary. A negative preliminary injury determination terminates the proceeding.

4. Preliminary Determination on Dumping by the Secretary

Normally the ITA will make its preliminary dumping determination within 160 days of the filing of a petition or commencement of a self-initiated investigation. If the ruling is affirmative, an estimated average amount of dumping margins will be included.

A preliminary determination under a waiver of verification is due within 90 days after commencement of an investigation. Under this procedure, within 75 days of the commencement of the investigation the Secretary reviews the information received in the first 60 days of the probe. Such information, if sufficient, is then disclosed to the petitioner and interested parties who have three working days to sign irrevocable waivers of verification of the information.

5. Extension of Time Period in Extraordinarily Complicated Cases

The procedure for extension of time may be initiated either by a request from the petitioner or by the Secretary, if the parties are cooperating. Under this procedure, the preliminary determination may be postponed until not later than the 210th day after the date of filing the petition or commencement of a self-initiated investigation. Also, parties must be notified of the postponement not later than 20 days before the date on which the determination would otherwise be required.

6. Effect of Preliminary Determination

If the preliminary determination is affirmative, the Secretary orders the suspension of liquidation of all entries. In addition, if the Secretary determines the existence of critical circumstances, suspension shall apply to all unliquidated entries of the merchandise entered or withdrawn from warehouse in the 90 days preceding the date on which the suspension was first ordered. The petitioner must have alleged critical circumstances in the original petition or by amendment filed more than 20 days before the date of a final determination by the Secretary.

7. Final Determination on Dumping by the Secretary

The final dumping determination is normally made within 75 days after the preliminary determination. A final determination may be postponed until not later than the 135th day after the preliminary determination if requested (a) by exporters who account for a significant proportion of the exports to the United States, if the preliminary determination was affirmative; or (b) by the petitioner if the preliminary determination was negative.

8. Final Commission Determination on Injury

Following an affirmative preliminary determination by the Secretary, the Commission undertakes a final injury determination which is due before the later of (a) the 120th day after the Secretary's preliminary determination, or (b) the 45th day after the Secretary's final determination. Following a negative preliminary determination and an affirmative final determination by the Secretary, the Commission's decision as to material injury or retardation is required within 75 days after the Secretary's final determination.

9. Publication of Antidumping Duty Order

Within seven days after notification by the Commission of an affirmative final injury determination, the Secretary must publish an antidumping duty order.

Under the Antidumping Law, the Secretary and the Commission perform their responsibilities simultaneously, except following a negative preliminary determination and an affirmative final determination by the Secretary. While the Secretary is investigating the possibility of dumping, the Commission is studying the question of injury. Each agency must promptly notify the other of any determination it makes, whether preliminary or final. All determinations, preliminary or final, must be published in the *Federal Register*, with a statement of the facts and conclusions of law on which based.

The following are some of the details as to the steps outlined in section B *supra.*

C. Processing by the Secretary

1. Initiation of Investigation; Preliminary Determination

The Secretary commences an investigation on his own motion, or on the basis of a petition filed by a domestic interested party that he has determined to be sufficient, *i.e.,* makes a *prima facie* case of dumping. This determination must be made on the basis of the petition and the petitioner's supporting data, and facts in the public domain, without soliciting or receiving information from other sources. *Roses Incorporated* v. *United States,* 3 CIT 110, 538 F. Supp. 418 (1982) 3 ITRD 1769. This ruling was affirmed by the CAFC which, however, reversed that part of the CIT decision requiring immediate commencement of an antidumpting investigation and remanded the case for further proceedings. *United States* v. *Roses Incorporated,* 706 F.2d 1563 (Fed. Cir. 1983) 4 ITRD 1841.

Section 609 of the 1984 Amendments amends Section 732(a) of the Tariff Act of 1930 (19 U.S.C. 1673a(a)) to give the Secretary the authority to establish a monitoring program for up to one year to detect persistent dumping with respect to imports of a class or kind of merchandise from countries regarding which no antidumping investigation (with respect to the class or kind of merchandise) is pending and no antidumping order is in effect, if:

(1) more than one antidumping order is in effect with respect to that class or kind of merchandise;

(2) there is reason to believe or suspect an "extraordinary pattern of persistent injurious dumping" from one or more additional countries; and

(3) this pattern is causing a serious commercial problem for the domestic industry.

The statute gives the Secretary discretion as to whether to establish a monitoring program. Once the program is established, however, the statute provides that the Secretary "shall" immediately commence an antidumping investigation whenever he determines there is sufficient evidence regarding an additional country, and that the proceedings in such cases shall be expedited "to the extent practicable" by the Secretary and Commission.

The Secretary publishes a notice of initiation of investigation in the *Federal Register.* All subsequent determinations in the proceeding must be similarly published.

The investigation is conducted by Commerce Department personnel in the United States and abroad. At the time of commencement of the investigation, the petitioner is sent a letter of notification in questionnaire form and similar letters are sent to the major manufacturers in the foreign country of the product alleged to be dumped. These letters contain detailed questions which the foreign manufacturers are required to answer within 30 days concerning their sales domestically and to U.S. producers.

a. Investigations Abroad

Investigations are conducted in foreign countries unless the foreign country objects. The answer to the manufacturers' questionnaires are carefully verified by the Secretary. The Commerce case analyst visits the manufacturers and goes over their books to check the validity of their answers to the questionnaire. Other checks are made in the foreign country. He also investigates in order to determine whether there is a relationship between the foreign manufacturers and the U.S. importers in order to determine whether the U.S. purchase price should be used for purposes of comparison or, if a relationship exists, the exporter's sales price should be used.

b. Investigations in the United States

In the meantime, other Commerce personnel in the United States gather data from a variety of sources. They may check with domestic importers to verify that the purchase information given by the foreign manufacturer in his response to the questionnaire was correct. Commerce also gathers data necessary for making the price adjustments mentioned above.

c. Waiver of Verification

The Secretary normally has 160 days after the commencement of the proceeding to make his preliminary determination as to whether there is a reasonable basis to believe or suspect that foreign merchandise which is the subject of the investigation is being sold or is likely to be sold at less than fair value. Frequently, it is in the interest of all parties, importers and domestic manufacturers alike, that the process of making the preliminary determination be expedited. Accordingly, the Law contains special provisions for a waiver of verification procedure pursuant to which the preliminary determination can be made within 90 days after the filing of the petition or commencement of the investigation.[31]

Under this procedure the Secretary reviews the information concerning the case developed during the first 60 days of the investigation and, if sufficient, discloses to the petitioner and any other party to the proceeding who requests disclosure, the available nonconfidential information and other confidential information which may be made available pursuant to protective orders. The petitioner and other parties aligned with the domestic industry are given three working days to furnish the Secretary with a waiver of further verification of the information and agreement to have the preliminary determination made on the basis of the record then available. Unless they all sign, the Secretary continues with the investigation and verifies the information. If they all sign, the Secretary makes the preliminary determination on the basis of the information then available.

d. Extraordinarily Complicated Cases

The time period for making the preliminary determination may be extended until not later than the 210th day after the date of filing of the petition or the commencement of the investigation in "extraordinarily complicated cases."[32] The postponement may be initiated by the Secretary or by the petitioner filing a request. The Secretary may determine a case to be extraordinarily complicated if the interested parties are cooperating in

---

[31]Section 733(b)(2), Tariff Act of 1930 (19 U.S.C. 1673b).
[32]Section 733(c)(1), Tariff Act of 1930 (19 U.S.C. 1673b).

the furnishing of information, and the Secretary finds that additional time is needed by reason of:

(1) the number and complexity of the transactions or adjustments to be considered;

(2) the novelty of the issues presented; or

(3) the number of firms whose activities must be investigated. In practice, a case in which it is necessary to determine the cost of production of the foreign merchandise has also been considered as extraordinarily complicated. Any decision to designate a case extraordinarily complicated must be made not later than 20 days before the date on which the preliminary determination would otherwise be required. Such a decision was subject to expedited judicial review until enactment of the 1984 Amendments (see Chapter 31, section VII).[33]

e. Opportunity for Consultation

Prior to making its preliminary determination, the Secretary will provide opportunities for consultation with all parties to the investigation concerning the information developed.

f. Effect of Preliminary Determination

As previously stated, if the Secretary makes an affirmative preliminary determination the Law requires the Secretary:

(1) to order the suspension of liquidation of all entries of such merchandise entered, or withdrawn from warehouse, for consumption on or after the date of publication of the notice of the determination in the *Federal Register*;

(2) to order the posting of a cash deposit, bond, or other security, as he determines appropriate, for each entry of merchandise equal to the estimated amount by which the foreign market value exceeds the United States price; and

(3) to make available to the Commission all information upon which the preliminary determination was based which may be relevant to the Commission's injury determination.[34]

g. Critical Circumstances Determinations

If the petitioner alleges critical circumstances in its original petition, or by amendment at any time more than 20 days before the date of the final determination, the Secretary may find the existence of such circumstances and direct that the liquidation of entries of the merchandise under investigation be suspended retroactively and applied to unliquidated entries of merchandise entered, or withdrawn from warehouse, for consumption on

---

[33]Section 516A, Tariff Act of 1930 (19 U.S.C. 1516a).
[34]Section 733(d), Tariff Act of 1930 (19 U.S.C. 1673b).

or after the date which is 90 days before the date of the original suspension of liquidation.[35] Under the timetable in 19 CFR 353.40, if the petitioner alleges critical circumstances not less than 30 days before the date the final determination is due, then the critical circumstances determination will be made a part of the preliminary determination unless the preliminary determination has already been made or is due within 20 days, in which case the critical circumstances determination will be made within one month after the allegation is received. If the allegation is made not more than 30 and not less than 20 days before the due date of the final determination, the critical circumstances determination will be included in the affirmative final determination. The Secretary may find the existence of critical circumstances if he has a reasonable basis for believing or suspecting that:

(1) there have been massive imports of the merchandise under investigation over a relatively short period; and

(2) there is a history of dumping in the United States or elsewhere, or the person by whom, or for whose account, the merchandise was imported, knew or should have known that the exporter was selling such merchandise at less than fair value. A negative critical circumstances decision is not by itself subject to judicial review. *Haarman & Reimer Corp.* v. *United States,* 1 CIT 148, 509 F. Supp. 1276 (1981) 2 ITRD 1305, *reh'g denied,* 1 CIT 207 (1981) 2 ITRD 1458.

h. Right to Hearing

Upon the request of any party to the proceeding, a hearing will be held during the course of the investigation (normally within 30 days after publication of the preliminary determination), at which interested persons may present views orally.[36] The hearing is not subject to the Administrative Procedure Act and does not involve examination and cross-examination of witnesses under oath.

2. Termination and Suspension of Investigation

The Secretary may terminate an investigation at any time upon withdrawal of the petition upon which it was based and after notification to all parties to the investigation, provided that under the 1984 Amendments if the termination is based upon an agreement to limit the volume of imports of the product into the United States (a quantitative restriction agreement), the Secretary must first determine that such a termination is in the public interest. Section 604(b) of the 1984 Amendments amends Section 734 of the Tariff Act of 1930 (19 U.S.C. 1673c) to provide that the Secretary, in making such a public interest determination, must consult, to the extent practicable, with potentially affected consuming industries and potentially

---

[35]Section 733 (e), Tariff Act of 1930 (19 U.S.C. 1673b).
[36]Section 774, Tariff Act of 1930 (19 U.S.C. 1677c); 19 CFR 353.47.

affected workers and producers in the U.S. domestic industry and must take into account:

(1) whether the agreement would more adversely affect U.S. consumers than would the imposition of antidumping duties,

(2) the relative impact on the U.S. international economic interests, and

(3) the relative impact on the competitiveness of the U.S. domestic industry producing the like merchandise.

As indicated *infra,* the Commission may also terminate an investigation upon withdrawal of a petition but not before a preliminary determination has been made by the Secretary.[37]

Notable use of the original authority to terminate an antidumping duty investigation was made by the Secretary of Commerce when he terminated on October 21, 1982, the remaining 18 antidumping investigations in the major carbon steel cases filed in January 1982, by the U.S. steel industry against exports from member countries of the European Community. The Secretary gave notice that the termination occurred upon the withdrawal by the petitioners of their petitions and upon the conclusion of agreements with respect to imports of the carbon steel products which were the subject of the investigations reached between the U.S. Government and the EC (47 FR 49058, October 29, 1982). The text of the agreements, which restricted imports to various percentages of U.S. consumption and required export licenses, was set forth in Appendix III of the *Federal Register* notice. In the investigations, preliminary affirmative determinations had been reached on August 9, 1982, 3 ITRD 2339. The International Trade Commission was therefore able to, and did, terminate its investigations in these carbon steel dumping cases (47 FR 49104, October 29, 1982). The Commerce Department and Commission terminations applied also to the companion countervailing duty investigations.[38]

The Secretary may terminate an investigation initiated by himself upon notice to all parties to the investigation, under authority added by Section 604 of the 1984 Amendments. Any termination of an investigation renders all determinations reached of no force or effect. It is to be distinguished from the suspension of an investigation upon acceptance of an agreement by the exporters of the merchandise under investigation which has the effects described below.

The Law also empowers the Secretary to suspend an investigation upon his acceptance of an agreement: (a) to eliminate sales at less than fair value completely or to cease exports of the merchandise, or (b) eliminating the injurious effect.[39]

---

[37]Section 734(a), Tariff Act of 1930 (19 U.S.C. 1673c).
[38]The requirements of the EC-US steel arrangement were enforced under the sanction of 19 U.S.C. 1626 in *Klockner, Inc.* v. *United States,* 8 CIT _____ , 590 F. Supp. 1266 (1984) 5 ITRD 2443.
[39]Section 734(b) and (c), Tariff Act of 1930 (19 U.S.C. 1673c).

a. Agreements to Eliminate Sales at Less than Fair Value or to Cease Exports

The Secretary may suspend an investigation if the exporters of the merchandise under investigation who account for substantially all the imports of that merchandise agree to cease all exports of that merchandise within six months or to revise prices to eliminate completely any dumping margin, *i.e.*, the amount by which the foreign market value exceeds the United States price. The phrase "substantially all" is interpreted to mean no less than 85 percent of total exports of the merchandise under investigation in the most recent representative period.[40]

b. Agreements Eliminating Injurious Effect

In the second category, the agreement does not have to provide for a complete cessation of the exports of the merchandise or for a complete elimination of any dumping margins. However, this category of agreement must provide assurances that steps have been taken and will be maintained to eliminate the injurious effect of the sales at less than fair value. This category of agreement may be accepted only:

(1) in "extraordinary circumstances," which are defined as circumstances in which the suspension of an investigation will be more beneficial to the domestic industry than continuation of the investigation (*e.g.*, because of the value of settling the case quickly or the certainty of prompt relief which the settlement provides), and

(2) if the case is "complex," for example, due to the large number of transactions and claims for adjustments, the novelty of the issues raised, or the large number of companies involved.

The Law states the agreement must provide that:

(1) the suppression or undercutting of price levels of domestic products by importers of the merchandise under the investigation will be prevented;

(2) for each entry of each exporter subject to the agreement the amount by which the estimated foreign market value exceeds the United States price will not exceed 15 percent of the weighted average amount by which the estimated foreign market value exceeded the United States price for all less-than-fair-value sales of the exporter examined during the course of the investigation; and

(3) the effect of such agreement is to eliminate completely the injurious effect of the imports of the merchandise subject to the investigation.

c. Conditions for Acceptance of an Agreement to Suspend

The Law and regulations provide that the Secretary shall not accept an agreement to suspend an investigation unless he has:

---

[40]19 CFR 353.42(c).

(1) consulted with the petitioner and notified all parties and the Commission not less than 30 days prior to the suspension;

(2) provided a copy of the proposed agreement to the petitioner at the time of notification together with an explanation of how the agreement will be carried out and enforced and of how the agreement will meet the requirements of the law; and

(3) permitted all parties to the investigation, as described in amended Section 771(9), to submit comments and information for the record before the date of suspension.[41]

In addition, the Secretary must not accept an agreement unless he is satisfied that suspension of the investigation is in the public interest, and that effective monitoring of the agreement by the United States is practicable.[42]

d. Monitoring of an Agreement

The regulations provide for effective monitoring of each agreement to suspend an investigation. The regulations and the agreements themselves were expected to include provisions with respect to entry, or withdrawal from warehouse, for consumption of merchandise which is the subject of an agreement.[43] However, they do not require the Secretary to ascertain or determine the level of domestic prices of the merchandise in monitoring compliance with an agreement or as a prerequisite to the acceptance of assurances.[44]

3. Effects of Suspension of an Investigation[45]

When the Secretary suspends an investigation he shall publish notice of that fact in the *Federal Register* and simultaneously issue and publish an affirmative preliminary determination with respect to the merchandise subject to the investigation unless such an affirmative preliminary determination has already been issued. Once an agreement to suspend is accepted, both the Secretary and the Commission shall suspend their investigations.

If the agreement accepted is one of those described in the first category above, *i.e.,* one which provides for the elimination of all dumping margins or the cessation of all exports there shall be no suspension of liquidation unless the liquidation of entries has already been suspended, in which case the suspension shall be terminated.

If the agreement to suspend an investigation is in the second category above, *i.e.,* an agreement to eliminate injurious effects, the liquidation of entries will be suspended to permit opportunity for a request for

---

[41]Section 734(e), Tariff Act of 1930 (19 U.S.C. 1673c) as amended in 1984; 19 CFR 353.42(h).

[42]Section 734(d), Tariff Act of 1930 (19 U.S.C. 1673c). For a discussion of the experience of Commerce with, and its reluctance to use, suspension agreements from 1980 to mid-1983, see Holmer and Bello, *Suspension and Settlement Agreements in Unfair Trade Cases,* 18 International Lawyer 683, Summer 1984.

[43]Administrative Statement, H.R. Doc. No. 96-153, Part II, p. 402.

[44]19 CFR 353.42(e).

[45]See Section 734(f), Tariff Act of 1930 (19 U.S.C. 1673c).

Commission review of the terms of the agreement. If no request is received, suspension of liquidation terminates on the 21st day after publication of the notice of suspension of the investigation.

4. Commission Review of Certain Agreements to Suspend Investigations

With respect to the second category of agreements described above, *i.e.*, agreements to eliminate injurious effects, the Law authorizes a review by the Commission.[46] An interested party which is a party to the investigation may file a petition with the Commission within 20 days after the suspension of investigation asking for a review of the suspension. Notice of this request must be given to the Secretary. The term "interested party" includes for this purpose a manufacturer, producer, or wholesaler in the United States of a like product; a certified union or recognized union or group of workers representative of an industry engaged in the manufacture, production, or sale at wholesale in the United States of a like product; a trade or business association, a majority of whose members manufacture, produce, or wholesale a like product in the United States; and, under the amendment made by Section 612(b)(2) of the 1984 Amendments in the suspension provisions, an association, a majority of whose members is composed of the foregoing domestic interested parties.[47]

Within 75 days after the filing of the petition, the Commission determines whether implementation of the agreement will eliminate the injurious effect of imports of the merchandise sold at less than fair value. If the Commission's determination is affirmative, the agreement to suspend the investigation remains in effect, the suspension of liquidation shall terminate, and any estimated dumping duties which may have been deposited or other security which may have been required shall be released. If the determination is negative, the agreement is set aside and the investigation is resumed, in which case the date of the preliminary determination by the Secretary is deemed to be the date of publication of notice of the Commission's negative determination.

5. Requests for Continuation of Investigation

Notwithstanding an agreement to suspend an investigation, it may be in the interest of certain interested parties that the investigation be continued in order that the questions raised in the proceeding may be finally disposed of at an early date. Accordingly, the Law provides that an interested party to the investigation eligible to file a petition for Commission review of a suspension of an investigation, or exporters accounting for a significant proportion of the exports to the United States of merchandise which is the subject of the investigation (which may be less than "substantially all"), may within the 20-day period following the date of publication of the notice of suspension request a continuation of the investigation. The term

---

[46]Section 734(h), Tariff Act of 1930 (19 U.S.C. 1673c); 19 CFR 353.42(k).
[47]Section 771(9), Tariff Act of 1930 (19 U.S.C. 1677), and Section 734(g), as amended by Pub. L. No. 98-573.

"interested party" for this purpose was expanded by the amendment made by Section 612(b)(2) of the 1984 Amendments to include an association, a majority of whose members is composed of the domestic interested parties described in Section 771(9)(C), (D), or (E) (19 U.S.C. 1677(9)) with respect to a like product.[48]

The request must be filed with both the Secretary and the Commission and both the Secretary and the Commission shall continue the investigation, notwithstanding the agreement, which may be of either type. If the final determination of the investigation by the Secretary or the Commission is negative, the agreement shall have no force or effect and the investigation shall be terminated. If the final determinations by both the Secretary and Commission are affirmative, the agreement remains in force. No antidumping order shall be issued so long as the agreement remains in force, the agreement continues to meet the requirements of the Law, and the parties continue to meet their obligations under the agreement.[49]

6. Violation of an Agreement

If the Secretary determines that an agreement suspending an investigation is being, or has been, violated or no longer meets the requirements of the Law, then the Secretary shall:

(a) suspend liquidation of unliquidated entries of the merchandise on the later of the date which is 90 days before the date of publication of the notice of suspension of liquidation, or the date on which the merchandise, the sale or export to the United States of which was in violation of the agreement, was first entered, or withdrawn from warehouse, for consumption;

(b) if the investigation was not completed, resume the investigation as if his affirmative preliminary determination were made on the day on which the investigation is resumed;

(c) if the investigation was completed, issue an Antidumping Duty Order, effective with respect to entries the liquidation of which was suspended upon the determination that the agreement had been violated; and

(d) if the violation is considered to be intentional, notify the Commissioner of Customs, who shall take appropriate action (a 1984 addition to the section); and

(e) notify the petitioner, interested parties who are or were party to the investigation, and the Commission, of his action, and publish notice of such action in the Federal Register.[50]

The regulations provide that parties to an agreement shall be notified at the earliest moment if there is reason to believe that the agreement no longer meets the requirements of the Law or that there has been a violation of the agreement (other than intentional violation) so that alternative or

---

[48]Section 734(g), Tariff Act of 1930 (19 U.S.C. 1673c), as amended by Pub. L. No. 98-573.
[49]Section 734(f)(3), Tariff Act of 1930 (19 U.S.C. 1673c); 19 CFR 353.42.
[50]Section 734(i)(l), Tariff Act of 1930 (19 U.S.C. 1673c).

amended agreements may be considered before the agreement is deemed violated.[51]

Any party intentionally violating an agreement on the basis of which an investigation has been suspended, may be subject to the penalties for fraud provided in Section 592 of the Tariff Act of 1930. (See 19 CFR 353.43(c).)

7. Final Determination by the Secretary

The Secretary must make his final determination as to whether the merchandise is being, or is likely to be, sold in the United States at less than fair value, *i.e.*, dumped, within 75 days after the date of his preliminary affirmative determination. However, the Secretary may postpone making his final determination until not later than the 135th day after publication of that determination under certain circumstances upon request by the exporters or the petitioner.[52]

a. Critical Circumstances Determinations

If the petitioner has alleged critical circumstances as indicated in section C.1.g *supra,* then the Secretary's affirmative determination must also contain a finding as to whether there is a history of dumping in the United States or elsewhere of the class or kind of merchandise which is the subject of the investigation, or the person by whom or for whose account the merchandise was imported knew or should have known that the exporter was selling the merchandise which is the subject of the investigation at less than its fair value; and there have been massive imports of the merchandise over a relatively short period.[53]

The 1984 Amendments, in Section 605(b), make it clear that under an affirmative critical circumstances determination the suspension of liquidation shall apply to all unliquidated entries entered, or withdrawn from warehouse, for consumption on or after the date which is 90 days before the date on which suspension of liquidation is first ordered, regardless of whether or not the preliminary determination was affirmative and, if so, even if the preliminary critical circumstances determination was negative.

b. Effect of Secretary's Final Determination

If the Secretary's final determination of the dumping petition is negative it is published in the *Federal Register,* the Commission is notified, and the antidumping proceeding is terminated. If the Secretary's final determination is affirmative, it is published in the *Federal Register,* the Commission is notified and proceeds to make its final determination on the question of existence or likelihood of material injury, or threat of injury, to an industry in the U.S., or material retardation of establishment of such industry.[54]

---

[51] 19 CFR 353.43(b).
[52] Section 735(a), Tariff Act of 1930 (19 U.S.C. 1673d).
[53] Section 735(a)(3), Tariff Act of 1930 (19 U.S.C. 1673d).
[54] Section 735(c), Tariff Act of 1930 (19 U.S.C. 1673d).

8. Issuance of Antidumping Order

Upon receipt of notice of an affirmative final determination by the Commission on the question of injury, the Secretary must within seven days publish an Antidumping Duty Order describing the merchandise to which it applies, and directing the Customs Service to require the deposit of estimated antidumping duties, pending liquidation, equal to the amount by which the foreign market value of the merchandise exceeds the United States price (the dumping margin), and thereafter to assess antidumping duties equal to the amount of the dumping margin determined or estimated by the Secretary following administrative review.[55]

The antidumping order must be limited to those articles which the ITC found to be causing injury and may not extend to other articles which were found by the ITA to be sold at less than fair value. *Badger-Powhatan, a Division of Figgie International, Inc.* v. *United States,* 9 CIT ___ , 608 F. Supp. 653 (1985) 6 ITRD 2324.

D. Processing by the Commission

The basic responsibilities of the Commission involve determinations on questions of whether dumping or alleged dumping causes or is likely to cause material injury, or threat thereof, to an industry in the United States or materially retard the establishment thereof. Policies and procedures in carrying out these responsibilities in antidumping cases (and countervailing duty cases as well) are elaborated principally in the regulations at 19 CFR Part 207. Some applicable requirements are also set forth in 19 CFR Part 201.

1. Preliminary Determination

In the first instance, it makes a preliminary determination within 45 days after the date of filing of the petition based on the best information available to it at that time as to whether there is a "reasonable indication" that an industry in the United States is materially injured, threatened with material injury, or its establishment is materially retarded by imports, or sales (or the likelihood of sales) for importation, of the merchandise in question. The Commission's regulations afford all parties to a proceeding an opportunity to present written views prior to its making a preliminary or final determination on the injury questions. A conference may be held prior to a preliminary determination.

The Court of International Trade has held that the 45-day time period for the preliminary determination was mandatory, not directory, with the consequence that the Commission's later reopening of a preliminary determination for additional evidence and reconsideration of its conclusion was void.[56]

---

[55]Section 736(a), Tariff Act of 1930 (19 U.S.C. 1673e); 19 CFR 353.48.

[56]*Babcock & Wilcox* v. *United States,* 2 CIT 74, 521 F. Supp. 479 (1981) 2 ITRD 1673.

The object of a preliminary determination, as stated by the CIT, is to find whether there are any facts raising the possibility of injury to the domestic industry. The evidentiary threshold is low. The resolution of conflicting facts is to be reserved for the final determination. *Republic Steel Corporation* v. *United States*, 8 CIT ____ , 591 F. Supp. 640 (1984) 5 ITRD 2433 (countervailing duty case), motion for reconsideration denied, 9 CIT ____ , Slip Op. 85-27 (1985) 6 ITRD 2039; *Jeannette Sheet Glass Co.* v. *United States*, 9 CIT ____ , 607 F. Supp. 123 (1985) 6 ITRD 2059 (antidumping case), *American Lamb Company* v. *United States*, 9 CIT ____ , 611 F. Supp. 979 (1985) 6 ITRD 2446.

2. Final Determination

After the Secretary has made a final affirmative determination as to the existence of sales at less than fair value, the Commission makes a final determination as to whether, "by reason of" imports, or sales (or the likelihood of sales) for importation, of the merchandise which has been dumped, an industry in the United States is materially injured, threatened with material injury, or its establishment is materially retarded.[57]

The Commission is required, as is the Secretary, by Section 774 of Title VII to hold a hearing in the course of an investigation, upon request of any party to the investigation, a right provided for under the Commission's regulations. However, under the amendment of Section 774 made by Section 616 of the 1984 Amendments, if antidumping and countervailing duty investigations are initiated within 6 months of each other (and before a final determination is made in either) with respect to the same merchandise from the same country, the Commission need not hold a hearing in the second investigation unless special circumstances exist.

Determinations by the Commission are on the basis of a majority vote of the Commissioners. If the Commissioners voting on a determination are evenly divided as to whether the determination should be affirmative or negative, the Commission shall be deemed to have made an affirmative determination. When the issue before the Commission is to determine whether there is:

(1) material injury to an industry in the United States,

(2) threat of material injury to such an industry, or

(3) material retardation of the establishment of an industry in the United States, an affirmative vote on any one of the issues shall be treated as a vote that the determination should be affirmative.[58]

Where the Commission determines the existence of only a threat of material injury, its final determination must include a finding as to whether, but for the suspension of liquidation of entries, material injury would have been found.

If the final determination of the Secretary found the existence of critical circumstances, the Commission must include in its final determination a

[57]Section 735(b)(1), Tariff Act of 1930 (19 U.S.C. 1673d).
[58]Section 771(11), Tariff Act of 1930 (19 U.S.C. 1677).

finding as to whether material injury is by reason of massive imports, as described in Section 735(a)(3), Tariff Act of 1930 (19 U.S.C. 1673d) to an extent that antidumping duties should be imposed retroactively to prevent the recurrence of such material injury.[59]

A negative preliminary or final determination by the Commission terminates the antidumping proceeding. If its final determination is affirmative it notifies the Secretary and all interested parties thereof, publishes its determination in the *Federal Register*, and the Secretary proceeds to publish an Antidumping Duty Order.[60]

3. *Definition of Industry*[61]

The Law defines industry to mean "the domestic producers as a whole of a like product, or those producers whose collective output of the like product constitutes a major proportion of the total domestic production of that product." A temporary exception to this definition was added by Section 612(a)(1) of the 1984 Amendments at the behest of the U.S. grape producers. The amendment provides that in the case of wine and grape products the domestic "industry" includes domestic producers of the principal raw agricultural product included in the like domestic product. Section 626(c) of the 1984 Amendments imposed a two-year time limit for a petition to be brought taking advantage of this special provision. The amendment resulted from a determination by the Commission that grape growers could not be included in the domestic wine industry in a combined antidumping and countervailing duty investigation of imported table wine. *Certain Table Wine from France and Italy,* Inv. Nos. 701-TA-210, 211 and 731-TA-167, 168 (Preliminary) (Pub. 1502, March 1984) 5 ITRD 2179. The Commission found that grape growers did not fit into the narrow circumstance in which agricultural producers could be combined with processors in one industry; namely, where the agricultural product was integrated into a single line of production resulting in one end product.

In certain categories of trade, substantial proportions of the total volume may take place between parties who are "related." For example, some domestic producers may be "related" to the exporters or importers or themselves be importers of the allegedly dumped merchandise. In these circumstances the Commission is authorized, in making its determinations, to exclude such producers from those included in that industry.

The Law also authorizes the Commission, in appropriate circumstances, to divide the United States into two or more product markets and to treat the producers within each market as a separate industry if

> (i) the producers within such market sell all or almost all their production of the like product in question in that market, and
> (ii) the demand in that market is not supplied to any substantial degree by producers of the product in question located elsewhere in the United States.[62]

---

[59]Section 735(b)(4), Tariff Act of 1930 (19 U.S.C. 1673d).
[60]Section 735(c)(2), Tariff Act of 1930 (19 U.S.C. 1673d).
[61]See Section 771(4), Tariff Act of 1930 (19 U.S.C. 1677).
[62]Section 771(4)(C), Tariff Act of 1930.

The Law provides that in these circumstances the Commission may find material injury, the threat thereof, or material retardation of the establishment of an industry even if the domestic industry as a whole or producers of a major proportion of the total domestic production of that product are not injured, if there is a concentration of subsidized or dumped merchandise imported into such an isolated market, and if the producers of all, or almost all, the production within that market are being materially injured or threatened by material injury or if the establishment of an industry is being materially retarded by reason of the subsidized or dumped imports. If the Commission defines a regional industry for purposes of injury determination, the absence of segregated profit and loss figures for a plant outside the region of the second largest regional producer is not so serious as to render the Commission's determination of injury unsupported by substantial evidence. *Atlantic Sugar Ltd.* v. *United States,* 744 F.2d 1556 (Fed. Cir. 1984) 6 ITRD 1170, *rev'g Atlantic Sugar, Ltd.* v. *United States,* 6 CIT _____ , 573 F. Supp. 1142 (1983) 5 ITRD 1294.

A regional market may be divided by the Commission into "sub-market" areas for evaluation of injury since the statute does not preclude this. *Gifford-Hill Cement Co.* v. *United States,* 10 CIT _____ , 615 F. Supp. 577 (1985) 7 ITRD 1041.

If available data permit the separate identification of production of a like product in terms of production process or producer's profits, the effect of subsidized imports shall be judged on this basis. If not, the effect "shall be assessed by the examination of the production of the narrowest group or range of products, which includes a like product, for which information can be provided."

In the *Babcock & Wilcox* decision (*supra* note 56) the Court of International Trade rejected the Commission's negative preliminary determination of injury as not in accordance with law because the Commission had not separately assessed the profitability of the various types of domestic boiler tubes and pipes in issue, even though multiple products were produced by the same production force.

4. Definition of Material Injury[63]

a. Factors to be Considered

The old law merely required the Commission to determine whether an industry is being "injured," etc. The new law changes the concept to "material injury" or the threat thereof or "material retardation" of the establishment of an industry. The Law defines material injury as "harm which is not inconsequential, immaterial, or unimportant."

The Law requires the Commission in making its determinations to consider, among other factors:

---

[63]See Section 771(7), Tariff Act of 1930 (19 U.S.C. 1677); 19 CFR 207.26 and 207.27.

(1) the volume of imports of the merchandise which is the subject of the investigation,

(2) the effect of imports of that merchandise on prices in the United States for like products, and

(3) the impact of imports of such merchandise on domestic producers of like products.

The Administrative Statement points out that the Law does not require the Commission in making its determinations to give particular balance or weight to any one or more of the various factors affecting an industry (H.R. Doc. No. 96-153, Part II, pp. 433–434). However, the Law spells out how the Commission will evaluate the factors listed above.

With respect to the volume of imports, the Law states that "the Commission shall consider whether the volume of imports of the merchandise, or any increase in that volume, either in absolute terms or relative to production or consumption in the United States, is significant." The Court of International Trade saw no "deficiency in reasoning" by the Commission in finding "significant" a maximum volume of imports into the region in focus of 4.5 percent of primary distribution, particularly since legislative history indicated this possibility. *Atlantic Sugar, Ltd.* v. *United States*, 2 CIT 18, 519 F. Supp. 916 (1981) 2 ITRD 1630. The Commission found import penetration of 0.2 percent clearly insignificant and incapable of causing material injury, in *Secondary Aluminum Alloy in Unwrought Form from the United Kingdom*, 731-TA-40 (Preliminary), May 1981, 2 ITRD 5515.

As to price, the Law directs the Commission to consider whether

(I) there has been significant price undercutting by the imported merchandise as compared with the price of like products of the United States, and

(II) the effect of imports of such merchandise otherwise depresses prices to a significant degree or prevents price increases, which otherwise would have occurred to a significant degree.[64]

Price depressing effect caused by imports was found by the Commission where underselling imports caused domestic prices to rise less than the cost of production. *Montan Wax from East Germany*, 731-TA-30 (Preliminary), October 1980, 2 ITRD 5334, and caused loss of sales. *Potassium Permanganate from Spain*, 731-TA-126 (Final) January 1984, 6 ITRD 1107.

As to the impact of imports on the domestic industry, the Law directs the Commission to

evaluate all relevant economic factors which have a bearing on the state of the industry, including, but not limited to:

(I) actual and potential decline in output, sales, market share, profits, productivity, return on investments, and utilization of capacity,

(II) factors affecting domestic prices, and

(III) actual and potential negative effects on cash flow, inventories, employment, wages, growth, availability to raise capital, and investments.[65]

---

[64]Section 771(7)(C)(ii), Tariff Act of 1930 (19 U.S.C. 1677).
[65]Section 771(7)(C)(iii), Tariff Act of 1930 (19 U.S.C. 1677).

The Commission examines the cause and effects of these various economic factors with extensive statistical analyses. See, *e.g., Precipitated Barium Carbonate from Federal Republic of Germany,* 731-TA-31 (Final) June 1981, 2 ITRD 5612; *Acrylic Sheet from Taiwan,* 731-TA-139 (Final) May 1984, 6 ITRD 2017.

The 1984 Amendments in Section 612(a)(2) also direct the Commission cumulatively to assess the volume and effect of imports of like products subject to investigation from two or more countries if such imports compete with each other and with like products of the domestic U.S. industry. This amendment appears to settle a long-standing difference of opinion among Commissioners as to whether, in simultaneous investigations of like products from more than one country, the injurious effects of the imports from all countries involved should be cumulated.

Cumulative assessment of injury was required by the CIT in *American Grape Growers Alliance for Fair Trade* v. *United States,* 10 CIT ____ , 615 F. Supp. 603 (1985) 7 ITRD 1065, reversing the ITC's negative preliminary determinations based on separate evaluation of effects of French table wines and Italian effervescent wines in companion countervailing duty and dumping investigations. Cumulative assessment was not necessary where imports affected segmented areas. *Gifford Hill Cement Co., supra* D.3.

b. Special Treatment of Agricultural Products

The Law points out that, with respect to agricultural commodities, the Commission should not make a negative finding on the question of material injury or threat thereof, "merely because the prevailing market price is at or above the minimum support price." It also directs the Commission, in the case of agricultural products, to "consider any increased burden on Government income or price support programs." In the *Atlantic Sugar* decision, *supra,* the court explained that this statutory provision was intended to insure that the injury analysis would not be distorted by the beneficial effects of the programs or the appearance of health in an industry sustained by government assistance.

c. Commission's Policy in Examining Threat of Material Injury

The Administrative Statement indicates that the Commission "will determine the likelihood of a particular situation developing into actual material injury." (H.R. Doc. No. 96-153, Part II, p. 434; see also 19 CFR 207.26(d).) It points out in this regard that an examination of trends will be important and cites as examples: "the rate of increase of the subsidized or dumped exports to the U.S. market, capacity in the exporting country to generate exports, and the likelihood that such exports will be to the U.S. market, taking into account the availability of other export markets." As under the old law the threat of material injury must be "real and imminent" and not based on "mere supposition or conjecture." *Asphalt Roofing Shingles from Canada,* 731-TA-29 (Preliminary), October 1980, 2 ITRD 5171; *Snow Grooming Vehicles from the Federal Republic of Germany,* 731-

TA-36 (Preliminary), December 1980, 2 ITRD 5344. This standard has now been codified in Section 771(7)(F) of the Tariff Act of 1930 (19 U.S.C. 1677(7)(F)) by Section 612(a)(2) the 1984 Amendments.

Prior to the 1984 Amendments the Law did not set out separate criteria to be considered in determinations of threat of material injury. The Commission is now directed by Section 771(7)(F) to consider eight economic factors, among others, as follows:

(1) the nature of any subsidy involved (particularly whether it is an export subsidy inconsistent with the Agreement);

(2) increased production capacity or increased idle capacity in the exporting country likely to increase U.S. imports;

(3) any rapid increase in U.S. market penetration;

(4) the probability that imports will enter the United States at prices which will suppress or depress U.S. prices;

(5) any substantial increase in U.S. inventories;

(6) idle capacity in the exporting country;

(7) any other demonstrable adverse trends that indicate the probability that imports will cause actual injury; and

(8) the potential for shifting foreign production facilities from other products already subject to investigations to the particular products under investigation.

d. Causal Relationship Between Dumped Imports and Material Injury

The Administrative Statement gives important insight into the interpretation of the statutory phrase "by reason of" in determining the causal relationship between the dumped imports and the existence of material injury or threat thereof (H.R. Doc. No. 96-153, Part II, pp. 434–435; see also 19 CFR 207.27). It states that these words

> express a causation link, but do not involve a weighing of injury by reason of subsidized imports or sales at less than fair value against the effects of other factors which may, at the same time, also be injuring the industry. The injury caused by subsidization or sales at less than fair value need not be the "principal" or a "major" or "substantial" cause of overall injury to an industry. Any such requirement has the undesirability of making relief more difficult to obtain for those industries facing difficulties from a variety of sources, although these may be precisely those industries that are most vulnerable to subsidized import competition and dumping.

The Administrative Statement points out, however, that notwithstanding the foregoing, the Commission will consider any information presented to demonstrate that the harm alleged by the petitioner is attributable to other factors such as the volume of imports not sold at less than fair value, contraction in demand or changes in patterns of consumption, trade restrictive practices or competition between the foreign and domestic producers, and export performance and productivity of the domestic industry. In summary, it is concluded in the Statement that the petitioner must demonstrate the positive to the Commission, that there is "the requisite causal link between the subsidization or dumping and material injury." But, the petitioner will not be required to demonstrate the negative, namely, that "the material injury is not by reason of such other factors as to which information has been introduced." 19 CFR 207.27.

By way of contrast, the Commission found injury caused by imports because of quantity, underselling, lost sales, and price depression, in *Certain Seamless Steel Pipes and Tubes from Japan,* 731-TA-87 (Final) February 1983, 5 ITRD 1042, but no causal link to imports because price decreases were initiated by domestic producers and occurred in areas not affected by imports, in *Portland Hydraulic Cement from Australia and Japan,* 731-TA-109 (Final) October 1983, 5 ITRD 2247.

E. Collection of Antidumping Duties

Upon the issuance of an antidumping duty order, antidumping duties are assessed and collected on imports of the merchandise which is the subject of the proceeding. The determination of the amount of the estimated duties to be paid initially and of the assessed duties is made by the Secretary. The section in Subtitle B of Title VII, Section 739 (19 U.S.C. 1673h), directing customs officers to ascertain and determine, or estimate, the foreign market value, the United States price, and other information was repealed by Section 610 of the 1984 Amendments.

No antidumping duty may be assessed on the portion of the margin between the foreign market value and the United States price which may be attributable to export subsidies. This prohibition derives from Art. VI.5 of the GATT, implemented by Section 772(d)(1)(D) of the Tariff Act of 1930 (19 U.S.C. 1677a(d)(1)(D)). Thus, the level of export subsidies determined in a countervailing duty order on certain products is subtracted from the dumping margin found for such products. See *Antidumping Order; Oil Country Tubular Goods from Spain,* 50 FR 21479, May 24, 1985.

1. Deposit of Estimated Antidumping Duties or Security

Pending the assessment of antidumping duties, and the liquidation of entries of the merchandise, the order requires the payment of estimated antidumping duties at the same time as estimated other customs duties are deposited, or if the Secretary is satisfied that an early determination of duties can be made, the posting of a bond or other security.[66] Such a determination is one made within 90 days of the publication of the antidumping duty order and determines the foreign market value and the United States price for all merchandise described in the order which was entered on or after the date of publication of the first affirmative determination by the Secretary and before the publication date of the affirmative final determination by the Commission. This early determination of duties under Section 736(c) of the Tariff Act constitutes in effect a review and determination of antidumping duties under Section 751 of that Act.[67]

---

[66]Section 736(a) and (c), Tariff Act of 1930 (19 U.S.C. 1673e); 19 CFR 353.48(b), 353.49.
[67]*Smith-Corona Group, Consumer Products Division, SCM* v. *United States,* 1 CIT 89, 507 F. Supp. 1015 (1980) 2 ITRD 1437.

2. Actual Duty Assessment

Following an antidumping duty order the actual assessment of the dumping duty is based upon an administrative review, either the early determination discussed in Paragraph 1 *supra,* or a periodic administrative review discussed in section F *infra.* The results of an administrative review serve as the basis for the dumping duty assessment with regard to entries covered by the review determination and for cash deposits of estimated duties for future entries. *Silver Reed America, Inc. and Silver Seiko, Ltd.* v. *United States,* 9 CIT _____ , Slip Op. 85-51 (1985) 6 ITRD 2330.

3. Application of the Order

a. Firms Excluded

Any firm which in the course of the investigation was found not to have been selling at less than fair value may be excluded from an antidumping order.[68] However, the order is a purely ministerial act and a first step in enforcement of the administrative determinations; it is not itself part of the determinations and cannot exclude from its scope a product covered by the determinations. *Royal Business Machines, Inc.* v. *United States,* 1 CIT 80, 507 F. Supp. 1007 (1980) 2 ITRD 1445.

b. Entries Subject to Assessment[69]—General Rule

If the Commission has found threat of material injury which but for the suspension of liquidation would have led to a finding of material injury, then all entries of the merchandise in question, the liquidation of which has been suspended, are subject to the imposition of the antidumping duties.

c. Entries Subject to Assessment—Special Rule

If the Commission finds threat of material injury other than that described in *b supra,* or material retardation of the establishment of an industry in the United States, then only merchandise entered, or withdrawn from warehouse, for consumption on or after the date of publication of the Commission's final determination shall be subject to the imposition of antidumping duties. All prior entries shall be liquidated without the imposition of antidumping duties, and the Secretary shall release any bond or other security and refund any cash deposit made to secure payment of antidumping duties with respect to such entries.

---

[68]Prerequisites to the exclusion of particular firms from an affirmative preliminary or final determination are set forth in 19 CFR 353.45.

[69]Section 736(b), Tariff Act of 1930 (19 U.S.C. 1673e).

4. Over- and Under-Collection of Estimated Antidumping Duties[70]

If the amount of estimated antidumping duties collected during the period of suspension of liquidation and before the Commission's final determination is different from the amount of antidumping duty determined pursuant to the antidumping order it shall be:

(1) disregarded, to the extent that the cash deposit is lower than the duty under the order, or

(2) refunded, to the extent that the cash deposit is higher than the duty under the order.

Thereafter, when estimated duties are deposited, pending finally determined antidumping duties, the amount of any underestimate shall be assessed, together with interest at the rates specified by the statute from the date of entry to the date of assessment, and the amount of any overestimate shall be refunded, together with interest at the rates specified from the date of overpayment to the date of refund.

Under Section 621 of the 1984 Amendments (19 U.S.C. 1677g) the rate of interest on overpayments and underpayments is the rate established under Section 6621 of the Internal Revenue Code (26 U.S.C. 6621). This rate is to be applied to overpayments and underpayments of amounts deposited on entries made on or after the date of publication of the antidumping duty order. The Customs Service construed Section 621 of the 1984 Amendments to require the compounding of interest as provided for in Section 6622 of the Internal Revenue Code, TD 85-93, 50 FR 21832, May 29, 1985. The Customs Service announced June 7, 1985, that it would publish twice a year in the *Federal Register* the rate of interest set under the statute semiannually (50 FR 23947).

5. Payment Conditions for Warehouse Withdrawal

A special section of the Law, Section 738 of Title VII (19 U.S.C. 1673g), provides the conditions governing the withdrawal from warehouse for consumption of merchandise subject to antidumping duties. The importer must deposit the estimated duty; furnish the information necessary for ascertaining the antidumping duty; maintain required records; state, if he is an exporter, the exporter's sales price; and agree to pay on demand the amount of antidumping duty imposed.

F. Administrative Review of Determinations

1. Review of Antidumping Orders[71]

Section 751 of the Law (19 U.S.C. 1675), as amended by Section 611 of the 1984 Amendments, requires the Secretary, if requested, once during each 12-month period, beginning on the anniversary of the date of the

---

[70]Section 737, Tariff Act of 1930 (19 U.S.C. 1673f); 19 CFR 353.50.
[71]Section 751(a), Tariff Act of 1930 (19 U.S.C. 1675).

issuance of an antidumping duty order, or a notice of suspension pursuant to an agreement, to review and determine:

(a) The amount by which the foreign market value exceeds the United States price, and

(b) The status of compliance with any agreement by which an investigation was suspended.

Upon completion of his review, the Secretary publishes the results of his review, with notice of any duty to be assessed, estimated duty to be deposited, or investigation to be resumed, and his determination of any revised margins of dumping, including the bases for the assessment of duties on the merchandise in question. The review determines the actual amount of dumping duties to be paid on prior entries and the cash deposits to be made on future entries, as described in section E.2 *supra.*

Revised regulations under Section 751, as amended in 1984, were issued by the Secretary, 50 FR 32556, August 13, 1985, which provided final procedures for requesting reviews of periods ending prior to September 1, 1985, covered by an order, finding, or suspension agreement published before September 1, 1984, and interim-final procedures for requesting reviews of later periods. The request must be made during the anniversary month of the publication of the order or finding and must specify, with reasons, the particular manufacturers, producers, or exporters sought to be reviewed. If no timely request is received, the Secretary will instruct the Customs Service to assess antidumping duties on merchandise entered during the unreviewed period, at rates equal to the cash deposits of estimated duties, and to continue to collect the cash deposits previously ordered.

In compliance with the original requirement of annual reviews, the International Trade Administration published a notice in the *Federal Register* March 28, 1980 (45 FR 20511) advising that it would review the 83 outstanding Treasury Department dumping orders, listed in the notice, during the 12-month period beginning with the anniversary date of the publication in the *Federal Register* of the finding under the 1921 Act. In the course of such a review the Commerce Department may review the scope of the Treasury's dumping determination. *Alsthom Atlantique* v. *United States,* 9 CIT ____ , 604 F. Supp. 1234 (1985) 6 ITRD 1814.

The undertaking by the Secretary of Commerce of an administrative review of the 1971 finding by the Treasury Department of dumping of television sets from Japan did not preclude his entering into a compromise agreement with the importers, under the authority of 19 U.S.C. 1617, settling the dumping claims. *COMPACT* v. *United States,* 2 CIT 208, 527 F. Supp. 341 (1981) 3 ITRD 1379, *aff'd,* 706 F.2d 1574 (Fed. Cir. 1983) 4 ITRD 1850, *cert. denied,* 104 S.Ct. 96 (1983).

In giving notice of review investigations, the ITA must publish notice of a specific date for commencement of an investigation. A statement of intent to conduct a review within 12 months, contained in the *Federal Register* notice of the duty order, was found by the Court of International Trade to be insufficient. *Hide-Away Creations, Ltd.* v. *United States,* 6 CIT ____ , 577 F. Supp. 1021 (1983) 5 ITRD 1539.

2. Other Review Upon Information or Request

The Secretary and the Commission are authorized to conduct a review of one of the final affirmative determinations specified in Section 751(b)(1) of the Law (19 U.S.C. 1675(b)(1)) or of an accepted agreement whenever they receive information or a request for review which shows changed circumstances sufficient to warrant such a review. For example, the Commission is authorized to consider whether, in the light of the changed circumstances, an agreement leading to the suspension of an investigation continues to eliminate completely the injurious effect of imports of the merchandise. If the Commission's determination is negative as to the continuing effectiveness of the agreement, the agreement will be treated as if it were not accepted as of the date of publication of the Commission's determination and the antidumping proceeding shall continue as if the agreement had been violated on that date, except that no antidumping duty shall be assessed on merchandise entered, or withdrawn from warehouse, for consumption before that date.[72] Certain agreements may not be reviewed in less than 24 months under this authority, in the absence of good cause shown.

The responsibility of the Commission in a review investigation is to assess the likely effect of revocation of an antidumping order, based on available evidence and logical assumptions; it cannot be certain of future events, *Matsushita Electric Industrial Co., Ltd.* v. *United States,* 750 F.2d 927 (Fed. Cir. 1984) 6 ITRD 1465.

The authority of the Commission under Section 751(b) of the Tariff Act to review an injury determination made under the 1921 Antidumping Act was confirmed by the Court of International Trade in *Matsushita Electric Industrial Co., Ltd.* v. *United States,* 2 CIT 263, 529 F. Supp. 670 (1981) 3 ITRD 1299.

3. Hearing Upon Request

If the Secretary or the Commission is conducting a review, he or it must under Section 751, upon the request of an interested party, hold a hearing on the record.

4. Revocation or Revision of Determination

The Secretary may revoke in whole or in part an antidumping duty order or terminate an investigation after review. Before doing so, he must publish a notice of his intention to revoke or terminate. Such action normally will not be considered except at the time of administrative reviews of determinations (see 19 CFR 353.54). A revocation or termination applies only to unliquidated entries ordinarily on and after the date of publication of the notice of Tentative Determination to Revoke or Terminate.[73]

---

[72]Section 751(b), Tariff Act of 1930 (19 U.S.C. 1675).
[73]Section 751(c), Tariff Act of 1930 (19 U.S.C. 1675); 19 CFR 353.54(f). See *American Cyanamid Company* v. *United States,* 8 CIT ___ (1984) 6 ITRD 1538.

A party seeking revocation of an order or finding or the termination of a suspended investigation must, under the regulation, request it and demonstrate that the imports have not been sold at less than fair value, ordinarily, for a two-year period subsequent to the publication of the order or finding or notice of suspension. Commerce Department officials advise that the ITA will consider revocation on the basis of no shipments of the covered merchandise for four years.

III. TREATMENT OF INFORMATION

The Law contains extensive provisions relating to information developed in an antidumping proceeding: verification, access, and maintenance of confidentiality.

A. Verification[74]

The Law requires the Secretary in making his determinations to verify all information relied upon whenever possible, except that, under Section 618 of the 1984 Amendments, no verification is required for determinations on administrative review more frequently than once every three years. Shortly before this amendment the CAFC had affirmed a CIT ruling that verification of information relied upon in a Section 751 review was necessary. *AL Tech Specialty Steel Corp.* v. *United States,* 745 F.2d 632 (Fed. Cir. 1984) 6 ITRD 1161, *aff'g* 6 CIT ___ , 575 F. Supp. 1277 (1983) 5 ITRD 1337.

However, verification is not required where it is waived under the procedure described in section II.C.1.c *supra.* Also if the Secretary is unable to verify the accuracy of information submitted, he is authorized to use the best information available to him, which may include the information submitted in support of the petition. Whenever a party or any other person refuses or is unable to produce information requested within the time or in the manner required, or otherwise significantly impedes an investigation, the Secretary and the Commission in making their respective determinations may, under 19 U.S.C. 1677e(b), use the best information otherwise available.

B. Access[75]

The Law contains extensive requirements for the maintenance of records and for providing possible access to information developed in proceedings. The Secretary and the Commission are required from time to time upon request to inform interested parties of the progress of investigations. They must maintain detailed records of *ex parte* meetings between interested parties or other persons providing factual information in connection with a proceeding and a person charged with making a determination and any

---

[74]Section 776, Tariff Act of 1930 (19 U.S.C. 1677e).
[75]Section 777(a), Tariff Act of 1930 (19 U.S.C. 1677f).

other person charged with making a final recommendation in connection with the proceeding, if, under the amendment made by Section 619(1) of the 1984 Amendments, information relating to that proceeding was presented or discussed at the meeting. The record of *ex parte* meetings is part of the record of a proceeding.

C. Treatment and Protection of Confidential Information[76]

The Law contains a basic requirement that the Secretary and the Commission shall not disclose to any person (except their own officers and employees) information which is designated as confidential by the person submitting it, without the latter's consent. As an exception Section 619(2) of the 1984 Amendments permits disclosure of confidential information to the Customs Service for investigation of fraud under Title VII.

Persons who wish the confidentiality of information submitted to be maintained should submit a nonconfidential summary in sufficient detail to be meaningful, or a statement that the information is not susceptible to summary. Such persons also must state whether or not they will agree to the release of the information under an appropriate administrative protective order, as described in section 2 *infra*. The Secretary and Commission may disclose any confidential information received in the course of a proceeding in a form which cannot be associated with, or otherwise used to identify operations of a particular person. Of course, the Secretary and the Commission are free to disclose any information which has not been designated as confidential. See 19 CFR Part 353, Subpart B, and 19 CFR Part 201.

The Department of Commerce, Import Administration, provided, as of September 1982, a statement on proprietary information describing information which is ordinarily protected from disclosure and that which usually is not protected, and outlining procedures for protecting proprietary information. See Appendix E.

1. Unwarranted Designation

If the Secretary or the Commission believes that the designation of any information as confidential is unwarranted and the person submitting it is unable to persuade the Secretary or the Commission to the contrary, the Secretary and the Commission may return it and such information will not be considered in the proceeding. The regulations set forth standards for determining the confidentiality of information.

2. Limited Disclosure Under a Protective Order[77]

The Law and the regulations set forth a procedure whereby upon application the Secretary and the Commission may make confidential

---

[76]Section 777(b), Tariff Act of 1930 (19 U.S.C. 1677f).
[77]Section 777(c), Tariff Act of 1930 (19 U.S.C. 1677f); 19 CFR 353.30 and 207.7.

information available under a protective order. The order shall contain such requirements as are deemed appropriate by the Secretary or the Commission for the protection of the information. The requirements for obtaining proprietary information under an administrative protective order and the procedures for release of such information under an order are described in the September 1982 publication of the Import Administration, Department of Commerce. The regulations of the Secretary and the Commission provide for sanctions including disbarment from practice before the agency in question for violation of a protective order.[78]

3. Disclosure Pursuant to Court Order

If the Secretary or the Commission denies a request for confidential information under a protective order, application may be made under Section 777(c)(2) (19 U.S.C. 1677f(c)(2)) to the Court of International Trade which is empowered, after notification of all parties and after an opportunity for a hearing on the record, to order that all or a portion of the information be made available under a protective order, setting forth sanctions for violation.[79]

The standards governing disclosure were elucidated by the Court of International Trade in two cases in which certain foreign steel producers sought injunctions to prevent disclosure by the Commerce Department to the domestic steel industry petitioners in an antidumping proceeding of information submitted by the producers in response to the Department's questionnaires. In the first case, *Sacilor, Acieries et Laminoirs de Lorraine, et al., v. United States, et al.* 3 CIT 191, 542 F. Supp. 1020 (1982) 3 ITRD 2225, the court issued the injunction on the ground that the Commerce Department had failed to follow the requirements of the statute, Section 777(c) of the Tariff Act of 1930, 19 U.S.C. 1677f(c), and of the Department's regulations, 19 CFR 353.30, in that it had decided to release the questionnaire information prior to the submission of the questionnaires, and thereby had not decided on the basis of a reasoned decision which carefully evaluated the needs of the applicant and the demands of confidentiality. Moreover, the petitioners had not followed the requirements that a party describe *with particularity* the information requested and provide *reasons* for the request (court emphasis). This ruling has been expressly overturned by Section 619 of the 1984 Amendments, which provides that the request for information under protective order may be made "before or after" receipt of the information requested.

In the second decision on the foreign steel producers' effort to prevent disclosure of their responses to the antidumping questionnaires, *ARBED, S.A. and Sacilor, Acieries et Laminoirs de Lorraine, et al.* v. *United States,* 4 CIT 132 (1982) 3 ITRD 2369, the court denied injunctive relief, finding

---

[78] 19 CFR 353.30(e); 19 CFR 207.7(e).

[79] The Customs Court allowed restricted disclosure of confidential business information received by the government to the lawyers for the petitioner, as "independent professionals and officers of the court" and not as "alter egos" of the petitioner. *Connors Steel Co.* v. *United States,* CRD 80-09, 80 Cust. Ct. 112 (1980) 2 ITRD 1129.

that the proper procedures had been followed, and that the "general need" by the petitioners "to examine, analyze, and comment on the data submitted" and the need of the agency to receive such comment justified the Department's discretionary decision to release it.

The CIT has developed a "balancing test" with respect to the relative needs for the disclosure of the confidential information in issue as opposed to the harm that might be caused by disclosure and inadvertent dissemination. See *Roquette Freres* v. *United States,* 4 CIT 239, 554 F. Supp. 1246 (1982) 4 ITRD 1388, and *Monsanto Industrial Chemicals Co.* v. *United States,* 6 CIT ____ (1983) 5 ITRD 1462. The balancing test was further discussed and applied with respect to the disclosure of exhibits to verification reports, ITA issue papers, and business correspondence with the ITA in *Jernberg Forgings Co.* v. *United States,* 8 CIT ____ , 598 F. Supp. 390 (1984) 6 ITRD 1602, directing disclosure with redactions.

The Court of Appeals for the Federal Circuit has given guidance to the CIT concerning the release of confidential information to in-house counsel. According to the CAFC, the risk of "inadvertent disclosure" of confidential information should not automatically bar access by in-house counsel. The court directed that "factual circumstances surrounding each individual counsel's activities, association, and relationship with a party, whether counsel be in-house or retained, must govern any concern for inadvertent or accidental disclosure." *U.S. Steel Corporation* v. *United States,* 730 F.2d 1465 (1984) 5 ITRD 1955. The CAFC reversed the CIT to provide full protection against disclosure of government documents containing attorney-client communications, attorneys' work product, and executive deliberations concerning issues in dumping settlement agreements. *Zenith Radio Corp.* v. *United States,* 764 F.2d 1577 (Fed. Cir. 1985) 6 ITRD 2377.

IV. PRICE MONITORING TO TRIGGER DUMPING ACTIONS

A. The Trigger Price Mechanism for Steel Imports

An unprecedented number of complaints by U.S. steel manufacturers alleging that steel mill products were being imported at less than fair value were filed with Customs during 1977. This led to the appointment by the President of an Interagency Task Force to study the problems of the U.S. steel industry. In its Report to the President the Task Force recommended, among other objectives, that the Treasury in administering the Antidumping Law set up a system of trigger prices based on the full costs of production of steel mill products by the most efficient foreign steel producers, currently the Japanese steel industry, which would be used as a basis for monitoring imports of steel and for initiating accelerated antidumping investigations of imports priced below the trigger prices. These investigations would be initiated by the Treasury Department but would not alter the existing rights of any person under the Antidumping Law, 1921.

This recommendation for a Trigger Price Mechanism (TPM), approved by the President, was effectuated by regulations, issued as an amendment of the entry regulations, 19 CFR 141.89(b), which required the presentation with each shipment of designated steel articles, valued over $2,500, of a Special Summary Steel Invoice, Customs Form 5520. The regulations became effective February 21, 1978.

The Treasury Department also announced January 3, 1978, the basic trigger prices to be used for certain importations of steel mill products and extras (January 9 and February 3, 1978, 43 FR 1464, 4703), effective for all covered entries made on or after February 21, 1978. The prices were based upon evidence made available to the Treasury Department by the Japanese Ministry of International Trade and Industry (MITI) concerning the current cost of producing steel in Japan. The products covered were steel mill products as defined by the American Iron and Steel Institute (AISI) and therefore did not extend to fabricated articles.

B. Treasury Administration; Special Summary Steel Invoice

The initial trigger prices covered the base products comprising the most significant imports, as produced by the six integrated Japanese firms. Additional trigger prices were announced for structural shapes, concrete reinforcing bars, pipes, and tubing and strips; for steel wire, cold finished bars, and certain rails, and for wire nails and heavy carbon steel rails. All announcements advised that the information on sales of these products would be kept as part of the monitoring system and would be available in the event that an antidumping petition was filed or that the Treasury Department initiated an antidumping proceeding. Revisions in trigger prices were announced quarterly, based upon changes in costs and exchange rates.

The Special Summary Steel Invoice, under a 1979 amendment to 19 CFR 141.89(b), was required for each shipment of $10,000 or over, including all expenses incident to preparation for shipment to the United States, and of $5,000 or over, if the shipment was from a contiguous country.

During the TPM period the Treasury continued to process various antidumping petitions challenging steel imports from Japan and from six European countries. The TPM, being only a monitoring mechanism, was held to have no effect on the importation of steel products in *United States v. Teraoka,* 669 F.2d 577 (CA 9 1982) 4 ITRD 1116. There the court determined that the falsification of an invoice covering Japanese nails to inflate their purchase price above the trigger price did not constitute a false entry subject to prosecution under 18 U.S.C. 542 because the entry could not be said to be by means of the false invoice.

C. Basis in the Antidumping Law, 1921

As indicated in the Task Force Report to the President, the Trigger Price Mechanism was developed from concepts expressed or implied in the Antidumping Law of 1921. Under an amendment of that Law, 19 U.S.C.

164(b), made by the Trade Reform Act of 1974, the home market prices of imported products might not be used to establish foreign market value if those prices had been, over an extended period of time, below the cost of production and were at levels at which costs would not be recovered within a reasonable period of time. By establishing the trigger prices for monitoring purposes at the cost of production of the most efficient steel producers, the Treasury became able to note and examine the likelihood of dumping where steel product imports were priced at levels below the recognized cost of production. It would be unlikely that many foreign manufacturers could sell steel products at less than the cost of production of the most efficient producers and still be selling at fair value.

D. Court Challenge

1. The Validity of the TPM

The Treasury position was challenged in a suit brought by the Davis Walker Corporation in March 1978, seeking declaratory and injunctive relief. The plaintiff claimed that the application of the TPM to steel wire rods contravened the Antidumping Law, that it was arbitrary and capricious, in violation of Section 10(e) of the Administrative Procedure Act, and that the TPM was invalid for failure to comply with the rulemaking provisions of the APA.

In May 1978, the court upheld the validity of the TPM against all three allegations.[80] It found the TPM to be consistent with the Antidumping Law, 1921, as it was simply a device to enable the Secretary to monitor imports and to provide sufficient information to enable him to determine whether to self-initiate an investigation; and further, the Secretary had authority under the 1921 Law to initiate an antidumping proceeding on his own motion. The rulemaking provisions of the APA were found not to be applicable since the trigger price announcements were policy statements and not rules imposing restrictions on regulated industries. The court noted that the Treasury had held hearings and received comments on aspects of the TPM at issue in this case and little would be gained from requiring additional hearings.

Finally, the court concluded that the application of the TPM to steel wire rod was not arbitrary or capricious either by reason of the application of the TPM to AISI steel mill products only, or by reason of the level of the prices set. The Treasury decisions were deemed to be rational and necessitated by the circumstances found to exist. The appeal of this suit was dismissed by the Court of Appeals of the District of Columbia July 14, 1978.

The government position was strengthened by the antidumping provisions included in Title VII of the Tariff Act of 1930, as added by the Trade Agreements Act of 1979. The Administering Authority was given explicit

---

[80]*Davis Walker Corporation* v. *Blumenthal,* 460 F. Supp. 283 (DC DC 1978) 1 ITRD 1745.

authority to commence an antidumping duty investigation on the basis of information available to it.[81] Moreover, the 1974 amendment of 19 U.S.C. 164(b) eliminating prolonged home market sales at less than cost of production from use in determining foreign market value, which provided the basis for the TPM, was reenacted in Title VII.[82]

2. Authority to Suspend the TPM

The Commerce Department's suspension of the TPM in March 1980 (see section E *infra*) was challenged by Korf Industries in the U.S. District Court for the District of Columbia on the grounds that (1) the suspension violated the government's contractual obligations; (2) the notice and comment procedures of 5 U.S.C. 553 were not complied with; and (3) the action violated principles of administrative fairness. The court rejected all three challenges to the suspension and found that the suspension was not arbitrary or capricious. *Korf Industries, Inc.* v. *Klutznick,* No. 80-0898 (DC DC 1980) 2 ITRD 1131.

E. Limited Reinstatement and Invoice Requirement

The Commerce Department, the administrator of the TPM since January 1, 1980, twice suspended the operation of the TPM because of the filing of major steel antidumping petitions. The TPM was fully reinstated after the 1980 suspension, upon withdrawal of the steel actions. The second suspension, January 11, 1982, continued except with respect to round stainless steel wire imports.[83] Neither suspension has affected the continuing requirement under the customs regulations (see section B *supra*) of the filing of the Special Summary Steel Invoice for each steel shipment of $10,000 or over, or if from a contiguous country, of $5,000 or over.

---

[81]Section 732(a), Tariff Act of 1930 (19 U.S.C. 1673a(a)).
[82]Section 773(b), Tariff Act of 1930 (19 U.S.C. 1677b)).
[83]Resumption of monitoring round stainless steel wire imports, 47 FR 16820, April 20, 1982. Monitoring terminated, 50 FR 25730, June 21, 1985.

13

Countervailing Duties

I. THE COUNTERVAILING DUTY LAW

The Countervailing Duty Law complements the Antidumping Law by providing a legal weapon to defend against a second frequently used foreign unfair trade practice: the foreign subsidization of exports. If the foreign manufacture, production, or export of merchandise is being subsidized, a domestic producer of a competing product may have a remedy under the Countervailing Duty Law. Likewise, an importer of foreign manufactured goods may be greatly affected by a countervailing duty proceeding.

As of October 1985, there were 64 countervailing duty orders outstanding against a wide variety of products from 28 countries around the world, the major target countries being Brazil (7) and Mexico (13). The list of these countervailing duty orders appears in Appendix J.

A. Title VII and Section 303 of the Tariff Act of 1930

1. The 1979 Trade Agreements Act[1]

Title I, Section 101 of the Trade Agreements Act of 1979, Public Law 96-39, added to the Tariff Act of 1930 a new Title VII—Countervailing and Antidumping Duties, 19 U.S.C. 1671–1677g. Subtitle A—Imposition of Countervailing Duties, replaces the countervailing duty law which is set forth in Section 303 of the Tariff Act of 1930, 19 U.S.C. 1303, as to exports from a "country under the Agreement." The effective date of the new provisions was January 1, 1980, since the two relevant Agreements on the implementation of certain articles of the General Agreement on Tariffs and Trade, approved by Section 2 of Public Law 96-39, had entered into force with respect to the United States as of that date.[2] The relevant agreements are the Agreement on Interpretation and Application of Articles VI, XVI, and XXIII of the General Agreement on Tariffs and Trade (relating to

---

[1]Where reference is made to the 1979 Law, the Tariff Act of 1930 section number will be given followed by the U.S. Code citation in parentheses.
[2]Section 107 of Pub. L. No. 96-39 (19 U.S.C. 1671 Note).

subsidies and countervailing measures) (see Appendix C) hereafter referred to as the Subsidy/CVD Code, and the Agreement on the Implementation of Article VI of the General Agreement on Tariffs and Trade (relating to antidumping measures) (see Appendix D).

Section 303 of the Tariff Act of 1930 applies to exports from a country not under the Agreement. However, Section 303 was amended by Section 103 of Title I of the Trade Agreements Act, effective January 1, 1980, to provide that countervailing duties shall be prescribed under that section under regulations of the administering authority "in accordance with Title VII" of the Tariff Act of 1930, added by Section 101 of the Trade Agreements Act. The regulations prescribed by the administering authority, 19 CFR Part 355 apply the same substantive and procedural law to Section 303 and Title VII cases, with exceptions discussed *infra.*

The Trade Agreements Act of 1979 also approved "Statements of Administrative Action" submitted by the Executive Branch along with the proposed new legislation. The statements refer to certain practices in the administration of the old law which will be continued, and to the substance of regulations to be issued in implementation of the new law. Information on countervailing duty administration provided in the Statement on "Title I—Countervailing and Antidumping Duties" is included *infra.* References to the Statement will be made to its publication in House Document No. 96-153, Part II.

2. The 1984 Amendments

Substantial amendments to Title VII were enacted by Title VI of the Trade and Tariff Act of 1984, Public Law 98-573, hereafter referred to as the 1984 Amendments. Many of these amendments applied to both countervailing duty and antidumping proceedings and are incorporated in Chapter 12 *supra,* as well as in this Chapter.

3. Countries Under the Agreement

As pointed out, Title VII applies to imports from a "country under the Agreement." This term is defined[3] as meaning a country:

(1) between which and the United States the Agreement on Subsidies and Countervailing Measures applies;

(2) which has assumed obligations with respect to the United States which are substantially equivalent to obligations under the Agreement, as determined by the President; or

(3) with respect to which the President determines that on June 19, 1979, and since, there is an agreement in effect between the United States and that country which requires "most-favored-nation" treatment with respect to articles imported into the United States, to which the General Agreement

---

[3]Section 701(b), Tariff Act of 1930 (19 U.S.C. 1671). The term "country" is defined in Section 771(3) (19 U.S.C. 1677(3)). The definition includes, for countervailing duty purposes, a customs union. The European Community must be investigated as a separate country where a petition alleged EC subsidies, *Republic Steel Corporation* v. *United States,* 4 CIT 33, 544 F. Supp. 901 (1982) 3 ITRD 2125.

on Tariffs and Trade does not apply, and where certain other specified conditions exist. The Administrative Statement indicates that initially this category of countries included Venezuela, Honduras, Nepal, North Yemen, El Salvador, Paraguay, and Liberia.[4]

In an initial determination of January 4, 1980 (45 FR 1181) the USTR, by delegation from the President, determined the countries recognized under Section 701(b)(1) as "countries under the Agreement" by virtue of acceptance of the Subsidies Agreement. By subsequent notices in the *Federal Register,* the USTR has reported additional countries having this status as signatories of the Agreement. Two countries have been recognized as "countries under the Agreement" under Section 701(b)(2) by virtue of having assumed obligations "substantially equivalent" to the obligations under the Agreement: Taiwan, initially, and Mexico, by USTR determination, published April 30, 1985 (50 FR 18355).

One country, New Zealand, was removed from the status of a "country under the Agreement" by the USTR in a notice of April 2, 1985 (50 FR 13111) which stated that notification had been given to the Director General of the GATT that the United States did not consent to the application of the Subsidies Code between it and New Zealand until further notice.

4. *Imports From Non-Agreement Countries*

As to the imports from any country which does not come under the definition of "country under the Agreement," Section 303, as amended in 1979, applies. The most important difference is that under Title VII injury determinations by the International Trade Commission (ITC) are required with respect to dutiable as well as non-dutiable imports subject to a countervailing duty proceeding. Under Section 303 injury determinations are not required as to dutiable imports.

Injury determinations are required, however, before countervailing duties may be imposed upon nondutiable merchandise if, as stated in Section 303(a)(2), such a determination is "required by the international obligations of the United States." This provision was added to Section 303 by Section 331 of the Trade Act of 1974, for the reason that, as explained in the Senate Finance Committee Report on H.R. 10710,[5] the extension being made of the countervailing duty law to duty-free merchandise carried the obligation of conformity to Article VI, Part II, of the GATT requiring a finding of injury before countervailing duties may be levied on subsidized imports. This obligation did not apply to dutiable merchandise which was countervailable without an injury test prior to the GATT and consequently excepted. An injury determination by the ITC under Title VII is therefore required respecting duty-free merchandise from any country which is a member of the GATT or from any country with which the United States has a bilateral agreement requiring most-favored-nation (MFN) treatment.

---

[4]H.R. Doc. No. 96-153, Part II, p. 394.
[5]S. Rep. No. 93-1298 on H.R. 10710, 1974 U.S. Code Cong. & Ad. News, 7186 at 7320.

Information as to the status of an exporting country may be obtained from the Director for Subsidies and Antidumping Policy, Office of the General Counsel, Office of the U.S. Trade Representative.

In addition, in Section 303 cases involving dutiable imports there can be no suspension of an investigation pursuant to an agreement to eliminate the injurious effect, as described in section II.C.2.b *infra;* and no determination as to the presence of critical circumstances, as described in section II.C.1.d *infra,* is required. See 19 U.S.C. 1303(b) and 19 CFR 355.0.

A major unifying provision in the application of Section 303 and Title VII is the definition in Title VII, Section 771(5), of "subsidy" as having the same meaning as the term "bounty or grant" in Section 303.

When the general terms "Countervailing Duty Law" or "Law" are used hereafter they refer to the law providing for countervailing duties as revised in 1979, without distinction between Title VII and Section 303.

B. The Administering Authority

The Countervailing Duty Law placed the authority and responsibility for its administration, other than injury determinations, upon the "administering authority" which was defined as "the Secretary of the Treasury, or any other officer of the United States to whom the responsibility for carrying out the duties of the administering authority under this title are transferred by law."[6]

Pursuant to the President's Reorganization Plan No. 3 of 1979,[7] and Executive Order 12188,[8] authority to administer the Countervailing Duty Law was transferred from the Secretary of the Treasury to the Secretary of Commerce, effective January 2, 1980. The exercise of that authority is under the general supervision of the Under Secretary for International Trade, and the immediate supervision of the Assistant Secretary for Trade Administration who, through the Deputy Assistant Secretary for Import Administration, supervises the administering agency, the International Trade Administration (ITA). Hereafter, references to the Secretary or to the ITA, as appropriate, will be made wherever the statutory reference is to the "administering authority." The U.S. Customs Service remains in the Treasury Department but assists Commerce in the administration of the law.

The International Trade Administration in January 1980 issued regulations, 19 CFR Part 355, governing countervailing duty procedures and determinations and access to information. The ITA reserved for later promulgation, on the basis of experience, the rules governing the determination and calculation of net subsidy and certain other matters.

The ITA provided advance notice of proposed rulemaking to incorporate the changes made by the 1984 Amendments and to codify existing administrative practices. 49 FR 45593, November 19, 1984. It issued proposed rules, with a request for comments, on June 10, 1985, 50 FR

---

[6]Section 771(1), Tariff Act of 1930 (19 U.S.C. 1677(1)).
[7]44 FR 69273, December 3, 1979, 5 U.S.C. App.
[8]45 FR 989, January 4, 1980.

24207, which would substantially revise Part 355, incorporating regulations to carry out the 1984 Amendments and to include and clarify existing administrative interpretations and practices. These regulations would also restate the effective dates of the provisions of the 1984 Amendments which the ITA had issued on an interim basis as Subpart E of Part 355 on February 12, 1985, 50 FR 5746. In addition, the ITA issued final and interim-final regulations providing procedures for requesting administrative reviews of countervailing duty orders under amended section 751 of the Tariff Act of 1930. 50 FR 32556, August 13, 1985. Significant provisions of the existing, revised, and proposed rules are referred to in this chapter.

C. Summary of Provisions

In essence, the Countervailing Duty Law provides that if (1) the Secretary determines that a country or a citizen or national thereof is providing, directly or indirectly, a subsidy of the manufacture, production, or exportation of merchandise imported, or (under Section 601 of the 1984 Amendments) merchandise sold (or likely to be sold) for importation, into the United States; and (2) when required, the Commission determines that an industry in the United States is materially injured, threatened with material injury, or its establishment is materially retarded by reason of imports of such merchandise, or by reason of sales (or the likelihood of sales) of such merchandise for importation, then a countervailing duty equal to the amount of the net subsidy shall be imposed upon such merchandise in addition to any other duty to which it is subject. For this purpose the 1984 Amendments provide that a sale includes a lease of merchandise equivalent to its sale.

The subsidy may emanate from government or private sources, including subdivisions of a foreign government. However, to date, all countervailing duty determinations have arisen out of foreign governmental actions and not private activities.

Countervailing duty cases are considered on a country basis, *e.g.,* passenger automobiles from West Germany, and countervailing duty orders call for the assessment and collection of countervailing duties on all imports of the merchandise originating in such country whether or not imported directly, unless a particular foreign manufacturer is expressly excluded. The 1984 Amendments in Section 607 provide that the level of duties shall presumptively be the same for all merchandise imported from the country investigated, but permit the ITA to provide for differing duties if it determines there is a significant differential between companies receiving subsidy benefits or if a State-owned enterprise is involved. The existing (1985) ITA regulations provide that in a final affirmative determination the amount of the net subsidy shall be estimated and stated and that if separate enterprises have received materially different benefits, such differences shall be estimated and stated (19 CFR 355.33(f)).

D. Standards for Determining the Existence of Subsidies

1. Definition of Subsidy

The term "subsidy" is defined in Title VII[9] as having the same meaning as the term "bounty or grant" in Section 303. However, for clarification, the law indicates that the term "subsidy" includes but is not limited to:

(A) Any export subsidy described in Annex A to the Agreement (relating to illustrative list of export subsidies).

(B) The following domestic subsidies, if provided or required by government action to a specific enterprise or industry, or group of enterprises or industries, whether publicly or privately owned, and whether paid or bestowed directly or indirectly on the manufacture, production, or export of any class or kind of merchandise:

(i) The provision of capital, loans or loan guarantees on terms inconsistent with commercial considerations.

(ii) The provision of goods or services at preferential rates.

(iii) The grant of funds or forgiveness of debt to cover operating losses sustained by a specific industry.

(iv) The assumption of any costs or expenses of manufacture, production, or distribution.

In addition, Section 613 of the 1984 Amendments adds a new Section 771A to Title VII which defines an "upstream subsidy" as an export or domestic subsidy (as defined above) provided by a foreign government with respect to an input product used in that country in the manufacture or production of the merchandise subject to the countervailing duty proceeding which has a significant effect on the cost of producing the merchandise and bestows a competitive benefit on the merchandise. Upstream subsidies are discussed separately under section I.D.6 *infra*.

The foregoing description in Subsections (A) and (B) of what a subsidy includes makes clear that a subsidy is a preferential benefit. An export subsidy is a benefit which prefers exports over products sold domestically, as the Illustrative List In Annex A to the Subsidies Agreement shows. A domestic subsidy is a benefit provided to a specific industry or group of industries, such as a regional group, in a manner inconsistent with normal commercial considerations. A nationwide government economic program, which is not an export subsidy, is not subject to countervailing duties by another government. This principle was confirmed by the Court of International Trade in its holding that the two Korean accelerated depreciation programs at issue were not countervailable, because the benefits accorded were not preferential but accorded generally to the entire business community. *Carlisle Tire and Rubber Company* v. *United States,* 5 CIT 229, 564 F. Supp. 834 (1983) 4 ITRD 2017. This principle is narrowed in *Bethlehem Steel Corp.* v. *United States,* 7 CIT ___ , 590 F. Supp. 1237 (1984) 5 ITRD 2337. But a generally available benefit may provide a *de*

---

[9]Section 771(5), Tariff Act of 1930 (19 U.S.C. 1677(5)). This definition is adopted by Section 702(b)(2) of the Trade Agreements Act to govern the periodic determination by the Secretary of Commerce of subsidies on articles of quota cheese under Section 702(a).

facto preference. *Cabot Corporation* v. *United States,* 10 CIT ＿＿ , Slip Op. 85-102 (1985) 7 ITRD ＿＿ .

Examples of export subsidies appear in the discussion of export tax rebate programs *infra.* Examples of domestic subsidies appear extensively in the ITA's final determinations in the major carbon steel products countervailing duty investigations, published September 7, 1982, 47 FR Part II. Domestic subsidies included cash grants, loan guarantees, real property tax exemptions, and other monetary benefits to companies locating in specified geographic areas or in economically depressed regions (Belgium, 47 FR 39304; France, 47 FR 39332; Federal Republic of Germany, 47 FR 39345; Italy, 47 FR 39356); and interest rebates and other financial assistance for the modernization of the particular industry, steel (Luxembourg, 47 FR 39364).

Several of the same programs providing financial assistance for investment in economically depressed areas had been recognized by the Customs Court and the Court of Customs and Patent Appeals as constituting bounties or grants requiring countervailing duty determinations, in decisions reversing Treasury Department determinations which had found the *ad valorem* value of less than 2 percent attaching to U.S. imports insufficient to justify countervailing duties where there was no distortion of international trade.[10]

In contrast to the regional and specific industry benefit programs, the ITA in the major carbon steel products determinations found that certain government benefits were not subsidies because the benefits were available generally; for example, labor assistance programs (Federal Republic of Germany, 47 FR 39345); infrastructure aid, including roads, water, and electricity (Luxembourg, 47 FR 39364), and energy and environmental incentives (Netherlands, 47 FR 39372).

The subsidies determined by the ITA to be provided to the major carbon steel products imported from the European Community were never countervailed because of the termination of the investigations upon withdrawal of the U.S. steel industry petitions October 21, 1982, as discussed under section II.C.2 *infra.*

The infusion of equity into the nationalized British steel corporation in the form of loans, capital, and forgiveness of debt was found to be countervailable, even though some funds specifically provided for the closure of redundant facilities and the layoff of unnecessary workers. *British Steel Corporation* v. *United States,* 9 CIT ＿＿ , 605 F. Supp. 286 (1985) 6 ITRD 1929.

2. Past Practice

The Administrative Statement indicates that since the term subsidy in the new law is defined to have the same meaning as the term "bounty or grant" in the old law, past policies and decisions as to what constitutes subsidy will

---

[10]*ASG Industries, Inc., et al.* v. *United States,* 67 CCPA 11, CAD 1237, 610 F.2d 770 (1979) 1 ITRD 1718, float glass from West Germany; *ASG Industries, Inc., et al.* v. *United States,* 85 Cust. Ct. 10, 495 F. Supp. 904 (1980) 2 ITRD 1388, float glass from Belgium.

continue to be relevant. In the past a wide variety of governmental actions were determined to constitute subsidy.[11]

In a landmark decision in 1973 on radial tires from Canada, the Treasury Department found that certain payments and benefits made to the Michelin Company as an inducement to build plants in Nova Scotia for the manufacture of tires constituted subsidy and countervailing duties were assessed.[12] The payments and benefits consisted of certain grants and accelerated depreciation under the income tax law afforded by the Canadian Government, and grants, a low interest rate, and property tax concessions afforded by the Province of Nova Scotia and its municipalities. A significant factor in this case was that the capacity of the proposed new plant was greatly in excess of the potential for consumption of radial tires in Canada. It was clear, therefore, that one of the primary purposes of this program was to stimulate the export of radial tires to the U.S. market.

The Treasury finding of bounties given was confirmed by the Court of International Trade in *Michelin Tire Corporation* v. *United States,* 2 CIT 143 (1981) 3 ITRD 1177. The court focused principally on the loan provided by Nova Scotia at 6 percent, finding a bounty in the difference between that percent and the 7.56 percent cost of a loan on the Eurobond market, and on the uncompensated deferral of principal payments, finding a bounty in an amount to be determined by conventional methods of financial analysis.

3. Application to Nonmarket Economies

After extensive consideration, the ITA concluded that bounties, grants, and subsidies could not be found in nonmarket economies. *Carbon Steel Wire Rod from Czechoslovakia, Final Negative Countervailing Duty Determination,* May 1, 1984, and *Carbon Steel Wire Rod from Poland, Final Negative Countervailing Duty Determination,* May 1, 1984, published in 49 FR 19370 and 19374, May 7, 1984; 6 ITRD 1176, 1209. The ITA explained this decision at length by contrasting the economic forces which function in market, as distinct from nonmarket, economies. It stated that in an NME system the government does not interfere in the market process but supplants it, leading to the conclusion that subsidies have no meaning outside the context of a market economy. The heart of the argument was given as follows:

> In a market economy, scarce resources are channeled to their most profitable and efficient uses by the market forces of supply and demand. We believe a subsidy (or bounty or grant) is definitionally any action that distorts or subverts the market process and results in a misallocation of resources, encouraging inefficient production and lessening world wealth.
>
> In NME's, resources are not allocated by a market. With varying degrees of control, allocation is achieved by central planning. Without a market, it is obviously meaningless to look for a misallocation of resources caused by

---

[11]See, *e.g.,* TD 78-295, August 16, 1978, 43 FR 37685; TD 75-300, November 24, 1975, 40 FR 55638; TD 78-181, June 13, 1978, 43 FR 25996; TD 78-446, November 8, 1978, 43 FR 53422; TD 78-444, November 7, 1978, 43 FR 53424; TD 76-173, June 14, 1976, 41 FR 24702, and TD 76-152, May 21, 1976, 41 FR 21766.

[12]TD 73-10, January 4, 1973, 38 FR 1018.

subsidies. There is no market process to distort [or] to subvert. Resources may appear to be misallocated in an NME when compared to the standard of a market economy, but the resource misallocation results from central planning, not subsidies.

Furthermore, the ITA found that Congress had made no effort to provide a means of evaluating economic factors which would be applicable to a countervailing duty determination of nonmarket economy imports, in contrast to its provision for surrogate country determinations in antidumping duty determinations.

The Court of International Trade rejected the ITA reasoning as "economic jargon" and "unlawful irrationality," holding that the countervailing duty law was plainly intended to apply to all countries and that the ITA definition of a subsidy as "a distortion of a *market* economy" failed to recognize the possibility of special preferences granted by an NME country. *Continental Steel Corp.* v. *United States* and *Amax Chemical, Inc. and Kerr-McGee Chemical Corp.* v. *United States,* Slip Op. 85-77, July 30, 1985, 7 ITRD 1001 (original emphasis). The Court proceeded to reverse and remand four ITA determinations based on the erroneous premise.

4. Effect of Tax Rebates

One of the earliest and still common forms of government incentives for increased manufacture and export of merchandise has been the granting of tax rebates to exporters. Many of the government assistance programs determined to be bounties or grants under the prior countervailing duty law also contained tax rebates. The Treasury determined that some tax rebates constituted bounties or grants while, in accordance with certain principles, others did not.

A principle followed by the Treasury since 1898 was that the nonexcessive remission of an indirect tax by reason of the export of products did not constitute a bounty or grant. A remission was considered "nonexcessive" if it did not exceed the amount of the tax paid or due. This interpretation of the law was upheld by the Supreme Court as reasonable and as constituting an administrative practice sanctioned by the Congress in the 1978 decision, *Zenith Radio Corporation* v. *United States.*[13] There the Supreme Court affirmed the decision reached by the Secretary of the Treasury and the Court of Customs and Patent Appeals (reversing the Customs Court) that Japan had not bestowed a bounty or grant upon the export of consumer electronic products by remitting a commodity tax on exports which was applied to the same products sold in Japan. The Supreme Court found reasonable the principle long followed by the Treasury Department that the Congress intended to require countervailing duties to be applied to a "net export bounty," *i.e.,* a tax advantage beyond a remission of an indirect tax upon export. The Supreme Court also noted that the historic position of the Treasury had been incorporated into the General Agreement on Tariffs and Trade, followed by every major trading nation in the world.

---

[13]437 U.S. 443, 57 L.Ed.2d 337, 1 ITRD 1634.

This established principle was stated by the Commerce Department, with distinctions and restrictions, in its Administrative and Interpretative Guidelines for Determination and Calculation of Subsidies, which form Annex I to its Countervailing Duties regulations. The Guidelines make four points: (1) under the "physical incorporation test" the rebate of fiscal charges on items physically incorporated in the exported product is not considered a subsidy, but rebated taxes on services, catalysts, and other nonincorporated items would be considered subsidies; (2) payment of a lump sum to an exporter which is identified as a nonexcessive rebate of an indirect tax may be treated as not a subsidy only if the government has reasonably calculated and documented the actual tax experience of the product under investigation; (3) drawback of duties paid or due on imported items physically incorporated in the export product is not regarded as a subsidy; and (4) the rebate or reduction of the amount of direct taxes, particularly income and social security taxes, imposed on an exported product is regarded as a subsidy.

These Guidelines have been applied in various informative Commerce Department decisions on countervailing duty petitions. In a series of determinations concerning the Cash Compensatory Support on Export (CCS) payments by the Government of India, the ITA found that the government had not met the standards for demonstrating a "clear link" between the indirect tax incidence and the CCS payments to exporters of industrial fasteners,[14] nor the standards of reasonable calculation and documentation in the export of iron-metal castings,[15] but had satisfied all evidentiary requirements in payments upon exports of certain textiles and textile mill products.[16] Similarly, the export tax rebate program, CEDI, of Mexico, although designed on its face to rebate indirect taxes, was found not to be clearly identified with the indirect tax incidence of the leather wearing apparel industry.[17] Also, the Pakistan Government was determined not to have supplied information demonstrating the necessary link between its export payment and the actual indirect tax incidence borne by the exported textiles.[18] In short, in only one of the five foregoing determinations did the government of the exporters

> present information that demonstrates to the Department's satisfaction (a) that indirect taxes paid have served as the official basis upon which the export rebate was calculated and (b) that there is, in fact, the requisite link between the export payment and the indirect tax incidence.[19]

The ITA requirement that there must be a "clear link" between eligibility for the Cash Compensatory Support on Export (CCS) program of India and the payment of indirect taxes and that the government must have reasonably calculated and documented the actual indirect tax incidence

---

[14]*Certain Fasteners from India,* 45 FR 48607, July 21, 1980, 2 ITRD 5166.

[15]*Certain Iron-Metal Castings from India,* 45 FR 55502, August 20, 1980, 2 ITRD 5161.

[16]*Certain Textiles and Textile Mill Products from India,* 45 FR 64611, September 30, 1980, 2 ITRD 5134.

[17]*Leather Wearing Apparel from Mexico,* 46 FR 21357, April 10, 1981, 2 ITRD 5433. See also, *Carbon Steel Wire Rod from Argentina,* 47 FR 30539, July 14, 1982, 4 ITRD 1277.

[18]*Certain Textile and Textile Products from Pakistan,* 45 FR 37873, June 5, 1980, 2 ITRD 5570.

[19]*Ibid.* 2 ITRD at 5572.

borne by the exporters of fasteners was upheld by both the Court of International Trade and the Court of Appeals for the Federal Circuit.[20]

5. Net Subsidy

Section 771(6) of the Law states that for the purpose of determining the net subsidy, the administering authority may subtract from the gross subsidy the amount of:

(A) any application fee, deposit, or similar payment paid in order to qualify for, or to receive, the benefit of the subsidy.

(B) any loss in the value of the subsidy resulting from its deferred receipt, if the deferral is mandated by Government order, and

(C) export taxes, duties, or other charges levied on the export of merchandise to the United States specifically intended to offset the subsidy received.

This specification of the offsets allowable was intended to reverse a Treasury Department practice of allowing as offsets the amount of nonexcessive indirect taxes which could have been, but were not, rebated. *Certain Textiles and Textile Mill Products from India, supra* note 16. After finding that India's CCS payments constituted a subsidy the ITA declined to find that the export inspection fee of 1 percent of the value of the exported castings was an allowable offset under Subsection (A), quoted *supra.* The reason stated was that the fee was payment by the exporter for the service of quality control, which was required for certain engineering products, whether or not the exports benefited from the CCS program. *Certain Iron-Metal Castings from India, supra* note 15. However, after finding that the reintegro, or rebate, program of the Government of Uruguay was a subsidy because it was designed to compensate exporters for both direct and indirect taxes, the ITA allowed as an offset the direct deduction by the government of 1 percent of the reintegro payment. The reason stated was that the 1 percent deduction was specifically intended to reduce the amount of the subsidy received and therefore was authorized by Subsection (C) of the law quoted *supra. Leather Wearing Apparel from Uruguay,* 46 FR 19288, March 30, 1981, 2 ITRD 5607.

Since under Section 771(b) an offset may be allowed only if it comes within one of the three categories of offsets specified, other kinds of offsets recognized prior to the Trade Agreements Act, such as the "disadvantages of location" analyzed in the *Michelin* case, *supra,* may no longer be considered in cases determined under Title VII or Section 303, as amended in 1979.

6. Upstream Subsidy

Prior to the 1984 Amendments, the term "subsidy" had never been defined explicitly to include or exclude subsidies bestowed on products at prior stages of manufacture or production. The 1984 Amendments in

---

[20]*Industrial Fasteners Group* v. *United States,* 2 CIT 181, 525 F. Supp. 885 (1981) 3 ITRD 1289; 3 CIT 58, 542 F. Supp. 1019 (1982) 3 ITRD 1724, *motion for reh'g denied,* 3 CIT 104 (1982) 3 ITRD 1991, 710 F.2d 1576 (Fed. Cir. 1983) 4 ITRD 2153.

Section 613 spell out the criteria concerning when and to what extent such so-called "upstream subsidies" will be countervailed. A countervailable upstream subsidy is defined as certain enumerated domestic subsidies within the meaning of existing law (namely, those set out as Item (i), (ii), or (iii) in section I.D.1 *supra*) bestowed by a foreign government with respect to an "input product" used in that country in the manufacture or production of the merchandise subject to the countervailing duty proceeding if that subsidy has a significant effect on the cost of producing the merchandise and bestows a competitive benefit on the merchandise. The law directs the ITA to find that a competitive benefit has been bestowed when the price paid by the producer for the input is below the price the producer otherwise would have paid for the input in an arms-length transaction. The amount of the benefit to be countervailed is the amount of the competitive benefit or the amount of the subsidy bestowed on the input, whichever is less. The 1984 law also provides for extensions in the statutory deadlines for conducting investigations when there is a reasonable basis to believe or suspect that an upstream subsidy has been bestowed.

When there is a single, continuous line of production resulting in one end product, as in the production of certain agricultural products, a subsidy granted at one stage of the production (to live swine) is not an upstream subsidy but a subsidy to the end product (pork products). *Preliminary Affirmative Countervailing Duty Determination; Live Swine and Fresh, Chilled and Frozen Pork Products from Canada,* 50 FR 13264, April 3, 1985. A 5 percent upstream subsidy is presumed significant. *Certain Agricultural Tools from Brazil*, 50 FR 34525, August 26, 1985.

7. Calculation of Subsidy

In calculating the value of a subsidy the Secretary will consider its value at the time received as well as the extent to which it is used by individual enterprises or classes of enterprises. Under Guideline 5 provided in Annex I of the Commerce Department regulations allowance may be made for the reduction in value of a subsidy due to currency fluctuations during delayed payment if the delay is officially mandated.

The Commerce Department announced the general principles applied in the allocation of the face value of the grants and other benefits found to be subsidies in the final affirmative determinations of the major carbon steel products cases published September 7, 1982, in a discussion in Appendix 2 to the determination in *Certain Steel Products from Belgium,* 47 FR 39316, 4 ITRD 1528. In early 1984, Commerce substantially revised this methodology in Appendix II to a preliminary determination involving *Certain Carbon Steel Products from Mexico,* 49 FR 5148, February 10, 1984, 6 ITRD 1199.

The 1982 and February 1984 Appendices were superseded by a Subsidies Appendix annexed to the final affirmative determination in *Cold-Rolled Carbon Steel Flat-Rolled Products from Argentina,* 49 FR 18006, April 26, 1984, 5 ITRD 2217 at 2234. The Subsidies Appendix is an extended and detailed explanation of the countervailing duty methodology which the ITA uses to examine and calculate the amount of grants, loans, loan guarantees, and equity, and which the ITA considers meets the sole directive on this matter in the legislative history, that of "reasonableness."

The Subsidies Appendix presents the general problem as follows:

> Funds provided under government direction or directly by the government provide a subsidy to the extent that the recipient pays less for the funds than it would on the market. In the case of a loan, this is the difference between the cash flows—the company's receipts and payments—on the loan under examination and the cash flows for a comparable commercial loan taken out by the same company. For equity, it is the difference between what the government paid for a share of the company and what the market would have paid for the share. For grants, the saving to the recipient is the face value of the grant; that is, the difference between what the company paid for the funds (nothing), and what it would have to pay on the market to receive the funds (the face value of the grant). The difference in cash flows can arise in a single moment, as with grants (complete receipt of the funds at once), or over several years, as with long-term loans (through periodic repayment).

The Appendix then provides a discussion of the reasons for its methods of selection of a discount rate for allocating money over time; of determining a reasonable shape and length for the stream of benefits; of constructing a comparable commercial loan at the appropriate market interest rate ("the benchmark"); of selecting an added risk premium for uncreditworthy companies; and of making an equity worthiness analysis.

If the calculation results in a *de minimis* amount, no countervailing duty is required. *Carlisle Tire & Rubber Co.* v. *United States.*, 1 CIT 352, 517 F. Supp. 704 (1981) 2 ITRD 1577.

E. Comparison of Coverage of Antidumping and Countervailing Duty Laws

There can be an overlap between the coverage of the Antidumping and the Countervailing Duty Law. Both can apply to the same merchandise imports in certain situations. However, the Treasury Department proceeded under one law or the other, not both at the same time. Under the 1979 law, simultaneous investigations are undertaken, as in the numerous steel cases filed January 11, 1982. The following examples illustrate the distinction between the areas of coverage of the two Acts.

Example 1: Singerfabrik, a German company, manufactures sewing machines. The price in Germany is $100. It sells the same machine in the United States for $75 (after adjustments for shipping, etc.). Singer gets no financial help from the German government in connection with the production or export of the machines. Only the Antidumping Law would apply since there is no element of subsidy.

Example 2: LaCarona, an Italian manufacturer, receives a government subsidy payment equivalent to $5 for each typewriter it exports. This enables it to sell its typewriters for $92.50 or the equivalent in both Italy and the United States. Were it not for the subsidy, the price would be $95 in both places. In this case, only the Countervailing Duty Law would apply because, although there is subsidy, there is no price discrimination.

Example 3: The Netherlands pays exporters of processed cheese an export subsidy of 2 cents per pound. Prochesse, a Dutch company, sells processed cheese for 37 cents a pound in the Netherlands and 35 cents (after adjustments) to the United States. A complaint could be filed with the Commerce Department asking for relief under either or both of these laws, because elements of both price discrimination and subsidy exist in this case. The added duty would, on the facts given, be the same under either law.

II. PROCESSING A COUNTERVAILING DUTY PROCEEDING

A. Starting the Proceeding

A countervailing duty proceeding can be initiated by the Secretary or by a petition filed by an interested party on behalf of a domestic industry. If the Secretary commences the proceeding, he promptly notifies the Commission. In a Title VII case, he will also notify and consult with the authorities of the foreign country concerned. Unless the petition pertains to dutiable merchandise from a nonagreement country, a petitioner must file the petition the same day with the Commission and so certify in submitting the petition to the Secretary. The petition and supporting documents must be in the form prescribed by the regulations (see 19 CFR 355.26).

The "interested parties" who may file a petition[21] in a countervailing duty proceeding are those described in the definition of "interested parties" in Section 771(9) (19 U.S.C. 1677(9)) as (C) a manufacturer, producer, or wholesaler in the United States of a like product; (D) a certified union or group of workers representative of an industry engaged in the manufacture, production, or wholesale in the United States of a like product; and (E) a trade or business association, a majority of whose members manufacture, produce, or wholesale a like product in the United States. This listing was not specifically amended by Section 612(b)(2) of the 1984 Amendments to include the association of interested domestic parties described in new Paragraph (F) of the interested party definition in Section 771(9), although the Conference Report indicates an intent to do so (H.R. Rep. No. 98-1156 at 175).

The Law requires that the petition allege the "elements necessary for the imposition of the [countervailing] duty." The regulations require that such information include to the extent reasonably available to the petitioner:[22]

(1) The name and address of the petitioner and any other person, firm, or association the petitioner represents, if appropriate;

(2) The industry on whose behalf the petition is filed, including the names of other enterprises included in such industry;

(3) A statement indicating whether the applicant has initiated proceedings pursuant to sections 337 and 732 of the Act [19 U.S.C. 1337, 1673a] or section 301 of the Trade Act of 1974 (19 U.S.C. 2411), or has filed, or is filing, for import relief pursuant to section 201 of the Trade Act of 1974 (19 U.S.C. 2251), or has initiated proceedings pursuant to section 232 of the Trade Expansion of

---

[21]Section 702(b), Tariff Act of 1930 (19 U.S.C. 1671a).
[22]19 CFR 355.26(a).

1962 (19 U.S.C. 1862), with respect to the merchandise which is the subject of the proceeding;

(4) A detailed description of the imported merchandise in question, including its technical characteristics and uses, and, where appropriate, its tariff classification under the Tariff Schedules of the United States;

(5) The name of the country or countries from which the merchandise is being, or is likely to be, exported to the United States and, if the merchandise is produced in a country other than that from which it is exported, the name of the country in which it is produced;

(6) The names and addresses of enterprises believed to be benefitting from the subsidy and exporting the merchandise so benefitted to the United States;

(7) All pertinent facts with regard to the alleged subsidy including, if known, the statutory or other authority under which it is provided, the manner in which it is paid and the value of such subsidy when received and used by producers or sellers of the merchandise;

(8) In addition to information concerning alleged subsidies, information as to individual sales (including customers) and prices thereof on sales by foreign manufacturers, producers or exporters to the United States during the period to be investigated;

(9) The volume and value of imports of the merchandise from the country in question in the most recent two-year period, and also other periods if the petitioner believes such other periods to be more representative, or, if the merchandise is not presently imported into the United States or is not imported in significant quantities, information as to the likelihood of its importation;

(10) The names and addresses of enterprises believed to be importing the merchandise;

(11) The names and addresses of the other enterprises in the United States engaged in the production, manufacture or sale of like merchandise. If numerous, information need not be provided with respect to any enterprises that accounted for less than 2 percent of domestic production, manufacture or sale of like merchandise during the most recent 12-month period;

(12) Information as to the material injury or threat thereof to, or the material retardation of the establishment of, a United States industry by reason of the imported merchandise alleged to be subsidized, as described in 19 CFR 207.11 and 207.26.

(13) If "critical circumstances" are alleged, information as to:

(i) Material injury which is difficult to repair;

(ii) Massive imports in a relatively short period; and

(iii) How the product benefits from an export subsidy which is inconsistent with the Agreement; and

(14) Any other documentation on which petitioner relies in making its petition.

Forms for the submission of petitions may be adopted from time to time. The use of such forms shall not be mandatory, provided the information required thereby and reasonably available to the petitioner is otherwise included in the petition.

The information called for under Paragraphs (12) and (13) need not be included if the petition is brought under Section 303 and concerns dutiable merchandise from a country not under the Agreement, as provided in Section 355.0(e) of the regulations.

The petition requirements in the regulations proposed June 10, 1985, are substantially the same except that provision is made for the information needed with an allegation of an upstream subsidy (Section 355.12(a)(8)) and for a petition based upon the derogation of an international undertaking on official export credits (Section 355.12(h)). Such a petition was provided for in an amendment of Section 702(b) of the Tariff Act of 1930 (19 U.S.C. 1671a) by Section 650 of Public Law 98-181, November 30, 1983.

Technical assistance in the filing of petitions was required by Section 221 of the 1984 Amendments to be provided to eligible small businesses by each agency administering a trade law, specifically including the agencies administering the antidumping and countervailing duty laws. An eligible small business was defined to mean any business concern which in the agency's unreviewable judgment has not the resources or financial ability to obtain qualified outside assistance in preparing and filing petitions. The agency is required to consult with any other agency which has provided this assistance to the business concerned and may consult the Small Business Administration. Assistance to eligible small businesses is provided for in Section 355.12(i) of the proposed regulations.

The Commission was also specifically required by Section 221 to establish a Trade Remedy Assistance Office to provide information to the public upon request on the remedies and benefits available under the trade laws and on petition and application procedures and filing dates.

B. Steps in the Processing of a Countervailing Duty Proceeding

There are several steps which have to be taken from the time of the initiation of a countervailing duty proceeding until the issuance of the final countervailing duty order. The following is an outline of these various steps, recognizing that no reference to the Commission is made of a Section 303 case involving dutiable merchandise:

1. Commencement of Proceeding

The proceeding can be commenced either by the Secretary of Commerce or by the filing of a petition by an interested party.

2. Determination of Sufficiency of Petition

Within 20 days of the filing of a petition, the Secretary must decide whether the petition contains sufficient information to initiate an investigation.

If the determination is affirmative, the Secretary publishes a notice of commencement of an investigation and notifies the Commission and the petitioner. If the determination is negative, the Secretary dismisses the petition, terminates the proceeding, notifies the Commission and petitioner, and publishes a notice of dismissal.

3. Preliminary Commission Determination on Injury

The Commission must make its preliminary determination within 45 days of the filing of the petition or of notification by the Secretary. A negative determination at this stage terminates the investigation.

4. Preliminary Determination on Subsidy by the Secretary

Normally the Secretary makes and publishes the preliminary determination on subsidy within 85 days of the filing of a petition or commencement of a self-initiated investigation. If the ruling is affirmative, it will include an estimated amount of net subsidy.

5. Extension of Time Period in Extraordinarily Complicated Cases

The procedure for extension of time may be initiated either by a request from the petitioner or by the Secretary, if the parties are cooperating. Under this procedure, the preliminary determination may be postponed until not later than the 150th day after the date of filing the petition or commencement of a self-initiated investigation. Also, parties must be notified of the postponement not later than 20 days before the date on which the determination would otherwise be required.

6. Extension of Time Period for Upstream Subsidy Investigation

(a) Extension may be granted when there is reasonable basis to believe or suspect upstream subsidy is being bestowed.

(b) Extension, if necessary, may be up to 250 days after filing of petition or commencement of a self-initiated investigation (up to 310 days in extraordinarily complicated cases).

7. Effect of Preliminary Determination

If the preliminary determination is affirmative, the Secretary orders the suspension of liquidation of all entries. In addition, if the Secretary determines the existence of critical circumstances, suspension shall apply to all unliquidated entries of the merchandise entered or withdrawn from warehouse in the 90 days preceding the date on which the suspension was first ordered.

8. Final Determination by the Secretary

A final determination on subsidy must be made by the Secretary within 75 days of the preliminary determination.

9. Extension of Time Period for Simultaneous Investigations

(a) When an antidumping duty investigation has been instituted simultaneously with the countervailing duty investigation and the petitioner requests an extension.

(b) Date of final determination shall be extended to coincide with the date of the final determination in the antidumping duty investigation.

10. Postpreliminary Extension of Time Period for
    Upstream Subsidy Investigation

(a) When ITA concludes after, but not before, the preliminary determination that there is reasonable basis to believe or suspect an upstream subsidy is being bestowed.

(b) ITA may postpone, if necessary, the final determination:

(1) where the preliminary determination was negative, up to 165 days (or up to 225 days in cases involving critical circumstances).

(2) where the preliminary determination was affirmative, at petitioner's option either up to 165 days or until the conclusion of the first administrative review. Under the 165-day option the suspension of liquidation resulting from the preliminary determination is terminated after 120 days and not resumed until publication of a Countervailing Duty Order.

11. Final Determination by the Commission

Following an affirmative preliminary by the Secretary, the Commission undertakes a final injury determination which is due before the later of (a) the 120th day after the Secretary's preliminary determination, or (b) the 45th day after the Secretary's final determination. Following a negative preliminary determination and an affirmative final determination by the Secretary, the Commission decision as to material injury or retardation is required within 75 days after the Secretary's final determination.

12. Publication of Countervailing Duty Order

(a) Within seven days after notification by the Commission of an affirmative final injury determination, the Secretary must publish a countervailing duty order.

Under the Countervailing Duty Law, the Secretary and the Commission perform certain of their responsibilities simultaneously. While the Secretary is investigating the possibility of subsidy, the Commission is studying the question of injury. Each agency must personally notify the other of any determination it makes, whether preliminary or final. A negative final determination by either of them (on the question of subsidy or injury) or a negative preliminary determination by the Commission will terminate the countervailing duty proceeding. All determinations, preliminary or final, must be reported in the *Federal Register*, with a statement of the facts and conclusions of law on which based.

(b) In Section 303 cases involving dutiable merchandise the affirmative final determination and CVD order are published simultaneously.

The following are some of the details as to the steps outlined above.

C. Processing by the Secretary

1. Preliminary Determination

If the Secretary initiates an investigation or considers a petition by an interested party to be sufficient, he commences an investigation. Prior to the publication of a notice of the initiation of an investigation in a Title VII case, the Secretary will, as required under the Subsidy/Countervailing Duty Code, notify and consult with the representative in Washington, D.C., of the foreign country or instrumentality concerned.[23] These consultations will continue throughout the investigation, but will not impede or delay it.

As indicated in section II.B *supra,* the time period for making the preliminary determination as to the existence of subsidy practices is normally within 85 days of the date of the filing of the petition or the commencement of a self-initiated investigation. Circumstances under which this 85-day time limit may be extended are discussed *infra.* The time may be reduced in the circumstances provided for by the amendment to Title VII made by Section 603 of the 1984 Amendments. This provides for an expedited preliminary determination on the basis of the unverified record developed during the first 50 days of the investigation if the record contains sufficient information upon which to make a decision and if all parties having interests aligned with the domestic industry, after reviewing this record, agree to waive verification.

When the Secretary has determined that the petition alleges elements necessary for the imposition of a countervailing duty and that it contains information reasonably available to the petitioner supporting the allegation, he is obligated to maintain the proceeding in a form which corresponds to the petition. Specifically, he must investigate alleged subsidies of the European Community as a separate country, and he must not fail to investigate alleged subsidies by deciding in passing upon the petitions that there were no or *de minimis* imports in recent years. *Republic Steel Corporation* v. *United States,* 4 CIT 33, 544 F. Supp. 901 (1982), 3 ITRD 2125.

During the course of an investigation information and written views may be submitted within established time periods. Copies are to be sent to counsel for each party or the alternative agent designated to receive service. The Secretary will transmit such copies if he determines that this action will be unduly burdensome to the submitting party. Further, an informal hearing will be provided, normally within 30 days after the preliminary determination, upon the request of a party to the proceeding. Notice of such a hearing will be provided in the *Federal Register.*[24]

---

[23] 19 CFR 355.26(g).
[24] Section 774, Tariff Act of 1930 (19 U.S.C. 1677c); 19 CFR 355.34 and 355.35.

a. Extraordinarily Complicated Cases

As indicated in section B *supra,* the time period for making the preliminary determination may be extended until not later than the 150th day after the date of filing of the petition or the commencement of the investigation in "extraordinarily complicated cases." The postponement may be initiated by the Secretary or by the petitioner filing a request. The Secretary may determine a case to be extraordinarily complicated if the interested parties are cooperating in the furnishing of information, and the Secretary finds that additional time is needed due to:

(1) the number and complexity of the alleged subsidy practices;

(2) the novelty of the issues presented;

(3) the need to determine the extent to which particular subsidies are used by individual manufacturers, producers, and exporters; or

(4) the number of firms whose activities must be investigated.[25]

Any decision to designate a case extraordinarily complicated must be made not later than 20 days before the date on which the preliminary determination would otherwise be required.[26] Until the 1984 Amendments such a decision was subject to expedited judicial review.[27]

b. Investigation of Upstream Subsidies

The upstream subsidy section added to Subtitle D of Title VII by Section 613 of the 1984 Amendments provides for extension of the time period for making the preliminary determination when the Secretary finds there is a reasonable basis to believe or suspect that an upstream subsidy is being bestowed. If an extension is found necessary, the extension may run until not later than the 250th day (or the 310th day, in extraordinarily complicated cases) after the date of filing of the petition or the commencement of a self-initiated investigation.

c. Effect of Preliminary Determination

As previously stated, if the Secretary makes an affirmative preliminary determination the Law requires the Secretary:

(1) to order the suspension of liquidation of all entries of such merchandise entered, or withdrawn from warehouse, for consumption on or after the date of publication of the notice of the determination in the *Federal Register;*

(2) to order the posting of a cash deposit, bond, or other security, as he determines appropriate, for each entry of merchandise equal to the estimated amount of the net subsidy; and

---

[25]Section 703(c), Tariff Act of 1930 (19 U.S.C. 1671b).
[26]19 CFR 355.28(b)(3).
[27]Section 516A, Tariff Act of 1930 (19 U.S.C. 1516a). See Chapter 31, section VII.

(3) to make available to the Commission all information upon which the preliminary determination was based which may be relevant to the Commission's injury determination.[28]

Where the duration of the suspension of liquidations would exceed the four-month limit specified in the Subsidies Code, because of the extension of the time for a final determination, the Secretary is justified in terminating the suspension. *U.S. Steel Corporation* v. *United States,* 10 CIT ____ , 614 F. Supp. 1241 (1985) 7 ITRD 1081.

d. Critical Circumstances Determinations

Except in Section 303 cases involving dutiable merchandise, if the petitioner alleges critical circumstances in its original petition in a Title VII case, or any time not less than 30 days before the date of the final determination, the Secretary may find the existence of critical circumstances and direct that the liquidation of entries of the merchandise under investigation be suspended retroactively and applied to unliquidated entries, entered, or withdrawn from warehouse, for consumption on or after the date which is 90 days before the date of the original suspension of liquidation.[29] The critical determination may be made at the time of the preliminary determination, unless the preliminary determination is due within 20 days or has already been made. In this case, the critical circumstances determination is made within one month of the making of the allegation or at the time of the final determination. The Secretary may find the existence of critical circumstances if he has a reasonable basis for believing or suspecting that:

(1) there have been massive imports of the merchandise under investigation over a relatively short period; and if so,

(2) the alleged subsidy is an export subsidy inconsistent with the Subsidy/Countervailing Duty Code.[30]

2. Termination and Suspension of Investigation

The Secretary may terminate an investigation at any time upon withdrawal of the petition upon which it was based and after a notification of all interested parties.[31] As indicated below, the Commission may also terminate an investigation upon withdrawal of a petition but not before the preliminary determination by the Secretary.

However, under Section 604 of the 1984 Amendments if the termination is based upon an agreement by the foreign government involved to limit the volume of imports of the product into the United States (a quantitative restriction agreement), the Secretary must first determine that such a termination is in the public interest. The 1984 Amendments provide that the Secretary, in making such a public interest determination, must consult,

---

[28]Section 703(d), Tariff Act of 1930 (19 U.S.C. 1671b); 19 CFR 355.28(e).
[29]Section 703(e), Tariff Act of 1930 (19 U.S.C. 1671b); 19 CFR 355.29.
[30]See the Agreement, Appendix C.
[31]Section 704(a), Tariff Act of 1930 (19 U.S.C. 1671c); 19 CFR 355.30.

to the extent practicable, with potentially affected consuming industries and potentially affected workers and producers in the U.S. domestic industry and must take into account:

(i) whether the agreement would more adversely affect U.S. consumers than would the imposition of countervailing duties,

(ii) the relative impact on the U.S. international economic interests, and

(iii) the relative impact on the competitiveness of the U.S. domestic industry.

The authority to terminate a countervailing duty investigation upon withdrawal of the underlying petition was effectively used by the Secretary in 1982 to terminate the remaining countervailing duty investigations concerning major carbon steel products imported from the European Community (as well as the remaining antidumping investigations of these imports) upon the withdrawal by the U.S. steel industry of their 22 countervailing duty petitions (47 FR 49058, October 29, 1982). Final determinations of subsidies had been reached in most of these investigations (47 FR 39304, September 7, 1982), and preliminary affirmative determinations on the others (47 FR 44818, October 12, 1983). The petition withdrawals and the termination followed upon the conclusion between the United States and the European Community of settlement agreements restricting the export of various carbon steel products from the European Community to designated percentages of the U.S. consumption and requiring EC export licensing. The text of the agreements, to be effective through December 31, 1985, was set forth in Appendix III of the *Federal Register* termination notice. The Commission likewise terminated its corresponding investigations upon the withdrawal of the petitions before it (47 FR 49104, October 29, 1983).

This part of the Law and regulations[32] also provide the extensive provisions, discussed *infra* through Subsection C.6, which permit the Secretary to suspend, rather than terminate, an investigation upon the consummation of an agreement or agreements meeting the requirements of the Law and regulations and to monitor their observance and effect. The Law authorizes two types of such agreements: (a) agreements to eliminate or offset completely a subsidy or to cease exports of subsidized merchandise; and (b) agreements eliminating injurious effect.

a. Agreements to Eliminate or Offset Completely a Subsidy or to Cease Exports of Subsidized Merchandise

Under this category, the Secretary may suspend an investigation if the government of the country in which the subsidy practice is alleged to occur agrees, or exporters who account for substantially all of the imports of the merchandise which is the subject of the investigation, agree:

(1) to eliminate the subsidy completely or to offset completely the amount of the net subsidy with respect to that merchandise exported

---

[32]Section 704, Tariff Act of 1930 (19 U.S.C. 1671c); 19 CFR 355.31.

directly or indirectly to the United States, within six months after the date on which the investigation is suspended, or

(2) to cease exports of that merchandise to the United States within six months after the date on which the investigation is suspended.

b. Agreements Eliminating Injurious Effect

Except in Section 303 cases involving dutiable merchandise, if the Secretary determines that extraordinary circumstances are present, he may suspend an investigation upon the acceptance of an agreement from the government or from exporters who account for substantially all of the imports of the merchandise, if the agreement will eliminate completely the injurious effect of exports to the United States of the merchandise which is the subject of the investigation. The agreement does not have to provide for a complete cessation of the exports of the merchandise or for a complete elimination of any subsidy. However, this category of agreement must provide assurances that steps have been taken and will be maintained to eliminate the injurious effect of the sales to the United States of the merchandise under investigation. This category of agreement may be accepted only in "extraordinary circumstances" which are defined as circumstances in which the suspension of an investigation will be more beneficial to the domestic industry than continuation of the investigation (*e.g.,* because of the value of settling the case quickly or the certainty of prompt relief which the settlement provides) and the case is "complex," for example, due to the large number of subsidy practices, the complexity of such practices, the novelty of the issues raised, or the large number of exporters involved.

The Law states the agreement must, except in the case of an agreement by a foreign government to restrict the volume of imports, provide that:

(1) the suppression or undercutting of price levels of domestic products by imports of the merchandise under investigation will be prevented; and

(2) at least 85 percent of the net subsidy will be offset.

c. Quantitative Restriction Agreements

Under the second category of agreement, the Secretary may accept an agreement by a foreign government to restrict the volume of imports of the merchandise which is the subject of the investigation, but the Secretary may not accept such an agreement with exporters. Under the special rules for quantitative restriction agreements added by Section 604 of the 1984 Amendments, such an agreement may not be accepted by the Secretary without consultations with potentially affected U.S. domestic producers, workers, and consuming industries, and a public interest determination based upon the same criteria as set out above for terminations based on quantitative restrictions.

d. Conditions for Acceptance of an Agreement to Suspend

The Law and regulations (19 CFR 355.31(h)) provide that the Secretary shall not accept an agreement to suspend an investigation unless he has:

(1) consulted with the petitioner and notified all parties to the proceeding and the Commission not less than 30 days prior to the suspension;

(2) provided a copy of the proposed agreement to the petitioner at the time of notification together with an explanation of how the agreement will be carried out and enforced and of how the agreement will meet the requirements of the Law; and

(3) permitted all parties to the investigation to submit comments and information for the record before the date of suspension.

In addition, the Secretary must not accept an agreement unless he is satisfied that suspension of the investigation is in the public interest, and that effective monitoring of the agreement by the United States is practicable. The Law further provides that an agreement eliminating injurious effects may not be accepted unless that agreement provides a means of ensuring that the quantity of the merchandise covered by that agreement exported to the United States during the period provided for elimination or offset of the subsidy or cessation of exports does not exceed the quantity of such merchandise exported to the United States during the most recent representative period determined by the Secretary.

When during the course of an investigation the subsidizing government eliminates the subsidy of its own accord and without negotiations, the ITA is required by the statute to suspend the investigation when suspension serves the interest of the public and the domestic industry affected, and follow suspension procedures, and may not decide instead to reach an immediate negative subsidy determination. *U.S. Steel Corporation* v. *United States,* 5 CIT 245, 566 F. Supp. 1529 (1983) 4 ITRD 2021.

3. Effect of Suspension of an Investigation

When the Secretary suspends an investigation he shall publish notice of that fact in the *Federal Register* and simultaneously issue and publish an affirmative preliminary determination with respect to the merchandise subject to the investigation unless such an affirmative preliminary determination has already been issued. Once an agreement to suspend is accepted, both the Secretary and the Commission shall suspend their investigations.

If the agreement is one of those described in the first category above, *i.e.,* one which provides for the elimination of all subsidies or the cessation of all exports, there shall be no suspension of liquidation. If the liquidation of entries has already been suspended, the suspension shall be terminated on the date of the notice of suspension and estimated countervailing duties shall be required and any bond or other security released.

If the agreement to suspend an investigation is in the second category above, *i.e.,* an agreement to eliminate injurious effects, the liquidation of entries will be or continue to be suspended but the security may be adjusted to reflect the agreement.

In practice the Secretary publishes the text of the suspension agreement in the notice of suspension of the investigation. Between March 1981, and February 1984, 22 countervailing duty investigations were suspended under an agreement. In these cases the exporters commonly agreed to renounce the benefits of subsidies or the exporting country undertook to impose an offsetting export tax.[33]

4. Review of Agreements to Suspend Investigations

a. By the Commission of Certain Agreements

With respect to the second category of agreements described above, *i.e.,* agreements to eliminate injurious effect, the Law authorizes a review by the Commission. Within 20 days after the suspension of an investigation pursuant to such an agreement, an interested party which is a party to the investigation may file a petition with the Commission asking for a review of the suspension. Notice of this request must be given to the Secretary. The term "interested party" includes for this purpose a manufacturer, producer, or wholesaler in the United States of a like product; a certified or recognized union or group of workers representative of an industry engaged in the manufacture, production, or wholesale in the United States of a like product; a trade or business association, a majority of whose members manufacture, produce, or wholesale a like product in the United States, and, under the amendment made by Section 612(b)(2) of the 1984 Amendments in the suspension provisions, an association, a majority of whose members is composed of the foregoing domestic interested parties.

Within 75 days after the filing of the petition the Commission determines whether implementation of the agreement will eliminate the injurious effect of imports of the merchandise subject to investigation. If the Commission's determination is affirmative the agreement to suspend the investigation remains in effect, the suspension of liquidation shall terminate, and any estimated duties which have been deposited or other security which was required shall be released. If the determination is negative, the agreement is set aside and the investigation is resumed, in which case the date of the preliminary determination by the Secretary is deemed to be the date of publication of notice of the Commission's negative determination. (See 19 CFR 355.31(k).)

b. By the Court of International Trade

The Court of International Trade has held that the provision in 19 U.S.C. 1516a(a)(2) authorizing an interested party to contest "any factual findings or legal conclusions" upon which a countervailing (or antidumping) determination is based, including the determination to suspend an investigation, extends its review of a suspension to "all determinations of fact and

---

[33]Holmer & Bello, *Suspension and Settlement Agreements in Unfair Trade Cases,* INT'L L., Summer 1984.

law embodied in the preliminary determination to which it relates." *U.S. Steel Corporation* v. *United States*, 4 CIT 257, 557 F. Supp. 590 (1982) 4 ITRD 1453. This ruling was issued upon a motion of domestic steel companies for an order declaring the scope of judicial review in their challenge to the suspension of a countervailing duty investigation of carbon steel plate from Brazil. Under the agreement Brazil was to offset the entire amount of the subsidies found by means of an export tax.

5. Requests for Continuation of Investigation

Notwithstanding an agreement to suspend an investigation, it may be in the interest of interested parties that the investigation be continued in order that the questions raised in the proceeding be disposed of once and for all at an early date. Accordingly, the Law provides that the petitioner, an interested party (if a party to the investigation), or the government of the country in which the subsidy practice is alleged to occur may within the 20-day period following the date of publication of the notice of suspension request a continuation of the investigation. The request must be filed with both the Secretary and the Commission. In this case, both the Secretary and the Commission shall continue the investigation, notwithstanding the agreement. If the final determination by the Secretary or the Commission is negative, the agreement shall have no force or effect and the investigation shall be terminated. If the final determinations by both the Secretary and Commission are affirmative the agreement remains in force. No countervailing duty order shall be issued so long as the agreement remains in force, continues to meet the requirements of the Law, and the parties continue to meet their obligations under the agreement. (See 19 CFR 355.311.)

6. Violation of an Agreement

If the Secretary determines that an agreement suspending an investigation is being, or has been, violated or no longer meets the requirements of the Act, then the Secretary shall:

(a) suspend liquidation of unliquidated entries of the merchandise on the later of the date which is 90 days before the date of publication of the notice of suspension of liquidation, or the date on which the merchandise, the sale or export to the United States of which was in violation of the agreement, was first entered, or withdrawn from warehouse, for consumption,

(b) if the investigation was not completed, resume the investigation as if his affirmative preliminary determination were made on the day on which the investigation is resumed,

(c) if the investigation was completed, issue a countervailing duty order, effective with respect to entries the liquidation of which was suspended upon the determination that the agreement had been violated; and

(d) if the violation is considered to be intentional, notify the Commissioner of Customs, who shall take appropriate action; and

(e) notify the petitioner, interested parties who are or were party to the investigation, and the Commission, of his action, and publish notice of his action in the *Federal Register.*

Any party intentionally violating an agreement on the basis of which an investigation has been suspended, may be subject to the penalties for fraud provided in Section 592 of the Tariff Act of 1930. (See 19 CFR 355.32(c).)

7. Final Determination by the Secretary

As indicated under section II.B *supra,* the Secretary must make his final determination on whether a subsidy is being provided within 75 days after the date of his preliminary determination, except in two situations for which extensions are provided by the 1984 Amendments. These exceptions, for simultaneous antidumping and countervailing duty investigations and for the investigation of upstream subsidies, are set out in section II.B.9 and 10 *supra.* A final determination is made with the following considerations and effects.[34]

a. Critical Circumstances Determinations

If the petitioner has alleged critical circumstances, as indicated in section C.1.c *supra,* then an affirmative determination must also contain a finding as to whether:

(1) the subsidy is inconsistent with the International Agreement, and

(2) there have been massive imports of the merchandise over a relatively short period.

The 1984 Amendments in Section 605(a) make it clear that under an affirmative critical circumstances determination the suspension of liquidation shall apply to all unliquidated entries entered, or withdrawn from warehouse, for consumption on or after the date which is 90 days before the date on which suspension of liquidation is first ordered, regardless of whether or not the preliminary determination was affirmative and, if so, even if the preliminary critical circumstances determination was negative.

b. Effect of Secretary's Final Determination

If the Secretary's final determination is negative, it is published in the *Federal Register,* the Commission is notified, and the countervailing duty proceeding is terminated. If the Secretary's final determination is affirmative, it is published in the *Federal Register,* the Commission is notified, and the Commission proceeds to make its final determination on the question of the existence, or likelihood thereof of material injury to an industry in the United States, or material retardation of the establishment of such an industry.

---

[34]Section 705, Tariff Act of 1930 (19 U.S.C. 1671d); 19 CFR 355.33.

8. Issuance of Countervailing Duty Order

Upon receipt of notice of an affirmative final determination by the Commission on the question of injury, the Secretary must within seven days publish a countervailing duty order describing the merchandise to which it applies, and directing the Customs Service to require the deposit of countervailing duties equal to the amount of the net subsidy determined or estimated to exist pending liquidation,[35] and thereafter to assess countervailing duties equal to the amount of the net subsidy determined or estimated to exist following annual review.

D. Processing by the Commission

The basic responsibilities of the Commission require determinations in Title VII cases and in Section 303 cases involving duty-free imports on questions of whether subsidies or alleged subsidies cause or are likely to cause material injury, or threat of material injury, to an industry in the United States or materially retard the establishment thereof. Policies and procedures in carrying out these responsibilities in countervailing duty cases (and antidumping cases as well) are elaborated principally in the Commission's regulations, 19 CFR Part 207. Some applicable requirements are also set forth in 19 CFR Part 201.

1. Preliminary Determination

In the first instance, it makes a preliminary determination within 45 days after the date of filing of the petition based on the best information available to it at that time as to whether there is a "reasonable indication" that an industry in the United States is materially injured, threatened with material injury, or its establishment materially retarded by imports, or sales (or the likelihood of sales) for importation, of the merchandise in question. Prior to making this determination, the Commission will afford a reasonable opportunity for presentation of views.[36]

The Commission was directed by the CIT not to weigh conflicting evidence in a preliminary determination but to accept a low threshold of evidence of a "reasonable indication" of injury, reserving the resolution of conflicting facts for the final determination. *Republic Steel Corporation* v. *United States*, 8 CIT _____ , 591 F.Supp. 640 (1984) 5 ITRD 2433.

2. Final Determination

Subsequently, after the Secretary has made a final affirmative determination as to the existence of subsidy practices, the Commission makes a final determination in accordance with the legislative directions[37] as to whether "by reason of" imports, or sales (or the likelihood of sales) for importation,

---

[35]Section 706, Tariff Act of 1930 (19 U.S.C. 1671e).
[36]19 CFR 207.15.
[37]Section 705(b), Tariff Act of 1930 (19 U.S.C. 1671d).

of the merchandise which has been subsidized an industry in the United States is materially injured, threatened with material injury, or the establishment thereof is materially retarded. If the Secretary's preliminary determination was affirmative, the Commission's determination must be made not later than the 120th day after the Secretary made his affirmative preliminary determination or the 45th day after the Secretary made his affirmative final determination. If the Secretary's preliminary determination was negative, then the Commission's determination must be made not later than the 75th day after the Secretary's affirmative final determination.

Where the Commission determines the existence of only a threat of material injury, its final determination must include a finding as to whether, but for the suspension of liquidation of entries, material injury would have been found.

If the final determination by the Secretary found the existence of critical circumstances, the final determination of the Commission shall include findings as to whether:

(1) there is material injury which will be difficult to repair, and

(2) the material injury was by reason of the massive imports of the subsidized merchandise over a relatively short period.

The Commission's regulations afford all parties to a proceeding an opportunity to present written views prior to its making a final determination on the injury questions. Under the Law and regulations a hearing will also be held upon the request of any party, or on the Commission's own motion, prior to such final determination.[38] Section 616 of the 1984 Amendments amends Title VII to require a hearing during an investigation upon the request of any party to the investigation with the exception that if antidumping and countervailing duty investigations are initiated within 6 months of each other (and before a final determination is made in either) with respect to the same merchandise from the same country, the Commission need not hold a hearing in the second investigation unless special circumstances exist.

A negative preliminary or final determination by the Commission terminates the countervailing duty proceeding.[39] If its final determination is affirmative it notifies the Secretary and all interested parties thereof, publishes its determination in the *Federal Register,* and the Secretary proceeds to publish a countervailing duty order.[40]

Determinations by the Commission are on the basis of a majority vote of the commissioners but provision is made for tie votes.[41] If the commissioners voting on a determination are evenly divided as to whether the determination should be affirmative or negative, the Commission shall be deemed to have made an affirmative determination. In this connection, when the issue before the Commission is to determine whether there is:

(1) material injury to an industry in the United States,

(2) threat of material injury to such an industry, or

---

[38] 19 CFR 207.22 and 207.23.
[39] Sections 703(a) and 705(c)(3), Tariff Act of 1930 (19 U.S.C. 1671b and 1671d).
[40] Section 705(c)(2), Tariff Act of 1930 (19 U.S.C. 1671d).
[41] Section 771(11), Tariff Act of 1930 (19 U.S.C. 1677(11)); 19 CFR 207.9.

(3) material retardation of the establishment of an industry in the United States,

an affirmative vote on any of the issues shall be treated as a vote that the determination should be affirmative.

3. Definition of Industry

The Law defines industry both for countervailing duty and dumping purposes to mean "the domestic producers as a whole of a like product, or those producers whose collective output of the like product constitutes a major proportion of the total domestic production of that product," with special provisions for regional industries, related parties, and product lines.[42] In certain categories of trade, substantial proportions of the total volume may take place between parties who are "related." For example, some domestic producers may be "related" to the exporters or importers or themselves be importers of the allegedly subsidized merchandise. In these circumstances the Commission is authorized in making its determinations to exclude such producers from those included in that industry. The Law also authorizes the Commission, in appropriate circumstances, to divide the United States into two or more product markets and to treat the producers within each market as a separate industry if:

(i) the producers within such market sell all or almost all of their production of the like product in question in that market, and
(ii) the demand in that market is not supplied, to any substantial degree by producers of the product in question located elsewhere in the United States.

The Law provides that in these circumstances the Commission may find material injury, the threat thereof, or material retardation of the establishment of an industry even if the domestic industry as a whole or producers of a major proportion of the total domestic production of that product are not injured, if there is a concentration of subsidized or dumped merchandise imported into such an isolated market and if the producers of all, or almost all of the production within that market are being materially injured or threatened by material injury or if the establishment of an industry is being materially retarded by reason of the subsidized or dumped imports.

The Commission found, for example, that the fishermen and fish processors in the Northeastern States constituted a regional industry, under the two criteria quoted above, against which the effects of the subsidized fish products from Canadian Atlantic sources should be measured; however, the Commission found no injury from the imports to the regional or national industry. *Fish, Fresh, Chilled or Frozen from Canada,* 701-TA-40 (Final) May 1980, 2 ITRD 5301.

If available data permit the separate identification of production of a like product in terms of production process or producer's profits, the effect of subsidized imports shall be judged on this basis. If not, the effect "shall be assessed by the examination of the production of the narrowest group or

---

[42] Section 771(4), Tariff Act of 1930 (19 U.S.C. 1677(4)).

range of products, which includes a like product, for which information can be provided." Only one domestic product, a projected commuter airplane of a particular capacity and capability, was found by the Commission, after a market survey, to be a "like product" to the allegedly subsidized projected foreign commuter planes. *Certain Commuter Airplanes from France and Italy,* Inv. 701-TA-174, 175, 47 FR 31632, July 21, 1982, 4 ITRD 1366, finding no reasonable indication of injury.

A temporary exception to the definition of industry was added to Title VII by Section 612(a)(1) of the 1984 Amendments at the behest of the U.S. grape producers. The amendment provides that in the case of wine and grape products the domestic "industry" includes domestic producers of the principal raw agricultural product included in the like domestic product. Section 626(c) of the 1984 Amendments imposed a two-year time limit for a petition to be brought taking advantage of this special provision. The amendment resulted from a determination by the Commission that grape growers could not be included in the domestic wine industry in a combined antidumping and countervailing duty investigation of imported table wine. *Certain Table Wine from France and Italy,* Inv. Nos. 701-TA-210, 211 and 731-TA-167, 168 (Preliminary) (Pub. 1502, March 1984) 5 ITRD 2179. The Commission found that grape growers did not fit into the narrow circumstance in which agricultural producers could be combined with processors in one industry; namely, where the agricultural product was integrated into a single line of production resulting in one end product.

4. Definition of Material Injury

a. Factors to be Considered

The law prior to the 1979 Act merely required the Commission to determine (with respect to subsidized nondutiable imports) whether an industry was being "injured," etc. The present law for Section 303, as well as Title VII, cases changes the concept to "material injury" or threat thereof or "material retardation" of the establishment of an industry. The Law defines material injury as "harm which is not inconsequential, immaterial, or unimportant" and requires the Commission in making its determinations to consider, among other factors:

> (i) the volume of imports of the merchandise which is the subject of the investigation,
> (ii) the effect of imports of that merchandise on prices in the United States for like products, and
> (iii) the impact of imports of such merchandise on domestic producers of a like product.[43]

The Administrative Statement points out that the Law does not require the Commission in making its determinations to give particular balance or weight to any one or more of the various factors affecting an industry.[44]

---

[43]Section 771(7), Tariff Act of 1930 (19 U.S.C. 1677(7)). See 19 CFR 207.26 and 207.27.
[44]Administrative Statement, H.R. Doc. No. 96-153, Part II, pp. 433, 434.

However, the statutory definition spells out how the Commission will evaluate the factors listed above.

With respect to the volume of imports, the definition states that "the Commission shall consider whether the volume of imports of the merchandise, or any increase in that volume, either in absolute terms or relative to production or consumption in the United States, is significant." In practice, the Commission found that the subsidized import of butter cookies from Denmark amounting to 0.3 percent, increasing to 0.6 percent, of the value of domestic cookie consumption (no separate butter cookie industry being found) was insufficient to cause injury to domestic cookie production, which in fact experienced price increases. *Butter Cookies from Denmark*, 701-TA-51 (Final) June 1980, 2 ITRD 5065.

As to price, the definition directs the Commission to consider whether:

> (I) there has been significant price undercutting by the imported merchandise as compared with the price of like products of the United States, and
> (II) the effect of imports of such merchandise otherwise depresses prices to a significant degree or prevents price increases, which otherwise would have occurred, to a significant degree.

The requirement that the Commission consider the existence of significant price undercutting "focuses solely on *prices* and does not mandate any *cost* analysis or adjustment of prices for cost factors" involved in the purchase of the imports. *British Steel Corporation* v. *United States*, 8 CIT _____ , 593 F.Supp. 405 (1984) 6 ITRD 1065 (emphasis in original).

A finding as to the effect of import prices may change completely from the preliminary to the final Commission determination. In the Investigation of *Plastic Animal Identification Tags from New Zealand*, 303-TA-14, the Commission found evidence of price suppression due to imports sufficient to base a finding of "reasonable indication of injury" (Preliminary) September 1980, 2 ITRD 5149; but in its final determination it concluded that the import prices which had held steady during the examined period did not seem to cause price suppression since domestic tag prices and sales continued to increase in that period. (Final) February 1981, 2 ITRD 5839.

As to the impact of imports on the domestic industry, the definition directs the Commission to

> evaluate all relevant economic factors which have a bearing on the state of the industry, including, but not limited to:
> (I) actual and potential decline in output, sales, market share, profits, productivity, return on investments, and utilization of capacity,
> (II) factors affecting domestic prices, and
> (III) actual and potential negative effects on cash flow, inventories, employment, wages, growth, availability to raise capital, and investments.

A careful examination of the foregoing economic factors caused the Commission to conclude in a series of cases that the impact of the subsidized imports did not cause injury to the affected industries because of the various healthy aspects of those industries. See *Dextrine and Starches from European Community*, 701-TA-11 and 701-TA-22 (Final) May 1980, 2 ITRD 5090; *Certain Nonquota Cheese from European Community*, 701-TA-52 (Final) June 1980, 2 ITRD 5097; *Textile and Textile Products of*

Cotton from Pakistan, 701-TA-62 and 63 (Final) July 1980, 2 ITRD 5070. Injury to the domestic industry was found in *Cotton Shop Towels from Pakistan,* 701-TA-202 (Final) February 1984, 6 ITRD 1494, in view of the declining state of the domestic industry and the impact of increasing imports.

The above-quoted list of economic factors was held by the CIT to be illustrative and not exclusive in a decision affirming the final negative determinations of the Commission in combined countervailing and anti-dumping investigations of prestressed concrete steel wire strand from four countries. *American Spring Wire Corporation* v. *United States,* 8 CIT ____, 590 F.Supp. 1273 (1984) 6 ITRD 1025, *aff'd sub nom. Armco Inc., et al.* v. *United States,* 760 F.2d 249 (Fed. Cir. 1985) 6 ITRD 2380. The Commission had found in four determinations that the domestic industry had increased production, shipments, capacity utilization, market share, etc., indicating a healthy state, despite a recent loss in profitability.

The definition of material injury in Section 771(7)(C), Tariff Act of 1930 (19 U.S.C. 1677(7)(C), was amended by Section 612(a)(2) of the 1984 Amendments to direct the Commission cumulatively to assess the volume and effect of imports from two or more countries of like products subject to investigation if such imports compete with each other and with like products of the domestic U.S. industry. This amendment appears to settle a long-standing difference of opinion among Commissioners as to whether, in simultaneous investigations of like products from more than one country, the injurious effects of the imports from the several countries involved should be cumulated.

Cumulative assessment of injury was required by the CIT in *American Grape Growers Alliance for Fair Trade* v. *United States,* 10 CIT ____, 615 F. Supp. 603 (1985) 7 ITRD 1065, reversing the ITC's negative preliminary determinations based on separate evaluation of the effects of French table wines and Italian effervescent wines in companion countervailing duty and dumping investigations.

b. Special Treatment of Agricultural Products

Further, the definition points out that, with respect to agricultural commodities, the Commission should not make a negative finding on the question of material injury or threat thereof, "merely because the prevailing market price is at or above the minimum support price." It also directs the Commission, in the case of agricultural products, to "consider any increased burden on Government income or price support programs."

c. Commission's Policy in Examining Threat of Material Injury

The Administrative Statement indicates that the Commission "will determine the likelihood of a particular situation developing into actual material injury."[45] It points out in this regard that an examination of trends will be important and cites, as examples:

the rate of increase of the subsidized or dumped exports to the U.S. market, capacity in the exporting country to generate exports, the likelihood that such exports will be to the U.S. market, taking into account the availability of other export markets, and the nature of the subsidy in question (*i.e.,* is the subsidy the sort that is likely to generate exports to the U.S.).

As it stated in its antidumping determinations, the Commission insists that a threat of material injury in a countervailing duty injury determination must be "real and imminent" and not based on "mere supposition and conjecture," *Textiles and Textile Products of Cotton from Pakistan, supra* 4.a. This standard has now been codified in Section 771(7)(F) of the Tariff Act of 1930 (19 U.S.C. 1677(7)(F)) by Section 612(a)(2) of the 1984 Amendments.

Prior to the 1984 Amendments the Law did not set out separate criteria to be considered in determinations of threat of material injury. The Commission is now directed, under the amendment of the definition of material injury in Section 771(7)(F) made by Section 612(a)(2) of the 1984 Amendments, to consider eight economic factors, among others, as follows:

(1) the nature of any subsidy involved (particularly whether it is an export subsidy inconsistent with the Agreement);

(2) increased production capacity or increased unused capacity in the exporting country likely to result in a significant increase in U.S. imports;

(3) any rapid increase in U.S. market penetration;

(4) the probability that imports will enter the United States at prices which will suppress or depress U.S. prices;

(5) any substantial increase in U.S. inventories;

(6) idle capacity in the exporting country;

(7) any other demonstrable adverse trends that indicate the probability that imports will cause actual injury; and

(8) the potential for shifting foreign production facilities from other products already subject to investigations to the particular products under investigation.

d. Causal Relationship Between Subsidized Imports and Material Injury

The Administrative Statement gives important insight into the interpretation of the statutory phrase "by reason of" in determining the causal relationship between the subsidized imports and the existence of material injury or threat thereof.[46] It states that these words

express a causation link, but do not involve a weighing of injury by reason of subsidized imports or sales at less than fair value against the effects of other factors which may, at the same time, also be injuring the industry. The injury caused by subsidization or sales at less than fair value need not be the "principal" or a "major" or "substantial" cause of overall injury to an industry. Any such

---

[45]*Ibid.* p. 434. See also 19 CFR 207.26(d).
[46]*Ibid.* pp. 434–435. See 19 CFR 207.27.

requirement has the undesirability of making relief more difficult to obtain for those industries facing difficulties from a variety of sources, although these may be precisely those industries that are most vulnerable to subsidized import competition and dumping.

The Administrative Statement points out, however, that notwithstanding the foregoing, the Commission will consider any information presented to demonstrate that the harm alleged by the petitioner is attributable to other factors such as the volume of imports not sold at less than fair value, contraction in demand or changes in patterns of consumption, trade restrictive practices or competition between the foreign and domestic producers, and export performance and productivity of the domestic industry.

In summary, it is concluded that the producer must demonstrate the positive to the Commission, that there is "the requisite causal link between the subsidization or dumping and material injury." But, the producer will not be required to demonstrate the negative, namely, that "the material injury is not by reason of such other factors as to which information has been introduced." See 19 CFR 207.27.

The understanding that the imports need not be the principal or major cause of injury but only one contributing cause has been expressed repeatedly in the ITC determinations and in the judicial review decisions. See *British Steel Corporation* v. *United States*, 8 CIT ____ , 593 F.Supp. 405 (1984) 5 ITRD 1065.

E. Collection of Countervailing Duties

Upon the issuance of a countervailing duty order, countervailing duties are to be assessed and collected on imports of the merchandise which is the subject of the proceeding in accordance with statutory directions.[47]

1. Temporary Payment of Estimated Countervailing Duties

Pending the assessment of countervailing duties, and the liquidation of entries of the merchandise, the order requires the payment of estimated countervailing duties at the same time as estimated normal duties are deposited.

The amount of the estimated countervailing duty cash deposit rate may not be reduced by the ITA outside the scope of the annual administrative review provided for in 19 U.S.C. 1675 (see section F *infra*). This was the holding of the Court of International Trade in *Ceramica Regiomontana, S.A.* v. *United States,* 5 CIT 23, 557 F. Supp. 596 (1983) 4 ITRD 1441. The court there denied an order of mandamus to require the ITA to reduce the estimated countervailing duty cash deposit rate on imports of ceramic tile

---

[47]Section 706, Tariff Act of 1930 (19 U.S.C. 1671e); Section 709, Tariff Act of 1930 (19 U.S.C. 1671h), added by the 1984 Amendments. See 19 CFR 355.36.

from Mexico by the percentage attributed to the CEDI subsidy discontinued on tile after the countervailing duty order.

2. Actual Duty Assessment

Assessment of the actual amount of countervailing duty due on the entries pending the liquidation which was suspended under the order and the preliminary determination, if affirmative, is made in the first administrative review under 19 U.S.C. 1675. Since such reviews are made under the 1984 Amendments only upon request, the ITA regulations issued under those amendments provide for automatic assessment of duties by the Secretary, if no request for administrative review is timely received, at rates equal to the cash deposits (Section 355.10(d), 50 FR 32560, August 13, 1985).

The duty assessed by an administrative review or by instruction of the Secretary serves as the amount for cash deposits of estimated duties on future entries.

3. Application of the Order

a. Firms Excluded

Any firm which in the course of the investigation was found not to have benefited from a subsidy found to have been granted to other firms may be excluded from a countervailing duty order on timely application therefor.[48] The regulations proposed June 10, 1985, provide for individual rates and for exclusion from the order of any producer or exporter that has timely made an irrevocable request for exclusion and that is found by the Secretary not to have received any net subsidies determined to be countervailable (Sections 355.21(b) and 355.22(d)).

b. Entries Subject to Assessment—General Rule

If the Commission has found threat of material injury which but for the suspension of liquidation would have led to a finding of material injury, then all entries of the merchandise in question the liquidation of which has been suspended are subject to the imposition of the countervailing duties.

c. Entries Subject to Assessment—Special Rule

If the Commission finds threat of material injury other than that described in *b supra,* or material retardation of the establishment of an industry in the United States, then only merchandise entered, or withdrawn from warehouse, for consumption on or after the date of publication of the Commission's final determination shall be subject to the imposition of

---

[48]Administrative Statement, H.R. Doc. No. 96-153, Part II, p. 409. See 19 CFR 355.38.

countervailing duties. All prior entries shall be liquidated without the imposition of countervailing duties, and the Secretary shall release any bond or other security and refund any cash deposit made to secure payment of countervailing duties with respect to such entries.

4. Over- and Under-collection of Estimated Countervailing Duties

If the amount of estimated countervailing duties collected during the period of suspension of liquidation and before the Commission's final determination is different from the amount of countervailing duty determined pursuant to the countervailing duty order it shall be:

(a) disregarded, to the extent that the cash deposit is lower than the duty under the order, or

(b) refunded, to the extent that the cash deposit is higher than the duty under the order.

Thereafter, when estimated duties are deposited, pending finally determined countervailing duties, the amount of any underestimate shall be assessed, together with interest at the rates specified by the statute from the date of entry to the date of assessment, and the amount of any overestimate shall be refunded, together with interest at the rates specified from the date of overpayment to the date of refund.[49]

The CIT had held that the provision for the payment of interest on overpayments and underpayments in 19 U.S.C. 1677g did not apply to the assessment of countervailing duties on merchandise from a country not under the Agreement. *Hide-Away Creations, Ltd.* v. *United States,* 7 CIT _____ , 584 F. Supp. 18 (1984) 5 ITRD 2152. This decision was overturned by Section 621 of the 1984 Amendments (19 U.S.C. 1677g) which expressly included Section 303 cases with Title VII cases under the interest provision and amended the date from which interest is payable to the date of publication of a countervailing or antidumping duty order under Title VII or Section 303, or the date of a finding under the Antidumping Act of 1921. On rehearing, the CIT reversed its denial of interest, without reference to the Section 621 amendment, and allowed interest for overpayments on entries made subsequent to the publication of the final affirmative countervailing duty determination in that case. *Hide-Away Creations, Ltd.* v. *United States,* 8 CIT _____ , 598 F. Supp. 395 (1984) 6 ITRD 1543.

Under Section 621 of the 1984 Amendments the rate of interest on overpayments and underpayments is the rate established under Section 6621 of the Internal Revenue Code (26 U.S.C. 6621). This rate is to be applied to overpayments and underpayments of amounts deposited on entries made on or after the date of publication of the countervailing duty order. The Customs Service construed Section 621 of the 1984 Amendments to require the compounding of interest as provided for in Section 6622 of the Internal Revenue Code, TD 85-93, 50 FR 21832, May 29, 1985.

---

[49]Section 707, Tariff Act of 1930 (19 U.S.C. 1671f). See 19 CFR 355.37.

The Customs Service announced June 7, 1985, that it would publish twice a year the rate of interest set under the statute semiannually (50 FR 23947).

5. Payment Conditions for Warehouse Withdrawal

A new Section 709 (19 U.S.C. 1671h) providing for the deposit of estimated countervailing duties as a condition for the withdrawal from warehouse for consumption of merchandise subject to such duties was added to Subtitle A of Title VII by Section 608 of the 1984 Amendments. The Section parallels Section 738 of Title VII providing identical provisions for warehoused merchandise subject to antidumping duties. The new section requires, in addition to the deposit, the furnishing of information necessary for ascertaining countervailing duties, the maintenance of required records, and agreement to pay on demand the countervailing duty imposed.

F. Administrative Review of Determinations

1. Review of Countervailing Duty Orders

The Law originally required the Secretary once during each 12-month period, beginning on the anniversary of the date of the issuance of the order under Title VII or Section 303, or of a notice of suspension of an investigation, to:

(1) review and determine the amount of any net subsidy; and

(2) review the current status of, and compliance with, any agreement by reason of which an investigation was suspended, and review the amount of any net subsidy involved in the agreement.[50] This requirement in Section 751 of Title VII was amended by Section 611(a)(2) of the 1984 Amendments to require an annual review only if a request for such a review is received.

Revised regulations under Section 751, as amended in 1984, were issued by the Secretary, 50 FR 32556, August 13, 1985, which provided final procedures for requesting reviews of periods ending prior to September 1, 1985, covered by an order, finding, or suspension agreement published before September 1, 1984, and interim-final procedures for requesting reviews of later periods. The request must be made during the anniversary month of the publication of the order or finding and must specify, with reasons, the particular manufacturers, producers, or exporters sought to be reviewed. If no timely request is received, the Secretary will instruct the Customs Service to assess countervailing duties on merchandise entered during the unreviewed period, at rates equal to the cash deposits of estimated duties, and to continue to collect the cash deposits previously ordered.

---

[50]Section 751(a), Tariff Act of 1930 (19 U.S.C. 1675(a)). See 19 CFR 355.41.

Upon completion of his review, the Secretary publishes his proposed determinations and affords interested parties an opportunity to comment thereon.

The Secretary's determination of the amount of the subsidies during the year under review must necessarily under Section 751 be retroactively applied to the imports during that year, and the liquidation of the entries covering those imports may properly be suspended pending the review under a proper interpretation of the statute placing time limitations on the liquidation of entries, 19 U.S.C. 1504. *Ambassador Division of Florsheim Shoe* v. *United States,* 748 F.2d 1560 (Fed. Cir. 1984) 6 ITRD 1422, *rev'g* 6 CIT ____ , 577 F. Supp. 1016 (1983) 5 ITRD 1531.

2. *Other Reviews Upon Information or Request*

The Secretary and the Commission are authorized to conduct a review of an affirmative determination of subsidy or injury, or a determination pursuant to an agreement whenever they receive information or a request for review which shows changed circumstances sufficient to warrant such a review.[51] For example, the Commission is authorized to consider whether, in the light of the changed circumstances, an agreement leading to the suspension of an investigation continues to eliminate completely the injurious effect of imports of the merchandise. If the Commission's determination is negative, the agreement will be treated as if it were not accepted as of the date of publication of the Commission's determination and the countervailing duty proceeding shall continue as if the agreement had been violated on that date, except that no countervailing duty shall be assessed on merchandise entered, or withdrawn from warehouse, for consumption before that date.[52] Certain agreements may not be reviewed in less than 24 months under this authority, in the absence of good cause shown.

3. *Revocation or Revision of Determination*

The Secretary may revoke in whole or in part a countervailing duty order or terminate an investigation, after review. Before doing so, he must publish a notice of his intention to revoke or terminate. Such action normally will not be considered except at the time of the review of determinations. A revocation or termination applies to unliquidated entries on and after a date determined by the Secretary.[53]

---

[51]Section 751(b), Tariff Act of 1930 (19 U.S.C. 1675(b)).
[52]Section 751(e), Tariff Act of 1930 (19 U.S.C. 1675(e)).
[53]Section 751(c), Tariff Act of 1930 (19 U.S.C. 1675(c)). See 19 CFR 355.42.

III. TREATMENT OF INFORMATION

The Law contains extensive provisions[54] relating to information developed in a countervailing duty proceeding: verification, access, and maintenance of confidentiality.

A. Verification

The Law requires the Secretary in making certain determinations to verify all information relied upon whenever possible. These determinations, as specified in the amendment to Section 776(a) of Title VII (19 U.S.C. 1677e(a)) made by Section 618 of the 1984 Amendments, are (1) a final determination in an investigation, (2) a revocation under Section 751(c), and (3) a review and determination under Section 751(a) if verification is requested by a domestic interested party and no verification was made during the two immediately preceding reviews of the same order, finding, or notice, unless good cause is shown. The Secretary is required when publishing notice of any action under (1), (2), or (3), to report the methods and procedures used to verify the information.

If the Secretary is unable to verify the accuracy of information submitted, he is authorized to use the best information available to him, which may include the information submitted in support of the petition. Whenever a party or any other person refuses or is unable to produce information requested within the time or in the manner required, or otherwise significantly impedes an investigation, the Secretary and the Commission in making their respective determinations may use the best information otherwise available.

B. Access

The Law contains extensive requirements for the maintenance of records and for providing possible access to information developed in proceedings. The Secretary and the Commission are required from time to time upon request to inform interested parties of the progress of investigations. They must maintain detailed records of *ex parte* meetings between interested parties or other persons providing factual information in connection with a proceeding and a person charged with making a determination and any other person charged with making a final recommendation in connection with the proceeding if relevent information was presented or discussed (Section 619(1) of 1984 Amendments). The record of *ex parte* meetings is part of the record of a proceeding.

Regulations governing access to, and protection of, information in countervailing duty proceedings are provided by the Secretary in 19 CFR Part 355, Subpart B, and by the Commission in 19 CFR Part 201, Subpart C.

---

[54]Sections 776, 777, Tariff Act of 1930 (19 U.S.C. 1677e, 1677f).

C. Treatment and Protection of Confidential Information

The Law contains a basic requirement that the Secretary and the Commission shall not disclose to any person (except their own officers and employees) information which is designated as confidential by the person submitting it, without the latter's consent. This restriction was amended by Section 619 of the 1984 Amendments to allow disclosure to an officer or employee of the Customs Service who is conducting a fraud investigation under Title VII.

Persons who wish the confidentiality of information submitted to be maintained are to submit a nonconfidential summary in sufficient detail to be meaningful, or a statement that the information is not susceptible to summary. Such persons must also state whether or not they agree to the release of the information under an administrative protective order, as described in section *2 infra*. The Secretary and the Commission may disclose any confidential information received in the course of a proceeding in a form which cannot be associated with, or otherwise used to identify, operations of a particular person. Of course, the Secretary and the Commission are free to disclose any information which has not been designated as confidential.

The Court of Appeals for the District of Columbia Circuit has ruled that the fact that information has been received from a foreign government in a countervailing duty investigation "in confidence" does not compel automatic classification of that information under exemption one in the Freedom of Information Act for national security matters classified under Executive Order. *Carlisle Tire & Rubber Co.* v. *U.S. Customs Service,* 663 F.2d 210 (CA DC 1980) 2 ITRD 1228. However, the court did not require the classified foreign government information to be disclosed in view of the representation by the Customs Service of identifiable damage to the national security resulting from disclosure. This conclusion was followed in *Ceramica Regiomontana, S.A.* v. *United States,* 4 CIT 168 (1982) 4 ITRD 1103.

1. Unwarranted Designation

If the Secretary or the Commission believes that the designation of any information as confidential is unwarranted and the person submitting it is unable to persuade the Secretary or the Commission to the contrary, the Secretary and the Commission may return it and such information will not be considered in the proceeding. The ITA regulations provide that the Secretary will ordinarily consider information to be confidential if its disclosure would (1) cause substantial harm to the competitive position of the person submitting the information; (2) have a substantial adverse effect upon the person supplying the information or upon the person from whom the information was obtained; or (3) impair the ability of the U.S.

Government to obtain in the future necessary information, not required by law, from the same person or others similarly situated.[55] The ITA has supplemented the regulations with a statement on proprietary information indicating the types of information usually protected or not protected. See Appendix E.

2. Limited Disclosure Under a Protective Order

The Law sets forth a procedure whereby upon application the Secretary and the Commission may make confidential information available under a protective order. The order shall contain such requirements as are deemed appropriate by the Secretary or the Commission for the protection of the information. The Secretary and the Commission are authorized to issue regulations providing for sanctions including disbarment from practice before the agency in question for violation of a protective order. The regulations of the Secretary (19 CFR 355.20) permit confidential information (other than national security information) to be made available under a protective order to an attorney or other representative in prescribed circumstances and upon a sworn statement promising nondisclosure and acknowledging the possibility of disbarment from practice before the agency in the event of a breach of the conditions of the order. The Commission's regulations provide that only independent attorneys, and not corporate counsel, economists, or other professionals, will have access to confidential information under protective order, and then only upon a showing of substantial need for such information.[56] Procedures for obtaining and releasing confidential information under an administrative protective order are described in the previously mentioned ITA publication reproduced in Appendix E.

3. Disclosure Pursuant to Court Order

If the Secretary or the Commission denies a request for confidential information under a protective order, application may be made under Section 777(c)(2) (19 U.S.C. 1677f(c)(2)) to the Court of International Trade which is empowered after notification of all parties and an opportunity for a hearing on the record to order that all or a portion of the information be made available under a protective order, setting forth sanctions for violation.

The principles governing the disclosure of exhibits to verification reports, ITA issue papers, and business correspondence with the ITA were discussed in *Jernberg Forgings Co.* v. *United States,* 8 CIT ____ , 598 F. Supp. 390 (1984) 6 ITRD 1602, directing disclosure with redactions. The Court of Appeals for the Federal Circuit advised the CIT that confidential information may not be denied to in-house counsel solely because of their status, and that disclosure to them is to be determined on the basis of the

---

[55] 19 CFR 355.19(a). The Commission regulations are similar. 19 CFR 201.6.
[56] 19 CFR 207.7, as revised, 47 FR 6182, February 10, 1982, with discussion of alternative provisions considered by the Commission.

factual circumstances in each case. *U.S. Steel Corporation* v. *United States,* 730 F.2d 1465 (Fed. Cir. 1984) 5 ITRD 1955. The court stated that this direction had no effect upon the regulations of the ICC prohibiting disclosure to in-house counsel in its administrative proceedings.

14

Quotas and Restraints

I. QUOTA ADMINISTRATION

A. Definition

A quota is a quantity control placed on imported merchandise by the Congress or by the executive branch under authorizing legislation. A quota that designates a maximum quantity of a commodity which may be imported in a stated period is called an "absolute quota." It may apply globally or to specified importations from specified countries. Another type of quota is a "tariff-rate quota" which permits entry of a specified quantity of imports from anywhere or from specified countries over a specified period at a preferential or reduced rate.

The Congress has prescribed quotas, or authorized the President to proclaim quotas, or authorized certain executive agencies to fix the amount of quotas in order to protect U.S. industry or agriculture, to safeguard the national security, to effectuate trade agreements, and, as added in the Trade Act of 1974, to stabilize the U.S. balance of payments or to provide temporary import relief.

An importer or business in any way dependent upon imported merchandise, will need to know whether the merchandise concerned is covered by a quota and, if so, for how long, what the quota terms are, and what agency administers the quota.

The existence of a statutory or proclaimed quota is shown in the Tariff Schedules of the United States Annotated (TSUSA) or in the TSUSA appendix.[1] If the quota has been fixed by the Congress, as most tariff-rate quotas and many absolute quotas are, the preferential rate and the total amounts are stated in the item in the TSUSA for the commodity covered. If the quota has been established by presidential proclamation under trade

---

[1] 19 U.S.C. 1202 (TSUS). The TSUSA is published annually, with periodic Supplements, by the U.S. International Trade Commission.

agreements legislation or under Section 22 of the Agricultural Adjustment Act,[2] the quota provision is given for the commodity in Part 2 or Part 3, respectively, of the TSUSA appendix, and reference to it is noted in the TSUSA by a footnote attached to the relevant commodity item, subpart, part, or schedule.

If the quantity control results from multilateral or bilateral agreements, information on the import restraints may appear in the TSUSA, as in the case of textiles control noted in the statistical headnotes to Schedule 3, or in the publication in the *Federal Register* of pertinent notices and regulations, as in the case of coffee quotas under the International Coffee Agreement. Quantitative restraints on imports under voluntary restraint agreements or suspension agreements, discussed in section VIII *infra,* are not reflected in the TSUSA.

B. Quotas Administered by the Customs Service

The Customs Service administers all quotas that are filled on a "first come first served" basis. This includes those quotas that are normally filled by entries made immediately upon the opening of the quota period. The customs procedure for filling such quotas on a pro rata basis is discussed *infra.* The following is a list of the commodities, identified by their TSUS numbers, subject to quotas set forth in the 1985 TSUSA, through Supplement 3, that are administered by the Customs Service:

Tariff-rate quotas
- Cattle, weighing less than 200 lbs. each (100.40).
- Cattle, weighing 700 lbs. or more each (other than dairy cows) (100.53).
- Whole milk, fluid, fresh or sour (115.10).
- Fish, fresh, chilled, or frozen, filleted, etc., cod, haddock, hake, pollock, cusk, and rosefish (110.50).
- Tuna fish (112.30).
- Potatoes, white or Irish:
  Certified seed (137.20).
  Other than certified seed (137.25).
- Whiskbrooms wholly or in part of broom corn (750.26).
- Other brooms wholly or in part of broom corn (750.29).

Absolute quotas under Section 22 of the Agricultural Adjustment Act
- Animal feeds containing milk or milk derivatives (950.17).
- Butter substitutes, containing over 45 percent of butterfat, provided for in Item 116.30 and butter oil (950.06).
- Buttermix over 5.5 percent but not over 45 percent by weight of butterfat (950.23).
- Chocolate (950.15, 950.16).
- Cheese, natural Cheddar, from Canada, made from unpasteurized milk and aged not less than nine months (950.08A, Appendix, Part 3, Headnote 3(a)).
- Ice cream (950.18).
- Milk and cream, fluid or frozen, fresh or sour (949.80).
- Milk and cream, condensed or evaporated (949.90).

---

[2]7 U.S.C. 624.

- Cotton having a staple length under 1⅛ inches (except harsh or rough cotton having a staple of under ¾ inches, and other linters) (955.01).
- Cotton (other than linters) having a staple length of 1⅛ inches or more (955.02–955.04).
- Cotton card strips made from cotton having a staple length, under 1³⁄₁₆ inches and comber waste, lap waste, silver waste, and roving waste, whether or not advanced (955.05).
- Fibers of cotton processed but not spun (955.06).
- Peanuts, shelled or not shelled, blanched, or otherwise prepared or preserved (except peanut butter) (951.00).
- Blended sirups described in Proclamation 5071 (958.10).
- Articles containing over 65 percent by dry weight of sugar described in Proclamation 5071 (958.15).
- Articles containing over 10 percent of dry weight of sugars described in Proclamation 5294, as modified by Proclamation 5340 (958.16, 958.17, 958.18).

Quotas under trade agreements legislation

- Sugars, sirups, and molasses covered by Proclamation 4941 (155.20 and 155.30).
- Motorcycles over 700 ccs covered by Proclamation 5050 through April 15, 1988 (tariff-rate quotas) (924.20).
- Certain stainless steel and alloy tool steel, covered by Proclamation 5074 through July 19, 1987 (926.00 through 926.23).

Quotas under temporary legislation

- (expired)

Quotas administered under international agreements

- Coffee from nonmember countries, under the International Coffee Agreement (see Chapter 23, section III.C.1) and ICA Act.
- Textile articles under bilateral textile agreements executed under the Multi-Fiber Arrangement (MFA) (see section IV *infra*).

The Customs Service issues a monthly report on the status of the various quotas established in the tariff schedules. The report states the total quota amount for each commodity and the amount thereof imported (as of the end of the previous month). In order to be placed on the mailing list, individuals should write to the Division of Public Information, U.S. Customs Service, Washington, D.C. 20229.

C. Quotas Administered by Other Agencies

Quotas on some commodities may be filled only on a licensing or allocation basis. This is true of a large variety of dairy products covered by quotas established by presidential proclamations under Section 22 of the Agricultural Adjustment Act, 7 U.S.C. 624, for which import licenses are issued by the Foreign Agricultural Service of the Department of Agriculture under regulations codified in 7 CFR Part 6. How these regulations work is described in section III *infra*. The quota for the free entry of watches that are the products of U.S. insular possessions, established under a formula in the TSUS explained in later paragraphs, is administered by the

Departments of Commerce and Interior. Sugar quotas are administered by the USTR and the Department of Agriculture, as described in section VII *infra.*

D. Changes Under the Trade Agreements Act

By Section 2 of Public Law 96-39, the Trade Agreements Act of 1979, 19 U.S.C. 2503, the Congress approved certain bilateral agreements on cheese, other dairy products, and meat, which affected existing quotas for these articles, and in Title VII of that Act, the Congress provided implementing legislation, as needed. This legislation affected the following quota programs.

1. The Cheese Import Program

The approved bilateral agreements resulted in a slight increase in the annual cheese import quota to 110,000 metric tons, and in quota coverage of approximately 85 percent, compared with the previous 50 percent, of cheese imports.[3] The President was directed to proclaim the new level of quotas under Section 22 of the Agricultural Adjustment Act, and the Department of Agriculture was directed to provide revised quota regulations to take effect January 1, 1980. These statutory requirements were met by the issuance of Proclamation 4708 of December 11, 1979 (44 FR 72069) amending Appendix 3 of the TSUS, effective January 1, 1980, and by the issuance December 20, 1979, by the Department of Agriculture's Foreign Agricultural Service of amended regulations covering: "Section 22 Import Quotas; Certain Dairy Products."[4] These regulations are discussed in section III *infra.*

The bilateral agreements also authorized counteractions by the importing country against cheese imports which are subsidized by the exporting country to the extent of undercutting the price of domestic products. The Act authorized the President to provide for compensatory fees against such imports or their exclusion from entry. Provision is made for findings on price undercutting by the Secretary of Agriculture and for complaints to be filed by interested parties. Before the President acts on a finding of price undercutting the USTR is to seek the elimination of the subsidy by the exporting country. Implementaion of these provisions is discussed in section III.H *infra.*

2. The Chocolate Crumb Quota

Bilateral agreements with Australia and New Zealand provided for their inclusion in the chocolate crumb quota and resulted in the increase of the U.S. quota by 2,000 metric tons.[5] Because the total quota has had a history

---

[3]Statements of Administrative Action, H.R. Doc. No. 96-153, Part II, p. 511.

[4]7 CFR Part 6, 44 FR 75594.

[5]Statements of Administrative Action, H.R. Doc. No. 96-153, Part II, p. 516.

of only partial use, Proclamation 4708 included no requirement for licensing these imports.

3. The Meat Import Law

Negotiations with meat-exporting countries resulted in bilateral agreements which required modification of the Meat Import Law of 1964.[6] Section 704 of the Trade Agreements Act implemented the agreements by amending the 1964 law to include a 1.2 billion pound minimum level of imports and to create new tariff classifications for certain types of meat. This legislation was superseded by Public Law 96-177, the Meat Import Act of 1979, which set a floor of 1.25 million pounds of meat import limitations and established a countercyclical formula to insure increased imports when domestic supplies were low and lower imports when domestic supplies were high.

Under the 1979 law the Department of Agriculture makes an estimate of meat imports before each calendar quarter to determine whether imports will exceed 110 percent of the trigger point. No restrictions on meat imports were imposed through the third quarter of 1985.

II. PROCEDURES FOR IMPORTING QUOTA GOODS

A. Importer's Eligibility

An importer wanting to import a commodity which is subject to an absolute quota or tariff-rate quota, i.e., "quota-class merchandise," needs to know how to become eligible to import the merchandise which is subject to such quota. The quotas administered by the Customs Service are governed by Part 132 of the customs regulations.[7] Under the regulations, eligibility and priority under an absolute quota are determined by the time, after the opening of the quota, when an importer formally files at the customhouse at any port of entry an entry summary for consumption (Customs Form 7501) or a document for the withdrawal of merchandise for consumption (Customs Form 7505) in proper form, together with a deposit of estimated duties. Eligibility and priority under a tariff-rate quota are determined the same way at the time of the opening of the quota period, but thereafter they are determined by the time of official acceptance of either document.

When these documents are filed, the customs officer notes the exact date, hour, and minute of presentation or of official acceptance, as the case may be. In the case of an absolute quota, if at the time of filing an entry summary or withdrawal document there is still an amount of the quota for the current year (or other specified period) remaining open, then it will achieve "quota priority," i.e., eligibility to import under the quota. The various ports are in close communication with customs headquarters as the time approaches when the quota nears capacity. At that time the

---

[6]78 Stat. 594, 19 U.S.C. 1202 note.
[7]19 CFR Part 132.

Commissioner of Customs may require that his approval be obtained before an entry summary or withdrawal for consumption is officially accepted. When the quota is filled an announcement is made to that effect. Thereafter in the case of an absolute quota, no imports of the commodity in question may be permitted until the opening of the next quota period. In the case of a tariff-rate quota, any entries or withdrawals filed after the closing of the quota are subject to the higher (nonquota) rate of duty. Merchandise imported in excess of either type of quota may be held for the opening of the next quota period by placing it in a foreign trade zone or by entering it for warehouse, or it may be exported or destroyed under customs supervision.

B. Special Procedures for Heavy Demand Quotas

The demand for imports under some quotas is so great in comparison to the quota amount that the quotas are filled almost immediately after they are opened. Where this situation exists or is expected, Customs provides that no entry summary or withdrawal for consumption may be accepted at any port before 12:00 noon, Eastern Standard Time, on the opening date (19 CFR 132.12). Special arrangements are made so that all importers may be present at that time and present their entry summary or withdrawal documents. In this situation under the regulations all such documents are considered to have been presented simultaneously. If the total exceeds the amount of the quota, then the Commissioner of Customs prorates the amount that each importer will be allocated against the total quota quantity so that each importer filing an entry summary or withdrawal document upon the opening of the quota will receive his fair share. The pro rata basis is the ratio between the quota quantity and the total quantity offered for entry.

After the opening day of a quota period Customs determines quota priority and quota status on the basis of the local time at the ports of entry at which entry summaries and warehouse withdrawals for consumption of quota class merchandise are presented or accepted. This procedure was made clear in a change of position statement, TD 78-228, made effective September 5, 1978, and published July 6, 1978.

C. Release and Rate of Duty Date

Merchandise subject to an absolute quota may not be released under the immediate delivery procedure unless it is perishable merchandise of a class approved by headquarters or headquarters has otherwise authorized the release. The general rule resulted from a clarification of 19 CFR 132.13 issued October 8, 1981, TD 81-260. The release must await the presentation of the entry summary. In the case of tariff-rate quota merchandise, it is possible to obtain a permit of delivery prior to a determination of quota status but only if estimated duties are deposited at the overquota rate of duty, and an appropriate bond is filed (19 CFR 142.21(e)). In this case, if it is subsequently determined that the entry has quota status, the excess duties which have been deposited are refunded.

The date for determination of the rate of duty is the date when the completed entry summary is filed. CSD 82-11, 16 Cust. Bull. 688.

III. QUOTAS ON DAIRY PRODUCTS

A. Section 22 Quotas and Licenses

Pursuant to Section 22 of the Agricultural Adjustment Act as amended,[8] quota limitations are maintained on a number of dairy products the unlimited importation of which it has been determined would interfere with the operation of domestic agricultural support and other programs. These quota limitations are set forth in Part 3 of the Appendix to the Tariff Schedules of the United States. Those which are administered by the Customs Service are included among the products subject to absolute quotas listed in section I.B, *supra.* The remainder, covering butter, various types of cheeses, and various dried milk products are administered under a licensing system by the Dairy, Livestock and Poultry Division, Foreign Agricultural Service, U.S. Department of Agriculture, Washington, D.C. 20250. The requirements for the importation of products covered by these quotas are set forth in Title 7 of the *Code of Federal Regulations.*[9] The list of the dairy products subject to Section 22 licenses and the annual import quotas for each quota year are in Appendixes 1 and 2 to the regulations.[10]

B. Changes Under Public Law 96-39

The President was required under Public Law 96-39, as explained in section I.D *supra,* to proclaim new country quotas on cheeses covered by the bilateral agreements approved by that Act. Proclamation 4708 authorized the issuance of licenses in accordance with previous procedures, designed to assure fair allocation and maximum utilization of the quotas. Consequently, the new regulations issued December 20, 1979, incorporated the existing system of licenses and provided for supplementary licenses to cover the additional quantities of quota cheese, which are listed in Appendix 2 to the regulations. Proclamation 4708 did not require licenses for the entry of three of the items covered by quotas, namely, Item 950.06 for certain butter substitutes and Items 950.15 and 950.16 for chocolate crumb. These quotas are administered on a first come, first served basis by the Customs Service.

Since the revised regulations continue the eligibility distinctions between historical and nonhistorical licenses, the following explanation of the existing system is in order. However, the former exception for "price-break" cheese is eliminated since the Act requires the total quantity of cheeses to be limited under quotas regardless of price.

---

[8]7 U.S.C. 624.
[9]7 CFR Part 6.
[10]7 CFR Part 6, Subpart-Section 22 Import Quotas, Appendixes 1 and 2.

C. Licensing Requirements

The Section 22 Quota Regulations, currently designated Import Regulation 1, Revision 7, provide that any person desiring to import an article which is subject to a quota license under Section 22 must obtain a license. There are three categories of exceptions to the licensing requirements: (1) articles imported by or for the account of any agency of the U.S. Government; (2) articles with an aggregate value not over $25 in any shipment, if imported as samples for taking orders, for the personal use of the importer, or for research; and (3) articles imported for exhibition, display, or sampling at a trade fair, or for research, if written approval of the licensing authority is obtained.[11]

D. Application for Licenses

To obtain a license, application must be made to the Head, Import Licensing Group, Dairy, Livestock and Poultry Division, Foreign Agricultural Service, U.S. Department of Agriculture, Washington, D.C. 20250. The application must specify the article subject to quota sought to be imported (including type in the case of cheese), the Part 3 TSUS Appendix Classification number, and the country of origin. Unpostmarked applications will not be approved. In applications for supplementary and nonhistorical licenses or licenses for portions temporarily reallocated, the size of the quota share desired must be stated. In addition to the license application, to participate in a Section 22 quota an importer must initially establish his eligibility.

Regulations requiring licensees to pay a license fee for each license, based upon an annual computation of the cost of administering the licensing program, were issued July 25, 1985, 50 FR 30261. Notice of the amount of the fee is to be given annually in the Federal Register.

1. Eligibility

There are two basic types of eligibility to participate in the dairy products quotas: historical eligibility and nonhistorical eligibility. Historical eligibility for license to enter quota shares of articles subject to quotas in effect as of November 20, 1978 (the effective date of Import Regulation 1, Revision 6), the adjusted quantities of which are set forth in Appendix 1, has been determined. Historical eligibility for license to enter a quota share of an article under Group II, III, or IV of Appendix 2 from a particular country of origin may be acquired only by persons eligible for a historical license to enter that article from that country under Appendix 1. Historical eligibility for license to enter quota shares of articles under Group V of Appendix 2, which articles were not subject to quota prior to January 1,

---

[11]7 CFR 6.23.

1980, is established by submitting the proof of prior imports set forth in 19 CFR 6.25(a)(2).

A portion of the quota amount for most of the specified dairy products is set aside for importers who cannot establish historical eligibility, or who have voluntarily surrendered such eligibility. If an importer is in this category, he can apply to establish his nonhistorical eligibility to import a portion of the quota amount which has been set aside for his particular group. The regulations provide that an importer must submit a notarized statement that he intends to be regularly engaged during the period covered by the license in the business of manufacturing or entering the specific articles and will maintain a *bona fide* business office within the United States; that he intends to use the specific articles entered in actual commerce and will submit proof thereof; and a certification that he is not a part of or an affiliate of any person or company eligible for an import license for which he is applying and is not an associate of any such business. Certain additional documentation is specified in the regulations.

2. Eligibility for Supplementary Licenses

As explained in the presentation of the 1979 rules in proposed form (44 FR 56944, October 3, 1979), eligibility to obtain a supplementary license will be established by meeting the same requirements for gaining nonhistorical eligibility. It will be established automatically for a given article from a given country of origin if the applicant already has historical eligibility for the same article from the same country of origin or if the licensee receives the endorsement of the government of the supplying country. Supplementary licenses will be issued on 50 percent or more of each quota listed in Appendix 2 of the regulation. Appendix 2 basically covers those portions of the Section 22 cheese quotas which are new or expanded. Appendix 1 covers the Section 22 quotas already in existence, with minor adjustments. A person with historical eligibility for a share of one of the absolute quotas, basically listed in Appendix 1, may obtain a prorated historical share of the quota for the same cheese in Appendix 2. Historical eligibility may also be established for the Swiss-type and Other cheeses listed in Group V of Appendix 2 by submitting to the Licensing Authority proof of importation of such cheeses free of quota restrictions (*i.e.,* so called price-break cheeses) during the base period July 1, 1978–June 30, 1979.

3. Other Eligibility Requirements and Provisions

Once an applicant has established eligibility to receive a license, the license will automatically be continued for subsequent quota years unless suspended or revoked, or surrendered. Eligibility to receive a license can be transferred. Thus, if an eligible company is purchased by another company, the new owner will be eligible provided the licensing authority has received satisfactory evidence that the entire dairy product business of the original eligible person has been transferred. Note, however, that if two or more companies are merged, the successor-in-interest company, with the historical eligibility of all the merged companies, shall nevertheless be considered only as one person for the purpose of determining eligibility for nonhistorical quota shares.

The allocation for a nonhistorical licensee, of course, cannot exceed the amount of the particular quota product requested in the license. The minimum annual quota share for an article is allocated as nearly as possible as shown in the Table in Section 6.26(b) of the regulations.

Subject to the foregoing, the total quota set aside will be divided proportionately among all of the eligible nonhistorical licensees.

4. Allocations to Historical Licensees

For historical licensees, the allocation of the annual quota amount was determined prior to the issuance of the current regulations. If an applicant acquired the business from a historical licensee and is actively operating it at the beginning of the quota year, then his allocation will be based on the average imports of his predecessor-in-interest.

If in the last quota year the licensee imported less than 85 percent of his authorized quota share, then in the forthcoming year his quota share will be reduced. Thereafter it will be no less than the amount of the imports during the preceding quota year. A licensee's original quota base will be reestablished if his quota share once again reaches or exceeds 85 percent of the reduced quota share during the quota year when the reduced quota share was established.

E. Limitations on the Uses of Licenses

1. Imports Pursuant to Licenses

Imports must comply strictly with the terms of the license. Thus, the article imported must be a product of the country of origin specified in the license. It must be accompanied by a through bill of lading from the country of origin named in the license, and it may be entered or withdrawn from warehouse only in the name of the licensee. The quantity entered must be charged against the license in effect on the date of entry.

An importer can sell part of his quota share of the product which is in transit but only if the transferee has a valid license to import the quota product in question and produces a properly endorsed through bill of lading and a certified copy of the bill of sale from the original consignee showing the amount paid and the date of purchase. For other details on requirements for the entry or withdrawal from warehouse of quota goods consult 7 CFR 6.27.

2. Suspension or Revocation

A licensee's eligibility to import quota shares may be suspended if he fails to import in any two consecutive quota years or three nonconsecutive quota years within a five-year period, or may be revoked if he violates the terms of his license or of the regulations.

If a quota article is imported contrary to the regulations, it may be charged against any import license that the importer holds or that may be issued to him in the future. Of course, for violations of the regulations or any provision of a license an importer may be subject to civil or criminal action. If the Licensing Authority believes that the importer has violated the provisions and the regulations or has filed false or incomplete information, it may, after providing notice, withhold for a period not to exceed three years the issuance of any further licenses to that party for a quota share of an article. An importer is entitled to a hearing on any proposed suspension or revocation of eligibility for a quota share.

F. Inability to Obtain Quota Share From Country of Origin

An importer who is unable to obtain his quota share of a particular product from the country of origin specified in his license, and who submits satisfactory proof to the Licensing Authority, may be authorized to obtain his quota share from other countries specified in the appendixes to the regulations or other countries whenever countries of origin for such article are not specified.

G. Quota Information on Dairy Products

Once monthly, usually in the second week, the Customs Service issues a press release setting forth the amount of the annual quota administered by it, for each category of dairy product remaining unfilled. These releases can be obtained by writing to the Division of Public Information, U.S. Customs Service, Washington, D.C. 20229. Information concerning licenses and other matters under the jurisdiction of the Department of Agriculture can be obtained by writing to the Dairy, Livestock and Poultry Division, Foreign Agricultural Service, Room 6616 South, U.S. Department of Agriculture, Washington, D.C. 20250.

H. Price-Undercutting by Quota Cheese

In conjunction with the authority given by Title VII of the Trade Agreements Act to the President to set quantitative quotas on specified cheese, Section 702 authorized the President to prohibit entry, or to impose a fee upon importation, of any quota cheese with respect to which it was determined (1) by the Secretary of Commerce that a foreign government had been providing a subsidy, and (2) by the Secretary of Agriculture that the duty-paid wholesale price of the cheese was below the domestic wholesale price of similar cheese produced in the United States. The regulations of the Department of Agriculture to govern the presentation of complaints of price-undercutting and the determination of relative prices by the Secretary of Agriculture are set forth in 7 CFR 6.40–6.44.

The Secretary of Commerce, through the ITA, publishes an annual list of foreign government subsidies on quota cheese, with quarterly updates of the type and amount of the subsidies.

IV. IMPORT CONTROLS ON TEXTILES

The Customs Service administers import controls which are the equivalent of quotas on cotton textiles and wool and man-made fiber textiles, and products manufactured therefrom. The controls are based on directives to Customs issued by the chairman of the Committee for the Implementation of Textile Agreements (CITA) established by Executive Order 11651, March 3, 1972, amended by Executive Order 11951, January 6, 1977. The committee is composed of representatives of the Departments of Commerce (chairman), Treasury, Labor, and State. Its directives are published in the *Federal Register* and the *Customs Bulletin.*

A. Presidential Authority and International Agreements

The law governing regulation of the importation of textiles and textile products, Section 204 of the Agricultural Act of 1956, 7 U.S.C. 1854, authorizes the President to negotiate with representatives of foreign governments to obtain agreements limiting their exports of textiles or textile products and the importation of these products into the United States. The President is authorized to issue regulations governing the entry or withdrawal from warehouse of any such products, to carry out an agreement. If a multilateral agreement is concluded among countries accounting for a significant part of world trade in textiles and textile products, the President may issue regulations governing the entry or withdrawal from warehouse of materials or products covered by the agreement, including those which are exported from countries not parties to the agreement.

Under this authority, the United States sponsored and entered into the Arrangement Regarding International Trade in Textiles negotiated under auspices of the GATT in 1973 and extended in 1977, also known as the Multi-Fiber Arrangement, or MFA, 25 U.S.T. 1001, TIAS No. 7840. A Protocol extending the MFA to July 31, 1986, TIAS 10323, was agreed to by the parties to the Arrangement on December 22, 1981, just prior to its expiration.

The MFA is a multilateral agreement between the principal countries importing textiles and textiles products and most of the countries exporting these products. It provides a framework within which the importing and exporting countries may enter into bilateral agreements to assure voluntarily orderly growth in textile trade. The MFA sets forth the principles to govern the application of restraint levels in bilateral agreements and provides a definition of the "market disruption" from imports which permits the importing country to invoke safeguard measures. It also establishes a dispute settlement and monitoring procedure. The aims of the

MFA, as expressed in the 1981 Protocol, are the liberalization of world trade in textiles and textile products, the avoidance of disruptive effects in individual markets, and the furtherance of the economic development of developing countries by providing a greater share for them in world trade.

Within the MFA framework the United States has negotiated bilateral textile agreements with countries which are major textile exporters, limiting the quantity of textiles in various categories which will be exported by them annually to the United States.

The CITA directives to Customs are for the implementation of these bilateral agreements. In most cases cotton, wool, and man-made fiber textiles are covered in one comprehensive agreement. The agreements are frequently amended and extended. The texts of the agreements, and amendments thereof, are published in *United States Treaties and Other International Acts Series* (TIAS). Until recently about 75 percent of the U.S. cotton, wool, and man-made fiber textile and apparel imports was covered by bilateral textile and apparel agreements. In January through June 1985, 61 percent was covered.

The following is a list of MFA and non-MFA signatory countries with which the United States had bilateral agreements with specific restraints pursuant to 7 U.S.C. 1854, covering cotton textiles only (*) or cotton, wool, and man-made textiles as of October 1985:

Bangladesh	Haiti	Malaysia	Poland
Brazil	Hong Kong	Maldives	Romania
China	Hungary	Mauritius	Singapore
Colombia	India	Mexico	Sri Lanka
Costa Rica	Indonesia	Pakistan*	Taiwan
Dominican	Japan	Panama	Thailand
Republic	Korea	Peru	Uruguay
Egypt	Macau	Philippines	Yugoslavia

Of the foregoing, all countries were MFA signatories except Costa Rica, Mauritius, and Taiwan. Consultation agreements without specific restraints were in effect as of October 1985 with one MFA signatory, Jamaica, and with five nonsignatories: Greece, Malta, Nicaragua, Portugal, and Spain. As new agreements are reached, or agreements amended, implementing directives are published in the *Federal Register*.

B. Enforcement of Textile Restraints

In order to assist foreign governments to manage their export quotas, CITA may provide in the directive to Customs that specific textiles from a particular foreign country shall not be permitted importation unless accompanied by a visa from the foreign government. Frequently, the CITA directive will ask Customs to enforce the absolute quotas on exports from a particular country. But in other cases, the agreement relies upon the foreign government to enforce the export quotas.

1. Textile Import Program Implementation

A number of actions were directed by the President in Executive Order 12475, 49 FR 19955, May 11, 1984, to implement the textile restraint program by preventing the growing circumvention of agreement restrictions through manipulation of the country of origin designation and other import stratagems. The Order provided for the issuance of interim regulations within 120 days by the Secretary of the Treasury governing the entry or withdrawal from warehouse for consumption of textiles and textile products subject to Section 204 of the Agricultural Act of 1956. The regulations were particularly to clarify or revise country of origin rules and manipulations in warehouses prior to entry. The Order also required the Commissioner of Customs to establish a Textile and Apparel Task Force in the Customs Service to coordinate enforcement of regulations concerning textile imports. CITA was directed to provide information and recommendations to the Task Force and the Treasury Department was directed to advise CITA of investigations and of pertinent requests for rulings, and to take into consideration comments received from CITA.

2. The Interim Country-of-Origin Regulations

Under the Executive Order, the Customs Service issued interim regulations effective September 7, 1984 (TD 84-171, 49 FR 31248, August 3, 1984), mandating that "country of origin" rules be applied in determining whether imported textile or textile products were subject to any of the textile agreements. Following protests by importers and retailers, the effective date was postponed to October 31, 1984, for merchandise exported from the country of origin, as defined in the regulations, which had been sold to a person in the United States pursuant to a written and binding contract executed prior to August 3, 1984 (49 FR 34199, August 29, 1984).

The regulations were applicable to all textiles and textile products subject to Section 204 of the Agricultural Act of 1956. In general, such products, as defined in the Multi-Fiber Arrangement, are those which are either in chief value or chief weight of cotton, wool, or man-made fibers, or which contain over 17 percent by weight of wool. The regulations applied to imports of such products from any source, whether or not the source country is covered by a bilateral agreement. A definition of the terms "Subject to cotton restraints," "Subject to wool restraints," and "Subject to man-made fiber restraints" for purposes of TSUS Schedules 3 and 7 was added to the Schedule 3 headnotes by section 2(b) of Annex I of Proclamation 5365, 50 FR 36220, September 5, 1985. See Headnote 10, Supplement 3, 1985 TSUSA.

The significant and controversial feature of the regulations was the provision governing articles which consist of materials originating in one country but which have been processed in a second country. In this situation, the regulations required that the article must be both substantially transformed in the second country into a new and different article, having a separate name, character, or use, and that this transformation must have been accomplished by a substantial manufacturing or processing operation.

To determine whether there has been a substantial manufacturing or processing operation in the second country, a comparison was to be made between the article or material before the manufacturing or processing operation and the article in its condition after such operation. Criteria to be used in this determination were spelled out in the regulations. To enable the district director to determine the country of origin under these requirements, the regulations required that imports be accompanied by a declaration, as set forth in the regulations, describing the manufacturing and processing operations, the materials used, the costs involved, and identifying the countries involved. The declaration was to be prepared by the manufacturer, producer, exporter, or importer and filed with the entry.

One purpose expressed in the explanation by the Customs Service for the regulations was to overcome the decision of the CIT in *Cardinal Glove Co. v. United States,* 4 CIT 41 (1982) 3 ITRD 2428, holding that gloves assembled in Haiti from front and back glove panels made in Hong Kong could be entered without regard to the limitation in the bilateral textile agreement between the United States and Hong Kong. Assembly was not recognized in the regulations as a substantial processing operation.

To assist the determination of the country of origin of entries for immediate transportation without appraisement, the regulations originally required the presentation of the visa or export license covering the merchandise before an in-bond movement was approved. This requirement was eliminated by TD 84-207 (49 FR 38245, September 28, 1984), and in lieu thereof there was required a listing of specific information to enable the district director to determine whether or not to approve an in-bond movement or to examine the merchandise.

The validity of the regulations was upheld by the CIT against a challenge on many legal grounds by a number of importers and retailers of textile products. *Mast Industries, Inc., et al.* v. *Donald T. Regan, Secretary of the Treasury, et al.,* 8 CIT _____ , 596 F. Supp. 1567 (1984) 6 ITRD 1225. The court made a number of rulings in the areas of constitutional and administrative law important to international trade: (1) Section 204 of the Agricultural Act of 1956 was not an unconstitutional delegation of legislative power to the President, since Congress gave a clear directive to the President on the regulation of textiles; (2) The President acted within his delegated authority in directing the promulgation of regulations governing the country of origin of restricted textile imports; (3) The regulations were not arbitrary and capricious under the judicial review provisions of 5 U.S.C. 706(2)(A); (4) Review in international trade matters extended only to the decisions whether the President acted within his delegated power, whether the statutory authority was properly construed, and whether the executive action was procedurally correct; (5) The requirements in the Administrative Procedure Act for notice and public comment on regulations prior to promulgation did not apply as the defining and altering of quantitative restrictions under international agreements was an exempted foreign affairs function and, to the extent the regulations gave discretion to customs officials over transportation of imported textiles in bond, the regulations constituted an exempt general statement of policy;

and (6) The extent of permitted manipulation of imported merchandise in bonded warehouses was left to the discretion of the Customs Service under the governing statute, 19 U.S.C. 1562.

Appeals of the CIT opinion to the CAFC, *Laura Ashley, Inc.* v. *United States,* Appeal No. 85-748; *Mast Industries, Inc.* v. *United States,* Appeal No. 85-835 were dismissed February 14, 1985.

3. The Final Country-of-Origin Regulations

The Customs Service issued its final regulations relating to textiles and textile products, TD 85-38, March 5, 1985, 50 FR 8710, effective April 4, 1985. The regulations adopted all parts of the interim regulations included in TD 84-171, as amended by TD 84-207, with expansion of Section 12.130 on country of origin. There were three major amendments in this section.

The first major change was the clarification and definition of the coverage of the regulations. Section 12.130(a) was expanded to provide that coverage under Section 204 of the Agricultural Act of 1956, as amended, included the textiles and textile products which were excluded from the provisions of the Caribbean Basin Economic Recovery Act, as spelled out in General Headnote (3)(g)(iii)(C)(1) and (2), and (E), of the TSUS. This statement of coverage is intended to make clear, as explained in the preamble to the regulations, 50 FR 8716–8717, that textiles and textile products covered under the Multi-Fiber Arrangement, and consequently excluded from CBERA coverage, are covered by Section 204 of the Agricultural Act of 1956 and are covered by the final regulations.

The major difference between the final and interim regulations is the extended clarification of the meaning of "substantial transformation," which is the criterion for determining the country of origin of the imported product, if the import is not wholly the growth, product, or manufacture of a single country. Section 12.130(b) provides the basic rule requiring substantial transformation in the country designated as the country of origin. Subsection (d) provides criteria for determining substantial transformation, with examples of manufacturing or processing operations which will generally result in substantial transformation and those which will not. These examples are designed to clarify the effect of marginal processing operations, particularly those involving cutting and assembly of textile materials.

A further change in the final regulations is a requirement for a declaration to cover the importation of textiles and textile products not subject to Section 204. The form for this declaration, denominated a "negative declaration," is set forth in Section 12.130(f)(3).

4. Invoice Information to the Country of Export

The Customs Service in a notice published February 27, 1985, 50 FR 8042, announced that under the authority of Section 204 of the Agricultural Act of 1956 Customs intended to provide, through CITA, to the government of Taiwan, pursuant to their request, copies of invoices which evidenced the use of a fraudulent dual-invoicing scheme. The release of invoice copies was considered necessary in the enforcement of the bilateral textile agreement made under the Act between the United States, acting through the American Institute of Taiwan, and Taiwan, acting through the Coordination Council of North American Affairs.

C. Nature of the Bilateral Agreements

The typical bilateral agreement provides that during a specific period of time the foreign government will limit its annual exports of the textile in question to a specified aggregate expressed in square yards equivalent. This is sometimes referred to as the "restraint level." Within the aggregate or restraint level, the agreements also provide for group and specific limits. Within the specific groups there are limits by numbers of articles or square yard equivalents.

D. Flexibility Within the Agreement

Countries are typically allowed considerable flexibility in operating under the terms of an agreement, subject to annual restrictive agreements. For example, the agreements may specify that the limits for each group of commodities may be exceeded by a specified percentage in any agreement year and also that within the group limits the specific limits for particular categories may be exceeded by a specified percentage. The agreements usually provide for growth in a country's exports of textiles. Thus, in the second and succeeding agreement years they allow for increases in the aggregate, group, and specific limits. From time to time the CITA issues notices increasing the level of restraint for a particular commodity.

If a foreign country does not use up its total quota for a given year, it may carry over to the next agreement year some of the shortfall within limits specified in the agreement. Similarly, a country can exceed aggregate group and specific limits by a specified amount in an agreement year and carry back the next year. Customarily there are specific limits on certain product categories within the aggregate and group limits but not on all product categories. These latter commodities are subject to what are called "consultation levels." If a foreign government wishes to permit exports to the United States in excess of the applicable consultation level, it is required to enter into consultations and unless agreement is reached is required to limit its exports to the specified level.

E. Market Disruption Restrictions

The United States, if it believes that imports not subject to specific limits are causing market disruption in the United States, generally may under a bilateral agreement request consultations with the exporting country. If the consultations do not result in a mutually satisfactory resolution, the United States may impose a restraint level based upon the previous year's import level. These provisions enable the United States to reduce surges in textile imports in "consultation level" categories. Market disruption, as defined in Annex A of the MFA, confirmed by the 1981 extension Protocol,

> must be based on the existence of serious damage to domestic producers or actual threat thereof caused by (1) a sharp and substantial increase or imminent increase of imports of particular products from particular sources and (2) the offering of these products at prices which are substantially below those prevailing for similar goods of comparable quality in the market of the importing country.

(*Associated Dry Goods Corp.* v. *United States,* 2 CIT 51, 56, 521 F. Supp. 473, 477 (1981) 2 ITRD 1625, 1628.)

The General Accounting Office analyzed 60 market disruption statements prepared in 1981 and 1982 which resulted in import restriction consultations with foreign governments, in a study requested by the House Ways and Means Subcommittee on Trade. The GAO report, released November 4, 1983, entitled "Implementation of Trade Restrictions for Textiles and Apparel," concluded that the CITA's decision-making process for restricting imports was generally adequate but that the data used for domestic production was usually outdated, that the preliminary informal consultations exclusively with the domestic industry were justified, but that market disruption statements should be published in the *Federal Register* when a call for consultation with the exporting countries is made.

Additional criteria for restricting textile imports in categories not presently controlled, if market disruption threatened, were announced by the President in a statement released December 16, 1983. The additional criteria to be used to determine a "presumption of market disruption or threat thereof" were:

> 1. Total growth in imports in that product or category is more than 30 percent in the most recent year, or the ratio of total imports to domestic production in that product or category is 20 percent or more; and
> 2. Imports from the individual supplier equal 1 percent or more of the total U.S. production of that product or category.

For countries already under bilateral trading arrangements, the statement provided that calls for consultation would be made on any product when export authorizations issued for the particular product reached 65 percent of the negotiated formula level. The call would only be made when the chairman of CITA determined that the item was in a category with an import-to-production ratio of 20 percent or more, or in categories in which there was a 30 percent or greater increase. Items restricted under the bilateral arrangements would remain so during the life of the agreement — generally about three to six years.

F. Court Review of Textile Restraints

The Court of International Trade has repeatedly recognized its jurisdiction to review the lawfulness of restraints on textile imports imposed by the CITA. *Associated Dry Goods Corp.* v. *United States,* 1 CIT 306, 515 F. Supp. 775 (1981) 2 ITRD 1493; 2 CIT 51, 521 F. Supp. 473 (1981) 2 ITRD 1625; 3 CIT 1, 533 F. Supp. 1343 (1982) 3 ITRD 1462. *Sanho Collections Ltd.* v. *Chasen,* 1 CIT 6, 505 F. Supp. 204 (1980) 2 ITRD 1374. In

American Association of Exporters and Importers, Textile and Apparel Group v. *United States,* 7 CIT ____, 583 F. Supp. 591 (1984) 5 ITRD 1891, the court took jurisdiction of a challenge to quantitative restrictions and calls for consultations by CITA on imports from China and determined that the broad delegation of authority to the President by Section 204 of the Agricultural Act of 1956 did not violate the delegation doctrine. However, the court held that the exercise of authority by the President and the factual bases for his action were nonjusticiable. The President need only take action rationally related to the statute's objectives. This decision was affirmed by the CAFC, 751 F.2d 1239 (1985) 6 ITRD 1593.

The restricted basis for judicial review of the President's direction of the regulation of restraints under international agreements was fully restated in *Mast Industries, Inc.* v. *Regan,* 8 CIT ____, 596 F. Supp. 1567 (1984) 6 ITRD 1225, discussed in section IV.B *supra,* appeal dismissed.

The court has also reviewed the correctness of the textile category classification made by the Customs Service under the textile quotas. *The Manhattan Shirt Company* v. *United States,* 2 CIT 270, (1981) 3 ITRD 1552; 2 CIT 332 (1981) 3 ITRD 1552 and 1554; *Wear Me Apparel Corp.* v. *United States,* 1 CIT 194, 511 F. Supp. 814 (1981) 2 ITRD 1385.

However, in each of the foregoing cases the court declined to issue a preliminary injunction because of the public interest involved in not preventing enforcement, before final determination, of a quantitative restriction of general application in order to accommodate one plaintiff, particularly as such an injunction would provide the plaintiff his ultimate relief of entry of his merchandise. The court pointed out in its first *Manhattan Shirt* opinion, quoting from its first *Associated Dry Goods* opinion, that lifting of the existing restriction to permit the plaintiff's importations to enter commerce throughout the United States would create incalculable market disruption repercussions affecting third parties and the public interest (3 ITRD 1553).

G. Importer Operation Under Textile Quota System

Except in cases of quotas enforced by the Customs Service, it is difficult for an importer to operate under the textile quota system because the controls are administered by the foreign government. If an importer wishes to import a particular textile commodity, essentially all he can do is to contact a foreign supplier concerning the placement of an order and he, after checking with his government, can inform the importer whether he can obtain a license or other form of official permission to export the commodity to the U.S. importer. The Customs Service publishes a monthly press release reporting on the status of textile quotas, but only those quotas which it enforces pursuant to a request from CITA. Information on quotas can be obtained by writing to the Division of Public Information, U.S. Customs Service, Washington, D.C. 20229, and by writing to the Committee for the Implementation of Textile Agreements, U.S. Department of Commerce, Washington, D.C. 20230.

H. Correlation of Textile Categories and TSUSA Numbers

The Office of Textiles of the Department of Commerce periodically publishes a schedule of textile and apparel categories. Category numbers are assigned to various textile products for use by the United States in monitoring import shipments. The categories are correlated with the Tariff Schedules of the United States Annotated (TSUSA) in a publication regularly issued by and obtainable without charge from the Office of Textiles. The correlation is also published in the TSUSA, a publication of the U.S. International Trade Commission available from the Government Printing Office. The correlation table appears as part of the statistical headnotes to Schedule 3 — Textile Fibers and Textile Products. The statistical headnotes also provide identification of the articles containing cotton, wool, or man-made fibers which are subject to restraints under textile agreements.

Where the bilateral agreement specifies limits for particular categories of textile commodities, an importer can check the CITA or TSUSA schedule for a description of what the category numbers cover. The CITA schedule also contains conversion factors for each category for converting into square yards. Thus, for example, the conversion factor for sweaters which are sold commercially by the dozen is 36.8. This means that for the purposes of implementing bilateral agreements one dozen sweaters is deemed to be the equivalent of 36.8 sq. yd.

V. QUOTAS ON WATCHES AND WATCH MOVEMENTS FROM INSULAR POSSESSIONS

A. Quotas on Free Entry for Foreign Component Products

Historically, under General Headnote 3(a), TSUS, and Headnote 6(b) of Schedule 7, Part 2, Subpart E of the TSUS, watches and watch movements from the Virgin Islands, Guam, and American Samoa, in which the foreign components did not exceed 70 percent of their value, could be entered free of duty in a quantity not exceeding one-ninth of the annual apparent U.S. consumption of watch movements. The International Trade Commission was required to determine as of April 1 of each year the apparent U.S. consumption of watch movements during the preceding year and then to publish this figure, together with an allocation of the number of watches and watch movements which might be entered free of duty from each of the three named possessions. In a determination published April 1, 1982, 47 FR 13935, the ITC determined that the apparent U.S. consumption of watch movements for 1981 was 90,610,000 units. In its division of one-ninth that number for free entry among the possessions, more than 8,000,000 of the units were designated for the Virgin Islands.

These historical provisions were amended by Section 110 of the Omnibus Tariff Act, Public Law 97-446, enacted January 12, 1983. The amendment removed the 70 percent limitation on the foreign component value and incorporated a new regulatory system for imports of insular possession watches and watch movements having any foreign components into Headnote 6 of Schedule 7, Part 2E of the TSUS. This system placed discretion in the Secretary of Commerce and Secretary of the Interior, acting jointly, to establish a limit on the quantity of watches and watch movements with foreign components which might be entered free of duty during any calendar year subsequent to 1983. They are to determine the limit in accordance with their consideration of the best interests of the insular possessions and of domestic and international trade policy. However, the limit may not exceed the greater of 10,000,000 units or one-ninth of the apparent domestic consumption as determined by the ITC as of April 1, beginning with the first year in which watch imports from the insular possessions exceed 9 million. Presently they are substantially below that level. For calendar year 1985, the total quantity of such articles to be admitted free of duty could not exceed 5,000,000 units (50 FR 7170).

B. Division of Quotas Between Possessions and Producers

Headnote 6(f) of Schedule 7, Part 2, Subpart E, TSUS divides the total number of units entitled to free entry in 1983 among the three insular possessions, assigning not more than 3,000,000 units to the Virgin Islands, 1,200,000 to Guam, and 600,000 to American Samoa. For subsequent calendar years the Secretaries of Commerce and the Interior are to establish new territorial shares of each year's total amount, taking into account the capacity of each territory to produce and ship its assigned amounts. Limitations are put on the amount of any annual reduction for any possession, with no territory to receive less than 500,000 units.

In accordance with previous responsibilities, the Secretary of the Interior and the Secretary of Commerce acting jointly must allocate on a fair and equitable basis among producers of watches and watch movements located in these possessions the quotas for each calendar year. This has been accomplished under the joint Commerce/Interior regulations on watches and watch movements[12] which provide for the application for, and allocation and reallocation of, quotas to producers and the issuance of licenses and shipment permits. In making reallocations the Secretaries consider the best interests of the economies of the insular possessions, taking into account factors such as wage and income tax contributions. If the Secretaries determine that new entrants offer the best prospects for added economic benefits, they publish in the *Federal Register* a notice offering an opportunity for new firms to participate in the quotas.

Although Public Law 94-241, March 24, 1976, approving the convenant to establish a political union with the Northern Mariana Islands, provided that imports from the NMI should have the same treatment as those from Guam, the first action to include watches from the NMI in the allocation of quotas was the amendment of the joint Commerce/Interior regulations

---

[12] 15 CFR Part 303.

proposed July 18, 1985, 50 FR 29232. This proposal responded to a request from the NMI.

For further informaton concerning the watch and watch movement quotas, inquiries may be directed to the Statutory Import Programs Staff, Department of Commerce, or the Office of Territorial Affairs, Department of the Interior, Washington, D.C. 20230 and 20240, respectively.

VI. FUEL OIL AND PETROLEUM PRODUCTS

Pursuant to a presidential proclamation of March 10, 1959, as amended,[13] the Department of Energy (DOE) administered an elaborate system of licensing and allocation controls over the importation of petroleum and petroleum products. This system was abolished by Proclamation 5141 of December 22, 1983, 48 FR 56929, which revoked Proclamation 3279 but required continued monitoring of imports.

VII. QUOTAS ON SUGARS, SIRUPS, AND MOLASSES

A. Quotas Proclaimed Under the Trade Expansion Act

1. Proclamations Prior to 1982

Proclamation 3822 of December 16, 1967, 82 Stat. 1455, added to the TSUS as Headnote 2 of Subpart A—Sugars, Sirups and Molasses—of Part 10 of Schedule 1 a sugar importation provision which was part of the Geneva (1967) Protocol of the General Agreement on Tariffs and Trade. The Geneva Protocol was a trade agreement executed under Section 201(a) of the Trade Expansion Act of 1962, 19 U.S.C. 1821(a). Headnote 2 applied to sugars, sirups, and molasses derived from sugar cane or sugar beets as described in Items 155.20 and 155.30, TSUS. Its proviso related to the termination of the Sugar Act of 1948, then in effect, by providing that the President might, within 90 days of such termination proclaim a tariff rate or quota limitation which would give due consideration to the interests in the U.S. sugar market of domestic producers and materially affected contracting members of the GATT. Such a proclamation was issued within 90 days of the expiration in 1974 of the Sugar Act, Proclamation 4334 of November 16, 1974, 39 FR 40739, proclaiming a duty rate and an annual quota, beginning January 1, 1975, of 7 million short tons, raw value on articles described in Items 155.20 and 155.30, TSUS. The quota provisions were added to Subpart A, Part 10, Schedule 1, as Headnote 3.

Headnote 3 was modified by Proclamation 4610 of November 30, 1978, 43 FR 56869, to bring the United States into conformity with provisions of the International Sugar Agreement, 1977 (ISA). The United States was applying the Agreement provisionally, by allocation of a large portion of the

---

[13] Proclamation 3279 as repeatedly amended; see 19 U.S.C.A. 1862 annotations. See also the Department of Energy Organization Act, 42 U.S.C. 7131.

sugar import quota to certain countries which were parties to the ISA. Proclamation 4663 of May 24, 1979, 44 FR 30663, again amended Headnote 3 to authorize the Secretary of State in consultation with the Secretary of Agriculture and the U.S. Trade Representative to allocate the sugar quota among supplying countries in conformity with the ISA. In 1980 after the signing of the ISA and the passage of the ISA Implementation Act, Public Law 96-236, Proclamation 4770 of July 1, 1980, placed in the USTR authority to prescribe regulations and limitations on sugar entry in conformity with the ISA and Public Law 96-236.

2. Proclamation 4941 of May 5, 1982, as Modified

This Proclamation, 47 FR 19657, rewrote Headnote 3 to establish country-by-country import quotas on sugars, sirups, and molasses described in Items 155.20 and 155.30, TSUS, and to limit the total entered between May 11, 1982, and June 30, 1982, to 220,000 short tons, raw value. Thereafter the total amount that might be imported was to be established quarterly by the Secretary of Agriculture. The Secretary was authorized, in consultation with the USTR and the Department of State to issue regulations establishing different quota periods, to modify the allocations of quotas governing the basket category, "Other specified countries and areas," and to review the operation of the sugar quota program annually as of September 1. The USTR was authorized, after consultation with the Secretary of Agriculture and the Department of State, to modify the allocation provisions for the named countries and issue regulations governing the entry of sugar. On issuing Proclamation 4941 the President announced that its purpose was to provide protection for the domestic sugar price support purchase program established under the Agriculture and Food Act of 1981 (Pres. Docs. Vol. 18, No. 18).

On the same day the President issued Proclamation 4940, 47 FR 19657, imposing import fees on the identical articles under the authority of Section 22 of the Agriculture Adjustment Act, 7 U.S.C. 624. Section 22 authorizes the imposition of fees or quotas to protect a domestic price support program. The validity of Proclamation 4941 was challenged by the U.S. Cane Sugar Refiners' Association on the ground, among others, that the President was not authorized to impose both quotas and fees in order to support a price support program. This contention was rejected by the Court of International Trade and, on appeal, by the Court of Customs and Patent Appeals which held that Proclamation 4941 was authorized by Section 201(a) of the Trade Expansion Act of 1962 and, consequently, the court would not examine the motive or purpose of the Presidential action. *U.S. Cane Sugar Refiners' Association* v. *Block,* 3 CIT 196, 544 F. Supp. 883 (1982) 3 ITRD 1963, *aff'd,* 69 CCPA 172, 683 F.2d 399 (1982) 3 ITRD 2121.

The need for Presidential action under Section 22 of the Agriculture Adjustment Act was confirmed by the International Trade Commission in its report to the President on Sugar, Inv. No. 22-45, 47 FR 26049, June 16, 1982, 4 ITRD 1226. The ITC found that sugars, sirups, and molasses provided for in Items 155.20 and 155.30 of the TSUS were being, or were practically certain to be, imported under such conditions and in such quantities as to render ineffective or materially interfere with the price support program of the Department of Agriculture for sugar cane and sugar beets. The ITC recommended that the President maintain the fee system set forth in Proclamation 4940, the duties set forth in Proclamation 4888, and the quota system set forth in Proclamation 4941 until such time as the duties and fees were again adequate to protect the price support program without the need for quotas. 19 U.S.C.A. 1862 annotations.

3. Operation of the Quotas

a. Modifications in 1982

The initial operation of the quotas under Proclamation 4941 on a first-come, first-served basis, and other aspects of the quota system were modified by issuances of both the USTR and the Secretary of Agriculture published in the *Federal Register* of August 11, 1982. These modifications included the following:

(1) Establishment of a Certificate of Eligibility system for imported sugar in order to facilitate the orderly purchasing and importing of foreign sugar. This was accomplished by the issuance of the USTR interim regulations as 15 CFR Part 2011, 47 FR 34777.

(2) Modification of the allocation provisions of the system. This was accomplished by the USTR notice, published at 47 FR 34870. The modifications included the removal of certain countries from the basket provision, the allocation to them of specific percentages, the deletion from the list of countries nonmembers of the ISA, and the inclusion of the Ivory Coast as an exporting member of the ISA.

(3) Modification of the allocation to the basket import quota for the "other specified countries or areas." This was covered by the regulations of the Secretary of Agriculture, 7 CFR Part 6, Subpart, Sugar Import Quotas, published at 47 FR 34969.

The modifications of August 11, 1982, also included the establishment of an annual quota period in lieu of quarterly periods. On September 15, 1982, the tentative annual quota for 1983 was established by the Secretary of Agriculture at 2.8 million short tons, raw value (47 FR 41407, September 20, 1982). For the 1984 sugar quota year the quota was raised to 3,052,000 short tons, raw value. For the 1985 quota year the limit was reduced to 2,552,000 short tons, raw value (49 FR 36669, September 19, 1984), and further reduced for the 1986 quota period to 1,722,000 short tons, raw value (50 FR 37887, September 18, 1985; corrected 50 FR 42198, October 18, 1985).

In his annual review of the sugar import system as of September 1, 1982, 47 FR 39223, September 7, 1982, the Secretary of Agriculture found that the program should be continued in view of the continuing imbalance between production and consumption of sugar and between foreign and domestic prices.

Similar findings were made September 1, 1983 (48 FR 40414, September 7, 1983), August 31, 1984 (49 FR 35162, September 6, 1984), and August 28, 1985 (50 FR 35588, September 3, 1985).

b. Specialty Sugars

In the *Federal Register* for June 23, 1983, the USTR and the Secretary of Agriculture published documents permitting and providing for the importation in excess of the quota of specialty sugars meeting certain criteria from 25 designated nonquota countries. The USTR Notice (48 FR 28771) determined that the importation from certain nonquota countries of specialty sugars not readily available in the United States should be permitted under Department of Agriculture certificates, and added a subparagraph of Headnote 3(c) of Subpart A, Part 10, Schedule 1, TSUS, to name the 25 countries given a quota of 80 short tons, raw value, each. USTR regulations, 15 CFR Part 2013, provided a certification system for the import of such specialty sugar (48 FR 28629). The Secretary of Agriculture issued a notice increasing the sugar quota for fiscal year 1983 to 2,802,000 short tons, raw value, to accommodate the 2,000 tons allowed for specialty sugars.

c. Proclamation 5002—Imports for Certain Exports

Proclamation 5002 of November 30, 1982, 47 FR 54269, added a further paragraph numbered (ij) to Headnote 3 of Subpart A, Part 10, Schedule 1 of the TSUS. This paragraph authorizes the Secretary of Agriculture to exempt from the quota system the entry of articles described in Items 155.20 and 155.30 of the TSUS on the condition that the articles are (1) to be used only for the production of polyhydric alcohols, except those for use as a substitute for sugar in human food consumption, or (2) to be reexported in refined forms or in sugar-containing products. Such exempt articles are to be entered under licenses issued under regulations of the Secretary of Agriculture.

Regulations providing procedures and conditions for the issuance of licenses permitting the importation exempt from quota of sugars, sirups, and molasses to be exported in refined form were published June 28, 1983, under 7 CFR Part 6, Subpart 6.100, 48 FR 29824, and enforcement provisions were tightened, 50 FR 36037, September 5, 1985. These regulations permit a refiner of sugar to import up to 28,000 short tons of sugar on the condition that an equivalent amount of refined sugar is exported within three months of the date of entry. Companion regulations, Subpart 6.200 tieing exempt imports to the export of sugar-containing products and the production of polyhydric alcohols, were issued January 25, 1984 (49 FR 3049 and 3054).

B. Quota Proclaimed Under Section 22 of the AAA

The President took emergency action on June 28, 1983, under Section 22 of the Agricultural Adjustment Act, to proclaim a zero quota on the import of certain sugars, blended sirups, and sugars mixed with other ingredients. The Proclamation, No. 5071, added to Appendix 3 of the TSUS a new Item 958.10 providing a zero quota for blended sirups provided for in TSUS Item 155.75, and a new Item 958.15 providing a zero quota for articles containing over 65 percent of designated sugars, covering articles provided for in TSUS Items 155.75, 156.45, 183.01, and 183.05.

The Proclamation was based upon a report by the Secretary of Agriculture that the covered sugar blends were being imported under such conditions and in such quantities as to render the sugar price support program ineffective, and requested the ITC to investigate the matter and report as soon as possible. The report was affirmative, USITC Pub. 1462, January 1984.

To stop entry of a blend of 65 percent or less sugar with corn sirup solids mixed solely for entry purposes the Customs Service in November 1984 required that all entered blends possess a valid commercial identity and use. A challenge to this requirement was rejected. *Arbor Foods, Inc.* v. *United States,* 9 CIT ____ , 607 F. Supp. 1474 (1985) 6 ITRD 2035.

A further Proclamation, No. 5294, of January 28, 1985, 50 FR 4187, was issued on the same emergency basis as Proclamation 5071, placing import quotas on certain other sugar-containing articles, and establishing Items 958.16, 958.17, 958.18, 958.20, 958.25, and 958.30 in Appendix 3 of the TSUS. Proclamation 5294 was modified by Proclamation 5340 of May 17, 1985 (50 FR 20881) pending the report of the ITC. The ITC instituted Investigation No. 22-48 on May 1, 1985 (50 FR 18584) to determine whether the importation of certain articles containing sugar in nine TSUS items was materially interfering with the sugar price support program. The ITC determined October 10, 1985, that most such articles were not injuring the program. USITC Press Release 85-096.

For such period as there is in effect a proclamation under Section 22 to protect the price support program for sugar the importation under the Caribbean Basin Initiative of sugars, sirups, and molasses provided for in Items 155.20 and 155.30, TSUS, is to be governed by Headnote 4 added to Subpart A, Part 10, Schedule 1 of the TSUS by Proclamation 5133 of November 30, 1983, implementing the Caribbean Basin Economic Recovery Act. Under Headnote 4 duty-free treatment shall be provided for all beneficiary countries, other than the Dominican Republic, Guatemala, and Panama, in the same manner as was provided under the General System of Preferences as of the effective date of the CBERA. However, the President may adjust upward the GSP value limitations. As an alternative treatment, the President may apply quantitative limitations on duty-free treatment for particular countries. Conditional duty-free treatment up to prescribed quantitative limits is provided for the three named excepted countries whose exports of sugars, sirups, and molasses were not eligible for GSP treatment in 1981.

VIII. NEGOTIATED IMPORT RESTRAINTS

A. Voluntary Restraint Agreements

In addition to quotas on imports formally imposed by action of the Congress or by proclamation of the President under trade legislation, which quotas are incorporated in the TSUSA, quantitative restrictions on imports are effected with respect to various key commodities through negotiations by the USTR with the countries deemed to be exporting these commodities in quantities injurious to domestic industry. These negotiations result in a Voluntary Restraint Agreement (VRA) or Voluntary Export Restraint (VER) which is enforced by the exporting country. An example of a Voluntary Export Restraint is that with Japan, initiated in 1981 and renewed through April 1985, restricting the export of Japanese automobiles initially to 1.68 million cars and subsequently to 1.85 million cars.[14] Other examples are the United States-European Community Arrangements for the restriction of certain EC carbon steel products and EC steel pipes and tubes which were reached October 21, 1982, in settlement of the 44 remaining antidumping and countervailing duty actions pending against EC steel products.

Quantitative restrictions may also be agreed upon with the exporting country involved in an antidumping or countervailing duty proceeding under the provisions for suspension agreements in the law. (See Chapters 12 and 13, section II.C.2. *supra.*)

B. Enforcement Authority

Voluntary Restraint Agreements or Voluntary Export Restraints are enforced by the exporting country. However, the Congress has provided to the President specific authority to enforce certain quantitative limitations reached in bilateral agreements through the requirement of export licenses as a condition of entry or other means of rejection by Customs of entries not within the restricted limits. A principal example of enforcement authority is that provided to the President by Section 204 of the Agricultural Act of 1956 (7 U.S.C. 1854), which authorizes him to promulgate regulations to prevent the entry of textiles covered by bilateral and multilateral agreements in excess of their limitations, as discussed in section IV *supra.*

The U.S.-EC Arrangements on Steel were supported by the enactment of Public Law 97-276 (19 U.S.C. 1626). This law authorized the Secretary of the Treasury upon receipt of a request from the President and a foreign government or customs union to require presentation of a valid export license or other document as a condition for entry of the steel mill products specified in the request. Requirements for the presentation of export certification to customs officials for EC steel subject to export licensing

---

[14] Table 7, Twenty-Seventh Annual Report of the President on the Trade Agreements Program, 1983, at 57.

were established under the Treasury and Commerce Department Agreement published in 48 FR 2488, January 19, 1983.

Further authority was given to the President by Section 805 of the Trade and Tariff Act of 1984, Public Law 98-573, 19 U.S.C. 2253 note, to enforce quantitative restrictions agreed to with steel-exporting nations by export license requirements and other means. This Section further provided with respect to the October 21, 1982, Arrangement on the export of EC steel pipes and tubes that the Secretary of the Treasury, at the request of the Secretary of Commerce after his finding of excessive imports under the Arrangement, shall take action to ensure limitation of the specified imports to the agreed restriction. Such action occurred in a November 27, 1984, directive from the Customs Service to port directors to prohibit entry of EC pipe and tube from November 29 through December 31, 1984 (1 ITR No. 21, November 28, 1984). A preliminary injunction against the ban on entry was denied. *American Institute for Imported Steel, Inc.* v. *United States,* 8 CIT ___ , 600 F. Supp. 204 (1984) 6 ITRD 1481.

Neither the enforcement authority provided in Section 805(b) of the Steel Import Stabilization Act nor any article of the United States-European Community Arrangement on the limitation of pipe and tube imports provides judicially enforceable rights for private parties. *Sacilor, Acieries et Laminoirs de Lorraine* v. *United States,* 613 F. Supp. 364, 9 CIT ___ , (1985) 6 ITRD 2441.

C. Additional Steel Import Restraints

Title VIII of the Trade and Tariff Act of 1984, entitled the Steel Import Stabilization Act, 19 U.S.C. 2253 note, authorized the President to negotiate bilateral restraint arrangements with steel-producing countries with the objective of containing the foreign share of the domestic steel market to the range of 17.0 to 20.2 percent, as the principal element in the development and carrying out of the national policy for the steel industry.

The national policy for the steel industry was defined by Title VIII as meaning the actions and elements described in Executive Communication 4046 dated September 18, 1984, printed as H.R. Doc. No. 98-263. As set forth in that document, the Administration rejected the types of import relief, including quotas, for carbon and certain alloy steel recommended by the ITC following an escape clause investigation, No. 201-TA-51, in order to avoid protectionism and injury to the steel fabricating and other consuming industries. The Administration undertook instead to implement a new steel policy under which the USTR would negotiate "surge control" arrangements and suspension agreements with countries whose steel exports to the United States had increased significantly in recent years to the detriment of the national economy. The USTR was also to reaffirm and to assure the effectiveness of agreements already reached for restraint levels on the export of steel, particularly the comprehensive 1982 Arrangements with the European Community, discussed *supra.*

A USTR announcement of June 4, 1985, reported 11 steel agreements signed, which in conjunction with the European Community Arrangement, provided coverage of approximately 77 percent of steel imports (2 ITR 758, June 5, 1985).

The title also authorized the Secretary of the Treasury to provide by regulation for the terms and conditions under which steel products may be denied entry into the United States.

The efforts with respect to making and strengthening bilateral agreements are to be the subject of study and periodic reports to the President and to the Congress. The continuation of the enforcement authority for an ultimate period of five years from the effective date of Title VIII, October 1, 1984, depends upon the annual submission by the President before each anniversary date of certain affirmative determinations respecting the steel industry. One necessary finding is that the major companies of the steel industry have during the 12-month period "committed substantially all of their net cash flow from steel product operations for purposes of reinvestment in, and modernization of, that industry through investment in modern plant and equipment, research and development, and other appropriate projects .... " Another determination must also assert that these companies have taken sufficient action to maintain their international competitiveness, including the production of price competitive and quality competitive products. A further condition on the continuance of the enforcement authority is the President's finding that each of the major companies has committed during the 12-month period not less than 1 percent of net cash flow to the retraining of workers. This latter requirement may be waived by the President for a noncomplying company if he finds unusual economic circumstances existing with respect to that company. The term "major company" is defined to mean an enterprise whose raw steel production in the United States during 1983 exceeded 1½ million net tons.

The President made the necessary affirmative determinations respecting the steel industry actions for the first twelve-month period, supported by a report to him by the ITC. 50 FR 40321, October 2, 1985.

D. Negotiations With Copper-Producing Countries

The Trade and Tariff Act of 1984 included in Section 247 a sense of Congress statement that the President should negotiate with the principal foreign copper-producing countries to conclude voluntary restraint agreements to effect "a balanced reduction of total annual foreign copper production for a period between three to five years." The statement was predicated on the unanimous ITC finding in Inv. No. 201-TA-52, July 16, 1984, that the U.S. copper-producing industry was being seriously injured by copper imports. HR 1520, legislation to mandate the negotiation of such arrangments, with imposition of a surcharge on imported copper if negotiation failed was reported by the House Interior Committee August 1, 1985.

15

Buy American Rules

I. SCOPE OF THE BUY AMERICAN ACT

The Buy American Act[1] requires the federal government to give preference to domestic materials and manufactures in the procurement of supplies and services and in public construction contracts. Certain other enactments require domestic procurement or prohibit procurement from certain areas abroad. The Buy American Act and its requirements are discussed first and the other provisions are discussed later in this Chapter.

A. Requirements

The first basic requirement of the Act is that only unmanufactured and manufactured articles, materials, and supplies produced in the United States shall be acquired for public use. In the case of manufactured articles the Act requires that they be produced substantially from unmanufactured articles, materials, and supplies produced in the United States.

This basic requirement has been much reduced as a result of the enactment of Title III of the Trade Agreements Act of 1979,[2] as discussed in section D *infra*.

A second basic requirement of the Buy American Act is that in the case of contracts for the construction, alteration, or repair of public buildings and public works, contractors, subcontractors, materialmen, and suppliers shall use only articles, materials, and supplies produced in the United States. The Act further provides for the blacklisting by the head of a department or agency of any contractor who has failed to comply with the Buy American requirements, with the result that for three years he shall not be eligible for any contract for the construction, alteration, or repair of any public building or public works in the United States or elsewhere.

---

[1] 41 U.S.C. 10a–10d.
[2] 19 U.S.C. 2511–2518, as added by Pub. L. No. 96-39 of July 26, 1979.

B. Exceptions and Limitations in the Act

The Buy American Act restrictions are declared not to be applicable to: (1) the acquisition of articles, materials, and supplies for use outside the United States; (2) the acquisition or use of articles which are not mined, produced, or manufactured in the United States "in sufficient and reasonably available quantities and of a satisfactory quality"; and (3) by regulation, reflecting a 1955 bilateral Memorandum of Understanding, the acquisition or use of articles, materials, and supplies mined, produced, or manufactured in the Republic of Panama (including construction materials) when purchased for use in the Canal Zone.

The Buy American Act provides that acquisition and use may be made without compliance with the Buy American restrictions if the head of the department or independent agency determines that a particular acquisition or use of domestic materials would be inconsistent with the public interest, or the cost of domestic materials in a particular case is unreasonable, or, in the case of a construction contract, the restrictions would be impracticable. This determination may be made after the contract has been awarded. *United States* v. *John T. Brady & Company,* 693 F.2d 1380 (Fed. Cir. 1982) 4 ITRD 1145.

C. Administration of the Act

On April 1, 1984, there took effect the Federal Acquisition Regulation (FAR)—issued jointly by the Secretary of Defense, the Administrator of the General Services Administration, and the Administrator of the National Aeronautics and Space Administration—setting forth the procedures and requirements for acquisition by all executive agencies, including compliance with the Buy American Act.[3] The FAR supersedes the Federal Procurement Regulations, issued by the GSA, and the Defense Acquisition Regulations, promulgated by the Defense Department. The old regulations continue to apply to procurement contracts made prior to April 1, 1984.

The governmentwide FAR is supplemented by individual agency regulations which together form the Federal Acquisition Regulations System (FARS). The FAR and the supplementary regulations are codified in Title 48 of the Code of Federal Regulations.

The FAR was extensively amended to implement the Competition in Contracting Act of 1984, Title VII of Public Law 98-369, by interim regulations (Federal Acquisition Circular 84-5) effective April 1, 1985, and published in 50 FR Part IV, January 11, 1985. Under the new provisions agencies are required to provide for full and open competition by soliciting sealed bids or requesting competitive proposals unless a statutory exception permits other action.

FAR Part 25 covers Foreign Acquisition and contains nine subparts. Subpart 1 contains the Buy American rules respecting contracts for

---

[3] 48 FR 42103, Book 2, September 19, 1983; amended, 49 FR 12972, March 30, 1984. The FAR is codified as 48 CFR Chapter 1.

supplies, and Subpart 2 those rules covering construction contracts. Other particularly pertinent parts are Subpart 4 on purchases under the Trade Agreements Act of 1979, Subpart 6 on customs and duties, and Subpart 8 on international agreements and coordination.

FAR Part 25 was amended by the interim regulations to implement the Competition in Contracting Act of 1984 to add a requirement in Section 25.402 that acquisitions of eligible products are subject to the competition requirements of Part 6 of the FAR.

D. Presidential Waivers Under International Agreements

Significant reduction of the applicability of the Buy American Act has resulted from the implementation by Title III of the Trade Agreements Act of 1979 of the Agreement on Government Procurement (AGP) and the Agreement on Trade in Civil Aircraft, which were approved among other MTN agreements by Section 2(c) of that Act.[4]. Title III implemented the AGP by authorizing the President on the effective date of the Agreement to waive with respect to eligible products of reciprocating or "least developed" countries the application of any U.S. law or regulation that treated foreign products less favorably than domestic products. Section 305 authorized the Secretary of the Treasury to provide for the prompt issuance of advisory rulings and final determinations on whether an article for import is an eligible product of a designated country. Procedures for this purpose were published January 11, 1983, as TD 83-13, 19 CFR Part 177, Subpart B.

Section 303 in Title III authorized the President to waive the provisions of the Buy American Act for the procurement of civil aircraft and related articles of a country or instrumentality which was a party to the Agreement on Trade in Civil Aircraft.

1. The Agreement on Government Procurement

The AGP, also known as the Government Procurement Code (for text see *International Trade Reporter* Reference File at 46:0801), requires its signatories (1) to administer specific procurement programs in a manner whereby eligible products and suppliers of products from reciprocating signatory countries are treated no less favorably than domestic products or suppliers; (2) to establish open or "transparent" procurement procedures; (3) to adopt common rules of procurement practices; and (4) to establish a dispute settlement procedure.

The AGP became effective January 1, 1981, pursuant to the declaration of the fulfillment of the requisite conditions made in Executive Order 12260 of December 30, 1980. The Executive Order authorized the U.S. Trade Representative to determine the signatory countries providing appropriate reciprocal government procurement opportunities, to determine the least developed countries privileged to have the benefit of the Agreement, and to

---

[4]19 U.S.C. 2503(c).

waivers with respect to 18 signatory countries and 26 least developed countries in his Determination and Waiver of January 1, 1981. This issuance also determined that the dollar equivalent for 1981 of the threshold purchase price of 150,000 Special Drawing Rights units was $196,000.

Under the FAR, Section 25.402, as amended 49 FR 12974, March 30, 1984, agencies are to evaluate offers of $161,000 or more for an eligible product without regard to the restrictions of the Buy American Act. The figure of $161,000 was the dollar equivalent determined by the USTR effective January 1, 1984 (48 FR 55790, December 15, 1983). The dollar equivalent determined by the USTR effective January 1, 1985, was $156,000 (49 FR 44959, November 13, 1984).

The current list of reciprocating or least developed countries, as determined by the USTR, is provided in 48 CFR 25.401, defining "designated country."

Aside from being limited to products from reciprocating or "least developed" countries, the waiver of Buy American Act restrictions authorized by Title III is subject to a variety of additional limitations, the most significant of which are:

(1) It applies only to the procurement of *goods.* It does not apply to government construction or service contracts.[5]

(2) It applies only to procurements made by those 53 U.S. government agencies which are listed in the Annex to Executive Order 12260. This list is set forth in 48 CFR 25.406.

(3) It applies only to purchases that exceed the dollar equivalent of 150,000 SDR units determined at least annually by the USTR and known as the "threshold for application of the Trade Agreements Act." This threshold was reduced to $50,000 for Israeli products by the U.S.-Israeli Free Trade Area Implementation Act, Public Law 99-47.

(4) It does *not* apply to the procurement of arms, ammunition, war materials, and procurements which are indispensable.

(5) It does not apply to purchases made under small business or minority business set-aside programs.

The United States did not include among the U.S. agencies covered by the Agreement certain departments and other agencies which purchase significant amounts of heavy electrical, telecommunications, and rail equipment. This withholding occurred because certain key negotiating countries, primarily the European Community, withheld their entities which were principal purchasers in these product sectors. For that reason Congress directed in Section 302(c) of the Trade Agreements Act that the USTR report to designated congressional committees on the economic effects of the refusal of developed countries to allow the AGP to cover certain government entities. On August 17, 1981, the USTR transmitted to

---

[5]The waiver can apply to services which are incidental to the purchase of goods but only if the value of the services does not exceed the value of the goods.

the congressional committees an extensive analytical report on this subject and on alternative means to obtain equity and reciprocity.

2. The Agreement on Trade in Civil Aircraft

In the President's determination of December 14, 1979, regarding acceptances of the MTN Agreements, he authorized the then Special Representative for Trade Negotiations to sign the Agreement on Trade in Civil Aircraft. Signature followed December 20, 1979.

By Executive Order 12188 of January 2, 1980, the President delegated the waiver authority conferred on him by Section 303 of the Trade Agreements Act to the USTR. On February 19, 1980, the USTR waived the requirements of the Buy American Act with respect to the procurement of civil aircraft and related articles of a country or instrumentality determined by him to be a party to the Agreement on Civil Aircraft and to be covered by such Agreement. The waiver was applied to all government agencies, in consultation with the USTR. This determination listed the countries covered by the Agreement. Subsequent determinations have added further covered countries.

In regulations published October 10, 1980, the GSA expanded its Federal Procurement Regulations on Foreign Purchases, 41 CFR Part 1–6, to cover procurement of "civil aircraft and related articles," as defined therein, under the Civil Aircraft Agreement. The FAR provisions are set forth in 48 CFR 25.104.

II. FAR BUY AMERICAN RULES

A. Supply Contracts—Procedures

1. Solicitations

The contracting officer is required by FAR 25.109(a) to insert the Buy American Certificate set out in FAR 52.225-1 in solicitations for the acquisition of supplies, or for services involving the furnishing of supplies, for use within the United States, except for acquisitions made under the Trade Agreements Act of 1979, as specified in FAR Subpart 25.4.

2. Evaluation

All offers for supply and service contracts must be evaluated in a specified manner as described in FAR 25.105. The basic rule has been that preference shall be given to domestic offers, *i.e.*, offers to supply domestic end products. If after evaluation of offers the price offered is identical between a domestic offer and an offer to supply foreign source materials, the award of the contract must be made to the domestic offer.

However, as a result of waivers authorized by Title III of the Trade Agreements Act of 1979, this evaluation process was altered, as of 1981.

Eligible products from countries which have been granted a waiver under that Act are treated as though they were domestic end products. See FAR 25.402. Thus, where used *infra,* the term "foreign offer" pertains only to an offer to supply foreign source materials that are not covered by such a waiver.

In the evaluation process the procuring agency has been required to add to the foreign offer (inclusive of duty) a factor of 6 percent, except that a factor of 12 percent is added if the firm submitting the low acceptable domestic offer is a small business concern, or a labor surplus area concern, or both. However, if an award of more than $100,000, raised to $250,000 by FAR 25.105(c), would be made to a domestic concern by applying the 12-percent factor to the foreign offer, but not by applying a factor of 6 percent, the regulations require that the matter be referred to the head of the department or agency for decision as to whether the award to the domestic offer would involve unreasonable costs. Where more than one item is submitted in response to a solicitation, the appropriate factor (6 percent or 12 percent) shall be applied on an item-for-item basis unless the solicitation specifically provides that the award is to be made on a particular group of items.

3. Mandatory Contract Clause

All contracts for supplies and for services involving furnishing supplies for use in the United States except for acquisitions made under the Trade Agreements Act of 1979, as specified in FAR Subpart 25.4, must, under FAR 25.109(c), include the Buy American clause set out in FAR 52.225-3. Principal provisions are:

(a) In acquiring end products, the Buy American Act (41 U.S.C. 10) provides that the government give preference to domestic end products.

"Components" means those articles, materials, and supplies incorporated directly into the end products.

A "domestic end product" means (1) an unmanufactured end product which has been mined or produced in the United States, or (2) an end product manufactured in the United States if the cost of its components mined, produced, or manufactured in the United States exceeds 50 percent of the cost of all its components. Components of foreign origin of the same class or kind as the products referred to in (b)(2) or (3) of this clause shall be treated as domestic.

"End products" means those articles, materials, and supplies which are to be acquired under the contract for public use.

(b) The contractor agrees that there will be delivered under the contract only domestic source end products, except end products:

(1) For use outside the United States;

(2) That the Government determines are not mined, produced, or manufactured in the United States in sufficient and reasonably available commercial quantities and of a satisfactory quality;

(3) For which the agency determines that the domestic preference would be inconsistent with the public interest; or

(4) For which the agency determines the cost to the Government to be unreasonable.

B. Construction Contracts

The basic rule is that only "domestic construction material" shall be used in the performance of contracts for construction in the United States entered into by executive departments and agencies. Domestic construction material is an unmanufactured construction material which has been mined or produced in the United States, or a manufactured construction material which has been manufactured in the United States if the cost of its components which are mined, produced, or manufactured in the United States exceeds 50 percent of the cost of all its components. See FAR 25.201.

The waivers of Buy American restrictions authorized by the Trade Agreements Act of 1979 do *not* apply to construction contracts.

1. Exceptions to Basic Rule

The regulations make certain exceptions to the requirement for the use of domestic construction materials. Such use is not required for a particular material as to which it is determined: (1) by the agency head, that to adhere to such a requirement (use of domestic construction material) is impracticable; (2) in accordance with agency procedures, that the domestic construction material is unavailable in sufficient and reasonably available commercial quantities and of a satisfactory quality; or (3) that to make such a requirement would unreasonably increase the cost. See FAR 25.202.

2. Evaluation

The FAR provides no formulas for evaluating offers. Section 25.203 states that the Buy American Act restrictions do not apply when the head of the agency determines that using a particular construction material would unreasonably increase the cost or would be impracticable.

3. Procedures

As in the case of supply and service contracts, solicitations on construction contracts require the inclusion of a standard clause regarding the Buy American Act. See FAR 25.205.

III. MILITARY ACQUISITION

A. The DoD FAR Supplement

The Department of Defense (DoD) FAR Supplement establishes uniform policies and procedures implementing and supplementing the Federal Acquisition Regulation for that Department. It is codified in 48 CFR

Chapter 2. Implementing provisions of the DoD FAR Supplement use the same part and section numbers as the FAR; thus, Part 25 of the FAR on Foreign Acquisition becomes Part 225 in the DoD FAR Supplement. Material which is new and supplementary to the FAR is promulgated with the use of the numbers 70 through 89 as new parts, subparts, sections, or subsections. Thus, Subpart 225.70 covers DoD appropriation act restrictions on foreign purchasing.

The DoD FAR Supplement supersedes the Defense Acquisition Regulations in effect prior to April 2, 1984, previously called the Armed Services Procurement Regulations (ASPR) codified in 32 CFR. The current regulations may be supplemented from time to time by Defense Acquisition Circulars.

Part 225—Foreign Acquisition, provides the DoD implementing regulations on the application of the Buy American Act to supply and construction contracts, on purchases under the Trade Agreements Act of 1979, and on other foreign purchase procedures covered by Part 25 of the FAR. It also provides special guidance for Military Assistance Program acquisition and foreign military sales, procedures to promote liaison with overseas activities, compliance with government-to-government agreements, and other uniquely military foreign acquisition concerns. Part 225 was published October 1, 1984, 49 FR 38550.

Some of the procurement for the Defense Department and its component departments and agencies is handled by the General Services Administration. Many administrative and office-type supplies are acquired from GSA stores, depots, or purchased from mandatory federal supply schedules. The departments and agencies of the Defense Department have the responsibility for compliance with the Act when they purchase a foreign end item from a mandatory federal supply schedule which includes a domestic source for that item or when they purchase a foreign end item from a nonmandatory federal supply schedule (48 CFR 225.107).

There is also a procedure within the federal government for coordinated procurement where one department may do the procuring of certain items on behalf of itself and a number of other departments (Chapter 1, Subpart 8; Chapter 2, Subpart 208). In this case, the regulations (Section 225.107) provide that compliance with the Buy American Act is the responsibility of the procuring department

except when the Requiring Department specifies a foreign end product; in which case the determination that a domestic source end product is not available, including consideration of foregoing the acquisition, or providing a U.S. substitute, shall be the responsibility of the Requiring Department.

B. Supply Contracts

The application of the Buy American Act to the acquisition of supplies is covered in Subpart 225.1. As in the case of civilian government procurement, the basic rule is that only domestic source end products shall be acquired for public use. In the case of Defense Department procurement exceptions are made for "Canadian end products" which receive specially favorable treatment (48 CFR 225.71), and for the products discussed in sections F and G *infra*.

C. Exceptions to the Basic Rule

The statute and regulations list several exceptions to the application of the basic rule: (1) The restrictions of the Buy American Act do not apply to articles, materials, or supplies acquired for use outside the United States. (2) The Act does not apply to articles, materials, or supplies of a class or kind which the government has determined are not mined, produced, or manufactured in the United States in sufficient and reasonably available commercial quantities and of a satisfactory quality. (3) The restrictions do not apply when it is determined by the Secretary of the department concerned that the cost of a domestic source end product would be unreasonable or that its acquisition would be inconsistent with the public interest. (4) The restrictions of the Act do not apply to subsistence supplies purchased for resale in domestic commissaries (48 CFR 225.102). Also excepted is scrap generated in, collected in, and prepared for processing in the United States (Section 225.108(d)).

In the case of exceptions 1 and 2 above, the required determinations may be made by the contracting officer without further approval in the following cases: (1) procurement of spare and replacement parts, if the procurement must be restricted to the original manufacturer or his supplier; and (2) procurement of foreign drugs by the Defense Personnel Support Center when the Chief of the Division of Technical Operations, Directorate of Medical Material, has determined that only the requested foreign drugs will fulfill the requirements (Section 225.102).

D. Level of Approval

The determination required for the nonavailability exception to the Buy American requirement may be made as follows: (1) at a level above the contracting officer, if the amount involved is estimated not to exceed $25,000; (2) by the chief of the contracting office concerned, if the procurement is estimated not to exceed $250,000; (3) by the head of the procuring activity or his immediate deputy or in the case of the Defense Advanced Research Projects Agency (DARPA), the director, DARPA, if the procurement is estimated not to exceed $2,000,000; or (4) by the secretary of the department concerned or his designee at a level no lower than a head of a contracting activity, if the procurement is estimated to exceed $2,000,000. The regulations require that the officer concerned, before granting such approval or making such determination, shall consider the feasibility of foregoing the requirements or providing a U.S. substitute (48 CFR 225.102).

E. Acquisition of Canadian End Items

The regulations provide for special treatment of acquisition involving Canadian end items (48 CFR 225.71). In accordance with the efforts since World War II to coordinate the economic efforts of the United States and Canada in the common defense it is DoD policy to assure Canada a fair opportunity to share in the production of military equipment and material and in related research and development. This policy requires (1) the exemption from the Buy American Act of acquisitions of supplies mined, produced, or manufactured in Canada, and (2) the insertion in Canadian contracts of provisions obtaining for DoD the same production rights, data, and information that the DoD would obtain if the Department were placing the contract with U.S. concerns.

F. Acquisition of Qualifying Country Components

Over the past several years the Department of Defense and several nations, particularly NATO countries, have concluded agreements which allow for the nonapplication of buy national laws. These countries include: (1) a foreign country which has a defense cooperation agreement and for which a Determination and Findings was made by the Secretary of Defense waiving the Buy American restrictions for a list of agreed items; (2) a foreign country which has an offset arrangement in conjunction with a Foreign Military Sale, which provides for a Buy American waiver on a case-by-case basis; and (3) a NATO country which has a Memorandum of Understanding or similar agreement under which a blanket waiver of the Buy American restrictions was made by the Secretary of Defense.

The procedures for procurement of end products from these qualifying countries are provided in Subparts 225.73, 225.74, and 225.75.

G. Acquisition Under the Trade Agreements Act

In order to implement the Agreement on Government Procurement, Title III of the Trade Agreements Act, Executive Order 12260 of December 30, 1980, and the USTR Determination of January 1, 1981, the DAR Council issued January 7, 1981, a new Part 6-1600 of Section VI, 32 CFR, which it entitled "Purchases Under the Trade Agreements Act of 1979."

Subpart 225.4 of the DoD FAR Supplement provides the regulations presently governing purchases under the Trade Agreements Act. It incorporates the FAR list in 48 CFR 25.401 of the designated reciprocating and least developed countries whose end products may be eligible for purchase by DoD (excepting the Corps of Engineers) under a Buy American Act waiver. Section 225.403 lists 99 Federal Supply Classification categories of items which may be eligible if the purchase price is above the threshold dollar amount determined by the USTR.

It should be reemphasized that waivers from Buy American Act restrictions granted under Title III of the Trade Agreements Act of 1979 do *not* extend to the procurement of arms, ammunitions, war materials, and other procurements deemed indispensable for national security or national defense purposes. However, the Department of Defense is a "covered agency" listed in Annex I to Executive Order 12260, so that such waivers from the Buy American Act, authorized as of January 1, 1981, will nonetheless extend to areas of military procurement not falling within the arms/ammunition/war materials categories.[6]

H. Buy American Procedures

1. Solicitations

Under 48 CFR 225.109 all solicitations require that each offer include a certificate set forth in 48 CFR 252.225-7000 as follows:

BUY AMERICAN–BALANCE OF PAYMENTS CERTIFICATE PROGRAM

The offeror hereby certifies that each end product, except the end products listed below, is a domestic end product (as defined in the clause entitled "Buy American Act and Balance of Payments Program") and that components of unknown origin have been considered to have been mined, produced, or manufactured outside the United States or a qualifying country:

2. Evaluation of Offers

The Secretary of Defense has made a determination establishing the use of certain formulas the application of which will result in an automatic determination as to whether the acquisition of domestic end products would be unreasonable in cost or inconsistent with the public interest. In making a comparison of offers involving domestic and foreign end items, each nonqualifying country offer (except Canadian) is adjusted as follows: (1) either exclude any duty from the price and add a factor of 50 percent of the offer to the remainder, or (2) add the duty to the nonqualifying country offer price and add a factor of 6 percent to the total. Whichever figure results in the greater evaluated price is used for purposes of comparison with the domestic offer.

In the second alternative above, a factor of 12 percent, instead of 6 percent, is added if: (1) the domestic offeror is a small business concern, or a labor surplus area concern, or both; (2) small purchase procedures are not used; or (3) an award to a domestic concern would result from applying the 12-percent factor but would not result from applying the 6-percent factor or the 50-percent factor and the contract would not exceed $100,000 (48 CFR 225.105).

---

[6]There are, however, further military procurement categories which are excluded from the coverage of the AGP and therefore from the waiver benefits of Title III as well. These excluded categories include all procurements for the Army Corps of Engineers and the federal supply classifications not listed in DoD issuance of January 7, 1981.

If under the same circumstances the contract would be more than $100,000, the regulations require the matter to be submitted to the Secretary of Defense for a determination of whether the award to the domestic concern "would involve unreasonable cost or inconsistency with the public interest." After the numerical adjustments have been made, in case of a tie between the domestic offer and the nonqualifying country offer, the domestic offer, of course, would win the award.

The regulations give a number of examples of the application of the formulas. In these examples the term "domestic offer—large" refers to an offeror which is not a small business concern or labor surplus area concern, and the term "domestic offer—small" refers to a concern which is a small business concern or a labor surplus area concern. The following are examples given in 48 CFR 225.105:[7]

EXAMPLE A

Nonqualifying Country Offer, including duty of $4,500 .... $14,500
Domestic Offer—Large 15,100
Domestic Offer—Small 15,110

Award on Domestic Offer—Large. Domestic Offer—Small is out because it is not the low acceptable domestic offer. Nonqualifying Country Offer, if adjusted by the 50-percent factor, would be $14,500 less $4,500 duty (*i.e.*, $10,000) plus 50 percent of $10,000 (*i.e.*, $5,000), or $15,000, but if adjusted by the 6-percent factor, it would be $14,500 plus 6 percent of $14,500 (*i.e.*, $870), or $15,370; therefore, the 6-percent factor is added and Domestic Offer—Large is the low evaluated offer.

EXAMPLE B

Nonqualifying Country Offer, including duty of $2,000 .... $12,000
Domestic Offer—Large 15,000

Award on Domestic Offer—Large. Nonqualifying Country Offer, adjusted by 50-percent factor, is $15,000; adjusted by 6-percent factor, it is $12,720. Therefore, Nonqualifying Country Offer is evaluated at $15,000, resulting in a tie and consequent award on the Domestic Offer—Large.

EXAMPLE C

Nonqualifying Country Offer, including duty of $3,500 .... $13,500
Domestic Offer—Large 17,000
Domestic Offer—Small 15,100

Award on Domestic Offer—Small. Nonqualifying Country Offer, adjusted by 50-percent factor is $15,000; adjusted by 12-percent factor, it is $15,120. Therefore, it is evaluated at $15,120, resulting in award on the Domestic Offer— Small.

---

[7] See Section 225.105 for additional examples.

EXAMPLE D

Nonqualifying Country Offer, including duty of $70,000 .... $270,000
Domestic Offer—Large 310,000
Domestic Offer—Small 302,000

Submit the case to the Secretary of the Department concerned. Nonqualifying Country Offer, adjusted by 50-percent factor, is $300,000; adjusted by 12-percent factor, it is $302,400; adjusted by 6-percent factor, it is $286,200. Therefore, Domestic Offer—Small is in line for possible award only because of the offeror's small business or labor surplus area status. But since the contract award would exceed $100,000, the matter requires Secretarial decision.

3. Required Contract Clause

As in the case of civilian procurement the DoD FAR Supplement requires that in all contracts for supplies (and services where applicable) there must be included a Buy American clause. The appropriate DoD clauses are provided in 48 CFR 252.225-7001 and 7002.

4. Excepted Articles, Materials, and Supplies

The secretaries of the component departments of the Defense Department have determined that certain articles, materials, and supplies are not mined, produced, or manufactured in the United States in sufficient and reasonably available commercial quantities of a satisfactory quality, or that it would be inconsistent with the public interest to apply the Buy American restrictions to the same. The list is included in 48 CFR 225.108(d). Items on the list are considered components of domestic origin "when required to be incorporated into end products or construction materials manufactured in the United States."

I. Military Construction Contracts

Subpart 225.2 implementing the Buy American restrictions with respect to military construction contracts closely parallels the regulations for civilian construction contracts described above. The basic rule is that use of domestic construction material is required. The same exception is made for materials not mined, produced, or manufactured in the United States in sufficient and reasonably available quantities and of a satisfactory quality. The same list of excepted materials mentioned above for supply contracts applies also to construction contracts. The Buy American restrictions do not apply to the use of the listed materials. The purchase of unlisted foreign construction materials must be approved: (1) by the Secretary of Defense, if the cost of such material is estimated to exceed $100,000; (2) by the head of the procuring activity, if the cost is under $100,000; (3) by the principal staff officer responsible for procurement, if the cost is $10,000 or under; or (4) by an official at a level above the contracting officer, if the cost is estimated not to exceed $2,500.

The Buy American restrictions do not apply if the Secretary of Defense determines that the use of a particular domestic construction material would unreasonably increase the cost or be impracticable. However, the procurement of nondomestic construction materials may be made under these circumstances only with the approval of the Secretary concerned.

IV. APPROPRIATION ACT RESTRICTIONS ON ACQUISITION OF FOREIGN SUPPLIES

A recurring provision in defense appropriation acts requires preference to be given to domestic articles in the procurement of food, clothing, cotton, wool, woven silk and woven silk blends, spun silk yarn for cartridge cloth, synthetic fabric, coated synthetic fabric, specialty metals, or hand or measuring tools; also a provision in Section 404 of Public Law 90-500 restricts the acquisition of foreign buses. These preferences are not affected by the waiver authority in the Trade Agreement Act of 1979. The current DoD appropriation act should be examined to determine the continued applicability of the appropriation act limitations.

The current regulations governing the interpretation and application of appropriation act restrictions are contained in 48 CFR 225.70. In a court challenge to the content and application of the predecessor regulations in 32 CFR 6.302, judicial review was held to be limited to a decision as to whether the DoD interpretation was a rational one. *Acme of Precision Surgical Co., Inc.* v. *United States,* 580 F. Supp. 490 (E.D. Pa. 1984) 5 ITRD 2486. In that case the court upheld the DoD interpretation of the appropriation act provision on specialty metals as applying only to the acquisition of specialty metals or articles made from specialty metals not melted in the United States.

A. Basic Requirement

The basic requirement is that supplies consisting in whole or in part of any of the items listed in the acts shall not be procured if they have not been grown or produced in the United States or its possessions. However, cotton or wool reprocessed or reused in the United States or its possessions and foods manufactured or processed in the United States may be procured.

B. Exceptions

The following exceptions are made to the foregoing basic requirement:
• Acquisitions outside the United States in support of combat operations.

- Acquisitions by vessels in foreign waters.
- Emergency acquisitions or acquisitions of perishable foods by establishments located outside the United States for the personnel attached thereto.
- Acquisitions of those supplies listed in FAR 25.108(d)(1) as to which the list does not make this part expressly applicable.
- Small purchases of items containing wool or cotton in amounts not exceeding $10,000. For the purposes of this exception, a small purchase in an amount not exceeding $10,000 shall mean an acquisition action involving a total dollar amount not in excess of $10,000, as distinguished from a single line item.
- Acquisitions of end items incidentally incorporating cotton, or wool, of which the estimated value is not more than 10 percent of the total price of the end item, provided that the estimated value does not exceed $10,000 or 3 percent of the total price of the end item, whichever is greater.
- Any articles of food or clothing of any form of cotton, woven silk and woven silk blends, spun silk yarn for cartridge cloth, synthetic fabric, coated synthetic fabric, or wool as to which the secretary concerned has determined that a satisfactory quality and sufficient quantity grown or produced in the United States or its possessions cannot be acquired as and when needed at U.S. market prices.
- Supplies purchased specifically for commissary resale.
- Purchases of specialty metals or any item incorporating specialty metals as to which the secretary concerned or his authorized designee has determined that a satisfactory quality and sufficient quantity melted in the United States or its possessions cannot be procured as and when needed at U.S. market prices.
- Purchases of specialty metals below the prime contract level for programs other than those for aircraft, missile and space systems, ships, tank-automotive, weapons, and ammunition.
- Purchases of specialty metals or chemical warfare protective clothing when such purchases are necessary to comply with certain agreements with foreign countries described in 225.7002(a)(11).

Where the procuring officer finds that prices for domestic supplies are unreasonable, he may refer the matter to the Secretary of Defense for determination as to whether foreign supplies should be procured.

C. Acquisition of Items Containing Wool (Except Mohair)

Special provisions in 48 CFR 225.7002(c) establish a formula for evaluating domestic and foreign bids in the acquisition of articles of wool. The formula relates to the Agriculture Department incentive prices for various types and grades of wool. In general a foreign offer, *i.e.,* an offer of an article containing foreign wool in whole or in part, will not be considered unless the average market price of domestic wools is more than 10 percent above prices which reflect the current incentive price of $.62 per pound grease basis converted to grade and type clean basis.

D. Acquisition of Foreign Buses

The purchase, lease, rental, or other acquisition of buses other than those manufactured in the United States is prohibited except where authorized by the Secretary of Defense under regulations designed to insure that compliance with the prohibitions will not result in an uneconomical procurement action or one which would adversely affect the national interest of the United States (Public Law 90-500). The regulations in 48 CFR 225.7006 authorize the use of foreign-manufactured buses where the Head of the Contracting Activity determines that the use of the U.S.-manufactured buses would be uneconomical or would adversely affect the national interest of the United States. Such a determination is not required, however, and foreign buses may be acquired in the following circumstances:

(1) When U.S.-manufactured buses are not available in time to satisfy requirements which cannot be postponed, foreign-manufactured buses may be used for a temporary period of time but not to exceed the lead time required for acquisition and delivery of U.S.-manufactured buses.

(2) When the requirement for buses is of a temporary nature to meet a special but nonrecurring requirement or where a recurring requirement is sporadic and infrequent, foreign-manufactured buses may be used for the temporary periods of time not to exceed the period of time needed to meet the nonrecurring or the recurring infrequent requirement.

(3) When foreign-manufactured buses are made available at no direct or indirect acquisition cost to the U.S. Government.

E. Acquisition of Hand and Measuring Tools

Public Law 97-377 and subsequent DoD appropriation acts provide restrictions on the acquisition of hand or measuring tools. Under 48 CFR 225.7003 the contracting officer is required to insert the Preference for Domestic Hand or Measuring Tools clause in Section 252.225-7013 in all small purchases of $10,000 or more and in all contracts for the delivery of hand or measuring tools.

V. MISCELLANEOUS

A. Acquisition for Use Abroad—Balance of Payments Program

Under a program announced for military purchases in February 1961 and made mandatory for GSA procurements in 1966 and for all civilian agencies in 1967, federal government agencies are required, in order to assist the U.S. balance of payments, to procure domestic materials for use abroad "unless the delivered cost of domestic materials is estimated to be 50 percent greater than the cost of like materials of foreign origin." However, this preferential formula is not applied with respect to foreign materials purchased under Title III of the Trade Agreements Act of 1979. The requirement does not apply to the Agency for International Development.

The balance of payments program also requires wherever feasible the use of excess foreign currencies for the procurement of articles, materials, supplies, and services for use outside the United States. When the use of such currencies is feasible, foreign articles, materials, supplies, and services can be procured.

The FAR in Section 25.3 provides for additional exceptions to the requirement of the procurement of domestic end products and services. These include:

• Where procurement is required to be made in accordance with a treaty or international agreement.

• Where the estimated cost of the product does not exceed the appropriate small purchase limitations in FAR Part 13.

• Where, in connection with the procurement of perishable subsistence items, it is determined that delivery from the United States would destroy or significantly impair their quality at the point of consumption. Such determinations shall be made by each agency in accordance with agency procedures.

• Where the agency head determines that a requirement can only be filled by a foreign end product or service, and that it is not feasible to forego filling the requirement or to provide a U.S. substitute for the requirement.

• Where procurements are paid for with excess or near-excess foreign currencies.

• Where the acquisition is for ice, books, utilities, communications, and other materials or services that by their nature, or as a practical matter, can only be acquired in the country concerned and a U.S. Government capability does not exist.

The balance of payments program in the DoD FAR Supplement, covered in 48 CFR Subpart 225.3, uses evaluation procedures similar to those implementing the Buy American Act. It incorporates, with variations and additions, the exceptions permitted under the FAR.

B. Purchases From Communist Areas

The FAR has a requirement that supplies originating from sources within Communist-controlled areas shall not be acquired for public use, and that government contractors and subcontractors shall not acquire any such supplies or services from such areas for use in the performance of government contracts (48 CFR 25.702). Communist-controlled areas are defined as including North Korea, Vietnam, Cambodia, and Cuba. The FAR in Section 25.703 and the DoD FAR Supplement in Section 225.703 implementing this general policy permit exceptions only in unusual circumstances, as in emergencies or when no suitable substitute is available, and only with the approval of the agency head concerned, except for small purchases.

C. Highway Improvement Act Buy American Limitations

The Highway Improvement Act of 1982, being Title I of the Surface Transportation Assistance Act of 1982, Public Law 97-424, January 6, 1983, prohibits in Section 169 the Secretary of Transportation from obligating any funds authorized to be appropriated under Title I, or any Act amended by Title I, or subsequently authorized to be appropriated to carry out Title I, or Title 23 (Highways) of the United States Code, the Urban Mass Transportation Act of 1964, or the Surface Transportation Assistance Act of 1978 "unless steel, cement, and manufactured products used in such project are produced in the United States." This prohibition carries the usual Buy American exception for a finding by the Secretary that (1) the application of the prohibition would be inconsistent with the public interest, or (2) that the materials are not produced in the United States in sufficient and reasonably available quantities and of a satisfactory quality.

A further exception is provided for the procurement of buses, other rolling stock, and certain support equipment where the cost of components produced in the United States is more than 50 percent of all components and final assembly occurs in the United States. Labor costs of the final assembly are not included in calculating component costs. Finally, the limitations imposed by the Secretary on assistance are not to restrict any State from imposing more stringent restrictions on the use of products of other countries on projects carried out with highway assistance funds.

16

Presidential Retaliation

I. RETALIATION AND RELIEF AGAINST FOREIGN UNFAIR TRADE RESTRICTIONS

An American producer of agricultural or manufactured goods or of services relating to international trade may encounter foreign import restrictions which prevent or limit sales of its product in one or more export markets. At the same time, producers in a foreign country which maintains these import restrictions may be benefiting from trade agreement concessions made by the United States to compete in the U.S. market, possibly in the sale of the same products whose import and sale are restricted abroad. Or a foreign country may give a tariff preference to competing products from another country. Or a foreign country may subsidize exports of a competing product to this country or to third country markets in which the American producer sells, or hopes to sell. Or a country may institute an export prohibition or limitation on a product which is essential to American business.

Title III of the Trade Act of 1974, as amended by the Trade Agreements Act of 1979,[1] contains broad authority (commonly referred to as "Section 301 authority") to enforce the rights of the United States under trade agreements, to retaliate against such restrictions and discriminatory acts and, indirectly, to provide relief to domestic producers and exporters who suffer therefrom.

The President's authority under Section 301 was extended by Section 304 of the Trade and Tariff Act of 1984, Public Law 98-573 (hereafter referred to as the 1984 Amendments), to the taking of action in response to unfair foreign practices on investment, as well as goods and services, and to the imposition of restrictions on access of foreign service firms to the United States.

Section 301 of the 1974 Trade Act was rewritten by Title IX of the Trade Agreements Act of 1979 to carry out the utilization of the consultation and

---

[1]Trade Act of 1974, Title III, ch. 1; amended by Pub. L. No. 96-39, Title IX—Enforcement of United States Rights and Section 304 of Pub. L. No. 98-573, 19 U.S.C. 2411–2416.

dispute settlement provisions incorporated during the Multilateral Trade Negotiations in the various trade agreement codes and in the framework agreement relating to obligations under the General Agreement on Tariffs and Trade. See *International Trade Reporter* Reference File, Section 75. The revised Section 301 consequently established a new dimension and new procedures in dealing with foreign trade practices determined to be inconsistent with the international codes.

The 1979 revision extended the definition of "commerce" subject to Section 301 consideration to include "services associated with international trade, whether or not such services are related to specific products." This definition was further clarified and extended by Section 304(f) of the 1984 Amendments by defining "services" as including "transfers of information" and by adding "foreign direct investments by United States persons with implications for trade in goods and services" (19 U.S.C. 2411(e)(1)).

A dramatic use of the Section 301 remedy for alleged unfair trade practices in services was the filing of a complaint in May 1984 by Transpace Carriers, Inc. charging that the member states of the European Space Agency and their instrumentalities were subsidizing the satellite launch services of the competing French company by two-tiered pricing policies and the provision of cost-free or below cost support in facilities, services, and personnel. The USTR initiated an investigation, No. 301-46, 49 FR 28643, July 13, 1984. The negative determination is discussed in section IV.C.2 *infra*.

A. Authority and Mandate to the President

If the President determines that action by the United States is appropriate because a foreign country
- has abrogated rights of the United States under any trade agreement; or
- is following a policy or practice injurious to U.S. trade, which is inconsistent with any trade agreement; or
- engages in other acts or policies which are unjustifiable, unreasonable, or discriminatory, and which burden or restrict U.S. commerce;

the President is mandated to "take all appropriate and feasible action within his power" to enforce U.S. rights and to eliminate such restrictions (19 U.S.C. 2411(a)). He may not grant tariff concessions in exchange for elimination of such unjustifiable restrictions.

Under the definitions added by the 1984 Amendments "unreasonable" describes a practice or policy deemed unfair or inequitable although not inconsistent with international legal rights; "unjustifiable" refers to a practice or policy which is inconsistent with legal rights, and "discriminatory" refers to a policy or practice which denies national or most-favored-nation treatment to U.S. goods, services, or investment.

B. Authorized Action by the President

Title III of the Trade Act as amended through 1984 provides that the President, in the case of any one of the above, in addition to treaty procedures,

• may suspend, withdraw, or prevent the application of, or may refrain from proclaiming, benefits of trade agreement concessions to carry out a trade agreement with such country or instrumentality; and

• may impose duties or other import restrictions on the goods of such foreign country or instrumentality, and may impose fees (notwithstanding any other provision of law) or restrictions on the services of such foreign country or instrumentality, for such time as he deems appropriate.

• may restrict in any manner appropriate, and notwithstanding any license or order providing access authorization, the terms and conditions of any service sector access authorization, or deny authorization.

The access provision, added by Section 304(c) of the 1984 Amendments, was drafted in recognition of the fact that foreign services, such as telecommunications, are subject to federal agency regulation and enter the United States not through ports but upon receipt of a license, permit, or other authorization from such agency (Conf. Rep., H.R. Rep. No. 98-1156 at 146).

C. Public and ITC Views on Import Restrictions

Before the President takes action to impose duties or other import restrictions on any foreign product or services his agent, the U.S. Trade Representative (USTR), is required by Section 304(b) of the Trade Act to provide opportunity for the expression of views on the matter, or if requested, public hearings, unless the need for expeditious action would make this procedure contrary to the national interest. In that event, opportunity for public comment must be provided after the action has been taken.

In addition, the USTR may request the ITC to advise as to the probable impact on the economy of imposing retaliatory restrictions on foreign articles or services. The ITC has provided regulations to govern such requested investigations.[2]

II. PRESIDENT'S DISCRETION

A. Extent

The President has virtually complete discretion as to whether or not to retaliate under these provisions of the Trade Act. The mandate to him is to "take all appropriate and feasible action" to enforce U.S. rights or to obtain the elimination of the restrictions or subsidies, but only if he determines

---

[2]19 CFR Part 205, Subpart B.

action to be appropriate. He is authorized to initiate action on his own motion in response to foreign action. Any retaliatory measures taken by the President may be removed by him whenever he deems it appropriate to do so. However, the President is under strong compulsion to act in the event of flagrant foreign acts because of the clear congressional intent that he do so.

Normally, the President would take retaliatory action only against the foreign country maintaining the import restrictions or other discriminatory measures. But the amended Trade Act continues to authorize him in his discretion to take action on a nondiscriminatory treatment basis against other countries other than the one whose restrictive actions led to the retaliation. In the words added by Section 304(a) to Section 301(a) of the Trade Act, the President may exercise his authority "with respect to any goods or sector ... without regard to whether or not such goods or sector were involved in the act, policy, or practice identified" as requiring retaliation. Thus, for example, he could raise the tariff on a given product for all imports.

Presidential retaliation on a nondiscriminatory basis was held by the Court of Customs and Patent Appeals to be implicitly authorized in the predecessor statute, Section 252(c) of the Trade Expansion Act of 1962, 19 U.S.C. 1882(c), repealed by the Trade Act of 1974, in *United States* v. *Star Industries, Inc.,* 59 CCPA 159, 462 F.2d 557 (1972) 1 ITRD 1369, *cert. denied,* 409 U.S. 1076 (1976). Thus, the present Section 301 provisions made explicit an authority previously implied.

B. Congressional Concern

The Trade Agreements Act eliminated the requirement in the Trade Act that whenever the President took action with respect to any country other than the one whose import restrictions or other discriminatory acts were the cause for taking action, he must report his action promptly to the Senate and House of Representatives setting forth his reasons for so doing. If within 90 days both sides of the Congress by a majority vote adopted a resolution of disapproval, then the retaliatory action was nullified except as to the country whose restriction or other discriminatory act was the cause for taking such action. However, the amended act continues to require semiannual reports to the House of Representatives and the Senate.

III. PROCEDURE

A. The Investigation Process

Proceedings under Title III, Chapter 1, of the amended Trade Act are basically governed by the provisions of Title IX of the Trade Agreements Act and by regulations of the Office of the USTR.[3] The 1979 amendatory provisions set time limits on the various duties of the USTR: 45 days to

---

[3] 15 CFR Parts 2001–2003 and Part 2006.

determine whether to initiate an investigation on a petition; 7 to 12 months to reach a recommendation on Presidential action, depending on the subject of the investigation.

The USTR regulations utilize the established "Section 301 Committee"[4] under the USTR's Trade Policy Staff Committee, whose functions are to receive and review complaints under Section 301 of the Trade Act and to afford an opportunity for interested parties to present oral and written statements concerning the operation of trade agreements and alleged foreign import restrictions or other discriminatory practices.

Under these regulations an interested person may file a written complaint setting forth certain specified information. Because the USTR in effect represents the petitioner in bilateral and multilateral negotiations, the USTR's office advises prospective petitioners to consult that office informally before filing a petition.

Section 304(g) of the Trade and Tariff Act of 1984 further amended Title III to provide procedures for obtaining confidentiality for information requested and received by the USTR in aid of any investigation, and to assure its nondisclosure except to federal employees engaged in a Section 301 investigation.

The USTR, within 45 days, makes an initial determination whether to initiate an investigation after receiving the advice of the Section 301 Committee. If his decision is negative, he must inform the petitioner of his reasons therefor and publish notice of his decision and a summary of the reasons in the *Federal Register.* One such negative decision was on the complaint of the American Iron and Steel Institute *et al.,* filed February 25, 1983, alleging that the Japanese agreement to limit steel exports to the European Coal and Steel Community was inconsistent with the GATT and with the U.S.-Japan Treaty of Friendship, Commerce and Navigation. The USTR decided against an investigation because the complaint failed to present evidence to demonstrate that U.S. benefits under the GATT were nullified or impaired (48 FR 8878, March 2, 1983). If he decides to initiate an investigation, he must publish notice of the investigation in the *Federal Register,* with the text of the petition, and provide opportunity for the presentation of views on the issue, including a public hearing.

As a matter of policy the USTR will not initiate a Section 301 complaint concerning a foreign government practice which is or has been the subject of investigation under any other provision of law, in order "to avoid redundant remedies and the waste of limited government resources." This policy was announced by the Chairman, Section 301 Committee, in terminating the complaint of the Industrial Union Department, AFL-CIO, No. 301-32, alleging subsidized financing by Canada of a subway car sale to the New York Metropolitan Transit Authority, because the alleged subsidy was being investigated by the Department of Commerce in response to a countervailing duty petition filed by The Budd Company and the Industrial Union Department. 47 FR 42059, September 23, 1982. Also, Roses, Inc. petition rejection, 50 FR 40250, October 2, 1985.

---

[4] 15 CFR 2002.3.

The USTR was authorized, under Section 304(d)(1) of the 1984 Amendments amending Section 302 of the Trade Act, to initiate an investigation in order to advise the President whether he should take action under Section 301. If the USTR does do so, he must publish his determination in the *Federal Register,* and the determination is to be treated as an affirmative determination to investigate. However, before making a determination to initiate an investigation the USTR is required by the amendment to consult with the appropriate advisory committees established under Section 135 of the Trade Act (19 U.S.C. 2155).

A public hearing will be held by the Section 301 Committee, if request therefor by the applicant or by other interested parties is made within time limits specified in the regulations.[5] If an interested party wishes to participate in the presentation of views at a public hearing or otherwise, he must submit a written brief within the time limits set forth in the published notice. An interested party may also request an opportunity to present oral testimony. The chairman of the Section 301 Committee notifies an applicant whether his request is granted and, if so, the time and place for his appearance and the amount of time allotted for his oral testimony. If the request to present oral testimony is denied, the letter from the chairman will state the reasons for the denial.

Upon receipt by the Section 301 Committee of a request for a public hearing which conforms with the stated requirements, the committee publishes in the *Federal Register* a notice of the hearing giving subject matter, time and place, and the period for submissions of briefs by other interested parties. All submissions are open to public inspection except for such pages as are marked "Business Confidential" and which the committee chairman determines should be protected from disclosure.

Review of a complaint may be terminated or suspended after receiving the advice of the Section 301 Committee. This USTR action is given effect by notification to the complainant and publication in the *Federal Register* of a notice and statement of reasons.

B. Bilateral and Multilateral Procedures

Section 303 requires the USTR, on the date of a determination to investigate, to request consultations with the foreign country or instrumentality concerned on issues raised in each petition accepted for investigation. If consultations prove fruitless and the subject involves a trade agreement, the USTR is required to request proceedings under the formal dispute settlement arrangements. If this occurs, the GATT or the signatories to the agreement establish a panel which hears the parties' positions and issues a formal report. In the course of this process the matter may be resolved by a voluntary change in the trade practice complained of.

Use of dispute settlement procedures has been specifically determined by the President to be the "appropriate and feasible" response under Section

---

[5] 15 CFR 2006.7.

301(a)(2) to various subsidy practices of the European Community and other countries. These Memorandums, issued in response to recommendations of the USTR for Presidential action, direct the USTR to initiate or continue to pursue diligently the dispute settlement provisions of the Subsidies Code or the GATT.

The effectiveness of dispute settlement operations under the GATT and under the MTN Agreements approved by the Trade Agreements Act of 1979 was made the subject of an ITC investigation, on request of the Senate Committee on Finance, Inv. No. 332-212, June 12, 1985 (50 FR 24716), with decision due December 31, 1985.

IV. EXPERIENCE UNDER SECTION 301

A. USTR Reports

The kinds of Section 301 cases investigated by the USTR and their disposition are reported in the Annual Reports of the President on the Trade Agreement Program and in the semiannual reports by the USTR to the Senate and House of Representatives. The report to the Senate and the House of April 16, 1985, reviewed the grounds of the complaints and the progress of USTR efforts toward resolution in the 12 Section 301 cases under investigation as of December 31, 1984.

The Office of the USTR also compiles as of April 1, a "Section 301 Table of Cases." This table provides the name of the petitioner and docket number of each petition filed, the substance of the complaint, the country against which the complaint is directed, and the disposition or pending status of each complaint. The Section 301 Table of Cases is kept current by the USTR's office. As of October 1985, there were 51 designated 301 cases which were under investigation or had been terminated.

B. Investigations Initiated

The USTR self-initiated, for the first time, investigations into trade and services barriers: Brazil's informatics policy, No. 301-49; Japan's tobacco import barriers, No. 301-50; and Korea's restrictions on insurance services, 50 FR 37608, September 16, 1985. In the 48 Section 301 investigations initiated by domestic industries through October 1985, the most common complaint was of export subsidies allowed for exports to the United States, or to third countries to which the United States sent competing exports, in violation of the Subsidies Code or of the GATT, or both. Other complaints were of one or more forms of import restrictions, such as a too-restrictive quota, excessive import tariffs, variable levies on, or restrictive requirements for, the contents of imports, and preferential import duties or restrictions. Several cases involved limitation by the foreign country of commercial transactions to its own insurance services or shipping facilities. Most of the complaints of unfair export subsidies were directed against the European Community or individual European countries.

C. Disposition of Cases

1. Consultation and Dispute Settlement Experience

The USTR reports show that generally the consultation process has been prolonged and inconclusive. In these cases the USTR recommends to the President and the President directs pursuit of the dispute settlement proceedings. The dispute settlement process is generally prolonged and difficult, requiring authorization and establishment of the panel by the authority designated in the applicable Agreement, hearings before the panel, and preparation of a report. Many of the Section 301 cases pending in 1985 were in this process.

A notable panel report favorable to the United States on the issue of EC subsidy of pasta products was issued May 19, 1983, by a panel authorized by the GATT Committee on Subsidies and Countervailing Measures. The panel determined that the EC subsidy of the durum wheat in the pasta products was not legitimate as a subsidy of a primary product under the Subsidies Code. The National Pasta Association investigation (Docket 301-25) was not terminated by this panel report pending acceptance of it and action under it by the Committee on Subsidies and Countervailing Measures, which had not occurred as of April 1985.

2. Suspension and Termination

The complaints against the USSR and Argentina for exclusivity in marine insurance (Dockets 301-14 and 18) were suspended pending favorable developments under accords. Several complaints have been terminated on the grounds that no action was needed or the evidence was insufficient. A change in U.S. law was found to be the appropriate solution in two cases (Dockets 301-15 and 21) and accomplished in the latter case. The investigation of the complaint of the Tanners' Council of America (Docket 301-24) was terminated and the petition withdrawn after consultations with Argentina showed that Argentina could not fulfill the agreement to reduce its export tax and consequently, by mutual consent, the U.S. import tax on cattle hides was raised by the President to the preagreement level (USTR Notice, 47 FR 53989, November 30, 1982). Also terminated after investigation and upon withdrawal of the petition were the petition alleging export subsidies of, and trademark infringement by, Korean steel wire rope imports, No. 301-39, and the petition alleging export subsidies of rice from Taiwan, No. 301-43.

The commercial satellite launching practices of the European Space Agency investigated in No. 301-46 were found by the President to be "not sufficiently different from U.S. practice in this field as to be considered unreasonable under Section 301." 50 FR 29631, July 22, 1985.

3. Alternative Relief

Investigation began in 1982 of the complaints of the Tool and Stainless Steel Industry and of the United Steel Workers of America that the European Community and six European countries were subsidizing the production of stainless steel and alloy tool steel (specialty steel), in violation of the obligations of the Subsidies Code (Dockets 301-27-31 and 33). Following consultation under that Code the USTR recommended, and the President directed on November 16, 1982 (47 FR 51717), that the USTR request the ITC to conduct an expedited investigation under the import relief provisions of Section 201 of the 1974 Trade Act and to take further consultation and monitoring actions. The ITC found that the specialty steel imports were a substantial cause of serious injury to four domestic producers and recommended three-year quota restrictions. On July 5, 1983, the President ordered higher tariffs on some specialty steel products and import quotas on others over a four-year period (48 FR 31177).

A group of U.S. border television broadcasters filed a complaint in 1978 alleging that certain provisions of the Canadian Income Tax Act were unreasonable in denying tax deduction to any Canadian taxpayer for the purchase of time from a U.S. broadcaster for advertising aimed at the Canadian market (Docket 301-15). After USTR hearings the President determined in 1980 and again in 1982 that the most appropriate response was legislation which would mirror in U.S. law the Canadian practice. Legislation providing for such a mirrored tax deduction denial was incorporated as Section 232 of the Trade and Tariff Act of 1984, Public Law 98-573, which added Subsection (j) to Section 162 of the Internal Revenue Code. That subsection provides that no tax deduction shall be allowed for expenses of advertising carried by a foreign broadcaster and directly aimed at the U.S. market where the foreign broadcaster is located in a country which denies a similar tax deduction for advertising on a U.S. broadcast aimed at the foreign market.

4. Increased Duties Imposed

The President utilized his authority to retaliate against denial of treaty rights and the unreasonable burdening of U.S. commerce, by imposing increased duties on the pasta articles provided for in Items 182.35 and 182.36, TSUS, which are the product of any member country of the European Economic Community. This was accomplished by Proclamation 5354 of June 21, 1985, 50 FR 26143, which added Items 945.80 and 945.82 to Subpart 2 of Part 2 of the Appendix to the TSUS, providing for additional duties of 40 and 25 percent *ad valorem,* respectively.

The Proclamation followed a Determination made in a Memorandum for the USTR of June 20, 1985, 50 FR 25685, reciting that preferential tariffs of the EC on imports of lemons and oranges from certain Mediterranean countries deny U.S. treaty rights and are unreasonable and discriminatory, and that the EC had proved unwilling after consultations since 1976 and a GATT dispute settlement panel decision favorable to the United States in

1984 to correct the unfair practice. This Proclamation concluded USTR Inv. No. 301-11 initiated November 1976 by Florida, California-Arizona, and Texas citrus organizations. However, Proclamation 5363 suspended the increased duties until November 1, 1985, to allow time for a mutually acceptable solution to be reached. 50 FR 33711, August 21, 1985.

17

ITC Protective Action

I. THE LAW

Section 337 of the Tariff Act of 1930 as amended[1] declares that "[u]nfair methods of competition and unfair acts in the importation of articles into the United States or in their sale . . . the effect or tendency of which is to destroy or substantially injure an industry, efficiently and economically operated, in the United States, or to prevent the establishment of such an industry, or to restrain or monopolize trade and commerce in the United States" are unlawful. When found by the U.S. International Trade Commission (ITC) to exist, such acts and methods may be dealt with by the issuance of a cease and desist order or an exclusion order. Appeal from a final order of the ITC is directly to the Court of Appeals for the Federal Circuit, as discussed in section II.I *infra.*

Most of the complaints filed under Section 337 prior to its 1974 amendment were by domestic companies alleging infringements of U.S. patents in the importation of merchandise manufactured abroad. However, as shown in section IV *infra,* Section 337 covers many unfair import practices not involving patent infringements. The experience of the ITC in attempting to apply the section to certain nonpatent infringement cases and the resulting 1979 amendment are discussed in section III *infra.* For further discussion of import infringement see Chapter 26 *infra.*

A. Requirements for Obtaining Relief Under Section 337

The requirements for obtaining relief under this section, both substantive and procedural, on paper appear quite forbidding. In the first place, the complainant must prove to the satisfaction of the ITC (1) the existence of an unfair method or act in the importation of merchandise; (2) that the effect or tendency of such unfair method or act is to destroy or substantially injure an industry in the United States; (3) that such industry is efficiently

---

[1]19 U.S.C. 1337.

341

and economically operated; or (4) that the effect of such unfair methods or act is to prevent the establishment of an industry in the United States, or to restrain or monopolize trade and commerce in the United States.

The complainant must also qualify as an "industry in the United States." The ITC held in *In re Certain Miniature, Battery-Operated, All Terrain, Wheeled Vehicles,* Inv. No. 337-TA-122, October 15, 1982, 4 ITRD 1920, that the petitioner was not entitled to relief because the term "industry in the United States" referred to production and the petitioner's toy vehicles were manufactured abroad. The petitioners appealed the ITC's determination to the Court of Appeals for the Federal Circuit, arguing that the determination was inconsistent with other determinations of what constituted a U.S. industry, particularly, *In re Certain Cube Puzzles,* Inv. No. 337-TA-112, December 30, 1982, 4 ITRD 2102. In the *Cube Puzzles* case the petitioner did not manufacture the merchandise in issue in the United States but engaged in extensive quality control, packaging, and repair operations in the United States, which the ITC found sufficient to constitute a U.S. industry.

However, in *Schaper Manufacturing Co.* v. *ITC,* 717 F.2d 1368 (Fed. Cir. 1983) 5 ITRD 1001, the CAFC upheld the ITC finding of no U.S. industry in the toy vehicles case. The CAFC stated that there is nothing in the statute to indicate that activities engaged in by the plaintiff—such as testing, advertising, and promotion—which do not involve either manufacture or production or servicing of the patented item, are meant to be protected by Section 337. The court added that Congress did not mean to protect American importers (like Schaper) who cause imports to be produced for them abroad and engage in a small amount of inspection and packaging in this country.

In determining whether infringing imports are injuring an industry in the United States, the ITC must decide on the basis of the condition of the industry at the time the complaint is brought and not at the time it considers the remedy. This direction was given to the ITC by the CAFC in *Bally/Midway Mfg. Co.* v. *U.S. International Trade Commission,* 714 F.2d 1117 (Fed. Cir. 1983) 4 ITRD 2309, holding that the ITC erred in finding no injury to the Rally-X audiovisual game because of the decline during the proceedings in the production and sales of the game.

B. Affirmative Finding—Exclusion of Article

If the ITC finds in the affirmative, it is required in Subsection (d) to direct that the articles concerned

> be excluded from entry into the United States, unless, after considering the effect of such exclusion upon the public health and welfare, competitive conditions in the United States economy, the production of like or directly competitive articles in the United States, and U.S. consumers, it finds that such articles should not be excluded from entry.

One such finding among 13 final determinations is reported in the ITC's Annual Report for fiscal year 1980. The ITC found that automatic crankpin grinders were in short supply so it declined to order exclusion of offending imports of such grinders. *In re Certain Automatic Crankpin Grinders,* Inv. No. 337-TA-60, December 17, 1979, 2 ITRD 5121.

Since an exclusion order is a remedy operating *in rem*, it is particularly appropriate where the respondents have no offices or assets in the United States. See *In re Certain Coin-Operated Audio-Visual Games,* Inv. No. 337-TA-68, June 25, 1981, 3 ITRD 1212 at 1224. The ITC there cited the CCPA holding in *Sealed Air Corp.* v. *U.S. International Trade Commission,* 68 CCPA 93, 645 F.2d 976 (1981) 2 ITRD 1353, that the ITC had authority under its *in rem* jurisdiction to exclude infringing products of a foreign concern not participating in the ITC investigation. In a later investigation of *Certain Coin-Operated Audiovisual Games,* Inv. No. 337-TA-105, July 1, 1982, 3 ITRD 1899, the ITC noted that it had jurisdiction of domestic respondents who were first purchasers of the imported products from the importers.

The ITC may issue a temporary exclusion order while it is investigating a complaint of unfair import practices. However, it has determined that it will not do so, even if it has found reason to believe that a violation of Section 337 has occurred, unless the complaint demonstrates that immediate and substantial harm will occur prior to final determination. *In re Certain Copper Rod Production Apparatus,* Inv. No. 337-TA-89, October 29, 1980, 2 ITRD 5597. In this determination the ITC discusses the legal standards governing issuance of a TEO. It states that it will balance the evidence of a violation, which need not be a preponderance of the evidence, and the evidence of immediate and substantial harm to the complainant, absent relief, against the evidence of adverse impact against other parties and the public interest (2 ITRD at 5600).

The section provides that any exclusion order shall not apply to imports made by or for the U.S. Government with its consent. Exclusion orders are implemented by the Secretary of the Treasury upon notification from the ITC.

C. Cease and Desist Order as an Alternative

In lieu of an exclusion order, the ITC may, under Subsection (f), issue a cease and desist order to any person violating the section. It may also decide not to issue such an order for the same reasons it may refrain from issuing an exclusion order.

The ITC may in a single case issue cease and desist orders against certain domestic respondents found to be engaging in unfair methods of competition in imported products and an exclusion order against the importation by other importers of infringing products (*In re Certain Airtight Cast-Iron Stoves,* Inv. No. 337-TA-69, December 31, 1980, 3 ITRD 1158). Separate cease and desist orders may be issued against different respondents tailored to fit the specific offenses found in a determination or the specific restrictions needed to provide an appropriate remedy. See, *e.g., In re Certain Apparatus for the Continuous Production of Copper Rod,* Inv. No. 337-TA-52, November 23, 1979, 2 ITRD 5006.

A civil penalty for violation of a cease and desist order was provided by Section 1105(b) of the Trade Agreements Act of 1979. The penalty consists of the greater of $10,000 for each day of the violation or the domestic value of the articles entered or sold on each such day. The penalty may be recovered in a suit by the ITC in a federal district court. The court may issue an injunction to require the relief sought by the ITC to the extent the court deems appropriate.

D. Presidential Power to Disapprove ITC Determination

The Act requires the ITC to publish in the *Federal Register* a notice of its determination of a violation of Section 337 or of an apparent violation justifying a temporary exclusion order, and to transmit a copy to the President with a statement of the action taken. The President has 60 days in which to disapprove the determination. If he disapproves, the proceeding is terminated and the action taken is nullified as of the date of his determination and notice thereof to the ITC.

The ITC has construed a Presidential disapproval of its determination as leaving the determination valid but unenforceable. *In re Certain Molded-In Sandwich Panel Inserts,* Inv. No. 337-TA-99, September 17, 1982, 4 ITRD 1822. In that determination the ITC modified the remedy provided in the earlier rejected determination to comport with the narrower remedy indicated in the President's disapproval. In *The Young Engineers, Inc.* v. *ITC,* 721 F.2d 1305 (Fed. Cir. 1983) 5 ITRD 1273, the Court of Appeals for the Federal Circuit upheld the ITC practice.

II. PROCEDURE

A. To Start a Proceeding Under Section 337

A proceeding under Section 337 is conducted in accordance with the extensive regulations for adjudicative investigations in 19 CFR Parts 210 and 211. It is commenced by filing a complaint with the U.S. International Trade Commission, Washington, D.C. 20436. A complaint may be filed by any interested person, partnership, association, or corporation. An original and 14 copies of the complaint are required by the ITC, plus one copy for each person alleged in the complaint to have violated Section 337. In addition, the ITC may commence a proceeding on its own initiative.

B. Content of Complaint

The requirements in 19 CFR 210.20 for the contents of a complaint were extensively revised by the amendment of Part 210 issued November 23, 1984, 49 FR 46123. In addition to the formal requirements set forth in 19 CFR 210.5 and 210.20 covering written submissions the complainant must provide full information, described in 19 CFR 210.20, covering the following matters:

- A statement of the facts constituting the alleged unfair methods of competition and unfair acts;
- Specific instances of all unlawful importations or sales, including the TSUS item number of the articles allegedly imported;
- The name, address and nature of the business of each person alleged to be violating Section 337;
- A statement as to any prior court or agency litigation concerning the alleged unfair methods of competition and unfair acts;
- A description of the domestic industry affected and, if restraint or monopolization is alleged, a description of the trade and commerce affected;
- A description of the complainant's business and his interests in the trade and commerce or the domestic industry affected;
- A specific theory underlying the general allegations regarding an effect or a tendency to destroy or substantially injure a domestic industry; to prevent the establishment of a domestic industry; or to have the effect or tendency to restrain or monopolize trade and commerce. The theory is to be supported by the kinds of specific information described in the regulation.

When a complaint is based upon the alleged infringement of a valid U.S. patent specific information is to be provided concerning the patent, its ownership, and each licensee; and of each foreign patent relevant to the allegations.

With the filing of the complaint there is to be submitted when practical and possible the involved articles as exhibits. If the complaint concerns the infringement of a patent, there must also be submitted three copies of each license agreement, and one certified copy and three additional copies of the Patent and Trademark Office file wrapper for each patent. If the complaint concerns a registered trademark, there shall be submitted a certified copy of the trademark registration. If the complaint concerns a nonfederally registered trademark, the submission is to include information concerning prior attempts to register, and the status of current attempts to register, the alleged trademark. If the complaint concerns the alleged infringement of a copyright, there shall be submitted one certified copy of the copyright registration.

The Court of Customs and Patent Appeals upheld the ITC's dismissal of a Section 337 complaint which failed to state facts, as required by 19 CFR 210.20(a)(2), showing the alleged monopolization and conspiracy and which was "no more than a theory built on suppositions," although the court noted that the allegations of less-than-fair-value pricing might support an antidumping claim. *Syntex Agribusiness, Inc.* v. *International Trade Commission,* 68 CCPA 141, 659 F.2d 1038 (1981) 3 ITRD 1194.

C. Preliminary Inquiry

After the ITC receives the complaint, it makes a preliminary inquiry to determine, within 30 days, whether the complaint is sufficient, whether there is good and sufficient reason for a full investigation, and, if so, and if a motion has been made therefor, whether the ITC should issue a temporary order of exclusion from entry. If the ITC determines that a full investigation is warranted, it will so order and publish in the *Federal Register* a notice of the commencement of an investigation. If it determines that a full investigation is not warranted, the complaint will be dismissed and complainant notified with the reasons therefor (19 CFR 210.12 and 210.13).

D. Investigation and Response

After the ITC determines upon a full investigation, it serves a copy of the complaint upon each person alleged to have violated Section 337 and gives each of them 20 days to make written answer under oath. Under the November 1984 amendment of 19 CFR 210.13 a copy of the complaint is served upon the government of each foreign country represented by a respondent, as well as upon the several federal agencies concerned with a public interest determination under Section 337 of the Tariff Act.

Each respondent must respond specifically to each allegation in the complaint and notice of investigation. The complainant is furnished copies of all the answers received by the ITC. Also, complainant and all other interested parties receive copies of all briefs that are submitted to the ITC.

The ITC must complete its investigations in not more than one year from the date of publication of the notice of investigation, except that 18 months are allowed in the more complicated cases. The ITC is required to publish in the *Federal Register* its reasons for designating any investigation as a more complicated investigation.

E. Formal Hearing and Initial Determination

The Act requires the ITC to make its determinations on the record after notice and opportunity for a hearing in conformity with the Administrative Procedure Act. Under Subparts E and F of the regulations the presiding officer is an ITC administrative law judge who conducts the hearing and writes an initial determination, including an opinion stating findings of fact and conclusions of law on all contested issues, on the basis of the record. The initial determination must be made within 9 months from the date of publication of the notice of the institution of the investigation, or within 14 months in a more complicated case. It becomes the ITC's determination 45 days after its filing unless the ITC orders review of the determination or certain issues therein.

It is not necessary that the ITC determine all issues in the initial determination; it may reach a "no violation" determination on the basis of a single dispositive issue, in which event the CAFC will review only that dispositive issue. *Beloit Corporation* v. *Valmet Oy,* 742 F.2d 1421 (Fed. Cir. 1984) 6 ITRD 1113; *cert denied,* 53 LW 3869 (1985).

Documents and testimony made subject to in camera orders are not, under 19 CFR 210.44, to be considered a part of the record of the proceedings. Otherwise, all information and testimony submitted and received will be considered part of the record of the proceedings of the ITC.

F. Ancillary Procedures

The ITC regulations provide for (where appropriate) the receipt, argument, and consideration of motions; discovery; the taking of depositions; interrogations; subpoenas; and prehearing conferences.

G. Termination and Consent Order Agreements

Any party may move at any time for an order to terminate an investigation in whole or in part as to any or all respondents, under the provisions in 19 CFR 210.51. Such a motion may be made on the basis of a licensing or other agreement between the complainant or complainants and one or more of the respondents, presented with a copy of the agreement and all supplemental agreements. After certification of these papers by the presiding officer with his initial determination to the Commission the ITC publishes a nonconfidential summary in the *Federal Register* for a 10-day comment period. An ITC order of termination based on an agreement is not a final determination of the question of violation of Section 337.

A consent order agreement submitted with a motion to terminate an investigation must be presented in conformity with the provisions on procedure and substance in Subpart B of Part 211. Upon proper compliance the ITC publishes the initial determination of the presiding officer in the *Federal Register* for a 10-day comment period and sends copies to the Department of Health and Human Services, the Department of Justice, the Federal Trade Commission, and any other agency appropriate to contribute to the ITC's determination of public interest considerations. The ITC thereafter accepts or rejects the initial determinations, or takes other action, and publishes its action in the *Federal Register.* An order of termination based upon a consent order agreement is not a final determination of the question of violation of Section 337.

H. ITC Review and Implementation of Orders

Any party may request a review by the ITC of an initial determination by filing a petition for review within 10 days after the service of the initial determination, or within 5 days of an initial determination concerning temporary relief, summary termination, or certain other ancillary matters. The ITC will order review if one of the Commissioners votes for it. On review the ITC may affirm, reverse, modify, set aside, or remand for further proceedings, the initial determination, in whole or in part.

A determination of a violation, or a believed violation, and the resulting action, is served upon each party, published in the *Federal Register,* and transmitted to the President, together with the record. An exclusion order is enforceable upon receipt by the Secretary of the Treasury. Other orders are enforceable upon receipt of notice by the affected party. The determination becomes final the day after the 60-day review period provided to the President, if he has not disapproved the determination, or, on the day on which the President notifies the ITC of an explicit approval.

I. Reconsideration and Appeals to the CAFC

Any party to an investigation may, within 14 days after service of an ITC determination, file a petition for reconsideration of the determination or action ordered, setting forth the relief requested and the grounds therefor, but only if the petition relates to new questions raised by the determination and action ordered. The filing of a petition does not affect the effective date of the determination or action ordered.

Any person adversely affected by a final determination of the ITC excluding articles from entry or issuing a cease and desist order may appeal to the Court of Appeals for the Federal Circuit. That court has the same jurisdiction to review determinations of the ITC as it does in appeals from the Court of International Trade. However, a determination of the ITC favorable to the complainant and directing the exclusion of articles imported or cease and desist action is not an appealable final determination until the ITC decision has been referred to the President and approved or disapproved within the statutory 60-day period.[2] A determination by the ITC unfavorable to the complainant is not referable to the President and may therefore be immediately appealed to the CAFC.

Because the ITC is acting in a judicial capacity in making a Section 337 determination, its determination is to be treated as *res judicata* in an action brought on the same issues by the unsuccessful ITC complainant in a U.S. district court. *Union Manufacturing Co., Inc.* v. *Han Baek Trading Co., Ltd.,* 763 F.2d 42 (CA 2 1985) 6 ITRD 2105. The Court of Appeals noted that the complainant should have appealed the negative ITC determination to the CAFC.

There appears to be little chance for court review of an interlocutory order of the ITC, as shown by the unsuccessful effort of the World-Wide Volkswagen Corporation to reverse an ITC order dismissing it from the ITC investigation of the importation of VWs with certain converters as an infringement of an Engelhard patent. The CCPA in the *Import Motors Limited* case, cited *supra* note 2, dismissed the appeal as the ITC order was not a final determination. On suit for an injunction against the ITC the District Court of the District of Columbia refused jurisdiction on the grounds that the judicial review provisions of the Administrative Procedure Act provided no "day to day supervision" of administrative agencies, especially where a special judicial tribunal was provided, and that review of the ITC order could await the CCPA's review of the final ITC investigation.[3]

The standard of review by the CAFC of findings of fact made by the ITC is the determination whether the findings are supported by substantial evidence. *American Hospital Supply Corporation* v. *Travenol Laboratories, Inc.,* 745 F.2d 1 (Fed. Cir. 1984) 6 ITRD 1366. In affirming the ITC determination the court there said that a finding of patent infringement under the doctrine of equivalents was a finding of fact.

---

[2] *Import Motors Limited, Inc.* v. *U.S. International Trade Commission,* 63 CCPA 57, CAD 1165, 530 F.2d 940 (1976) 1 ITRD 1506.
[3] *World-Wide Volkswagen Corp.* v. *U.S. I.T.C.,* 414 F. Supp. 713 (DC DC 1976) 1 ITRD 1529.

J. Enforcement, Modification, and Revocation

The provisions governing the enforcement, modification, and revocation of final ITC actions, including exclusion, cease and desist, and consent orders, are set forth in Subpart C of Part 211 of the ITC regulations. Important here is the power of the ITC to require sworn reports from any person relevant to compliance with its orders, whether as part of a final order or independently thereof. A requirement of a report is enforceable by civil action in a U.S. district court under 19 U.S.C. 1333.

Enforcement of a final order may be accomplished by initiation by the ITC of a civil action in a U.S. district court under Section 337(f) requesting a civil penalty or a mandatory injunction. The ITC may also institute its own enforcement proceeding, with a hearing discretionary, and decide upon a modification of an order, a substitution of an exclusion order for a cease and desist or a consent order, or the initiation of a civil action.

Modification or dissolution of an ITC order may be requested by motion by any person, or initiated by the ITC, upon the basis of changed conditions of fact or law or the public interest. Before final action the ITC publishes notice of a provisionally accepted motion or a self-initiated action in the *Federal Register,* serves copies upon interested parties, and provides, if appropriate, a public hearing.

K. Award of Attorney Fees—Regulations Lapsed

To implement the Equal Access to Justice Act, 5 U.S.C. 504, the ITC published Part 212 of its regulations on March 5, 1982, as final regulations effective to September 30, 1984, the termination date of the Act. The regulations provided for the award of attorney fees to an eligible party who prevailed in an adversary proceeding brought by the ITC upon its own complaint. Eligibility was limited to the five types of applicants specified in Section 212.04. The regulations have lapsed.

III. RELATION TO ANTIDUMPING AND COUNTERVAILING DUTY INVESTIGATIONS

A. Experience Prior to Public Law 96-39

Prior to enactment of the Trade Agreements Act[4] almost all the complaints investigated under Section 337 had involved allegations of infringements by imports of U.S. letters patent, with two notable exceptions. These two concerned allegations of predatory pricing of imports, and their handling by the ITC caused considerable administrative conflict.

In the first such case GTE Sylvania, Inc. and Philco Consumer Electronics Corp. alleged predatory pricing in the sale of certain Japanese color television sets.[5] The Treasury Department advised the ITC that it did

---

[4]Pub. L. No. 96-39, July 26, 1979.
[5]Inv. No. 337-TA-23, filed January 15, 1976.

not properly have jurisdiction over the investigation of allegations falling within the antidumping and countervailing duty areas. After hearing oral arguments on its jurisdiction as well as on the merits of the allegations, the ITC terminated its investigation with the issuance of consent orders accepted by all parties to the investigation.[6] These orders conceded ITC jurisdiction and prohibited predatory pricing and special purchase inducements in the sale of color television receivers, and combinations to fix prices.

In the second such case the ITC ordered certain manufacturers, exporters, and importers of Japanese welded stainless steel pipe and tube to cease and desist from selling such products in the United States at prices below the average variable cost of production without commercial justification.[7] The President disapproved this cease and desist order because of its detrimental effect on the national economic interest and on international economic relations but also because of the "need to avoid conflicts in the administration of the unfair trade practice laws of the United States."[8] He found such duplication to be wasteful of private and public resources and an irritant to foreign governments as a departure from internationally agreed procedures for dealing with below-cost sales. He pointed out that sales below cost of welded steel pipe and tube had been the subject of three antidumping investigations by the Treasury Department, the last of which resulted in a determination of sales at less than fair value by six producers of about 85 percent of the imports.

B. Directives Provided by Public Law 96-39

The authority of the ITC in investigations involving alleged acts or effects within the purview of the Antidumping or Countervailing Duty Laws was clarified by Section 1105 of the Trade Agreements Act, 19 U.S.C. 1337(b)(3). That section directs the ITC to notify the Secretary of the Treasury, or other administering authority, when the ITC believes that a matter under investigation involves such alleged acts or effects and to terminate or not institute an investigation which is based solely on such alleged acts or effects. The section authorizes the ITC to suspend its investigation, where the matter is based in part on such alleged acts or effects, during the time the Secretary or administering authority is making a final decision under those laws. The suspension time is excluded from the maximum periods allowed the ITC in reaching a determination in that part of the investigation which concerns the alleged acts or effects violative of Section 337 of the Tariff Act of 1930, and not covered by the antidumping or countervailing duty determination.

In view of the discretionary authority inherent in 19 U.S.C. 1337(b)(3) the ITC may not be mandated to initiate and then suspend an investigation of a complaint based in part on allegations of dumping activities. *Syntex Agribusiness, Inc.* v. *U.S. International Trade Commission,* 659 F.2d 1038

---

[6]42 FR 39492, August 4, 1977.
[7]Inv. No. 337-TA-29, 1 ITRD 5245.
[8]Presidential Determination of April 22, 1978, 43 FR 17789, April 26, 1978.

(CCPA 1981) 3 ITRD 1194; *In re CF Industries, Inc.,* CAFC No. 83-845, April 25, 1983, 5 ITRD 1447.

IV. EXTENDED APPLICATION OF SECTION 337

Since latter 1979 the ITC has determined an increasing number of investigations of complaints alleging a variety of unfair practices in import trade other than patent infringement. Among these are the following:

A. Infringement of U.S. Registered Trademark

In its major investigation, *In re Certain Airtight Cast-Iron Stoves,* Inv. No. 337-TA-69, December 30, 1980, 3 ITRD 1158, involving originally 52 respondents and numerous types of alleged unfair acts, the ITC determined that infringement had occurred of the U.S. registered trademark of the complainant, Jotul, by certain of the respondents who had sold stoves carrying the same or similar word. Infringement of the U.S. registered trademark of the complainant was also found by the ITC in the case of *In re Certain Rotatable Photographic Display Units,* Inv. No. 337-TA-74, November 21, 1980, 3 ITRD 1011, with the statement that likelihood of customer confusion was properly the test of trademark infringement.

B. Infringement of Common Law Trademark

In both of the foregoing cases the ITC also found infringement of the complainant's common law trademark. It approved the administrative law judge's determination that the complainant had proved the necessary elements of such infringement; namely, that the imports were an imitation of the physical details and design of the complainant's product which caused consumer confusion, and that the features imitated were nonfunctional in character and had acquired a secondary meaning, namely, public association of the features with the product.

In a more elaborate statement of the elements of common law trademark infringement, *In re Certain Coin-Operated Audio-Visual Games,* Inv. No. 337-TA-68, June 25, 1981, 3 ITRD 1212, the ITC listed the following five elements (3 ITRD 1212 at 1216):

1. The mark must be distinctive;
2. The mark must be arbitrary or created for the express purpose of serving as a trademark;
3. The mark, if a design, must be nonfunctional;
4. The mark must have achieved secondary meaning, unless the mark is either "suggestive" or non-descriptive, i.e. arbitrary and fanciful;
5. There must be likelihood of confusion. [footnotes omitted]

The ITC, applying these tests, concluded that the complainant's trademark "Galaxian" was infringed by the use by certain of the respondents of variations of that name. Restating these tests, the ITC found a violation of common law trademark in *In re Sneakers with Fabric Uppers and Rubber Soles,* Inv. No. 337-TA-118, March 9, 1983, 5 ITRD 1226.

After an extensive examination of the elements necessary to prove common law trademark infringement the ITC concluded that such infringement was not proved in *In re Certain Vacuum Bottles,* Inv. No. 337-TA-108, October 29, 1982, 4 ITRD 1937. See also *In re Certain Vertical Milling Machines,* Inv. No. 337-TA-133, March 22, 1984, 6 ITRD 1259, in which the ITC concluded in a thorough analysis of the attributes of common law trademark that the overall appearance of complainant Textron's vertical milling machine had not acquired a secondary meaning and was functional in character. This determination was affirmed by the CAFC in an opinion reviewing the law on common law trademark protection. *Textron, Inc.* v. *U.S. International Trade Commission,* 753 F.2d 1019 (1985) 6 ITRD 1742.[9] See also *New England Butt Co.* v. *ITC,* 756 F.2d 874 (Fed. Cir. 1985) 6 ITRD 1939.

C. Infringement of Copyright

In the 1981 determination of the *Coin-Operated Audio-Visual Games* investigation the ITC also found infringement of the complainant's registered copyright in the Galaxian play mode and attract mode. It concluded that the complainant had met the two requirements to sustain a claim of copyright infringement in the federal courts: ownership of the copyright in question and copying by the defendant. The requirements for protection of common law trademarks and of copyrights were found to be satisfied in a subsequent investigation by the ITC under the same title, and for the same complainant, *In re Certain Coin-Operated Audiovisual Games,* Inv. No. 337-TA-105. It found infringement of the complainant's common law trademark in the term "PAC-MAN" and infringement of the complainant's copyright in the PAC-MAN audiovisual work, issuing as temporary relief a cease and desist order against 18 respondents, January 15, 1982, 3 ITRD 1899, and a final general exclusion order, July 1, 1982, 4 ITRD 1403. The failure of the ITC to include the Rally-X game in this relief was the subject of the CAFC remand in the *Bally/Midway Mfg. Co.* decision discussed in section I.A *supra.*

D. Passing or Palming Off

In the *Certain Airtight Cast-Iron Stoves* determination, section IV.A *supra,* the ITC recognized as a separate violation of Section 337 the offense of passing off which it described as the leading of a customer to believe that he was buying the product of another. This offense was committed by certain respondents passing off Taiwanese stoves as complainant's stoves. The ITC noted that this practice was prohibited in domestic commerce under the prohibitions against false designations of origin and false

---

[9]Common law trademark and unfair competition were federalized by Section 43(a) of the Lanham Act, 15 U.S.C. 1125(a), prohibiting "any false description or representation." Palmeter, *The U.S. International Trade Commission at Common Law,* 18 J. WORLD TRADE No. 6, November-December 1984.

descriptions of goods and services in Section 43(a) of the Lanham Act and the Federal Trade Commission Act.

E. Copying Trade Dress

Another unfair method of import competition under Section 337 found by the ITC is the copying of the trade dress of complainant's products. Trade dress refers to a product's distinctive packaging or design features. This offense is similar to an infringement of a common law trademark in that necessary elements are that the trade dress must include nonfunctional features, *i.e.,* features not serving any function but to distinguish the product, and the trade dress must have acquired a secondary meaning in the public's mind, *i.e.,* the public associates a particular trade dress with the particular product using it. Also, there must be a likelihood of consumer confusion. These elements were found proven by the complainant in *In re Certain Novelty Glasses,* Inv. No. 337-TA-55, July 11, 1979, 2 ITRD 5400, and in *In re Certain Miniature Plug-in Blade Fuses,* Inv. No. 337-TA-114, January 13, 1983, 4 ITRD 2417, with resulting exclusion orders. In *CBS, Inc.* v. *Logical Games,* 719 F.2d 1237 (CA 4 1983) 5 ITRD 1467, the court found that the importer, CBS, Inc., having the exclusive right to import and sell the trademarked Rubik's Cube, was entitled to enjoin the sale of a competitive puzzle using a similar trade dress.

F. False and Deceptive Advertising

Another unfair act found to have been engaged in by certain respondents in the *Certain Airtight Cast-Iron Stoves* case, section IV.A *supra,* was the false advertising of stoves imported from Taiwan as Scandinavian. The ITC noted that the proof of falsification was sufficient to show violation of Section 337 without showing that consumer confusion had occurred. In the *Certain Vertical Milling Machines* case, *supra,* the ITC found false advertising in the use of a photograph of a competitor's product to advertise another manufacturer's product, and that such falsity was a violation of Section 43(a) of the Lanham Act.

G. Misappropriation of Trade Secrets

Cease and desist orders were issued against the respondents in *In re Certain Apparatus for the Continuous Production of Copper Rod,* Inv. No. 337-TA-52, November 23, 1979, 2 ITRD 5006, found to have misappropriated trade secrets. The complainant was held to have proved the following four elements necessary to establish an unfair act respecting trade secrets under Section 337 (*Id.* at 5022):

(1) the existence of a trade secret which is not in the public domain, (2) that the complainant is the owner of the trade secret or possesses a proprietary interest therein, (3) that the complainant disclosed the trade secret to respondent while in a confidential relationship or that the respondent wrongfully took the trade secret by unfair means, and (4) that the respondent has used or disclosed the trade secret causing injury to the complainant.

18

Other Restrictive Action

Chapters 12, 13, 16, and 17 discuss the U.S. laws which are of principal use in combating foreign unfair trade practices. However, there are other statutes which, depending upon the circumstances, may be applicable and useful.

I. FOREIGN COUNTRY DISCRIMINATION

A. Section 338 of the Tariff Act of 1930

This section[1] authorizes the President to proclaim new or additional duties upon the products of a country when he finds that the country in question is discriminating against U.S. products in any of a variety of ways. Such new duties are fixed at a rate determined by the President adequate to offset the burden or disadvantage on U.S. commerce, not to exceed 50 percent *ad valorem* or its equivalent.

After the President issues such a proclamation, if the foreign country maintains or increases its discrimination against U.S. products, the President is authorized to issue a further proclamation directing that such products of said country or such articles imported in its vessels shall be excluded from importation into the United States. Importations in violation of a presidential proclamation issued under this section are subject to forfeiture. The ITC is required by Subsection (g) to ascertain whether the proscribed discriminatory practices exist, but has no regulations implementing this statute. There is no current record of ITC or Tariff Commission or Presidential action under these provisions of the statute.

Subsection (e) of this section further authorizes the President to offset by additional duties the advantage which may accrue to the industry of one country by reason of the discrimination against U.S. commerce by a second country. The Customs Court has pointed out that this subsection resulted

---

[1] 19 U.S.C. 1338.

from a 1922 recommendation by the Tariff Commission that statutory authority be made available to reach the situation where colonies of colonial powers were furnishing raw materials to their mother countries on terms which discriminated against third countries, thereby giving the products of the mother country an unfair advantage; this situation could not be remedied under the countervailing duty statute which applied only where one country bestowed a bounty or grant upon its own products.[2] However, there is no record of a presidential proclamation or of a finding by the U.S. Tariff Commission or the successor agency, the International Trade Commission, issued under this section.

Section 338 has been described as an "obscure and never-used provision of the law.[3] It is superseded for all practical purposes by Section 301 of the Trade Act of 1974, as amended (see Chapter 16).

II. UNFAIR METHODS OF COMPETITION

A. Sections 800 to 803 of the Revenue Act of 1916, as Amended[4]

Section 800 defines the scope of Sections 801–803 to include persons, partnerships, corporations, and associations.

1. The "Antidumping Act of 1916"

Section 801, 15 U.S.C. 72, sometimes called the Antidumping Act of 1916, makes it unlawful to import, sell, or cause to be imported or sold articles from a foreign country at a price, after adjustments for transportation costs, substantially less than the actual market value or wholesale price of such articles, at the time of exportation to the United States, in the principal markets of the country of production or third countries to which they are commonly exported, provided such acts are done

> with the intent of destroying or injuring an industry in the United States, or of preventing the establishment of an industry in the United States, or of restraining or monopolizing any part of trade and commerce in such articles in the United States.

Violators are subject to a fine not exceeding $5,000 or imprisonment not exceeding one year or both. The section further provides that any person injured by reason of a violation of, or combination or conspiracy to violate, the section may sue in a District Court of the United States and recover treble damages plus costs and attorneys' fees. The latter treble damage provision can be an important remedy for persons damaged by illegal price-cutting by foreign manufacturers and exporters, or importers.

After almost 60 years of disuse the Zenith Radio Corporation brought action under this statute in 1974 against Japanese manufacturers of

---

[2]See *Hammond Lead Products, Inc.* v. *United States,* CD 3915, 306 F. Supp. 460, 471 (1969), *rev'd on other grounds,* CAD 1017, 440 F.2d 1024 (1971) 1 ITRD 1334, *cert. denied,* 404 U.S. 1005.

[3]MTN Studies No. 6, Pt. 1, p. 48, reported in McGovern, INTERNATIONAL TRADE REGULATION, (1982), at 354. A pertinent customs regulation, 19 CFR 159.42, remains.

[4]15 U.S.C. 71–74.

electronics products and their importers and sellers to recover treble damages. The defense contended that the following terms in the statute were void for vagueness: (1) "commonly and systematically"; (2) "substantially less"; (3) "actual market value or wholesale price"; and (4) "other charges and expenses necessarily incident to the importation and sale thereof in the United States." The court denied the defendants' motion to dismiss, deciding that, even under a strict construction of the statute, the terms were not unconstitutionally vague.[5]

The *Zenith Radio* v. *Matsushita* litigation burgeoned into extensive, complex, and numerous decisions on procedural and substantive questions, involving the Sherman Antitrust Act and the Wilson Tariff Act, discussed *infra,* as well as the Antidumping Act of 1916. With respect to the latter Act, the district court decided that the Act imposed substantially similar legal requirements relating to price discrimination as those imposed by the Clayton Antitrust Act of 1914 on domestic business and could not be applied to articles not strictly similar to the domestic articles. Finding that the consumer electronic products (CEPs) manufactured in Japan were not similar to such products manufactured in the United States, the court granted the defendants' motion to dismiss all claims under the Antidumping Act of 1916, with minor exceptions, and certified its order for interlocutory appeal to the Third Circuit.[6] Because of the exceptions to the dismissal, the court proceeded to determine that the 1953 Treaty of Friendship, Commerce and Navigation between the United States and Japan did not repeal the Antidumping Act of 1916.[7] Before the Court of Appeals resolved the interlocutory appeal the district court dismissed Zenith's residual dumping claims and entered a final judgment.[8]

In a comprehensive opinion deciding all the issues in this litigation under the Antidumping Act of 1916, the Court of Appeals for the Third Circuit, determined, in brief, that (1) the 1953 Treaty of Friendship, Commerce and Navigation was not violated by the 1916 Act; (2) product comparability was not on a functional or generic basis, but the district court had erred in finding that the necessary technological differences between CEPs in Japan and the United States made them noncomparable; (3) issues of fact existed as to whether the defendants conspired to sell their CEPs at lower prices in the United States than in Japan; and (4) as to whether the conspiracy had predatory intent. The Court of Appeals reversed the dismissals of the dumping claims against all of the defendants except Sony Corporation, Motorola, Inc., and Sears, Roebuck & Co., and remanded for further proceedings.[9]

---

[5]*Zenith Radio Corp.* v. *Matsushita Electric Industrial Co., Ltd.,* 402 F. Supp. 251 (ED Pa. 1975) 1 ITRD 1464, *petition denied,* 521 F.2d 1399 (1975).

[6]*Zenith Radio Corp.* v. *Matsushita Electric Industrial Co., Ltd.,* 494 F. Supp. 1190 (ED Pa. 1980) 2 ITRD 1001.

[7]*Zenith Radio Corp.* v. *Matsushita Electric Industrial Co., Ltd.,* 494 F. Supp. 1263 (ED Pa. 1980).

[8]*Zenith Radio Corp.* v. *Matsushita Electric Industrial Co.,* 513 F. Supp. 1100 (ED Pa. 1981) 3 ITRD 1081.

[9]*In re Japanese Electronic Products Antitrust Litigation* (DC MDL No. 189), Appeal Nos. 80-2080, 81-2331, 81-2332, 81-2333, December 5, 1983, 723 F.2d 319, 5 ITRD 1616, *cert. granted,* April 1, 1985, No. 83-2004, with review limited to two questions. See 2 ITR 487, 53 LW 3696.

In 1977 the Outboard Marine Corporation brought suit for treble damages under this statute and various provisions of the Sherman Antitrust Act against a Polish foreign trade organization, called Pezetel, and its U.S. sales corporation, for the importation and sale below cost of electric golf carts made in Poland exclusively for sale to the United States. The court granted the defendants' motion to dismiss this pricing claim because the Antidumping Act of 1916 could not be applied where the merchandise was not sold in the market of production or in any other foreign country and had no market value to provide a basis of comparison with the sales price in the United States.[10]

The question of standing to sue under the Antidumping Act of 1916 has received different answers. A plaintiff wholesaler was held not to have standing to sue the American distributor of Japanese electronic products on the ground that the 1916 Act was intended to protect only American manufacturers. *Schwimmer* v. *Sony Corporation of America,* 471 F. Supp. 793 (ED NY 1979) 2 ITRD 1125, *aff'd on other grounds,* 637 F.2d 41 (CA 2 1980). However, in *Jewel Foliage Co.* v. *Uniflora Overseas Florida, Inc.,* 497 F. Supp. 513 (DC Fla. 1980), the court distinguished the *Schwimmer* case on the ground that the plaintiff there was outside the target area and recognized the standing of the Jewel Co., an importer, to sue a competing importer, since the 1916 Act provided a remedy to "any person" without reference to domestic manufacturers.

After a review of the question of standing to sue the Court of Appeals for the Ninth Circuit held that a domestic competitor of a domestic buyer of dumped goods did not have standing under the 1916 Act because the purpose of the Act was to protect domestic producers of the competing dumped goods. *Western Concrete Structures Co., Inc.* v. *Mitsui & Company (USA), Inc.,* 760 F.2d 1013 (CA 9 1985) 7 ITRD 1070.

2. Restrictive Sales Agreements

Sections 802 and 803, 15 U.S.C. 73, 74, authorize the imposition, under regulations of the Secretary of the Treasury, of a special duty double the amount of the regular duty if a foreign article is imported under any agreement, understanding, or condition that the importer of the article will not use, purchase, or deal in the articles of any other person. Excluded from this penalty are importations under arrangements with a foreign producer for an exclusive agency for the sale of the foreign product without further restriction. The customs regulation under these sections[11] requires the district director to report to the Commissioner of Customs and await further instructions whenever it appears that imported articles may be subject to these special duties.

---

[10]*Outboard Marine Corp.* v. *Pezetel,* 461 F. Supp. 384 (D Del. 1978). After a counterclaim and a series of motions, the court allowed the plaintiff to amend its complaint to include a predatory pricing claim, limiting discovery to six months, 535 F. Supp. 248 (D Del. 1982) 3 ITRD 1917. In January 1984, the plaintiff was directed to file a new response brief to a motion for summary judgment. D Del. No. 77-51 MMS, January 26, 1984, 1984-1 Trade Cas. (CCH) ¶65,891.
[11]19 CFR 159.44.

B. Federal Trade Commission Act

This Act[12] declares unlawful unfair methods of competition in commerce among the several states and with foreign countries and unfair or deceptive acts or practices in such commerce. It authorizes the Federal Trade Commission (FTC) to issue cease and desist orders, subject to appeal to a U.S. Court of Appeals, to bring civil actions for recovery of civil penalties up to $10,000 for each violation, to sue to enjoin violations, and to investigate business practices, including trade conditions in and with foreign countries where trade combinations or practices may affect U.S. foreign trade.

The FTC has extensively implemented this Act through regulations published in Title 16 of the Code of Federal Regulations which provide guides as to practices considered unfair or deceptive and those considered conducive to sound business, trade practice rules for specific industries, and other interpretations of the law. The FTC requirements are in addition to any similar requirements imposed by the Customs Service. Importers were not successful in contending that their compliance with the country-of-origin marking requirements of Customs relieved them from compliance with the country-of-origin marking required by the FTC.[13]

The FTC increasingly appears before the ITC on antitrust issues in import competition determinations.

III. RESTRAINT OF TRADE

A. Sherman Antitrust Act of 1890, as Amended

This Act[14] declares to be illegal every contract, combination in the form of trust or otherwise, or conspiracy in restraint of trade or commerce among the several states or with foreign nations. Violation of this provision, or of the further provision prohibiting any monopoly or combination or conspiracy to monopolize interstate or foreign commerce, is now a felony. Conviction carries a penalty of a fine not exceeding $1,000,000 if the guilty party is a corporation, or if any other person $100,000 or imprisonment not exceeding three years or both such punishments. Furthermore, any property owned under any contract or by any combination or pursuant to any conspiracy which is illegal as a prohibited restraint of trade, being in interstate or foreign transportation, is subject to seizure and forfeiture.

The Act has been held to apply to U.S. persons who carry out a conspiracy formed in a foreign country where the effect is to restrain the importation and sale of foreign goods in the United States.[15]

---

[12]15 U.S.C. 41–58.

[13]*Baldwin Bracelet Corp.* v. *FTC*, 325 F.2d 1012 (DC Cir. 1963); *W.M.R. Watchcase Corp.* v. *FTC*, 343 F.2d 302 (DC Cir. 1965).

[14]15 U.S.C. 1–7.

[15]*Timken Roller Bearing Co.* v. *United States*, 341 U.S. 593 (1951); *United States* v. *Sisal Sales Corp.*, 274 U.S. 268 (1927); *Mannington Mills Inc.* v. *Congoleum Corp.*, 595 F.2d 1287 (CA 3 1979); *United States* v. *R.P. Oldham Co.*, 152 F. Supp. 818 (DC Cal. 1957).

The extended antitrust claims of the Zenith Radio Corporation under Sections 1 and 2 of the Sherman Act against the Matsushita Company were reviewed in a 234-page opinion and dismissed, with summary judgment for the defendants.[16] The district court determined that, in spite of "millions of documents" inspected "in nine years of discovery," the plaintiffs had not proved that the Japanese business cartels, their system of export customer allocations, and other alleged predatory practices constituted a conspiracy in restraint of trade. This was the decision which dismissed the remaining claims under the Antidumping Act of 1916. See section II.A.1 *supra*.

The Court of Appeals for the Third Circuit, in a companion opinion to its December 5, 1983, opinion rejecting the dismissal of the Antidumping Act of 1916 claims, reversed the summary judgment which the district court had issued in favor of the defendants, but affirmed the judgment in favor of Sony Corporation, Motorola, Inc., and Sears, Roebuck & Co.[17] The reversal extended to the summary judgment against the remaining 21 defendants on all the plaintiffs' claims under Sections 1 and 2 of the Sherman Act, under the Wilson Tariff Act, under Section 7 of the Clayton Act, under the Robinson-Patman Act, addressed to discriminatory sales to American customers, and under Section 16 of the Clayton Act respecting injunctive relief. The Court of Appeals found that the plaintiffs had presented sufficient evidence to raise genuine issues of material fact of a conspiracy for price stabilization in Japan which permitted the conspirators to cut prices in the American market and to allocate American customers.

The Court of Appeals for the Ninth Circuit found that a complaint stated a cause of action under the restraint-of-trade provisions of Section 1, and the antimonopoly provisions of Section 2, of the Sherman Act, which alleged that the defendants intended to injure competitors and drive them out of the market through the sale of imported steel strand at illegal low prices. *Western Concrete Structures Co., Inc.* v. *Mitsui & Company (USA) Inc.,* 760 F.2d 1013 (1985) 7 ITRD 1070. The court considered the import prices illegal because they were below the price fixed by the Trigger Price Mechanism, discussed in Chapter 12, Section VI.

B. Sections 73 and 74 of the Wilson Tariff Act of 1894, as Amended

These provisions[18] declare combinations, conspiracies, trusts, agreements, or contracts which are intended to operate in restraint of lawful trade or free competition or to increase the market price of imported articles, or of products into which such imported articles enter, to be contrary to public policy, illegal, and void. Persons engaged in the importation of goods or commodities in violation of the section or who participate in conspiracies or combinations to violate the section are subject to a fine of up to $5,000 and,

---

[16]*Zenith Radio Corp.* v. *Matsushita Electric Industrial Co., Ltd., supra* note 8.

[17]*In re Japanese Electronics Products Antitrust Litigation* (DC MDL No. 189), Appeal Nos. 81-2331, 81-2332, 81-2333, December 5, 1983, 723 F.2d 238, 5 ITRD 1593, *cert. granted,* April 1, 1985, No. 83-2004. See *supra* note 9.

[18]15 U.S.C. 8, 9.

in the court's discretion, imprisonment up to 12 months. The district courts are empowered to prevent and restrain violations.

This statute specifically applying the Sherman Antitrust Act to import trade does not supersede that Act and has been held to be coextensive with Section 1 of the Sherman Act in the international context.[19] They are so treated by the district court and the Court of Appeals in the *Japanese Electronic Products Antitrust Litigation,* discussed *supra.* Both acts may be applied in a criminal action charging illegal restraint of import trade.[20] Since the penalties under the Wilson Tariff Act have not been increased to match those available under the Sherman Act, the United States may more frequently invoke the Sherman Act to assure free competition in the import trade.

In the treble damage suit brought against the Polish manufacturer of electric golf carts, discussed *supra,* Outboard Marine Corporation sued under this statute charging an attempt to monopolize the electric golf cart market, as well as under 15 U.S.C. 72 for predatory pricing. The court denied the defendants' motion to dismiss the monopoly complaint, in view of the plaintiff's showing that the defendants' share of the market had grown from zero in 1970 to 35 percent in 1975 through low prices and restricted territorial sales.[21]

---

[19]*Zenith Radio Corp.* v. *Matsushita Electric Industrial Co., Ltd., supra* note 8; *Western Concrete Structures Co., Inc.* v. *Mitsui & Company (USA), Inc.,* 760 F.2d 1013 (CA 9 1985) 7 ITRD 1070.
[20]See cases *supra* note 15.
[21]See 1978 decision cited *supra* note 10.

19

Escape Clause (Safeguards)

The Trade Act of 1974 provides expanded and liberalized procedures whereby industries, firms, workers, and (ended 1982) communities which are injured by import competition can obtain relief during an adjustment period.[1] Title II of the Act, as amended by the Trade Agreements Act of 1979, Public Law 96-39, and the Trade and Tariff Act of 1984, Public Law 98-573, which affords relief from injury by import competition from any one or more non-Communist countries, provides for two forms of relief from foreign import competition: (1) import relief, and/or (2) adjustment assistance (see Chapter 20). The Act also contains provisions for relief when imports of an article which is a product of a Communist country cause market disruption.[2] The relief provided (see Chapter 21) is only in the form of "import relief." Adjustment assistance is not available in cases where imports of products of Communist countries cause market disruption.

I. BASIC PROVISIONS FOR RELIEF FROM INJURY FROM IMPORT COMPETITION

The provisions of Title II are designed to provide, on a temporary basis, flexible and appropriate forms of relief and assistance to domestic industries which are being injured as the result of import competition. These provisions largely replace the old escape-clause provisions under earlier trade agreements legislation and represent also an effort to simplify and make more effective the provisions for adjustment assistance in such legislation. The term "escape clause" refers to a provision in the legislation that allows relief from tariff concessions which are causing injury to domestic industry.

---

[1] 19 U.S.C. 2251–2394; Section 2395, Judicial Review, was added by Pub. L. No. 96-417.
[2] 19 U.S.C. 2436.

A. Not Necessary to Prove Foreign Competition Unfair

These provisions are in addition to other provisions in the 1974 Trade Act and in other statutes which afford relief from unfair foreign trade practices and which are discussed in Chapters 12, 13, 16, 17, and 18. The provisions discussed here relate to import competition, whether fair or unfair, which meets certain tests for establishing the existence of injury to a domestic industry.

B. Not a Protectionist Provision

The philosophy of this title of the law is not to provide permanent protection against foreign imports but to assist workers and firms to make adjustments to increased imports which are substantially injurious. Thus, import restrictions imposed are to be of limited duration; and adjustment assistance to workers and firms is authorized in some cases as an alternative to import restrictions, where appropriate to remedy the problem.

C. Who Makes the Decision

The decision on whether to grant import relief is made by the President after an investigation and a finding by the U.S. International Trade Commission (ITC) that an article is being imported "in such increased quantities as to be a substantial cause of serious injury, or the threat thereof, to the domestic industry producing an article like or directly competitive with the imported article." The President's decision is subject to review by the Congress (see section III.G *infra*).

The decision on adjustment assistance is made by the Secretary of Labor in the case of a petition by workers, and by the Secretary of Commerce in the case of a petition by a domestic firm or, until 1982, a community.

II. IMPORT RELIEF

The Act provides that import relief shall be afforded if the ITC finds that an article is causing injury and recommends that import relief be afforded.[3] The imports causing the injury need not be dutiable and the injury need not be attributable to a trade agreement concession, in whole or in part.

A. Forms of Relief Obtainable

If the injury standard is met, the President is required (unless he determines that to do so would be contrary to the national economic interest) to provide one of the following types of relief:

(1) Increases in, or imposition of, duties;
(2) Tariff-rate quotas;

---

[3] 19 U.S.C. 2251–2253.

(3) Quantitative restrictions;

(4) Orderly marketing agreements; or

(5) Any combination of the above.

Under the first alternative above, the President may impose a duty where none now exists or he may increase the rate of an existing duty. In the case of tariff-rate quotas, the President fixes a maximum annual amount of imports of the article in question which shall receive the existing rate of duty and provides that any imports above that amount shall carry a higher rate of duty. Quantitative restrictions (otherwise known as quotas) are provisions for a fixed annual amount of imports of a specified article and thereafter no more imports of such article may be entered in that year. Orderly marketing agreements are agreements whereby foreign countries undertake to limit the annual amount of their exports of a given article to the United States, usually under their own controls by licensing, visas, or otherwise.

It should be noted that the import relief provisions of the Trade Expansion Act of 1962 did not allow for a combination of the foregoing types of relief.

B. Procedure for Obtaining Import Relief

An American business seeking import relief under these provisions of the Trade Act, starts by filing a petition with the ITC under Section 201 of the Act.[4] A petition can be filed by a group "which is representative of an industry." This includes trade associations, firms, certified or recognized unions, or groups of workers. The law states that the petition should set forth the purpose of the petition for import relief, *i.e.,* should describe the petitioner's plan for adjusting to the import competition and how the relief sought relates to this adjustment. The filing of the petition commences an investigation by the ITC of the question of injury to a domestic industry. The investigation may also be started upon the request of the President or the U.S. Trade Representative, or upon resolution by the House Ways and Means Committee or the Senate Finance Committee, or by the ITC itself upon its own motion.

C. What to Include in the Petition

A petitioner needs to make out a *prima facie* case for import relief in the petition. That is, it should present facts as to imports of the competitive product and as to the effects of these increased imports in causing or threatening to cause serious injury which will support the findings of the ITC discussed *infra*. The ITC's regulations set forth specific requirements as to the contents of petitions.

The ITC requires that a petition contain the following:[5]

---

[4] 19 U.S.C. 2251. The regulations of the International Trade Commission are in 19 CFR Part 206, Subparts A and B.

[5] 19 CFR 206.9.

(1) Name and precise description of the imported article and the tariff classification and current tariff treatment thereof, and the name and a precise description of the like or directly competitive domestic article;

(2) Petitioning firm's name and location and the location of its production facilities;

(3) Name and addresses of other known producers not represented in the petition;

(4) Import data for the most recent five years "forming the basis of the claim that there has been an increase in imports, either actual or relative to domestic production," of the foreign article;

(5) Data on total U.S. production of the domestic article for the most recent five years;

(6) Data showing injury as described in the language from the Trade Act quoted in section D *infra;*

(7) An enumeration and description of the causes of injury, or threat thereof, and the extent to which increased imports are such a cause;

(8) Purpose of petition, *e.g.,* to facilitate orderly transfer of resources to alternative uses, other means of adjustment to increased competition, etc.; and

(9) A description of efforts by firms and workers to compete more effectively.

Assistance in the filing of petitions is available from the ITC which, under Section 221 of the Trade and Tariff Act of 1984, is required to set up a Trade Remedy Assistance Office to provide information on request concerning petition and application procedures, and is obligated, as are other trade agencies, to provide technical assistance to small businesses.

D. ITC Findings

Once the ITC starts a proceeding, it gathers facts from all available sources on the question of increased imports and their impact on domestic industry. It must reach findings determining (1) the domestic industry affected, (2) the extent of its injury, (3) whether increasing imports are the substantial cause, and (4) the appropriate relief, if relief is indicated.

1. The Industry Affected

Section 201(b)(2) provides that in the case of a domestic producer who also imports, the ITC may treat as part of such domestic industry only the producer's domestic production, and may in the case of a domestic producer who produces more than one article, treat as part of such domestic industry only that portion or subdivision of the producer which produces the "like or directly competitive" article.

The meaning of "like or directly competitive" was extensively examined by the ITC in its determination of serious injury to the canned mushroom industry from imports of mushrooms "prepared or preserved" under Item 144.20 TSUS, Inv. No. TA-201-43, August 1980, 2 ITRD 5209. After review of the interpretation of these modifiers under earlier escape clause legislation the ITC concluded that where producers of a "like" article can be treated as a separate industry from producers of an unlike but "directly competitive" product it should consider which of the two industries presents more compelling arguments for relief. It found that processors of mushrooms were a separate industry from producers of mushrooms and had demonstrated a threat of serious injury from the imported canned mushrooms. In reaching this conclusion the ITC noted that "like" has to do with the physical identity of the articles themselves, whereas "directly competitive" relates more to commercial interchangeability.

The subsection further provides that the ITC may, in the case of one or more domestic producers located in a major geographic area of the United States and whose production facilities in such area for such article constitute a substantial portion of the domestic industry and primarily serve the market in such area, and where the imports are concentrated in such area, treat as such domestic industry only that segment of the producer located in such geographic area.

2. The Extent of Injury

To recommend Section 201 relief the ITC must find that the increasing imports are a substantial cause of "serious injury," or the "threat thereof." Section 201(b)(2) lists as guidelines various economic factors which the ITC may take into account, as follows:

> with respect to serious injury, the significant idling of productive facilities in the industry, the inability of a significant number of firms to operate at a reasonable level of profit, and significant unemployment or underemployment within the industry;

and with respect to the threat of serious injury,

> a decline in sales, a higher and growing inventory, and a downward trend in production, profits, and wages, or employment (or increasing underemployment) in the domestic industry concerned.

As pointed out in the determination of injury to *Footwear*, Inv. No. TA-201-7 (1976), these factors are not all inclusive nor singly decisive (1 ITRD 5178, 5183). The ITC weighs the economic data pertaining to all these factors. Transitory factors are discounted and the closing of a few facilities may not be significant. *Bolts, Nuts, and Screws of Iron or Steel,* TA-201-2 (1975) 1 ITRD 5142.

The emphasis put by the ITC in a subsequent negative *Footwear* determination, Inv. No. 201-TA-50 (See section IV.A *infra*), on the profitability of the surviving firms in the industry led to the inclusion in the Trade and Tariff Act of 1984, of one of several amendments proposed by the Senate in the Section 201(b)(2) guidelines. (Conf. Rep. 98–1156 at 139–142). The amendment, Section 249 of Public Law 98-573, provides that "the presence or absence of any factor which the Commission is required to evaluate ... shall not necessarily be dispositive" in determining whether imports are a substantial cause of serious injury or threat of serious injury to the domestic industry. Section 249 further provides that the term "significant idling of productive facilities" includes the closing of plants or the underutilization of production capacity.

3. Imports the Substantial Cause

The economic factors mentioned in Section 201(b)(2) to guide the ITC determination as to whether the imports are a "substantial cause" of injury are

> an increase in imports (either actual or relative to domestic production) and a decline in the proportion of the domestic market supplied by domestic producers.

The subsection also provides a definition of "substantial cause" as follows:

> the term "substantial cause" means a cause which is important and not less than any other cause.

In applying this definition the ITC stated at the outset that where the increased imports are just one of many causes of equal weight it is unlikely that they would constitute important cause of the serious injury, but where such imports are one of two factors of equal weight, they probably constitute an important cause. *Wrapper Tobacco,* Inv. No. TA-201-3 (1975) 1 ITRD 5137 (no injury); *Stainless Steel and Alloy Tool Steel,* Inv. No. TA-201-5 (1976) 1 ITRD 5404 (injury to certain products). The increased imports must, of course, precede the serious economic condition of the industry. *Birch Plywood Door Skins,* Inv. No. TA-201-1 (1975) 1 ITRD 5121 (no injury).

Where the quantity and value of imports increased markedly over a three-year period without other significant contributing factors, import relief was recommended. *Leather Wearing Apparel,* Inv. No. TA-201-40 (1980) 1 ITRD 5455. However, the substantial increase from 1975 to June 1980, of imported automobiles and light trucks was found not to be a substantial cause of the economic plight of the domestic automobile industry, in view of the more important causes within the industry which would not be remedied by decreased imports. *Certain Motor Vehicles and Certain Chassis and Bodies Therefor,* Inv. No. TA-201-44 (1980) 2 ITRD 5241.

4. Appropriate Relief

A review of the import relief recommended by the ITC in determinations made to October 1985, is provided in section IV.A *infra.*

E. Hearing Required

The law requires the ITC to hold a public hearing during the proceeding at which interested parties will be provided an opportunity to be present, to present evidence, and to be heard. The hearing proceeding may be crucial in shaping the outcome. A domestic producer either alone or in cooperation with other members of the domestic industry and with counsel should marshal and present to the ITC all facts that can demonstrate that increased imports are a substantial cause of serious injury or the threat thereof.

An importer of the product under consideration needs either alone or in cooperation with other importers and the foreign exporters and with counsel to marshal all the facts and arguments that can demonstrate that imports have not increased actually or relative to the size of the market or that the increased imports are not a substantial cause of serious injury, *i.e.,* that other factors are more important causes of the plight of the domestic industry.

F. ITC Report

The Act requires the ITC to report to the President its findings, including any dissenting or separate views. Its report must be made not later than six months from the date of the filing of the petition. The ITC is required to publish its report promptly.

G. Negative Determination

If the ITC finds that increased imports are not a substantial cause of serious injury or the threat thereof to the domestic industry, that terminates the proceeding. If the ITC makes a negative determination, then a new proceeding on the same imported product may not be started until one year has elapsed, unless the ITC determines that there is good cause to consider the question again in less time. See section III.F.1 *infra.*

H. Affirmative Determination

If the ITC finds serious injury or threat thereof, it is also required to find "the amount of the increase in, or imposition of, any duty or other import restriction on such article which is necessary to prevent or remedy" such injury. The ITC is also required to report on efforts made by firms and workers in the industry to compete more effectively with imports. If the ITC's investigation gives reason to believe that there have been foreign unfair trade practices in connection with the imports in question, such as violation of the Antidumping Act or Countervailing Duty Law, the ITC must refer the matter to the Commerce Department so that it can act under the applicable statute. If the ITC determines that adjustment assistance can effectively remedy the serious injury, it must include such a finding and recommendation in its report.

I. Parallel Studies by Secretaries of Labor and Commerce

Whenever the ITC commences an investigation, it must immediately notify the Secretary of Labor, who must immediately begin a study of (1) the number of workers in the domestic industry producing the like or directly competitive article who have been or are likely to be certified as eligible for adjustment assistance; and (2) the extent to which the adjustment of such workers to the import competition may be facilitated through the use of existing programs. The Secretary of Labor's report must be made to the President not more than 15 days after the date when the ITC's report is due (19 U.S.C. 2274).

Likewise the ITC must immediately notify the Secretary of Commerce of the commencement of an import relief investigation. That Secretary undertakes a study, also due 15 days after the ITC report, of the number of domestic firms producing like or directly competitive articles likely to be certified as eligible for adjustment assistance and the extent to which adjustment may be facilitated by existing programs (19 U.S.C. 2354).[6] In making his decision, the President must consider these reports.

III. PRESIDENTIAL ACTION

A. Requirements

The Act requires the President within 60 days after receiving a report from the ITC containing an affirmative finding to do the following:

• Determine what method and amount of import relief he will provide or determine that the provision of such relief is not in the national economic interest of the United States, and whether he will direct expeditious consideration of adjustment assistance, and publish in the *Federal Register* that he has made such determination; or

• If the ITC's report recommends the provision of adjustment assistance, publish in the *Federal Register* his order to the Secretary of Labor and Secretary of Commerce for expeditious consideration of petitions.

In making these determinations, the Act says that he may take into account any other considerations that he deems relevant, including:

• The probable effectiveness of import relief as a means to promote adjustment, the efforts being made or to be implemented by the industry concerned to adjust to import competition, and other considerations relative to the position of the industry in the nation's economy;

• The effect of import relief on the international economic interests of the United States;

• The impact on U.S. industries and firms as a consequence of any possible modification of duties or other import restrictions which may result from international obligations with respect to compensation;

• The geographic concentration of imported products marketed in the United States;

• The extent to which the U.S. market is the focal point for exports of such article by reason of restraints on exports of such article to, or on imports of such article into, third country markets; and

---

[6]Executive Order 11913, 41 FR 17721, April 26, 1976, requires the ITC to provide to the Secretaries of Commerce and Labor the factual data it collects from firms seeking import relief on their "sales, production, employment, and financial experience," for use solely for performance of their adjustment assistance functions.

• The economic and social costs which would be incurred by taxpayers, communities, and workers if import relief were or were not provided.

B. Limitations on the President's Action

Once the President determines to grant import relief, he is required to issue a proclamation within 15 days establishing the restrictions he has selected, unless he announces on that date his intention to negotiate an orderly marketing agreement. If the President determines to grant relief via the tariff or tariff-rate quota route, he may not proclaim or increase a rate of duty which is more than 50 percent *ad valorem* above the existing rate. If he imposes a quantitative restriction on imports of the article (quota), it must permit the importation of a quantity or value of the article at least equal to the amount normally imported in a representative period.

C. Orderly Marketing Agreements

If the President selects orderly marketing agreements as the best method of dealing with the increased imports, the law allows 90 days in which to negotiate such agreements during which time the effectiveness of an initial proclamation imposing increased duties or quantitative restrictions can be suspended. As an alternative, the President may proclaim an increase in duties, a tariff-rate quota, or quantitative restriction initially, then proceed to negotiate and carry out orderly marketing agreements, and, after such agreements take effect, suspend or terminate, in whole or part, the import restrictions. On the other hand, if an orderly marketing agreement does not continue to be effective, he can at any time proclaim another form of import relief.

D. Equivalents of Increases in Duty

The Trade Act provides that suspension with respect to an article under Item 806.30 or 807.00 of the tariff schedules or suspension of the designation of an article under Title V of the Act (GSP) shall be treated as an increase in duty. The President may proclaim such a suspension only if the ITC determines in its report that the serious injury results from the application of Items 806.30, 807.00, or the designation under Title V. Items 806.30 and 807.00 of the tariff schedules afford duty benefits on certain articles exported for further processing or packaging and returned to the United States. Title V of the Trade Act authorizes the President to extend tariff preferences on designated articles from developing countries under certain conditions.

E. Duration and Level of Import Relief

Any import relief proclaimed by the President shall terminate after five years, unless extended. If the import relief proclaimed is for more than three years, it shall be phased down during the period it is in effect starting not later than three years from the date the relief starts. The duration of a proclamation can be extended by the President for one period of not more than three years and only at the level existing at the time he extends it.

F. ITC Reinvestigation and Review of Relief

1. Reinvestigation Under Section 201

No reinvestigation of the need for import relief for articles which were the subject of a Section 201 investigation is to be made within one year of the ITC's original report to the President except for "good cause determined by the Commission" (Section 201(e)). In a suit brought by importers of footwear restricted by orderly marketing agreements resulting from a second investigation under Section 201 begun within eight months of a prior report to the President, the U.S. district court held that a resolution of the Senate Finance Committee calling for a new investigation constituted good cause.[7] The court further held that no notice or hearing was necessary prior to a good cause determination since the rights of the parties were protected by the notice and hearing provisions within the investigation process.

No investigation under Section 201 is to be commenced with respect to an article which has received import relief unless two years have elapsed since the last day on which import relief was provided (Section 203(j)).

2. Review and Relief Continuance Under Section 203(i)

The ITC is required to keep under review developments respecting an industry receiving import relief under the Trade Expansion Act as well as the 1974 Act, including the industry's efforts and progress toward adjusting to the import competition. It reports these developments to the President upon his request; and upon the President's request or its own motion, it advises the President under either Act on the probable economic effect upon the protected industry of the extension, reduction, or termination of the import relief which was provided.

Six to nine months before the initial period of import relief is to expire, the affected domestic industry can petition the ITC for an extension. The ITC will advise the President, after holding a hearing, and the President will decide whether an extension is warranted taking into account the objectives of the Act. The President can, after consulting with the Secretaries of Commerce and Labor, reduce or terminate import relief at any time he considers it in the national interest.

The ITC investigations undertaken to provide advice on relief continuation are identified as Section 203(i) investigations, since they are authorized by that section of the Trade Act (19 U.S.C. 2253(i)), as distinguished from the original investigations of the need for relief under Section 201 of the Act

---

[7]*Sneaker Circus, Inc.* v. *Carter*, 457 F. Supp. 771 (ED NY 1978), *aff'd,* 614 F.2d 1290 (1979).

(19 U.S.C. 2251). A survey of the ITC's advice under this section is included in section IV.B *infra*.

G. Reports to the Congress and Congressional Veto Procedure[8]

Whatever the President decides with respect to a petition for import relief, he must report promptly to the Congress. If he decides to take an action which differs from the action recommended by the ITC, or if he decides that he will not provide import relief, the action recommended by the ITC shall take effect upon enactment of a joint resolution within 90 days of the transmission of the President's report. The provision for "enactment of a joint resolution" was substituted in Section 203(c) of the Trade Act of 1974 for a prior provision for a majority vote of each House of Congress for a disapproving concurrent resolution, by Section 248 of the Trade and Tariff Act of 1984.

Under an amendment of Section 330 of the Tariff Act by the Tax Reform Act of 1976 (Section 1801, Public Law 94-455)[9] the Congress may also override presidential action which is contrary to a plurality of three votes in the ITC, or which supports one side in a tie vote, or which differs from both sides in a tie vote. These provisions apply not only to escape clause import relief findings but also to findings on relief from market disruptions by imports from Communist countries.

H. Compensatory Concessions

Section 123 of the Trade Act of 1974 (19 U.S.C. 2133), consistent with GATT rules, provides that whenever import relief has been provided increasing or imposing any duty or other import restriction the President may enter into trade agreements with foreign countries to grant new concessions as compensation in order to maintain the general level of reciprocal and mutually advantageous concessions. To carry out any such agreement the President may proclaim modification or continuance of any existing duty or treatment as appropriate. However, the section places limits on the extent of any decrease in the rate of duty and requires adherence to substantially the same time schedule for reduction as is applicable to the relevant import relief for which compensation is being given.

Compensatory compensation takes the form of a Presidential Proclamation modifying Schedule XX annexed to the GATT, the schedule of United States concessions, and adding to Subpart C of Part 2 of the TSUS Appendix the list of TSUS items on which rates of duty are temporarily reduced. As stated in Presidential Proclamation 5140 of December 19, 1983 (48 FR 56553), issued under Section 123, the TSUS items upon which rates of duty were reduced were determined upon through negotiations with the foreign countries affected by the import relief granted under the escape

---

[8]Note *Immigration and Naturalization Service* v. *Chadha,* 103 S.Ct. 2764 (1983), holding unconstitutional the invalidation of Executive actions by a House of Congress.

[9]19 U.S.C. 1330(d).

clause provisions. In that Proclamation the negotiations had been with the governments of Japan and Spain to effect compensation for the adverse result of Proclamation 4713 of January 16, 1980, temporarily increasing the rates of duty on certain nonelectric cooking ware of steel. The compensatory rate reduction proclaimed was in the Column 1 rate of duty available to the products of all countries eligible for Column 1 rates.

IV. OPERATION OF THE RELIEF PROVISIONS

A. Relief Obtained Under Section 201

During the 10 years ending December 31, 1984, since the effective date of Section 201 of the Trade Act of 1974, the ITC completed 53 investigations brought under this section.[10] It recommended relief in 31 of these cases. In 16, or just about half, of the 31 affirmative determinations the President provided for some relief to the domestic industry: adjustment assistance in 5 instances and import relief in the form of increased duties, quotas, or orderly marketing agreements in 11 instances. The President rejected relief in 15 cases on the ground, in most instances, that relief would not be in the national economic interest because of increased costs to consumers, improvements occurring in the industry, the probability of foreign retaliation, or adverse impact on U.S. efforts to obtain international reduction of trade barriers.

The relatively low percentage of achievement of Section 201 relief through 1980 may provide one reason why only one investigation was instituted during 1981, *Fishing Rods and Parts Thereof,* Inv. No. TA-201-45. This resulted in an ITC determination of no serious injury substantially caused by imports.[11] The previous decision on November 10, 1980, in the investigation of *Certain Motor Vehicles and Certain Chassis and Bodies Therefor,* Inv. No. TA-201-44, had found that increased imports of automobiles and light trucks were not a substantial cause of serious injury to the U.S. industry.[12]

In 1982 the ITC again reached a negative finding of serious injury substantially caused by imports, in its investigation of *Tubeless Tire Valves,* Inv. No. TA-201-46.[13] In 1983, however, the ITC found that serious injury to domestic industry was substantially caused by imports in its investigations of *Heavyweight Motor Cycles,* Inv. No. TA-201-47,[14] and *Stainless Steel and Alloy Tool Steel,* Inv. No. TA-201-48.[15] The President then determined to provide import relief for the heavyweight motorcycle industry in the form of declining tariff rate quotas, starting at 45 percent *ad*

---

[10]Data in this subpart A are drawn in part from USITC "Summary of Investigations Under Section 201 of the Trade Act of 1974" and USITC Annual Report 1980.

[11]46 FR 57777, November 25, 1981, 3 ITRD 1819.

[12]45 FR 85194, December 24, 1980, 2 ITRD 5241.

[13]47 FR 42852, September 29, 1982, 4 1TRD 1986.

[14]48 FR 6043, February 9, 1983, 4 1TRD 2469.

[15]48 FR 22373, May 18, 1983, 5 ITRD 1411.

valorem, during a five-year period, to be under review by the USTR as to its continuing necessity.[16] For the specialty steel industry the President determined to provide more extended and diversified relief than recommended by the ITC, namely, declining tariff increases for certain types of steel, as well as quotas for other types, over a four- rather than a three-year period.[17] The USTR was directed to undertake an annual review of the necessity for and effectiveness of the import relief. Country allocations of the quotas and modifications of the TSUS made by the USTR were published in the *Federal Register* for October 21, 1983, 48 FR 48888, and modified, January 20, 1984, 49 FR 2567.

In 1984 the ITC reported to the President that imports of *Stainless Steel Table Flatware,* Inv. No. 201-TA-49, were not being imported in such increased quantities as to be a substantial cause of serious injury. 49 FR 24459, June 13, 1984, 6 ITRD 1032. It made a similar negative report respecting *Nonrubber Footwear,* Inv. No. 201-TA-50, 49 FR 29161, July 18, 1984, 6 ITRD 1992. However, the ITC found that imports were a substantial cause of serious injury in *Carbon and Certain Steel Products,* Inv. No. 201-TA-51, and in *Unwrought Copper,* Inv. No. 201-TA-52, reported, respectively, to the President July 24, 1984, 49 FR 30807, August 1, 1984, 6 ITRD 2236, and July 16, 1984, 49 FR 30026, July 25, 1984, 6 ITRD 1708.

The President declined to adopt the recommendations for relief made by the ITC in the carbon steel and unwrought copper determinations because of the national interest in free trade, 49 FR 36813, September 20, 1984. However, he proposed quantitative restrictions to be negotiated with steel-exporting countries, which proposal became "the national policy for the steel industry" embodied in the Steel Import Stabilization Act, Title VIII of the Trade and Tariff Act of 1984. The provisions of that Act are discussed in Chapter 14, section VIII *supra.* The Congress also provided in the Trade and Tariff Act, Section 247, that the President should negotiate voluntary restraint agreements with the principal foreign copper-producing countries.

In the fifth and last escape clause investigation in 1984, *Certain Canned Tuna Fish,* Inv. No. TA-201-53, the ITC found imports not to be a substantial cause of serious injury. 49 FR 34310, August 29, 1984, 6 ITRD 2464. A further negative determination was issued in 1985: *Potassium Permanganate,* Inv. No. TA-201-54, 50 FR 19497, May 8, 1985, 7 ITRD ———.

At the request of the Senate Committee on Finance, the ITC instituted in January 1985, a fourth Section 201 investigation of *Nonrubber Footwear,* Inv. No. TA-201-55. It reached an affirmative determination of injury and recommended to the President the imposition of quotas for a five-year period. 50 FR 30245, July 24, 1985, 7 ITRD ———. However, the President determined that import relief was not in the national interest. 50 FR 35205, August 30, 1985.

---

[16]48 FR 17179, April 21, 1983. Proclamation 5050, 48 FR 16639, April 19, 1983.
[17]48 FR 31177, July 7, 1983. Proclamation 5074, 48 FR 33233, July 21, 1983.

Certain products which ultimately received import relief went through the Section 201 process several times. Imports of *Bolts, Nuts, and Screws of Iron or Steel* were the subject of Inv. Nos. TA-201-2 (negative injury, 1975), TA-201-27 (affirmative ITC finding 1977, rejected by the President February 10, 1978), and TA-201-37, initiated at the request of the House Committee on Ways and Means, and resulting in retained or increased duties over a three-year period.[18] The investigation of *Nonrubber Footwear* in 1975, Inv. No. TA-201-7, resulted in the provision of adjustment assistance, but a second investigation in 1976 at the instance of the Senate Finance Committee, Inv. No. TA-201-18, resulted in orderly marketing agreements with various producing countries.[19] The third investigation reached a negative result, TA-201-50, but the fourth found injury, TA-201-55. *High-Carbon Ferrochrome* was the subject of Inv. No. TA-201-28, in 1977, which reached an affirmative determination rejected by the President in 1978 for reasons of national economic interest. A second investigation, Inv. No. TA-201-35, in 1978, culminated in a three-year increase in duties.[20] The importation of *Mushrooms* has received three investigations, Inv. No. TA-201-10, resulting in adjustment assistance, Inv. No. TA-201-17, resulting in Presidential rejection, and Inv. No. TA-201-43, 2 ITRD 5209, resulting in a three-year increase in duties.[21]

B. Continuation of Relief Under Section 203(i)

Through June 30, 1985, the ITC conducted 14 investigations under Section 203(i) of the Trade Act of 1974, Inv. Nos. TA-203-1 through TA-203-14, to determine the need for continuance of the relief provided, in the case of Inv. No. TA-203-1 under the Trade Expansion Act, and in the other instances, under Section 201 of the Trade Act. For certain articles more than one investigation was made.

These investigations resulted in recommendations by the ITC for continuance of relief, in existing or modified form, for all or a portion of the commodities covered, in 10 of the 14 cases. Continuance of relief as recommended, or with modification, was provided by the President, or permitted to continue without change, in 9 of these 10 cases. One investigation, Inv. No. TA-203-14, was terminated shortly after institution.

Certain Ceramic Articles. Inv. No. TA-203-1, 1976, found that termination of the increased rates of duty would have an adverse effect upon the competitive portion of the industry. Proclamation 4436 of April 30, 1976, then extended and modified the increased rates for certain ceramic articles and terminated them for others. Inv. No. TA-203-4, 1978, advised that termination of relief would probably have a minimal effect. Relief was then terminated by Proclamation 4604, published in the *Federal Register* of October 5, 1978.

---

[18]Proclamation 4632, January 4, 1979.
[19]Proclamation 4510, June 24, 1977, 42 FR 32430, see section III.F *supra.*
[20]Proclamation 4608, November 15, 1978.
[21]Proclamation 4801, October 29, 1980.

Stainless Steel and Alloy Tool Steel. Three investigations involved continuance of the quotas protecting stainless steel and/or alloy steel imposed by the President in 1976 and 1977, Inv. No. TA-203-2 (USITC Pub. 805, 1977), Inv. No. TA-203-3 (USITC Pub. 838, 1977), and Inv. No. TA-203-5 (USITC Pub. 968, 1979). Termination of the annual quotas for certain alloy tool steel (bearing steel) was recommended by the ITC in Inv. No. TA-203-2, February 24, 1977. Those quotas were terminated by Proclamation 4509.[22] A divided ITC in Inv. No. TA-203-3 advised continuation of all remaining quotas. Two products were then removed from quotas. The second overall investigation resulted in a split recommendation for and against termination of all quotas for stainless steel and alloy tool steel, Inv. No. TA-203-5, April 24, 1979. The result was the issuance of Proclamations 4665[23] and 4668[24] modifying part and extending other parts of the existing quotas to February 13, 1980.

TV and Footwear Orderly Marketing Agreements. The ITC recommended limited continuance of the orderly marketing agreements with Taiwan and Korea covering color television receivers and subassemblies, Inv. No. TA-203-6 (45 FR 37781, June 4, 1980), and a two-year continuance for most nonrubber footwear, Inv. No. TA-203-7 (46 FR 24036, 2 ITRD 5549, April 29, 1981). Modified coverage of color TV products was extended through June 30, 1982, by Proclamation 4769 of June 30, 1980.[25] No extension was provided respecting nonrubber footwear, and the restraint period terminated June 30, 1981.

High-Carbon Ferrochrome. Inv. No. TA-203-8 (46 FR 49683, 3 ITRD 1171, October 7, 1981) advised the President that termination of tariff relief would have an adverse effect on the domestic industry. The increase of duty was continued for one year by Proclamation 4884 of November 13, 1981.[26]

Certain Mushrooms. Inv. No. TA-203-9 (46 FR 47892, 3 ITRD 1707, September 30, 1981) recommended termination of tariff relief respecting certain specified products and continuation respecting the remainder. This recommendation was carried out in Proclamation 4904 of February 27, 1982.[27]

Porcelain-on-Steel Cooking Ware. Inv. No. TA-203-10 (46 FR 55163, November 6, 1981) recommended continuation of tariff relief for the remaining two years of the four-year period ending January 1984, provided in Proclamation 4713. No action by the President was needed or taken.

Bolts, Nuts, and Large Screws of Iron or Steel. Inv. No. TA-203-11 (46 FR 56950, November 19, 1981) recommended termination of the increased duties scheduled to terminate January 5, 1982. No extension was provided by the President.

---

[22]42 FR 30829, June 17, 1977.
[23]44 FR 34089, June 14, 1979.
[24]44 FR 40873, July 13, 1979.
[25]45 FR 45237, July 2, 1980.
[26]46 FR 56407, November 17, 1981.
[27]47 FR 8753, March 2, 1982.

Clothespins. Inv. No. TA-203-12, 46 FR 62338, December 22, 1981, advised continuation for three years of the existing quota relief due to terminate February 22, 1982. Proclamation 4901 of February 22, 1982[28] continued quota relief at the existing levels for two years.

Certain Mushrooms. Inv. No. TA-203-13, 47 FR 18197, April 28, 1982, advised against termination of the relief provided for canned frozen mushrooms broiled in butter or butter sauce, as termination would have an adverse effect on an industry improving its capability.

Certain Mushrooms. Inv. No. TA-203-14 was instituted May 12, 1983, 48 FR 22373, covering mushrooms provided for in Item 144.20, TSUS, and terminated June 23, 1983, on the withdrawal of the petition, 48 FR 29962, June 29, 1983.

V. JUDICIAL REVIEW

A. Jurisdiction

In *Sneaker Circus, Inc.* v. *Carter,* 457 F. Supp. 771 (ED NY 1978), *aff'd,* 614 F.2d 1290 (CA 2 1979), referred to in section III.F *supra,* the district court had been directed by the Court of Appeals for the Second Circuit to take jurisdiction of a challenge to the validity of orderly marketing agreements resulting from the ITC determination in Inv. No. TA-201-18, section IV.A *supra,* because such agreements were enforced abroad, giving the importer plaintiffs no opportunity to challenge the restraints by protest in the Customs Court, 566 F.2d 396 (CA 2 1977) 1 ITRD 1647. With the enactment of the Customs Courts Act of 1980 the Court of International Trade appears to have jurisdiction of such a challenge under its exclusive jurisdiction given in 28 U.S.C. 1581(i) over questions arising from quantitative restrictions on the importation of merchandise. In *Sneaker Circus,* the district court held that the importers claiming injury to their business had standing to sue executive officers alleged to have exceeded their statutory authority.

In *Maple Leaf Fish Co.* v. *United States,* 5 CIT 275, 566 F. Supp. 899 (1983) 4 1TRD 2173 the Court of International Trade took jurisdiction, through a protest against liquidation, of a challenge to the action by the ITC and the President under Section 201, claiming that frozen buttered and breaded mushrooms had improperly been included in the ITC findings and recommendations of import relief (Inv. No. TA-201-43, 2 ITRD 5209, section IV.A *supra*) and the Proclamation of increased duties. Jurisdiction was found in 28 U.S.C. 1581(a) since the plaintiff had protested the increased duties. The court later upheld the President's action. *Maple Leaf Fish Co.* v. *United States,* 8 CIT ____ , 596 F. Supp. 1076 (1984) 6 ITRD 1019, *aff'd,* 762 F.2d 86 (Fed Cir. 1985), 6 ITRD 2186.

---

[28]47 FR 7997, February 24, 1982.

B. Extent of Review

The district court held in *Sneaker Circus* that its review of the ITC good cause determination underlying its investigation could be only to determine if it was arbitrary, capricious, or an abuse of discretion, and that its review of the President's action could be only for its conformity to statutory authority. No abuse or invalidity was found. Likewise, in the *Maple Leaf Fish Co.* case the CIT and the CAFC restricted their review to the same limits.

20

Adjustment Assistance

I. SCOPE OF RELIEF

The Trade Act of 1974, in its Title II covering import relief, provided for adjustment assistance to workers, firms, and communities determined to be adversely affected by import competition, whether fair or unfair.[1] The Title II provisions were intended to enhance and expedite the trade adjustment assistance to workers and firms first made available in the Trade Expansion Act of 1962, and to extend assistance to communities impacted by trade dislocation. The adjustment assistance program was designed to provide transition assistance to alternative work, enterprise, and development. The authority to provide adjustment assistance extended to September 30, 1982.

Title XXV of the Omnibus Budget Reconciliation Act of 1981[2] extended the authority to provide adjustment assistance to workers and firms through September 30, 1983. It restricted and revised the adjustment assistance provided to workers, as described in section II *infra,* and added a provision authorizing the Secretary of Commerce to provide technical assistance to industrywide programs for new product development, new process development, export development, or other uses consistent with import relief.[3] Public Law 98-120, October 12, 1983, extended adjustment assistance to workers and firms to September 30, 1985. The Deficit Reduction Act of 1984, Public Law 98-369, enabled workers to receive up to 26 additional weeks of trade readjustment allowance (TRA) under certain conditions. Adjustment assistance was extended to November 15, 1985, while legislation for further extension was being considered.

Special provisions contemplating adjustment assistance for workers in communities adversely affected by imports of steel products and assuring industry-financed retraining for workers of the major steel companies were enacted as part of the Steel Import Stabilization Act, Title VIII of the Trade and Tariff Act of 1984, Public Law 98-573. See section II.E *infra.*

---

[1] 19 U.S.C. 2271–2394; Part 2 (workers) 2271–2322; Part 3 (firms) 2341–2354; Part 4 (communities) 2371–2374. For purposes of the program see S. Rep. No. 93-1298, November 26, 1974.
[2] Pub. L. No. 97-35, August 13, 1981, 95 Stat. 881.
[3] 19 U.S.C. 2355.

Adjustment assistance may come about as a result of a petition for import relief if the President on the recommendation of the U.S. International Trade Commission (ITC), or on his own determination, directs the Secretary of Labor or the Secretary of Commerce to give expeditious consideration to petitions for adjustment assistance. But it is not necessary to petition for import relief to be eligible for adjustment assistance.

II. ADJUSTMENT ASSISTANCE FOR WORKERS

A. Petition

The petition for certification of eligibility to apply for adjustment assistance may be filed with the Secretary of Labor by a group of workers or by their certified or recognized union or other authorized representative.[4] The Secretary must then promptly publish in the *Federal Register* notice of receipt of the petition and initiation of an investigation. Any interested person may, within 10 days after the *Federal Register* notice, request the Secretary of Labor to provide a public hearing on the question of eligibility.

B. Criteria for Approval

The Secretary of Labor is required to certify a group of workers as eligible to apply for adjustment assistance if he determines that:
- A significant number or proportion of the workers in such workers' firm, or an appropriate subdivision of the firm, have become totally or partially separated or are threatened to become totally or partially separated;
- Sales and/or production of such firm or subdivision have decreased absolutely; and
- Increases of imports of articles like or directly competitive with articles produced by such workers' firm, or an appropriate subdivision thereof, contributed importantly to such total or partial separation, or threat thereof, and to such decline in sales or production.

The Act defines "contributed importantly" as meaning "a cause which is important but not necessarily more important than any other cause." This test of "contributed importantly" was reinstated by Public Law 98-120, October 12, 1983, after this provision in the original statute was supplanted under the 1981 Act by a "substantial cause" test.

C. Time Limit

The Secretary is required to make a determination on the question of eligibility within 60 days from the date of filing of the petition and to

---

[4]The regulations covering the certification of eligiblity to apply for worker adjustment assistance are in 29 CFR Part 90; the regulations pertaining to applications by individuals to state -gencies for adjustment assistance, after certification of eligibility of the group of workers, are in 29 CFR Part 91. The termination date applicable to Part 91 of September 30, 1982, was removed October 1, 1982, 47 FR 43375.

publish his determination in the *Federal Register,* stating his reasons. A certificate of eligibility will not apply to any worker whose last separation from the firm occurred more than a year before the date of the petition or more than six months before the effective date of the Trade Act. When conditions change so that the Secretary of Labor determines that adjustment assistance is no longer appropriate he may publish a notice of termination of the certification of eligibility.

D. Types of Adjustment Assistance Available

A worker covered by a certificate of eligibility may apply for a trade readjustment allowance and, in addition, may be eligible for reemployment services, including job training and job search and relocation allowances. Adjustment assistance is administered and provided by the state agency which administers the state's unemployment compensation law, but in accordance with the regulations, and with use of the forms, provided by the Secretary of Labor.

The kind and extent of trade adjustment assistance available to workers under the Trade Act of 1974, as amended by the 1981 Act, together with the eligibility and procedural requirements, are set forth in the proposed regulations of the Employment and Training Administration of the Department of Labor, 20 CFR Part 635, published March 4, 1983, 48 FR 9444, and proposed amendments, published April 15, 1985, 50 FR 14720. These regulations are to be issued as Part 617 of Title 20, CFR. They will supersede the regulations on this subject in 29 CFR Part 91. The responsibility for directing trade adjustment assistance available to workers after certification was placed in the Employment and Training Administration of the Department of Labor in 1981.

1. Trade Readjustment Allowance

A worker covered by a certificate of eligibility may apply to a state agency and qualify for a trade readjustment allowance (TRA) if his separation occurred within the two-year period prior to the date of certification and on or after the impact date determined in the certification, and if his work duration satisfies the requirements of the regulations. The 1981 Act revised the prior law on eligibility for a TRA to prohibit payment of a TRA until a worker has exhausted all rights to state or federal unemployment insurance. That Act also restricted the amount of the weekly TRA payment to that equal to the unemployment insurance weekly benefit. Previously, workers could receive a combination of benefits within certain limits. Eligibility for TRA extends for 52 weeks after exhaustion of unemployment benefits, but may extend up to 26 weeks further if the worker is in approved training. A further 26 weeks was authorized in the 1984 Deficit Reduction Act. During the eligibility period the worker not in training must be actively searching for work in order to receive the TRA.

2. Reemployment Services, Including Training

State agencies are responsible for providing to adversely affected workers a variety of reemployment services, including counseling, listing, placement, supportive services, job search and relocation assistance, and training. Training costs are paid by the federal government if funds are available and the training is approved under the Trade Act, as amended. Training is approved if there is no suitable employment available and if there is a reasonable expectation of employment as a result of the training. A worker in training outside his commuting area receives subsistence and transportation payments within prescribed limits.

3. Job Search Allowance

An affected worker covered by a certification, who has been totally separated from his job, can also apply to the appropriate state agency for a job search allowance. If approved, the worker may receive 90 percent of his necessary job search expenses up to a maximum of $600. The job search allowance may be approved only:

- To assist an adversely affected worker in securing a job within the United States;
- Where the state agency determines that such worker cannot reasonably be expected to secure suitable employment in the community area in which he resides; and
- Where the worker has filed an application for such allowance with the state agency no later than one year after the date of his last total separation or (in the case of a worker who has been referred to training) within a reasonable period of time after the conclusion of such training period.

4. Relocation Allowance

The law authorizes an adversely affected worker covered by a certification to apply for a relocation allowance. The state agency may approve the application if the worker has obtained employment affording a reasonable expectation of long-term duration in the area in which he wishes to relocate or if he has obtained a *bona fide* offer of such employment. The allowance may be granted only if the worker is under a certificate in the week in which he files his application or would be entitled to but for the fact that he has obtained the employment.

The relocation must occur within a reasonable period after filing the application or completion of an authorized training program. The relocation allowance is 90 percent of the reasonable and necessary expenses incurred in transporting the worker and his family, if any, and household effects to the place of the new job, plus a lump sum equal to three times his average weekly wage up to a maximum of $600.

E. Additional Assistance to Steel Workers

Title VIII, entitled Steel Import Stabilization Act, of the Trade and Tariff Act of 1984, Public Law 98-573, provided enforcement authority for the national policy for the steel industry. This national policy was identified as Executive Communication 4046 dated September 18, 1984 (H.R. Doc. No. 98-263) containing the President's proposal to reduce foreign steel imports under bilateral agreements. This proposal was the President's substitute for providing the steel import relief under Section 201 of the Trade Act of 1974, following the affirmative finding of injury, recommended by the ITC in Inv. No. 201-TA-51 in July 1984. The Act provided to the President for five years authority to enforce the quantitative limitations in bilateral agreements on the condition that the major companies of the steel industry during each 12-month period commit substantially all of their net cash flow for modernization of the industry and commit not less than 1 percent of net cash flow to the retraining of workers. The provisions of the Act are more fully discussed in Chapter 14, section VIII, *supra.*

In addition, Section 807 provided that the Secretary of Labor shall prepare and submit to Congress a proposed plan of action for assisting workers in communities that are adversely affected by imports of steel products. The assistance is to include retraining and relocation for former workers of the steel industry not likely to return to that employment. The plan of action reported is to be based upon existing authorities for providing adjustment assistance but is to be accompanied by recommendations for additional statutory authority as considered necessary to carry out the purposes of the plan.

III. ADJUSTMENT ASSISTANCE FOR FIRMS

Chapter 3 of Title II of the Trade Act of 1974, as amended by Subtitle B of Title XXV of the 1981 Act, and Section 4 of Public Law 98-120, provides for financial assistance to firms adversely affected by imports, which are certified to be eligible for adjustment assistance, and technical assistance to such firms and for the establishment of certain productive industrywide programs.[5]

A. Assistance Procedure

The procedure for a firm to obtain adjustment assistance is parallel to that for workers' groups.[6] A firm starts by filing a petition for a certification of eligibility with the Secretary of Commerce. The Secretary publishes a notice in the *Federal Register* of the receipt of the petition and initiation of an investigation. Anyone who has a substantial interest in the proceedings can within 10 days request a public hearing and an opportunity to be

---

[5] 19 U.S.C. 2341–2355.

[6] The applicable regulations of the Department of Commerce, Economic Development Administration are in 13 CFR Part 315. The program was transferred to the International Trade Administration in September 1981.

present to produce evidence and be heard. The functions of the Secretary of Commerce are performed by the Deputy Assistant Secretary for Trade Adjustment Assistance.

1. Criteria for Certification

A firm may be certified as eligible to apply for adjustment assistance if the Secretary determines that:
- A significant number or proportion of the workers in such firm have become totally or partially separated or are threatened to become totally or partially separated;
- Sales and/or production of such firm have decreased absolutely; and
- Increases of imports of articles like or directly competitive with articles produced by such firm contributed importantly to such total or partial separation, or threat thereof, and to decline in sales or production.

The Secretary is required to make a decision on the eligibility question within 60 days from the date of the filing of the petition.

2. Application After Certification

At any time within two years after a firm has been certified as eligible it may file an application with the Secretary of Commerce for adjustment assistance. Along with its application it must include a proposal setting forth specifically how it plans to adjust to the problem of increased imports.

3. Action by the Secretary

The Secretary of Commerce can deny the application or he can approve the granting of adjustment assistance in the form of technical assistance or financial assistance or a combination of both. The law provides that the Secretary shall approve the application only if he finds that:
- The firm has no reasonable access to financing through the private capital market; and
- The firm's adjustment proposal (1) is reasonably calculated materially to contribute to the economic adjustment of the firm, (2) gives adequate consideration to the interests of the workers of such firm, and (3) demonstrates that the firm will make all reasonable efforts to use its own resources for economic development.

Once the Secretary determines that a firm no longer requires adjustment assistance, he terminates the certification of eligibility and publishes a notice to this effect in the *Federal Register.*

B. Technical Assistance

Technical assistance can be furnished to a firm to help develop its proposal for its economic adjustment, to assist in the implementation of such proposal, or both. The technical assistance can be furnished through existing government agencies or through private individuals, firms, or institutions or intermediary organizations, including Trade Adjustment Assistance Centers. If it is furnished through private sources, the government shares the cost up to 75 percent.

C. Financial Assistance

The Secretary of Commerce may provide to a firm appropriate financial assistance which can be in the form of direct loans or guarantees of loans. A loan can be made in the form of the assumption of an outstanding indebtedness of the firm, with or without recourse.

1. Criteria for Loans or Guarantees

The Secretary may make loans or guarantees of loans only for the purpose of making funds available to a firm (1) for the acquisition, construction, installation, modernization, development, conversion, or expansion of land, plant, buildings, equipment, facilities, or machinery; or (2) to supply such working capital as may be necessary to enable the firm to implement its adjustment proposal.

2. Conditions for Financial Assistance

Financial assistance shall not be provided by the Secretary unless he determines that (1) the funds required are not available from the firm's own resources, and (2) there is reasonable assurance of repayment of the loan. In the case of guaranteed loans the guaranteed portion of the loan may not bear interest at a rate higher than the maximum rate approved by the Small Business Administration for loans to small businesses which it guarantees. The rate of interest on direct loans shall be a rate approved by the Secretary of the Treasury taking into account the average cost of money, administrative costs, etc. Moreover, if funds can be obtained from private sources at or below the maximum SBA rate, the Secretary shall not provide the financial assistance. Maximum maturity on loans or guarantees by the Secretary is 25 years or the useful life of the fixed assets, if shorter. The Secretary may not guarantee more than 90 percent of a loan.

The conditions for financial assistance were amended by Section 4 of Public Law 98-120, October 12, 1983, to provide that the Secretary shall give preference to firms having employee stock ownership plans which meet specified requirements.

3. Funds Authorized

The law authorizes direct loans for adjustment assistance outstanding at any time not to exceed the aggregate amount of $1,000,000 to any firm and guarantees for such purpose outstanding at one time not to exceed the aggregate amount of $3,000,000 to any firm.

D. Industrywide Programs

The 1981 Act added Section 265 to Chapter 3 of Title II of the 1974 Trade Act (19 U.S.C. 2355) providing for technical assistance, on such terms as the Secretary of Commerce deems appropriate, for the establishment of industrywide programs "for new product development, new process development, export development or other uses consistent with the purposes" of Title II. The technical assistance may be provided through existing agencies or private channels or by grants, contracts, or cooperative arrangements to associations, unions, or other nonprofit industry organizations in which a substantial number of firms have been certified as eligible to apply for adjustment assistance. Expenditures were authorized up to $2,000,000 annually per industry.

To be eligible for technical assistance of this character evidence of actual or potential trade impact against the industry must exist, including declining sales and increased imports.[7] Assistance projects are developed, monitored, and coordinated by various agencies in the Department of Commerce.

E. Report of Assistance Programs Available

The Secretary of Commerce is required by Section 264 of the Trade Act of 1974, whenever the ITC commences a Section 201 import relief investigation, to study the number of firms likely to be certified for adjustment assistance and the facilitation of their adjustment through the use of existing programs. If the ITC makes an affirmative finding of injury, the Secretary is to make available to the firms in the industry information about programs which may facilitate their orderly adjustment to import competition and to provide assistance in preparing petitions and applications.

After the ITC made its affirmative finding of injury in its investigation of *Carbon and Certain Steel Products,* Inv. No. 201-TA-51, the ITA published a statement advising that industry that four federal agencies have financial or technical assistance programs which might assist orderly adjustment. These included the ITA's trade adjustment assistance and industrywide programs, the Commerce Department's Public Works and Economic Development Act loans and guarantees, and the Farmers Home Administration and Small Business Administration programs. 49 FR 36670, September 19, 1984. A report on the nonrubber footwear industry was announced August 22, 1985, 50 FR 33993.

---

[7]TWENTY-SIXTH ANNUAL REPORT OF THE PRESIDENT OF THE UNITED STATES ON THE TRADE AGREEMENTS PROGRAM, 1981–82, at 210.

IV. ADJUSTMENT ASSISTANCE FOR COMMUNITIES

The Trade Act of 1974 also provided adjustment assistance for communities adversely affected by increased imports.[8] Those eligible to apply were: a political subdivision of a state (a community), a group of communities, or the state itself on behalf of a group of communities. No funding was provided for this program in 1981.[9] This part of the adjustment assistance law was not extended by the 1981 Act beyond the September 30, 1982, termination date.

V. COORDINATION AND MONITORING OF THE ADJUSTMENT ASSISTANCE PROGRAM

The Trade Act placed responsibility for coordination of the adjustment assistance policies, studies, and programs of the Departments of Labor and Commerce and the Small Business Administration in an Adjustment Assistance Coordinating Committee.[10] The committee is to be chaired by a Deputy Special Trade Representative and composed of officials charged with responsibilities for the program in the several agencies. Its purpose is to promote the efficient and effective delivery of benefits.

The Trade Act also directed the Comptroller General to conduct a study of the program and report the results to the Congress no later than January 31, 1980.[11] The report was to include an evaluation of the effectiveness of the program and of the coordination of the administration of the program with other government programs which provide unemployment compensation and relief to depressed areas.

Moreover, the Secretaries of Commerce and Labor were directed to maintain a program to monitor imports of articles, which would reflect changes in volume, the relation of imports to changes in domestic production and employment, and the concentration of changes in specific geographic areas.[12]

VI. ACTIVITY UNDER THE PROGRAM[13]

A. Assistance to Workers

From April 3, 1975, the effective date of the program, through 1979, an estimated 561,195 workers had been certified as eligible for adjustment assistance and 340,267 denied eligibility. The industries with the most workers certified were: primary metal industries (principally steel), trans-

---

[8] 19 U.S.C. 2371–2374.
[9] ANNUAL REPORT, *supra* note 7 at 209.
[10] 19 U.S.C. 2392.
[11] 19 U.S.C. 2391. See GAO REPORT, H.R. Doc. No. 80-11, January 15, 1980.
[12] 19 U.S.C. 2393.
[13] Information provided in the TWENTY-FOURTH ANNUAL REPORT OF THE PRESIDENT OF THE UNITED STATES ON THE TRADE AGREEMENTS PROGRAM—1979; TWENTY-SIXTH ANNUAL REPORT 1981-82, APPENDIXES J AND K; AND TWENTY-SEVENTH ANNUAL REPORT, APPENDIX J, THROUGH JUNE 1983, AND APPENDIX K, THROUGH 1982.

portation equipment, apparel and other finished products made from fabrics, electrical and electronic machinery equipment and supplies, and leather and leather products.

Following the certification process, state employment security agencies provided benefits during 1979 to approximately 140,000 workers from a total of 185,000 who applied, approximately 75 percent. The benefits paid in 1979 totaled $285 million, and averaged about $2,036 per claimant.

Program activity slowed during 1981 due to the fewer petitions investigated by the Labor Department and to the higher rate of petition denial. The number of workers covered by certified petitions decreased to 29,073, down 95 percent. Similar patterns continued during the first half of 1982. The decline in program activity was largely due to the decrease in the number of petitions and workers certified in the automobile industry. Nevertheless, the largest number of certified workers since the program's commencement in April 1975, through December 1981, was in the automotive equipment product group, followed in number by apparel and fabric workers, and by those in the primary metals industries. Workers in all 50 states, the District of Columbia, and Puerto Rico, have received adjustment assistance since April 1975.

Through June 1983 program activity continued to slow, with the receipt by the Labor Department of fewer petitions. The largest number of certified workers continued to be found in the automobile, fabric, and primary metals industries. Over 1.4 million workers had been certified from April 1975, through June 1983, and nearly 1 million workers had been denied certification.

B. Assistance to Firms

During 1979 a total of 329 firms were certified eligible to apply for trade adjustment assistance, and only 3 were denied. Approximately 60 percent were members of the footwear, apparel, textile, and handbag industry. The Economic Development Administration in the Commerce Department approved during 1979 the adjustment proposals of 90 certified firms and authorized financial assistance totaling $104,200,000.

In response to a directive from the President on April 1, 1977, to provide an expanded and more effective assistance program to the nonrubber footwear industry, the Commerce Department announced on July 20, 1977, a three-year, $56 million program to revitalize the affected segments of the industry. During 1979 the EDA provided over $6 million of trade adjustment technical assistance to benefit 80 trade-impacted footwear firms. By the end of 1979 the EDA had provided under the program $31.5 million in loan obligations to 39 certified footwear firms.

To provide technical assistance generally to firms seeking financial assistance the EDA funded during 1979 10 Trade Adjustment Assistance Centers (TAACs) across the United States.

In 1981 the ITA awarded cooperative agreements totaling $12.6 million to the operations of the then 11 TAACs. From the establishment of the TAACs in September 1978, through December 1981, they assisted more than 1,400 petitioning firms, almost 95 percent of the firms certified, and provided implementation assistance to over 900 certified firms. During 1981 the Department of Commerce authorized financial assistance totaling $45.9 million, including direct loans amounting to $27.0 million and guaranteed loans with face values totaling $18.9 million. This represented a 26 percent decrease from the financial assistance authorized in 1980.

During 1982 trade-impacted producing firms submitted 366 petitions for certification of eligibility, 14 percent more than in 1981. Of these, 238 firms were certified eligible to apply for trade adjustment assistance. The large majority were producers of apparel, metal products, machinery and equipment, sporting goods, textiles, giftware, transportation equipment, and wood products. Of 33 firms applying for financial assistance, the ITA approved 12 firms, with assistance totaling $16.5 million. In 1982 ITA awarded cooperative agreements totaling $10.5 million to fund the 13 TAACs.

C. Assistance to Communities

Because of the practical inability of most communities to gather data necessary to show their qualification for adjustment assistance under the Trade Act criteria, EDA encouraged their application for aid under the Public Works and Economic Development Act of 1965, as amended (PWEDA), which provided loans and grants for public works and facilities and direct and indirect loans to businesses in the community. During 1979 EDA funded 10 grants totaling nearly $4.5 million designed to offset dislocations resulting principally from import competition.

As stated in section IV *supra,* the program was not funded in 1981 and was terminated September 30, 1982.

D. Assistance to Industrywide Programs

During 1981 three technical assistance cooperative agreements totaling over $1 million were awarded to a joint labor/management organization, a public nonprofit organization, and an apparel industry trade association to help the U.S. apparel and textile industries recover from the adverse effects of imports. These agreements were directed toward the development of new technical and managerial systems to reduce costs and increase markets.

After the expiration of the three-year footwear program begun in 1977, technical assistance continued to be provided. During 1980 and 1981 funding was provided to the American Shoe Center in Philadelphia to promote industrywide adoption of new technology and management systems, and to provide information and services to footwear firms.

During 1982 $3.2 million of technical assistance funds were used for export promotion, improving manufacturing productivity and marketing for five trade-impacted industries, including apparel and footwear.

VII. JUDICIAL REVIEW

A. Jurisdiction and Extent of Review

The Trade Act of 1974 provided for judicial review in the U.S. circuit courts of determinations by the Secretary of Labor on the eligibility of workers for certification.[14] The Customs Courts Act of 1980 revised judicial review of adjustment assistance and enlarged its scope by providing for review in the U.S. Court of International Trade, with appeal to the Court of Customs and Patent Appeals (now the Court of Appeals for the Federal Circuit) of not only determinations respecting workers but of determinations by the Secretary of Commerce on the eligibility of firms and communities for adjustment assistance.[15] Under both statutes, the findings of fact by the Secretary were conclusive if supported by substantial evidence.

The CIT reviews a decision by the Secretary of Labor denying a petition for certification of eligibility for trade adjustment assistance to assure that the decision is in accordance with law and supported by substantial evidence, and will accept the Secretary's methodology if the resulting findings are not arbitrary and are based on substantial evidence. *Abbott* v. *Donovan,* 6 CIT _____ , 510 F. Supp. 41 (1983) 5 ITRD 1194. Similarly, the nature and extent of the investigation of eligibility are matters within the discretion of the administration. *Cherlin* v. *Donovan,* 7 CIT _____ , 585 F. Supp. 644 (1984) 5 ITRD 2281. However, the CIT required a comparative analysis of a plant's departments, after remand, in *Abbott* v. *Donovan*, 7 CIT _____ , Slip Op. 84-64 (1984) 5 ITRD 2467.

Challenges to the administrative denial of benefits by the state agencies administering adjustment assistance under the guidelines of the Secretary of Labor may not succeed in a federal court without joinder of the state agencies; the attempt to require reversal of state agency denials through a federal court mandate to the Secretary of Labor to require him to revise his guidelines is inappropriate in view of Section 239(d) of the Trade Act of 1974 (19 U.S.C. 2311(d)) providing for review of state agency decisions under state law. *UAW* v. *Donovan,* 746 F.2d 839 (CA DC 1984) 6 ITRD 1297, *rev'g UAW* v. *Donovan,* 568 F. Supp. 1047 (D DC 1983) 5 ITRD 1134.

The Secretary of Labor may not be required to allocate funds for adjustment assistance training from a lump sum appropriation covering a number of training programs since the disposition of a lump sum appropriation is a matter left to agency discretion. *UAW* v. *Donovan,* 746 F.2d 855 (CA DC 1984) 6 ITRD 1289, *rev'g UAW* v. *Donovan,* No. 82-1458 (D DC 1983) 4 ITRD 2441.

---

[14]19 U.S.C. 2322, repealed, Pub. L. No. 96-417, Section 612, October 10, 1980.
[15]19 U.S.C. 2395.

B. Rights and Obligations

It has been determined that the 60-day statute of limitations on the filing of a petition for review of an eligibility determination must be strictly enforced. *Brunelle* v. *Donovan,* 3 CIT 76 (1982) 3 ITRD 2013; *Washko* v. *Donovan,* 4 CIT 271, Slip Op. 82-121 (1982) 4 ITRD 1439. However, this is not true where the Secretary of Labor has failed in his duty to advise the worker whose petition has been rejected of the address and phone number of the Court of International Trade and the availability of further information for filing an appeal and the date of the disclosure of the negative determination. *Tyler* v. *Donovan,* 3 CIT 62, 535 F. Supp. 691 (1982) 3 ITRD 1797. Moreover, the Secretary of Labor has a duty to investigate the facts concerning eligibility before rejecting a workers petition alleging that the employer, an automobile dealership, is a producer as well as distributor of automobiles. *Woodrum* v. *Donovan,* 4 CIT 130 (1982) 4 ITRD 1080. It has also been held that neither the employer nor the union representing the workers has a duty to the employees to file a claim for adjustment assistance. *Coleman* v. *Louisville Pants Corp.,* 691 F.2d 762 (CA 5 1982) 4 ITRD 1118.

The authority of the Secretary of Labor to recover overpayments to workers not obtained through fraud has been disputed. Prior to the 1981 Act, the statute provided no provision for such recoupment but the regulations of the Secretary of Labor did so. In *Collins* v. *Donovan,* 661 F.2d 705 (1981) 3 ITRD 1494, the Court of Appeals for the Eighth Circuit, reversing the district court, upheld the validity of the regulations under common law. However, the 1981 Act added a section, 19 U.S.C. 2315, providing for recovery of such overpayments with a proviso that the Secretary may waive such payments if he or the state agency determines "in accordance with guidelines prescribed by the Secretary" that the payment was made without fault on the part of the worker and the recoupment would be contrary to equity and good conscience. In view of the proviso, the District Court for the District of Columbia determined that the Secretary may not obtain repayment when he has not issued guidelines to cover the application of the proviso. *United Automobile, Aerospace, and Agricultural Implement Workers of America* v. *Donovan,* 554 F. Supp. 1172 (1983) 4 ITRD 1580.

C. Import Requirements

There can be no eligibility for adjustment assistance unless the increasing imports which are alleged to justify adjustment assistance are found to be "like" or "directly competitive with" the product manufactured by the petitioning workers or firm, *Morristown Magnavox Former Employees* v. *Marshall,* 671 F.2d 194 (CA 6 1982) 3 ITRD 1859; *UAW Local 834* v. *Donovan,* 8 CIT _____ , 592 F. Supp. 673 (1984) 6 ITRD 1098. Similarly, workers engaged in repair and maintenance in one shipyard are not eligible for adjustment assistance available to workers engaged in ship construction in another shipyard, owned by the same parent company, by reason of increased foreign construction of new ships. *Pemberton* v. *Marshall,* 639 F.2d 798 (CA DC 1981) 2 ITRD 1243. Furthermore, there is no constitutional defect in the statutory provision of assistance only to workers who "produce" articles and not to those in independent new car dealerships. *Woodrum* v. *United States,* 737 F.2d 1575 (CAFC 1984) 5 ITRD 2495, *aff'g Woodrum* v. *Donovan,* 5 CIT 190, 564 F. Supp. 826 (1983) 4 ITRD 2176.

21

Market Disruption
by Communist Countries

I. THE 1974 TRADE ACT PROVISIONS

Title IV of the Trade Act of 1974 covers two main facets of trade relations with Communist countries. Most of the provisions set forth the prerequisites and procedures for entering into a bilateral commercial agreement with a Communist country and the resulting extension to it of nondiscriminatory treatment of its products imported into the United States. Nondiscriminatory treatment consists of the application to imports of the duty rates in column 1 of the TSUS, which apply generally, rather than the higher rates in column 2 which apply to imports from Communist countries.[1]

The second concern of Title IV is the provision in Section 406[2] of ways and means to afford import relief to American industry where investigation by the International Trade Commission establishes that Communist imports are causing market disruption. Section 406 relief is available even if the imports come from a Communist country enjoying nondiscriminatory treatment, but in this case the President is to initiate consultations with that country under the safeguard provisions of the commercial agreement.

Section 406 defines "market disruption" as existing within a domestic industry whenever imports of a like or directly competitive article are increasing rapidly so as to be a significant cause of material injury, or threat thereof to that industry. The importation need not constitute an unfair trade practice.

---

[1]See General Headnotes 3(d) and (f) of the Tariff Schedules, 19 U.S.C. 1202, 1985 TSUSA, Supplement 3, reprinted in Appendix A.
[2]19 U.S.C. 2436.

II. PROCEDURE TO OBTAIN RELIEF

A. Title IV Procedure

The procedure under Section 406 parallels the one under Title II for coping with import injury caused by imports of products of foreign countries in general. A petition may be filed by any interested party, or the investigation by the U.S. International Trade Commission (ITC) may be initiated at the request of the President, or the U.S. Trade Representative, or upon resolution of the House Ways and Means Committee or the Senate Finance Committee, or the ITC may start an investigation on its own motion.[3]

Upon completion of its investigation, the ITC reports to the President as in the case of investigations under Title II. In its report, the ITC determines whether market disruption exists with respect to an article produced by a domestic industry, and, if it so determines, the amount of the increase in, or imposition of, any duty or other import restriction on such article which is necessary to prevent or remedy such market disruption.

B. Differences From Title II Requirements and Procedure

The Section 406 requirement that increased imports must be found to be a "significant cause of material injury, or threat thereof" in order to justify relief is a less demanding requirement than that in Section 201(b)(1). Under Section 201(b)(1) the ITC must find that the increased imports are "a *substantial* cause of *serious* injury, or threat thereof" in order to justify relief. The ITC regulations reflect the less stringent test for "market disruption" than "import injury" in the reduced requirements for data showing injury.[4] To prove market disruption it is necessary to show only an idling of productive facilities, not a "significant" idling of productive facilities, required to prove import injury; the inability of a number of firms to operate at a reasonable level of profit, not a "significant" number of firms; and unemployment or underemployment in the industry, not "significant" unemployment and underemployment.

There are a number of other differences, between the provisions of Section 406 and the provisions under Title II. In the first place, adjustment assistance to workers or industry or communities affected is *not* an alternative where market disruption is caused by imports of products of a Communist country. Only import relief of some sort may be resorted to in order to deal with the problem.

Moreover, action must be taken more promptly than in the case of proceedings under Title II. For example, the report of the ITC must be made not later than three months after the date on which a petition is filed

---

[3]The ITC regulations covering market disruption investigations are in 19 CFR Part 206, Subpart C.

[4]Compare Section 206.9(f) and Section 206.14(f). See ITC comparison in *Anhydrous Ammonia-USSR* (1979), Inv. No. TA-406-5, 1 ITRD 5270, and in *Certain Ceramic Kitchenware and Tableware-China* (1982), Inv. No. TA-406-8, 4 ITRD 1470. See also Senate Finance Committee Report, S. Rep. No. 93-1298, 93d Cong., 2d Sess., 1974 at 212.

or a request or resolution is received (as compared with six months in proceedings under Title II). Also, where the remedy prescribed is an orderly marketing agreement, such an agreement must be entered into within 60 days after the import relief determination date (as compared with 90 days in proceedings under Title II). Finally, the President, if he finds that emergency action is necessary, can proclaim import relief without waiting for the determination of the ITC. If he takes emergency action, it is terminated or altered if subsequently the ITC makes a negative determination on market disruption or recommends a different form or amount of import relief and the President makes a determination pursuant thereto.

C. Difference From Unfair Trade Practice Standards

Both Section 406 and Title II of the Trade Act of 1974 provide remedies against imports causing injury to domestic industry even though the importation may not be challengeable as unfair. The ITC had occasion to set forth the difference in standards to determine whether the imports complained of had the necessary causal connection to the injury experienced, as applied in an antidumping investigation as contrasted with a Section 406 investigation. In a unanimous preliminary affirmative determination the ITC found reasonable indication that an industry in the United States is "materially injured or threatened with material injury by reason of" imports of canned mushrooms from the People's Republic of China (Inv. No. 731-TA-115 (Preliminary), 47 FR 55336, December 8, 1982). Two months previously the ITC had divided 2-2 on the question whether canned mushrooms from the People's Republic of China were "a significant cause of material injury or threat thereof" (Inv. No. TA-406-9, 47 FR 45981, October 4, 1982, 4 ITRD 2061).

The commissioners who had reached a negative determination in the Section 406 case explained that "section 406 is a fair trade provision which requires the Commission to weigh the various causes of material injury," and that the "significant cause" standard of Section 406 "has been interpreted to require a more direct causal connection than the contributing cause standard applied in antidumping investigations." The commissioners cited *Pasco Terminals, Inc.* v. *United States,* 477 F. Supp. 201 (Cust. Ct. 1979) 2 ITRD 1101, *aff'd,* 634 F.2d 610 (CCPA 1980) 2 ITRD 1401, on injury causation under the Antidumping Act of 1921, and the Senate Report on the Trade Agreements Act of 1979. The Senate Report was quoted as stating that "injury caused by unfair competition...does not require as strong a causation link to imports as would be required in determining the existence of injury under fair trade import relief laws."

III. EXTENSION OF NONDISCRIMINATORY TREATMENT TO THE PRODUCTS OF COMMUNIST COUNTRIES

Sections 404 and 405 of Title IV of the Trade Act of 1974 authorize the conclusion of bilateral commercial agreements providing for nondiscriminatory tariff treatment, subject to congressional approval.[5] These agreements shall initially be for a period of three years and shall contain specified provisions protective of U.S. industry and commerce. The principal objective of these agreements is to develop balanced and mutually beneficial trade relations.

However, before entering into any commercial agreement with a Communist country the President is required by Section 402 of Title IV (19 U.S.C. 2432), popularly known as the Jackson-Vanik amendment, either to report to Congress that the Communist country is not in violation of that section's free emigration provisions or, for limited periods, to waive compliance with those provisions and report to Congress that the waiver will promote the objectives of the section. A favorable concurrent resolution is required.

Under this authority the President proclaimed in April 1975,[6] the signing of an Agreement on Trade Relations with the Socialist Republic of Romania, to become effective after approval by the Congress of the extension of nondiscriminatory treatment to the products of Romania. This approval having been given, the agreement became effective August 3, 1975. It was renewed by Memorandum of the President of June 2, 1978,[7] upon his determination under Section 405(b)(1) that a satisfactory balance of concessions in trade and services had been maintained and that actual or foreseeable reductions in U.S. tariff and nontariff barriers to trade would be satisfactorily reciprocated. A similar agreement with the Hungarian People's Republic was proclaimed April 7, 1978,[8] which became effective July 7, 1978. The President continued the waivers of the Jackson-Vanik amendment applicable to Romania and Hungary in periodic determinations.

Under the procedures a trade agreement with China was signed July 7, 1979, and submitted to Congress. In Proclamation 4697 of October 23, 1979, the President proclaimed that the agreement would become effective and nondiscriminatory tariff treatment would be provided on the date on which the Contracting Parties exchanged notifications of the completion of legal procedures. The U.S. Trade Representative in a *Federal Register* notice of January 30, 1980, announced that the effective date of the agreement was February 1, 1980, and that as of that date (then) General Headnote 3(f) of the Tariff Schedules of the United States was amended to delete therefrom "China (any part of which may be under Communist domination or control)" and "Tibet" (45 FR 6882).

---

[5] 19 U.S.C. 2434, 2435. Note *Immigration and Naturalization Service* v. *Chadha,* 103 S.Ct. 2764 (1983) holding unconstitutional the provisions in 8 U.S.C. 1254(c)(2) for Congressional invalidation of Executive Branch action.

[6] Proclamation 4369, 40 FR 18389, April 24, 1975.

[7] 43 FR 25983, June 16, 1978.

[8] Proclamation 4560, 43 FR 15125, April 11, 1978.

Where a trade agreement has been negotiated, Section 406 provides that a petition can be filed by an interested party requesting the President to initiate consultations if such an interested party believes that imports of the products of the country in question may be causing market disruption. The petition can request the President to initiate consultations under the safeguard arrangements contained in the agreement, looking toward a resolution of the problem. And, of course, if a satisfactory resolution cannot be agreed upon, the President can take action under Section 406 to initiate import relief.

IV. MARKET DISRUPTION INVESTIGATIONS

In 1978 the ITC completed the first four investigations of market disruption under the authority of Section 406. The first case concerned certain gloves from the People's Republic of China, Inv. No. TA-406-1, and resulted in a negative determination (Pub. 867, 1 ITRD 5371, not published in the *Federal Register*). The next three were combined investigations, undertaken on petition of the domestic industry, relating to clothespins from the People's Republic of China (Inv. No. TA-401-2), from the Polish People's Republic (Inv. No. TA-401-3), and from the Socialist Republic of Romania (Inv. No. TA-401-4). On August 3, 1978, the ITC reported to the President an affirmative determination respecting clothespin imports from the People's Republic of China, recommending quota restrictions, and negative determinations in the other two cases.[9]

In a Memorandum of October 2, 1978,[10] the President denied import relief respecting clothespin imports from the People's Republic of China, stating that other foreign sources accounted for 73 percent of U.S. imports and that third country imports would take up the excess resulting from restrictions on imports from one country. He noted that the ITC had commenced an investigation under Section 201 of import injury resulting from clothespin imports generally.

The general ITC investigation of clothespin imports (Inv. No. TA-201-36) resulted in an affirmative determination of injury, reported to the President December 12, 1978[11] and his proclamation February 23, 1979, of a three-year global quantitative limitation on importations.[12]

Under his emergency authority in Section 406(c) the President, on January 18, 1980, proclaimed a one-year quota of one million tons on imports of certain anhydrous ammonia from the Soviet Union (Proclamation No. 4714, 45 FR 3875, January 21, 1980). He cited as the factual basis for his action the ITC investigation of these imports and its October 1979 recommendation of three-year relief to meet market disruption, Inv. No. TA-406-5, 1 ITRD 5270. Although the President found in December 1979 that the recommended relief was not in the national interest, the one-year quota was imposed in January 1980 in the light of intervening altered

---

[9]43 FR 35757, August 11, 1978, 1 ITRD 5435.
[10]43 FR 45547, October 3, 1978.
[11]43 FR 59445, December 20, 1978.
[12]44 FR 19073, February 26, 1979.

international economic conditions. As a result of the emergency action, the ITC, in accordance with Section 406(c) procedure, instituted a new investigation into the question whether market disruption existed due to these imports. It then determined that the imports were not causing market disruption and so reported to the President on April 11, 1980, Inv. No. TA-406-6, 1 ITRD 5355. This report automatically terminated the quota restraint. Notice of this termination was published by the USTR in the *Federal Register* of April 30, 1980, 45 FR 28847.

The next Section 406 determination by the ITC was in January 1982, in the case of *Unrefined Montan Wax from East Germany,* Inv. No. TA-406-7, 3 ITRD 2058. The ITC found that the imports were not disrupting the U.S. market because they were not increasing rapidly. The ITC's eighth Section 406 investigation, that in *Certain Ceramic Kitchenware and Tableware from the People's Republic of China,* Inv. No. TA-406-8, published August 30, 1982, 47 FR 38220, 4 ITRD 1470, was also negative. The ITC noted that there was substantial foreign competition before importation from China began, that one domestic manufacturer was prospering due to its innovations of production, and that U.S. producers had generally failed to upgrade and update their products.

In *Canned Mushrooms from the People's Republic of China,* Inv. No. TA-406-9, the ITC split 2-2 on the question whether prepared or preserved mushrooms, not frozen, were causing market disruption. The affirmative opinion recommended to the President the imposition of a three-year quantitative import restriction limited to 21 million pounds per annum (47 FR 45981, October 14, 1982).

In the event of an evenly divided ITC Section 406 determination the President has the option under 19 U.S.C. 1330(d)(1) to accept either decision. The President accepted the negative finding because certain canned mushrooms from all sources were under an import relief program under Section 203 of the Trade Act of 1974, and because the increased imports from China were offset by decreased imports from other countries.[13] However, he directed the USTR to monitor imports from China for possible future action.

In *Ferrosilicon from the USSR,* Inv. No. TA-406-10, 6 ITRD 1319, the ITC concluded by a 3-1 vote that the subject imports were not causing market disruption in the United States (49 FR 4857, February 8, 1984).[14] The ITC found that the first two criteria for determining market injury were proved, namely, that the Soviet imports were increasing rapidly, and that the domestic industry was injured or threatened with injury, but that the third criterion was not proved, namely, that the increasing Soviet imports were the significant cause of material injury. The reasons given were that the industry's problems antedated Soviet imports; the demand for ferrosilicon had declined, and imports from other sources had increased.

---

[13]USTR Press Release 82/22, November 30, 1982.
[14]USITC Pub. 1484, 1984.

Part IV

Negotiations

22

Trade Agreement Authority

I. THE PRESIDENT'S AUTHORITY

A. The 1934 Reciprocal Trade Agreements Act

Since the enactment of the Reciprocal Trade Agreements Act in 1934,[1] the President has had broad and explicit authority delegated by the Congress to enter into trade agreements. On the basis of this authority the United States participated in the General Agreement on Tariffs and Trade (GATT),[2] which became effective January 1, 1948. The GATT is an international agreement subscribed to by almost all of the nations of the free world, including all of the major industrial nations, laying down rules for the conduct of international trade. Under such trade agreement authority the United States has participated in several rounds of multilateral negotiations which have reduced our tariffs to very low levels in comparison to the original levels of the Tariff Act of 1930, and the tariffs of other nations of the world have been reduced to comparable levels.

In the early days of the Trade Agreements Program, tariff reductions were accomplished by bilateral negotiations and agreements. However, any tariff concession made by the United States in a bilateral agreement is available to all other free world countries, as reflected in the most-favored-nation (MFN) clause of the Tariff Act of 1930 (19 U.S.C. 1881). Since the 1950s, the major tariff reductions have been accomplished pursuant to periodic multilateral tariff agreements negotiated under the auspices of the GATT.

---

[1]19 U.S.C. 1351–1354.
[2]61 Stat. Parts 5 and 6, 8 U.S.T. Part 2, 1768. See Appendix B for the text of the GATT.

B. The 1974 Trade Act Authority

1. Tariff Changes

The Trade Act of 1974 conferred upon the President broad new authority for a period of five years from January 3, 1975, to negotiate multilateral and bilateral trade agreements involving the reduction or raising of tariffs and the elimination of nontariff barriers to trade.[3] The Act also provided "residual authority" permitting tariff reductions during the two-year period commencing on January 3, 1980. It also authorized the President to extend duty-free treatment to so-called "beneficiary developing countries" with respect to imports of products on lists to be proclaimed by the President.

The legislation authorized the President during the five-year period commencing January 3, 1975, to reduce tariffs a maximum of 40 percent from existing rates. On products whose 1975 rate of duty was not more than 5 percent *ad valorem,* the President might reduce the duty to zero.[4] If the total reduction in the rate of duty on any article exceeded 10 percent of the existing rate, then the reduction agreed to must take place in gradual stages over a period of time according to a formula set forth in the Trade Act.[5]

During the two-year period of "residual authority" to reduce duties, commencing January 3, 1980, the President could reduce duties to a rate no less than 80 percent of the existing rate. However, in any one-year period this authority could not be used to reduce duties on any product which in a representative period constituted more than 2 percent of the value of total U.S. imports.[6]

The President was authorized to raise the tariff on an item that had been reduced by a previous trade agreement to an amount no more than 50 percent above the original Tariff Act of 1930 rate or 20 percent above the *ad valorem* rate existing on January 1, 1975.[7] This might be done if an American industry was suffering from foreign competition, and a tariff concession on another item might be given in exchange. Continuance of existing tariff rates, popularly called "bindings," are frequently of considerable value to foreign countries producing a given item and such countries might be willing to accord tariff concessions in order to obtain such bindings. However, the authority to reduce tariffs in exchange for other countries' tariff reductions has been the most widely used.

2. Nontariff Barriers

For the first time presidential authority to enter into trade agreements providing for the harmonization, reduction, or elimination of nontariff barriers to trade was also contained in the 1974 Act (Section 102). The barriers in question could be those of the United States or of foreign countries or both. Presumably, tariff concessions could be given in exchange

---

[3]19 U.S.C. 2102–2213.
[4]Section 101, 19 U.S.C. 2111.
[5]Section 109, 19 U.S.C. 2119.
[6]Section 124, 19 U.S.C. 2134.
[7]Section 101, 19 U.S.C. 2111.

for agreements to eliminate or modify nontariff barriers. The use of this authority was subject to special provisions for congressional review both before and after the negotiation of the agreement. These procedures are described *infra.*

C. The 1979 Trade Agreements Act Authority

Under the authority of the 1974 Act, the United States, through the Special Representative for Trade Negotiations, completed in early 1979 the latest in the series of Multilateral Trade Negotiations (MTN), known as the "Tokyo Round" because of its commencement in that city in 1973. This round of negotiations resulted in a comprehensive series of trade agreements for the elimination of nontariff barriers to trade and agreements for the reduction of tariffs. In Public Law 96-39 of July 26, 1979, the Trade Agreements Act, the Congress approved the trade agreements resulting from the Tokyo Round and authorized the President to accept them on behalf of the United States. The legislation provided that no agreement might apply between the United States and any other country unless that country had accepted the obligations of the agreement with respect to the United States and was not otherwise denying the United States adequate trade benefits including substantially equal competitive opportunities to the extent required under Section 126(c) of the Trade Act of 1974 (19 U.S.C. 2136(c)). Moreover, the President was not authorized to accept any of the trade agreements unless he determined that each major industrial country was also accepting the agreement.

However, the Act further provided that in a case where only one major industrial country was not accepting the agreement the President might nevertheless accept the agreement on behalf of the United States if he determined that the agreement by that country was not essential to the effective operation of the agreement, and if

(1) that country was not a major factor in trade in the products covered by that agreement;

(2) the President had authority to deny the benefits of the agreement to that country and had taken steps to do so; or

(3) a significant portion of U.S. trade would benefit from the agreement notwithstanding such non-acceptance, and the President determined and reported to the Congress that it was in the national interest of the United States to accept the agreement.[8]

D. Authority to Negotiate Further Trade Agreements

1. To Reduce Trade Barriers

The basic authority in the Trade Act of 1974 to enter into trade agreements for the reduction of tariffs expired on January 3, 1980. The

---

[8]Section 2, Pub. L. 96-39, 19 U.S.C. 2503.

Trade Agreements Act of 1979 contained no new authority for agreements to reduce tariffs. However, the residual authority remained in effect until the end of 1981. The 1979 Act continued for eight years the authority in Section 102(b) of the Trade Act of 1974 (19 U.S.C. 2112) to enter into trade agreements providing for the harmonization, reduction, or elimination of nontariff barriers to trade.[9]

Section 102(b) of the Trade Act of 1974 was amended by Section 401(b) and (c) of the Trade and Tariff Act of 1984, Public Law 98-573, to remove the word "nontariff" from the term "nontariff barriers" in the title to Section 102, and to include in the definition of the term "barrier" in Section 102(g) of the 1974 Act the words "any duty or other import restriction." These amendments were made in view of the incorporation into Section 102 of the 1974 Act by Section 401 of the 1984 Act of authority to the President to negotiate a trade agreement with Israel providing for the elimination or reduction of any duty imposed by the United States, as discussed *infra*.

The expansion of Section 102 of the 1974 Act by the 1984 Act to include negotiations for duty reductions also permitted the President to enter into trade agreements with countries other than Israel for the elimination or reduction of any U.S. duty. However, an agreement with another country may be made only if such country requested the negotiation of such an agreement and the President provided a 60-day longer than usual written notice to the Senate Committee on Finance and the House Committee on Ways and Means, consulted with such committees regarding the negotiations, and neither committee disapproved of the negotiations during the extra 60-day advance notice period.

2. Duty Reduction Agreement With Israel

The authority to negotiate the reduction or elimination of U.S. duties on Israeli articles provided by Section 401(a) of the 1984 Act was restricted by the proviso that an agreement with Israel must take fully into account any product that benefits from a discriminatory preferential tariff arrangement between Israel and a third country if the preference has been challenged by the United States under Section 301 of the Trade Act of 1974 and the GATT (see Chaper 16 *supra*). The reduction or elimination of U.S. duties may apply only to eligible articles which meet the same rule-of-origin requirements as are required of articles which are eligible for free entry under the Caribbean Basin Initiative (see Chapter 10, section I.E *supra*).

A duty reduction trade agreement with Israel is subject to the same special provisions in Section 102 of the 1974 Act for Congressional review and approval of trade agreements, except that advance consultation with the congressional committees and the 90-day prior notification requirements would not apply. The remaining necessary provisions are the submission by the President to the Congress of the agreement, an

---

[9]Section 1101, Pub. L. No. 96-39.

implementing bill, and an administrative statement of action proposed to implement the agreement, and the enactment of the implementing bill.

A bilateral free trade agreement with Israel was signed April 22, 1985, and necessary implementing legislation was enacted June 11, 1985, as Public Law 99-47. Under this authority the President issued Proclamation 5365 of August 30, 1985 (50 FR 36220, September 5, 1985), providing (1) for duty-free treatment of Israeli products under the TSUS items enumerated in Annex VIII, (2) for staged duty-reduction for such products under the TSUS items in Annex IX, and (3) for duty-free treatment after January 1, 1995, for such products under the TSUS items set forth in Annex X.

3. Compensatory Duty Reduction Agreements

The Trade Act of 1974 contained authority for the President to enter into agreements to reduce duties to compensate for increases in other duties effected under the escape clause (or safeguard) provisions to protect domestic industries from serious injury or the threat thereof. There was no time limit on this authority and it remains in effect.[10]

4. With Canada and Northern Western Hemisphere Countries

A special obligation was placed upon the President by Section 612 of the Trade Act of 1974, expanded by Section 1104(a) of the 1979 Act (19 U.S.C. 2486), to enter into trade agreements with Canada and other countries of the northern portion of the western hemisphere to promote economic growth of the United States and such countries. Negotiations with Canada were authorized looking toward the establishment of a free trade area covering Canada and the United States. Such negotiations are in progress, as is a possible trade agreement with Mexico.

E. The 1984 Trade and Tariff Act Title III Authority

The Trade and Tariff Act of 1984, Public Law 98-573, provided in its Title III extended definition of new negotiating objectives to govern U.S. trade negotiations in three emerging trade areas and explicit authority to the President to enter into bilateral or multilateral agreements to achieve these objectives. Title III is cited as the "International Trade and Investment Act."

1. Negotiating Objectives

The definition of negotiating objectives was provided in a new Section 104A (19 U.S.C. 2114a) added to Chapter 1 of Title I of the Trade Act of 1974 by Section 305 of the 1984 Act. These objectives are directed toward: (a) trade in services, (b) U.S. foreign direct investment, and (c) high technology products.

---

[10]19 U.S.C. 2133.

(a) With respect to trade in services, the principal negotiating objectives are to reduce or eliminate barriers to, and distortion of, international trade in services, and to develop internationally agreed trade rules, including dispute settlement procedures, consistent with the commercial policies of the United States. In negotiations to accomplish these objectives, the U.S. negotiators are required to take into account legitimate U.S. domestic objectives, including the protection of health or safety, essential security, environmental, consumer, or employment opportunity interests.

(b) With respect to foreign direct investment, the principal negotiating objectives are to reduce or eliminate trade distorting barriers to foreign direct investment, to expand the principle of national treatment, and to develop internationally agreed rules, including dispute settlement procedures, to help insure a free flow of foreign direct investment. Here also, U.S. negotiators are to take into account the legitimate U.S. domestic objectives described with respect to trade in services.

(c) With respect to high technology products, the United States negotiating objectives are sevenfold:

• To obtain openness with respect to international trade and investment in high technology products and related services;

• To obtain the elimination or reduction of, or compensation for, distorting effects of foreign government acts and practices which have been identified by the USTR in the required study, discussed *infra*;

• To obtain official commitment against the discouragement of government or private procurement of foreign high technology products and related services;

• To obtain the reduction or elimination of tariffs on, and barriers to, U.S. exports of high technology products and related services;

• To obtain commitments to foster national treatment;

• To obtain commitments to foster the pursuit of joint scientific cooperation and assure access by all participants to the results of cooperative efforts; and

• To provide minimum safeguards for the acquisition and enforcement of intellectual property rights and the property value of proprietary data.

2. Analyses of Trade Barriers

As a basis for pursuing these negotiating objectives, Section 303 of the 1984 Act amended Title I of the 1974 Trade Act by adding a new Chapter 8 entitled "Barriers to Market Access" (19 U.S.C. 2241). This chapter, which consists of new Section 181, requires the USTR through the Trade Policy Committee (described in section II.A *infra*), to identify and analyze acts, policies, or practices which constitute significant barriers to, or distortions of, U.S. exports of goods or services, including agricultural commodities and intellectual property, and of foreign direct investment by U.S. persons, especially if such investment has implications for trade in goods or services. In making these analyses and estimates of the trade-distorting impact of the barriers on U.S. commerce, the USTR is directed to take into account specified considerations, including private sector advice. A report by the

USTR on the required analyses and estimates is to be made annually to the Committee on Finance of the Senate and the Committee on Ways and Means of the House of Representatives. These reports are to include information on the action taken to eliminate any of the acts of policies or practices identified in the analysis.

3. Negotiation in Three Trade Areas

a. Trade in Services

The 1984 Act in Section 306 (19 U.S.C. 2114b) provides a broad and multifaceted program to promote international trade in services. This program includes direction to the Secretary of Commerce (1) to establish "a service industries development program" designed to establish federal policies to increase the competitiveness of U.S. service industries in foreign commerce and to develop data relating thereto; (2) to collect and analyze information on international operations concerning U.S. service industries, including the policies of foreign governments toward such industries; federal, state, and local regulation of both foreign and U.S. suppliers of services; the tax treatment of services; the treatment of services under international agreements; and antitrust policies affecting the competitiveness of U.S. firms; and (3) to conduct a program of research and analysis, including forecasts and industrial strategies, together with sectoral studies of domestic service industries. The information collected by the Secretary of Commerce under this program is to be reported biennially to the Congress and to the President.

Section 306 provides a definition of the term "services" as meaning economic activities "whose outputs are other than tangible goods." Specifically, the term includes, but is not limited to, "banking, insurance, transportation, communications and data processing, retail and wholesale trade, advertising, accounting, construction, design and engineering, management consulting, real estate, professional services, entertainment, education, health care."

The reporting on trade in services is strengthened and expanded by the amendment made by Section 306(b) in the International Investment Survey Act of 1976 (22 U.S.C. 3101), to include reporting on trade in services. The title of the Act is amended to read "International Investment and Trade in Services Survey Act." The reporting required under the amended act extends to transactions with unaffiliated, as well as affiliated, foreign persons. The Executive Order providing for administration of the Act, No. 11961, is appropriately amended by Executive Order 12518 of June 3, 1985, 50 FR 23661.

The USTR is directed under Section 306(c) (19 U.S.C. 2114c), through the Trade Policy Committee, to develop and coordinate the implementation of U.S. policies concerning trade in services. In this connection, each department or agency of the government responsible for the regulation of any service sector industry is to report the treatment afforded that service sector in foreign markets and any allegations of unfair practices by foreign governments to that service sector. Further, in this connection, the President is required to consult with state governments on issues of trade policy related to trade in services and to provide to such governments information concerning U.S. policies on international trade in services. Intergovernmental advisory committees are to be established to facilitate this exchange.

b. Foreign Direct Investment

Section 307(a) of the 1984 Act amends the definition of "international trade" in Section 102(g)(3) of the 1974 Trade Act (19 U.S.C. 2112(g)(3)), to include "foreign direct investment by United States persons, especially if such investment has implications for trade in goods and services." Section 307(b) (19 U.S.C. 2114d) directs the USTR, with the advice of the Trade Policy Committee, to seek to obtain the reduction and elimination of export performance requirements which he has determined adversely affect the economic interest of the United States, through consultations and negotiations with the foreign countries concerned. The USTR is also authorized to impose duties or other import restrictions on the products or services of the foreign countries providing export performance requirements, and to prevent their entry, for such time as he determines appropriate. Note that this is the first instance in trade legislation when the authority to impose duties, restrictions, and prohibitions on entry of foreign goods of services has been given to any official other than the President.

c. Trade in High Technology

To carry out the negotiating objectives with respect to trade in high technology, Section 308(a) of the 1984 Act (19 U.S.C. 2114e) authorizes the President to enter into bilateral or multilateral agreements. Under that section, the President may also, to carry out any such agreement, proclaim the modification, elimination, or continuance of any existing duty, duty-free, or excise treatment, or impose additional duties (19 U.S.C. 2138). However, this authority is to be exercised only with respect to the high technology products described in seven items of the Tariff Schedules of the United States. These seven items are the following:

(1) Transistors (provided for in Item 587.70 [687.70 intended], Part 5, Schedule 6).
(2) Diodes and rectifiers (provided for in Item 687.72, Part 5, Schedule 6).
(3) Monolithic integrated circuits (provided for in Item 687.74, Part 5, Schedule 6).
(4) Other integrated circuits (provided for in Item 687.77, Part 5, Schedule 6).
(5) Other components (provided for in Item 687.81, Part 5, Schedule 6).
(6) Parts of semiconductors (provided for in Item 687.85, Part 5, Schedule 6).
(7) Parts of automatic data-processing machines and units thereof (provided for in Item 676.52, Part 4G, Schedule 6) other than Parts incorporating a cathode ray tube.

Action was initiated, both by the USTR and the International Trade Commission, to examine the effect upon domestic industry of the elimination of duties on the products falling within the seven TSUS items. By a notice in the *Federal Register* of October 29, 1984 (49 FR 43519), the USTR announced a Trade Policy Staff Committee hearing on the possible modification, elimination, or continuance of duties on the designated high technology products, as a basis for negotiating international agreements. On October 31, 1984 (49 FR 43811), the ITC initiated an investigation under Section 332 of the Tariff Act of 1930 into the probable economic effect of providing duty-free treatment for U.S. imports of these designated products. On November 7, 1984, this notice was amended to designate the investigation as one under Title I of the Trade Act of 1974 (49 FR 44564).

Duties on the high technology products listed in Items (2) through (6) *supra* were removed, effective for entries on or after March 1, 1985, by Proclamation 5305 of February 21, 1985, 50 FR 7571. The Proclamation provided for removal of duties on the products covered by Item (1) following legislation correcting the TSUS item number, and authorized the USTR to make duty-free treatment effective for the remaining articles in the seven items listed.

II. OFFICE OF THE UNITED STATES TRADE REPRESENTATIVE

Primary responsibility under the President for developing and for coordinating international trade policy was placed upon the USTR by the Reorganization Plan No. 3 of 1979, which reorganized government functions relating to international trade. The Trade Representative and his Office were made the successors, with enhanced authority, to the Special Representative for Trade Negotiations (STR) and his Office, which were established by the Trade Act of 1974 and by Executive Order 11846 of March 27, 1975. Under the Plan the Trade Representative serves as principal advisor to the President on international trade policy and on the impact of other policies of the U.S. Government on international trade. He has lead responsibility for the conduct of international trade negotiations, including commodity and direct investment negotiations in which the United States participates.

Additional responsibilities set forth in the Reorganization Plan and supplemented in Executive Order 12188 of January 2, 1980,[11] are to provide policy guidance, with the advice of the Trade Policy Committee, to other departments and agencies on matters concerning the GATT and the implementation of the MTN agreements, the OECD and UNCTAD; the expansion of exports, international trade policy research; U.S. policy concerning unfair trade practices and the enforcement of countervailing and antidumping duty functions; bilateral trade and commodity issues; and trade issues involving energy. The USTR was given broader rulemaking

---

[11]45 FR 989. The organization and functions of the office of the USTR are provided for in 15 CFR Parts 2001–2007.

power and other administrative authority by Public Law 97-456, January 12, 1983, 19 U.S.C. 2171.

Responsibility for the direction and execution of the new negotiating authorities respecting trade in services, U.S. foreign direct investment, and high technology products, outlined in section I.E *supra*, was placed in the USTR by Title III of the Trade and Tariff Act of 1984. The carrying out of this responsibility was facilitated by the additional provisions placed in new Section 181 of the 1974 Trade Act, added by Section 303 of the 1984 Act (19 U.S.C. 2241(c)), requiring the head of each department and executive or independent agency of the government to furnish the USTR upon request such data, reports, and other information as he may need for his functions, and authorizing the departments and agencies to detail personnel and furnish services, with or without reimbursement, as the USTR may request.

Additional provisions in Section 181 (19 U.S.C. 2241(b)) required the USTR to keep the Senate Committee on Finance and the House Ways and Means Committee currently informed of trade policy priorities for the purposes of expanding market opportunities, as well as to report annually to them the analyses and estimates of trade barriers directed by Section 181.

A. Organization of the Office

Serving under the Trade Representative are three Deputy Trade Representatives, also with the rank of ambassador, and a professional and nonprofessional staff. The Trade Representative is chairman of the interdepartmental Trade Policy Committee. Its members are, under Executive Order 12188: the Secretaries of the Departments of Commerce (Vice-Chair), State, Treasury, Defense, Interior, Agriculture, Labor, Transportation, and Energy, the Attorney General, the Director of the Office of Management and Budget, the Chairman of the Council of Economic Advisors, the Assistant to the President for National Security Affairs, and the Director of the U.S. International Development Cooperation Agency.

The Trade Policy Committee has the statutory functions placed in an interagency organization by Section 242 of the Trade Expansion Act of 1962, as amended by the Trade Act of 1974,[12] namely, to advise the President on basic trade policy issues, on recommendations of the ITC on import relief, on presidential determinations concerning unfair trade practices, and on other functions designated by executive order or directed by the President. The Trade Policy Committee has a subordinate body called the Trade Policy Committee Review Group composed of representatives at the subcabinet level of the departments and agencies that are members of the Trade Policy Committee. This group reviews materials and recommendations developed at the staff level and initiates recommendations to the Trade Representative and members of the Trade Policy Committee.

---

[12] 19 U.S.C. 1872. The various functions of the committee are set forth in Executive Order 11846, and 15 CFR Part 2002.

At the staff level it is the interdepartmental Trade Policy Staff Committee, with much the same agency membership as the Trade Policy Committee, that does the initial spade work on tariff negotiations as described below and initiates other policy recommendations on trade agreements and tariff matters for review and approval by the Trade Policy Review Group or the Trade Policy Committee on their way to the President. There is also an interagency Section 301 Committee, subordinate to the Trade Policy Staff Committee, which is responsible for conducting reviews and providing for the presentation of public views on complaints filed under Section 301 of the Trade Act of foreign discrimination and other unfair trade restrictions.[13]

The TPSC Subcommittee on Intellectual Property, in preparation of a report to the Congress on trade barriers related to intellectual property, identified such barriers and requested information on individual country practices falling within the scope of such barriers, 50 FR 3853, January 28, 1985.

A subcommittee of the Trade Policy Committee was established by Executive Order 12188. This is the Trade Negotiating Committee created to advise the USTR on the management of all trade negotiations. It is composed of the Trade Representative, as Chair, and the Secretaries of State, Treasury, Agriculture, Commerce, and Labor.

B. Advice From the International Trade Commission

With respect to any proposal for tariff negotiations or to compensate foreign countries for an escape clause increase in duties, Section 131 of the Trade Act of 1974 required the President from time to time to publish in the *Federal Register* and to furnish to the International Trade Commission lists of articles which might be considered for modification of their present rate of duty.[14]

The ITC was given six months to study and report to the President, with respect to each article, its judgment as to the "probable economic effect of modifications of duties on industries producing like or directly competitive articles and on consumers."

In addition, the ITC was required by Section 131 of the 1974 Act to make investigations and reports, as requested by the President, to assist his determination of whether to enter into any trade agreement with a foreign country providing for the harmonization, reduction, or elimination of nontariff barriers to international trade. This ITC responsibility continues throughout the period to January 3, 1988, during which such agreements may be made. The investigations and reports are to include advice on the probable economic effects of modifications of trade barriers on domestic industries and purchasers, and on prices and quantities of domestic articles.

---

[13] 19 U.S.C. 2411. Regulations governing procedures under Section 301 are contained in 15 CFR Part 2006. See Chapter 16.

[14] 19 U.S.C. 2151. Implementing regulations are 19 CFR Part 205, Subpart A.

The foregoing responsibilities of the ITC extend to the consideration of the tariff and trade agreements undertaken pursuant to Titles III and IV of the Trade and Tariff Act of 1984, discussed in sections I.D and E *supra*.

C. Opportunities for Interested Parties to Be Heard

The Trade Act of 1974 provided numerous and expanded opportunities for interested parties to present their views at every step of the way on the conduct of international tariff and trade negotiations, particularly to the ITC and the STR, now the USTR.[15]

1. ITC Hearings

In connection with its investigations under Section 131 of the 1974 Act, applicable to investigations under the 1984 Act, the ITC is required to hold public hearings. The hearings provide the first opportunity for importers and domestic producers, processors, and manufacturers of articles affected to protect their interests. Section 131 requires the commission to:

- Investigate conditions, causes and effects relating to competition between the foreign industries producing the articles in question and the domestic industries producing the like or directly competitive articles; and
- Analyze the production, trade, and consumption of each like or directly competitive article, taking into consideration employment, profit levels, and use of productive facilities with respect to the domestic industries concerned, and such other economic factors in such industries as it considers relevant, including prices, wages, sales, inventories, patterns of demand, capital investment, obsolescence of equipment, and diversification of production.

The commission's regulations governing hearings on a proposed tariff negotiation list are set forth in 19 CFR Part 205.

2. Trade Policy Staff Committee Hearings

The Trade Act requires the President in connection with any proposed trade agreement to afford an opportunity for any interested person to present his views concerning any article on the list for trade agreement negotiations, any article which should be listed, any concession which should be sought by the United States, or any other matter relevant to such proposed trade agreement. The Trade Policy Staff Committee, chaired by a Deputy Trade Representative, is the agency of the U.S. Government designated by the President to hold such hearings.

---

[15] 19 U.S.C. 2155.

3. Advisory Committees

Members of the public and interested parties have a third opportunity for presenting their views on impending tariff and trade negotiations via the numerous advisory committees established pursuant to the Trade Act of 1974.[16] The Act required the President to establish an Advisory Committee for Trade Negotiations "to provide overall policy advice on any trade agreement."

The responsibility of this committee, and of the other private sector advisory committees, was enlarged by the Trade Agreements Act of 1979 to include the provision of advice "with respect to the operation of any trade agreement once entered into, and with respect to other matters arising in connection with the administration of the trade policy of the United States.[17]

The Advisory Committee for Trade Negotiations, chaired, under the 1979 Act, by an elected member, is composed of up to 45 individuals and must include representatives of government, labor, industry, agriculture, small business, service industries, retailers, consumer interests, and the general public.

The President is authorized by the 1974 Act, as amended by the 1979 Act, to establish general policy advisory committees for agriculture, industry, labor, or services, to provide policy advice on trade agreements. The 1974 Act also authorized the establishment of sector advisory committees for the purpose of considering more precisely the impact of contemplated tariff and trade agreements upon particular sectors of agriculture, industry, and labor.

The 1979 Act authorized, in addition, the establishment of advisory committees along functional lines, such as to advise on the operation of a particular trade agreement code.

Title III of the 1984 Act authorized the President not only to consult with state governments on issues of trade policy, including those affecting their regulatory authority or procurement, but to establish one or more intergovernmental policy advisory committees to serve as a forum for state and local governments (Section 306(c)(2), 19 U.S.C. 2114c(2)). The advisory committee provisions of the 1974 Act were revised to cover representatives from "the non-Federal governmental sector" (19 U.S.C. 2155).

Communications may be sent to these committees and information concerning their work may be obtained from the Departments of Agriculture, Commerce, and Labor, respectively, or the Office of the U.S. Trade Representative, which provides overall management.

The 1974 and 1979 Acts require the USTR and the Secretaries of Agriculture, Commerce, and Labor to establish procedures for obtaining the views of the various advisory committees on a continuing and timely basis. The committees are to be provided with information concerning (1)

---

[16]Advisory committee provisions are in Section 135, 19 U.S.C. 2155, as amended by Section 1103 of Pub. L. No. 96-39.

[17]Section 1103, Pub. L. No. 96-39.

significant issues and developments and (2) overall negotiating objectives and positions of the United States and other parties on trade policy. While the USTR is not bound by the advice that he gets from the advisory committees, he is required to inform them when he fails to accept their advice or recommendations, and the President in his reports to the Congress relating to the trade program must give information concerning consultations with the advisory committees and the reasons why their advice and recommendations were not accepted in certain instances.

Procedures are also established through which private organizations and groups may submit data and other trade information, as well as recommendations relevant to trade agreement policy to the Office of the Special Trade Representative.

Committees were established and meetings were held periodically in connection with the Tokyo round of tariff and trade negotiations.

Forty-five committees, with over 950 members played a significant role in developing the U.S. position in the MTN.

The post-MTN private sector advisory committees include, as a second level under the Advisory Committee for Trade Negotiations, the policy advisory committees in the specific areas of industry, agriculture, labor, defense, services, investments, steel, and commodities. Then there are, as reported by the President, April 1984,

> technical and sectoral advisory committees, that are composed of experts from their respective fields. The ATACs (Agricultural Technical Advisory Committees), ISACs (Industry Sector Advisory Committees), and Labor Advisory Subcommittees provide specific and technical information on problems within the private sector (such as automobiles, steel, wheat, export finance, aircraft, or poultry) which are being affected by trade policy. New sectoral committees from areas not represented during the MTN have been formed including energy, small and minority business, and services. In addition, functional committees have been established to monitor various Codes of Conduct which were negotiated during the Tokyo Round.

The private advisory committees, other than the statutory Advisory Committee on Trade Negotiations, are chartered for two-year periods. Notices of the establishment and renewal of the policy advisory committees appear in the *Federal Register.*

III. CONGRESSIONAL ROLE

The Trade Act of 1974 requires[18] that 10 members of the Congress be designated as official advisors to the U.S. delegations to international conferences, meetings, and negotiating sessions relating to trade agreements—five members from the House of Representatives and five from the Senate, with no more than three in the same party from each side of Congress. Additional members and staff members may be designated by the chairmen of the House Ways and Means Committee and the Senate Finance Committee.

---

[18]Section 161, 19 U.S.C. 2211.

Trade agreements that involved merely tariff adjustments did not require congressional approval. But if the President exercises the authority to enter into trade agreements for the harmonization, reduction, or elimination of nontariff barriers to trade, or the trade agreements authorized by Titles III and IV of the Trade and Tariff Act of 1984, he must adhere to certain procedures calling for congressional approval, with such variations as were stated in sections I.D.1 and 2 *supra*. Generally,[19] before entering into any such agreement, the President must consult with the House Ways and Means Committee, the Senate Finance Committee, and all other committees having jurisdiction concerning such a trade agreement and its implementation. Second, he must, not less than 90 days before the day on which he enters into such a trade agreement, notify the House and the Senate of his intention to enter into such an agreement and publish a notice of such intention in the *Federal Register*. Then, after he has entered into the agreement, he must submit the agreement to the House and the Senate with a draft of an implementing bill, supporting material, and a statement of how the agreement serves the interest of U.S. commerce. Thereafter, the implementing bill must be enacted into law by the Congress in order for the trade agreement to become effective.

These procedures were followed with respect to the Tokyo Round. The President notified the Congress on January 4, 1979, of his intent to enter into several international agreements, dealing mainly with nontariff trade matters, following the 90-day notice period. On June 19, 1979, the President submitted the texts of the agreements reached and proposed legislation to approve and implement them, together with statements of administrative action necessary or appropriate.[20] Consideration by the Congress of this submission resulted in the enactment on July 26, 1979, of the Trade Agreements Act of 1979.

---

[19]Sections 151–154, 19 U.S.C. 2191–2194, as amended by Sections 902 and 1106 of Pub. L. No. 96-39.
[20] H.R. Doc. No. 96-153, Parts I and II.

23

International Trade Agreements

I. THE GENERAL AGREEMENT ON TARIFFS AND TRADE

A. The GATT and Its Functions

In 1947 the United States and seven other major trading nations entered into the General Agreement on Tariffs and Trade (GATT), effective January 1, 1948.[1] This agreement froze tariffs at their then-current levels and laid down internationally agreed trading rules, including the "most-favored-nation principle." Pursuant to this principle, each GATT signatory country agreed to afford to every other country, with certain minor exceptions, the lowest tariff rates it afforded to the products of any country.

Today, almost all of the trading nations of the free world, accounting for four-fifths of the world's trade, have adhered to the GATT. Under the GATT's auspices, seven rounds of multilateral tariff negotiations have been completed, reducing tariffs to comparatively low levels and, in the seventh round, modifying trade barriers and establishing certain trading codes. An eighth round of multilateral trade negotiations to expand trade and competition has been called for by the United States.

The GATT has become the primary international forum for the settlement of trade disputes and disagreements between countries, as well as for conducting multilateral trade negotiations. In theory, the GATT is nothing but an agreement to meet for discussions. (The Congress refused on a number of occasions to authorize U.S. membership in a proposed formal international trade organization.) In reality, the GATT is an international organization, headquartered in Geneva, Switzerland, with 90 member countries and a large professional staff. Thus the GATT is an organization of the contracting parties to the agreement, *i.e.,* those countries which have agreed to freeze their tariffs, provide most-favored-nation treatment to the other contracting parties, and abide by the trading rules, as provided in the agreement.

---

[1] 61 Stat. Parts 5 and 6, TIAS No. 1700. For the current text of GATT see Appendix B. A description of the GATT for the private sector is provided in the USTR publication *A Preface to Trade,* 1982.

The GATT meets once a year in Geneva, and its subsidiary commissions and committees meet throughout the year. It acts as a mediator of trade disputes between member countries and on occasion makes decisions and takes disciplinary actions against members found to be violating the trading rules. Decisions of the contracting parties are by a majority vote, with each member country having one vote. As described in Chapter 16, several of the Section 301 complaints against foreign government restrictions or subsidies limiting U.S. exports have been acted upon by GATT panels or referred through the GATT procedures to the Multilateral Trade Negotiation Agreements panels for resolution.

In preparation for multilateral trade negotiations, each country has in the past drawn up a list of articles on which it would like to obtain concessions in exchange for others. Through a complicated process the GATT staff determined which countries would benefit from a tariff reduction of a given amount on each item under consideration in the negotiations and the value in terms of increased trade annually to each country so benefiting. The negotiations therefore became an effort to achieve a balance around the world, where each country benefiting from the numerous tariff concessions which are granted by other countries gives in return tariff concessions of approximately equal value.

During its first 25 years the GATT conducted six major trade negotiations directed largely to the reduction of tariffs. The tariff rates for thousands of items in world commerce were reduced or bound against increase, resulting in an impressive increase in world trade. The trade negotiations also resulted in a reduction of quantitative restrictions, which had been historically major obstacles to world trade. The GATT contains a provision generally prohibiting quantitative restrictions, with exceptions limited as to duration and purpose.

B. The Tokyo Round of Multilateral Trade Negotiations

The seventh (Tokyo) round of multilateral tariff and trade negotiations conducted under the aegis of the GATT was begun in 1973 and completed in 1979. The Trade Agreements Act of 1979 provided congressional approval of the many trade agreements listed *infra* which were completed in the negotiations, as well as certain tariff reductions and adjustments not covered by prior delegation of authority to the President.[2] Two other agreements remain under negotiation, an agreement on Safeguards and one on Commercial Counterfeiting. They will be submitted to the Congress for approval under the same procedure for trade agreement consideration as was followed for the approved agreements.

MTN Trade Agreements approved in the Trade Agreements Act of 1979 are as follows:

(1) The Agreement on Implementation of Article VII of the General Agreement on Tariffs and Trade (relating to customs valuation) (see Appendix F);

---

[2]Section 2 and Title V, Pub. L. No. 96-39; 19 U.S.C. 2503 and 1202. See Chapter 10, section III.C.

(2) The Agreement on Government Procurement (see *International Trade Reporter* Reference File, Section 46);

(3) The Agreement on Import Licensing Procedures (see *International Trade Reporter* Reference File, Section 82);

(4) The Agreement on Technical Barriers to Trade (relating to product standards) (see *International Trade Reporter* Reference File, Section 82);

(5) The Agreement on Interpretation and Application of Articles VI, XVI, and XXIII of the General Agreement on Tariffs and Trade (relating to subsidies and countervailing measures) (see Appendix C);

(6) The Agreement on Implementation of Article VI of the General Agreement on Tariffs and Trade (relating to antidumping measures) (see Appendix D);

(7) The International Dairy Arrangement (see *International Trade Reporter* Reference File, Section 75);

(8) Certain bilateral agreements on cheese, other dairy products, and meat;

(9) The Arrangement Regarding Bovine Meat (see *International Trade Reporter* Reference File, Section 75);

(10) The Agreement on Trade in Civil Aircraft (see *International Trade Reporter* Reference File, Section 75);

(11) Texts Concerning a Framework for the Conduct of World Trade (see *International Trade Reporter* Reference File, Section 75);

(12) Certain Bilateral Agreements to Eliminate the Wine Gallon Method of Tax and Duty Assessment;

(13) Certain other agreements to be reflected in Schedule XX of the United States to the General Agreement on Tariffs and Trade, including Agreements

(A) To Modify United States Watch Marking Requirements, and to Modify United States Tariff Nomenclature and Rates of Duty for Watches;

(B) To Provide Duty-Free Treatment for Agricultural and Horticultural Machinery, Equipment, Implements, and Parts Thereof; and

(C) To Modify United States Tariff Nomenclature and Rates of Duty for Ceramic Tableware;

(14) The Agreement with the Hungarian People's Republic.

C. Signature and Acceptance of the MTN Agreements

The congressional approval of the MTN agreements provided by Section 2 of the Trade Agreements Act authorized the President to accept for the United States the final texts of the trade agreements, if only nonsubstantive changes were made since presentation to the Congress, on condition that he determined that each major industrial country was also accepting the agreement, or, if only one major industrial country was not so accepting, that certain factors existed which made acceptance by the United States in the national interest.

The President made these determinations in a document dated December 14, 1979 (44 FR 74781, December 18, 1979), addressed to the Special Representative for Trade Negotiations, to be transmitted by him to the Speaker of the House and the President of the Senate. The Presidential

Determination Regarding the Acceptance and Application of Certain International Trade Agreements authorized the STR to sign and accept the seven multilateral agreements listed in section B *supra* as (3), (4), (5), (6), (7), (9), and (10). The Determination further authorized the STR to sign the Government Procurement Agreement ((2) *supra*), subject to completion of the negotiations on entity coverage, and the Valuation Agreement ((1) *supra*), subject to acceptance.

The seven multilateral agreements accepted by the United States were also signed December 17, 1979, by the European Community and by Sweden. Canada signed all but the Dairy Arrangement, and several other countries, notably Brazil and Switzerland, signed most of them. Japan signed the Dairy and Bovine Arrangements, and, subject to ratification by the Japanese Diet, the other seven agreements.

On the basis of these signatures the STR (now the U.S. Trade Representative) issued a notice December 28, 1979 (45 FR 1181, January 4, 1980) making the determinations as to application of the agreements to other countries required by Section 2(b) of the 1979 Trade Agreements Act and by Section 701(b) of the Tariff Act of 1930, as amended by Section 101 of the 1979 Act. The notice listed the signatory countries to each U.S. signed and accepted multilateral agreement which had accepted the Agreement with respect to the United States and which should not be denied its benefits. The notice further listed five additional countries, Austria, Finland, Japan, Norway, and Taiwan, which had assumed "substantially equivalent" obligations under the Countervailing Duty Agreement and were therefore entitled to the benefits of the injury determination provision of the new countervailing duty subtitle of the Tariff Act of 1930. The "substantially equivalent" obligations were the undertaking of retroactive application to January 1, 1980, of subsequent legislative ratification of the Countervailing Duty Agreement. The notice also advised on the status of the other multilateral and bilateral agreements listed in Section 1(c) of the Trade Agreements Act.

Charts on the current status of the signature and acceptance of the MTN Agreements by GATT and non-GATT members are published periodically by the USTR Office of GATT Affairs. See Appendix K.

D. Effective Date: January 1, 1980; Legal Consequences

Each of the seven multilateral agreements signed and accepted by the United States entered into force with respect to the United States on January 1, 1980, as stated in the USTR's notice of December 28, 1979. As a consequence of the entering into force of the Countervailing and Antidumping Duty Agreements, new Title VII of the Tariff Act of 1930, entitled "Countervailing and Antidumping Duties," enacted by Section 101 of the 1979 Trade Agreements Act, became effective under Section 107 of that Act as of January 1, 1980. As a further consequence, the new Judicial Review provisions enacted by Title X of the Trade Agreements Act also became effective January 1, 1980.

Further, the entering into force of the Agreement on Technical Barriers to Trade brought into effect as of January 1, 1980, Title IV of the Trade

Agreements Act, entitled "Technical Barriers to Trade (Standards)" under Section 454 of that Act. The Agreement on Import Licensing Procedures became simultaneously effective. Under the findings made in Section 1e of the Presidential Determination of December 14, 1979, the tariff changes called for by the Agreement on Trade in Civil Aircraft, after signature and acceptance of that Agreement, took effect as of January 1, 1980.

The Valuation Agreement came into effect July 1, 1980, in accordance with Title II of the 1979 Trade Agreements Act and the President's Proclamation 4768 of June 28, 1980. The Agreement on Government Procurement entered into force January 1, 1981, with respect to the countries which had accepted it. See the USTR Determination of January 1, 1981 (46 FR 1657, January 6, 1981), and Executive Order 12260.

It should be noted that the approved trade agreements are subordinate to U.S. law. Under Section 3(a) of the Trade Agreements Act, 19 U.S.C. 2504(a), no provision of an approved trade agreement, nor its application to any person or circumstance, which is in conflict with any U.S. statute shall be given effect. However, Section 3(c), 19 U.S.C. 2504(c), directs the President to propose legislation, in accordance with the stated procedures, when necessary to implement any requirement of, amendment to, or recommendation under any approved trade agreement.

II. OTHER INTERNATIONAL TRADE AGREEMENTS

A. Organization for Economic Cooperation and Development

Major decisions on world trade and monetary policies are largely made in the Organization for Economic Cooperation and Development (OECD). Based in Paris, this organization was originally formed in 1948 as the Organization for European Economic Cooperation (OEEC) to help administer aid coming from the United States under the Marshall Plan. The OEEC was instrumental in liberalizing European trade and payments and promoting the growth of European economic prosperity. In 1961, when the United States, Japan, and Canada joined the original 17 Western European nations, the organization was transformed into the present-day OECD.

Today, the 24 industrialized nations which make up the OECD are actively concerned with the harmonization of tax, fiscal, and other policies among the member countries.[3] An important achievement was the identification of a wide range of trade issues significant in the 1980s and the presentation of a proposal for action to the OECD ministers in June 1982. These issues concerned maintenance of an open world economy and its extension to newly important areas of trade, including services, trade-related investment, and high technology, and the strengthening of multilateral trade cooperation with developing countries. In 1983 the United States initiated a study of high technology problems and related governmental

---

[3]The OECD member countries are: Australia, Austria, Belgium, Canada, Denmark, Federal Republic of Germany, Finland, France, Greece, Iceland, Ireland, Italy, Japan, Luxembourg, Netherlands, New Zealand, Norway, Portugal, Spain, Sweden, Switzerland, Turkey, United Kingdom, and United States. The European Community, as a unit, participates, as does Yugoslavia, an associate member. A liaison committee with Mexico was established in 1982.

policies, focusing on government developmental funding; access limitation; joint research and development; and discriminatory trade measures.[4]

B. United Nations Conference on Trade and Development

The United Nations Conference on Trade and Development (UNCTAD) is a permanent organ of the General Assembly of the United Nations. Its basic purpose is to encourage international trade, and particularly to look out for the interests of the developing countries. It recommends policies and courses of action on trade and economic development. It is an important sounding board for the complaints of the developing countries, and therefore has a degree of political influence. The UNCTAD meets twice a year. See section III. D *infra* for UNCTAD's activity in commodities policies.

C. Customs Cooperation Council

The Customs Cooperation Council is an international technical body created under a 1950 Convention for the purpose of securing the highest degree of harmony and uniformity in customs systems and of studying and recommending solutions to the problems inherent in customs administration. As of October 1985, the council consisted of 96 member countries. The United States joined in 1970. A member may adhere to the CCC Convention without adhering to particular conventions sponsored by the council. The Treasury Department through the Customs Service represents the United States on the council.

The council operates principally through the following committees which have coordinating responsibilities in major areas of customs operations:

The Nomenclature Committee supervises the operation of the 1950 Convention on Nomenclature for the Classification of Goods in Customs Tariffs. It passed upon the chapters of the proposed Harmonized Code as they were prepared by the Harmonized System Committee.

One of the two Valuation Committees supervises the operation of the 1950 convention on the Valuation of Goods for customs purposes. This convention adopted the Brussels Definition of Value. The other Valuation Committee, known as the Technical Committee on Valuation, was established under the 1979 MTN Valuation Code to advise on and facilitate the acceptance and operation of that Code.

The Harmonized System Committee developed a Harmonized Commodity Description and Coding System to meet the needs for uniform and consistent classification of merchandise for purposes of customs administration, trade statistics, and world trading operations. The System and the convention for its adoption were approved by the council in June 1984, and opened for signature.

The U.S. International Trade Commission had the responsibility, given by Section 608(c) of the Trade Act of 1974, to participate in the U.S.

---

[4]TWENTY-SIXTH ANNUAL REPORT OF THE PRESIDENT OF THE UNITED STATES ON THE TRADE AGREEMENTS PROGRAM, November 18, 1982 at 66, and TWENTY-SEVENTH ANNUAL REPORT, 1983 at 91.

contribution to the technical work of this committee, to assure recognition of the needs of the U.S. business community in the development of the Harmonized Code reflecting sound principles of commodity identification and modern producing methods and trading practices.

In 1983, after investigations and hearings, the U.S. International Trade Commission, as part of the U.S. contribution to the work of the committee, released a four-volume report to the President entitled "Conversion of the Tariff Schedules of the United States Annotated Into the Nomenclature Structure of the Harmonized System" (USITC Pub. 1400). This report is under consideration for submission to the Congress. A fuller discussion of the proposed system and the work of the ITC and the USTR is set forth in Chapter 8, section II.F *supra.*

The permanent Technical Committee seeks to promote mutual administrative assistance between customs administrations, particularly in technical matters and in law enforcement. Its activities led to the adoption in 1977 by the council of the International Convention on Mutual Administrative Assistance for the Prevention, Investigation and Repression of Customs Offences. A recommendation for accession by the United States to this convention, known as the Nairobi Convention, remains under administration consideration. The International Convention on the Simplification and Harmonization of Customs Procedures, the Kyoto Convention, provides basic principles covering major customs procedures. The U.S. Senate ratified this convention June 21, 1983.

III. INTERNATIONAL COMMODITY STABILIZATION AGREEMENTS

A. Character, Purposes, and Mechanisms

International commodity stabilization agreements (ICSAs) are agreements between governments of producing and consuming countries designed to stabilize the price and assure the supply of particular commodities. These objectives result from general dissatisfaction with relatively severe instability of the price of commodities and from concern over possible limitations on supplies. The agreements impose certain restrictions on the free movement of commodities in international trade and usually operate to support prices above the lowest free market levels. Commodity exports account for about 50 percent of the total exports of developing countries (excluding energy exports), and the percentage is higher for many of the least developed countries.[5] Consequently, stabilization of commodity prices is of great importance to the economies of those countries.

An ICSA is distinguished from other trade agreements by having all the following characteristics: (1) It is multilateral in membership; (2) membership includes producer and consumer countries; (3) the subject is one

---

[5] Information in subsection A is largely drawn from INTERNATIONAL COMMODITY AGREEMENTS, A Report of the USITC to the Subcommittee on International Trade of the Committee on Finance, U.S. Senate, USITC Pub. 741, November 1975.

commodity or two related commodities which are internationally traded; (4) it has objectives such as the stabilization of prices, the assurance of adequate supplies, and the facilitating of economic development; (5) it contains specific economic mechanisms; and (6) it is administered by a central body representing the members. Generally exporting and importing countries as separate groups are equally represented by the same number of votes, which votes, within each group, are usually roughly proportionate to volume of trade.

The economic mechanisms used include buffer stocks, export quotas, and long-term multilateral contracts. Buffer stocks are used to stabilize prices between maximum and minimum levels. Managers of the buffer stocks buy up the commodity when the price falls near the minimum and sell the commodity when the price approaches the maximum. This mechanism requires considerable capital to acquire and maintain the stock. Export quotas are most commonly used to maintain price stability, but the allocation of quota shares tends to reward inefficient producers and penalize efficient ones, and reallocation of shares is historically difficult. A system of multilateral contracts creates a negotiated price range. Consumer countries agree to purchase quantities at no less than the minimum price, and producer countries agree to supply stipulated quantities at no more than the maximum price. The inherent problems in this system are enforcement and the anticipation of the correct price range.

The importance of ICSAs was enhanced in the mid-1970s as a result of the efforts of developing countries to improve their economic posture and of the concern of the consuming countries to moderate commodity price rises and to assure adequate supplies. The United States became more receptive in this period to commodity agreements while insisting that the agreement provide economic benefits to consuming as well as producing countries.

B. Presidential Authority

The President has authority to enter into an ICSA as an executive agreement, as a treaty ratified by a two-thirds majority of the Senate, or in implementation of specific legislative authority.[6] The commodity agreements discussed in section C *infra* in which the United States is, or has been, a member, have been effected by treaty. The Trade Act of 1974 provides no specific authority for entering into an ICSA, although such action might be consistent with the direction to the President in Section 102, 19 U.S.C. 2111, to take appropriate steps, including trade agreements, to harmonize, reduce, or eliminate nontariff barriers and other distortions of international trade. Further, Section 108, 19 U.S.C. 2118, states that one objective of Section 102 negotiations is the assurance of fair and equitable access at reasonable prices to supplies of articles which are important to the economic requirements of the United States. An ICSA may be one means of helping to assure this objective. However, an ICSA is inherently a limited distortion of trade.

---

[6]See USITC Pub. 741, *supra* note 5, for discussion of Presidential authority.

C. Current Agreements

During the third quarter of 1985 there remained in effect four commodity stabilization agreements—those covering coffee, tin, natural rubber, and cocoa. The United States then belonged to two: the coffee and natural rubber agreements. The stabilization agreement covering sugar, which the United States had ratified and implemented in 1980, expired in December 1984, but an agreement for the exchange of information on sugar remains in effect until January 1986. A sixth agreement concerning wheat and other grains originally had the attributes of an ICSA but since 1971 has lacked economic provisions and has been essentially an organization for economic exchange and negotiation. Also in operation was the Multi-Fiber Arrangement (MFA), discussed in Chapter 14, section IV, which differs from other commodity agreements by establishing a framework under which bilateral agreements provide for control of supplies.

Not included among the international commodity stabilization agreements are the International Dairy Arrangement and the Arrangement Regarding Bovine Meat which were among the multilateral trade agreements approved by Section 2(c) of the Trade Agreements Act of 1979. These arrangements do not contain a specific stabilization mechanism, which is one of the distinguishing features of an ICSA. The arrangements provide for the development by their International Councils of possible solutions for such serious market disequilibrium as the councils may find, for consideration by governments.

1. The International Coffee Agreement

On October 1, 1976, the United States became a member of the 1976 ICA which, like its 1962 and 1968 predecessors was "essentially an agreement among the major coffee exporting and importing countries to regulate the amount of coffee entering international trade." This information is given in the U.S. International Trade Commission's "Summary of Trade and Tariff Information—Coffee" (Pub. 841, June 1978) which reported membership of 42 exporting countries, accounting for 99 percent of green coffee exports, and 24 importing countries, accounting for about 91 percent of green coffee imports. The ITC stated that the administering agency, the International Coffee Council, "attempts to establish a basic demand-supply balance through a system of export quotas and production goals." Export quotas come into effect when prices fall to a given range and are suspended when prices are sustained for 20 consecutive market days above the ceiling range. The Agreement was extended to September 30, 1983. The trigger prices and the export quota totals are adjusted periodically through the International Coffee Organization (ICO).

To carry out the obligations of the United States under the ICA the Congress enacted Public Law 96-599, approved December 24, 1980, 19 U.S.C. 1356k–n, and extended its expiration date to October 1, 1983, by Section 154 of Public Law 97-446. This Act authorized the President during the effective life of the 1976 ICA to regulate the importation of coffee when ICA export quotas are in effect by limiting entry from non-ICA members and by prohibiting entry from ICA members without the documentation required by the ICA. The USTR, acting under Executive Order 12297, notified the Acting Comissioner of Customs by letters dated March 16, 1981, that the ICO had placed export quotas in effect and that the Customs Service was directed to prohibit entry of coffee from ICA members without proper certification and to limit entry of coffee from non-ICA members to 121,860 bags of 60 kilos each for the coffee year 1980–81 (46 FR 17946, March 20, 1981). The Customs Service thereupon issued TD 81-58 providing background information on the ICA and on Public Law 96-599 and Customs Guidelines and Instructions for administering the quota system, effective March 24, 1981 (46 FR 18427, March 24, 1981).

A new six-year agreement entered into force October 1, 1983. The new agreement provides for periodic updating of the formula for distributing quotas among exporting countries. The Senate unanimously approved the extended agreement in July 1983. The President's authority to enforce the agreement was extended to October 1, 1986, by Public Law 98-120, October 12, 1983, amending 19 U.S.C. 1356k–n.

The quota limit on imports of coffee from non-ICA members for the 1984–85 coffee year was reduced to 74,710 60–kilogram bags and was confined to imports from February 1 to September 30, 1985 (USTR Notice, 49 FR 47344, December 3, 1984). In the same notice the USTR announced that the United States, acting under the privilege of importing ICA members to establish lower levels than the quota figure, was setting a zero quota on non-ICA member coffee for the year 1985–86.

2. International Tin Agreement

The Fifth ITA, which became definitively effective in June 1977, was entered into by the United States with Senate approval in September 1976. This was the first membership by the United States in an international tin agreement although international arrangements for the control of trade in tin had existed since 1921 (USITC Pub. 741, p. 8). The Agreement, administered by an International Tin Council, operates through the purchase and sale of buffer stocks, consisting of at least 20,000 metric tons or money equivalent. The stocks are financed largely by the producer countries. As the price of tin approaches the fixed ceiling, sales of the stocks are made to reduce the price. Conversely, as the price falls to the fixed minimum, purchases are made to stabilize the price.

The Fifth Agreement expired in July 1982. The text of a Sixth Agreement was agreed upon at a meeting of producing and consuming countries in Geneva June 26, 1981, but the United States declined to accept the pact because the text did not adequately provide for the central role of the buffer stock and its assured financing. The United States insisted upon a fully financed buffer stock of 50,000 metric tons. The agreed pact provided for a buffer stock of 30,000 metric tons financed by cash and a further 20,000 metric tons to be financed through the use of stock warrants and government guarantees. Financing would be provided by both producing and consuming countries. To become effective the new agreement must be ratified by 65 percent of the consuming nations and 65 percent of the producing nations.

The decision of the United States not to join the Sixth Agreement was confirmed in a press release of the Office of the USTR of October 9, 1981, stating that the requirement of balance between consumer and producer interest had not been achieved. However, the release announced that the United States would continue an active role in the Fifth Agreement and close cooperation with tin producers and consumers.

The Sixth Agreement was brought into effect July 1, 1982, by the ratifying countries for a five-year period. Because of the depressed prices, the International Tin Council imposed export cutbacks on members and operates two buffer stocks of almost 60,000 MT.

3. International Natural Rubber Agreement

The United States adhered provisionally to this Agreement following Senate approval in May 1980 and the passage of legislation in June 1980, authorizing the appropriation of $88 million for the U.S. contribution to the 550,000 metric ton buffer stock. The Agreement entered into force provisionally on October 23, 1980. The United States became a full member in May 1981, and Congress appropriated the $88 million contribution.

The Agreement seeks to stabilize prices of natural rubber through the buffer stock mechanism and to expand supplies. Market forces are to operate so long as the price varies no more than 15 percent above or below the reference price, initially set at 45 cents per pound, but subject to periodic review. The buffer stock may be bought or sold to stabilize prices if the market price rises or falls between 15 or 20 percent, and must be bought or sold if the price rises or falls 20 percent or more in relation to the reference price. The buffer stock is financed equally by importing and exporting members, with commitments covering the entire buffer stock.

The Agreement includes provisions designed to foster the expansion of natural rubber supplies through measures to be proposed by the International Natural Rubber Council.

The provisional ratification of the Agreement was for 18 months; in April 1982, it became effective to October 1985, upon ratification by countries representing 80 percent of exports and imports, and has been extended to 1987. At the first meeting in November 1980, of the International Natural Rubber Council, which designated Kuala Lumpur, Malaysia, as its headquarters, it was noted that this Agreement was the first new commodity agreement since UNCTAD established its integrated program for commodities in 1976 (see section D *infra*).

4. International Cocoa Agreement

The 1980 International Cocoa Agreement (ICCA) came into force on August 18, 1981, despite the refusal of the Ivory Coast, the world's largest cocoa producer, and the United States, the world's largest cocoa consumer, to accept the accord. The United States participated in the negotiating discussions but expressed reservations about the economic and financial viability of the Agreement. The Agreement was due to expire July 3, 1984, but has been continued in effect through September 1986 while negotiations for renewal were in process.

The Agreement provides for a buffer stock of 250,000 tons, to be financed by export levies and borrowings based on stock warrants. It does not provide for export quotas but contains a semiautomatic price adjustment mechanism for a decrease or increase in intervention prices as buffer stock purchases or sales are made.

The 1980 Agreement succeeded the cocoa agreements of 1972 and 1976 which successfully operated through export quotas and buffer stocks to keep prices within target range (USITC Pub. 741, p. 13).

5. International Wheat Agreement

This Agreement, first effective in 1949 and periodically renewed, was originally a multilateral sales and purchases arrangement. Both the United States and Canada, accounting for about two-thirds of the world's exports, have been members. The failure of the 1967 Agreement to prevent selling below minimum prices led to the abandonment of control arrangements. (USITC Pub. 741, p. 15.)

The current 1971 Agreement, extended beyond its expiration date in 1979, has no economic provisions but its International Wheat Organization provides a forum for discussion, exchange of information, and the gathering of statistics. Negotiating sessions since 1979, instigated under UNCTAD auspices, have sought to establish a more comprehensive agreement with economic provisions. Unresolved issues concern the size and allocation of national reserve shares. A Special Committee was set up to examine alternative approaches.

The 1971 Agreement comprised not only the Wheat Trade Convention but also a Food Aid Convention (FAC). Negotiations in 1980 resulted in a new FAC effective July 1, 1980, which increased the guaranteed level of cereals (wheat, coarse grains, and rice) food aid available globally, and provided for greater sharing of the food aid burden among donors. In March 1981, both the FAC and the Wheat Trade Convention were extended until June 30, 1983. They have been further extended to July 1, 1986.

D. Integrated Program for Commodities

In 1976 the Fourth UNCTAD Ministerial Conference in Nairobi adopted a resolution establishing the Integrated Program for Commodities (IPC). The IPC provides a framework for producer-consumer discussions on 18 commodities, including rubber, copper, cocoa, sugar, tropical timber, jute, tea, and cotton. The IPC provided for preparatory meetings on a Common Fund for commodities which would facilitate the financing of commodity stabilization measures. The meetings resulted in an agreement in March, 1979 on essential elements of a Common Fund.[7]

---

[7]TWENTY-FOURTH ANNUAL REPORT OF THE PRESIDENT ON THE TRADE AGREEMENTS PROGRAM, 1979, at 96.

A revised agreement on a Common Fund, worked out in the Spring of 1980, contained provisions favorable to positions taken by the United States. Voting power is to be distributed 47 percent to the Third World, 42 percent to the developed countries, 8 percent to the Soviet bloc, and 3 percent to China. However, key questions are to be decided by a 75 percent vote. A directly contributed fund of $470 million is to be produced by members paying one-third of their assessments immediately upon their ratification of the agreement. As of November 1981, 69 countries, including the United States, had signed the Common Fund Agreement, and 12 had ratified it. Congressional authorization is required for U.S. ratification. The fund is to come into force when 90 countries, accounting for two-thirds or more of the total $470 million, have ratified the Agreement. The United States declines to participate because of doubt as to its feasibility (*Gist,* State Department, August 1985).

The UNCTAD Deputy Secretary General reported in April 1985 that 84 countries had ratified the Common Fund Agreement and that the target of 90 countries would be met shortly. However, there was little chance of reaching the target of two-thirds of the contributed capital without ratification by "certain major countries," meaning the United States and the Soviet Union (2 ITR 623, May 1, 1985).

The Sixth UNCTAD Ministerial, held in Belgrade, June 1983, approved five resolutions concerning commodities. These resolutions treated the Common Fund; the implementation of the Integrated Program for Commodities (IPC); the processing, marketing, and distribution of commodities; the resumption of negotiation of an international wheat agreement; and the compensatory financing of export earnings shortfalls in commodity trade. The United States joined the consensus approving all of these resolutions except for the last (although in several cases strong reservations were made).[8]

At a meeting of January 25, 1985, UNCTAD established a committee to work on increased international cooperation in the fields of processing, marketing, and distributing 13 individual unprocessed commodities which had been the subject of study by the UNCTAD Secretariat. The United States, joined by Canada, criticized the studies as inadequate and unbalanced and as attacking the market economies from which benefits were expected and had been obtained (2 ITR 242, February 13, 1985).

---

[8]TWENTY-SEVENTH ANNUAL REPORT OF THE PRESIDENT ON THE TRADE AGREEMENTS PROGRAM, 1983, at 93.

Part V

Regulated Trade

24

Standards

I. U.S. IMPORT STANDARDS

In addition to the general requirement that imports be marked with the country of their origin, there are a host of additional statutory provisions placing standards requirements upon the import of special classes of merchandise. These requirements are briefly listed by class of merchandise in Appendix G.

A. Purposes and Scope

Federal laws impose these requirements for a variety of purposes, which are readily apparent from the context. There are requirements designed to protect the health of people, animals, and plants in the United States from diseases, infections, and infestations from abroad. An example of such a provision is found in the Federal Seed Act (7 U.S.C. 1551–1611) which governs the importation into the United States of agricultural or vegetable seeds and screenings of seeds other than certain seeds not imported for seeding purposes. Other laws are designed to protect against unsafe substances, devices, and vehicles, and to protect the environment from pollution or contamination. An example of such a law is found in the Act of July 1, 1944, as amended (42 U.S.C. 262), controlling the importation of any virus, therapeutic serum, toxin, antitoxin, vaccine, blood, blood component or derivative, allergenic product, or analogous product. Some of the requirements are directed against commercial practices not permitted in this country, such as inadequate labeling of fur, wool, and textile products. Other requirements are designed to aid the revenue, *i.e.*, the collection of tobacco, alcohol, and other special taxes. See, for example, the Act of June 25, 1948, as amended (18 U.S.C. 1263), and 19 CFR 12.37–12.38 concerning labeling and other requirements in connection with the importation of alcoholic beverages.

Finally, there are import requirements intended to assist enforcement of laws both in this country and in other countries, which may, for example, forbid the export of certain classes of rare or endangered items. Examples include the Fur Seal Act of 1966 (16 U.S.C. 1151–1175) prohibiting the importation of certain skins of fur seals; and the provisions of Public Law 92-587 (19 U.S.C. 2091–2095) and of 19 CFR 12.105-12.109 prohibiting the importation of certain pre-Columbian art. A more recent addition to such laws is the Convention on Cultural Property Implementation Act, Title III of Public Law 97-446, 19 U.S.C. 2601–2613. That Act authorizes the President to enter into a bilateral (or multilateral) agreement with a State Party to the Convention to impose restrictions on the import of archaeological or ethnological materials over 250 years old which that State finds to be in danger of pillage.

The federal law permitting the import under federal license of an endangered species article was held to preempt the California law prohibiting any trade in parts or products of such species. *Man Hing Ivory and Imports, Inc.* v. *Deukmejian,* 702 F.2d 760 (CA 9 1983) (elephant ivory) 4 ITRD 1716, and *H.J. Justin & Sons, Inc.* v. *Deukmejian,* 702 F.2d 758 (CA 9 1983) (elephant hide boots) 4 ITRD 1721, *cert. denied,* 104 Sup. Ct. 91 (1983) 5 ITRD 1208.

Publication in this country of foreign laws prohibiting the exportation of wildlife, and culpable intent on the part of an importer who imports in violation of foreign laws, are not necessary predicates to the enforcement of U.S. law prohibiting such importations. *United States* v. *Fifty-Three Eclectus Parrots,* 685 F.2d 1131 (CA 9 1982) 4 ITRD 1346.

B. Agencies

The various statutory requirements are carried into operation by a corresponding variety of regulatory agencies. Each particular import requirement is carried out by the agency responsible for the domestic administration of the program. Appendix G lists over a dozen regulatory agencies. Three are independent agencies: the Federal Trade Commission, the Environmental Protection Agency, and the Consumer Product Safety Commission. The rest are bureaus and offices in seven of the cabinet departments.

C. Chart of Federal Import Standards for Special Classes of Merchandise

The chart in Appendix G lists the special classes of merchandise subject to import requirements and indicates briefly the nature of the requirements. The regulations are those of the regulatory agency that set forth and describe the requirements and that should be consulted in any case prior to importation. The chart also makes reference to those Customs Service regulations which supplement the basic regulations.

II. WORKING RELATIONS WITH CUSTOMS

Since the customs entry process is the net through which foreign articles must pass to enter this country, the Customs Service has the primary obligation to assure that articles do not enter which do not comply with all the import requirements applicable to them. To accomplish this, customs officers are assisted to a greater or lesser extent by officers of the regulatory agencies, depending largely on the type of import requirement to be enforced.

A. Marks, Labels, and Stamps

When the import requirement is fulfilled by the affixation of a proper mark, label, or stamp, customs officers generally determine compliance with the requirement on the basis of their own knowledge of the governing regulations and their own inspection and testing, with recourse, as necessary for advice or participation, to local or regional officers of the regulatory agency.

B. Inspection, Samples, and Permits

Many import standards, particularly in areas involving public health and safety, call for inspection of the total importation or of a sample from the importation to determine conformity with the law and regulations. This type of inspection is performed by officers of the regulatory agency. The importation subject to inspection generally is held by Customs pending the investigation or may be released under bond. Where a permit to import, or to carry on the business of importing particular classes of merchandise is required, the permit is issued by the regulatory agency.

C. Joint Regulations

In recognition of the close and complex working relationship necessary between the Customs Service and the regulatory agency when sampling and inspection must be carried out by the regulatory agency, certain statutes call for joint prescription of regulations by the Secretary of the Treasury and the head of the regulatory agency. This is true of the Federal Food, Drug and Cosmetic Act,[1] and the Federal Hazardous Substances Act.[2] In these instances the joint regulations are published among the regulatory agency's regulations. The Federal Insecticide, Fungicide, and Rodenticide Act[3] requires that the import regulations of the Secretary of the Treasury be promulgated in consultation with the Administrator of the Environmental Protection Agency.

---

[1] 21 U.S.C. 371.
[2] 15 U.S.C. 1269.
[3] 7 U.S.C. 1360.

III. THE MTN STANDARDS CODE

One of the agreements resulting from the Tokyo Round of Multilateral Trade Negotiations and approved by Congress in the Trade Agreements Act of 1979, 19 U.S.C. 2501, was the Agreement on Technical Barriers to Trade (relating to product standards),[4] known as the Standards Code.

A. Purposes

The principal purpose of the Agreement, as recited in its Preamble, is "to ensure that technical regulations and standards, including packaging, marking and labeling requirements, and methods for certifying conformity with technical regulations and standards do not create unnecessary obstacles to international trade." The Agreement is also intended to facilitate the international consideration of the definition and application of product standards and to aid developing countries in conforming to such standards. Nevertheless, the Agreement recognizes the right of each signatory party to take measures to ensure the quality of its exports, to protect its human, animal, and plant life or health, its environment, and national security, and to guard against deceptive practices, avoiding unjustified discriminations between countries.

B. Procedures

To advance these purposes the signatory parties undertake to follow open and public procedures, as far as possible, in the promulgation of standards for products and to follow, insofar as feasible, internationally developed standards. They also agree that in the application of their standards to imports from the territory of another signatory party, the imports shall be accorded treatment no less favorable than that accorded to domestic products. The parties agree to seek to ensure that their local governing bodies will follow similar internationally guided and nondiscriminatory practices. They further agree to establish a central inquiry point for information on their standards for products and to follow the dispute procedures established in the Agreement for the settlement of complaints of discrimination.

C. Developments

1. Activities of the Code Committee

In conformity with the Standards Code, a Committee on Technical Barriers to Trade has been established to facilitate and supervise activities under the code. It is composed of representatives from each of the parties to

---

[4]For text of Agreement, see *International Trade Reporter* Reference File, Section 82.

the Agreement. The committee meets at least three times a year at the GATT headquarters in Geneva.

The activities of the committee, as recorded in the three-year report to Congress referred to in section IV.C *infra,* have two principal thrusts: first, to monitor the implementation of the Agreement by the members, and second, to discuss ways in which the working of the Agreement could be improved. These activities have led to more consistent administration of the Standards Code by signatories. At a meeting in May 1982, the proposals of the United States for simplifying and accelerating communications between national inquiry points were unanimously adopted.

The following issues have been under discussion by the committee: (1) the application of the dispute settlement procedures to requirements based upon process and production methods; (2) the compliance with the procedural requirements of the code by regional standardizing and certifying bodies; (3) the activities of private standardizing and certification bodies; (4) guidelines to govern the comment period to be provided for consideration of mandatory standards; and (5) possible accession to the Agreement by non-Gatt members and particularly a nonmarket economy country. Experience under the dispute settlement provisions has shown a disposition by signatories to resolve the problems prior to reference for committee consideration.

2. Membership in the Code

As of October 1, 1985, the Agreement on Technical Barriers to Trade, the Standards Code, had been signed by 37 states including the European Community and its 10 member states. Of the 37 signatories, 32, including the United States, had fully accepted the Agreement without reservations.

IV. TITLE IV OF THE TRADE AGREEMENTS ACT

A. General Provisions

The Standards Code is implemented by Title IV of the 1979 Act, 19 U.S.C. 2531–2573, which reflects the objectives of the code. Each federal agency is directed to ensure in applying standards-related activities to imported products that such products are treated no less favorably than are domestic or other imported products. The treatment referred to includes testing, fees charged, release of test results, location of testing facilities, and treatment of confidential information. In developing standards, federal agencies shall consider and use as appropriate any international standards promulgated by international standards organizations.

The Act further states that it is the sense of the Congress that no state agency and no private person should engage in standards-related activity that creates unnecessary obstacles to the foreign commerce of the United States.

While the Act establishes these protections for imports against discriminatory standards, it is recognized that American exporters will benefit significantly from corresponding assurance of nondiscriminatory treatment of their exports in signatory countries and from access to information and complaint procedures in those countries.[5]

B. Functions of Federal Agencies

The administration of Title IV of the Act requires no new government agency. Rather, the Trade Agreements Act places specific responsibilities on existing agencies, with the lead being given to the U.S. Trade Representative.

1. The USTR

The development and coordination of international trade policy as it relates to technical barriers to trade are the responsibility of the USTR, as is the representation of the U.S. position in consultation on standards questions with trading partners. See USTR regulations, 15 CFR Part 2009. He must consult also with federal agencies having expertise on the pertinent standards. He is to submit triennial reports to Congress on the operation of the Agreement.

2. The Secretaries of Commerce and Agriculture

Each of these Secretaries is to maintain technical offices to keep adequately informed regarding international standards in the commercial or agricultural areas, respectively; to assure adequate representation of the U.S. interests in international standards organizations; and to coordinate consideration of standards-related activities with the USTR. Each Secretary and the USTR may make grants and contracts with other federal agencies, state agencies, or private persons to encourage compliance with the objectives of Title IV and of the Standards Code and to increase awareness of standards-related activities in the United States and in other signatory countries.

3. The Standards Information Center

This center, required under the code, is to be maintained in the Department of Commerce. It is to serve as the national collection facility for information relating to standards, certification systems, and related activities, whether public or private, domestic or foreign, or international, regional, national, or local. It is to make this information available, at reasonable fees and with translations as needed, to the public, referring to the Agriculture Department technical agricultural standards matters.

---

[5]Statement of Administrative Action, H.R. Doc. No. 96-153, Part II, pp. 491–492.

C. U.S. Implementation and Use of Code

The actions taken by the U.S. Government to implement the Standards Code and Title IV of the Trade Agreements Act and the activities pursued under the code are described at length in the Report to Congress covering the three-year period, January 1, 1980, through December 31, 1982, made in March 1983, by the four government agencies concerned. These agencies are the Office of the U.S. Trade Representative; the Department of Agriculture through the Foreign Agricultural Service; the Department of Commerce through the International Trade Administration and the National Bureau of Standards; and the Department of State through the Economic and Business Affairs Bureau.

The following information is a synopsis of the highlights of the information in this report:

1. U.S. Objectives

The Standards Code was initiated by the United States at the request of the private sector to secure openness in the development of product standards in other countries, similar to the open procedures followed in the United States, and to assist U.S. exporters in providing input into the development of foreign product standards and in obtaining information concerning such standards and certification systems. The report sets forth the principles and objectives of the Standards Code, as given in section III. A–B *supra,* and notes the further objective of encouraging the specification of technical regulations and standards in terms of performance of the product, rather than in terms of design and descriptive characteristics.

2. Bilateral Standards Discussions

The code encourages the resolution of standards-related problems bilaterally. The U.S. Government has raised both code-covered and non-code-covered problems with a number of other signatories, with useful results. These problems have been concerned principally with transparency provisions to obtain open information on standards-setting activities; the setting of international standards in accordance with those adopted by international organizations; the nonacceptance by importing countries of test data generated in the United States; and the denial of access to certification systems under the same conditions as access is provided to producers in importing countries. The countries with which such discussions have been carried on are Japan, the Federal Republic of Germany, France, the United Kingdom, and the Commission of the European Communities.

3. Multilateral Standards Discussions

Discussions on the development of international standards have been productively conducted on a multilateral basis on the subjects of access to telecommunications interconnect equipment, and the property value of pesticide data submitted under national regulations. This latter discussion involved consultations with the Food and Agriculture Organization and the Organization for Economic Cooperation and Development.

4. Implementing Agencies

In accordance with the requirement in the Standards Code and in Title IV, a U.S. Inquiry Point was established in the National Bureau of Standards, responsible for reporting to the GATT Secretariat all proposed U.S. regulations which might significantly affect international trade. This Inquiry Point also receives and maintains files on all foreign notifications issued by the GATT Secretariat, and disseminates the foreign notifications through several domestic media and directly to interested U.S. groups. The U.S. Inquiry Point is the focal point for inquiries about proposed domestic and foreign regulations and comments upon them. This operation is part of the Standards Code and Information (SCI) Program, in the Office of Products Standards Policy in the National Bureau of Standards. Interested persons may request from the SCI a copy of the full text of a proposed foreign regulation and an English translation, on a cost-recovery basis.

A further part of the Standards Code and Information Program is the National Center for Standards and Certification Information (NCSCI). This center is the national repository of standards documents. It responds to more than 5,000 inquiries annually on U.S. voluntary standards, regulations, federal specifications, and foreign national and international standards.

Also in conformity with the requirements of the code and the Act, a Technical Office has been established by the Secretary of Commerce in the National Bureau of Standards for industry assistance, and by the Secretary of Agriculture in the Department of Agriculture for activities concerning agricultural products. These offices help to meet the obligations and to acquire the benefits envisaged by the code. The offices assist the private sector in the technical aspects of analyzing and commenting upon proposed foreign standards and coordinate comments received from several sources. They assure that all comments are transmitted by U.S. embassies to the foreign agencies which drafted the proposed regulations. The offices work closely with the offices of the USTR, the ITA, and the State Department, providing technical assistance for bilateral discussions.[6]

Further, to implement the Federal Standards Policy, the National Bureau of Standards published three guidelines documents developed by the Interagency Committee on Standards, 49 FR 5792, February 15, 1984. These documents were: Guidelines for Participation by U.S. Government Agencies, Employees or Representatives in International Standards-Related Activities; Guidelines for Federal Agency Use of Private Sector Third-Party

---

[6]The activities of the National Bureau of Standards are reported in a publication, *GATT Standards Code Activities of the National Bureau of Standards — 1983,* Special Publication 678, available from the NBS Office of Products Standards Policy, Gaithersburg, MD 20899.

Certification Programs, and Guidelines for Federal Agency Use of Self Certification by Producer or Supplier.

5. *Voluntary Guidelines*

The activities described above have involved principally the mandatory central government standards which are the main concern of the Standards Code and Title IV. However, the code is also concerned with international consideration of proposed standards by internal state, local, and private bodies. To facilitate this objective, the ITA has issued voluntary procedural guidelines for state, local, and private bodies involved in developing standards, testing products, and operating certification systems which affect international trade. These guidelines were published in the *Federal Register* on December 7, 1982, 47 FR 54990.

Guidelines have also been provided by the American National Standards Institute to assist in developing the U.S. positions for technical standards work of the International Organization for Standardization and the International Electrotechnical Commission (1 ITR 243, August 29, 1984).

V. THE MTN AGREEMENT ON IMPORT LICENSING PROCEDURES

This Agreement,[7] also approved under Section 2 of the 1979 Act, complements the Standards Agreement in its purpose to remove the technical barrier to trade created by discriminatory licensing procedures. The Agreement requires that rules for import licensing shall be neutral in application and administered in a fair and equitable manner, and that the rules and implementing procedures be published, together with the eligibility requirements and the lists of products subject to licensing. Further, application forms and procedures shall be as simple as possible, and the administering agencies kept to a minimum number.

In the case of automatic import licensing, *i.e.,* where licenses are freely granted, legally qualified applicants shall be equally eligible to apply for and obtain such licenses. In nonautomatic licensing, as for the division of quotas, no additional trade restrictions not caused by the import restriction are to be applied.

This Agreement became effective in the United States January 1, 1980, since the President determined that each major industrial country, as defined in 19 U.S.C. 2136(d), with the permissible exception of Japan, accepted the Agreement.

No legislation specifically implementing this Agreement was necessary since the U.S. practices and procedures in import licensing conform to the code requirements. Complaints by U.S. business that other signatories have violated their obligations under the Agreement may be resolved under the provisions of Section 301 of the Trade Act of 1974, as amended, 19 U.S.C.

---

[7]For text of Agreement, see *International Trade Reporter* Reference File, Section 82.

2411, authorizing Presidential retaliation for violation of a trade agreement.[8]

As of October 1985, the Agreement on Import Licensing had been signed without reservation by 21 states in addition to the European Community, accepting for its 10 member states. See Appendix K.

---

[8]See *A Preface to Trade,* Office of the USTR, 1982 at 99 and Chapter 16.

25

Marking

I. COUNTRY OF ORIGIN MARKING REQUIRED

A. Tariff Law and Other Provisions

Section 304 of the Tariff Act of 1930[1] imposes a country of origin marking requirement that is applicable to all imported merchandise not exempted. Other U.S. laws place marking, labeling, certification, and similar requirements on certain classes and kinds of imported merchandise to protect American health, welfare, or business practices. Section 304 provides that "every article of foreign origin" or, in authorized circumstances, its container, with specified exceptions, "shall be marked in a conspicuous place as legibly, indelibly, and permanently as the nature of the article (or container) will permit in such manner as to indicate to the ultimate purchaser in the United States the English name of the country of origin of the article." The section authorizes the Secretary of the Treasury to provide in regulations the methods by which the requirement may be met and the conditions for applying the categories of exceptions listed in the law.

Section 207 of the Trade and Tariff Act of 1984, Public Law 98-573, enacted October 30, 1984, amended Section 304 to mandate the marking without exceptions of certain metal objects, as described in section G *infra.*

The 98th Congress also amended certain sections of the Textile Fiber Products Identification Act (15 U.S.C. 70b) and the Wool Products Labeling Act (15 U.S.C. 68b) to provide that the products covered by those acts shall be considered to be falsely or deceptively advertised in any mail order catalog or mail order promotional material used in direct sales unless the product description states clearly and conspicuously that the product is processed or manufactured in the United States, or imported, or both. (Sections 303 and 305 of Public Law 98-417, enacted September 24, 1984.) These provisions were effective 90 days after enactment. All textile fiber

---

[1]19 U.S.C. 1304.

441

products covered by the Identification Act which are imported are misbranded if not labeled or tagged with the name of the country where processed or manufactured (15 U.S.C. 70b(b)(4)).

B. Purpose

The purpose of the country of origin requirement is to give the ultimate purchaser in the United States the option of buying or not buying merchandise from a particular country.[2] The country of origin is to be designated by its English name. A clear abbreviation or a variant spelling is acceptable. Any other marking to indicate the English name must be specifically authorized by the Commissioner of Customs, and notice of the authorized marking must be published in the *Federal Register* and *Customs Bulletin.*

C. Key Words—"Ultimate Purchaser"

The customs regulations[3] amplifying 19 U.S.C. 1304 provide definitions of the key words. "Country" means a political entity known as a nation. Colonies, possessions, or protectorates outside the boundaries of the mother country are considered separate countries. "Country of origin" means the country of manufacture, production, or growth. Substantial transformation of an article in another country must occur to render that other country the country of origin. See TD 85-158, 50 FR 37842, September 18, 1985.

The meaning of the term "ultimate purchaser" is crucial because the acceptability of the marking depends upon whether the ultimate purchaser can determine the country of origin. The regulations state that the "ultimate purchaser" is "generally the last person in the United States who will receive the article in the form in which it was imported." Of the four clarifying examples provided in the regulations,[4] two concern the most litigated circumstance, the use of the imported articles in manufacturing. Example 1 advises that the manufacturer may be the ultimate purchaser if he subjects the imported article to a process resulting in the substantial transformation of that article, even though no new or different article may result. Example 2 advises that if the manufacturing process is merely a minor one, which leaves the identity of the imported article intact, then the consumer or user of the article, subsequent to the processing, will be regarded as the ultimate purchaser.

To assure that the ultimate purchaser is aware of the country of origin even if marked imports are repacked in this country the Customs Service amended its regulations to require importers to certify that: (1) if the importer does the repacking he must not conceal the country of origin on the article or the container; or (2) if the article is sold or transferred, the importer must notify the purchaser or repacker in writing that any

---

[2] *Globemaster, Inc.* v. *United States,* 68 Cust. Ct. 77, CD 4340, 304 F. Supp. 974 (1972) 1 ITRD 1358.
[3] 19 CFR Part 134.
[4] 19 CFR 134.1(d).

repacking must reveal the country of origin. Section 134.26, added by TD 84-127, 49 FR 22793, June 1, 1984.

In the *Uniroyal, Inc.* litigation, the importer from Indonesia of footwear uppers which formed complete shoes except for the absence of soles, maintained that the ultimate purchaser was the U.S. manufacturer who attached the uppers to soles, thereby substantially transforming the uppers and making unnecessary the marking of the uppers themselves. Their containers had been marked with the country of origin. The Court of International Trade, after reviewing prior litigation, concluded that the attachment of the uppers to the soles was a minor manufacturing process which left the identity of the uppers intact, and that consequently the individual uppers required marking with the country of origin. *Uniroyal, Inc.* v. *United States,* 3 CIT 219, 542 F. Supp. 1026 (1982) 3 ITRD 2193. The Court of Appeals for the Federal Circuit agreed with the CIT's analysis, *Uniroyal, Inc.* v. *United States,* 702 F.2d 1022 (Fed. Cir. 1983) 4 ITRD 1702.

In a dispute between an importer and the Customs Service as to whether imported merchandise in a marked container is delivered to the ultimate purchaser before the unmarked merchandise is removed from the container, it was held to be the responsibility of the importer to prove customer usage and sales and to provide the evidence of who is the ultimate purchaser.[5] In this connection it should be noted that the marking adequate to reach and inform the ultimate purchaser must be adequate to reach substantially all the ultimate purchasers and not just a few of them.[6]

D. Consequences of Not Marking

If at the time of importation an article (or its container, when acceptable) is not marked as required by Section 304, it must be exported or destroyed or properly marked under customs supervision. Otherwise, a duty of 10 percent *ad valorem* will be levied on the article, in addition to any other duties and whether or not the article is exempt from ordinary customs duties. Moreover, Section 304 provides that no imported article held in customs custody shall be delivered until it and every other article in that importation which may have been released have been properly marked. Because of this prohibition on the delivery of improperly marked importations, the payment of the 10-percent additional duty does not give an importer the right to have his merchandise released to him without the required marking.[7] Penalties are provided in the section for defacement, removal, or obliteration of markings with intent to conceal the information required.

---

[5]*Noel R. Chapin Co.* v. *United States,* 74 Cust. Ct. 66, CD 4586, 388 F. Supp. 551 (Cust. Ct. 1975) 1 ITRD 1456; *Midwood Industries, Inc.* v. *United States,* 64 Cust. Ct. 499, CD 4026, 313 F. Supp. 951 (1970) 1 ITRD 1286. See 19 CFR 134.35 on the manufacturer as the ultimate purchaser.

[6]*U.S. Wolfson Bros. Corp.* v. *United States,* CAD 856, 52 CCPA 46 (1965).

[7]*Supra* note 2.

E. General Exceptions

The Congress provided that articles coming within 10 general categories might be exempted from the marking requirement under regulations issued by the Treasury Department. The customs regulations increase the exempt general categories to 15. These categories recognize the circumstances in which the country of origin marking of articles would be impractical, unfeasible, or unnecessary, as is apparent from the following listing:[8]

(1) Articles that are incapable of being marked;

(2) Articles that cannot be marked prior to shipment to the United States without injury;

(3) Articles that cannot be marked prior to shipment to the United States except at an expense economically prohibitive of their importation;

(4) Articles for which the marking of the containers will reasonably indicate the origin of the articles;

(5) Articles which are crude substances;

(6) Articles imported for use by the importer and not intended for sale in their imported or any other form;

(7) Articles to be processed in the United States by the importer or for his account otherwise than for the purpose of concealing the origin of such articles and in such manner that any mark contemplated by this part would necessarily be obliterated, destroyed, or permanently concealed;

(8) Articles for which the ultimate purchaser must necessarily know the country of origin by reason of the circumstances of their importation or by reason of the character of the articles even though they are not marked to indicate their origin;

(9) Articles which were produced more than 20 years prior to their importation into the United States;

(10) Articles entered or withdrawn from warehouse for immediate exportation or for transportation and exportation;

(11) Products of American fisheries which are free of duty;

(12) Products of possessions of the United States;

(13) Products of the United States exported and returned;

(14) Articles exempt from duty under 19 CFR 10.151 through 10.153, 145.31, or 145.32 (importations not over $5 and gifts not over $50); and

(15) Articles which cannot be marked after importation except at an expense that would be economically prohibitive unless the importer, producer, seller, or shipper failed to mark the articles before importation to avoid meeting the requirements of the law.

F. J-List Exceptions

The Congress also authorized in Subsection (a)(3)(J) of Section 304 the exemption from marking of articles of a class or kind which were imported in substantial quantities during the five-year period immediately preceding

---

[8] 19 CFR 134.32.

January 1, 1937, and were not required to be marked during that period, and for which the Secretary of the Treasury has given notice by publication in *Treasury Decisions.* Over 80 classes and kinds of articles under this so-called J-list exception are now listed in the customs regulations.[9] The list contains a wide variety of articles not readily marked, such as artworks, beads, bolts and nuts, chemicals, cigars and cigarettes, eggs, firewood, flowers and plants, ribbon, and sponges. However, to the extent that any of these articles are imported in containers, the outermost container in which the article reaches the ultimate purchaser must be marked with the country of origin.

Moreover, if J-list articles or articles incapable of being marked are to be repacked after importation in new containers for sale to an ultimate purchaser, the amended regulations require the importer to make the certification regarding marking after repacking as is now required for marked articles which are to be repacked (see section C *supra*), 19 CFR 134.25, added by TD 83-155, 48 FR 33860, July 26, 1983.

G. Required Marking of Certain Metal Objects

Section 304 of the Tariff Act of 1930 was amended by Section 207 of the Trade and Tariff Act of 1984, Public Law 98-573, to insert as Subsections (c), (d), and (e), provisions prohibiting exception from the marking requirements of the following specific kinds of metal objects:

Pipes of iron, steel, or stainless steel, pipe fittings of steel, stainless steel, chrome-moly steel, or cast and malleable iron (Subsection (c)).

Compressed gas cylinders designed to be used for the transport and storage of compressed gases, whether or not certified prior to exportation to have been made in accordance with the safety requirements in 49 CFR 178.36 through 178.68 (Subsection (d)).

Manhole rings or frames, covers, and assemblies thereof (Subsection (e)). The subsections require that these objects be marked with an English name of the country of origin by means of die-stamping, cast-in-mold lettering, etching, or engraving, or, with respect to the gas cylinders, raised lettering, or an equally permanent method of marking. Subsection (e) further required marking of the manhole objects on the top side.

These provisions originated in the Senate version of H.R. Doc. No. 3398 which became, after conference, Public Law 98-573 (Conf. Rep. 98-1156 at 34). The Senate version, entitled "Miscellaneous Tariff, Trade, and Customs Matters," was reported in S. Rep. No. 98-308. The report notes (at 32) that iron and steel pipes and pipe fittings were presently on the J-list and that metal pressure containers were subject to the marking requirement except when certified as not intended for resale. It stated further that there appeared to have been significant evasion of the laws with regard to the articles covered by the proposed amendment and provided, as an example, the fact that manhole covers, rings, and assemblies had been marked on

[9]19 CFR 134.33.

their underside which became embedded in concrete obscuring the marking. The report concluded that these covers should be marked on the surface for the inspection of the public which was the ultimate purchaser and user of these items.

The amendment made by Section 207 was effective November 14, 1984, being 15 days after enactment. On that date the Customs Service issued a directive permitting for a period of 120 days the marking of pipes of iron or steel (except for cast or malleable iron) by means of paint stenciling, or tagging of small diameter pipe in bundles, during which period guidelines would be developed for determining which pipe and pipe fittings, owing to their nature, may not be marked in the ways specified in the statute. The Customs Service then solicited public comments as to precisely which pipe and tube fittings of iron and steel could be marked by any of the prescribed methods without rendering them unfit for their intended purposes. (50 FR 1064, January 9, 1985; corrected 50 FR 4524, January 31, 1985.) The Section 207 objects were removed from the J-List July 23, 1985, 50 FR 29954.

The Customs Service announced a change of practice in the requirements for the marking of certain imported rotary metal cutting tools, in TD 84-214, 49 FR 40802, in response to complaints by domestic manufacturers that the unmarked imported tools were being removed from marked containers prior to sale. Under the change of practice rotary metal cutting tools 3/16 of an inch or over must be individually marked unless packaged in containers of a kind virtually certain to reach ultimate purchasers.

II. CONTAINER MARKING

A. Substitute for Content Marking

The requirement that the outermost container in which the imported article reaches the ultimate purchaser be marked with the country of origin applies whenever the imported article is exempted from the marking requirement, with a few exceptions. Three exceptions are for containers of articles in the exempted categories (6), (7), and (8), listed *supra,* where container marking would apparently be unnecessary. Whenever the container is marked in lieu of the marking of the imported article, the container marking must state the country of origin of the contents in addition to any other marking indicating the origin or return address for the container itself.

B. Containers as Imported Articles[10]

Containers or holders for imported merchandise which are themselves subject to treatment as imported merchandise under General Headnote 6, Tariff Schedules of the United States,[11] must be marked to show clearly their own country of origin in addition to any marking required for the

---

[10]19 CFR 134.22, 134.23.
[11]19 U.S.C. 1202.

country of origin of the contents. General Headnote 6 provides that containers or holders are to be treated as imported articles if they are imported empty or if they are imported full and are designed for, or capable of, reuse as containers or for other purposes. Containers which are treated as imported articles may come within an exemption from marking applicable to imported articles. When disposable empty containers are imported for sale and packed and sold in multiple units, their outermost container may be marked with the country of origin in place of marking the individual containers.

III. METHOD AND LOCATION OF MARK

A. Legibility and Permanence

To assure the statutory objective that the marking of the country of origin be "legible, indelible, and permanent," the customs regulations[12] provide that as a general rule the best method of marking is by working the marking into the article at the time of manufacture. But any method is acceptable which insures conspicuous country of origin marking, except for articles noted in sections B and C *infra* or the subject of a special customs ruling. The degree of permanence should be sufficient to insure that the marking will remain on the article through all reasonably foreseeable circumstances until it reaches the ultimate purchaser, unless deliberately removed. If paper stickers, pressure-sensitive labels, or tags are used, they must be attached in a conspicuous place and in a manner which assures that they will, unless deliberately removed, remain on the articles until the articles reach the ultimate purchaser.

The ITC in its investigation under Section 337 of the Tariff Act of unfair trade practices in the importation of caulking guns considered the inadequacy of the marking of the guns with their country of origin under 19 U.S.C. 1304. It found that the marking with a sticker, "a paper label, whose adhesive is comparatively unreliable, fails to meet the §1304(a) requirement that a mark shall be placed as 'indelibly, and permanently as the nature of the article ... will permit'." *In re Certain Caulking Guns,* Inv. No. 337-TA-139 (Pub. 1507, February 1984) 6 ITRD 1432, 1451.

If the words "United States," "America," or some variation thereof, or if the name of a city or locality in the United States, is marked, the article must bear legibly and permanently in close proximity and in at least a comparable size the name of the country of origin. When souvenir articles bear the name of the United States, America, or some variation thereof, the country of origin must be marked on the article in close proximity thereto or in some other conspicuous location. The ultimate purchaser must be able to find the mark easily and read it without difficulty.

The major countries from which supplies have come should be marked on labels where bulk imports from various countries have been blended or mixed in the United States without producing a new or different article.

---

[12] 19 CFR Part 134, Subpart E.

CSD 84-44 (blended honey) and CSD 84-50 (fertilizer), published in 18 Cust. Bull. No. 23, June 6, 1984.

B. Certain Glass and Metal Instruments

The regulations list some 11 illustrative articles, covered in more than 50 specifically designated tariff schedule items, including such items as knives, shears, surgical instruments, scientific and laboratory instruments, pliers, vacuum containers and parts thereof, etc., that must be marked by die-stamping, cast-in-the-mold lettering, etching, engraving, or by means of metal plates.

C. Watch, Clock, and Timing Apparatuses

The country of origin is one of several points of information which Schedule 7, Part 2, Subpart E, Headnotes 4 and 5, of the tariff schedules requires to be disclosed by marking on any imported movement, case, or dial of watches, clocks, and timing apparatuses. The name of the manufacturer or purchaser must also be marked in watch and clock movements, and watch case origin and the number of jewels must be marked in watch and clock movements. For watch movements there must also be marked the number and classes of adjustments, or, if unadjusted, the word "unadjusted." All markings must be conspicuously and indelibly made by cutting, die-sinking, engraving, or stamping.

IV. COMPLIANCE PROCEDURES

A. Notice and Options

When articles or containers are found upon examination not to be legally marked, the district director notifies the importer on Customs Form 4647 to arrange with the district director's office to properly mark the articles or containers or to return all released articles to customs custody for marking, exportation, or destruction.[13] The importer then has 30 days to properly mark the delivered merchandise and examination packages held by Customs or to redeliver the released merchandise for customs action.

B. Certified Marking by Importer

The district director is authorized to accept from importers or actual owners certificates of marking, supported by samples (unless sample submission is waived), certifying that the requisite marking of the articles or containers has been accomplished. The district director notifies the importer when the certificate is accepted. The director is authorized to spot check the marking before accepting the certificate. A false certificate

---

[13]Compliance procedures are set forth in 19 CFR Part 134, Subpart F.

subjects the articles to seizure or creates a claim of forfeiture value and renders the importer liable to criminal penalities. The district director may require physical supervision by a customs officer whenever he determines such action to be necessary.

C. Compliance Under Customs Supervision

When the marking, verification of marking, exportation, or destruction of improperly marked articles is accomplished under customs supervision, it is done at the expense of the importer. He will be billed by Customs for all periods devoted to supervision and for all periods during which customs officers or employees are away from their regular posts for supervision purposes.

D. Penalty for Failure to Comply

If an importer fails within 30 days from the date on the notice Form 4647 either to properly mark the merchandise previously released to him or to redeliver it for customs marking, exportation, or destruction, the director demands liquidated damages under the entry bond in an amount equal to the entered value of the articles not returned, plus any estimated duty thereon. The importer may petition the Commissioner of Customs for relief under the regulations governing liquidated damages.[14] Any relief is contingent upon deposit of the 10-percent additional duty and the decision of the district director that the importer was not guilty of negligence or bad faith in permitting the distribution of the illegally marked imported merchandise.

E. Nondisclosure as an Unfair Trade Practice

In its investigation under Section 337 of the Tariff Act (19 U.S.C. 1377) of unfair trade practices in the importation of caulking guns, referred to in section III.A *supra,* the ITC found that failure to disclose the country of origin of imported goods, as required under 19 U.S.C. 1304, was a "tacit misrepresentation" that the goods were of domestic origin and therefore actionable under Section 43(a) of the Lanham Act, 19 U.S.C. 1125(a), citing *Bohsei Enterprises Co.* v. *Porteous Fastener Co.,* 441 F. Supp. 162 (CD Cal. 1977). *In re Certain Caulking Guns,* Inv. No. 337-TA-139 (Pub. 1507, February 1984) 6 ITRD 1432, 1451.

As stated by the ITC in the *Caulking Guns* case, a violation of Section 43(a) of the Lanham Act is also an unfair trade practice under Section 337 of the Tariff Act. However, a violation of Section 43(a) of the Lanham Act was not found by the ITC in that determination because the complainant had not proved that the unmarked goods had caused customer confusion or mistake, as required under the Lanham Act.

---

[14]19 CFR Part 172.

26

Infringement

I. PROTECTIVE IMPORT LAWS

The laws and regulations of the United States provide concrete ways in which the U.S. owners of trademarks, trade names, copyrights, and patents may protect their interests in such properties from spurious and infringing imports. In brief, the laws provide an opportunity for American owners (and other owners covered by treaties) to record their trademarks, trade names, and copyrights with the Treasury Department, which is authorized to prevent importation of goods bearing unauthorized marks or names or constituting unauthorized or piratical copies. Furthermore, the law gives to American industry the opportunity to complain to the U.S. International Trade Commission (ITC) of infringing imports and to initiate procedures looking toward the exclusion of such imports.

There follows a description of the laws and regulations administered through the Customs Service, offering protection to the holders of registered trademarks, trade names, and copyrights from unauthorized importations. The protection to owners of trademarks, trade names, and copyrights against unfair practices in import trade provided under Section 337 of the Tariff Act of 1930, 19 U.S.C. 1337, through formal ITC proceedings, which may result in an exclusion or cease and desist order, is discussed in Chapter 17 *supra*. The application of Section 337 specifically to patent-infringing imports is discussed in section IV *infra*, as well as in Chapter 17 *supra*.

A. Trademark Protection

1. Unauthorized Importation of Trademarked Merchandise

Section 526 of the Tariff Act of 1930, 19 U.S.C. 1526, makes it unlawful to import foreign merchandise if it or its label, sign, or wrapper bears a trademark owned by a U.S. citizen, association, or corporation registered in the Patent and Trademark Office under trademark provisions of the

Lanham Trade-Mark Act, 15 U.S.C. 1051–1127, and if a copy of the certificate of registration has been filed with the Secretary of the Treasury (under 15 U.S.C. 1124), unless written consent of the owner is produced at the time of entry. The consequences of violation of this law may be the seizure and forfeiture of the merchandise, an injunction against dealing in such merchandise in the United States, a requirement to export or destroy the merchandise or obliterate the trademark, and liability for damages and profits resulting from wrongful use of the mark. The Customs Procedural Reform and Simplification Act of 1978, in Section 211, provided an exemption for the importation of articles accompanying a person arriving in the United States which are for his personal use and not for sale, within restrictions imposed by the Secretary of the Treasury (19 U.S.C. 1526(d)).

2. Counterfeit Marks in Commerce in Goods or Services

The "Trademark Counterfeiting Act of 1984," Ch. XV, Title II of Public Law 98-473, enacted October 12, 1984, provided criminal penalties and additional civil remedies for the use of counterfeit marks in the sale, transfer, or distribution of goods and services. The scope of the Act would include the import of goods and services covered by counterfeit marks, although importation is not specifically mentioned.

The criminal penalties are set forth in new Section 2320 of Title 18 of the U.S. Code entitled "Trafficking in Counterfeit Goods and Services." They consist of a fine for an individual of not more than $250,000 and for a corporation of not more than $1,000,000, and imprisonment of up to five years for an individual, with or without a fine, for the first offense, with increases for a second offense. The offense is described as intentionally trafficking or attempting to traffic in goods or services and knowingly using a counterfeit mark on or in connection with the goods or services.

The new civil remedy provisions are amendments to the Lanham Act. The injunction provisions of 15 U.S.C. 1116 are amended to authorize the court in a civil action brought under 15 U.S.C. 1114, under certain conditions, to grant an order upon *ex parte* application for the seizure of the goods and counterfeit marks involved in the violation, the means of making the marks, and the records of manufacture, sale, and receipt of things involved in the violation. The recovery provisions in 15 U.S.C. 1117 are amended to direct judgment for triple damages or profits and attorneys fees, unless the court finds extenuating circumstances, on proof of intentional counterfeiting.

The definitions of "counterfeit mark" in the criminal and civil provisions differ in phraseology but both refer to the counterfeit or spurious reproduction of a mark registered on the principal register of the U.S. Patent and Trademark Office, whether or not the defendant knew of such registration, but do not include a mark authorized by the holder of the mark to be used in the manufacture or production in question.

B. Trade Name and Mark Protection

The Trade-Mark Act of 1946 extends to trade names as well as trademarks protection against unauthorized imports through Treasury Department recordation. 15 U.S.C. 1124 provides that no article shall be imported which copies or simulates a name of any domestic manufacturer or trader, or of any manufacturer or trader of a foreign country which by treaty or law affords similar privileges to U.S. citizens, or which copies or simulates a trademark registered under U.S. laws. To enable Customs to enforce this prohibition the statute permits any domestic manufacturer or trader or an eligible foreign manufacturer or trader to have his commercial name and trademark and relevant information on manufactures and trade recorded with the U.S. Customs Service. Copies are then transmitted to the proper customs officers.

C. Copyright Protection

1. Infringing Importations

Section 501 of the copyright law, Title 17 of the U.S. Code, provides that anyone who imports copies or phonorecords in violation of Section 602 is an infringer of the copyright. Section 602 provides that importation without the authority of the owner of a copyright under Title 17 of copies or phonorecords acquired outside the United States is an infringement of the owner's exclusive right of distribution. There are three important exceptions: namely, importation for the use of the federal or state governments, importation for private use of the importer, and importation of a limited number for nonprofit religious or educational purposes.

To carry out these provisions the Secretary of the Treasury and the U.S. Postal Service are authorized in Section 603 to make regulations separately or jointly. These regulations may require the person seeking exclusion of importations to prove a valid copyright and a violation of Section 602 and to furnish a surety bond covering any unjustified injury to the importer. The Treasury regulations may also set up a procedure whereby, for a specified fee, the copyright owner may obtain notification by the Customs Service of the importation of apparent copies or phonorecords of his work.

The Treasury regulations extend protection against unauthorized imports through recordation with Treasury of claims to copyrights not registered in the U.S. Copyright Office but covered by the Universal Copyright Convention (UCC), signed at Geneva in 1952. More than 80 countries, including the United States, have become parties to this convention which provides reciprocal protection to the copyrights registered in member countries.

2. Non-American Manufacture

Until July 1, 1986,[1] the importation of copies of a work in the English language consisting predominantly of nondramatic literary material, which is covered by U.S. copyright, is prohibited unless the material has been manufactured in the United States or Canada. This prohibition applies whether or not the copyright owner has consented to the foreign manufacture. There are numerous exceptions to this prohibition set forth at length in Section 601, including importations for governmental or educational or religious purposes, importations of a single copy for personal use, importations of copies printed in braille, importations of no more than 2,000 copies on certain certifications, and importations of works first printed abroad. The regulatory authority of the Treasury Department and the Postal Service extends to the enforcement of this manufacturing restriction.

The Customs Service does not, however, have "unfettered discretion" to determine whether a book is "preponderantly" of nondramatic literary material based on the district director's judgment of the relative "importance" of the text to the pictorial material. The test is the objective, mechanical one of whether more than half of the book's surface area, exclusive of margins, consists of English language text. *Stonehill Communications, Inc.* v. *Martuge,* 512 F. Supp. 349 (SD NY 1981) 2 ITRD 1667. This test is to be applied at the port of entry. CSD 85-43, 19 Cust. Bull. No. 37, September 11, 1985.

After review of the legislative history and congressional intent behind the manufacturing clause, the Customs Service ruled that the clause did not apply to literary material on labels and packaging, generally, but was primarily aimed at periodicals and books. CSD 84-80, 18 Cust. Bull. No. 39, September 26, 1984.

II. CUSTOMS RECORDATION REGULATIONS

The regulations of the Customs Service, 19 CFR Part 133, designed to afford the protection authorized by the foregoing tariff, trademark, and copyright laws cover the following provisions and procedures.

A. Recordation

There may be recorded with the Customs Service, under the customs regulations, Subparts A, B, and D: (1) trademarks currently registered by the U.S. Patent and Trademark Office, other than those registered on the supplemental register compiled under 15 U.S.C. 1096; (2) a name or trade style used for at least six months to identify a manufacturer or trader (this generally must be the complete business name and may not be a trademark); and (3) a claim to a subsisting copyright registered in the U.S.

---

[1] This "manufacturing clause" was extended four years from July 1, 1982, by Pub. L. No. 97-215, July 13, 1982.

Copyright Office or an unregistered claim to copyright in a work entitled to protection under the UCC.

B. Application

Applications for recordation are to be addressed to the Commissioner of Customs, U.S. Customs Service, Washington, D.C. 20229. The application to record a trademark or a trade name must include the name, complete business address, and citizenship of the owner; the name and principal business address of each foreign business entity authorized to use the mark or name, with a statement of the use authorized; the identity of any foreign company under common ownership or control; and, in the case of a trademark application, the places of manufacture of goods bearing the mark. In the case of a trade name recordation application there must also necessarily be given the name or trade style to be recorded and a description of the merchandise with which the name is associated.

An application to record a claim to copyright may be made not only by the copyright proprietor but also by "any person claiming actual or potential injury by reason of actual or contemplated importations of copies of eligible works." If the applicant is such a person, he must state the circumstances of such actual or potential injury. Besides the basic information of the name and address of the copyright owner or owners and of any foreign entity authorized to use the copyright, with the extent of such use, the applicant for copyright recordation must also include the foreign title of the work, if different from the U.S. title. Further, if claim is made by virtue of the UCC, the applicant must state the name of the author, his citizenship and domicile at the time of first publication, the date and country of such publication, a description of the work and its title, and a statement that all copies bore the UCC notice from first publication.

A simplified procedure has been provided for recording a copyright in a sound recording because such a recording may be readily identified by title, author, performing artist, or other identifying names. The application need provide only a statement setting forth the name(s) of the performing artist(s) and any other identifying names appearing on the surface of the reproduction or on its label or container.

C. Accompanying Documents and Fee

Each application must be accompanied by the essential record, which includes:

● A status copy of the certificate of trademark registration, certified by the U.S. Patent and Trademark Office, showing present ownership in the applicant, with five copies thereof;

● A statement of the owner of a trade name, corroborated by two others having actual knowledge, that the applicant has used the name for the class of merchandise described for at least six months, that it is not identical or confusingly similar to another trade name used for that class of merchandise, and that the applicant has sole or exclusive right to the use of such name; or

- An "additional certificate" of copyright registration issued by the U.S. Copyright Office, with five copies, and a certified copy of any assignment, exclusive license, or other document recorded in the Copyright Office, and five photographic copies of any copyrighted work not readily identifiable by title and author, and not a sound recording (as amended, TD 84-133, 49 FR 26570, June 28, 1984).

Each application is to be accompanied by a fee of $190 payable to the U.S. Customs Service.

D. Effective Date

Recordation of a trademark or copyright is effective from the date the application is approved. Since a trade name has not been officially recognized previous to the application for recordation, the application is published in the *Federal Register* with a notice specifying a procedure and time period within which interested parties may oppose the recordation. Notice of final approval or disapproval is published in the *Federal Register* after consideration of the response, if any.

E. Term and Termination

Recordation and protection thereunder remain in force:
- For a trademark, concurrently with the 20-year current registration period or last renewal thereof in the Patent and Trademark Office. When a trademark is renewed, the trademark owner may continue uninterrupted customs protection by written application to Customs to renew recordation, not later than three months after expiration of the current 20-year registration issued by the Patent and Trademark Office, accompanied by a copy of the renewal certification, a statement of ownership, and a fee of $80.
- For a trade name, as long as the trade name is used or until cancellation is requested by the recordant. Continued use is subject to question by the Commissioner of Customs from time to time.
- For a copyright, under the new law, for the life of the author plus 50 years, if the work was created on or after January 1, 1978, or if created prior to that date but not theretofore in the public domain or copyrighted. Renewal may be obtained for 47 years of subsisting copyrights in their first terms and for 75 years from the original copyright date for subsisting copyrights in their renewal term.

Recordation of a trademark or copyright is canceled if its registration is canceled or revoked by the office which registered it or upon request of the recordant.

F. Change in Ownership or Name of Owner

A change in ownership or the name of the owner of a registered trademark or copyright requires submission of documents to the Commissioner of Customs and the payment of a fee of $80 to continue the protection of recordation. If there is a change in ownership, the new owner must submit an original application, describe any time limit on the rights of ownership transferred, and submit a certified copy of the certificate of registration or of the assignment, license, or other document showing the acquisition of ownership interest. If there is a change of the name of the owner, without a transfer of ownership, the written notice to the Commissioner of Customs is to be accompanied by a certified copy of the new certificate of registration from the Patent and Trademark Office or of the document recorded in the Copyright Office showing the change in name.

III. CUSTOMS ENFORCEMENT

The Customs Service proceeds to protect the recorded trademarks, trade names, and copyrights through procedures set forth in Subparts C and E of 19 CFR Part 133, applied by customs officers at the ports of entry. These officers are kept apprised of recordations and of the foreign entities authorized to use them.

A. Articles Denied Entry

Articles denied entry are articles of foreign or domestic manufacture bearing a mark or name which copies or simulates a recorded trademark or trade name; or, in other words, a mark or name which is an actual counterfeit or so resembles the recorded mark or name as to be likely to mislead the public. Also denied entry are foreign-made articles bearing a trademark identical to the U.S.-owned and recorded one; and articles bearing a false notice of copyright and pirated copies of a recorded copyrighted work, these latter being actual or substantial copies of such a work imported in contravention of the owner's rights.

However, under 19 CFR 133.21(c), issued under 19 U.S.C. 1526, entry is not denied where both the foreign and domestic trademark or name are owned by the same entity, or are owned by entities having common ownership or control; or where use of the mark or name on foreign articles is authorized by the U.S. owner, or where the foreign article is imported by the recordant himself or his designate. Furthermore, entry is not denied if the offending foreign mark or name is completely removed or obliterated before importation, or if the recordant gives consent to the otherwise unacceptable importation.

1. Gray Market Import Litigation

The exceptions in Section 133.21(c) of the regulations to the ban on U.S. trademarked imports where the domestic and foreign trademarks are under common ownership or control permit the importation of so-called "gray market goods" or "parallel imports." These are articles manufactured abroad bearing genuine trademarks but imported without the consent of the registered U.S. trademark owner. These exceptions have given rise to extensive litigation in which the legislative history and purpose of 19 U.S.C. 1526 have been repeatedly examined. Recent decisions in the CIT, the CAFC, and the district courts of the District of Columbia, and, in 1984 and 1985, of the Eastern District, New York, have upheld the refusal of Customs to ban the gray market imports where the American owner of the registered trademark had control over its use by the foreign manufacturer, leaving the owner to pursue private remedies. A brief review of the controversies follow:

The customs regulation was rejected by a U.S. district court in a complicated case of competing noncounterfeit imports, *Bell and Howell: Mamiya Co.* v. *Masel Supply Co.,* 548 F. Supp. 1063 (ED NY 1982) 4 ITRD 1006. The district court held that the plaintiff, an American corporation, the owner of a U.S. trademark used on goods manufactured by its Japanese owner which the plaintiff exclusively imported from Japan and sold in the United States could bar the entry of the same goods, with the same trademark, manufactured by the Japanese owner, but purchased by the defendant elsewhere. The Japanese owner held worldwide rights to the use of the trademark but the district court, after extended review of U.S. trademark law, upheld the territorial exclusiveness of the U.S. trademark.

On appeal, the Second Circuit addressed only the issuance of the preliminary injunction banning the imports. According to the appeals court, the lower court had not properly discussed the irreparable injury issue, and noted the apparent genuineness of Masel's goods. The preliminary injunction was vacated. *Bell & Howell: Mamiya Co.* v. *Masel Supply Co.,* 719 F.2d 42 (1983) 5 ITRD 1209. The district court thereupon found irreparable injury to the plaintiff, then Osawa & Co., in customer confusion, damage to the trademark, and loss of business due to the imports and issued an injunction against the gray market importations. *Osawa & Co.* v. *B & H Photo,* 589 F. Supp. 1163 (SD NY 1984) 6 ITRD 1124. See also *Selchow & Righter Co.* v. *Goldex Corp.,* 612 F. Supp. 19 (SD Fla. 1985) 6 ITRD 2022.

The CIT, however, upheld the customs regulation in *Vivitar Corporation* v. *United States,* 8 CIT _____ , 593 F. Supp. 420 (1984) 6 ITRD 1074, after an extended review of the legislative purpose and administrative interpretations of 19 U.S.C. 1526(a). There the plaintiff owned the U.S. rights to the Vivitar trademark and licensed its application by foreign manufacturers. The CAFC affirmed the CIT decision, 761 F.2d 1552 (1985) 6 ITRD 2169; petition for *cert.* filed, September 10, 1985. The U.S. District Court of the District of Columbia also upheld the Customs Service rule and refused to ban imports of a variety of trademarked products manufactured by foreign subsidiaries or licensees of the U.S. trademark owners, which did not authorize the imports. This court also considered the customs regulation reasonable in the light of the legislative history and acquiescence and the judicial decisions. It found its jurisdiction in the provisions of 28 U.S.C. 1338(a) relating to trademarks and in the Lanham Trademark Act. *Coalition to Preserve the Integrity of American Trademarks* v. *United States,* 598 F. Supp. 844 (DC DC 1984) 6 ITRD 1474. A similar conclusion was reached in *El Greco Leather Products Co., Inc.* v. *Shoe World, Inc.,* 599 F.

Supp. 844 (ED NY 1984), and *Olympus Corp.* v. *United States,* No. CV-84-0920 (ED NY 1985) 7 ITRD _____ .

2. The Gray Market Import Study

Because of the considerable controversy on the question of "gray market goods" the Cabinet Council on Commerce and Trade's Working Group on Intellectual Property has undertaken a study for which the Customs Service and the Patent and Trademark Office issued questions for public comment. 49 FR 21453, May 21, 1984. The opportunity for public comment was extended to September 19, 1984. As of June 1985 the WGIP was preparing options to present to the Economic Policy Council, into which the Cabinet Council on Commerce and Trade was merged.

B. Detention Period

Articles denied entry are subject to seizure and forfeiture. However, before such action is taken, a detention period is instituted by notice to the importer allowing him 30 days to establish that the articles in question are entitled to entry, but the regulations make no provision for such a notice and detention period for articles bearing a false notice of copyright. However, in the case of suspected pirated copies, if the importer files a denial within the 30-day period, notice is then given to the copyright owner, with a representative sample of the imported articles, advising him that the importation will be released to the importer unless the owner within 30 days files with the district director a written demand for exclusion of the entry and a bond which will recompense the importer in the event the Commissioner of Customs determines that the article is not a pirated copy. If the copyright owner does demand exclusion of the copy in question, he and the importer are given 30 days to submit evidence and briefs or other pertinent material, and the file is then sent to the Commissioner of Customs for determination of the issue. If the copyright owner is sustained, the pirated copy is seized and forfeited. If he is not, his bond is transmitted to the importer.

Under 19 CFR 133.43(c)(4) the district director may permit the copyright owner to withdraw his bond and may release the detained articles to the importer if both the owner and the importer file statements agreeing to hold the Customs Service harmless for the consequences. The copyright owner may enjoin the Customs Service from releasing his bond and the articles to the importer where the importer has not filed the required statement and the shipment is acknowledged to contain piratical copies. *Schaper Manufacturing Co.* v. *Regan,* 5 CIT 97 (1983) 4 ITRD 1854.

C. Seizure and Forfeiture

Articles denied entry on the ground that their importation would violate the trademark and trade name laws are detained for 30 days from the date of notice to the importer to permit him to prove that the import restrictions should not apply for a specified reason, given in the regulations, including the permanent obliteration or removal of the offending mark or name. However, any article bearing a counterfeit mark must be seized unless the owner of the mark gives written consent to entry. Any article bearing an otherwise unacceptable mark not released within the 30-day detention period must also be seized and forfeited. All forfeitures are subject to the importer's right to petition for relief under 19 CFR Part 171.

The Customs Service may be mandated to forfeit imported articles which it has found to carry a mark infringing the plaintiff's registered trademark, using the average purchaser's test, but which it did not find to be a counterfeit mark, using the standards of experts. *Montres Rolex, S.A.* v. *Snyder* (oral opinion) SD NY, No. 82 Civ. 1692, April 7, 1982, 3 ITRD 1775. The court said that since the purpose of 19 U.S.C. 1526 was to protect the public as well as the trademark owner the Customs Service did not have the right to establish a criterion different from the average purchaser's perception for determining a mark to be counterfeit, with required forfeiture. The Second Circuit affirmed the use of the "average purchaser" test. *Montres Rolex, S.A.* v. *Snyder,* 718 F.2d 524 (1983) 5 ITRD 1065, *cert. denied,* 80 L.Ed.2d 126 (1984) 5 ITRD 1944.

D. Relief From Forfeiture

An importer notified of the seizure of merchandise is likewise notified of his right to petition for relief from, or cancellation of, a forfeiture under the trademark or copyright laws, or for relief from a customs claim for liquidated damages for failure to redeliver merchandise which may have been released to him under special provisions. Such petitions are made and considered under the provisions of 19 CFR Parts 171 and 172.

In response to a petition for relief from forfeiture in a trademark or copyright case, relief may be granted under Subpart F of Part 133 in appropriate cases (other than counterfeit marks) conditioned on (1) the export or destruction under customs supervision and at no cost to Customs of the prohibited articles; (2) the removal or obliteration of all offending trademarks or trade names; or (3) if books or periodicals have been manufactured abroad contrary to the American manufacturing requirements of 17 U.S.C. 601, the submission of satisfactory evidence that a statement of abandonment has been recorded in the Copyright Office by the copyright owner and the notice of copyright has been completely obliterated from the books or periodicals.

IV. PATENT PROTECTION LAW AND REGULATIONS

A. The Law

The statute offering protection against patent-infringing imports places a much greater burden upon the American patent owner than the laws discussed *supra* place upon American holders of recorded trademarks, trade names, and copyrights. The patent owner must establish not only that the questioned imports are unauthorized but that they are injuring or may injure his U.S. business and that this business is efficiently and economically operated. Moreover, these contentions must be established in a formal adversary hearing called by the International Trade Commission.

The statute providing these requirements and the possibilities for relief, if infringing imports are proved, is Section 337 of the Tariff Act, as amended by the Trade Act of 1974 and the Trade Agreements Act of 1979, 19 U.S.C. 1337. This section states that

> unfair methods of competition and unfair acts in the importation of articles into the United States or in their sale—the effect or tendency of which is to injure an industry, efficiently and economically operated, in the United States, or to prevent the establishment of such an industry or to restrain or monopolize trade and commerce in the United States

are unlawful and when found by the ITC to exist are to be dealt with in one of alternative specified ways. This statute, directed at any and all types of unfair import activity, is fully discussed in Chapter 17. Historically most of the complaints filed under Section 337 have been by domestic companies alleging infringements of U.S. patents in importations of merchandise manufactured abroad. Increasingly, complaints are also filed under that section by domestic companies alleging infringement of their trademarks, trade names, and copyrights.

If the ITC finds that patent infringement does exist, it is required to issue either an exclusion order, excluding the merchandise from entry, or a cease and desist order to any person violating the section. But the ITC may refrain from issuing either an exclusion or a cease and desist order if it finds that such action should not be taken after consideration of the public health and welfare, competitive conditions in the U.S. economy, U.S. production of like or competitive articles, and the interests of U.S. consumers. Further, the statute permits the President to veto any final ITC action within 60 days. During the course of its investigation, the ITC may issue an order excluding articles from entry, except under bond, if it finds there is reason to believe that there is a violation of Section 337.

B. ITC Regulations

The regulations issued by the ITC to carry out the amendments of the statute made by the Trade Act of 1974 are set forth in 19 CFR Parts 210 and 211. The regulations describe the full and formal complaint, under oath, required to initiate a proceeding and the specific matters to be included in a complaint based upon an alleged unauthorized importation or sale of an article covered by, or produced under a process covered by, the claims of a valid U.S. patent. Also, the regulations outline the further steps taken by the ITC if it determines, after preliminary inquiry, that the complaint is sufficient and that there is good and sufficient reason for a full investigation. These steps include (1) the institution of an investigation, with notice provided in the *Federal Register,* and with service of a copy of the complaint upon each respondent named therein or later discovered; (2)

the determination during the course of its proceedings, off the record, of what action the ITC should take (exclusion from entry, exclusion from entry except under bond, or a cease and desist order) and the taking of such action, where appropriate; and (3) consultation with the Department of Health and Human Services, the Department of Justice, the Federal Trade Commission, and such other agencies as may be concerned in the subject of the complaint, as required by Section 337.

While the investigation of the complaint is in progress, the ITC proceeds with the formal adversary hearing, providing full opportunity to the parties for exchange and amendment of pleadings, the submission of motions, use of discovery, compulsory process, and depositions and interrogatories. The parties may also apply for the issuance of subpoenas and for the holding of prehearing conferences. The hearing is followed by an initial determination by the presiding officer and a review by the ITC on the record, with ultimate appeal to the Court of Appeals for the Federal Circuit.

C. Customs Enforcement and Assistance

The Customs Service enforces an ITC order excluding infringing articles from entry or from entry without bond in accordance with its regulations issued under Section 337 of the Tariff Act.[2] Any bond required is to be a single entry bond on Customs Form 301, containing the basic importation and entry bond conditions of 19 CFR 113.62 in an amount determined by the ITC.

The Customs Service offers to U.S. patent owners a means to determine whether merchandise is being imported which infringes upon their patents. A patent owner believing such infringement is occurring may apply for a survey to provide him with the names and addresses of importers of merchandise appearing to infringe upon his patent.[3] The application, made to the Commissioner of Customs, provides information concerning the patent owner, the suspected merchandise, and the country of manufacture, along with a certified copy of the patent registration and three additional copies. The fee for this service depends upon the requested duration of the survey, being $1,000 for a two-month period, $1,500 for a four-month period, and $2,000 for a six-month period. The duration is at the option of the applicant.[4]

V. INTERNATIONAL DEVELOPMENTS

The United States participates in a number of international organizations and efforts working toward international rules on trademarks, copyrights, and patents.

---

[2] 19 CFR 12.39, as amended by TD 84-213, 49 FR 41152, October 19, 1984.
[3] 19 CFR 12.39a, as amended 49 FR 26571, June 28, 1984.
[4] 19 CFR 24.12(a)(3).

A. Patents and Copyrights

From time to time the State Department announces open meetings of the International Industrial Property Panel or the International Copyright Panel of its Advisory Committee on International Intellectual Property, setting forth the agenda of topics under international consideration. The agendas have included the following topics, among others, relating primarily to copyrights and patents:

• Consideration of U.S. Adherence to the Berne Convention for the Protection of Literary and Artistic Works;

• Recent Developments to Suppress International Copyright Piracy;

• Revision of the Paris Convention for the Protection of Industrial Property;

• The Draft International Code of Conduct on the Transfer of Technology;

• Report on the 4th Session of the Universal Copyright Convention/Intergovernment Copyright Committee;

• International Activities relating to Computer Uses of Copyrighted Works.

Information on these matters may be obtained from the Office of Business Practices at the State Department.

B. Trademarks

An international agreement to protect against trademark and trade name piracy by requiring the forfeiture of counterfeit merchandise was sought by the United States in the Tokyo Round of Multilateral Trade Negotiations; as of October 1979, a draft sponsored by the United States and the European Communities was being circulated among other countries to broaden the base of support.

The Office of the U.S. Trade Representative has the lead role in pursuing the completion of this code. As yet, the code has not been formally adopted and has not gained significant backing beyond the United States and the EC. It has been under study by the GATT Secretariat.[5]

---

[5]Twenty-Seventh Annual Report of the President of the United States on the Trade Agreements Program (1983) at 54.

27

Prohibited Transactions and Embargoed Merchandise

I. PROHIBITED TRANSACTIONS WITH SPECIFIED COUNTRIES

A. Trade Controlled Under the Trading With the Enemy Act and the National and International Emergencies Acts of 1976 and 1977

The Trading With the Enemy Act of 1917 as amended over the years, 50 U.S.C. App. 5, has been used in a variety of instances to prohibit or restrict imports from, exports to, and financial transactions with many countries whose interests are considered inimical to those of the United States. These controls are administered primarily by the Office of Foreign Assets Control (FAC) of the U.S. Treasury Department.

Under this authority, at least in part, the Office of Foreign Assets Control has been administering three sets of regulations which prohibit trade and financial transactions without a license from the Treasury with certain designated foreign countries. These regulations are:

1. Foreign Assets Control Regulations, prohibiting transactions with North Korea, Cambodia, North and South Vietnam, and, until January 31, 1980, China, 31 CFR Part 500;

2. Regulations prohibiting transactions involving the shipments of certain merchandise between foreign countries, specifying 19 Communist-dominated countries, 31 CFR Part 505; and

3. Cuban Assets Control Regulations, prohibiting trade and transactions with Cuba and Cuban nationals, 31 CFR Part 515.

Also under authority of the Trading With the Enemy Act the FAC administers the Foreign Funds Control Regulations which control the remaining property blocked under the World War II foreign funds control, 31 CFR Part 520.

The continuation of the authority for these regulations was limited by Public Law 95-223, enacted December 28, 1977,[1] to two years from the date of enactment of the National Emergencies Act of 1976,[2] namely, September 14, 1978. However, the President was given authority to extend the exercise of the authority for one-year periods upon a determination for each such extension that the exercise of the authority with respect to the specific country was in the national interest of the United States. The continuation of the authority for the regulations described *supra* for the years following September 14, 1978, has been provided in annual memorandums from the President to the Secretary of State and the Secretary of the Treasury.[3]

Public Law 95-223 not only limited the continuing authority of controls administered under the Trading With the Enemy Act but confined the President's authority under the governing Section 5(b) of that Act to action during time of war, striking out his authority "during any other period of national emergency" declared by him. Title II of the Public Law, entitled the "International Emergency Economic Powers Act," granted new but more restricted authority to the President to control foreign trade and financial transactions with any foreign country or national thereof.

The Congress enacted Public Law 95-223 and the earlier National Emergencies Act, which delimited Presidential action in domestic national emergencies, in order to exert greater congressional control over the proclamation and duration of national emergencies. In particular, Congress was concerned with the extensive use made by Presidents of Section 5(b) of the Trading With the Enemy Act "to regulate both domestic and international economic transactions unrelated to a declared state of emergency."[4] But Congress excluded the four sets of FAC trade and fund control regulations described *supra,* issued under Section 5(b) authority, from the 1976 National Emergencies Act in order that they might receive further study and the special consideration which eventuated in Public Law 95-223.

The FAC regulations consequently remain in effect and must be strictly observed. In fact, Public Law 95-223 increased the maximum fine in 50 U.S.C. App. 16 for violation of any regulation or license issued under Section 5(b) of the Trading With the Enemy Act to $50,000 from $10,000, retaining the existing other penalties of imprisonment for a maximum of 10 years and forfeiture of the property concerned. Since the controls are highly technical and sanctions for violations are severe, extreme caution should be exercised in connection with engaging in any transaction involving any of the designated countries. In the event of any question as to the legitimacy of a proposed transaction, the prudent course is to seek a ruling from the

---

[1] 50 U.S.C. 1701; 50 U.S.C. App 5, and 5 note.

[2] 50 U.S.C. 1601.

[3] See, *e.g.,* 49 FR 35927, September 11, 1984; 50 FR 36563, September 9, 1985.

[4] S. Rep. No. 95-466, October 3, 1977, 1977 U.S. Code Cong. & Ad. News 4541. The authority of the President under Section 5(b) to impose a 10 percent surcharge on dutiable imports during a balance-of-payments crisis was upheld in *United States* v. *Yoshida International, Inc.,* 526 F.2d 560 (CCPA 1975) 1 ITRD 1483. The supplemental duty paid was held not recoverable under Section 9(a) of the Act, that section allowing only for recovery of property vested during wartime under Section 5(b). *Alcan Sales Division* v. *United States,* 693 F.2d 1089 (Fed. Cir. 1983) 4 ITRD 1097, *cert. denied,* No. 82-1384, May 23, 1983, 77 L.Ed.2d 1300, 4 ITRD 2152.

Office of Foreign Assets Control, Treasury Department, Washington, D.C. 20220.

1. Foreign Assets Control Regulations: North Korea, Cambodia, North and South Vietnam

The FAC regulations of the Treasury Department, instituted at the time of the Korean War and continued and extended through the Vietnam conflict and up to the present time, restrict trade and financial transactions involving North Korea, Cambodia, and North and South Vietnam. In the case of the People's Republic of China no coverage remains except a requirement for the maintenance and furnishing of records of previously covered transactions.[5] In the case of the other countries the control amounts to an almost complete embargo. The restrictions on trade with North Korea, Cambodia, and North and South Vietnam are described first, followed by a summary of the removal of restrictions on trade with the People's Republic of China.

a. Basic Prohibitions

The FAC regulations prohibit, except as specifically authorized by the Secretary of the Treasury or his designee, all payments, transactions in foreign exchange, and transfers of credit with respect to any property subject to the jurisdiction of the United States by any person subject to such jurisdiction if the transactions are by or on behalf of or pursuant to the direction of a designated country or a national thereof, or such transactions involve property in which a designated country or a national thereof has at any time since the effective date had an interest. The designated countries and effective dates are as follows:

- North Korea, *i.e.,* Korea north of the 38th parallel of north latitude—December 17, 1950;
- Cambodia—April 17, 1975;
- North Vietnam, *i.e.,* Vietnam north of the 17th parallel of north latitude—May 5, 1964; and
- South Vietnam, *i.e.,* Vietnam south of the 17th parallel of north latitude—April 30, 1975.

The regulations further prohibit all dealings in any such property, including transfers, withdrawals, or exportations, by any person subject to U.S. jurisdiction, except as specifically authorized by the Treasury Department. Finally, the regulations prohibit, except as authorized by a general or specific license, any person subject to the jurisdiction of the United States from purchasing, transporting, importing, or otherwise dealing in or engaging in any transaction with respect to any merchandise outside the United States, the country of origin of which is North Korea, Cambodia, North Vietnam, or South Vietnam.

---

[5]31 CFR 500.201(d). See Subsection (c) for the deletion of the PRC.

If an article of merchandise is manufactured in a nondesignated country from raw materials originating in one of the designated countries, there is no prohibition on its importation into the United States or on any other dealings with respect to it. However, the regulations specify a list of processes such as shredding, slicing, peeling, scraping, etc., that are deemed not to alter the character of the merchandise insofar as the prohibition against importation or other dealings is concerned. Also, an article manufactured elsewhere is deemed to be a product of one of the designated countries if there has been added to it such articles as embroidery, needlepoint, petit point, lace, or any other article or adornment which is the product of one of the designated countries.

There is a basic prohibition, therefore, on all direct trade with the designated countries or on transactions involving property in which any of them or their nationals have an interest. Moreover, the supplying of petroleum products to any vessel bound to or from North Korea, Cambodia, North Vietnam, South Vietnam, or Cuba is prohibited.

The FAC issued General License 31 CFR 500.563, effective March 21, 1977, which is applicable generally to all persons and has two functions:

• It authorizes persons who visit North Korea, North Vietnam, South Vietnam, or Cambodia

(1) To pay their transportation and maintenance expenses (meals, hotel bills, taxis, etc.) and

(2) To buy a maximum of $100 worth of goods (at foreign market value) for personal use and not for resale. This allowance is usable only once every six months. Goods purchased must be brought back by the traveler in his baggage.

• It authorizes news gatherers, documentary filmmakers, researchers, and others who visit for similar purposes to acquire and pay for films, magazines, books, and similar publications for professional use and not for resale.

Single copies of any publication may be released by Customs to addressees. 50 FR 5753, February 12, 1985.

An additional general license, 31 CFR 500.565, authorizes persons in the United States to send up to $300 in any three months to close relatives in Vietnam and an additional $750 on a one-time basis for one person for purposes of emigration, provided the funds do not come from a blocked account.

b. Foreign Residents and Subsidiaries

The basic prohibition applies to U.S. citizens or residents of the United States wheresoever located and in a limited way to foreign subsidiaries and branches of U.S. corporations. Subsidiaries that are foreign corporations are subject to foreign law and not U.S. law. Branches operating abroad are also subject to local law, but FAC has ruled that American parent corporations have an obligation to direct their foreign subsidiaries and branches not to engage in prohibited transactions.

American citizens or residents serving as officers, directors, and managerial personnel are prohibited from participating in prohibited transactions. Moreover, FAC has ruled that they have a positive duty to prevent the foreign subsidiary or branch from engaging in the prohibited transaction if at all possible. In the case of a director this means that he must cast his vote against the proposed transaction. This policy of FAC frequently brings American citizens and foreign subsidiaries and branches into conflict with policies of foreign governments and foreign laws concerning the duties and responsibilities of corporate officers and directors. These are not academic questions, however, as FAC has authority, such as the blocking of assets, which it may use to secure compliance with its policy, not to mention the possibility of criminal sanctions against responsible individuals.

A general license, 31 CFR 500.564, permits American-owned or American-controlled foreign firms to pay expenditures for travel to and in North Korea, North or South Vietnam, or Cambodia by their foreign national employees.

c. Deletion of Prohibitions Applicable to the People's Republic of China

Pursuant to general licenses issued in 1971 and 1975,[6] all customary trade and related financial transactions with mainland China were authorized with certain limitations.

Two agreements between the United States and the People's Republic of China, executed in 1979, resulted in the removal of China from coverage under the Foreign Assets Control Regulations as of January 31, 1980.[7] The Agreement Concerning the Settlement of Claims, signed on May 11, 1979, as amended, provided for the unblocking on January 31, 1980, of assets blocked, as described *supra,* by reason of an interest held by China or its nationals between December 17, 1950, and May 6, 1971.[8] Further, the Agreement on Trade Relations, done at Peking, July 7, 1979, provided for the mutual accord of most-favored-nation status in trade relations and unrestricted financial dealings. This agreement came into force February 1, 1980, for a three-year period on the exchange of notifications that each contracting party had completed legal procedures for this purpose.[9] The agreement provided for extensions for successive three-year periods unless either party gave timely notice of termination.

---

[6] 31 CFR 500.541, 500.546, and 500.547, deleted January 31, 1980.
[7] 45 FR 7224, January 31, 1980.
[8] 44 FR 56434, October 1, 1979. Notice of the Office of Foreign Assets Control.
[9] 45 FR 6882, January 30, 1980.

d. Other Exports Prohibited

The export of the following is prohibited: (1) merchandise, regardless of origin, of a type included in the commodity control list of the U.S. Department of Commerce[10] and identified by the code letter "A" following the export control commodity number; and (2) merchandise of a type the unauthorized exportation of which is prohibited by regulations issued under Section 414 of the Mutual Security Act of 1954 relating to arms, ammunition, and implements of war, or under Sections 53(a), 62, 82(c), 103, and 104 of the Atomic Energy Act as amended relating to atomic energy facilities or materials for use for nonmilitary purposes.

2. Transaction Control Regulations

The Treasury Department's FAC also administers the transaction control regulations prohibiting certain transactions involving the shipment of certain merchandise between certain foreign countries without Treasury authorization. These regulations, first issued in 1953, 31 CFR Part 505 prohibit persons within the United States from buying commodities abroad or facilitating the purchase of commodities abroad for the purpose of shipment to a list of designated Communist countries if the merchandise is included in the Commerce Department's commodity control list referred to in 15 CFR Part 399 and is identified on that list by the letter "A" in the column titled "special provisions list"; or if the merchandise is of a type that is prohibited exportation under the Commerce Department's export regulations.

The list of Communist countries to which these controls apply is as follows: Albania, Bulgaria, Cambodia, Czechoslovakia, Estonia, German Democratic Republic, East Berlin, Hungary, Latvia, Lithuania, North Korea, Outer Mongolia, People's Republic of China, Poland and Danzig, Romania, Tibet, the Union of Soviet Socialist Republics, and Vietnam.

3. Cuban Assets Control Regulations

Pursuant to both Section 5(b) of the Trading With the Enemy Act of 1917 as amended, and Section 620(a) of the Foreign Assistance Act of 1961,[11] authorizing the President to establish and maintain a total embargo on all trade with Cuba, and pursuant to Proclamation 3447 of February 6, 1962, the Treasury Department issued the Cuban Assets Control Regulations effective July 8, 1963. These regulations essentially prohibit all trade and financial transactions with Cuba and Cuban nationals in Cuba, except pursuant to a license issued by the Treasury Department's FAC, 31 CFR Part 515.

Treasury regulations prohibit all unlicensed transactions in foreign exchange by any person within the United States and all transfers of credit

---

[10] 15 CFR Part 399.
[11] 22 U.S.C. 2370(a).

and all payments through any banking institutions with respect to property subject to U.S. jurisdiction, if they are by or on behalf of or pursuant to the direction of Cuba or if a Cuban national has at any time on or since July 8, 1963, had an interest in such property. They also prohibit all dealings in property or evidences of ownership of property by any person subject to U.S. jurisdiction, if the transactions involve property in which Cuba or any national of Cuba has at any time on or since July 8, 1963, had any interest.

a. General Licenses

General License 31 CFR 515.560, effective April 20, 1982, authorized various transactions incident to travel in Cuba but only by officials of the United States or of a foreign government or of an intergovernmental organization of which the United States is a member, by news-gatherers, by persons engaged in professional research, and by persons traveling to visit close relatives in Cuba. Current authorized transactions include:

(1) All transportation-related transactions ordinarily incident to travel to and from Cuba;

(2) All transactions ordinarily incident to travel within Cuba;

(3) Purchase of a maximum of $100 worth of goods (at foreign market value) for personal use and not for resale. This allowance is usable only once every six months. Goods purchased must be brought back by the traveler in his baggage.

(4) Transactions by any person incident to arranging or assisting travel to or from Cuba;

(5) Transactions on behalf of aircraft or vessels incidental to nonscheduled passage to and from Cuba, not involving carriage of commercial merchandise;

(6) Transactions incident to the processing and payment of checks and credit cards for authorized expenditures in Cuba, within specified limitations;

(7) The acquisition and import into the United States by news-gatherers, documentary filmmakers, researchers, and others in Cuba for similar purposes, of films, books, magazines, and similar publications related to their professions; and

(8) The receipt of a single copy of any Cuban publication. 50 FR 5753, February 12, 1985.

The General License applicable to persons engaged in professional research was restricted in July 1982, to persons engaged in full-time professional researching in areas specifically related to Cuba, with full-time work schedules in Cuba, 47 FR 32060, July 23, 1982.

The 1982 amendment of Regulation 560 restricted the 1977 general license permitting travel-related economic transactions, including tourist travel (47 FR 17030, April 20, 1982). The purpose was to reduce Cuba's hard currency earnings from travel by U.S. persons to and within Cuba. This restriction on general travel was challenged as invalid under the International Emergency Economic Powers Act of 1977 (IEEPA), which curtailed the authority of the President to act under Section 5(b) of the

Trading With the Enemy Act (TWEA), and on constitutional grounds as abridging the right to travel. The challenge, rejected by the District Court, was upheld by the Court of Appeals for the First Circuit, *Wald* v. *Regan,* 708 F.2d 794 (1983). However, the Supreme Court held by a 5–4 decision that the TWEA authority to regulate all property transactions with Cuba, including travel-related transactions, was being, in effect, "exercised" at the time of the adoption of the IEEPA and was therefore "grandfathered" under the exception in the IEEPA for existing TWEA authority. The decision also determined that the constitutional right to travel could be curtailed on weighty grounds of foreign policy. *Regan* v. *Wald,* 104 S.Ct. 3026.

A further general license added to the regulations, Section 515.563, is similar to that provided under the FAC regulations described *supra.* It permits persons in the United States to send up to $500 in any three months to any one payee or household in Cuba and up to $500 once to one person for emigration.

In addition, Section 515.564 authorizes a Cuban national with a visa to travel from the United States to places outside Cuba, and Section 515.565 provides specific licenses for participation by Cuban nationals in public exhibitions or performances in the United States and for U.S. nationals engaging in similar performances in Cuba.

Exports from the United States to Cuba are governed by the export administration regulations of the Department of Commerce. Treasury regulations provide a general license, subject to various conditions, for all exports licensed by Commerce[12] so it is not necessary to seek an FAC license for exporting.

b. Specific Licensing Policy

The Treasury Department's FAC has stated[13] that it is not inclined to issue specific licenses for the importation of goods of Cuban origin unless the applicant for the license submits satisfactory documentary proof that the goods were located outside Cuba prior to July 8, 1963, and that no Cuban national has had an interest in such goods since that date. Generally speaking, affidavits from the manufacturer or shipper of the goods will not be enough to satisfy the proof requirements. The FAC does state that it will issue specific licenses for the importation of:

• Cuban-origin books, films, phonograph records, tapes, photographs, microfiche, and posters (1) by universities, libraries, and research and scientific institutions if the materials are for specific educational or research programs of such institutions which have the approval of the Librarian of Congress or the National Science Foundation; and (2) for commercial purposes, but only on condition that payment for the materials is deposited in a blocked account in a domestic bank; and

---

[12]31 CFR 515.533.
[13]31 CFR 515.543.

• Cuban-origin newspapers, magazines, photographs, films, tapes, and other news material by news-gathering agencies in the United States or by journalists traveling to Cuba under a valid passport, if such materials are necessary for their journalistic assignments.

c. Nickel and Nickel Products

The Castro government nationalized without compensation a U.S. nickel mine and has endeavored to market production from this mine throughout the world. To prevent Cuba from benefiting from the nationalization, the FAC published a provision which stated that nickel and nickel-bearing materials purchased outside the United States were presumptively of Cuban origin, and the importation of such materials into the United States was authorized only if there was presented to the district director of customs an appropriate certificate of origin from a government approved by FAC for issuance of such certificates.[14] Thus, the purchase for importation of nickel, nickel-bearing materials, or stainless steel containing more than 2.50 percent nickel is a risky proposition. Before any contracts are made for the importation of such materials, careful attention should be given to the current Cuban Assets Control requirements.

From time to time, the FAC issues notices which are published in the *Federal Register* concerning the importation of nickel and nickel-bearing materials. For example, a notice issued on September 27, 1984 (49 FR 38217), stated that certificates of origin were available from the Japanese Ministry of International Trade and Industry attesting that nickel-bearing material from the Shunan Works did not contain nickel of Cuban origin, and that importation of such material covered by such a certificate would be permitted.

d. Foreign Subsidiaries or Branches of American Firms

The FAC is prepared to issue specific licenses "for certain categories of transactions between U.S.-owned or -controlled firms in third countries and Cuba, where local law requires, or policy in the third country favors, trade with Cuba."[15] Direct trade between the United States and Cuba continues embargoed. Moreover, the specific licenses issued do not authorize any person in the United States to engage in, participate in, or be involved in a licensed transaction with Cuba.

The categories of transactions FAC is prepared to license include:
• Exportation to Cuba of commodities produced in the authorized trade territory, as defined *infra,* provided:
(1) The commodities to be exported are nonstrategic;
(2) U.S.-origin technical data (other than maintenance, repair, and operations data) will not be transferred;

---

[14] 31 CFR 515.536(c).
[15] 31 CFR 515.559.

(3) If any U.S.-origin parts and components are included therein, such inclusion has been authorized by the Department of Commerce;

(4) If any U.S.-origin spares are to be reexported to Cuba in connection with a licensed transaction, such reexport has been authorized by the Department of Commerce;

(5) No U.S. dollar accounts are involved; and

(6) Any financing or other extension of credit by a U.S.-owned or U.S.-controlled firm is granted on normal short-term conditions which are appropriate for the commodity to be exported.

• Importation of goods of Cuban origin into countries in the authorized trade territory, provided the licensee thereunder is itself located in the importing country.

The term "strategic goods" means any item, regardless of origin, of a type included in the commodity control list of the U.S. Department of Commerce[16] and identified by the code letter "A" following the export control commodity numbers, or of a type the unauthorized exportation of which from the United States is prohibited by regulations issued under Section 414 of the Mutual Security Act of 1954[17] relating to arms, ammunitions, and implements of war, or under Sections 53(a), 62, 82(c), 103, and 104 of the Atomic Energy Act of 1954[18] relating to atomic energy facilities or materials for nonmilitary purposes.

The authorized trade territory referred to includes all countries of the free world other than the United States, plus Yugoslavia.

In addition, General License 515.561 authorizes payment or reimbursement by American-owned or American-controlled foreign firms of expenditures incidental to travel to Cuba, and incidental to travel and maintenance in Cuba by their foreign national employees.

4. Iranian Assets Control Regulations

a. Transaction Prohibitions Imposed

In response to the Iranian seizure of hostages at the U.S. Embassy in Tehran, and the developing crisis in relations with the Iranian Government, the President of the United States on November 14, 1979, in Executive Order 12170 (44 FR 65729) ordered the blocking of property of the Government of Iran, its instrumentalities and controlled entities, and the Central Bank of Iran. The action was taken under authority of the International Emergency Economic Powers Act, 50 U.S.C. 1701, the National Emergencies Act, 50 U.S.C. 1601, and 3 U.S.C. 301. Property of Iranian citizens and private Iranian business firms was not blocked. The President delegated to the Secretary of the Treasury authority to implement the Order. Previously, on November 12, 1979, in Proclamation 4702, the President had, in response to the same threat, prohibited the importation of Iranian crude oil (44 FR 65581).

---

[16] 15 CFR Part 399.
[17] 68 Stat. 848, 22 U.S.C. 1934.
[18] 68 Stat. 1921, 42 U.S.C. 2011–2296.

Effective November 14, 1979, the Office of Foreign Assets Control issued the Iranian Assets Control Regulations implementing the blocking order (31 CFR Part 535). As stated by the Treasury:

> The effect of the Regulations is that transactions in property subject to the jurisdiction of the United States or which is in the possession or control of persons subject to the jurisdiction of the United States in which Iran or its instrumentalities or controlled entities has or has had an interest on or after the effective date of these Regulations are prohibited in the absence of a license from the Treasury Department.

The regulations were amended to provide general licenses authorizing various types of transactions, including export transactions under certain conditions, and payments of obligations to persons in the United States from nonblocked accounts (44 FR 65988, 66591, 66832, 67617).

Prohibitions on exports to, or imports from Iran, whether to Iranian Government entities or private citizens, were added by Executive Orders 12205 of April 7, 1980, and 12211 of April 17, 1980, 45 FR 24099, 26685. The regulations were amended accordingly to prohibit without general or specific license the import into the United States of any goods or services of Iranian origin and the sale or transfer of any commodities, except food and medical supplies, to any person in Iran by any person subject to the jurisdiction of the United States (31 CFR 535.204–207).

b. Termination of Prohibitions

The prohibitions on exports to or imports from Iran and related transactions were revoked by Executive Order 12282 of January 19, 1981, 46 FR 7925, January 23, 1981 as part of the implementation of agreements with the Government of Iran (the "Algiers Accords") relating to the release of the U.S. hostages and the resolution of claims of U.S. nationals against Iran. The pertinent regulations added to the Iranian Assets Control Regulations in April 1980, were removed therefrom (46 FR 14337, February 26, 1981).

c. Transfer of Assets

Companion Executive Orders of January 19, 1981, Nos. 12276-12285, 46 FR Part XXII, January 23, 1981, ordered the transfer to and through the Federal Reserve Bank of New York to accounts established under the international agreements the blocked Iranian assets held in U.S. domestic and overseas banks. These Executive Orders were also implemented in the amendments to the Iranian Assets Control Regulations published February 26, 1981. The amendments nullified any attachments, injunctions, or other action secured in litigation subsequent to November 14, 1979, and prohibited further judicial action respecting disposition of the blocked accounts. This nullification and prohibition were supplemented by Executive Order 12294, February 24, 1981, 46 FR 14111, suspending all claims which might be presented to the Iran-United States Claims Tribunal except as presented to that Tribunal. The time limits for compliance with the required transfers of Iranian assets subject to judicial attachment were suspended pending review by the Supreme Court of the President's authority in the premises, 46 FR 31630, June 16, 1981. On July 2, 1981, the Supreme Court held in *Dames & Moore* v. *Regan,* 453 U.S. 654, that the President had authority under the International Emergency Economic Powers Act, 50 U.S.C. 1701, to nullify the attachment and order transfer of the Iranian assets. The transfer to the Federal Reserve Bank of New York was thereupon ordered to be completed by July 10, 1981. 46 FR 35106, July 7, 1981.

d. Continuation of National Emergency

On November 7, 1984, the President issued a notice, such as had been issued in November 1981, 1982, and 1983, continuing the national emergency declared November 14, 1979, under the National Emergencies Act, on the ground that the process of implementing the January 19, 1981, agreements with Iran was still under way (49 FR 44741, November 9, 1984).

5. Nicaraguan Trade Control Regulations

Under the authority of the International Emergency Economic Powers Act (50 U.S.C. 1701 *et seq.*) the President issued Executive Order 12513 of May 1, 1985, declaring a national emergency to deal with the Nicaraguan threat to the national security; prohibiting all imports of goods and services of Nicaraguan origin, all exports of goods and services to Nicaragua, except those destined for the organized democratic resistance, and the entry into the United States of Nicaraguan aircraft and vessels; and delegating to the Secretary of the Treasury the authority to carry out the order (50 FR 18629, May 2, 1985).

Executive Order 12513 was promptly implemented by the issuance by the Office of Foreign Assets Control of the Nicaraguan Trade Control Regulations as 31 CFR Part 540, effective May 7, 1985 (50 FR 19890, May 10, 1985). The regulations prohibit, except as may be authorized by regulations or licenses, the import of goods and services of Nicaraguan origin, directly or through third countries (unless substantially transformed), or into bonded warehouses or foreign trade zones.

Section 540.504 of the regulations provides a general license for the import of Nicaraguan goods completely paid for prior to May 1, 1985, and, upon application, for specific licenses for such goods partially paid for, and for services previously fully or partly paid for. General licenses are also provided for the import of Nicaraguan publications, gifts valued at no more than $100, and accompanied baggage. Licenses are provided also for various exports, particularly medical supplies.

6. South African Trade Control Regulations

Under the authority of the International Emergency Economic Powers Act and other legislation, the President issued Executive Order 12532 of September 9, 1985, 50 FR 36861, September 10, 1985, finding that the policies and actions of the Government of South Africa constitute a threat to the foreign policy and economy of the United States and declaring a national emergency to deal with that threat. The Executive Order prohibited generally a number of transactions, with described exceptions to be governed by agency regulations. The prohibitions extended to (a) loans by U.S. financial institutions to the South African Government or its entities, (b) exports of computers and computer technology to military and police agencies, (c) the issuance of any license for the export to South Africa of nuclear goods, and (d) the import of any South African arms, ammunition or military vehicles.

The Executive Order affirmed the policy of the United States to encourage adherence by U.S. firms in South Africa to fair labor principles and directed the Secretary of State to provide procedures for registration by U.S. firms of their adherence to the principles set forth in the Order. U.S. government agencies operating in South Africa were required to follow these principles and to assist South African business enterprises having more than 50-percent beneficial ownership by disadvantaged persons.

Prohibition of the importation of South African Krugerrands was decreed by Executive Order 12535, 50 FR 40325, October 3, 1985, and implemented by regulations of the Office of Foreign Assets Control, 31 CFR Part 545, 50 FR 41682, October 15, 1985.

B. Trade Controlled Under the U.N. Participation Act

By Executive Order 12183 of December 16, 1979 (44 FR 74787), the President terminated the then current limitations relating to trade and other transactions involving Zimbabwe-Rhodesia. The order revoked, with respect to subsequent transactions, the three prior Executive Orders under which the Rhodesian Sanctions Regulations were promulgated by the Treasury Department but continued in force and effect until terminated by appropriate authority the existing regulations, determinations, rulings, and licenses, etc., and continued the application of the orders to acts done or omitted prior to December 16, 1979.

The Rhodesian Sanctions Regulations were amended December 17, 1979 (44 FR 74841) to remove all formerly prohibited transactions with Rhodesia from Treasury control, but to retain certain relevant sections, including the recordkeeping, reporting, and penalties provisions. Consequently, the legal basis for, and scope of, the Rhodesian Sanctions Regulations remain important.

In implementation of United Nations Security Council Resolutions of 1966 and 1968 on Rhodesia (officially designated Southern Rhodesia) and pursuant to Section 5 of the United Nations Participation Act of 1945, as amended,[19] and Executive Orders 11322 of 1967 and 11419, of 1968, as amended by Executive Order 11978 of 1977, the Treasury Department maintained and administered the Rhodesian Sanctions Regulations, 31 CFR Part 530. The regulations amounted to a total embargo of all trade and related financial transactions with Rhodesia by any person subject to the jurisdiction of the United States. Thus, the following were prohibited except pursuant to a general or specific license issued by the Treasury Department's FAC:

● The importation into the United States of any merchandise of Rhodesian origin;

● Transfers of property which involved merchandise outside the United States of Rhodesian origin;

● Transfers of property which involved merchandise destined to Rhodesia or to or for the account of business nationals thereof.

Between 1966 and 1968 there was less than a total embargo. In that period there was a prohibition on the importation of certain commodities whose origin was Rhodesian. In July 1968, in implementation of a second United Nations Resolution, the embargo was made total.

On January 24, 1972, Treasury's FAC issued a general license, 31 CFR 530.518, authorizing the importation of certain critical materials originating in Rhodesia and also licensing the payment transactions in connection with such importations. But, effective March 18, 1977, pursuant to the amendment of 22 U.S.C. 287c in Public Law 95-12, the authorization for the importation of critical materials was canceled, except for chromium then in transit, and the total embargo of Southern Rhodesia was reinstated.[20]

C. Trade Controlled Under Congressional Finding

In Section 5 of Public Law 95-435, enacted October 10, 1978,[21] the Congress made the finding that "the Government of Uganda, under the regime of General Idi Amin, has committed genocide against Ugandans." It provided as a consequence that after the date of enactment of the Act

no corporation, institution, group or individual may import, directly or indirectly, into the United States or its territories or possessions any article grown, produced, or manufactured in Uganda until the President determines and certifies to the Congress that the Government of Uganda is no longer committing a consistent pattern of gross violations of human rights.

Exports to Uganda were also prohibited until the Presidential determination and certification.

The President determined and certified that the Government of Uganda was no longer committing a consistent pattern of gross violations of human rights, in a memorandum of May 15, 1979, to the Secretaries of State,

---

[19]22 U.S.C. 287c.

[20]Executive Order 11978, March 18, 1977; 31 CFR 530.202 (1977 ed.), and other amendments; 42 FR 18073, April 5, 1977.

[21]22 U.S.C. 2151 note.

Treasury, and Commerce, which requested the Secretary of State to so advise Congress (44 FR 28773).

II. PROHIBITED IMPORTS

A. Embargoed Merchandise

The Tariff Schedules of the United States contain a number of absolute prohibitions on the importation of certain merchandise. Imports of the following are prohibited:

- Ermine, fox, kolinsky, marten, mink, muskrat, and weasel fur skins which are the product of the USSR (Schedule 1, Part 5B, Headnote 4);
- Pepper shells, ground or unground (Schedule 1, Part 11B, Headnote 4);
- White phosphorous matches (Schedule 7, Part 9A, Headnote 1);
- Impure tea, except for use in manufacturing caffeine and other chemical products under specified conditions (Schedule 1, Part 11A, Headnote 3; Schedule 8, Part 5D); and
- Eggs of wild birds, except eggs of game birds imported for propagating purposes under regulations prescribed by the Secretary of the Interior, and specimens imported for scientific collections (Schedule 1, Part 4E, Headnote 1).

In addition to the foregoing, there is a prohibition on the importation of the feathers or skin of any bird. The prohibition does not apply to domesticated chickens, turkeys, guinea fowl, geese, ducks, pigeons, ostriches, rheas, English ring-necked pheasants, or pea fowl. Nor does it apply to the importation of fully manufactured artificial flies used for fishing, or to the importation of live birds or game birds killed abroad and imported for noncommercial purposes. There are exceptions in the form of quotas for skin-bearing feathers for use in the manufacture of artificial flies used for fishing of not more than 5,000 skins of gray jungle fowl and not more than 1,000 skins of mandarin ducks. Also, for use in the manufacture of artificial flies used for fishing, or for millinery purposes, not more than 45,000 skins total may be imported of the following species of pheasant: Lady Amherst, golden, silver, Reeves, blue-eared, and brown-eared. In order to import one of the articles listed above as an exception to the prohibition, it is necessary to obtain a permit from the Secretary of the Interior (Schedule 1, Part 15D, Headnote 2(d)).[22]

B. Prohibition of Importation of "Immoral Articles"

Section 1305 of Title 19, U.S. Code, prohibits the importation of so-called immoral articles. These include: (1) any book, other printed matter, or picture or illustration advocating or urging treason or insurrection against the United States, or forcible resistance to any law of the United States, or

---

[22]See Appendix G.

containing any threat to take the life or inflict bodily harm upon any person in the United States; (2) any obscene book, other writing, picture or illustration, or other article which is obscene or immoral; (3) any drug or medicine or other article for causing unlawful abortion; and (4) any lottery ticket or any printed paper that may be used for a lottery ticket, or any advertisement of any lottery.

Any such articles are subject to seizure along with the entire contents of the package in which they were contained unless the Customs Service is satisfied that they were contained in the package without the knowledge or consent of the importer, owner, agent, or consignee.[23] The statute makes an exception for the Secretary of the Treasury in his discretion to admit the so-called classics or books of recognized and established literary or scientific merit, but books in this category may be imported only for noncommercial purposes in the discretion of the Secretary.

The obscenity of imported merchandise is determined by the community standards of the port of entry, not the place of destination, and if found obscene, seizure is not avoided because the merchandise is for private and personal use and possession only, or because it was made from sources produced in the United States. *United States* v. *Various Articles of Obscene Merchandise,* 536 F. Supp. 50 (DC SNY 1981).

C. Convict or Forced Labor Made Goods

Section 1307 of Title 19, U.S. Code, prohibits the importation of all articles mined, produced, or manufactured wholly or in part in any foreign country by convict labor and/or forced labor and/or indentured labor under penal sanctions. An exception is made for articles which are not mined, produced, or manufactured in such quantities in the United States as to meet the consumptive demands of the United States.[24]

In response to a request by the Senate Finance Committee on December 21, 1983, the ITC investigated the extent of imports made by compulsory labor in the Soviet Union and China. The ITC report to the Finance Committee of December 19, 1984, concluded, on the basis of available evidence, that the United States is not importing large quantities of such goods, although some merchandise of specified types believed to be made by convict labor in each country could be entering international trade (2 ITR 10, January 2, 1985).

In January 1985 the Secretary of the Treasury determined that there was no reasonable basis to prohibit the entry of certain goods from the Soviet Union. On the basis of that determination, the CIT dismissed as moot a suit by certain members of Congress and others to require denial of entry of the Soviet imports. *Representative Stewart B. McKinney et al.* v. *United States Department of the Treasury, et al.,* 10 CIT ____ , 614 F. Supp. 1226 (1985) 7 ITRD 1009. The Court also held that only plaintiffs who were workers or producers affected by the imports had standing to sue.

---

[23]The implementing regulations are in 19 CFR 12.40, 12.41.
[24]The implementing regulations are in 19 CFR 12.42–12.45.

D. Limitation on Importation of U.S. Foreign Excess Property

Since 1949 Congress has prohibited[25] the sale of U.S. foreign excess property (FEP), sometimes called "surplus property," without a condition forbidding its importation into the United States unless the Secretary of Agriculture, in the case of any agricultural commodity, or the Secretary of Commerce, in the case of other property, determines that the importation of that property "would relieve domestic shortages or otherwise be beneficial to the economy of this country." However, in 1976 Congress authorized the return after October 17, 1977, of FEP for handling as federal excess or surplus property when an executive agency head, or the General Services Administration in consultation with the agency head, determined the return to be in the interest of the United States.[26]

The Commerce Department has issued extensive and explicit regulations to carry out this statute by providing procedures for applying for determination as to whether the importation of foreign excess property would be permitted by the statute and for the issuance of import authorizations.[27] The regulations define foreign excess property as including any property, other than agricultural commodities, outside the United States under the control of a federal agency but not required by it, or which has been disposed of by it, notwithstanding changes in ownership.

To obtain import authorization for such property any interested person may apply to the Deputy Assistant Secretary for Trade Regulation of the Industry and Trade Administration, Commerce Department, for a determination that the importation of particular foreign excess property would relieve domestic shortages or otherwise be beneficial to the U.S. economy. The regulations provide criteria under which this determination is to be made. If the determination is affirmative, it is published in the *Federal Register*. Until the determination is amended or withdrawn by notice published in the *Federal Register*, the Foreign Excess Property Officer will issue FEP import authorizations on applications conforming to the requirements in the regulations. If foreign excess property is to be imported in bond for reexport, the importation is handled by the Customs Service and not the Commerce Department.

Requests for importation of U.S. agricultural commodities are so infrequently made that the Department of Agriculture has not found it necessary to promulgate regulations. Any individual requests are handled by the Office of the Secretary on a case-by-case basis.

E. Fish and Fish Products From Country Seizing American Vessels

Under the Fishery Conservation and Management Act of 1976 (16 U.S.C. 1801 *et seq.*) the State Department certifies to the Treasury Department a determination that a fishing vessel of the United States has been seized by a foreign nation while fishing in waters over which that

---

[25] 40 U.S.C. 512.
[26] 40 U.S.C. 512(c). Implementing regulations are in 41 CFR Subpart 101-43.5.
[27] 15 CFR Part 302.

nation claims jurisdiction but such jurisdiction is not recognized by the United States. Upon receipt of this certification the Treasury Department is required to take appropriate action to prohibit the importation of fish and fish products from the fishery involved, until such time as the State Department notifies Treasury that the reasons for its determination no longer prevail.

F. Imports Threatening to Impair National Security

Section 232 of the Trade Expansion Act of 1962, 19 U.S.C. 1862, authorizes the Secretary of Commerce to make an investigation to determine the effects on the national security of the import of an article concerning which investigation is requested by the head of a department or agency or by an interested party, or is initiated upon his own motion. If he finds that the article is being imported "in such quantities or under such circumstances as to threaten to impair the national security," he so advises the President, and the President is then authorized to adjust the import of such article to remove the threat.

An investigation under this section is pursued in accordance with the regulations of the Secretary of Commerce in 15 CFR Part 359. These regulations set forth the criteria for determining the effects on the national security stated in the statute, including such considerations as the domestic production needed for projected national defense requirements, and the capacity of domestic industries to meet these requirements.

The major action taken under this authority was the adjustment of the import of petroleum and petroleum products, originating in Proclamation 3279 of March 10, 1959, and subsequently amended at least once or twice annually.[28] The adjustment consisted principally of restricting imports to persons licensed by the Secretary of Energy in accordance with regulations and the allocation under regulations of quantities of imports by Districts of the United States. Amendment of Proclamation No. 3279, as amended, was used as the vehicle for the embargo on the importation of Iranian crude oil during the Iranian holding of American hostages.[29] More recently, the President issued Proclamation 4907 of March 10, 1982, prohibiting the importation of crude oil from Libya. Exempted from the embargo was crude oil loaded aboard maritime vessels prior to March 12, 1982.

Proclamation 3279 was revoked as serving no current purpose by Proclamation 5141 of December 22, 1983, 48 FR 56929, which directed the continued monitoring of imports of petroleum and petroleum products, and which prohibited any imports of crude oil from Libya.

A negative determination under Section 232 was announced by the Office of Industrial Resource Administration of the International Trade Administration in 48 FR 8842, March 2, 1983, after the completion of an investigation of the effects on the national security of imports of bolts, nuts,

---

[28]March 10, 1959, 24 FR 1781. The several score amending Executive Orders and Proclamations are listed in the annotation in 19 U.S.C.A. 1862 of Proclamation 3279.

[29]Embargo imposed by Proclamation 4702, November 12, 1979 (44 FR 65581) and revoked by Executive Order 12282 of January 19, 1981.

and large screws of iron or steel. The Department of Defense concurred in the negative report sent by the Secretary of Commerce to the President February 10, 1983. A negative determination was also reached on ferroalloys. 49 FR 21391, May 21, 1984.

G. Designated Archaeological or Ethnological Material

Section 307 of Public Law 97-446, enacted January 12, 1983, 19 U.S.C. 2606, prohibits the importation of certain archaeological or ethnological material designated by the Secretary of the Treasury under Section 305, 19 U.S.C. 2604. The latter section directs the Secretary to promulgate a list of the archaeological or ethnological material of a State Party to the Convention on Cultural Property, which is covered by an agreement between that State Party and the United States or which comes under the emergency protection provisions of Section 304, 19 U.S.C. 2603. The convention is identified in Section 301, 19 U.S.C. 2061, as the convention on the means of prohibiting and preventing the illicit import, export, and transfer of ownership of cultural property adopted by the General Convention of UNESCO at its sixteenth session. Under Section 301 an archaeological object which may be protected must be at least 250 years old, and discovered through excavation or exploration. An ethnological one must be the product of a tribal or nonindustrial society and important to the cultural heritage of a people.

Implementing customs regulations are in 19 CFR 12.104 through 12.104i.

III. IMPORT AND EXPORT OF CERTAIN MONETARY INSTRUMENTS

A. Reports Required

The Currency and Foreign Transactions Reporting Act of 1970, Public Law 91-508, in Section 231,[30] required any person or his agent or bailee to file a report, as required by the Secretary of the Treasury, whenever he transported monetary instruments of more than $5,000 at one time from a place in the United States to a place outside the United States or to a place in the United States from or through a place outside the United States. The figure of $5,000 was raised to $10,000 by Section 901(c) of the Crime Control Act of 1984, Public Law 98-473. Violation of the reporting requirements was made subject to the penalty of forfeiture and specified civil and criminal penalties. The Act defined "monetary instruments," in Section 203,[31] to mean United States coin and currency, and, as the regulations of the Secretary of the Treasury prescribed, coins and currency of a foreign country, travelers' checks, bearer negotiable instruments, and other bearer securities.

---

[30]Codified at 31 U.S.C. 5316, formerly 31 U.S.C. 1101.
[31]Codified at 31 U.S.C. 5312, formerly 31 U.S.C. 1052.

The Treasury regulations in 31 CFR Part 103 require a report from each person who physically transports, mails, or ships, or causes to be transported, mailed, or shipped, monetary instruments, defined broadly, into or out of the country, and prescribe the content and timing of the reports. The regulations also delegated to the Commissioner of Customs the responsibility for the obtaining of the reports upon the import or export of the instruments.

B. Customs Enforcement

The enforcement of the reporting requirements by Customs is in accordance with the general customs procedures, including the opportunity to petition for remission or mitigation of forfeitures. This method of operation was explicitly upheld in litigation involving the seizure and forfeiture of imported currency not reported as required. *Ivers* v. *United States,* 581 F.2d 1362 (CA 9 1978).

The authority of customs officers to make searches of persons, conveyances, and other transport was enhanced by the amendment made by Section 901(d) of Public Law 98-473 which authorized search without a warrant by a customs officer if he had reasonable cause to believe a violation of the reporting requirement was occurring. In addition, Section 901(d) authorized rewards for informants up to $150,000 if the information led to the recovery of more than $50,000.

Part VI

Administration and Enforcement

28

Administering Agencies
and Industry Participation

I. THE ADMINISTERING AGENCIES

The President and several departments and agencies of the federal government execute and administer the customs, tariff, and trade laws of the United States.

A. The President

1. Range of Authority

The President, as the chief executive officer, directs and lays down policies for the departments and agencies of the government. In addition, by legislation the Congress has invested him with powers to take various actions and make a variety of determinations in the customs, tariff, and trade fields. Actions and determinations by the President are made customarily by the issuance of proclamations, executive orders, and memorandums, which are published in the *Federal Register.*

The historic authority of the President to negotiate trade agreements with foreign countries for the modification of duties and other import restrictions was broadly structured and enlarged by the Trade Act of 1974,[1] and was enlarged again and further directed by the Trade and Tariff Act of 1984.[2] Under the Trade Act of 1974 the President had authority for a maximum period of seven years to enter into trade agreements raising, lowering, or continuing existing rates of duties, and has continuing authority, to January 3, 1987, to negotiate trade agreements, harmonizing, reducing, or eliminating nontariff barriers to trade and, under the 1984 Act, tariff barriers also.

The President has authority, for a variety of purposes relating to the welfare of the country, to adjust rates of duty, withdraw trade agreement

---

[1] 19 U.S.C. 2101–2487.
[2] Pub. L. No. 98–573, October 30, 1984, 98 Stat. 2948.

concessions, and take various other actions affecting trade. For balance-of-payments reasons he has authority in Section 122 of the 1974 Trade Act to proclaim temporary import surcharges or temporary import quotas, on the one hand, or to proclaim temporary reduction of duties or liberalization of import restrictions, on the other hand (19 U.S.C. 2132).

He may take action to provide import relief for a period not exceeding five years or adjustment assistance to domestic workers and industries being injured by import competition. Import relief can take the form of increased or new tariff duties, absolute quotas, tariff-rate quotas, or the conclusion of orderly marketing agreements with foreign countries. The President also has authority to combat and counteract various forms of foreign discrimination and other unfair trade practices. If foreign countries impose import restrictions or institute subsidies on exports to third-country markets of the United States, the President may suspend trade agreement concessions and impose duties or other restrictions.

The President may take certain import relief actions if imports from Communist countries are causing market disruption in the United States. He reviews determinations of the International Trade Commission finding foreign countries guilty of unfair practices in import trade and issuing cease and desist orders or import exclusion orders. The President is empowered to disapprove such orders of the commission. The President is empowered to enter into bilateral commercial agreements and extend most-favored-nation treatment to "nonmarket economy" countries subject to certain conditions laid down by the Congress. He proclaims those countries deemed to be beneficiary developing countries eligible to receive duty-free preferences and the commodities from such countries which may receive duty-free treatment from the United States.

The Trade Agreements Act of 1979, Public Law 96-39, which approved the listed multilateral and bilateral agreements negotiated under the President's authority in the 1974 Trade Act, gave the President authority to accept the final text of each multilateral agreement on the condition that the other major trading partners of the United States were also accepting the agreement (19 U.S.C. 2503).

The Trade and Tariff Act of 1984 amended the negotiating authority of the President given by the Trade Act of 1974 to expand it in various ways and to direct its use into important new fields. The 1984 Act revived the lapsed authority in the 1974 Act to negotiate, with Congressional consultation, duty reductions, with specific reference to negotiations with Israel. Title III of the 1984 Act, entitled International Trade and Investment Act, defined new negotiating objectives directed toward: (1) the reduction or elimination of trade barriers to international trade in services and the development of international rules to ensure open international trade in services; (2) the reduction or elimination of barriers to, and the development of international rules promoting, foreign direct investment; and (3) the obtaining of openness in international trade and investment in high technology products and services and the reduction of distorting effects of foreign government policies and practices affecting U.S. exports of those products and services. The scope and purposes of the expanded negotiating authority given to the President are discussed more fully in Chapter 22 *supra.*

2. The Trade Representative

In carrying out all of these functions the President's chief agent is the U.S. Trade Representative, established under that name by Reorganization Plan No. 3 of 1979, and Executive Order 12188 of January 3, 1980 (45 FR 989). He was formerly designated the Special Representative for Trade Negotiations. The United States Trade Representative is an advisor to the President in the executive office of the President with the rank of an ambassador. He is the chief representative of the United States in all the trade negotiations and the principal coordinator of all tariff and trade agreement activities in the executive branch of the government and the principal liaison with the Congress and congressional committees and staffs on such matters. The United States Trade Representative and his office are referred to as the "USTR."

The President provided in Reorganization Plan No. 3 that the USTR should have primary responsibility, with the advice of the interagency committee established under 19 U.S.C. 1872, the Trade Policy Committee, for developing and coordinating international trade policy. This responsibility includes policy oversight over the application of import remedies; the establishment of antidumping and countervailing duty coordination with other trade policies; leadership in East-West trade matters, and in international investment and commodity policies; coordination of energy trade matters; and policy oversight of export expansion. The USTR represents the United States in international trade, commodity, and direct investment negotiations.

All the provisions of the Reorganization Plan were put into effect as of January 1, 1980, by Executive Order 12188, except those transferring to the Secretary of Commerce the trade promotion and commercial functions of the Secretary of State. This latter transfer took effect April 1, 1980. Public Law 97-456, January 12, 1983, 19 U.S.C. 2171, gave to the USTR the authority to promulgate rules and regulations, as necessary to carry out his powers and duties, as well as functions, and other administrative powers and increased the number of Deputy USTRs from two to three.

Title III of the Trade and Tariff Act of 1984 placed the responsibility in the USTR for direction and coordination of the accomplishment of the new negotiating objectives respecting trade in services, U.S. foreign direct investment, and high technology products and services, discussed in Chapter 22, section I.E. *supra.* As a first priority the USTR was directed, through the Trade Policy Committee, to identify and analyze acts, policies, and practices which constitute significant barriers to, or distortions of, U.S. exports of goods and services, including property protected by trademarks, patents, and copyrights, and of foreign direct investment by U.S. persons, and to estimate the trade-distorting impact on U.S. commerce of the matters identified. The USTR was further directed to report his analysis and estimate to the Congress by October 30, 1985, and updates of the report annually thereafter. To assist the USTR, the heads of departments and agencies were directed to furnish him, upon request, such data, reports, and other information as he may need and to provide such personnel and services, with or without reimbursement as he may request.

Titles VIII and IX of the Trade and Tariff Act of 1984 placed added responsibility on the USTR for certain industry-specific negotiations. Title VIII, entitled the "Steel Import Stabilization Act," required the President (in practice, the USTR) to implement the national steel policy by negotiations to ensure that the foreign share of the domestic steel market did not exceed a designated percentage (see Chapter 14, section VIII). Title IX of the 1984 Act, cited as the "Wine Equity and Export Expansion Act of 1984," required the USTR to enter into consultations with the major wine-trading countries, identified by him, to seek reduction or elimination of tariff and nontariff barriers to trade in U.S. wine. The USTR was also required to report to the Congress on actions taken or proposed, with recommendations for any additional legislative authority, and, for the purposes of Title IX, to consult with the wine and grape industries in the United States.

3. Other Executive Agencies

Many departments and agencies of the U.S. Government have functions and responsibilities in the customs, tariff, and trade field. In addition to the USTR, the agencies with the most comprehensive operating responsibilities have been the Department of the Treasury and its Customs Service and the U.S. International Trade Commission. Under Reorganization Plan No. 3 the Department of Commerce has now become the "focal point of operational responsibilities in the non-agricultural trade area," using the description in the President's Message to Congress submitting the plan, September 24, 1979.

B. Department of the Treasury

The Secretary of the Treasury is a member of the interdepartmental Trade Policy Committee, redefined by the Trade Act of 1974, and recomposed and reorganized by Executive Order 12188, to assist the President in trade expansion and import relief questions, and the Department of the Treasury is represented on subsidiary bodies of that committee.[3] He has laid down general policy guidelines and, through his Assistant Secretary (Enforcement and Operations), supervises, among other things, the activities of the U.S. Customs Service and the Office of Foreign Assets Control.

Responsibility for the administration of the antidumping and the countervailing duty law was transferred to the Secretary of Commerce.[4]

---

[3] This includes the Trade Negotiating Committee established by Executive Order 12188.
[4] Reorganization Plan No. 3 of 1979, Section 5.

C. U.S. Customs Service

The U.S. Customs Service is an agency of the U.S. Treasury Department under the supervision of the Assistant Secretary of the Treasury (Enforcement and Operations). Its primary function is the administration and enforcement of the customs and navigation laws of the United States. This involves the classification and valuation of imports, the determination of the proper rates of duty or taxes applicable to imports, and the assessment and collection of customs duties and taxes.

The Customs Service supervises the entry and unlading of vessels, vehicles, and aircraft, and enforces numerous other provisions relating to vessels, vehicles, and aircraft arriving and departing. It is responsible for the enforcement of laws prohibiting the importation of various types of goods and materials, the prevention of smuggling of contraband, the administration of quotas and of a variety of health, safety, environmental, and commercial restrictions on various types of imports. Until Reorganization Plan No. 3 of 1979 became effective, it had the primary administration and enforcement of the antidumping and countervailing duty laws relating to unfair practices in the import trade. Under the plan the Customs Service retains the acceptance of deposits, bonds, or other security, as deemed appropriate by the Secretary of Commerce, and the imposition and collection of antidumping and countervailing duties.

The Customs Service is headed by the Commissioner of Customs and has its national headquarters in Washington, D.C. The Customs Service is decentralized, with most of the individual determinations and decisions being made initially in the field. However, customs headquarters maintains a close control over policy.

The service is divided into regions each headed by a regional commissioner of customs. The number of regions was reduced from nine to seven by TD 82–118, published June 25, 1982 and their structure was realigned by TD 83-125, published June 6, 1983, in order to obtain more efficient use of personnel, facilities, and resources, and to provide better services to carriers, importers, and the public. The regions are divided into customs districts, each district being headed by a district director. As of October 1, 1985, there were 45 customs districts. Within the customs districts there are ports of entry and customs stations.[5] The Customs Service maintains foreign field offices in Bonn, Brussels, Hong Kong, London, Mexico City, Montreal, Paris, Rome, and Tokyo.

Prior to initiating any major field reorganization through fiscal year 1985 the Commissioner of Customs was required to notify the Senate Committee on Finance and the House Committee on Ways and Means at least 90 days in advance. This notification requirement extended to any action which would result in a significant reduction in force of employees, otherwise than by attrition; the elimination or relocation of any district, regional, or border office, or the significant reduction of the number of employees at any such

---

[5]See customs regulations governing the authority of customs officers and providing lists of customs regions and districts and the ports of entry and customs stations within each region and district, 19 CFR Part 101.

office. This notification provision in Section 237 of the Trade and Tariff Act of 1984 was the final version of several proposals before the 98th Congress to restrict the reorganization activity of the Commissioner of Customs.

The present form of customs administration through regional offices, with all local officials appointed under the civil service laws and all administrative authority centralized in the Secretary of the Treasury and delegated by him to the Commissioner of Customs and by the latter, as appropriate, to regional and local officials, was brought about through approval by the Congress of the President's Reorganization Plans No. 26 of 1950 and No. 1 of 1965.[6]

Throughout the history of customs administration the Secretary of the Treasury was given a wide area of discretion to supplement the customs laws with regulations "to secure a just, impartial, and uniform appraisement of imported merchandise and the classification and assessment of duties thereon" and otherwise to implement the customs laws.[7]

D. U.S. International Trade Commission

The Trade Act of 1974 greatly expanded the responsibilities of the U.S. International Trade Commission (ITC) (formerly the U.S. Tariff Commission).[8] The ITC has a continuing responsibility for studying and making reports on the status of U.S. trade, the impact of imports upon the U.S. economy, and the relationship of U.S. tariffs to the health of U.S. trade. As required, it investigates the comparative costs of production of U.S.- and foreign-made articles and the effects of imports on agricultural programs. It has responsibilities in certain statistical aspects of the classification of commodities and in analyzing statistics on international trade. It has a particular responsibility for establishing a system to monitor and develop statistics on East-West trade. It is charged with making studies and developing reports on tariff and trade matters at the request of the President, the Congress, the House Ways and Means Committee, and the Senate Finance Committee.

In connection with international trade agreements the ITC investigates, holds hearings, and reports on the probable effect of tariff concessions which might be made by the United States. It investigates, holds hearings, and advises the President on the question of which articles should be made eligible for duty-free treatment when imported from designated beneficiary developing countries.

Upon receipt of a petition from a trade association, firm, certified or recognized union, or group of workers the ITC investigates, holds hearings, and determines whether an article is being imported into the United States in such increased quantities as to be a substantial cause of serious injury, or the threat thereof, to the domestic industry producing a like or directly competitive article, and advises the President as to the form and amount of relief, if any, which it recommends be afforded by the President. Where

---

[6]5 U.S.C. App.
[7]19 U.S.C. 3, 1502, 1624, 1646a.
[8]19 U.S.C. 2231, 2232.

relief from import injury has been afforded by the President, the ITC periodically reviews the additional protection provided to determine the adequacy and necessity thereof.

In antidumping proceedings and certain proceedings under the countervailing duty law, the ITC has the responsibility for determining whether the price discrimination or subsidy actions of foreign countries are causing or threatening to cause injury to a domestic industry or to prevent the establishment of a domestic industry. It receives petitions and investigates and reports to the President its determination as to whether market disruption exists because of imports of an article produced in a Communist country. Its determination and advice to the President may result in the proclamation by the President of some form of tariff or other import protection to the domestic industry concerned.

A Trade Remedy Assistance Office was established in the ITC by Section 221 of the Trade and Tariff Act of 1984, which added a new Section 339 to the Tariff Act of 1930 (19 U.S.C. 1339). The office is required to provide full information to the public, upon request, concerning remedies and benefits under the trade laws, and petition and application procedures and filing dates related to the remedies and benefits.

In all its investigations the ITC has subpoena power for the attendance of witnesses and the production of documentary evidence, enforceable by order of a U.S. district court (19 U.S.C. 1333).

E. Department of Commerce

The Department of Commerce has been assigned, under Reorganization Plan No. 3 of 1979, general operational responsibility for major nonagricultural international trade functions of the government, including export development, commercial representation abroad, the administration of the antidumping and countervailing duty laws, export controls, and monitoring compliance with the international trade agreements to which the United States is a party.

Furthermore, under Title IV of the Trade Agreements Act of 1979, which implements the international Standards Code, the Commerce Department must establish and maintain supervision of the development and application of technical standards applicable to nonagricultural products imported and exported, including standards developed by international organizations. The Commerce Department must also maintain a Standards Information Center called for by the Code and by Title IV.

To meet its expanded responsibilities under the Reorganization Plan the Commerce Department established an International Trade Administration, headed by an Under Secretary for International Trade. The Under Secretary operates through an Assistant Secretary for International Economic Policy, an Assistant Secretary for Trade Administration, and an Assistant Secretary for Trade Development.

The Department provides research and analysis in the formulation of international economic and commercial programs and policies relating to trade, finance, and investment. As a member of the interdepartmental

Trade Policy Committee its representatives participate in international trade negotiations. It provides commercial, economic, and marketing information on export prospects and methods of marketing goods. The Department of Commerce administers existing provisions providing for adjustment assistance for firms and (until 1982) communities suffering from import competition. It conducts research and gathers data on fibers, textiles, and apparel and the effect of imports thereof on domestic industry. The Department of Commerce, as the head of an interdepartmental committee, implements and administers the provisions of restraint agreements with foreign countries limiting the export to the United States of textiles and textile products.

As part of the emphasis on the fostering of international trade in services embodied in Title III of the Trade and Tariff Act of 1984, the Secretary of Commerce is required by Section 306 of that Act to establish a service industries development program. That program is intended to develop policies regarding services designed to increase the competitiveness of U.S. service industries in foreign commerce; to develop a data base for assessing the adequacies of government policies and actions pertaining to services; to collect and analyze, in consultation with appropriate agencies, information on the international operations and competitiveness of U.S. service industries; to conduct research and analysis of service-related issues and problems; and to conduct sectoral studies of domestic service industries. The information collected is to be prepared in biennial reports submitted to the Congress and to the President. Section 306 defines the term "services" to mean "economic activities whose outputs are other than tangible goods." Under the definition, the term includes, but is not limited to, "banking, insurance, transportation, communications and data processing, retail and wholesale trade, advertising, accounting, construction, design and engineering, management consulting, real estate, professional services, entertainment, education, and health care."

To facilitate the obtaining of data with respect to services, Section 306(b) amends the International Investment Survey Act of 1976, 22 U.S.C. 3101 *et seq.* to add "trade in services" to "international investment" in the various provisions defining the required surveys and reports. The administration of the surveys and reports on trade in services under this Act is accomplished by the Commerce Department in connection with its related responsibility with respect to international direct investment.

In conjunction with the Department of the Interior, Commerce administers quotas on the importation of watches and watch movements from territories of the United States. Together with the Departments of the Treasury and Health and Human Services, it administers provisions authorizing duty-free importations of scientific and technical equipment and materials by nonprofit institutions in the United States. It administers provisions of law concerning the establishment and operation of foreign trade zones and importations for use in trade fairs. Commerce administers export controls instituted under the Export Administration Act and conducts research and analysis on opportunities for trade with Communist nations. The Bureau of the Census, a part of Commerce, compiles and publishes import and export statistics.

F. Other Departments and Agencies Having Important Responsibilities

There are a number of departments and agencies in addition to those discussed *supra* which have important responsibilities in the customs and international trade field.

1. Department of State

The Secretary of State heads the nonpresiding cabinet officers who are members of the Trade Policy Committee. The Department of State, in conjunction with the office of the USTR, conducts a wide variety of international trade negotiations. Through its embassies and consulates it is the spokesman for the United States abroad except that commercial representation abroad is the responsibility of the Commerce Department under Reorganization Plan No. 3 of 1979 as of April 1, 1980. The State Department administers provisions of law controlling the exportation of munitions and implements of war.

2. Department of Labor

The Department of Labor, whose secretary is a member of the Trade Policy Committee, administers provisions of law authorizing adjustment assistance to workers injured by foreign import competition.

3. Department of Agriculture

The Department of Agriculture initiates investigations of the need for, and administers import quotas on, various agricultural commodities and processed agricultural products necessary to protect domestic agricultural support programs and groups of American producers from injury from import competition. The Secretary of Agriculture serves on the Trade Policy Committee. With respect to the supervision and development of international standards for imports and exports the Secretary of Agriculture has the same responsibility for agricultural products as the Secretary of Commerce has for nonagricultural products under the international Standards Code and Title IV of the Trade Agreements Act of 1979.

4. Department of Defense

The Department of Defense is concerned with the effect of foreign economic policies on international security. The Department administers the provisions of the Buy American Act restricting the military procurement of foreign-made goods and materials and the modifications under the Trade Agreements Act. The Secretary of Defense is a member of the Trade Policy Committee.

5. General Services Administration

The General Services Administration administers provisions of the Buy American Act limiting the procurement of foreign goods and materials for civilian government purposes.

G. Trade Assistance to Small Business

Each agency responsible for administering a trade law is obligated to provide technical assistance to eligible small businesses to enable them to prepare and file petitions and applications to obtain the remedies and benefits available under the trade law which it administers. This obligation was imposed by Section 339 of the Tariff Act of 1930 (19 U.S.C. 1339) added by Section 221 of the Trade and Tariff Act of 1984.

Section 339(c) defines "eligible small business" to mean any business which in the agency's unreviewable judgment has inadequate internal resources and financial ability to obtain qualified outside assistance. In determining eligibility the agency may consult with the Small Business Administration and must consult with any other agency which has provided trade assistance under Section 339 to the business concerned. The "trade laws" covered are the laws relating to:

- Relief from import competition, and adjustment assistance under Title II of the Trade Act of 1974;
- Relief from foreign unfair trade practices under Title III of the Trade Act of 1974;
- Relief under the Antidumping and Countervailing Duty Laws;
- Safeguarding national security under Section 232 of the Trade Expansion Act, 19 U.S.C. 1862;
- Exclusion of infringing and unfairly traded goods under Section 337 of the Tariff Act of 1930.

II. INDUSTRY PARTICIPATION OPPORTUNITIES

Of first importance to American industry concerned with international trade is the extent to which it can participate in the making of governing laws—the trade and tariff acts, the negotiation of trade treaties and agreements, and the rulemaking and decision making by the controlling agencies. Of like importance is the extent to which it can obtain needed information held by the government and protect confidential information supplied to the government.

The increasing opportunities for business interests to participate in the governmental process and to obtain information from the government are indicated in the following discussion of the relevant laws and regulations. In recent years the Congress has accelerated the requirements placed upon itself and the executive agencies to provide the public with notice and opportunity to participate in the processes of lawmaking. Executive agencies have occasionally also taken the initiative in providing such notice and opportunity in important policy making. The coming into effect of the Freedom of Information Act on July 4, 1967, and its strengthening by 1974 amendments,[9] made it much easier for business interests to learn about and obtain copies of agency opinions, interpretations, decisions, and records of interest to them.

The principal formal opportunities for industry to contribute directly to the law-, treaty-, and rulemaking processes are (1) giving testimony before committees of the Congress; (2) serving on advisory committees established to facilitate industry representation; and (3) responding to published invitations for oral or written comments on pending proposals.

A. Testimony Before Congressional Committees

The committees concerned with legislation on tariffs and trade are primarily the House Ways and Means Committee, operating initially through its Subcommittee on Trade, and the Senate Finance Committee, with its Subcommittee on International Trade. Since all bills relating to revenue must originate in the House of Representatives, the Ways and Means Committee has original jurisdiction of legislation pertaining to customs duties and administration and trade agreements. Other standing committees with jurisdiction over matters importantly affecting trade are the Committees on Agriculture, Energy and Commerce, Foreign Affairs, and Government Operations in the House, and the Committees on Agriculture, Nutrition, and Forestry, on Commerce, Science, and Transportation, on Foreign Relations, and on Governmental Affairs in the Senate. The important point is that hearings are held on legislative proposals being shaped by the committees into bills reported for floor action. Any interested business may send representatives to attend and to speak at these hearings.

The Legislative Reorganization Act of 1970[10] made regular the giving of notice of committee sessions and their openness to the public. The Act required meetings of the standing committees for the transaction of business to be open to the public, except during executive sessions for the marking up of bills, for voting, or when by a majority vote an executive session is ordered. As for committee hearings, the Act required one week's advance notice of hearings of any standing, select, or special committee and required that hearings be open to the public except when the committee determined that the testimony might relate to a national security matter, or reflect adversely on the character or reputation of an individual, or divulge matters deemed confidential under law or regulation.

B. Trade Negotiation Advisory Committees

The Trade Act of 1974 required the President "to seek information and advice from representative elements of the private sector with respect to

---

[9] 5 U.S.C. 552.
[10] 84 Stat. 1140, 2 U.S.C. 190a–k.

negotiating objectives and bargaining positions" before entering into any trade agreement authorized by the Act to be negotiated for the adjustment of duties or nontariff barriers to trade. He was to obtain this information and advice from the network of advisory committees provided for in the Act. The Trade Agreements Act of 1979 continued these trade advisory committees and gave them responsibility for consideration of the operation of trade agreements.

The provisions in the Trade Act of 1974 for information and advice from the private sector were amended by Section 306(c)(2) of the Trade and Tariff Act of 1984 to include specifically information and advice from "the non-Federal governmental sector," meaning any state, territory, or U.S. possession, the District of Columbia, or any subdivision or agency thereof. The President was directed, as appropriate, to consult with state governments on trade policy issues affecting regulatory authority of nonfederal governments, or their procurement of goods and services, and to establish intergovernmental advisory committees on trade.

All of the advisory committees operate within the framework of the Federal Advisory Committee Act,[11] except that meetings of all the committees other than those of the Advisory Committee on Trade Negotiations may be exempted from the publicity provisions, and special protection is provided for the information submitted in confidence to these committees and to government employees.

Each of these trade negotiation advisory committees had been influential in advising in advance of the negotiation of the approved trade agreements, and continue important in assessing the extent to which the trade agreements entered into during that period "serve the economic interests of the United States."

C. Notice and Opportunity for Comment

All sectors of business can generally count on an opportunity to file written comments on regulations of federal agencies before they are finally promulgated. In fact, they may be invited to present oral arguments when a particular regulation will deal with a novel or controversial matter. Since the Administrative Procedure Act of 1946, it has been the law that agencies generally are required to publish proposed regulations in the *Federal Register* with a statement of the time and place for submitting comments and of the authority under which the rule is proposed.[12]

The only subject areas excepted from this general requirement are military or foreign affairs functions, matters relating to agency management or personnel or to public property, loans, grants, benefits, or contracts, and rules of agency organization, procedure, or practice. Furthermore, an agency may promulgate a final regulation without the usual notice and opportunity for public comment when it finds, and publishes this finding, that notice and public procedure would be impracticable, unnecessary, or

---

[11]5 U.S.C. App. I.
[12]5 U.S.C. 553.

contrary to the public interest. Even in such an instance an agency often invites comment on a regulation which by necessity has been published without prior notice.

D. Required Hearings Under 1974 Trade Act, as Amended in 1979 and 1984

The Trade Act of 1974 was remarkable in the extent to which it required all government agencies operating under it, including even the President, to provide an opportunity for public discussion before taking actions or making decisions affecting economic interests. Because of the eight-year extension of the President's authority to enter into nontariff barrier agreements, provided by the Trade Agreements Act of 1979, and the redefinition of the term "barrier" to include "any duty" made by Section 401(b) of the Trade and Tariff Act of 1984, there is described *infra* each statutory requirement for a public hearing, after reasonable notice, with reference to the applicable provisions of the U.S. Code and the regulations.

1. Title I. Trade Negotiations

The ITC is required to hold public hearings in preparing its advice to the President with respect to the probable economic effect of modifications of any trade barrier on domestic industries and on consumers (19 U.S.C. 2151(e); 19 CFR Part 205).

An agency or an interagency committee designated by the President is required to hold public hearings for presentation of views as to any matter relevant to a proposed trade agreement (19 U.S.C. 2153). The interagency committee designated for this purpose by the Special Trade Representative (STR) under authority of Executive Order 11864 was the STR's Trade Policy Staff Committee (15 CFR Parts 2001, 2002, 2003). This committee continues under the USTR.

The Secretary of the Treasury was required "if it is appropriate" to hold public hearings in connection with his investigation of the effect on national security of imports of any article (19 U.S.C. 1862(b); 31 CFR Part 9). An investigation with the benefit of public comment was conducted under this authority by the Treasury Department in 1978–79, culminating in a published report to the President[13] on the effects on national security of oil imports. The responsibility for national security investigations was transferred to the Secretary of Commerce by Reorganization Plan No. 3 of 1979, 5 U.S.C. App. Commerce Department regulations providing for public hearings appear in 15 CFR Part 359.

---

[13]44 FR 18818, March 29, 1979.

2. Title II. Relief From Injury Caused by Import Competition

The ITC is required to hold public hearings in the course of any investigation to determine whether an article is being imported in such increased quantities as to be a substantial cause of injury, or threat thereof, to an industry producing a competitive article (19 U.S.C. 2251(c); 19 CFR Part 206).

The Secretary of Labor must provide a public hearing, if requested, on a petition for certification of eligibility to apply for adjustment assistance for workers (19 U.S.C. 2271(b); 29 CFR Parts 90, 91).

The Secretary of Commerce must provide a public hearing, if requested, on a petition for certification of eligibility to apply for adjustment assistance for firms (19 U.S.C. 2341; 13 CFR Part 315).

The Secretary of Commerce had to provide a public hearing, if requested, on a petition for certification of eligibility for adjustment assistance for communities (19 U.S.C. 2371(b); 13 CFR Part 315).

3. Title III. Relief From Unfair Trade Practices

The President is required to provide "an opportunity for the presentation of views" concerning unjustifiable or unreasonable tariff or other import restrictions maintained by a foreign country, or foreign instrumentality; foreign discriminatory acts and policies; foreign subsidies on exports; or unreasonable foreign restrictions on access to commodities or products (19 U.S.C. 2411(d)(1)). This responsibility was delegated by Executive Order 11846 to the STR, now the USTR, who also has the statutory duty to provide public hearings upon complaint of any such foreign practices or policies at the request of the complainant (19 U.S.C. 2411(d)(2); 15 CFR Part 2006).

The Secretary of Commerce and the ITC must, before making their respective final determinations in an antidumping or countervailing duty proceeding, provide a hearing upon the request of any party to the proceeding. (19 U.S.C. 1677c. See 19 CFR 207.23, 353.47, and 355.35).

The ITC must make its determination that an unfair method of competition has been practiced in the import trade not only after a hearing but on the basis of the record made at a hearing, which has all the formalities of an adjudicatory hearing under the Administrative Procedure Act where a finding of an unfair practice would result in exclusion of the imported article from entry or from entry except under bond (19 U.S.C. 1337; 19 CFR Part 210;

4. Title IV. Trade Relations With Communist Countries

The ITC is required to hold a public hearing in the course of an investigation to determine whether an import from a Communist country is causing market disruption with respect to an article produced by a domestic industry (19 U.S.C. 2436(a)(2); 19 CFR Part 206).

5. Title V. Generalized System of Preferences

The President is required to follow all the public participation procedures required under Title I of the Trade Act of 1974 for trade negotiations (except the use of advisory committees) in making provisions for duty-free treatment for eligible articles from developing countries. This includes hearings before the ITC on eligible articles and hearings before the USTR's Trade Policy Staff Committee on various economic issues (19 U.S.C. 2463; 15 CFR Part 2007; 19 CFR Part 205). This requirement was not modified by the extension and amendment of the GSP by Title V of the 1984 Act.

E. Effects of Imports on Agricultural Programs

Any interested person may, with a statement of his reasons, request an investigation by the Secretary of Agriculture into the need for the imposition of import quotas or fees under Section 22 of the Agricultural Adjustment Act.[14] The Secretary may then hold a hearing to secure information (7 CFR Part 6). If he finds grounds for action under Section 22, he recommends to the President that the ITC investigate the need for Section 22 protective action. If the President so directs, the ITC makes an investigation with a public hearing, as required by Section 22 (19 CFR Part 204).

F. Administrative Change of Practice or Position

The Customs Service has undertaken to give public notice and an opportunity to comment before publication of a ruling having the effect of changing a uniform practice or position of the service. Part 177 of the customs regulations provides in 19 CFR 177.10(c) that notice will be published in the *Federal Register* when there is under consideration (1) a ruling which will change a practice and will result in the assessment of a higher rate of duty, or in the assessment of a lower rate of duty if the headquarters office determines that the lower assessment involves the interests of domestic industry, or (2) a ruling which will change a position of the service and will result in a restriction or prohibition, or in the removal of a restriction or prohibition if the headquarters office determines that the removal involves the interests of the general public. In each case the notice will provide an opportunity for interested parties to make written submissions with respect to the correctness of the contemplated change.

These regulations are a substantial enlargement of the opportunity previously allowed interested parties to participate in the consideration of changes in established customs rulings. Previously, this opportunity was given only when the Commissioner of Customs was considering a change of practice that would result in a higher rate of duty.

---

[14] 7 U.S.C. 624. See Chapter 14.

The notice and opportunity for comment requirements in 19 CFR 177.10(c) do not apply to a ruling letter issued under 19 CFR 177.9 which relates to methods of appraisement for valuation purposes because that matter does not involve a "rate of duty or charge" to which the uniform practice rule in 19 CFR 177.10(b) applies. *American Air Parcel Forwarding Co., Ltd.* v. *United States,* 7 CIT ____ , 587 F. Supp. 550 (1984) 5 ITRD 2212. Consequently, the CIT held in that case, the ruling letter on methods of appraisement could be overruled by a later ruling letter without regard to the uniform practice rule.

G. Antitrust Consent Judgment Proposals

The opportunity for businessmen to comment on proposed government action affecting them was extended to proposed antitrust consent decrees by the Antitrust Procedures and Penalties Act of 1974.[15] This Act requires the Department of Justice to file with the district court and to publish in the *Federal Register* at least 60 days prior to the effective date of the judgment the proposal for a consent judgment and, thereafter, any written comments and any responses of the government. A competitive impact statement is to accompany the proposal when filed and published, unless the court instructs otherwise.

III. ACCESS TO GOVERNMENT-HELD INFORMATION

A. Freedom of Information Act

The Freedom of Information Act, as amended in 1974 (FOIA),[16] in brief, requires federal agencies to publish in the *Federal Register* their substantive and procedural regulations and organizational arrangements; to make available for inspection and copying their orders, opinions, precedential interpretations, and staff manuals; and to make available to any person any record identified by him and requested in accordance with agency regulations stating the time, place, fees, and procedures to be followed. However, no such information need be provided if it comes within one or more of the nine specific exemptions enumerated in the Act. Prompt resort to a U.S. district court is provided for the purpose of challenging an agency's refusal of information.

The 1974 amendments were intended "to contribute to the fuller and faster release of information" by the agencies (H.R. Rep. No. 93-876). Among other provisions, they require agency action upon initial requests within 10, and upon appeals within 20, working days and substantially restrict the exemption for investigatory files. They require promulgation of uniform fees by an agency for all constituent units.

---

[15] 15 U.S.C. 16.
[16] 5 U.S.C. 552.

1. Treasury Regulations and Customs Service Procedures

The Treasury Department promulgated as of February 20, 1975, departmentwide regulations (31 CFR Part 1, Disclosure of Records, Subpart A) under the FOIA as amended. They apply to all units of the department and supersede any bureau or other unit's regulations inconsistent therewith, and they authorize each unit to reprint the departmental regulations with applicable supplementary regulations. The department regulations set forth the controlling standards governing disclosure and exemption, the requisites for an identifiable request, the procedures to be followed in processing requests and appeals from denials, and the fees to be charged for searches and copies. Each Treasury unit is assigned a place in the appendix to the regulations for listing the headquarters and field locations of public reading rooms where documents will be made available for inspection and copying, the officers designated to make initial and appellate determinations on requests, the officer designated to receive service of process, and the addresses for delivery of requests, appeals, and service of process. This operational information respecting the Customs Service is set forth in Appendix C to Subpart A of the Treasury regulations.

2. Specific Customs Documents

a. Disclosure Provided

The extent to which customs material is available to the public will be appreciated by noting the listing the Customs Service has provided in its availability of information regulations (19 CFR Part 103) of its available staff manuals and instructions and its other classes of records, with the notation that certain individual documents or portions thereof may be exempt (19 CFR 103.11).

Section 112 of the Customs Procedural Reform and Simplification Act of 1978, 19 U.S.C. 1625, required the Customs Service to publish all precedential decisions, including ruling letters, internal advice memoranda, and protest review decisions within 120 days of their issuance. While some of these customs determinations were published by the Service in the *Customs Bulletin* when the Service considered them to be of general interest, the requirement in the 1978 Act assures a much more extensive revelation to the public of how the Service applies the laws and regulations to given situations.

b. Information on Vessel Manifests

Specific information is required by law to be included on vessel manifests, or their attached documents, and submitted to Customs prior to vessel clearance, in the case of outward manifests, by 46 U.S.C. 92, 93, and prior to entry, in the case of inward manifests, by 19 U.S.C. 1431. Historically, the Customs Service has treated this information as confidential, although permitting limited access by accredited representatives of the press.

46 U.S.C. 93 was amended in 1980 to make available for public disclosure, unless the Secretary of the Treasury makes a specific negative finding or the information is classified by Executive Order, and only in accordance with access regulations: (1) the name and address of the shipper, unless the shipper has made a biennial certification claiming confidential treatment pursuant to procedures adopted by the Secretary of the Treasury; (2) the general character of the cargo; (3) the number of packages and gross weight; (4) the name of the vessel or carrier; (5) the port of exit; (6) the port of destination; and (7) the country of destination. The April 1984 Customs Service regulations made this information available to press representatives by examination of the manifests and indirectly to the public who were not permitted examination of the manifests. Importers might, on request, obtain permanent protection of their names from disclosure (19 CFR 103.14).

The regulations governing the disclosure of inward manifests were amended in May 1984 to allow representatives of the press to examine, copy, and publish all information appearing on the cargo declaration, Customs Form 1302, except where the Secretary of the Treasury made an affirmative finding on a shipment-by-shipment basis that such disclosure would pose a threat of personal injury or property damage. TD 84-111, 49 FR 19952, May 10, 1984, amended 49 FR 23339, June 6, 1984. This enlargement of disclosure was based upon a consent decree in the U.S. District Court of the District of Columbia in litigation brought by the Twin Coast Newspapers Inc., as discussed in TD 84-111.

In order to bring the disclosure of information on inward manifests more in line with that governing outward manifests, Section 203 of the Trade and Tariff Act of 1984 amended 19 U.S.C. 1431 to provide new Subsection (c) on the availability of information on inward manifests (House Ways and Means Committee Print 98-39 at 12). Subsection (c) provides, in effect, that, with specified exceptions, the types of information on an inward manifest similar to the disclosable information on an outward manifest shall be available for public disclosure. The exceptions are (1) for an affirmative finding by the Secretary of the Treasury on a shipment-by-shipment basis that disclosure is likely to pose a threat of personal injury or property damage, and (2) for information exempt from disclosure under the national security exemption in 5 U.S.C. 552(b)(1). The subsection directs the Secretary to establish access procedures which are to include provisions for adequate protection against the public disclosure of information not made available for disclosure under the law.

3. Commerce Department and ITA Regulations

The Commerce Department, like the Treasury Department, provides departmentwide rules for the disclosure of information, setting forth policies, procedures, applicable fees, and the location of public reading rooms (15 CFR Part 4). These rules may be supplemented by department units. The International Trade Administration provides rules on access to information in antidumping and countervailing duty proceedings in Subsection B of 19 CFR Parts 353 and 355.

4. ITC Records

The records of the International Trade Commission that are available under the FOIA are described in the commission's regulations (19 CFR Part 201, Subpart C), which include request and appeal procedures. Requests are addressed to the Secretary of the ITC. If he denies a request, appeal may be made to the full commission. Available information includes applications, petitions, transcripts of testimony, and exhibits submitted at hearings. Reports to the President and congressional committees are available only if authorized by the recipient of the report.

5. USTR Records

The regulations governing the availability and release of records in the office of the U.S. Trade Representative are found in 15 CFR Parts 2004 and 2008. Requests are to be addressed to the Freedom of Information Officer and appeals may be made to the FOI Appeals Committee established in the regulations. Of special interest is the procedure to obtain review of classified materials under Executive Order 12065 by the Classification Review Committee established in the regulations to make determinations of the applicability of the exemption for records to be kept secret under executive order in the interests of national defense or foreign policy.

Special protection from disclosure was provided for confidential business information furnished to the USTR in investigations under Title III of the Trade Act of 1974 (Enforcement of United States Rights) by Section 304(g) of the Trade and Tariff Act of 1984. Section 304(g) amended Section 305 of the 1974 Act to provide that notwithstanding the Freedom of Information Act or any other law no information requested or received by the USTR in any investigation under Title III shall be made available to any person if the provider has certified that the information is business confidential, that the disclosure of it would endanger trade secrets, or profitability, and that the information is not generally available. The USTR must determine that the certification is well founded, and the provider of the information must, to the extent required by regulation, provide an adequate nonconfidential summary of the information. The USTR or any employee of the federal government may use the information in a Title III investigation but no other use is permitted. The information may be made available generally if in a form which cannot be associated with, or otherwise identify, the provider of the information.

B. Exemptions From Disclosure Rules

1. General

The basic principles of disclosure are clearly set forth in the Treasury regulations (31 CFR 1.2). They are: (1) The public will be afforded access to information or records in the possession of any constituent Treasury unit, subject only to the specific exemptions; (2) if parts of a record are exempt, any "reasonably segregable portion" of the record will be provided after deletion of exempt portion; and (3) any Treasury unit may in a given case elect not to apply an exemption, although fully applicable, without prejudicing application of the exemption in other cases.

The nine exemptions, revised in accordance with the 1974 amendments, and an amendment made by the Government in Sunshine Act of 1976, 5 U.S.C. 552b, are set forth in 31 CFR as follows:

§1.2(c) *Exemptions*— (1) *In general.* Under 5 U.S.C. 552(b), the disclosure requirements of section 552(a) do not apply to certain matters which are:

(i)(A) Specifically authorized under criteria established by an Executive order to be kept secret in the interest of the national defense or foreign policy and (B) are in fact properly classified pursuant to such Executive order (See 31 CFR Part 2);

(ii) Related solely to the internal personnel rules and practices of an agency;

(iii) Specifically exempted from disclosure by statute (other than 5 U.S.C. 552b): Provided, that such statute (A) requires that the matters be withheld from the public in such a manner as to leave no discretion on the issue, or (B) establishes particular criteria for withholding or refers to particular types of matters to be withheld;

(iv) Trade secrets and commercial or financial information obtained from a person and privileged or confidential;

(v) Inter-agency or intra-agency memorandums or letters which would not be available by law to a party other than an agency in litigation with the agency;

(vi) Personnel and medical files and similar files the disclosure of which would constitute a clearly unwarranted invasion of personal privacy;

(vii) Investigatory records compiled for law enforcement purposes, but only to the extent that the production of such record would (A) interfere with enforcement proceedings, (B) deprive a person of a right to a fair trial or an impartial adjudication, (C) constitute an unwarranted invasion of personal privacy, (D) disclose the identity of a confidential source and, in the case of a record compiled by a criminal law enforcement authority in the course of a criminal investigation, or by an agency conducting a lawful national security intelligence investigation, confidential information furnished only by the confidential source, (E) disclose investigative techniques and procedures, or (F) endanger the life or physical safety of law enforcement personnel;

(viii) Contained in or related to examination, operating or condition reports prepared by, on behalf of, or for the use of an agency responsible for the regulation or supervision of financial institutions; or

(ix) Geological and geophysical information and data, including maps, concerning wells.

2. Confidential Business Information Exemption in Particular

For businessmen the exemption of utmost concern is Item (iv) *supra.*[17] The importance of this exemption increases with growing demands for information by the government upon businesses and with greater opportunities provided by the government, as in the 1974, 1979, and 1984 trade acts, for the business community to participate in the administrative process by providing information and views in hearings, written comments, and informal advice on proposed regulations and determinations, and in investigations and negotiations.

---

[17] 5 U.S.C. 552(b)(4).

The term "trade secret" has a well-recognized and fairly concrete meaning, normally transcribed as any formula, patent, device, plan, or compilation of information used in a business which gives it a competitive advantage. The remainder of the exemption has been the subject of much judicial interpretation. It has now been established that the commercial or financial information protected from disclosure must have been obtained from outside the government and must be either privileged or confidential. The categories of "privileged" information, e.g., an attorney's work product, are fairly well defined in the evidentiary rules of litigation but the scope of the term "confidential" is amorphous.

Guidelines for determining what is confidential, commercial, or financial information submitted to the government by business were definitively laid down by the Court of Appeals of the District of Columbia in *National Parks and Conservation Association* v. *Morton,* 498 F.2d 765, 770 (CA DC 1974). This was a suit seeking to require the Interior Department to permit inspection and copying of audits of national park concessionaires, their annual financial statements filed with the National Park Service, and other financial information.[18] The court concluded after discarding earlier formulas:

> To summarize, commercial or financial matter is "confidential" for purposes of the exemption if disclosure of the information is likely to have either of the following effects: (1) to impair the Government's ability to obtain necessary information in the future, or (2) to cause substantial harm to the competitive position of the person from whom the information was obtained.

Applying these guidelines to the case before it, the court decided that the first alternative was not likely since the concessionaires were required to provide the information to the government, but that the concessionaires should have an opportunity to prove to the district court that the disclosure sought would substantially harm their competitive position.

3. Definition in ITC Regulations

The court of appeals guidelines quoted *supra* were incorporated by the ITC into its definition of "confidential business information" in its regulations on this subject, 19 CFR 201.6 (as amended, 49 FR 32571, August 15, 1984). The definition enumerates some of the types or categories of confidential business information which have been used in statutory provisions prior to the Freedom of Information Act and adds, in the 1984 amendment, the general clause "other information of commercial value." Such other information is intended to cover copyrighted material and similar material of commercial value not otherwise covered by the definition, according to the ITC's amendment statement. Because the

---

[18]The Court of Appeals, after considering the trial court evidence, determined in applying the guidelines, that disclosure of the information requested would cause competitive injury to five concessionaires, but not to two, with resultant disclosure concerning these two. *National Parks and Conservation Ass'n* v. *Kleppe,* 547 F.2d 673 (CA DC 1976). These guidelines have been extensively followed in subsequent cases and by seven other circuits.

definition controls the protection of information submitted in connection with all ITC investigations of injury to domestic industry from import trade, fair or unfair, and from Communist countries, the text is quoted in full:

§201.6 Confidential business information.

(a) *Definition.* Confidential business information is information which concerns or relates to the trade secrets, processes, operations, style of works, or apparatus, or to the production, sales, shipments, purchases, transfers, identification of customers, inventories, or amount or source of any income, profits, losses, or expenditures of any person, firm, partnership, corporation, or other organization, or other information of commercial value, the disclosure of which is likely to have the effect of either (1) impairing the Commission's ability to obtain such information as is necessary to perform its statutory functions, or (2) causing substantial harm to the competitive position of the person, firm, partnership, corporation, or other organization from whom the information was obtained, unless the Commission is required by law to disclose such information.

4. Procedure for Identifying Confidential Business Information

A basic pattern has been developed by the Treasury and Commerce Departments, the Customs Service, the ITC, and other agencies for obtaining a clear identification and separation of information submitted as confidential and for rejecting the information or its characterization as confidential where the agency disagrees with the submitter. This pattern, developed in more or less detail in regulations governing submission of comments on public rulemaking and of data for investigations and adjudications, requires the submitter to divulge any information he wants treated as confidential separately and clearly and with an explanation of the nature of the information and of the reasons to consider it confidential. If the agency disagrees with the characterization, it may reject and refuse to consider that portion of the submission unless the submitter agrees to its public disclosure.

A submitter needs to refer to the regulations governing the particular proceeding or type of information to ascertain the precise procedures. The ITC confidential business information regulations provide procedures elaborate enough to include appeal to the full commission of any rejection at staff level of a claim of confidentiality. The International Trade Administration regulations on the availability of information in antidumping and countervailing duty proceedings[19] set forth the kinds of information ordinarily regarded as appropriate for disclosure and those ordinarily regarded as confidential.

In antidumping and countervailing duty proceedings administrative and judicial protective orders are available as a means for the disclosure of confidential information.

---

[19] 19 CFR 353.29 and 355.19.

C. Relation of the FOIA and the Privacy Act

The Privacy Act of 1974 (5 U.S.C. 552a) was enacted at the same session of the Congress as were the amendments to the FOIA, discussed *supra,* which enlarged and facilitated access to government records. However, the Privacy Act had the different objective of restricting access to government records on individuals, held in systems of records, without the consent of the individual concerned, except in specific circumstances. It intended to allow an individual more control over the acquisition, dissemination, and correctness of records pertaining to himself compiled by the government.

The relation between the Privacy Act and the FOIA in areas where they overlap and have been found to conflict is discussed at length, with analysis of their legislative histories and textual provisions, in *Greentree* v. *U.S. Customs Service,* 674 F.2d 74 (CA DC 1982). That circuit court concluded, contrary to opinions in the Fifth and Seventh Circuits, that records unavailable under the Privacy Act were not per se unavailable under the FOIA. Specifically, the restriction in the Privacy Act upon release of certain criminal investigatory information to the individual concerned was not found to come within the FOIA exemption, Section 552(b)(3), for information specifically exempted from disclosure by another statute, since the Privacy Act was not, under its provisions, to be used as a barrier to FOIA disclosure.

D. Open Agency Meeting

In enacting The Government in the Sunshine Act in 1976 (5 U.S.C. 552b) the Congress decided to provide the public not only with access to specific information in the government files but with access to the decision-making process itself, where that process was carried on by two or more members as a "collegial body." The basic statutory requirement is that every portion of every meeting of such an agency must be open to public observation except where the agency determines that the public interest requires it to apply one or more of the 10 exemptions specified in the Act to public access to the entire meeting or any portion thereof.

Exemptions (1), (2), (3), (4), (6), (7), and (8) correspond with the identically numbered exemptions in the Freedom of Information Act. Exemption (5) prevents disclosures which would "involve accusing any person of a crime, or formally censoring any person." Exemption (9) would protect agencies which regulate currencies, securities, commodities, or financial institutions from premature destabilizing disclosures, or any agency from disclosures frustrating implementation of agency action. Exemption (10) applies to an agency's litigation or adjudication functions.

As in the case of the FOI Act, the statute gives the U.S. District Courts jurisdiction of actions to compel agency compliance. The statute gave the agencies six months to promulgate implementing regulations, and specified various time limits and procedures for public notices of agency meetings.

The ITC is the only agency with major responsibilities for customs, tariffs, and trade which is headed by a collegial body. The ITC published on

February 28, 1977, its regulations under the Act in 19 CFR Part 201 as Subpart E, entitled "Opening Commission Meetings to Public Observation Pursuant to 5 U.S.C. 552b." These regulations describe the meetings governed by the Act, which may even include conference calls, and for the various procedures for notices of meetings and explanations of any closed sessions or portions thereof. The regulations also provide for the listening to recordings of meetings and for copying at the cost of transcription.

29

Inspection, Search, and Seizure; Recordkeeping

I. CUSTOMS ENFORCEMENT AUTHORITY

A. Statutory and Constitutional Authority

Customs officers have had authority since the original revenue acts to stop and search vessels for dutiable and illegally imported merchandise. For over 100 years they have also had authority to stop, search, and examine "any vehicle, beast, or person" on which or whom they suspect there is such merchandise, or to search "any trunk or envelope, wherever found," in which they may have "a reasonable cause to suspect there is merchandise which was imported contrary to law." Further, if such merchandise is found, they have authority to seize and secure it.[1] The Tariff Act of 1930 and later legislation amplified this basic and still functional authority, specifying extensive inspection, search, and seizure authority in various enforcement areas.

Persistent litigation has established that, in the interests of policing national boundaries, the traditional Fourth Amendment prohibitions on unreasonable searches and seizures and on search warrants not based on probable cause do not inhibit border searches by customs officers of persons, articles, or vehicles, entering or leaving the country. The limitations on such searches are primarily statutory. 19 U.S.C. 482, quoted from *supra*, requires reasonable suspicion of illegal activity under the customs laws, but other statutes authorize random searches in certain circumstances.

The Supreme Court upheld as constitutional the random boarding of a vessel, without articulable suspicion, and its search by customs officers, under the authority of 19 U.S.C. 1581(a), because of the governmental interest in assuring compliance with documentation requirements, particu-

---

[1] 19 U.S.C. 482.

larly in waters providing access to the sea where deterrence of smuggling is great. *United States* v. *Jose Reynaldo Villamonte-Marquez,* 462 U.S. 579, 77 L.Ed. 2d 22 (1983). See also *United States* v. *Helms,* 703 F.2d 759 (CA 4 1983), allowing random boarding in inland waters if the vessel has probably crossed the border, and *United States* v. *Montoya de Hernandez,* 87 L. Ed. 2d 381 (1985), allowing detention of an incoming traveler on reasonable suspicion of drug smuggling.

B. Vessels, Vehicles, Aircraft, Passengers, and Cargo

The comprehensive provision[2] in the Tariff Act of 1930, applied in part in the *Jose Reynaldo* case, authorizes customs officers to board any vessel or vehicle, to examine the manifest and other documents, to inspect and search the vessel or vehicle and any person, trunk, package, or cargo on board, and for this purpose to hail and stop the vessel or vehicle and use all necessary force to compel compliance. Such action may be carried out any place in the United States or within customs waters[3] or, as the customs officers may be authorized, within a customs enforcement area established under the Anti-Smuggling Act,[4] and against any American vessel on the high seas regardless of probable cause to believe that the vessel is violating U.S. laws.[5] Customs officers may also seal the hatches or other outlets of a vessel or vehicle, as necessary to protect the revenue; cause the unlading of a vessel or vehicle if that operation is delayed more than 25 days; and inspect, examine, and search persons, baggage, and merchandise even though previously inspected and searched by Customs.[6]

Customs officers have had the same authority over civil aircraft arriving at airports that are ports of entry as over vessels or vehicles at other ports of entry under the federal aviation laws (49 U.S.C. 1509) and customs regulations (19 CFR 162.5). However, both the Comprehensive Crime Control Act of 1984 and the Trade and Tariff Act of 1984[7] amended the seizure and forfeiture statutes in the Tariff Act of 1930 (19 U.S.C. 1602–1618) and the informer award provision (19 U.S.C. 1619) to specifically include reference to aircraft as well as vehicles.

The foregoing legislation authorizes customs officers to seize any vessel, vehicle, aircraft, or merchandise which appears from their inspection and search to be liable to forfeiture, fine, or other penalty for breach of U.S. laws. Seizure for forfeiture purposes is also authorized for everything used to "facilitate" the illegal introduction of "any article,"[8] and for every vessel used for smuggling.[9] Excepted from seizure authority are common carriers, which may not be delayed in clearance or seized unless the master, owner,

---

[2]19 U.S.C. 1581.
[3]Customs waters are defined in 19 U.S.C. 1401(m) and 1709(c) as four leagues off the U.S. coast unless altered by a treaty covering the vessel concerned.
[4]19 U.S.C. 1701–1711.
[5]19 CFR 162.3.
[6]19 U.S.C. 1455, 1457, 1467.
[7]Pub. L. No. 98–473, October 12, 1984, in Title II, Chapter III, Part D, 98 Stat. 2053; Pub. L. No. 98–573, October 30, 1984, in Section 213, 98 Stat. 2984.
[8]19 U.S.C. 1595a.
[9]19 U.S.C. 1703.

driver, or other person in charge was a consenting party or privy to the illegal act.[10]

C. Baggage

Other provisions of the Tariff Act of 1930 focus specifically on the baggage of persons coming into ports of entry. A customs officer may examine the baggage of any such person, even though a declaration and entry have been made,[11] and may require closed containers to be opened.[12] If the owner fails to open the container, the customs officer may force the opening, and, if any article in the container is found subject to duty, all the contents and the container may be forfeited.[13] If a dutiable article is not declared, it is subject to forfeiture and a penalty equal to its value is assessed as well.[14]

D. Imported Merchandise

1. Examination of Merchandise

Imported merchandise must be inspected, examined, and appraised in order to determine the duty due, if any, and compliance with applicable restrictions on imports, such as health and safety regulation. The Treasury Department has broad authority to determine the time, place, and method of examination of imports[15] and has provided governing regulations.[16] Customs will not release merchandise from customs custody, except under bond, until examination has proved correct invoicing and compliance with regulations. If merchandise has been released under bond prior to completion of the examination of the samples provided for this purpose, and the merchandise proves to be inadmissible, Customs may recall the merchandise. If recall is not, or cannot be, effected, recourse is had to the bond.

2. Examination of Books and Witnesses

The Customs Service was given greatly enhanced authority by Section 105 of the Customs Procedural Reform and Simplification Act of 1978, Public Law 95-410, to examine records and documents pertaining to compliance with the customs laws and to require the testimony of importers and other persons with relevant information of customs transactions. Under amended 19 U.S.C. 1509 and TD 84-170 (49 FR 31188, August 3, 1984) a customs officer not below the rank of a district director or special agent in charge may in an investigation of customs laws compliance:

---

[10]19 U.S.C. 1594.
[11]19 U.S.C. 1496.
[12]19 U.S.C. 1461.
[13]19 U.S.C. 1462.
[14]19 U.S.C. 1497.
[15]19 U.S.C. 1202, General Headnote 12; 19 U.S.C. 1499.
[16]19 CFR Part 151.

(a) Upon reasonable notice examine any record, statement, declaration, or other document described with reasonable specificity in the notice which is relevant to the investigation;

(b) Upon reasonable notice summon the importer, his agent or employee, or a person having custody of his records, or any other person deemed proper, to appear, produce records, and give testimony; and

(c) Take relevant testimony under oath.

The requirements surrounding service of a summons, particularly the procedures for third-party summonses, are described in section II *infra*.

3. Restrictions on Seizure

Customs officers have authority to seize illegally imported merchandise, but their authority under 19 U.S.C. 1592 to seize merchandise believed to be falsely or fraudulently entered was restricted by Section 110 of the 1978 Act to circumstances in which seizure may be necessary to protect the revenue or prevent the introduction of prohibited or restricted merchandise.

E. Customs Officers' Arrest Authority

Until October 1984, the statutory authority of customs officers to make arrests was limited. Under 19 U.S.C. 1581(b), customs officers could make arrests for breach of the navigation laws and, under 26 U.S.C. 7607, they could make arrests for violations of the narcotic drug and marijuana laws. Otherwise, customs officers needed to rely on the citizen arrest authority or peace officer status given under state laws or upon deputization as U.S. marshals (see H.R. Doc. No. 98–1030, September 17, 1984, on H.J. Res. 648 (Public Law 98–473) at 220).

This inadequate and confusing authority was rectified by both the Comprehensive Crime Control Act of 1984 and the Trade and Tariff Act of 1984.[17] Section 320 of the Crime Control Act added Section 589 to the Tariff Act of 1930 (19 U.S.C. 1589) authorizing a customs officer to make an arrest without a warrant for any offense against the United States committed in the officer's presence or for any federal felony committed outside his presence if he has reasonable grounds to believe the person to be arrested has committed or is committing the felony. This new Section 589 in identical language was also added to the Tariff Act of 1930 by Section 213(a)(17) of the Trade and Tariff Act which, under Section 214(a) of that Act, was made effective October 15, 1984, three days after the effective date of the Crime Control Act. Both Section 320 of the Crime Control Act and Section 213 of the Trade and Tariff Act incorporated in new Section 589 the authority in 26 U.S.C. 7607 for customs officers to carry firearms, and extended the authority in that section to execute and serve warrants to the execution and service of any order, warrant, subpoena, summons, or other process issued under U.S. authority. Both sections repealed 26 U.S.C. 7607,

---

[17]Pub. L. No. 98–473 and 98–573, cited *supra* note 7.

and authorized customs officers to "perform any other law enforcement duty that the Secretary of the Treasury may designate."

II. CUSTOMS PROCEDURAL REQUIREMENTS

Customs laws and regulations place certain procedural obligations and requirements upon officers undertaking inspection, examination, investigation, search, and seizure. Among these are the following.

A. Identification

One of the oldest requirements is that a customs officer performing a search or seizure must make known his official capacity, if questioned.[18] A customs vessel requiring another vessel to stop must display proper insignia.[19]

B. Search Warrant

Customs officers do not need to obtain a search warrant for the search of vessels, vehicles, passengers, cargo, baggage, and imported merchandise authorized by the statutes described *supra.* However, they do need to obtain a search warrant for searches and seizures in any dwelling house, store, or other building, and they must have reasonable cause to suspect that there may be merchandise therein imported contrary to law.[20] Nevertheless, a customs officer who is lawfully on any premises and is able to identify merchandise which has been imported contrary to law may seize the merchandise without a warrant.[21] In search of illegally imported merchandise a customs officer may, if he deems it necessary, pass through lands, enclosures, and buildings other than a dwelling house without a search warrant.[22]

A warrant to search rooms in a building occupied by persons named or described in the warrant is limited to the rooms so occupied and no search is to be made of other rooms not so occupied. Further, a warrant to search for and seize merchandise does not authorize the removal of letters and other documents and records unless they are instruments of crime and are seized as an incident to a lawful arrest.[23]

C. Service of Warrant

A search warrant must be served in person by the officer to whom it was issued, and this officer is to leave a copy of the warrant with the person in

---

[18] 19 U.S.C. 507.
[19] 19 U.S.C. 1581(d).
[20] 19 U.S.C. 1595(a).
[21] 19 CFR 162.11.
[22] 19 U.S.C. 1595(b).
[23] 19 CFR 162.13 and 162.14.

charge of the premises. In the absence of any person the copy is to be posted in a conspicuous place on the premises.[24]

D. Seizure Requisites, Limitations, and Remedies

A customs officer seizing property is required to give a receipt for it to the person from whom it was taken or, if the property was taken under a search warrant, to the person in charge of the premises searched; but in the absence of any person the receipt is to be posted in a conspicuous place.[25] The customs officer is required to report the seizure immediately to the appropriate customs officials and, if court action will be required, report is also to be made to the U.S. attorney.[26] Seized property is to remain in the custody of a customs officer in the district where it was seized, but it may be stored outside the district in a convenient and appropriate place.[27]

Customs is also required to give written notice of any liability for forfeiture of seized property to each party that the facts indicate has an interest in the seized property. The notice must provide information on the law alleged to be violated, the basis of the alleged violations, and the avenues of relief available to the party.[28]

A new Section 600 was added to the Tariff Act of 1930 (19 U.S.C. 1600) by Section 323 of the Comprehensive Crime Control Act of 1984, providing that the seizure procedures set forth in the Tariff Act enforcement provisions, 19 U.S.C. 1602 through 1619, shall apply to seizures of any property effected by customs officers under any law enforced or administered by the Customs Service, unless that law specifies different procedures. This new section was not duplicated in the 1984 Trade and Tariff Act.

Where property has been legitimately seized and detained by a customs officer and negligently damaged, the owner has no recourse for damages against the United States under the Federal Tort Claims Act because of the exclusion in that Act, 28 U.S.C. 2680(c), of any claim arising in respect of "the detention of any goods or merchandise by any officer of customs." *Kosak* v. *United States,* 679 F.2d 306 (CA 3 1982) 4 ITRD 1583. This decision was affirmed by the Supreme Court, *Kosak* v. *United States,* No. 82-618 (1984) 5 ITRD 1945. However, the exclusion in that Act was held by the Supreme Court not to prevent an action against the United States in the Court of Claims under the Tucker Act for breach of an implied contract of bailment arising from the loss of goods while held by the Customs Service after seizure for customs violations. *Hatzlachh Supply Co., Inc.* v. *United States,* 444 U.S. 460 (1980) 1 ITRD 1705.

Where the importer claims that his merchandise was illegally seized for false entry under 19 U.S.C. 1592, he has adequate administrative and judicial relief through petition under 19 U.S.C. 1618 or forfeiture proceedings, which coexist and work in tandem, and no equity relief is

---

[24] 19 CFR 162.12.
[25] 19 CFR 162.15, 162.21.
[26] 19 U.S.C. 1602, 1603.
[27] 19 U.S.C. 1605.
[28] 19 CFR 162.31.

appropriate. *Hector Rivera Siaca* v. *United States,* 754 F.2d 988 (Fed. Cir. 1985) 6 ITRD 1803.

E. Investigation of Records

1. In General

Important procedural requirements were placed by the amendments to 19 U.S.C. 1509, made by Section 105 of Public Law 95-410, on customs officers conducting an investigation or inquiry to determine the correctness of an entry, liability for duty or taxes, or compliance with law and regulations. As stated in section I.D *supra,* only a qualified customs officer may examine books and records and only upon reasonable specification of the documents to be examined. Also, a summons to appear to testify and to produce records must provide reasonable notice. Further, the appearance must be at a place within 100 miles of the service of the summons.

2. Third-Party Summonses

Under amended 19 U.S.C. 1509 a customs officer not below the rank of a district officer or special agent in charge may summon a "third-party recordkeeper" to appear, produce records required to be kept, and testify in an inquiry or investigation concerning an import transaction. A third-party recordkeeper is defined as any customhouse broker, any attorney, and any accountant. If the summons requires testimony concerning, or the production of records of an identified person other than the person summoned, notice of the summons must be provided, unless a court determines otherwise, to that identified person within a reasonable time before the required appearance. The notice is to include a copy of the summons and directions for staying compliance. The identified person then has the right to intervene in the proceedings and to stay compliance with the summons by giving notice in writing to the person summoned not to comply and by giving a copy of such notice by registered or certified mail to that person and to the proper office of the Customs Service. Thereafter no examination of the records which are the subject of the notice not to comply shall be made until the expiration of the period allowed for the notice not to comply or except upon order of a court of competent jurisdiction.

III. RECORD REQUIREMENTS

The Customs Procedural Reform and Simplification Act of 1978 introduced into the tariff laws a general requirement that records be kept by importers of importations into the United States. Added Section 19 U.S.C. 1508 requires any owner, importer, consignee, or agent thereof who imports goods into the United States or knowingly causes goods to be imported, to make, keep, and render for examination and inspection records, including statements, declarations, and other documents, which pertain to an importation and are normally kept in the ordinary course of business. The records are to be kept for such period of time, not exceeding five years from the date of entry, as the Secretary of the Treasury shall prescribe.[29]

A person ordering merchandise from an importer is not considered to "knowingly cause merchandise to be imported" unless he controls the terms and conditions of the importation or unless he furnishes technical data, equipment, components, or other production assistance with knowledge that they will be used in the manufacture or production of the imported merchandise.

The fact that records were not required to be kept prior to the enactment of the 1978 law was no excuse for not providing prior records where they existed. *Matter of Clubman, Inc.,* 532 F. Supp. 92 (DC PR 1982) 3 ITRD 1862. However, the court in that case required the Customs Service to correct the summonses issued to specify the time period for which records were required, although the respondent was aware of the period in issue.

In a decision consistent with the *Clubman* holding the Court of Appeals for the Second Circuit affirmed a district court's enforcement of customs summonses for relevant records more than five years old, stating that the five-year recordkeeping requirement in 19 U.S.C. 1508(b) did not limit the summons authority in 19 U.S.C. 1509. *United States* v. *Frowein,* 727 F.2d 227 (CA 2 1984) 5 ITRD 1801.

---

[29]Section 162.1c of 19 CFR Part 162, issued June 4, 1979, requires records to be kept for five years unless a different period is provided for a specific type of record.

30

Penalties, Forfeitures, and Mitigation

I. PENALTIES ENFORCED BY CUSTOMS

A. Customs Control

The Customs Service has an unusual advantage in enforcing the laws and regulations over which it has supervision, not shared by many other government agencies, namely, its direct control over the means and procedures whereby persons and merchandise enter the United States. It has actual or constructive custody of merchandise being imported or exported; under the customs and the navigation laws[1] it has control over commerce in ports of entry and the lading and unlading of merchandise and the embarkation and disembarkation of persons on and from vessels, vehicles, and aircraft. It has authority to seize and detain such means of transportation and the merchandise transported in or from them in order to forestall or terminate illegal traffic. Under the Anti-Smuggling Act[2] customs officers may board, seize, and arrest vessels, merchandise, and persons engaged in smuggling not only in the customs waters of the United States[3] but also in a customs enforcement area adjacent to such waters, as declared by the President. The Customs Service, because of its advantageous practical and legal position, is authorized to impose civil penalties, in accordance with the prescribed procedures discussed in this Chapter.

B. Types of Penalties

Various provisions of the Tariff Act of 1930 place monetary penalties upon persons failing to comply with its requirements. Thus a master of a

---

[1] Principally included in various portions of Titles 19 and 46 of the United States Code; 19 CFR Parts 4 and 6.

[2] 19 U.S.C. 1701–1711.

[3] Defined in 19 U.S.C. 1401(m) and 1709(c) as four leagues off the U.S. coast unless altered by a treaty covering the vessel concerned.

vessel arriving from a foreign port and, absent necessity, departing without making entry is liable to a penalty of $5,000.[4] A master of a vessel or the person in charge of an incoming vehicle who does not produce the manifest for a customs officer is liable to a penalty of $500 and, as the statute was extended by the Customs Procedural Reform and Simplification Act of 1978, those persons, or the owners, or any person directly or indirectly responsible for a discrepancy in the manifest, is liable for a penalty of the lesser of $10,000 or the domestic value of the merchandise found not to be included in the manifest.[5]

An important and characteristic penalty imposed under the Tariff Act of 1930 is forfeiture of the vessel, vehicle, or merchandise involved in a violation or of the value of that property.[6] The enforcement provisions of that Act dealing with seizure and forfeiture procedures, 19 U.S.C. 1602, 1615, 1618, and 1619, were amended by both the Comprehensive Crime Control Act of 1984, Public Law 98-473, and the Trade and Tariff Act of 1984, Public Law 98-573, to insert "aircraft" following every reference to "vehicles" subject to forfeiture (see Chapter 29, section I.B *supra*). Some penalty statutes call for forfeiture of the merchandise concerned *and* a penalty of the value of the forfeited merchandise. This unusually severe double penalty applies, for example, where a person arriving in the United States has not declared an article required to be declared, prior to customs examination.[7]

There are other penalties enforced against merchandise under the control of the Customs Service appropriate to the particular customs violations. Thus, an importer who is in contempt of court for failing to comply with a Customs Service summons may be prohibited from further importation, and delivery to him of merchandise already imported may be withheld and, after one year of his recalcitrance, the merchandise may be sold at public auction.[8] Merchandise remaining in customs custody for one year without estimated duties and charges paid is considered to be unclaimed and abandoned to the government and is appraised and sold at public auction.[9] Abandoned or forfeited merchandise subject to internal revenue tax which is considered to be of less value than the amount of the taxes is to be destroyed.[10]

The penalties for fraud, gross negligence, and negligence in the entry of merchandise with false documentation were restated in the revision of Section 592 of the Tariff Act (19 U.S.C. 1592) made by Section 110 of the 1978 Act. This revision resulted from prolonged legislative effort by importers and other business interests seeking to eliminate from Section 592 the penalty of forfeiture of the merchandise and to provide greater procedural safeguards in the administrative consideration of penalty claims and more substantive judicial review. Revised Section 592 is described in section IV *infra*.

---

[4] 19 U.S.C. 1585.
[5] 19 U.S.C. 1584.
[6] See, *e.g.*, 19 U.S.C. 1526(e), 1527(b), 1585, 1586, 1595a.
[7] 19 U.S.C. 1497.
[8] 19 U.S.C. 1510.
[9] 19 U.S.C. 1491.
[10] 19 U.S.C. 1492.

II. ENFORCEMENT PROCEDURES

A. Notice

Customs has been obligated under its regulations[11] to provide written notice of any fine or penalty incurred, as well as of any liability to forfeiture, to each party that the facts of record indicate has an interest in the claim or seized property. The notice also provided information on the right of an interested party to apply for relief through mitigation of penalties or remission of forfeiture under 19 U.S.C. 1618, discussed *infra,* or other relief statute.

Until amendment in October 1984, the statutory requirement for notice of seizure and liability to forfeiture of property subject to summary forfeiture by the Customs Service (then property valued at $10,000 or less), 19 U.S.C. 1607, was for publication of notice for three successive weeks. The amendment of Section 1607 made in nearly identical terms by Section 311 of the Comprehensive Crime Control Act of 1984 and by Section 213(a)(4) of the Trade and Tariff Act of 1984 requires written notice of seizure of property subject to summary forfeiture, together with information on the applicable procedures, to be sent to each party who appears to have an interest in the seized article, in addition to the three-week publication requirement. This amendment puts into statutory form an obligation held to be a constitutional requisite under the due process clause. *Winters* v. *Working,* 510 F. Supp. 14 (D W.Tex. 1980).

B. Enforcement Timing

If the person subject to a fine, penalty, or forfeiture fails to petition for relief or fails to pay or arrange to pay the fine within 60 days from the date of the notice, unless he was absent from the country for more than 30 days, or has other justified excuse, the case is referred to the U.S. attorney for appropriate action.[12]

Prompt action by the Customs Service and the Justice Department is required in taking all steps between the seizure of private property and administrative or judicial forfeiture proceedings. However, applying the balance of factors rule the Supreme Court held that the 18 months taken prior to civil forfeiture proceedings for consideration of remission and criminal and civil proceedings was reasonable. *United States* v. *Eight Thousand Eight Hundred Fifty Dollars ($8,850.00) in U.S. Currency,* 461 U.S. 555 (1983), *rev'g* 645 F.2d 836 (CA 9 1981). See *United States* v. *$10,755.00 in U.S. Currency,* 523 F. Supp. 447 (D Md. 1981) holding, contrary to the Ninth Circuit, that delay in a currency forfeiture was not prejudicial since currency was not a wasting asset.

---

[11] 19 CFR 162.31.
[12] 19 CFR 162.32.

C. Appraisement of Seized Property

Any vessel, vehicle, aircraft, merchandise, or baggage seized under the customs laws is, by statute and regulation,[13] to be appraised at its domestic value. This value is the price at which the same or similar merchandise is freely offered for sale at the time and place of appraisement. Where the property involved is not seized but its value is the measure of the penalty, the appraisement is of its domestic value as of the date of the violation.

D. Release on Payment of Appraised Value

A person with a substantial interest in seized property may obtain its release upon payment of its appraised domestic value.[14] The written offer to make payment is to be addressed to the Commissioner of Customs if the value exceeds $50,000. A district director may accept a written offer for payment for property of less value.

E. Summary Forfeiture

The seized property which is subject to summary forfeiture was redefined in nearly identical terms by the amendments cited in section A *supra,* made in Section 607 of the Tariff Act of 1930, 19 U.S.C. 1607, by the Comprehensive Crime Control Act of 1984 and the Trade and Tariff Act of 1984. Under the amended section the subject property is property in one of the following three categories:

(1) The value of the seized vessel, vehicle, aircraft, merchandise, or baggage does not exceed $100,000;

(2) The seized merchandise consists of articles the importation of which is prohibited; or

(3) The seized vessel, vehicle, or aircraft was used to import, export, transport, or store any controlled substance.

Prior to the amendment, the property now in Category (1) was property having a value not exceeding $10,000. With respect to Category (2), the prior section provided that for the purposes of the statutory forfeiture provisions merchandise, the importation of which was prohibited, should be held not to exceed $10,000 in value. Category (3) represents a new category of property subject to summary forfeiture. With respect to this category, the amended section provides that the term "controlled substance" has the meaning given that term in Section 102 of the Controlled Substances Act (21 U.S.C. 802).

Property subject to summary (administrative) forfeiture may be sold at public auction after the prescribed notice has been given, if no petition for relief has been filed or, if filed, the petition has been denied, and if no claim was filed under 19 U.S.C. 1608 and penal bond posted.[15] A filing of a claim under that statute within 20 days of the first publication of notice of intent

---

[13] 19 U.S.C. 1606; 19 CFR 162.43(a).
[14] 19 U.S.C. 1614; 19 CFR 162.44.
[15] 19 U.S.C. 1609; 19 CFR 162.45–162.48.

to forfeit and sell the property stops the summary forfeiture procedure and causes the case to be transferred to the U.S. attorney for condemnation proceedings.[16] Seized property which is perishable may be sold at the earliest possible date following its advertisement for sale, and the proceeds may be held subject to the claims of parties in interest (19 U.S.C. 1612).

F. Customs Forfeiture Fund

The Comprehensive Crime Control Act, by Section 317, and the Trade and Tariff Act, by Section 213(a)(11), each added a new section, 613A, to the Trade and Tariff Act of 1930, to establish a Customs Forfeiture Fund to be available, subject to appropriations, from the date of enactment to September 30, 1987, for enumerated purposes. The provisions in the Trade and Tariff Act are more comprehensive concerning the uses and sources of the fund. That Act provides that the fund may be used for the payment (1) of the expenses of seizure, forfeiture, and sale of property, (2) of awards of compensation to informers, (3) for the satisfaction of liens against seized property, (4) of amounts authorized with respect to remission and mitigation, (5) for equipping for law enforcement functions, forfeited vessels, vehicles, and aircraft, retained for official customs use, and (6) of claims of parties in interest to property disposed of under the provisions of 19 U.S.C. 1612 for summary sale of perishable goods. In addition, the fund is to be available for purchases by the Customs Service of evidence of smuggling of controlled substances, and of violations of the currency and foreign transaction reporting requirements in 31 U.S.C. Chapter 53, if there is substantial probability that the violation of those requirements are related to the smuggling of controlled substances. Further, the amounts in the fund may be used to reimburse the Coast Guard for related expenses incurred by it.

There is to be deposited in the fund all proceeds from forfeiture under any law enforced or administered by the Customs Service and all earnings on amounts invested under the authorization for investment of amounts in the fund not currently needed, in obligations of, or guaranteed by, the United States. Annual reports are to be transmitted to the Congress on receipts and disbursements no later than four months after the end of each fiscal year. Both 1984 Acts authorized the appropriation from the fund for each fiscal year of not more than $10 million. At the end of the final fiscal year, any amount remaining in the fund is to be deposited in the general fund of the Treasury and the fund will cease to exist.

---

[16]19 U.S.C. 1608. The amendment of 19 U.S.C. 1608 by Section 312 of the Comprehensive Crime Control Act provided for the giving of a penal sum of $5,000 or 10 percent of the value of the claimed property, whichever is lower. However, the corresponding amendment of Section 1608 made by Section 213(a)(5) of the Trade and Tariff Act specifies a penal sum of $2,500 or 10 percent of the value of the claimed property, whichever is lower. Since the effective date of Section 213 is October 15, 1984, subsequent to the effective date, October 12, 1984, of the Comprehensive Crime Control Act, the amendment made by Section 213(a)(5) appears to govern.

G. Judicial Forfeiture Proceedings

Where property has been seized and no petition for relief has been filed, or if the filed petition has been denied, or any mitigated amount not paid, or no offer to pay the appraised value has been received within a reasonable time, and the property is not subject to summary forfeiture, the district director reports the facts to the U.S. attorney for the judicial district in which the seizure was made for the institution of proceedings for the condemnation of the property.[17]

III. REMISSION OR MITIGATION OF PENALTIES

A. Authority for Relief

The Customs Service is authorized to remit or mitigate the fines, penalties, or forfeitures it may impose upon the filing of a proper petition for relief if it finds that any such penalty "was incurred without willful negligence or without any intention on the part of the petitioner to defraud the revenue or to violate the law" or finds "the existence of such mitigating circumstances as to justify" remission or mitigation.[18] This authority, placed by the statute in the Secretary of the Treasury, was delegated by him to the Commissioner of Customs, who in turn redelegated his authority to the Director, Office of Regulations and Rulings and also authorized each district director to remit or mitigate a penalty on such terms and conditions as he deems appropriate under the law and circumstances when the total amount of penalties in any one offense, other than under 19 U.S.C. 1592, together with the total value of the merchandise or other article subject to forfeiture or to a claim for forfeiture value, does not exceed $100,000.[19] By TD 85-25 the Customs Service raised the maximum to $100,000, except with respect to penalties or forfeitures incurred under Section 592 of the Tariff Act of 1930 (19 U.S.C. 1592) where the total value remained $25,000. 50 FR 7335, February 22, 1985.

The statutory reference to a "fine, penalty, or forfeiture" does not include a voluntary payment by an importer to the Customs Service made in the course of an investigation of his entries for fraud under Section 592. *Carlingswitch, Inc.* v. *United States,* 85 Cust. Ct. 63, CD 4873, 500 F. Supp. 223 (1980) 2 ITRD 1257, *aff'd,* 68 CCPA 49, 651 F.2d 768 (1981) 2 ITRD 1529, *new action dismissed,* 5 CIT 70 (1983) 4 ITRD 1699.

B. Petition for Relief

A petition for the remission or mitigation of a fine, penalty, or forfeiture incurred under any law administered by the Customs Service is to be addressed to the Commissioner of Customs and filed with the district director for the district in which the property was seized or the fine or

---

[17]19 U.S.C. 1603, 1610, as amended by Section 213(a)(10) of the Trade and Tariff Act of 1984; 19 CFR 162.32, 162.49, 162.50.
[18]19 U.S.C. 1618; 19 CFR Part 171.
[19]19 CFR 171.21.

penalty imposed within 60 days of the date of mailing of the notice of that penalty (under TD 84-60, 30 days for certain seized conveyances). The Customs Service proposed reducing the petition time from 60 to 30 days in proposed regulations issued June 27, 1985, 50 FR 26588.

The petition must contain a description of the property involved, the date and place of the violation or seizure, the facts and circumstances deemed to justify remission or mitigation, and when relief from forfeiture is sought, the interest of the petitioner in the property, with supporting evidence. If the seized property was in the possession of another person who was responsible for or caused the act resulting in the seizure, evidence must be submitted as to how the property came into that other person's possession and showing that the petitioner prior to parting with the property did not know nor have reasonable cause to believe that the property would be used to violate the law or that the violator had a criminal record or general reputation for commercial crime.

C. Action on Petition for Relief

Within the total value limitations described *supra* the district director may act on the petition as he deems appropriate. A decision to mitigate a penalty or remit a forfeiture upon condition that a stated amount is paid is generally effective for not more than 60 days. Unless the amount is paid or a supplemental petition is filed, the full penalty becomes effective and is to be enforced. A petitioner may have his supplemental petition to the district director considered and decided by the regional commissioner. A supplemental petition to the Commissioner of Customs is decided by him, unless it concerns a penalty assessed under Section 592 and is accepted for review by the Secretary of Treasury, as described *infra*.

Guidelines for the administrative disposition of violations of 19 U.S.C. 1497, providing penalties for the failure of travelers to declare articles brought into the United States, issued as TD 82-35, and Revised Penalty Guidelines under 19 U.S.C. 1592 issued as TD 84-18, are published as Appendices A and B to the penalty regulations, 19 CFR Part 171. These guidelines specify mitigating and aggravating factors which affect the decrease or increase of penalties.

IV. PENALTIES FOR FALSE ENTRY OF MERCHANDISE: SECTION 592

A. Definition of Offenses

Section 592 of the Tariff Act of 1930 (19 U.S.C. 1592) provides that no person may by fraud, gross negligence, or negligence, enter or attempt to enter any merchandise into the commerce of the United States by means of "any document, written or oral statement, or act which is material and false," or "any omission which is material," or aid or abet any other person in such a violation. Clerical errors or mistakes of fact are not violations unless they are part of a pattern of negligent conduct. A violation does not depend upon whether or not the United States is deprived of part or all of lawful duty.

Section 592 was held to apply to the presentation to Customs of importation papers proper in form but based upon an import license falsely obtained from the Interior Department. *United States* v. *Ven Fuel, Inc.,* 758 F.2d 741 (CA 1 1985) 6 ITRD 2197.

B. Penalties Matched to Violations

The penalties for violation of the offenses described are civil monetary penalties and are graded in accordance with the seriousness of the offense. However, merchandise falsely entered may be seized, and upon assessment of a monetary penalty, forfeited unless the penalty is promptly paid, if the Secretary of the Treasury has reason to believe that the violator is insolvent or beyond the jurisdiction of the United States or that seizure is otherwise essential to protect the revenue. Furthermore, if a violation has caused a loss of duties, those duties must be paid whether or not a monetary penalty is assessed.

The maximum penalties allowed under Section 592, and set forth in 19 CFR 162.73, are the following:

• For a fraudulent violation, an amount not to exceed the domestic value of the merchandise. Congress considered domestic value to be "generally equivalent to retail value."[20]

• For a grossly negligent violation, an amount not to exceed (1) the lesser of the domestic value of the merchandise or four times the loss of lawful duties, or (2) if the violation did not affect the assessment of duties, 40 percent of the dutiable value of the merchandise. Congress considered dutiable value to be "generally equivalent to wholesale value."[21]

For a negligent violation, an amount not to exceed (1) the lesser of the domestic value of the merchandise or two times the loss of duties, or (2) if the violation did not affect the assessment of duties, 20 percent of the dutiable value of the merchandise.

C. Advantage of Prior Disclosure

The maximum penalties are reduced and seizure of merchandise is prohibited if the person concerned discloses to Customs the circumstances of a violation before, or without knowledge of, the commencement of a formal investigation of the violation. However, the person asserting lack of knowledge of the investigation's commencement has the burden of proof in establishing his lack of knowledge. The regulations applicable to prior disclosure cases are 19 CFR 162.74. The Customs Service proposed to amend these regulations to make clear that a person is presumed to have had knowledge of the commencement of a formal investigation if any

---

[20]Senate Report on H.R. 8149, S. Rep. No. 95-778 at 20.
[21]*Ibid.*

customs officer, not just an investigation agent, having reasonable cause to believe a Section 592 violation has occurred, so notifies the person concerned (50 FR 27829, July 8, 1985).

The maximum penalties which may be assessed for a violation which has been voluntarily disclosed may not exceed:

• For a fraudulent violation, an amount equal to 100 percent of the loss of duties, if that amount is tendered at the time of disclosure or within 30 days thereafter (or after notice of the unpaid amount calculated by the customs officer), or if the violation did not affect the assessment of duties, 10 percent of the dutiable value.

• For a negligent or grossly negligent violation, an amount equal to the interest on the loss of duties if the violator tenders the amount of the loss of duties at the time of disclosure or within 30 days or such longer period as the customs officer provides after notice of his calculation of duties lost. The amount of the interest is computed from the date of liquidation and is at the rate applied under the Internal Revenue Code to underpayments of federal income tax.

D. The Penalty Process

Before final determination of a penalty, the importer or other person whose entry is under investigation has at least two opportunities to present his case: first, in response to a prepenalty notice and second, in petitioning for remission or mitigation of the penalty claimed.

1. The Prepenalty Notice

The 1978 revision of Section 592 enacted the prepenalty notice procedure initiated by the Customs Service in 1975 for use in Section 592 cases[22] with specific requirements. If a customs officer determines that there are reasonable grounds for proceeding with a Section 592 charge he must issue a written notice to the person concerned of his intention to issue a claim for a monetary penalty. The notice must (a) describe the merchandise; (b) set forth the details of the entry or attempted entry; (c) specify the laws and regulations allegedly violated; (d) disclose the material facts; (e) state whether the alleged violation occurred as a result of fraud, gross negligence, or negligence; (f) state the estimated loss of duties, if any, and the proposed penalty; and (g) inform the person of his opportunity to make representations, both oral and written, as to why the penalty should not be issued in the amount stated.

This prepenalty notice is not required if the importation in issue is noncommercial in nature, or if the amount of the penalty claim is $1,000 or less.

---

[22]19 CFR 171.1(b) (1983 Ed.) applicable to claims for forfeiture value. The prepenalty notice regulations applicable to claims under revised Section 592 appear in 19 CFR 162.74, 162.77, as amended by TD 84-18.

2. The Penalty Claim

After considering any representations made following the prepenalty notice the customs officer determines whether any violation of Section 592 has occurred. If not, he so advises the person concerned in writing. Otherwise he must issue a penalty claim specifying any changes in the information provided in the prepenalty notice.

3. Petition for Remission or Mitigation of the Penalty

Under the statute the recipient of the penalty claim must have "a reasonable opportunity" to make oral or written representations to the Customs Service for remission or mitigation of the penalty under 19 U.S.C. 1618. The customs regulations and procedures discussed in section III *supra* allow such opportunity and describe the steps for the petitioner to take.

The administrative provisions of revised Section 592 became effective 90 days after the date of enactment, which date was October 3, 1978. However, most changes in these provisions did not apply to alleged intentional violations involving television receivers from Japan subject to antidumping proceedings if the alleged violation occurred prior to the date of enactment and was then under investigation by Customs.

E. Disclosure of Violation Information

Although the Freedom of Information Act[23] exempts from disclosure government information in active investigatory files, the Customs Service determined in 1974 that persons against whom Section 592 penalties had been assessed and their attorneys were entitled to certain information necessary to prepare petitions for relief. This information included a list of all the entries involved; the loss of revenue attributable to each and how this was determined; the specific bases for assessing the penalty, *e.g.*, undervaluation; and proper identification of the merchandise under each entry for which forfeiture value is claimed.[24] This disclosure was made mandatory in the revision of Section 592, as described in section D.1 *supra*.

F. Appeal to the Secretary of the Treasury

A further procedural advantage provided by the Customs Service is the possibility of appeal to the Secretary of the Treasury from an unfavorable decision of the Commissioner of Customs on a petition for relief in a Section 592 case. Treasury Department Order No. 219-2[25] provides that a petitioner filing a supplemental petition under 19 CFR 171.33 from a decision of the commissioner on a Section 592 liability may request that it be considered an appeal to the Secretary of the Treasury, and that the

---

[23]5 U.S.C. 552.
[24]ORR Ruling 74-0203, June 21, 1974, issued by the Office of Regulations and Rulings, Customs Service.
[25]41 FR 8192, February 25, 1976.

Secretary will accept such an appeal if he finds that the petition raises a sufficiently important question of fact, law, or policy. If he does not accept it, the commissioner's decision on the supplemental petition will be final. In these matters the Assistant Secretary (Enforcement and Operations) or his delegate acts for the Secretary.

G. Judicial Enforcement

The Customs Procedural Reform and Simplification Act of 1978, Public Law 95-410, accomplished changes in the court enforcement of penalties long advocated by the importing industry. Before the Act, the U.S. Attorney could bring suit to enforce an unpaid customs penalty under 19 U.S.C. 1604. If the court found the violation to have occurred, it had no choice but to impose the full penalty. Under Section 592(e), added in 1978, the court may consider all issues, including the amount of the penalty, in a trial *de novo.* Subsection (e) was held, however, not to apply in a case in which the administrative proceedings had begun prior to October 3, 1978, the effective date of Public Law 95-410. *United States* v. *F.A.G. Bearings, Ltd.,* 8 CIT ____ , 598 F. Supp. 401 (1984) 6 ITRD 1588.

Moreover, the provisions fixing the burden of proof require the United States in a fraud charge to establish the violation by clear and convincing evidence. If the charge is gross negligence, the United States has the burden of proof to establish all elements of the alleged violation. If the penalty is based on negligence the United States must establish the act or omission, and the alleged violator has the burden of proof that the act or omission did not occur as a result of negligence.

The Customs Courts Act of 1980 transferred jurisdiction of actions by the United States to recover monetary penalties under Section 592 to the Court of International Trade. That court held in a Memorandum opinion, *United States* v. *Digital Equipment Corp.,* 3 CIT 52 (1982) 3 ITRD 1763, that its jurisdiction was *in personam* only and that a penalty for false entries prior to Public Law 95-410 must be sought by an *in rem* action in a U.S. district court. That decision was vacated by the court, 4 CIT 83 (1982) 3 ITRD 2338, in light of its decision in *United States* v. *Accurate Mould Co., Ltd.,* et al., 4 CIT 81, 546 F. Supp. 567 (1982) 3 ITRD 2337.

In the *Accurate Mould* case, the court determined that it had exclusive jurisdiction over all actions for civil penalties commenced after January 30, 1981, the effective date of the Customs Courts Act of 1980, without limitation as to whether the action was brought under Section 592 as revised in 1978 by Public Law 95-410 or the prior section providing only for an *in rem* action. Moreover, the court determined that the U.S. district courts were relieved of all jurisdiction over Section 592 penalty cases by the Customs Courts Act. This decision has been repeatedly confirmed by decisions of the court taking jurisdiction of actions for penalties for false statements or omissions made in entries filed prior to 1978. *United States* v. *Shineman,* 4 CIT 129 (1982) 4 ITRD 1069; *United States* v. *Appendagez,* 5 CIT 74 (1983) 4 ITRD 1817; and *United States* v. *Murray,* 5 CIT 102 (1983) 4 ITRD 1857.

The penalty of forfeiture may be applied under Section 592 only for the purposes stated in the statute. *United States* v. *Gold Mountain Coffee,* 8 CIT _____ , 597 F. Supp. 510 (1984) 6 ITRD 1408.

The CIT will not issue an order in the form of mandamus to direct Customs to "institute" a Section 592 action nor will the court provide a declaratory judgment that a plaintiff has not violated Section 592. *Seaside Realty Corp.* v. *United States,* 9 CIT _____ , Slip Op. 85-40 (1985) 6 ITRD 2190.

V. STATUTE OF LIMITATIONS

When a fine, penalty, or forfeiture matter is referred to the U.S. attorney for enforcement, he must bring a civil action within five years after the time when the alleged offense was discovered, except in Section 592 cases not involving fraud. This is the statute of limitations on suits for penalties arising under the customs law provided in Section 621 of the Tariff Act of 1930.[26] A proviso was added to this statute by Section 110 of the 1978 Act to provide that in a case of alleged violation of Section 592 arising out of gross negligence or negligence an action shall not be instituted more than five years after the date the alleged violation was committed.

Aside from the partial Section 592 exception, the customs case time limit is more favorable to the enforcement of customs penalties than the general statute of limitations is to the enforcement of other civil fines, penalties, and forfeitures. The general statute[27] provides a limit of five years "from the date when the claim first accrued." (Both statutes exclude the time of absence from the United States of the person or property charged.) The customs enforcement time limit, thus, does not begin to run from the date of the alleged offense, which is when the claim accrues, but from the date of the discovery of the alleged offense. So if the falsity of an invoice covering merchandise entered July 1, 1975, is not discovered until July 1, 1981, the U.S. Government has until June 30, 1986, to bring suit to recover the value of that merchandise. See *United States* v. *Joan and David Halpern Co., Inc.,* 9 CIT _____ , Slip Op. 85-64 (1985) 6 ITRD 2491. The unavailability of old evidence would generally prevent prosecution of an action a great many years after an offense had been alleged to have been committed.

In a fraud penalty action the government must plead the facts relating to discovery. *United States* v. *Gordon,* 7 CIT _____ , Slip Op. 84–68 (1984) 5 ITRD 2501.

VI. AWARDS TO INFORMERS

Any person not an officer of the United States who furnishes original information to a U.S. attorney or a Treasury or customs officer concerning any fraud upon the customs revenue, or a violation of the customs or

---

[26] 19 U.S.C. 1621.
[27] 28 U.S.C. 2462.

navigation laws, which leads to a recovery of any duties withheld, or of any fine, penalty, or forfeiture incurred, may be paid by the Secretary of the Treasury a compensation of 25 percent of the net amount recovered, not to exceed $250,000 in any case.[28] When a vessel, vehicle, aircraft, merchandise, or baggage is forfeited to the United States and thereafter is disposed of otherwise than by sale, an informer may be awarded by the Secretary compensation of 25 percent of the appraised value of the article, subject to the same limitation.

Under Section 319(b) of the Comprehensive Crime Control Act of 1984, the Secretary of the Treasury may not delegate the authority to pay an award over $10,000 to an official below the level of the Commissioner of Customs.

The Court of Claims, however, has held that this award provision refers to the service of furnishing information rather than the number and value of recoveries affected thereby.[29] The court held that an informer who had furnished original information relative to various cases of customs law violations by 19 trading companies through the use of false invoices was entitled to an informer's award at the maximum of $50,000 under the statutory phrase "in any case," rather than the sum arrived at by taking a statutory 25 percent of recoveries against all 19 companies, limited to $50,000 for any one company. Provisions for the filing with customs officials of claims for awards, their payment, and the protection of informers' identities are contained in 19 CFR Part 161, Subpart B.

VII. CRIMINAL PENALTIES

A. Range of Customs Crimes

Import activities which constitute a fraud on the revenue are subject to criminal penalties enforced by the Department of Justice as well as to civil penalties enforced by the Customs Service, backed by the Department of Justice wherever civil litigation is required. The Federal Criminal Code contains 12 sections defining customs-related crimes.[30] Included are sections placing criminal penalties on entries of goods falsely classified or entered by means of false statements, on smuggling into the United States and into foreign countries, on relanding goods after export without entry, on removing or attaching customs seals without authority, on concealing or destroying invoices, books, and other import documents, and on false claims for refunds. An officer of the revenue may be penalized for exacting less than the legal duty or for aiding the importation of obscene, immoral, or treasonable material; and all customs officers are covered by the statute against bribery.[31]

---

[28]19 U.S.C. 1619, as amended by Section 213(a)(15) of the Trade and Tariff Act of 1984 to raise the prior maximum amount of $50,000 to $250,000, effective October 15, 1984. Section 319(a) of the Comprehensive Crime Control Act of 1984, effective October 12, 1984, raised the maximum award to $150,000.

[29]*Cornman v. United States,* 409 F.2d 230 (Ct.Cl. 1969), *cert. denied,* 396 U.S. 960 (1969).

[30]18 U.S.C. 541–552.

[31]18 U.S.C. 201.

B. Entry Under False Statement

The most important statute in customs criminal law enforcement is 18 U.S.C. 542 making it an offense to enter goods by means of a false invoice, declaration, or other false statement. It is the criminal law counterpart to the civil penalty statute, Section 592 of the Tariff Act of 1930, discussed *supra*. The Customs Service has found that alleged violations of 18 U.S.C. 542 "frequently involve complex legal and technical issues" and, consequently, internal legal review of such cases is desirable before the case is referred to the U.S. attorney for consideration of criminal prosecution.[32] To provide such internal review all criminal case reports concerning an alleged violation of 18 U.S.C. 542 are to be reviewed by the appropriate regional counsel of customs before referral to the U.S. attorney, unless there is an imminent running of the statute of limitations, in which event the case report is to go simultaneously to the regional counsel and the U.S. attorney.

---

[32]Customs Service Circular ENF-3-CC, June 10, 1975. See 19 CFR 161.3.

31

Judicial Review

I. THE COURTS OF REVIEW

In 1980 and 1982 the courts designated by the Congress to review customs and international trade questions were renamed, reconstituted, and invested with expanded jurisdiction and powers. The U.S. Customs Court became the U.S. Court of International Trade with the full powers of a U.S. district court by the Customs Courts Act of 1980, Public Law 96-417, effective generally on November 1, 1980.[1] The authority and functioning of this court, often referred to as the CIT, are discussed in sections II through VII *infra*.

Under the Federal Courts Improvement Act of 1982, Public Law 97-164, effective October 1, 1982,[2] a new appellate court named the Court of Appeals for the Federal Circuit (CAFC) began operations with the full powers of a U.S. circuit court. This court has jurisdiction of all appeals from the CIT, of appeals from certain administrative international trade decisions, patent and trademark decisions, and of a variety of other federal questions. The authority and functioning of this Court of Appeals are discussed in section VIII *infra*.

The Trade and Tariff Act of 1984, Public Law 98–573, enacted October 30, 1984, amended a number of the provisions defining the jurisdiction of the CIT, particularly with regard to the review of antidumping and countervailing duty administrative determinations, detailed in section VII *infra*.

---

[1] 94 Stat. 1727, 28 U.S.C. 251 *et seq.;* effective date amendment Pub. L. No. 96-542.
[2] Pub. L. No. 97-164, April 2, 1982, 96 Stat. 25, 28 U.S.C. 41 *et seq.*

II. THE U.S. COURT OF INTERNATIONAL TRADE

A. Clarification of Powers and Jurisdiction

A major purpose of the transformation of the Customs Court into the Court of International Trade, an Article III court under the U.S. Constitution, was to "create a comprehensive system of judicial review of civil actions arising from import transactions," and simultaneously to increase the effectiveness of judicial review by granting to the new court "all the powers in law and equity of, or as conferred by statute upon, a district court of the United States."[3]

Restatement and enlargement of the jurisdiction of the Customs Court were necessitated, first, because of the long-experienced confusion in jurisdiction between the Customs Court and the district courts over international trade matters, the latter having jurisdiction over cases not within the exclusive jurisdiction of the Customs Court. This confusion caused much wasted litigation, and loss of relief.[4] Secondly, changes were required because of the increased judicial review of trade issues provided for in the Trade Agreements Act of 1979,[5] without provision for implementing procedures. That Act also expanded the definition of interested persons with standing to sue on various import issues.[6]

B. Composition

Section 101 of Public Law 96-417 amended 28 U.S.C. 251 to provide that the President shall appoint, with the advice and consent of the Senate, nine judges to constitute the U.S. Court of International Trade, not more than five of whom shall be from the same political party. Further, the President was to appoint one judge under 70 years of age as chief judge, who might serve until he reached the age of 70. A single judge may exercise the power of the court. The continuation of the then judges of the Customs Court was assured by Section 703 of Public Law 96-417, which provided that the Act shall not affect their status, except for the 70-year age limit on the chief judgeship.

C. Location of Trials

The offices of the court are located in New York, N.Y., under Section 251(c) of Title 28. However, under Section 256, the chief judge may designate a judge or judges to preside at a trial or hearing at any port or place within the jurisdiction of the United States, or upon application of a

---

[3] S. Rep. No. 96-466 on S.1654, the Customs Courts Act of 1979, 96th Cong. 1st Sess. at 3.

[4] See, e.g., Thompson Toyota, Inc. v. Chasen, Civ. No. 80-2089 (DC DC 1980) 2 ITRD 1130; Flintkote Company v. United States, 596 F.2d 51 (CA 2 1979); Consumers Union of United States, Inc. v. Committee for Implementation of Textile Agreements, 561 F.2d 872, 1 ITRD 1602 (DC Cir.), cert. denied, 435 U.S. 933 (1977); SCM Corporation v. United States, 549 F.2d 812 (DC Cir. 1977) 1 ITRD 1594; Sneaker Circus, Inc. v. Carter, 566 F.2d 396 (CA 2 1977) 1 ITRD 1647.

[5] Pub. L. No. 96-39, July 26, 1979, 93 Stat. 146, 19 U.S.C. 2501 et seq.

[6] See, e.g., 19 U.S.C. 1516 and 1516a.

party or upon his own initiative and a showing that the interests of economy, efficiency, and justice will be served, the chief judge may issue an order authorizing a judge to preside in an evidentiary hearing in a foreign country which does not prohibit it. An appeal from such an order may be taken to the Court of Appeals for the Federal Circuit.

III. JURISDICTION AND STANDING TO SUE

The jurisdiction of the Court of International Trade is defined, as was that of the Customs Court, by specifying the civil actions of which the court has jurisdiction. The important changes lie in the increased number of specified actions enumerated in the amendment of 28 U.S.C. Chapter 95, made by Section 201 of the 1980 law and in the larger number of persons entitled to commence these actions described in the amendment of 28 U.S.C. 2631, made by Section 301 of that law.

The civil actions of which the new court has exclusive jurisdiction are set forth in Sections 1581, 1582, and 1583 of 28 U.S.C., as amended by Section 201 of Public Law 96-417.

A. Section 1581. Civil Actions Against the United States and Agencies and Officers Thereof

This section grants exclusive jurisdiction of nine classes of civil actions, designated in Subsections (a) through (i), and denies any jurisdiction, in Subsection (j), over any civil action arising under Section 305 of the Tariff Act of 1930. Section 305, 19 U.S.C. 1305, prohibits importation of immoral or subversive articles.

The persons who may bring the permitted nine types of civil actions are designated in the corresponding provisions of Subsections (a) through (i) of 28 U.S.C. 2631, and are therefore covered in this discussion of the nine permitted types of civil actions against the United States.

1. Contesting the Denial of a Protest: Sections 1581(a) and 2631(a)

Primary exclusive jurisdiction in the CIT, as in the Customs Court, is of a civil action commenced to contest the denial of a protest, in whole or in part, under Section 515 of the Tariff Act of 1930, 19 U.S.C. 1515. This action may be brought by the person who filed the protest against the customs decision under 19 U.S.C. 1514, or by a surety on the transaction which is the subject of the protest. The action may not contest any matter unrelated to the administrative decision protested. *Gray Tool Co.* v. *United States,* 6 CIT ____ (1983) 5 ITRD 1697. In this case the court ruled that a challenge to the protested valuation of the imports could not be enlarged to a challenge also to the classification of the imports which had not been protested.

The CIT took jurisdiction under Section 1581(a) of a challenge to the inclusion of frozen mushrooms (alleged not to be the subject of an ITC investigation of injury to the canned mushroom industry) in the President's Proclamation imposing import relief supplemental duties on certain mushrooms since the plaintiff had protested the imposition of the supplemental duties. *Maple Leaf Fish Co.* v. *United States,* 5 CIT 275, 566 F. Supp. 899 (1983) 4 ITRD 2173. A protest filed by the plaintiff prior to liquidation is premature and may not serve as the basis of jurisdiction under Section 1581(a). *Lowa, Ltd.* v. *United States,* 5 CIT 81, 561 F. Supp. 441 (1983) 4 ITRD 1900, *aff'd,* 727 F.2d 121 (Fed. Cir. 1984) 5 ITRD 1757.

2. Contesting the Denial of a Petition: Sections 1581(b) and 2631(b)

The CIT has exclusive jurisdiction of a civil action commenced under Section 516 of the Tariff Act of 1930, 19 U.S.C. 1516. Under Section 516, as amended by the Trade Agreements Act, any "interested party" may petition the Secretary of the Treasury to challenge the appraised value, the classification, or rate of duty of an import. The "interested party" may be a U.S. manufacturer, producer, or wholesaler of a like product, a representative union or business association of producers or wholesalers of such products, and under the amendment made by Section 612(a)(3) and (b)(1) of the Trade and Tariff Act of 1984, an association the majority of whose members is composed of the foregoing interested parties. This amendment added such an association as (F) to the definition of interested parties in 19 U.S.C. 1677(9) referred to in 19 U.S.C. 1514 and 1516. Any interested party who filed the petition may bring a civil action contesting an adverse determination by the Secretary.

3. Countervailing and Antidumping Duty Actions: Sections 1581(c) and 2631(c)

The CIT took the Customs Court's exclusive jurisdiction of civil actions seeking judicial review under the special provisions for review of preliminary and final countervailing and antidumping duty determinations by the International Trade Administration and the International Trade Commission, given by Section 516A of the Tariff Act (19 U.S.C. 1516a), which was added by Title X of the Trade Agreements Act. These special review provisions, as amended by the Trade and Tariff Act of 1984, are discussed in section VII *infra.* An action under Section 516A may be brought by any interested party who was a party to the administrative proceeding.

4. Adjustment Assistance Eligibility: Sections 1581(d) and 2631(d)

Transferred from the circuit courts of appeal to the new court was exclusive jurisdiction to review a final determination of the Secretary of Labor denying certification of eligibility of workers for adjustment assistance or a final determination of the Secretary of Commerce denying certification of eligibility for such assistance to a firm or a community. See Chapter 20. The action for review may be brought by the aggrieved party.

5. Buy American Exemption: Sections 1581(e) and 2631(e)

The CIT has exclusive jurisdiction of an action to review the final determination of the Secretary of the Treasury under Section 305(b)(1) of the Trade Agreements Act (19 U.S.C. 2515) of whether an imported article is the product of a country or instrumentality which the President has found eligible for the benefits of the MTN Government Procurement Code, as permitted by Section 301 of the Trade Agreements Act (19 U.S.C. 2511). An eligible foreign product is exempt from the application of the Buy American Act. The action may be commenced by any person who was a party in interest to the Secretary's determination.

6. Confidential Countervailing or Antidumping Duty Information: Sections 1581(f) and 2631(f)

The exclusive jurisdiction of the Customs Court, granted by Title X of the Trade Agreements Act, was continued in the new court to issue an order under Section 777(c)(2) of the Tariff Act of 1930 for protective disclosure of confidential information submitted by a party to a countervailing duty or antidumping proceeding. An action to obtain such an order may be brought by any interested party whose application for the information was denied.

In *American Spring Wire Corp.* v. *United States,* 4 CIT 210 (1982) 4 ITRD 1308, the CIT determined that the Trade Agreements Act intended that it have jurisdiction to review the treatment of confidential information by the ITC. In this case the court reviewed the propriety of the release by the ITC of the confidential information of countervailing duty petitioners, as well as the refusal of the ITC to release to the petitioners the ITC's confidential staff report.

7. Customs Broker's License Suspension or Revocation or Monetary Penalty: Sections 1581(g) and 2631(g)

Prior to the amendment of these sections by Section 212(b) of the Trade and Tariff Act of 1984, any civil action to review the denial, suspension, or revocation by the Secretary of the Treasury of a customhouse broker's license, under then-existing Section 641(a) or (b) of the Tariff Act (19 U.S.C. 1641 (a) or (b)), was within the exclusive jurisdiction of the new court. It might be brought by the person whose license was denied, suspended, or revoked. These provisions remain effective as to any proceeding brought prior to October 30, 1984, the effective date of the 1984 Act.

Section 212(a) of the 1984 Act amended the 1930 Tariff Act provisions on customhouse brokers, 19 U.S.C. 1641, to establish new license and permit provisions for customs brokers and to authorize the Secretary of the Treasury to impose monetary penalties as an alternative to the revocation or suspension of licenses. The jurisdictional provisions in 28 U.S.C. 1581(g) were accordingly amended to give exclusive jurisdiction to the CIT of any civil action to review any decision of the Secretary of the Treasury to deny or revoke or suspend a customs broker's license or permit or impose a monetary penalty in lieu thereof under various revised subsections of 19 U.S.C. 1641. The provisions concerning the persons entitled to bring the action were similarly revised, 28 U.S.C. 2631(g), to provide that a civil action to review any of the foregoing decisions of the Secretary of the Treasury may be commenced by the person whose license or permit was denied or revoked, or by the person against whom the decision revoking or suspending a license or permit or imposing a monetary penalty was issued.

8. Administrative Rulings: Sections 1581(h) and 2631(h)

The CIT has exclusive jurisdiction of any civil action commenced to review, prior to the importation of the goods involved, a ruling issued by the Secretary of the Treasury, or a refusal to issue or change such a ruling, relating to classification, valuation, rate of duty, marking, restricted merchandise, entry requirements, drawbacks, vessel repairs, or similar matters, but only if the party commencing the civil action demonstrates to the court that he would be irreparably harmed unless given an opportunity to obtain judicial review prior to such importation. This action may be brought by a person who could bring an action to contest the denial of a protest if he imported the goods involved and filed a protest which was denied.

Section 1581(h) does not provide jurisdiction to review a general administrative ruling or interpretative guidelines; the ruling must relate to specific importations of specific goods. *Pagoda Trading Co.* v. *United States,* 6 CIT ____, 577 F. Supp. 22 (1983) 5 ITRD 1628.

The CAFC affirmed a decision of the CIT, based upon the legislative history of Section 1581(h), that the term "ruling" did not include "internal advice" or a request for "further review" because both those procedures relate to completed import transactions. *American Air Parcel Forwarding Company, Ltd.* v. *United States,* 718 F.2d 1546 (Fed. Cir. 1983) 5 ITRD 1129, *aff'g* 5 CIT 8, 557 F. Supp. 605 (1983) 4 ITRD 1492.

However, in order to inform the public "of its right to judicial review," the Customs Service amended its regulations on requests for advice by importers, 19 CFR 177.11 to add Subsection (b)(8) providing that a refusal by Headquarters to consider the questions raised by an importer in a request for internal advice may be appealed to the CIT if he would be irreparably harmed without judicial review prior to the importation of the merchandise. TD 85-90, 50 FR 21431, May 24, 1985.

9. Other Revenue, Tariff, or Quota Laws, and Enforcement Generally: Sections 1581(i) and 2631(i)

The foregoing specific jurisdictional provisions are followed by a broad grant of exclusive jurisdiction over questions arising from revenue, tariff, and trade restriction laws, and customs administration generally. This grant reads as follows:

[T]he Court of International Trade shall have exclusive jurisdiction of any civil action commenced against the United States, its agencies, or its officers, that arises out of any law of the United States providing for—

(1) revenue from imports or tonnage;

(2) tariffs, duties, fees, or other taxes on the importation of merchandise for reasons other than the raising of revenue;

(3) embargoes or other quantitative restrictions on the importation of merchandise for reasons other than the protection of the public health or safety; or

(4) administration and enforcement with respect to the matters referred to in paragraphs (1)-(3) of this subsection and subsections (a)-(h) of this section.

Such a civil action may be commenced by any person adversely affected or aggrieved by agency action within the meaning of Section 702 of Title 5 (5 U.S.C. 702), a provision of the original Administrative Procedure Act. This broad residual grant of jurisdiction was evidently designed to assure that the new court, rather than the district courts, takes jurisdiction of any justiciable action challenging the administration of laws affecting import trade.

a. Jurisdiction Accepted

Among the cases in which jurisdiction has been accepted under this residual provision are:

(1) Actions challenging the reduction of textile quotas and the exclusion of merchandise under textile quota restrictions, *Sanho Collections Ltd.* v. *Chasen,* 1 CIT 6, 505 F. Supp. 204 (1980) 2 ITRD 1374; *Wear Me Apparel Corporation* v. *United States,* 1 CIT 194, 511 F. Supp. 814 (1981) 2 ITRD 1385; *American Association of Exporters and Importers (TAG)* v. *United States,* 7 CIT ____ , 583 F. Supp. 591 (1984) 5 ITRD 1891, and the President's authority to impose fees and quotas on sugar, *U.S. Cane Sugar Refiners' Association* v. *Block,* 69 CCPA 172, 683 F.2d 399 (1982) 3 ITRD 2121;

(2) An action to recover supplemental duties paid under Proclamation 4074 imposing a 10 percent duty surcharge, *International Fashions* v. *Buchanan,* 2 CIT 321, 543 F. Supp. 828 (1981) 3 ITRD 1398;

(3) An action to enjoin the Customs Service from denying the plaintiff's immediate delivery privilege and from refusing to accept documentation with uncertified checks, *American Air Parcel Forwarding Co., Ltd.* v. *United States,* 1 CIT 293, 515 F. Supp. 47 (1981) 2 ITRD 1497;

(4) An action challenging the denial of a customhouse cartman's license, *Di Jub Leasing Corp.* v. *United States,* 1 CIT 42, 505 F. Supp. 1113 (1980) 2 ITRD 1236; *United States* v. *Bar Bea Truck Leasing Co., Inc.,* 713 F.2d 1563 (Fed. Cir. 1983) 4 ITRD 2369;

(5) An action to enjoin disclosure of confidential information submitted by foreign steel producers to the Commerce Department, *Sacilor, Acieries et Laminoirs de Lorraine* v. *United States,* 3 CIT 191, 542 F. Supp. 1020 (1982) 3 ITRD 2225;

(6) An action seeking a mandamus order to require the ITA to reduce the estimated countervailing duties imposed under a CVD order, since the

denial of a reduction is not an ITA determination subject to review under 19 U.S.C. 1516a and 28 U.S.C. 1581(c). *Ceramica Regiomontana, S.A.* v. *United States,* 5 CIT 23, 557 F. Supp. 596 (1983) 4 ITRD 1441;

(7) An action by a trademark owner for a mandatory order directing the Customs Service to exclude from entry "gray market goods" bearing owner's trademark, imported without his consent. *Vivitar Corporation* v. *United States,* 7 CIT ____ , 585 F. Supp. 1415 (1984) 5 ITRD 2030;

(8) An action contesting the President's designation of GSP status for man-made fiber flat goods covered by the international textile agreement known as the Multi-Fiber Arrangement, *Luggage and Leather Goods Manufacturers of America, Inc.* v. *United States,* 7 CIT ____ , 588 F. Supp. 1413 (1984) 5 ITRD 2201;

(9) An action for review of a Commerce Department letter ruling excluding a personal electronic computer from an antidumping duty order covering personal electronic typewriters, which ruling would not be subject to a Section 751 administrative review or court review under Section 516A of the Tariff Act of 1930. *Smith-Corona Group, SCM Corporation* v. *United States,* 8 CIT ____ , 593 F. Supp. 415 (1984) 6 ITRD 1241. Section 516A has since been amended by the Trade and Tariff Act of 1984 to provide for a timely review of a determination by the Commerce Department as to whether a particular kind of merchandise is covered by an antidumping order. See section VII.A *infra.*

(10) An action to compel Customs to render a decision on an applicant's four-year-old application for a customs broker's license. *Allen* v. *Regan,* 9 CIT ____ , 607 F. Supp. 133 (1985) 6 ITRD 2120.

b. Jurisdiction Denied

However, as pointed out in the *International Fashions* and other cases cited *supra,* the residual provision is not all inclusive of matters concerning importations and international trade but is limited to the four specifically enumerated areas. Accordingly, the Court of International Trade has rejected jurisdiction of a number of actions brought under Section 1531(i), including:

(1) The complaints of tortious government action included in the *Bar Bea Truck Leasing Co.* case *supra;*

(2) An action brought by the United States for tonnage duties, *United States* v. *Biehl & Company,* 3 CIT 158, 539 F. Supp. 1218 (1982) 3 ITRD 1881;

(3) Any challenge to an administrative action which may be reviewed as part of a final agency action appealable under a specific jurisdictional grant. Thus, for example, a challenge under Section 1581(i) to a Customs Service ruling on country-of-origin marking was rejected as the merits could be determined on review of a denial of a protest under Section 1581(a). *United States* v. *Uniroyal, Inc.,* 69 CCPA 179, 687 F.2d 467 (1982) 3 ITRD 2265. This ruling was followed in the *American Air Parcel Forwarding Company* decisions of the CIT and CAFC, cited in subsection 8 *supra,* rejecting jurisdiction under Section 1581(i) of a challenge to the lawfulness of a

change by the Customs Service in the basis of its valuation of the plaintiff's importations because the plaintiff failed to exhaust its administrative remedy of protest under 19 U.S.C. 1514, with court review thereafter under 28 U.S.C. 1581(a). Also, a challenge under Section 1581(i) of a Commerce Department failure to grant a disclosure conference in a review of an antidumping duty order was rejected on the ground that the Department's interlocutory decision would be considered a part of any judicial review of the final determination. *PPG Industries, Inc.* v. *United States,* 2 CIT 110, 525 F. Supp. 883 (1981) 3 ITRD 1304.

(4) An action for return of imported merchandise alleged to be wrongfully seized by the Customs Service, *Hector Rivera Siaca* v. *United States,* 7 CIT _____ , Slip Op. 84-5 (1984) 5 ITRD 1812, *rehearing denied,* 7 CIT _____ , 585 F. Supp. 668 (1984), *aff'd,* 754 F.2d 988 (Fed. Cir. 1985) 6 ITRD 1803.

In exceptional circumstances where the exhaustion of administrative remedies through proceeding by protest and appeal under Section 1581(a) would be a useless formality, particularly where the Customs Service would be foreclosed from granting relief from the Presidential Proclamation challenged, the CIT will accept jurisdiction under Section 1581(i). *United States Cane Sugar Refiners' Association* v. *Block,* 3 CIT 196, 544 F. Supp. 883 (1982) 3 ITRD 1963, *aff'd,* 69 CCPA 172, 683 F.2d 399 (1982) 3 ITRD 2121. In its opinion the CCPA noted that the delay in relief through proceeding by protest and appeal in the special circumstances of the case, involving irreparable harm to an industry and substantial impact on the national economy, made that remedy manifestly inadequate.

If the Court of International Trade does not have jurisdiction of an action under Section 1581(i) or other specific subsection of Section 1581, it does not acquire subject matter jurisdiction from Section 1585, giving the CIT the powers of a district court in law and equity, nor from 5 U.S.C. 702. *Kidco, Inc.* v. *United States,* 4 CIT 103 (1982) 4 ITRD 1071.

B. Section 1582. Civil Actions Commenced by the United States

Prior to Public Law 96-417 the United States brought suit on customs, as on other, matters exclusively in the U.S. district courts, under 28 U.S.C. 1345. The exclusive jurisdiction now given to the Court of International Trade over civil actions commenced by the United States is defined as those arising out of an import transaction and brought for one of the purposes discussed below.

1. Action To Recover a Civil Penalty Under Section 592, and Other Provisions of the Tariff Act of 1930

Section 592, 19 U.S.C. 1592, is the statute providing for penalties for fraud, gross negligence, and negligence in the entry of merchandise which was extensively revised by the Customs Procedural Reform and Simplification Act of 1978, Public Law 95-410, with provisions governing civil actions for recovery of penalties in the U.S. district courts. See Chapter 30. Section

609 of Public Law 96-417 transferred those proceedings to the Court of International Trade.

After some uncertainty as to its jurisdiction over actions brought on fraudulent entries made prior to the 1978 Act when the civil penalty was exclusively an *in rem* forfeiture proceeding, the CIT determined that 28 U.S.C. 1582 gave it exclusive jurisdiction of *any* civil action by the United States to recover a civil penalty under Section 592, either before or after its amendment in 1978. *United States* v. *Accurate Mould Co., Ltd.,* 4 CIT 81, 546 F. Supp. 567 (1982) 3 ITRD 2337, overruling *United States* v. *Digital Equipment Corp.,* 3 CIT 52 (1982) 3 ITRD 1763.

An action brought by the United States in the CIT to recover a penalty under 19 U.S.C. 1592 for false entry does not prevent the Customs Service from obtaining a summons in the federal district court requiring the importer to produce financial records for the investigation of the entry. *United States* v. *Frowein,* 727 F.2d 277 (CA 2 1984) 5 ITRD 1801.

Other provisions of the Tariff Act of 1930 originally specified under Section 1582(1) were Sections 704(i)(2) or 734(i)(2), identified *infra.* To these were added by the amendment made by Section 212(b)(2) of the Trade and Tariff Act of 1984, Section 641(d)(2)(A) of the Tariff Act of 1930, as amended by Section 212(a) of the 1984 Act.

Section 641(d)(2)(A) provides procedures for imposition by the Customs Service of a monetary penalty upon a customs broker, where no action to revoke or suspend his license has been taken, and after the conclusion of consideration by the Secretary of the Treasury of any petition for remission or mitigation of the penalty under 19 U.S.C. 1618.

Section 704(i)(2), 19 U.S.C. 1671c(i)(2), provides that any person who intentionally violates an agreement to eliminate subsidies or their injurious effect approved in a countervailing duty proceeding shall be subject to a penalty assessed under the same procedure as a Section 592 penalty.

Section 734(i)(2), 19 U.S.C. 1673c(i)(2), provides for the same penalty assessment in the event of intentional violation of an agreement to eliminate sales at less than fair value or their injurious effect approved in an antidumping proceeding.

*2. Action To Recover Upon a Bond Relating to the Importation
   of Merchandise Required by U.S. Law or by the Secretary
   of the Treasury*

The CIT held that it did not have jurisdiction under this paragraph of an action brought by the United States to recover under the bond of a shipowner's agent additional tonnage taxes and light money alleged to be due on the entry of a vessel, for the reason that the action did not arise out of an import transaction and the bond did not relate to the importation of merchandise. *United States* v. *Biehl & Company,* 3 CIT 158, 539 F. Supp. 1218 (1982) 3 ITRD 1881.

3. *Action To Recover Customs Duties*

This explicit jurisdiction has no statutory antecedent.

C. Section 1583. Counterclaims, Cross-Claims, and Third-Party Actions

Exclusive jurisdiction is given to the court to render judgment in any civil action upon any counterclaim, cross-claim, or third-party action of any party, if (1) the claim or action involves the imported merchandise that is the subject of the civil action, or (2) the claim or action is to recover upon a bond or customs duties relating to such merchandise. Counterclaims based upon the Federal Torts Claim Act or the Tucker Act are outside the jurisdiction of the CIT. *United States* v. *Federal Insurance Co.,* 6 CIT ____ , (1983) 5 ITRD 1625.

Under this section the CIT provided relief in a surety's cross-claim and third-party action seeking indemnification on an import bond upon which the United States brought action for liquidated damage penalties. *United States* v. *Saul Mizrahie and Safeco Insurance Co. of America,* and *Safeco Insurance Co. of America* v. *Rebecca Mizrahie,* 9 CIT ____ , 606 F. Supp. 703 (1985) 6 ITRD 2085.

Section 1583 is a new provision since the Customs Court could not entertain counterclaims.[7] The Senate Report on this legislation points out that under this new jurisdiction the court will be able to require a plaintiff, who proves that the valuation of his merchandise was incorrect, to pay duties on a higher valuation if the United States demonstrates that such alternative valuation is correct.[8]

D. Transfers of Jurisdiction

Section 1584, repealed by Section 135 of Public Law 97-164, had directed the U.S. district court in which a civil action is commenced, which is within the exclusive jurisdiction of the Court of International Trade, to transfer the action to that court. Likewise, the section directed the Court of International Trade to transfer to a U.S. district court, a court of appeals, or the Court of Customs and Patent Appeals, as appropriate, a civil action not within its own exclusive jurisdiction. These transfer provisions are superseded by Section 1631, entitled "Transfer to cure want of jurisdiction," added to Title 28 of the U.S. Code by Section 301 of Public Law 97-164. Section 1631 directs any U.S. court, if in the interest of justice, to transfer any civil action or appeal filed with it of which it does not have jurisdiction to a court where it could have been brought, there to proceed as from the date of filing in the original court.

---

[7] S. Rep. No. 96-466, *supra* note 2 at 12–13.
[8] *Ibid.* at 13.

IV. PROCEDURE

A. Extent of Change

Section 301 of Title III, Procedure, of Public Law 96–417 rewrote the provisions on procedure governing the Customs Court, Chapter 169 of Title 28, U.S.C., and expanded the provisions to encompass the multiplicity of actions of which the Court of International Trade has exclusive jurisdiction. Chapter 169 of Title 28 now includes 17 sections—2631 through 2647—which are too detailed to restate here, and which require close examination by the practitioner. The court incorporated and implemented many of these provisions in its rules. The major provisions are described below.

Section 302 amended Chapter 121 of Title 28, U.S.C., "Juries; Trial by Jury," to allow for trials by jury in the new court.

B. Pretrial Procedure

1. Section 2631. Persons Entitled to Commence a Civil Action and to Intervene

The persons described in Section 2631(a) through (i) who are entitled to bring the civil actions described in the amended Section 1581(a) through (i) of Title 28, U.S.C., have been identified in the discussion of Section 1581 in section III.A *supra.*

Section 2631(j) designates the persons who may intervene in a pending civil action, by leave of court. Any person who would be adversely affected or aggrieved by the court's decision may do so, with three exceptions: (A) no person may intervene in an action contesting the denial of a protest or a petition; (B) in a countervailing or antidumping duty action only an interested party who was a party to the proceeding in issue may intervene, and he may do so as a matter of right; and (C) in an action for disclosure of confidential countervailing or antidumping duty information only a party to the investigation may intervene, and he may do so as a matter of right.

Exception (B) was construed and applied in *Matsushita Electric Industrial Co., Ltd.* v. *United States,* 2 CIT 254, 529 F. Supp. 664 (1981) 3 ITRD 1295, denying motions to intervene in an action challenging an affirmative injury antidumping determination of the ITC. The court found that the applicant intervenor COMPACT, a group of 14 concerned industries and unions, did not meet any of the definitions of an "interested party" in the antidumping law, that applicant Imports Committee, a group of electronic manufacturers, did not have a majority of members producing a "like product" as required by the "interested party" definition, and that the applicant three unions were disqualified as not being parties to the proceeding. It concluded that the term "party" was limited to those who have an independent and unitary participation in the administrative proceeding.

In a subsequent action for judicial review of an ITA antidumping finding both COMPACT and the Imports Committee were disqualified as plaintiffs. *Zenith Radio Corp.* v. *United States,* 5 CIT 155 (1983) 4 ITRD 1950. The court stated that standing to bring actions under Section 516A of the Tariff Act of 1930 and standing to intervene in them are exactly the same.

The class of persons having standing to bring countervailing and antidumping duty actions was broadened by the amendment of the definition of "interested party" in Section 771(9) of the Tariff Act of 1930 made by Section 612(a)(3) of the Trade and Tariff Act of 1984. The amendment added a class (F), being "an association, a majority of whose members is composed of interested parties described in subparagraph (C), (D), or (E)," the parties interested in a like domestic product. The purpose of the amendment was to overturn the CIT decision in the 1981 *Matsushita Electric Industrial Co.* case, discussed *supra.*

2. *Section 2632. Commencement of a Civil Action*

The general rule is that an action is commenced by the concurrent filing with the clerk of the court of a summons and complaint in the form and style prescribed by the rules of the court. The exceptions are two: (1) a civil action contesting the denial of a protest or petition, and (2) a countervailing or antidumping duty action for review of a determination on the record, as listed in Section 516A(a)(2) of the Tariff Act of 1930. In these exceptional cases the action is commenced by filing of a summons only. When any action is commenced, an Information Statement, Form 5, must be filed under the court's rules.

3. *Section 2633. Procedure and Fees*

The court's rules on filing fees under this section require a $50 filing fee to be paid to the clerk of the court when an action is commenced, except that a $10 filing fee is to be paid when the action contests a denial of a protest or petition under 28 U.S.C. 1581(a) or (b). In such an action a $25 fee is to be paid when the complaint is filed.

4. *Section 2635. Filing of Official Documents*

This section specifies the particular documents to be produced by the government following service of summons, with or without complaint, in civil actions contesting the denial of a protest or petition, in a countervailing or antidumping duty action, in an action for disclosure of confidential information, and in any other action in which review is based upon the agency record.

5. *Section 2636. Time for Commencement of Action*

This section specifies the time limits within which the nine types of action must be brought, ranging from 10 days after the denial of confidential information to 2 years after a cause of action accrues under the general jurisdiction given the court by Section 1581(i) of Title 28 U.S.C., discussed in section III.A *supra*.

As to the effect of the two-year limitation for Section 1581(i) causes of action arising prior to the enactment of Section 2636, the decisions of the CIT conflict. Cf. *International Fashions* v. *Buchanan*, 2 CIT 321, 543 F. Supp. 828 (1981) 3 ITRD 1398, and *O'Hare Services, Inc.* v. *United States*, 3 CIT 77 (1982) 3 ITRD 1927.

6. Section 2637. Exhaustion of Administrative Remedies

Under Section 2637 an action to contest the denial of a protest may be commenced only if all liquidated duties, charges, or exactions have been paid, and an action to contest the denial of a petition may be brought only by a person who has exhausted his administrative remedies under 19 U.S.C. 1516. An action to review an administrative ruling may be brought under 28 U.S.C. 1581(h) only if the plaintiff demonstrates the irreparable harm required by the section. The court is to require the exhaustion of administrative remedies in other actions where appropriate. See discussion of *United States* v. *Uniroyal, Inc.* in section III.A.9.b *supra*.

C. Trial Procedure

1. Section 2639. Burden of Proof; Evidence of Value

Except in civil actions brought by the United States, the decision of the Secretary of the Treasury or the administering authority (the International Trade Administration) or the International Trade Commission is presumed to be correct in actions to contest the denial of a protest or petition or to challenge a decision in a countervailing or antidumping duty proceeding. The burden of proving otherwise rests upon the challenger.

This statutory presumption of the correctness of the Customs Service's classification does not apply where the classification encompasses multiple categories under one TSUS provision, and is thus an "equivocation." Historically, the importer needed to prove the correctness of the classification he urged. *United States* v. *Miracle Exclusives, Inc.*, 69 CCPA 42, 668 F.2d 498 (1981) 3 ITRD 1497, *aff'g Miracle Exclusives, Inc.* v. *United States*, 1 CIT 158, 516 F. Supp. 33 (1981) 2 ITRD 1348. Since the CAFC decision in *Jarvis Clark Co.* v. *United States*, 733 F.2d 873 (Fed. Cir. 1984) 5 ITRD 2137, the plaintiff need prove only the incorrectness of the government's classification. The CIT will decide the correct classification or remand the matter to the Customs Service.

Where the value of merchandise is in issue, reports or depositions of U.S. officials and depositions and affidavits of other persons not reasonably able to attend may be admitted into evidence when served upon the opposing party. Price lists and catalogs, duly authenticated, relevant and material, may also be admitted into evidence.

2. Section 2640. Scope and Standard of Review

a. Trial de Novo

Subsection (a) requires the Court of International Trade to make its determination "upon the basis of the record made before the court" in the following categories of actions:

(1) To contest the denial of a protest under 19 U.S.C. 1515;

(2) To contest the denial of a petition under 19 U.S.C. 1516;

(3) To review a final determination of the Secretary of the Treasury on the eligibility of a foreign article for Buy American exemption under Section 305(b)(1) of the Trade Agreements Act of 1979;

(4) To obtain an order for protective disclosure of confidential information in a countervailing or antidumping duty proceeding under 19 U.S.C. 1677f(c);

(5) To review any decision of the Secretary of the Treasury under Section 641 of the Tariff Act of 1930 with the exception of decisions under Section 641(d)(2)(B) (concerning revocation or suspension of a license or permit), which are governed by Subsection (d) of Section 2640, applying to other civil actions. This paragraph incorporates the amendment made by Section 212(b)(5) of the Trade and Tariff Act of 1984;

(6) Commenced by the United States to make the recoveries specified under Section 1582.

b. Countervailing and Antidumping Duty Actions

Court review is to be provided in accordance with Section 516A(b) of the Tariff Act of 1930, 19 U.S.C. 1516a(b). See section VII *infra.*

c. Adjustment Assistance Eligibility

Court review is to be provided in accordance with Section 284 of the Trade Act of 1974, 19 U.S.C. 2395, added by Section 613 of Public Law 96-417. This section provides for review of the determination made by the Secretary of Labor or by the Secretary of Commerce upon the basis of the administrative record. The Secretary's findings of fact are to be conclusive, if supported by substantial evidence.

d. Other Civil Action

Court review is to be provided in accordance with the judicial review provisions of the Administrative Procedure Act, 5 U.S.C. 706. These provisions call for judicial review on the basis of the agency record. Where the record before the CIT is inadequate or incomplete, the court will hold proceedings in abeyance until the appropriate customs officer transmits the essential documents and information. *Bar Bea Truck Leasing Co., Inc.* v. *United States,* 4 CIT 138 (1982) 4 ITRD 1060.

3. Section 2641. Witnesses; Inspection of Documents

a. Trial Proceedings

Except as otherwise provided by law, each party shall have an opportunity to introduce evidence, to hear and cross-examine the other party's witnesses, and to inspect samples and papers offered as evidence. The Federal Rules of Evidence are to apply to all actions except as provided in Section 2639(b) or the rules of the court. Section 2639(b) provides that in actions challenging an administrative ruling the plaintiff has the burden of demonstration of irreparable harm by clear and convincing evidence.

b. Confidential Information

The court may order disclosure, under prescribed terms and conditions, of trade secrets, confidential and privileged commercial or financial information, or information from foreign governments or persons. This provision restates decisional law of the Customs Court.[9]

4. Section 2642. Analysis of Imported Merchandise

The court may order an analysis of imported merchandise and reports thereon by laboratories and U.S. agencies.

D. Trial by Jury

Provisions for a trial by jury in the Court of International Trade are added by Section 302 of Public Law 96-417 to the provisions for jury trials in the U.S. district courts in 28 U.S.C. Chapter 121. A new Section 1876 entitled "Trial by jury in the Court of International Trade" is added at the end of the chapter. It provides that the jury is to be selected in accordance with the chapter provisions and under the procedures set forth in the jury selection plan of the district court for the judicial district in which the case is to be tried.

When the Court of International Trade conducts a jury trial the clerk of the district court for the district in which the court is sitting, or an authorized deputy, is to act as clerk of the court for summoning and selecting the jurors. The qualifications for, and compensation of, the jurors are to be the same as for U.S. district court jurors. The provisions in Section 1862 against discrimination on account of race, color, religion, sex, national origin, or economic status are expressly made applicable. Each party in the civil action may challenge jurors in accordance with the provision for civil case challenges in Section 1870.

---

[9]S. Rep. No. 94-466, *supra* note 3 at 20. For decisions by the Court of International Trade on disclosure of confidential information see, *e.g.: COMPACT* v. *United States,* 3 CIT 59 (1982) 3 ITRD 1777, and 3 CIT 60 (1982) 3 ITRD 1778; *National Latex Products Co.* v. *United States,* 3 CIT 49 (1982) 3 ITRD 1794; *ARBED S.A.* v. *United States,* 4 CIT 132 (1982) 3 ITRD 2369.

A motion for a jury trial was conditionally granted in *United States* v. *Priority Products, Inc.,* 10 CIT ____ , 615 F. Supp. 593 (1985) 7 ITRD 1144.

V. JUDGMENTS AND ORDERS

A. Relief Authorized Under Section 2643

1. Money Judgment

The court may enter a money judgment for or against the United States in any civil action brought under 28 U.S.C. 1581 or 1582 (see section III *supra*), and for or against the United States or any other party in any counterclaim, cross-claim, or third-party action under 28 U.S.C. 1583. The United States may obtain a default judgment in an action for penalties assessed under Section 592 of the Tariff Act of 1930 where the defendant has not responded to the complaint or motion. *United States* v. *Servitex, Inc.,* 3 CIT 65, 535 F. Supp. 695 (1982) 3 ITRD 1855.

This provision for money judgment changes preexisting law in two major respects:[10] (1) If the judgment is in favor of the importer, the judgment will be paid as any other judgment against the United States, thus avoiding the previous procedure of return of the papers to the Customs Service for reliquidation of the entry; (2) the Customs Court could not enter a money judgment in favor of the United States. The Court of International Trade must be able to do so as it has jurisdiction of counterclaims of the United States and of actions brought by the United States to recover fines and penalties, duties, and obligations under bonds.

2. Retrial or Remand

If on the basis of the evidence presented in any civil action the court is unable to determine the correct decision, it may order a retrial or rehearing or such further administrative or adjudicative procedures as it deems necessary. This provision permits the court to remand a classification or valuation case to the Customs Service for a correct decision instead of dismissing the case where the importer has proved the classification or valuation made to be incorrect but has been unable to prove the correct decisions.[11]

3. Other Relief; Injunctions, etc.

In accord with a major purpose of Public Law 96-417, the court has a general grant of authority to issue or order any form of appropriate relief; *i.e.,* declaratory judgments, orders of remand, injunctions, and writs of mandamus and prohibition, with the following three exceptions:

---

[10]*Ibid.* at 20.
[11]*Ibid.* at 20. For remand decisions see Chapter 9, section V *supra*.

(1) No injunction or writ of mandamus may issue in any action challenging the decision of the Secretary of Labor or of Commerce on certification of eligibility for adjustment assistance.

(2) In an action seeking disclosure of confidential countervailing or antidumping duty information the court may issue an order of disclosure only with respect to the information requested.

(3) In an action challenging an administrative ruling the court may order only declaratory relief.

The Court of International Trade refused to issue an extraordinary writ under the All Writs Act to require the ITC to continue terminated antidumping and countervailing duty investigations, where there was no threat to the court's jurisdiction and no demonstration that the possibility of relief was precluded. *U.S. Steel Corp.* v. *United States,* 3 CIT 106 (1982) 3 ITRD 1929.

4. Relief to a Surety

In an action by a surety he may recover only the amount of the liquidated duties, charges, or exactions paid on the entries included in the action. Any excess of recovery is to be paid to the importer.

A surety may, however, in a cross-claim and third-party action obtain a writ of attachment on California real estate, in accordance with state law to protect recovery upon its claim, under the equity powers of the CIT. *United States* v. *Saul Mizrahie and Safeco Insurance Company of America,* and *Safeco Insurance Company of America* v. *Rebecca Mizrahie,* 9 CIT _____ , 606 F. Supp. 703 (1985) 6 ITRD 2085.

B. Interest

Under Section 2644 if a plaintiff in an action contesting the denial of a protest obtains monetary relief by a judgment or under a stipulation agreement, interest is to be allowed at an annual rate established under Section 6621 of the Internal Revenue Code, 26 U.S.C. 6621, which is based on the prime interest rate. This provision for interest follows upon the provision for a money judgment in Section 2643(a). It is not affected by the revised provision on interest in other federal courts, 28 U.S.C. 1961, made by Section 302 of Public Law 97-164, which applies the current Treasury coupon issue yield.

The interest runs from the date of the summons filed in the protest action covered by the judgment order. For the information of the Customs Service, which determines the amount of interest to be paid upon reliquidation, the date of the summons should be included in the judgment order.

The Customs Service determined in TD 85-93, 50 FR 21832, May 29, 1985, to apply the compounding of interest provisions in 26 U.S.C. 6622 to the refund of duties allowed under 28 U.S.C. 2644, in order to establish consistency with the provisions for interest on overpayments and underpayments of antidumping and countervailing duties enacted in Section 621 of the Trade and Tariff Act of 1984 (19 U.S.C. 1671), which Customs found in TD 85-93 to require compounding of interest under 26 U.S.C. 6622.

C. Decisions

A final decision in a contested action or a decision granting an injunction must, under Section 2645, be supported by (1) a statement of findings of fact and conclusions of law, or (2) an opinion stating the reasons and facts upon which the decision is based. After judgment the court may amend its findings and the decision and judgment, upon motion of a party or upon its own motion, made not later than 30 days after entry of the judgment.

Under Subsection (c), as amended by Section 141 of Public Law 97-164, a court decision is final and conclusive unless a retrial or rehearing is granted under Section 2646 or an appeal is taken to the Court of Appeals for the Federal Circuit "by filing a notice of appeal with the Clerk of the Court of International Trade within the time and in the manner prescribed for appeals to United States courts of appeals from the United States district courts."

D. Powers in Law and Equity

The judicial power of the court is summed up in new Section 1585 of Title 28 U.S.C., which provides that the Court of International Trade "shall possess all powers in law and equity of, or as conferred by statute upon, a district court of the United States."

VI. PRECEDENCE OF CASES

Section 2647 of Title 28 U.S.C., as amended by Public Law 98-573, Section 623(b), provided that among the actions pending before it the court was to give precedence to, and expedite in every way, the following civil actions:

(1) An action involving the exclusion of perishable merchandise or the redelivery of such merchandise;

(2) An action contesting the denial of a protest involving the exclusion or redelivery of merchandise;

(3) An action commenced under Section 516 or 516A of the Tariff Act of 1930.

These precedence requirements were eliminated by Section 1657 of Title 28 U.S.C., added by Section 401(a) of Public Law 98–620, November 8, 1984. Section 1657 provides that notwithstanding any other provision of law each U.S. court is to determine the order in which civil actions are heard and determined, with four expediting requirements, two of which are applicable to import litigation. One is any action for a temporary or preliminary injunction. The second is any action if good cause is shown. Good cause is shown if a right under the U.S. Constitution or a federal statute (including the Freedom of Information Act) "would be maintained in a factual context that indicates that a request for expedited consideration has merit." The U.S. Judicial Conference is given authority to modify court priority rules to establish consistency among the judicial circuits.

VII. JUDICIAL REVIEW OF COUNTERVAILING AND ANTIDUMPING DUTY DETERMINATIONS—"SECTION 516A"

A. Determinations Subject to Review

Specific provisions for extensive judicial review of preliminary and final administrative determinations in countervailing and antidumping proceedings were enacted in Title X of the Trade Agreements Act of 1979. This title added Section 516A to the Tariff Act of 1930, 19 U.S.C. 1516a, to correlate judicial review provisions with the revised provisions for countervailing and antidumping duty determinations made in the new Title VII of the Tariff Act of 1930, added by Title I of the Trade Agreements Act. See Chapters 12 and 13. Judicial review of these proceedings is placed in the exclusive jurisdiction of the Court of International Trade under Section 1581(c) of Title 28 U.S.C., as amended by Section 201 of Public Law 96-47.

Prior to the enactment of the Trade and Tariff Act of 1984, Public Law 98-573,[12] Section 516A(a) divided the administrative determinations which were subject to judicial review into two groups: (1) "certain determinations," which were five initial or preliminary determinations, and (2) "determinations on record," which were five determinations which were either final or halting of the proceedings. Section 608 of Public Law 96-417 further subdivided the first group, "certain determinations" into those allowed a 30-day review initiation period, (A), and those allowed only a 10-day review initiation period, (B).

Section 623(a) of the Trade and Tariff Act of 1984 eliminated judicial review of the two administering agency interlocutory determinations which had been listed under (1)(B), the 10-day review initiation period. These were determinations in countervailing or antidumping duty cases: (i) that the case was extraordinarily complicated (Section 703(c) or 733(c), 19 U.S.C. 1671b(c) or 1673b(c)), and (ii) a negative preliminary determination (Sections 703(b) or 733(b), 19 U.S.C. 1671b(b) or 1673b(b)). As stated in the House Committee Print, WMCP 98-39 at 33, all challenges to agency determinations "would be combined and reviewable by the court after final agency action has been taken."

Section 623(a) also eliminated judicial review of certain determinations not to undertake an administrative review under Section 751(b) of the Tariff Act due to changed circumstances. These were a determination by the administering authority not to review an affirmative determination described in Section 751(b), or by either the administering authority or the commission not to review an agreement under which an investigation was suspended.

---

[12]Act of October 30, 1984, 98 Stat. 2948.

The 1984 provisions continued the division of reviewable determinations in Section 516A(a) between (1) "Review of Certain Determinations," to be initiated by filing concurrently a summons and complaint, and (2)(B) "Reviewable Determinations" (formerly entitled "Review of determinations on record"), to be initiated by filing a summons, and within 30 days thereafter a complaint. The list of remaining determinations subject to review under (1) or (2)(B) remained basically the same, with clarifications in (2)(B) designed to meet problems found in litigation.

However, Section 623(a) eliminated from both review listings all of the determinations made under Section 303 (19 U.S.C. 1303), the former countervailing duty act still applicable to countries not under the Subsidies Agreement. Presumably, Section 303 cases will be subject to review under the residual court jurisdiction in 28 U.S.C. 1581(i). Further, a sixth type of determination was added to the list of reviewable determinations under (2)(B). This was a determination by the administering authority "as to whether a particular type of merchandise is within the class or kind of merchandise described in an existing finding of dumping or antidumping or countervailing duty order."

As amended by Section 623(a), the lists of determinations subject to review read as set forth below.

1. "Certain Determinations" and Their Commencement

Provisions concerning the first division of determinations are as follows:

(1) REVIEW OF CERTAIN DETERMINATIONS.—Within 30 days after the date of publication in the Federal Register of—

(A) a determination by the administering authority, under 702(c), or 732(c) of this Act [19 U.S.C. 1671a(c), 1673a(c)], not to initiate an investigation,

(B) a determination by the Commission, under Section 751(b) of this Act [19 U.S.C. 1675(b)], not to review a determination based upon changed circumstances, or

(C) a negative determination by the Commission, under Section 703(a) or 733(a) of this Act [19 U.S.C. 1671b(a), 1673b(a)], as to whether there is reasonable indication of material injury, threat of material injury, or material retardation,

an interested party who is a party to the proceeding in connection with which the matter arises may commence an action in the United States Court of International Trade by filing concurrently a summons and complaint, each with the content and in the form, manner, and style prescribed by the rules of that Court, contesting any factual findings or legal conclusions upon which the determination is based.

2. "Reviewable Determinations" and Their Commencement

An interested party who is a party to the administrative proceeding may obtain court review of any of the following six determinations on the record, as set forth in Section 516A(a)(2)(B) of the Tariff Act of 1930, as amended:

(i) Final affirmative determinations by the administering authority and by the Commission under section 705 or 735 of this Act [19 U.S.C. 1671d, 1673d], including any negative part of such a determination (other than a part referred to in clause (ii)).

(ii) A final negative determination by the administering authority, or the Commission under section 705, or 735 of this Act [19 U.S.C. 1671d, 1673d], including, at the option of the appellant, any part of a final affirmative determination which specifically excludes any company or product.

(iii) A determination, other than a determination reviewable under paragraph (1), by the administering authority, or the Commission under Section 751 of this Act [19 U.S.C. 1675].

(iv) A determination by the administering authority, under section 704 or 734 of this Act [19 U.S.C. 1671c, 1673c], to suspend an antidumping duty or a countervailing duty investigation, including any final determination resulting from a continued investigation which changes the size of the dumping margin or net subsidy calculated, or the reasoning underlying such calculations, at the time the suspension agreement was concluded.

(v) An injurious effect determination by the Commission under section 704(h) or 734(h) of this Act [19 U.S.C. 1671c(h), 1673c(h)].

(vi) A determination by the administering authority as to whether a particular type of merchandise is within the class or kind of merchandise described in an existing finding of dumping or antidumping or countervailing duty order.

The addition of the inclusive phrases in Clauses (i) and (ii) *supra* was designed to clarify when negative portions of affirmative determinations may be reviewed (a point of contention in the *Bethlehem Steel Corporation* decisions discussed *infra*), and that any portion of a final affirmative determination which specifically excludes any company or product may, at the option of the appellant, be treated as a final negative determination. This is the explanation given in the Conference Report, 98-1156 at 179 on HR 3398, the Trade and Tariff Act of 1984, of the intent of the House provision which was agreed to by the conference. Under this explanation an appellant may apparently at his option challenge the exclusion of any company or product within 30 days after publication of an affirmative determination, under Clause (ii), or within 30 days after publication of an antidumping or countervailing duty order under Clause (i), but may not raise this challenge twice.

It is important to note that under Section 516A(a)(2)(A), as technically amended in 1984, it remains necessary for an interested party challenging a determination listed under Clauses (ii) through (v) of Section 516A(a)(2)(B) to file the summons within 30 days after publication in the *Federal Register* of the determination, and for an interested party challenging a final determination described in Clause (i) of that section to await the issuance of the resulting antidumping or countervailing duty order and file the summons within 30 days after publication in the *Federal Register* of the order. A challenge to the determination described in Clause (vi) with respect to merchandise must be brought within 30 days of the date of its mailing.

A challenge to a final affirmative countervailing duty determination of the ITA begun prior to the publication of the countervailing duty order, although within 30 days of publication of the determination, is premature and must be dismissed. *British Steel Corporation* v. *United States,* 6 CIT _____ , 573 F. Supp. 1145 (1983) 5 ITRD 1350.

For purposes of judicial review the affirmative and negative determinations in an ITA final determination had been held to be separable. In *Bethlehem Steel Corporation* v. *United States,* 6 CIT ____ , 571 F. Supp. 1265 (1983) 5 ITRD 1346, the Court refused to take jurisdiction of a challenge to a negative subsidy determination which was part of a final countervailing duty determination resulting in a CVD order because it was filed later than 30 days after the publication of the final determination although within 30 days after publication of the CVD order. The CAFC reversed and remanded this decision, holding that domestic interests may challenge the negative finding of a subsidy which is part of an affirmative finding of subsidies underlying a countervailing duty order within 30 days after the order. *Bethlehem Steel Corporation* v. *United States,* 742 F.2d 1405 (1984) 6 ITRD 1054. This holding is now incorporated into Clause (i) in the list of Reviewable Determinations in Section 516A(a)(2)(B), as amended in 1984, as quoted *supra.*

In *Huffy Corporation* v. *United States,* 9 CIT ____ , 604 F. Supp. 1250 (1985) 6 ITRD 2049, the CIT discussed the judicial treatment of negative findings included in affirmative dumping and subsidy determinations and the applicability of the 1984 provisions, in undertaking to review the exclusion of 11 Taiwanese bicycle producers from the ITA's final determination of sales at less than fair value. See also *Can-Am Corp.* v. *United States,* 9 CIT ____ , Slip Op. 85-70 (1985) 6 ITRD 2496.

An action which challenges a determination made by the administering authority or the commission under Section 516A must be brought under 28 U.S.C. 1581(c) and within the limited time allowed for such actions, although Congress recognized that there were occasions when some aspect of an antidumping (or countervailing duty) determination might come within the more general jurisdiction of the CIT under Section 1581(i) and within the two-year limit for such actions. So stated the CCPA in *Royal Business Machines, Inc.* v. *United States,* 69 CCPA 61, 669 F.2d 692 (1982) 3 ITRD 1321, in holding that the plaintiff's suit under Section 1581(i) to compel the Customs Service to exclude the "Administrator" typewriter from the reach of an antidumping duty order must be dismissed as the suit was actually a challenge to the correctness of the determinations by the Commerce Department and the ITC in an antidumping proceeding. The difficulty encountered by the importer plaintiff in this case in obtaining judicial review of the inclusion of specific merchandise in a determination and order is obviated by new Clause (vi) of Section 516A(a)(2)(B).

Further, Section 1581(i) does not provide jurisdiction to review a preliminary negative determination by the Commerce Department as to "critical circumstances" in an antidumping proceeding, which is not a determination reviewable under Section 1581(c), because the omission of such a determination from reviewable determinations listed in Section 516A was not unintentional. *Haarman & Reimer Corporation* v. *United States,* 1 CIT 148, 509 F. Supp. 1276 (1981) 2 ITRD 1305.

B. Standards of Review and Review Record

Section 516A(b) confines judicial review of the specified administrative determinations to the record before the agency. It does not permit *de novo* proceedings. The scope of the review depends on whether the determination is one of the "certain determinations" listed in Subsection (a)(1) or a "reviewable determination" listed in Subsection (a)(2)(B).

In an action brought under Subsection (a)(1) the court is to hold unlawful any determination, finding, or conclusion found to be "arbitrary, capricious, an abuse of discretion, or otherwise not in accordance with law."

In an action brought under Subsection (a)(2) any determination, finding, or conclusion is to be held unlawful if the court finds that it is "unsupported by substantial evidence on the record, or otherwise not in accordance with law."

The record for review, unless otherwise stipulated by the parties is to consist of:

> (i) a copy of all information presented to or obtained by the Secretary, the administering authority, or the Commission during the course of the administrative proceeding, including all governmental memoranda pertaining to the case and the record of ex parte meetings required to be kept by Section 777(a)(3) [19 U.S.C. 1677f(a)(3)]; and
> (ii) a copy of the determination, all transcripts or records of conferences or hearings, and all notices published in the *Federal Register.*

Documents not considered by the ITA and not part of the administrative record are not part of the record for review even if they should have been considered in the administrative proceeding. *PPG Industries, Inc.* v. *United States,* 5 CIT 282 (1983) 4 ITRD 2446. Moreover, the court will not allow the plaintiff to supplement the record in the final negative determination of the Commerce Department under judicial review with the record of the proceedings in the case before the ITC. *Melamine Chemicals, Inc.* v. *United States,* 2 CIT 113 (1981) 3 ITRD 1307.

In applying the substantial evidence rule, the CIT has stated that it may not weigh the evidence concerning specific factual findings of the ITC nor substitute its judgment for that of the commission. *SCM Corporation* v. *United States,* 4 CIT 7, 544 F. Supp. 194 (1982) 3 ITRD 2198. In an extensive review of the application of the substantial evidence rule the CIT reversed a finding by the ITC, in a Section 751 review of an antidumping finding, of continuing threat to the domestic industry which was based upon presumptions and conjectures. *Matsushita Electric Industrial Co., Ltd.* v. *United States,* 6 CIT _____ , 569 F. Supp. 853 (1983) 4 ITRD 2321. The CIT was itself reversed by the CAFC which found that the necessarily circumstantial evidence before the ITC was substantial evidence. *Matsushita Electric Industrial Co., Ltd.* v. *United States,* 750 F.2d 927 (Fed. Cir. 1984) 6 ITRD 1465.

C. Liquidation of Entries Subject to Judicial Review

Unless liquidation is enjoined by the Court of International Trade, entries of merchandise covered by a contested determination of the Secretary, the administering authority, or the commission are to continue, under Section 516A(c), to be liquidated in accordance with the agency determination until a notice of a decision of that court or of the Court of Appeals for the Federal Circuit not in harmony with that determination is published in the *Federal Register.* Such notice is to be published by the agency concerned within 10 days from the issuance of such a decision.

Upon review of a "reviewable determination," formerly a "determination on record" the Court of International Trade may enjoin the liquidation of some or all of the entries of merchandise covered by the contested determination upon a request by an interested party and a proper showing that the requested relief should be granted.

To obtain a preliminary injunction pending review of the results of an administrative review of an antidumping order the plaintiff must have met the requirements then set forth in Section 516A(c)(2), the court stated in *Smith-Corona Group* v. *United States,* 1 CIT 89, 507 F. Supp. 1015 (1980) 2 ITRD 1437. The four requirements in Section 516A(c)(2) were deleted by the Customs Courts Act of 1980 but are still applied. *American Spring Wire Corporation* v. *United States,* 7 CIT _____ , 578 F. Supp. 1405 (1984) 5 ITRD 1758; *Atlantic Steel Company* v. *United States,* 8 CIT _____ , 592 F. Supp. 679 (1984) 6 ITRD 1303.

However, where an injunction is sought pending court review of an administrative review determination under Section 751, the courts recognize that the prospect of liquidation prior to the judicial decision may constitute irreparable harm with respect to the entries liquidated under the administrative review because there is no relief available for reliquidation if the moving party were to succeed in its challenge to the review determination. *Ceramica Regiomontana, S.A.* v. *United States,* 7 CIT _____ , 590 F. Supp. 1260 (1984) 6 ITRD 1039. This holding follows the CAFC decision in *Zenith Radio Corp.* v. *United States,* 710 F.2d 806 (1983) 4 ITRD 2159, which reversed the CIT holding that liquidation could not constitute irreparable injury absent a showing of specific commercial injury. *Zenith Radio Corp.* v. *United States,* 4 CIT 217 (1982) 4 ITRD 1249. The CAFC concluded on the appeal that the liquidation effect in that case was sufficient establishment of irreparable injury to require the trial court to consider all appropriate factors in deciding to grant or deny an injunction.

D. Final Disposition

If the final disposition by the court is not in harmony with the contested determination, the court is to remand the matter to the administering authority, or the commission, as appropriate, for disposition consistent with the decision of the court.

VIII. COURT OF APPEALS FOR THE FEDERAL CIRCUIT

A. Organization and Purposes

The Court of Appeals for the Federal Circuit (CAFC), the thirteenth Federal Court of Appeals, was established by Public Law 97-164[13] and commenced operations on October 1, 1982. The CAFC is an amalgamation of the Court of Customs and Patent Appeals and the Court of Claims, both of which courts were abolished. Public Law 97-164 provided for the continuance on the CAFC of all of the serving judges of the abolished courts, thereby establishing a new court of 12 judges.

The major purposes of the Court of Appeals are to provide "an appellate forum capable of exercising nationwide jurisdiction over appeals in areas of the law where Congress determines there is a special need for nationwide uniformity"; to centralize appeals in patent cases; and to provide an upgraded forum for government claims cases.[14] The CAFC thus differs from other Federal Courts of Appeal in that its jurisdiction is defined in terms of subject matter rather than geography.

Section 103 of Public Law 97-164, amending 28 U.S.C. 46, authorized the hearing and determination of appellate cases by panels and directed the CAFC to determine by rule a procedure for the rotation of judges from panel to panel to insure that all the judges sit on a representative cross section of the cases heard. The section further provided that the CAFC panels should consist of not less than three judges. The CAFC provided by rule that cases will be heard and determined by panels of an odd number of judges, not less than three, and by practice assigns to each panel at least one judge from each of the prior courts. The CAFC holds regular sessions in the District of Columbia and may hold sessions in any other place in which one of the circuit Courts of Appeals is located, as the CAFC may direct by rule. The rules of the CAFC, issued effective October 1, 1982, supplement the Federal Rules of Appellate Procedure, which govern appeals to the CAFC.

B. Appellate Jurisdiction

The exclusive jurisdiction of the CAFC is defined in a new Section, 1295, added to Title 28 of the United States Code by Section 127 of Public Law 97-164. This definition embraces substantially all the jurisdiction previously held by the Court of Claims and the Court of Customs and Patent Appeals. The areas of customs jurisdiction taken over from the CCPA are (designated by the paragraphs in Section 1295):

(5) An appeal from a final decision of the United States Court of International Trade;

(6) Review of the final determinations of the U.S. International Trade Commission relating to unfair practices in import trade, made under Section 337 of the Tariff Act of 1930 (19 U.S.C. 1337); and

---

[13]Federal Courts Improvement Act of 1982, April 2, 1982, 96 Stat. 25.
[14]S. Rep. No. 97-275, November 18, 1981, 1982 U.S. CODE CONG. & AD. NEWS at 11.

(7) Review, by appeal on questions of law only, of findings of the Secretary of Commerce under Headnote 6 to Schedule 8, Part 4 of the Tariff Schedules of the United States (relating to importation of instruments or apparatus).

In its first appeal under Paragraph (7) the CAFC held that the function of the Secretary of Commerce under the TSUS was only to determine whether a domestic apparatus had the equivalent capabilities of the imported apparatus which were desired by the importing nonprofit institution, and not to pass upon the value of the import to the institution, and that his determination must be based upon substantial evidence, not a conclusory statement. *University of North Carolina* v. *U.S. Department of Commerce,* 701 F.2d 942 (Fed. Cir. 1983) 4 ITRD 1577.

In *M.M. & P. Maritime Advancement, Training, Education & Safety Program* v. *Department of Commerce,* 729 F.2d 748 (Fed. Cir. 1984) 5 ITRD 1881, the Court of Appeals held that the Department of Commerce had acted arbitrarily in denying duty free treatment to a scientific article imported by an educational institution because it was to be used for vocational purposes and not "for scientific research or formal science-oriented education."

Section 1292(c) of Title 28, United States Code, added by Section 125 of Public Law 97-164, gives the CAFC exclusive jurisdiction of an appeal from an interlocutory order or decree in any case over which the court has jurisdiction of an appeal under Section 1295.

Section 1296 of Title 28, U.S. Code, added by Section 127, Public Law 97-164, provides for the giving of precedence to civil actions in the CAFC in such order as applicable law requires and the court by rule establishes. The rules of the court, effective October 1, 1982, do not provide for precedence of particular types of cases. The precedence provided for specified civil actions in the CCPA by 28 U.S.C. 2602 is repealed. Section 1296 is consistent with the federal courts civil priorities provisions in Section 1657 added to 28 U.S.C. by Section 401(a) of Public Law 98-620, described in section VI *supra.*

C. Proceedings

Any matter pending before the CCPA on the effective date of the Act was transferred to the CAFC by Section 403(b) of Public Law 97-164.

The rules of the CAFC, as amended, together with a Procedural Handbook detailing the information needed to process appeals, are available from the Clerk of the Court, 717 Madison Place, N.W., Washington, D.C. 20439.

In its first appeal heard and its first published opinion the CAFC, sitting *en banc,* adopted as governing precedent the holdings of its predecessor courts, the U.S. Court of Claims and the U.S. Court of Customs and Patent Appeals, in order to maintain uniformity and stability, *South Corporation* v. *United States,* 690 F.2d 1368 (1982) 4 ITRD 1049. This decision affirmed a decision of the Court of International Trade upholding the assessment of duties upon repair in a foreign country of an oceanographic vessel. The

CAFC opinion recognized that when the court was sitting *en banc* it was in a position to overturn a precedent of a prior court when reason compelled it.

In *Asberry* v. *U.S. Postal Service*, 692 F.2d 1378 (1982) 4 ITRD 1323, an appeal from a decision of a Merit Systems Protection Board which was found to be frivolous, the CAFC warned that frivolous appeals would in the future be subject to the imposition of damages and costs upon the appellant.

IX. CUSTOMS SERVICE ACQUIESCENCE

The Customs Classification and Appraisement regulations provide that unless the Commissioner of Customs otherwise directs the principles of any court decision adverse to the government (except for a decision upholding an American manufacturer's petition) shall be applied to unliquidated entries and protested entries not denied in which the same issue is involved as soon as the time for further court action has expired.[15] If the court decision upholds an American manufacturer's petition under Section 516 of the Tariff Act of 1930, the principles of the decision are to apply to all merchandise of that character entered or withdrawn for consumption after the date of publication of the court's decision in the *Customs Bulletin*.[16]

The regulations on Administrative Rulings make clear that the application of a court decision may be limited by a published ruling to the specific article under litigation, to a specific class or kind of such merchandise, or to the particular circumstances or entries which were the subject of the litigation.[17] If the Customs Service does not issue such a limited ruling within the prescribed time limit, the Service has in effect acquiesced in the decision. If the Customs Service does acquiesce in an adverse decision, it accepts the conclusions reached by the court for general application to transactions not specifically the subject of the litigation.

The Customs Service has published a uniform procedure to inform customs officers and the public that the general application of a final decision adverse to the government will be recognized unless a limiting ruling is published in the *Customs Bulletin*.[18] Liquidation of entries other than those covered by the decision or action on protests which are pending, if affected by the decision, will be suspended for 180 days. A limiting ruling, if found necessary, will be published in the *Customs Bulletin* within 180 days of the final decision of the court.

---

[15] 19 CFR 152.16(e).
[16] 19 CFR 152.16(d).
[17] 19 CFR 177.10(d).
[18] TD 78-481, 43 FR 57208, December 6, 1978.

Part VII

Appendices

Appendix A

TSUS General Headnotes
and Rules of Interpretation

Title 19, U.S. Code

§1202. Revised Tariff Schedules

General Headnotes and Rules of Interpretation*

1. *Tariff treatment of imported articles* — All articles imported into the customs territory of the United States from outside thereof are subject to duty or exempt therefrom as prescribed in general headnote 3.

2. *Customs territory of the United States* — The term "customs territory of the United States", as used in the schedules, includes only the States, the District of Columbia, and Puerto Rico.

3. *Rates of duty* — The rates of duty in the "Rates of Duty" columns numbered 1 and 2 and the column designated Special of the schedules apply to articles imported into the customs territory of the United States as hereinafter provided in this headnote:

(a) *Products of Insular Possessions:*

(i) Except as provided in headnote 6 of subpart E of part 2 of schedule 7, and except as provided in headnote 3 of subpart A of part 7 of schedule 7, articles imported from insular possessions of the United States which are outside the customs territory of the United States are subject to the rates of duty set forth in column numbered 1 of the schedules, except that all such articles the growth or product of any such possession, or manufactured or produced in any such possession from materials the growth, product, or manufacture of any such possession or of the customs territory of the United States, or of both, which do not contain

*As revised by Proclamation 5365, August 30, 1985, 50 FR 36220, September 5, 1985, and issued in Supplement 3, TSUSA, September 1, 1985.

foreign materials to the value of more than 70 percent of their total value, (or more than 50 percent of their total value with respect to articles described in section 213(b) of the Caribbean Basin Economic Recovery Act), coming to the customs territory of the United States directly from any such possession, and all articles previously imported into the customs territory of the United States with payment of all applicable duties and taxes imposed upon or by reason of importation which were shipped from the United States, without remission, refund, or drawback of such duties or taxes, directly to the possession from which they are being returned by direct shipment, are exempt from duty.

(ii) In determining whether an article produced or manufactured in any such insular possession contains foreign materials to the value of more than 70 percent, no material shall be considered foreign which either—

(A) at the time such article is entered, or

(B) at the time such material is imported into the insular possession,

may be imported into the customs territory from a foreign country, other than Cuba or the Philippine Republic, and entered free of duty; except that no article containing material to which (B) of this subdivision applies shall be exempt from duty under subdivision (i) unless adequate documentation is supplied to show that the material has been incorporated into such article during the 18-month period after the date on which such material is imported into the insular possession.

(iii) Subject to the limitations imposed under sections 503(b) and 504(c) of the

Trade Act of 1974 [sections 2463(b) and 2464(c) of this title], articles designated eligible articles under section 503 of such Act [section 2463 of this title] which are imported from an insular possession of the United States shall receive duty treatment no less favorable than the treatment afforded such articles imported from a beneficiary developing country under title V of such Act [section 2461 et seq. of this title].

(iv) Subject to the provisions in section 213 of the Caribbean Basin Economic Recovery Act [section 2703 of this title], articles which are imported from insular possessions of the United States shall receive duty treatment no less favorable than the treatment afforded such articles when they are imported from a beneficiary country under such Act.

(b) *Products of Cuba* — Products of Cuba imported into the customs territory of the United States, whether imported directly or indirectly, are subject to the rates of duty set forth in column numbered 1 of the schedules. Preferential rates of duty for such products apply only as shown in the said column 1.[1]

(c) *Products of Canada*

(i) Products of Canada imported into the customs territory of the United States, whether imported directly or indirectly, are subject to the rates of duty set forth in column numbered 1 of the schedules. The rates of duty for a Canadian article, as defined in subdivision (c)(ii) of this headnote, apply only as shown in the said column numbered 1.

(ii) The term "Canadian article", as used in the schedules, means an article which is the product of Canada, but does not include any article produced with the use of materials imported into Canada which are products of any foreign country (except materials produced within the customs territory of the United States), if the aggregate value of such imported materials when landed at the Canadian port of entry (that is, the actual purchase price, or, if not purchased, the export value, of such materials, plus, if not included therein, the cost of transporting

such materials to Canada but exclusive of any landing cost and Canadian duty) was —

(A) with regard to any motor vehicle or automobile truck tractor entered on or before December 31, 1967, more than 60 percent of the appraised value of the article imported into the customs territory of the United States; and

(B) with regard to any other article (including any motor vehicle or automobile truck tractor entered after December 31, 1967), more than 50 percent of the appraised value of the article imported into the customs territory of the United States.

(d) *Products of Communist Countries* — Notwithstanding any of the foregoing provisions of this headnote, the rates of duty shown in column numbered 2 shall apply to products, whether imported directly or indirectly, of the following countries and areas pursuant to section 401 of the Tariff Classification Act of 1962, to section 231 or 257(e)(2) of the Trade Expansion Act of 1962, or to action taken by the President thereunder, or pursuant to Presidential Proclamation 4991, dated October 27, 1982[2]

Albania,
Bulgaria,
Cuba[3]
Czechoslovakia,
Estonia,
German Democratic Republic and East Berlin
Indochina (any part of Cambodia, Laos, or Vietnam which may be under Communist domination or control),

---

[1] By virtue of section 401 of the Tariff Classification Act of 1962, the application to products of Cuba of either a preferential or other reduced rate of duty in column 1 is suspended. See general headnote 3(d), *infra.*

[2] In Proclamation 4697, dated October 27, 1979, the President, acting under authority of Title IV of the Trade Act of 1974, amended general headnote 3(e) [predecessor of 3(d)] by deleting "China (any part of which may be under Communist domination or control)" and "Tibet", effective February 1, 1980, the date on which written notices of acceptance were exchanged, following adoption on January 24, 1980 by the Congress of a concurrent resolution of approval extending nondiscriminatory treatment to the products of the People's Republic of China.

[3] In Proclamation 3447, dated Feb. 3, 1962, the President, acting under authority of section 620(a) of the Foreign Assistance Act of 1961 (75 Stat. 445), as amended, prohibited the importation into the United States of all goods of Cuban origin and all goods imported from or through Cuba, subject to such exceptions as the Secretary of the Treasury determines to be consistent with the effective operation of the embargo.

Korea (any part which may be under Communist domination or control),

Kurile Islands,

Latvia,

Lithuania,

Outer Mongolia,

Polish People's Republic

Southern Sakhalin,

Tanna Tuva,

Union of Soviet Socialist Republics and the area in East Prussia under the provisional administration of the Union of Soviet Socialist Republics.

(e) *Products Eligible for Special Tariff Treatment.*

(i) The "Special" column reflects rates of duty available under one or more special tariff treatment programs which are provided for in subdivision (e) of this headnote and which are identified in parentheses immediately following the rate(s) of duty set out in such column. Upon application in proper form by a person who possesses the right to make entry for the imported article, a special rate shall be applied to such article only if —

(A) it is classified in an item for which a special rate (or rates) is set out in the "Special" column opposite such item;

(B) it is imported from a country —

(1) which is designated as an eligible country with respect to such item under a program designated in the "Special" column opposite such item, and

(2) which is otherwise eligible for column 1 rates of duty; and

(C) it has satisfied all other requirements for eligibility for such program or programs.

(ii) Programs under which special tariff treatment may be provided to imported articles, and the corresponding symbols for such programs as they are indicated in the "Special" column, are as follows:

Generalized System of Preference .. A or A*

Least Developed Developing Countries .... D

Caribbean Basin Economic Recovery Act ....E or E*

United States-Israel Free Trade Area Implementation Act of 1985 I

(iii)(A) Articles which are eligible for the special tariff treatment provided for in subdivision (e) of this headnote and which are subject to temporary modification under any provision of part 1 of the Appendix to these schedules shall be subject, for the period indicated in the "Effective Period" column in the Appendix, to rates of duty as follows:

(1) if the "Special" column in the Appendix is blank, the rate of duty in column numbered 1 therein shall apply;

(2) if a rate of duty for which the article may be eligible is set forth in the "Special" column in the Appendix followed by one or more symbols described above, such rate shall apply in lieu of the rate followed by the corresponding symbol(s) set forth for such article in the "Special" column in schedules 1 to 8; or

(3) if "No change" followed by one or more symbols described above appears in the "Special" column in the Appendix and subdivision (iii)(A)(2) above does not apply, the rate of duty in column numbered 1 in the Appendix or the applicable rate(s) of duty set forth in the "Special" column in schedules 1 to 8, whichever is lower, shall apply.

(B) Unless the context requires otherwise, articles which are eligible for the special tariff treatment provided for in subdivision (e) of this headnote and which are subject to temporary modification under any provision of parts 2 or 3 of the Appendix to these schedules shall be subject, for the period indicated in the Appendix, to the rates of duty in column numbered 1 therein.

(iv) Whenever any rate of duty set forth in the "Special" column in schedules 1 to 8 is equal to, or higher than, the corresponding rate of duty provided in column numbered 1 in such schedules, such rate of duty in the "Special" column shall be deleted; except that, if the rate of duty in the "Special" column is an intermediate stage in a series of staged rate reductions for that item, such rate shall be treated as a suspended rate and shall be set forth in the "Special" column, followed by one or more symbols described above, and followed by an "s" in parentheses. If no rate of duty for which the article may be eligible is provided in the "Special" column for a particular item in schedules 1 to 8, the rate of duty provided in column numbered 1 shall apply.

(v) *Products of Countries Designated Beneficiary Developing Countries for Purposes of the Generalized System of Preferences (GSP):*

(A) The following countries, territories, and associations of countries eligible for treatment as one country (pursuant to section 502(a)(3) of the Trade Act of 1974 (19 U.S.C. 2462(c)(3)) are designated beneficiary developing countries for the purposes of the Generalized System of Preferences, provided for in Title V of the Trade Act of 1974, as amended (19 U.S.C. 2461 *et seq.*):

Independent Countries[4]

Angola
Antigua and Barbuda
Argentina
Bahamas
Bahrain
Bangladesh
Barbados
Belize
Benin
Bhutan
Bolivia
Botswana
Brazil
Brunei Darussalem
Burkina Faso
Burma
Burundi
Cameroon
Cape Verde
Central African Republic
Chad
Chile
Colombia
Comoros
Congo
Costa Rica
Cyprus
Djibouti
Dominica
Dominican Republic
Ecuador
Egypt
El Salvador
Equatorial Guinea
Fiji
Gambia
Ghana
Grenada

Guatemala
Guinea
Guinea Bissau
Guyana
Haiti
Honduras
India
Indonesia
Israel
Ivory Coast
Jamaica
Jordan
Kenya
Kiribati
Korea, Republic of
Lebanon
Lesotho
Liberia
Madagascar
Malawi
Malaysia
Maldives
Mali
Malta
Mauritania
Mauritius
Mexico
Morocco
Mozambique
Nauru
Nepal
Nicaragua
Niger
Oman
Pakistan
Panama
Papua New Guinea
Paraguay
Peru
Philippines
Portugal
Romania
Rwanda
Saint Lucia
Saint Vincent and the Grenadines
Sao Tome and Principe
Senegal
Seychelles
Sierra Leone
Singapore
Solomon Islands
Somalia
Sri Lanka
Sudan
Suriname
Swaziland
Syria
Taiwan

---

[4] Pursuant to section 4(b)(i) of the Taiwan Relations Act (22 U.S.C. 3303(b)) the reference to countries includes Taiwan.

Tanzania
Thailand
Togo
Tonga
Trinidad and Tobago
Tunisia
Turkey
Tuvalu
Uganda
Uruguay
Vanuatu
Venezuela
Western Samoa
Yemen Arab Republic (Sanaá)
Yugoslavia
Zaire
Zambia
Zimbabwe

Non-Independent Countries & Territories

Anguilla
Bermuda
British Indian Ocean
    Territory
Cayman Islands
Christmas Island
    (Australia)
Cocos (Keeling) Islands
Cook Islands
Falkland Islands
(Islas Malvinas)
French Polynesia
Gibraltar
Heard Island and McDonald
    Islands
Hong Kong
Macau
Montserrat
Netherlands Antilles
New Caledonia
Niue
Norfolk Island
Pitcairn Islands
Saint Christopher-Nevis
Saint Helena
Tokelau
Trust Territory of the
    Pacific Islands
Turks and Caicos Islands
Virgin Islands, British
Wallis and Futuna
Western Sahara

Associations of Countries (treated as one country)

Member Countries of the Cartagena Agreement (Andean Group)

Consisting of:

Bolivia
Colombia
Ecuador
Peru
Venezuela

Association of South East Asian Nations (ASEAN)

Consisting of:

Brunei
Indonesia
Malaysia
Philippines
Singapore
Thailand

Member Countries of the Caribbean Common Market (CARICOM)

Consisting of:

Antigua and Barbuda
Bahamas
Barbados
Belize
Dominica
Grenada
Guyana
Jamaica
Montserrat
Saint Christopher-Nevis
Saint Lucia
Saint Vincent and the Grenadines
Trinidad and Tobago

(B) The following beneficiary countries are designated as least-developed beneficiary developing countries pursuant to section 504(c)(6) of the Trade Act of 1974, as amended:

Bangladesh
Benin
Bhutan
Botswana
Burkina Faso
Burundi
Cape Verde
Central African Republic
Chad
Comoros
Djibouti
Equatorial Guinea
Gambia
Guinea
Guinea-Bissau

Haiti
Lesotho
Malawi
Maldives
Mali
Nepal
Niger
Rwanda
Sao Tome and Principe
Sierra Leone
Somalia
Sudan
Tanzania
Togo
Uganda
Western Samoa
Yemen Arab Republic (Sanaá)

Whenever an eligible article is imported into the customs territory of the United States directly from one of the countries designated as a least-developed beneficiary developing country, it shall be entitled to receive the duty-free treatment provided for in subdivision (e)(v)(C) of this headnote without regard to the limitations on preferential treatment of eligible articles in section 504(c) of the Trade Act, as amended (19 U.S.C. 2464(c)).

(C) Articles provided for in an item for which a rate of duty appears in the "Special" column followed by the symbols "A" or "A*" in parentheses are those designated by the President to be eligible articles for purposes of the GSP pursuant to section 503 of the Trade Act of 1974. The symbol "A" indicates that all beneficiary developing countries are eligible for preferential treatment with respect to all articles provided for in the designated TSUS item. The symbol "A*" indicates that certain beneficiary developing countries, specifically enumerated in subdivision (e)(v)(D) of this headnote, are not eligible for such preferential treatment with regard to any article provided for in the designated TSUS item. Whenever an eligible article is imported into the customs territory of the United States directly from a country or territory listed in subdivision (e)(v)(A) of this headnote, it shall be eligible for duty-free treatment as set forth in the "Special" column, unless excluded from such treatment by subdivision (e)(v)(D) of this headnote; provided that, in accordance with regulations promulgated by the Secretary of the Treasury the sum of (1) the cost or value of the materials produced in the beneficiary developing country or any 2 or more countries which are members of the same association of countries which is treated as one country under section 502(a)(3) of the Trade Act of 1974, plus (2) the direct costs of processing operations performed in such beneficiary developing country or such member countries is not less than 35 percent of the appraised value of such article at the time of its entry into the customs territory of the United States.

(D) Articles provided for in an item for which a rate of duty appears in the "Special" column followed by the symbol "A*" in parentheses, if imported from a beneficiary developing country set opposite the TSUS item numbers listed below, are not eligible for the duty-free treatment provided in subdivision (e)(v)(C) of this headnote:

[For list of TSUS item numbers under (D) see Proclamation 5365, Annex I, 50 FR 36220 at 36228-31, or the TSUSA, Supplement 3.]

(vi) *Products of Least Developed Developing Countries.*

(A) The following countries are designated least developed developing countries (LDDC's):

Bangladesh
Benin
Bhutan
Botswana
Burkina Faso
Burundi
Cape Verde
Central African Republic
Chad
Comoros
Gambia
Guinea
Haiti
Lesotho
Malawi
Maldives
Mali
Nepal
Niger
Rwanda
Somalia
Sudan
Tanzania
Uganda
Western Samoa
Yemen Arab Republic (Sanaá)

(B) Products of such countries imported into the customs territory of the United States, whether imported directly or indirectly, and entered under an item for which a rate of duty appears in the "Special" column followed by the symbol "D" in parentheses are eligible for full tariff reductions without staging, as set forth in the "Special" column, in accordance with section 503(a)(2)(A) of the Trade Agreements Act of 1979 (93 Stat. 251).

(vii) *Products of Countries Designated as Beneficiary Countries for Purposes of the Caribbean Basin Economic Recovery Act (CBERA).*

(A) The following countries and territories or successor political entities are designated beneficiary countries for the purposes of the CBERA, pursuant to section 212 of that Act (19 U.S.C. 2702):

Antigua and Barbuda
Bahamas
Barbados
Belize
Costa Rica
Dominica
Dominican Republic
El Salvador
Grenada
Guatemala
Haiti
Honduras
Jamaica
Montserrat
Netherlands Antilles
Panama
Saint Christopher-Nevis
Saint Lucia
Saint Vincent and the Grenadines
Trinidad and Tobago
Virgin Islands, British

(B)(1) Unless otherwise excluded from eligibility by the provisions of subdivisions (e)(vii)(D) or (e)(vii)(E) of this headnote, any article which is the growth, product, or manufacture of a beneficiary country shall be eligible for duty-free treatment if that article is provided for in an item for which a rate of duty appears in the "Special" column followed by the symbols "g" or "E*" in parentheses, and if —

(i) that article is imported directly from a beneficiary country into the customs territory of the United States; and

(ii) the sum of (A) the cost or value of the materials produced in a beneficiary country or two or more beneficiary countries, plus (B) the direct costs of processing operations performed in a beneficiary country or countries is not less than 35 per centum of the appraised value of such article at the time it is entered. For purposes of determining the percentage referred to in (ii)(B) above, the term "beneficiary country" includes the Commonwealth of Puerto Rico and the United States Virgin Islands. If the cost or value of materials produced in the customs territory of the United States (other than the Commonwealth of Puerto Rico) is included with respect to an article to which subdivision (e)(vii) of this headnote applies, an amount not to exceed 15 per centum of the appraised value of the article at the time it is entered that is attributed to such United States cost or value may be applied toward determining the percentage referred to in (ii)(B) above.

(2) Pursuant to subsection 213(a)(2) of the CBERA, the Secretary of the Treasury shall prescribe such regulations as may be necessary to carry out subdivision (e)(vii) of this headnote including, but not limited to, regulations providing that, in order to be eligible for duty-free treatment under the CBERA, an article must be wholly the growth, product, or manufacture of a beneficiary country, or must be a new or different article of commerce which has been grown, produced, or manufactured in the beneficiary country, and must be stated as such in a declaration by the appropriate party; but no article or material of a beneficiary country shall be eligible for such treatment by virtue of having merely undergone —

(i) simple combining or packaging operations, or

(ii) mere dilution with water or mere dilution with another substance that does not materially alter the characteristics of the article.

(3) As used in subdivision (e)(vii)(B) of this headnote, the phrase *direct costs of processing operations* includes, but is not limited to —

(i) all actual labor costs involved in the growth, production, manufacture, or assembly of the specific merchandise, including fringe benefits, on-the-job training and the cost of engineering, supervisory, quality control, and similar personnel; and

(ii) dies, molds, tooling, and depreciation on machinery and equipment which are allocable to the specific merchandise. Such phrase does not include costs which are not directly attributable to the merchandise concerned or are not costs of manufacturing the product, such as (i) profit, and (ii) general expenses of doing business which are either not allocable to the specific merchandise or are not related to the growth, production, manufacture, or assembly of the merchandise, such as administrative salaries, casualty and liability insurance, advertising, and salesmen's salaries, commissions or expenses.

(C) Articles provided for in an item for which a rate of duty appears in the "Special" column followed by the symbols "E" or "E*" in parentheses are those designated by the President to be eligible articles for purposes of the CBERA pursuant to section 213 of that Act. The symbol "E" indicates that all articles provided for in the designated TSUS item are eligible for preferential treatment. The symbol "E*" indicates that some articles provided for in the designated TSUS item are not eligible for preferential treatment, as further described in subdivision (e)(vii)(D) of this headnote. Whenever an eligible article is imported into the customs territory of the United States in accordance with the provisions of subdivision (e)(vii)(B) of this headnote from a country or territory listed in subdivision (e)(vii)(A) of this headnote, it shall be eligible for duty-free treatment as set forth in the "Special" column, unless excluded from such treatment by subdivisions (e)(vii)(D) or (e)(vii)(E) of this headnote.

(D) Articles provided for in an item for which a rate of duty appears in the "Special" column followed by the symbol "E*" in parentheses shall be eligible for the duty-free treatment provided for in subdivision (e)(vii) of this headnote, except —

(1) articles of beef or veal, however provided for in subpart B of part 2 of schedule 1, and sugars, syrups, and molasses, provided for in items 155.20 or

155.30, if a product of the following countries, pursuant to section 213(c) of the CBERA:

Antigua and Barbuda
Montserrat
Netherlands Antilles
Saint Lucia
Saint Vincent and the Grenadines

(2) sugars, syrups, and molasses, provided for in items 155.20 or 155.30, to the extent that importation and duty-free treatment of such articles are limited by headnote 4, subpart A, part 10, schedule 1, pursuant to section 213(d) of the CBERA; or

(3) textile and apparel articles —

(i) in chief value of cotton, wool, man-made fibers, or blends thereof in which those fibers, in the aggregate, exceed in value each other single component fiber thereof; or

(ii) in which either the cotton content or the man-made fiber content equals or exceeds 50 percent by weight of all component fibers thereof; or

(iii) in which the wool content exceeds 17 percent by weight of all component fibers thereof; or

(iv) containing blends of cotton, wool, or man-made fibers, which fibers, in the aggregate, amount to 50 percent or more by weight of all component fibers thereof; *provided,* that beneficiary country exports of handloom fabrics of the cottage industry, or hand-made cottage industry products made of such handloom fabrics, or traditional folklore handicraft textiles products, if such products are properly certified under an arrangement established between the United States and such beneficiary country, are eligible for the duty-free treatment provided for in subdivision (e)(vii) of this headnote.

(E) The duty-free treatment provided under the CBERA shall not apply to watches, and watch parts (including cases, bracelets, and straps), of whatever type including, but not limited to, mechanical, quartz digital, or quartz analog, if such watches or watch parts contain any material which is the product of any country with respect to which column 2 rates of duty apply.

(viii) *United States-Israel Free Trade Area Implementation Act of 1985.*

(A) The products of Israel described in Annex 1 of the Agreement on the Establishment of a Free Trade Area between the Government of the United States of America and the Government of Israel, entered into on April 22, 1985, are subject to duty as provided herein. Products of Israel, as defined in subdivision (e)(viii)(B) of this headnote, imported into the customs territory of the United States and entered under an item for which a rate of duty appears in the "Special" column followed by the symbol "I" in parentheses are eligible for tariff treatment, as set forth in the "Special" column, in accordance with Section 4(a) of the United States-Israel Free Trade Area Implementation Act of 1985 (99 Stat. 82).

(B) For purposes of subdivision (e)(viii) of this headnote, articles imported into the customs territory of the United States are eligible for treatment as "products of Israel" only if —

(1) that article is the growth, product, or manufacture of Israel or is a new or different article of commerce that has been grown, produced, or manufactured in Israel;

(2) that article is imported directly from Israel into the customs territory of the United States; and

(3) the sum of —

(i) the cost or value of the materials produced in Israel, plus

(ii) the direct costs of processing operations performed in Israel, is not less than 35 percent of the appraised value of such article at the time it is entered. If the cost or value of materials produced in the customs territory of the United States is included with respect to an article to which subdivision (e)(viii) of this headnote applies, an amount not to exceed 15 percent of the appraised value of the article at the time it is entered that is attributable to such United States cost or value may be applied toward determining the percentage referred to in subdivision (e)(viii)(B)(3) of this headnote.

(C) No article may be considered to meet the requirements of subdivision (e)(viii)(B)(1) of this headnote by virtue of having merely undergone —

(1) simple combining or packaging operations; or

(2) mere dilution with water or mere dilution with another substance that does not materially alter the characteristics of the article.

(D) As used in subdivision (e)(viii) of this headnote, the phrase "direct costs of processing operations" includes, but is not limited to —

(1) all actual labor costs involved in the growth, production, manufacture, or assembly of the specific merchandise, including fringe benefits, on-the-job training and the cost of engineering, supervisory, quality control, and similar personnel; and

(2) dies, molds, tooling, and depreciation on machinery and equipment which are allocable to the specific merchandise.

Such phrase does not include costs which are not directly attributable to the merchandise concerned, or are not costs of manufacturing the product, such as (i) profit, and (ii) general expenses of doing business which are either not allocable to the specific merchandise or are not related to the growth, production, manufacture, or assembly of the merchandise, such as administrative salaries, casualty and liability insurance, advertising, and salesmen's salaries, commissions or expenses.

(E) The Secretary of the Treasury, after consultation with the United States Trade Representative, shall prescribe such regulations as may be necessary to carry out subdivision (e)(viii) of this headnote.

(f) *Products of All Other Countries* — Products of all countries not previously mentioned in this headnote imported into the customs territory of the United States are subject to the rates of duty set forth in column numbered 1 of the schedules.

4. *Modification or Amendment of Rates of Duty* — Except as otherwise provided in general headnote 3(e) or in the Appendix to the Tariff Schedules—

(a) a statutory rate of duty supersedes and terminates the existing rates of duty in both column numbered 1 and column numbered 2 unless otherwise specified in the amending statute;

(b) a rate of duty proclaimed pursuant to a concession granted in a trade agreement shall be reflected in column numbered 1 and, if higher than the then existing rate in column numbered 2, also in the latter column, and shall supersede but not terminate the then existing rate (or rates) in such column (or columns);

(c) a rate of duty proclaimed pursuant to section 336 of the Tariff Act of 1930 [19 U.S.C. 1336] shall be reflected in both column numbered 1 and column numbered 2 and shall supersede but not terminate the then existing rates in such columns; and

(d) whenever a proclaimed rate is terminated or suspended, the rate shall revert, unless otherwise provided, to the next intervening proclaimed rate previously superseded but not terminated or, if none, to the statutory rate.

5. *Intangibles* — For the purposes of headnote 1—

(a) corpses, together with their coffins and accompanying flowers,

(b) currency (metal or paper) in current circulation in any country and imported for monetary purposes,

(c) electricity,

(d) securities and similar evidences of value,

(e) records, diagrams, and other data with regard to any business, engineering, or exploration operation whether on paper, cards, photographs, blueprints, tapes, or other media,

(f) articles returned from space within the purview of section 484a of the Tariff Act of 1930; and

(g) vessels which are not "yachts or pleasure boats" within the purview of subpart D, part 6, of schedule 6, are not articles subject to the provisions of these schedules.

6. *Containers or Holders for Imported Merchandise* — For the purposes of the tariff schedules, containers or holders are subject to tariff treatment as follows:

(a) *Imported Empty* — Containers or holders if imported empty are subject to tariff treatment as imported articles and as such are subject to duty unless they are within the purview of a provision which specifically exempts them from duty.

(b) *Not Imported Empty* — Containers or holders if imported containing or holding articles are subject to tariff treatment as follows:

(i) The usual or ordinary types of shipping or transportation containers or holders, if not designed for, or capable of, reuse, and containers of usual types

ordinarily sold at retail with their contents, are not subject to treatment as imported articles. Their cost, however, is, under section 402 or section 402a of the tariff act, a part of the value of their contents and if their contents are subject to an ad valorem rate of duty such containers or holders are, in effect, dutiable at the same rate as their contents, except that their cost is deductible from dutiable value upon submission of satisfactory proof that they are products of the United States which are being returned without having been advanced in value or improved in condition by any means while abroad.

(ii) The usual or ordinary types of shipping or transportation containers or holders, if designed for, or capable of, reuse, are subject to treatment as imported articles separate and distinct from their contents. Such holders or containers are not part of the dutiable value of their contents and are separately subject to duty upon each and every importation into the customs territory of the United States unless within the scope of a provision specifically exempting them from duty.

(iii) In the absence of context which requires otherwise, all other containers or holders are subject to the same treatment as specified in (ii) above for usual or ordinary types of shipping or transportation containers or holders designed for, or capable of, reuse.

7. *Commingling of Articles:*

(a) Whenever articles subject to different rates of duty are so packed together or mingled that the quantity or value of each class of articles cannot be readily ascertained by customs officers (without physical segregation of the shipment or the contents of any entire package thereof), by one or more of the following means—

(i) sampling,

(ii) verification of packing lists or other documents filed at the time of entry, or

(iii) evidence showing performance of commercial settlement tests generally accepted in the trade and filed in such time and manner as may be prescribed by regulations of the Secretary of the Treasury, the commingled articles shall be subject to the highest rate of duty applicable to any part thereof unless the consignee or his agent segregates the articles pursuant to subdivision (b) hereof.

(b) Every segregation of articles made pursuant to this headnote shall be accomplished by the consignee or his agent at the risk and expense of the consignee within 30 days (unless the Secretary authorizes in writing a longer time) after the date of personal delivery or mailing, by such employee as the Secretary of the Treasury shall designate, of written notice to the consignee that the articles are commingled and that the quantity or value of each class of articles cannot be readily ascertained by customs officers. Every such segregation shall be accomplished under customs supervision, and the compensation and expenses of the supervising customs officers shall be reimbursed to the Government by the consignee under such regulations as the Secretary of the Treasury may prescribe.

(c) The foregoing provisions of this headnote do not apply with respect to any part of a shipment if the consignee or his agent furnishes, in such time and manner as may be prescribed by regulations of the Secretary of the Treasury, satisfactory proof—

(i) that such part (A) is commercially negligible, (B) is not capable of segregation without excessive cost, and (C) will not be segregated prior to its use in a manufacturing process or otherwise, and

(ii) that the commingling was not intended to avoid the payment of lawful duties.

Any article with respect to which such proof is furnished shall be considered for all customs purposes as a part of the article, subject to the next lower rate of duty, with which it is commingled.

(d) The foregoing provisions of this headnote do not apply with respect to any shipment if the consignee or his agent shall furnish, in such time and manner as may be prescribed by regulations of the Secretary of the Treasury, satisfactory proof—

(i) that the value of the commingled articles is less than the aggregate value would be if the shipment were segregated;

(ii) that the shipment is not capable of segregation without excessive cost and

will not be segregated prior to its use in a manufacturing process or otherwise; and

(iii) that the commingling was not intended to avoid the payment of lawful duties.

Any merchandise with respect to which such proof is furnished shall be considered for all customs purposes to be dutiable at the rate applicable to the material present in greater quantity than any other material.

(e) The provisions of this headnote shall apply only in cases where the schedules do not expressly provide a particular tariff treatment for commingled articles.

8. *Abbreviations* — In the schedules the following symbols and abbreviations are used with the meanings respectively indicated below:

$	dollars.
¢	cents.
%	percent.
+	plus.
ad val	ad valorem.
bu	bushel.
cu	cubic.
doz	dozen.
ft	feet.
gal	gallon.
in	inches.
lb	pounds.
oz	ounces.
sq	square.
wt	weight.
yd	yard.
pcs	pieces.
prs	pairs.
lin	linear.
I.R.C.	Internal Revenue Code.

9. *Definitions* — For the purposes of the schedules, unless the context otherwise requires—

(a) the term "entered" means entered, or withdrawn from warehouse, for consumption in the customs territory of the United States;

(b) the term "entered for consumption" does not include withdrawals from warehouse for consumption;

(c) the term "withdrawn for consumption" means withdrawn from warehouse for consumption and does not include articles entered for consumption;

(d) the term "rate of duty" includes a free rate of duty; rates of duty proclaimed by the President shall be referred to as "proclaimed" rates of duty; rates of duty enacted by the Congress shall be referred to as "statutory" rates of duty; and the rates of duty in column numbered 2 at the time the schedules become effective shall be referred to as "original statutory" rates of duty;

(e) the term "ton" means 2,240 pounds, and the term "short ton" means 2,000 pounds;

(f) the terms "of", "wholly of", "almost wholly of", "in part of" and "containing", when used between the description of an article and a material (e.g., "furniture of wood", "woven fabrics, wholly of cotton", etc.), have the following meanings:

(i) "of" means that the article is wholly or in chief value of the named material;

(ii) "wholly of" means that the article is, except for negligible or insignificant quantities of some other material or materials, composed completely of the named materials;

(iii) "almost wholly of" means that the essential character of the article is imparted by the named material, notwithstanding the fact that significant quantities of some other material or materials may be present; and

(iv) "in part of" or "containing" mean that the article contains a significant quantity of the named material.

With regard to the application of the quantitative concepts specified in subparagraphs (ii) and (iv) above, it is intended that the *de minimis* rule apply.

10. *General Interpretative Rules* — For the purposes of these schedules—

(a) the general, schedule, part, and subpart headnotes, and the provisions describing the classes of imported articles and specifying the rates of duty or other import restrictions to be imposed thereon are subject to the rules of interpretation set forth herein and to such other rules of statutory interpretation, not inconsistent therewith, as have been or may be developed under administrative or judicial rulings;

(b) the titles of the various schedules, parts, and subparts and the footnotes therein are intended for convenience in reference only and have no legal or interpretative significance;

(c) an imported article which is described in two or more provisions of the schedules is classifiable in the provision which most specifically describes it; but, in applying this rule of interpretation, the following considerations shall govern:

(i) a superior heading cannot be enlarged by inferior headings intended under it but can be limited thereby;

(ii) comparisons are to be made only between provisions of coordinate or equal status, i.e., between the primary or main superior headings of the schedules or between coordinate inferior headings which are subordinate to the same superior heading;

(d) if two or more tariff descriptions are equally applicable to an article, such article shall be subject to duty under the description for which the original statutory rate is highest, and, should the highest original statutory rate be applicable to two or more of such descriptions, the article shall be subject to duty under that one of such descriptions which first appears in the schedules;

(e) in the absence of special language or context which otherwise requires—

(i) a tariff classification controlled by use (other than actual use) is to be determined in accordance with the use in the United States at, or immediately prior to, the date of importation, of articles of that class or kind to which the imported articles belong, and the controlling use is the chief use, i.e., the use which exceeds all other uses (if any) combined;

(ii) a tariff classification controlled by the actual use to which an imported article is put in the United States is satisfied only if such use is intended at the time of importation, the article is so used, and proof thereof is furnished within 3 years after the date the article is entered;

(f) an article is in chief value of a material if such material exceeds in value each other single component material of the article;

(g) a headnote provision which enumerates articles not included in a schedule, part, or subpart is not necessarily exhaustive, and the absence of a particular article from such headnote provision shall not be given weight in determining the relative specificity of competing provisions which describe such article;

(h) unless the context requires otherwise, a tariff description for an article covers such article, whether assembled or not assembled, and whether finished or not finished;

(ij) a provision for "parts" of an article covers a product solely or chiefly used as a part of such article, but does not prevail over a specific provision for such part.

11. *Issuance of Rules and Regulations* — The Secretary of the Treasury is hereby authorized to issue rules and regulations governing the admission of articles under the provisions of the schedules. The allowance of an importer's claim for classification, under any of the provisions of the schedules which provide for total or partial relief from duty or other import restrictions on the basis of facts which are not determinable from an examination of the article itself in its condition as imported, is dependent upon his complying with any rules or regulations which may be issued pursuant to this headnote.

12. The Secretary of the Treasury is authorized to prescribe methods of analyzing, testing, sampling, weighing, gauging, measuring, or other methods of ascertainment whenever he finds that such methods are necessary to determine the physical, chemical, or other properties or characteristics of articles for purposes of any law administered by the Customs Service.

* * *

General Agreement on Tariffs and Trade

---

* Text reproduced from Committee Print 96-5, 96th Cong. 1st Sess., Committee on Finance, U.S. Senate, at pages 37 *et seq.* Original text, 61 Stat. Part 5. TIAS 1700.

THE GENERAL AGREEMENT ON TARIFFS AND TRADE

The Governments of the Commonwealth of Australia, the Kingdom of Belgium, the United States of Brazil, Burma, Canada, Ceylon, the Republic of Chile, the Republic of China, the Republic of Cuba, the Czechoslovak Republic, the French Republic, India, Lebanon, the Grand-Duchy of Luxemburg, the Kingdom of the Netherlands, New Zealand, the Kingdom of Norway, Pakistan, Southern Rhodesia, Syria, the Union of South Africa, the United Kingdom of Great Britain and Northern Ireland, and the United States of America:

Recognizing that their relations in the field of trade and economic endeavour should be conducted with a view to raising standards of living, ensuring full employment and a large and steadily growing volume of real income and effective demand, developing the full use of the resources of the world and expanding the production and exchange of goods,

Being desirous of contributing to these objectives by entering into reciprocal and mutually advantageous arrangements directed to the substantial reduction of tariffs and other barriers to trade and to the elimination of discriminatory treatment in international commerce,

Have through their Representatives agreed as follows:

Part I

Article I.—GENERAL MOST-FAVOURED-NATION TREATMENT

1. With respect to customs duties and charges of any kind imposed on or in connection with importation or exportation or imposed on the international transfer of payments for imports or exports, and with respect to the method of levying such duties and charges, and with respect to all rules and formalities in connection with importation and exportation, and with respect to all matters referred to in paragraphs 2 and 4 of Article III, any advantage, favour, privilege or immunity granted by any contracting party to any product originating in or destined for any other country shall be accorded immediately and unconditionally to the like product originating in or destined for the territories of all other contracting parties.

2. The provisions of paragraph 1 of this Article shall not require the elimination of any preferences in respect of import duties or charges which do not exceed the levels provided for in paragraph 4 of this Article and which fall within the following descriptions:

(a) preferences in force exclusively between two or more of the territories listed in Annex A, subject to the conditions set forth therein;

(b) preferences in force exclusively between two or more territories which on July 1, 1939, were connected by common sovereignty or relations of protection or suzerainty and which are listed in Annexes B, C and D, subject to the conditions set forth therein;

(c) preferences in force exclusively between the United States of America and the Republic of Cuba;

(d) preferences in force exclusively between neighbouring countries listed in Annexes E and F.

3. The provisions of paragraph 1 shall not apply to preferences between the countries formerly a part of the Ottoman Empire and detached from it on July 24, 1923, provided such preferences are approved under paragraph 5 of Article XXV,[1] which shall be applied in this respect in the light of paragraph of Article XXIX.

4. The margin of preference of any product in respect of which a preference is permitted under paragraph 2 of this Article but is not specifically set forth as a maximum margin of preference in the appropriate Schedule annexed to this Agreement shall not exceed:

(a) in respect of duties or charges on any product described in such Schedule, the difference between the most-favoured-nation and preferential rates provided for therein; if no preferential rate is provided for, the preferential rate

---

[1]Pending the entry into force of the Protocol Amending Part I and Articles XXIX and XXX, this reference to Article XXV actually reads "sub-paragraph 5(a) of Article XXV," although paragraph 5 is no longer divided into sub-paragraphs (a), (b), etc., as was formerly the case. The present text of paragraph 5 was formerly sub-paragraph 5(a) of Article XXV.

shall for the purposes of this paragraph be taken to be that in force on April 10, 1947, and, if no most-favoured-nation rate is provided for, the margin shall not exceed the difference between the most-favoured-nation and preferential rates existing on April 10, 1947;

(b) in respect of duties or charges on any product not described in the appropriate Schedule, the difference between the most-favoured-nation and preferential rates existing on April 10, 1947.

In the case of the contracting parties named in Annex G, the date of April 10, 1947, referred to in sub-paragraphs (a) and (b) of this paragraph shall be replaced by the respective dates set forth in that Annex.

Article II.—SCHEDULES OF CONCESSIONS

1. (a) Each contracting party shall accord to the commerce of the other contracting parties treatment no less favourable than that provided for in the appropriate Part of the appropriate Schedule annexed to this Agreement.

(b) The products described in Part I of the Schedule relating to any contracting part, which are the products of territories of other contracting parties, shall, on their importation into the territory to which the Schedule relates, and subject to the terms, conditions or qualifications set forth in that Schedule, be exempt from ordinary customs duties in excess of those set forth and provided for therein. Such products shall also be exempt from all other duties or charges of any kind imposed on or in connection with importation in excess of those imposed on the date of this Agreement or those directly and mandatorily required to be imposed thereafter by legislation in force in the importing territory on that date.

(c) The products described in Part II of the Schedule relating to any contracting party which are the products of territories entitled under Article I to receive preferential treatment upon importation into the territory to which the Schedule relates shall, on their importation into such territory, and subject to the terms, conditions or qualifications set forth, in that Schedule, be exempt from ordinary customs duties in excess of those set forth and provided for in Part II of that Schedule. Such products shall also be exempt from all other duties or charges of any kind imposed on or in connection with importation in excess of those imposed on the date of this Agreement or those directly and mandatorily required to be imposed thereafter by legislation in force in the importing territory on that date. Nothing in this Article shall prevent any contracting party from maintaining its requirements existing on the date of this Agreement as to the eligibility of goods for entry at preferential rates of duty.

2. Nothing in this Article shall prevent any contracting party from imposing at any time on the importation of any product:

(a) a charge equivalent to an internal tax imposed consistently with the provisions of paragraph 2 of Article III in respect of the like domestic product or in respect of an article from which the imported product has been manufactured or produced in whole or in part;

(b) any anti-dumping or countervailing duty applied consistently with the provisions of Article VI;

(c) fees or other charges commensurate with the cost of services rendered.

3. No contracting party shall alter its method of determining dutiable value or of converting currencies so as to impair the value of any of the concessions provided for in the appropriate Schedule annexed to this Agreement.

4. If any contracting party establishes, maintains or authorizes, formally or in effect, a monopoly of the importation of any product described in the appropriate Schedule annexed to this Agreement, such monopoly shall not, except as provided for in that Schedule or as otherwise agreed between the parties which initially negotiated the concession, operate so as to afford protection on the average in excess of the amount of protection provided for in that Schedule. The provisions of this paragraph shall not limit the use by contracting parties of any form of assistance to domestic producers permitted by other provisions of this Agreement.

5. If any contracting party considers that a product is not receiving from

another contracting party the treatment which the first contracting party believes to have been contemplated by a concession provided for in the appropriate Schedule annexed to this Agreement, it shall bring the matter directly to the attention of the other contracting party. If the latter agrees that the treament contemplated was that claimed by the first contracting party, but declares that such treatment cannot be accorded because a court or other proper authority has ruled to the effect that the product involved cannot be classified under the tariff laws of such contracting party so as to permit the treatment contemplated in this Agreement, the two contracting parties, together with any other contracting parties substantially interested, shall enter promptly into further negotiations with a view to a contemplated adjustment of the matter.

6. (a) The specific duties and charges included in the Schedules relating to contracting parties members of the International Monetary Fund, and margins of preference in specific duties and charges maintained by such contracting parties, are expressed in the appropriate currency at the par value accepted or provisionally recognized by the Fund at the date of this Agreement. Accordingly, in case this par value is reduced consistently with the Articles of Agreement of the International Monetary Fund by more than twenty per centum, such specific duties and charges and margins of preference may be adjusted to take account of such reduction; *Provided* that the Contracting Parties (i.e., the contracting parties acting jointly as provided for in Article XXV) concur that such adjustments will not impair the value of the concessions provided for in the appropriate Schedule or elsewhere in this Agreement, due account being taken of all factors which may influence the need for, or urgency of, such adjustments.

(b) Similar provisions shall apply to any contracting party not a member of the Fund, as from the date on which such contracting party becomes a member of the Fund or enters into a special exchange agreement in pursuance of Article XV.

7. The Schedules annexed to this Agreement are hereby made an integral part of Part I of this Agreement.

Part II

Article III.—NATIONAL TREATMENT ON INTERNAL TAXATION AND REGULATION

1. The contracting parties recognize that internal taxes and other internal charges, and laws, regulations and requirements affecting the internal sale, offering for sale, purchase, transportation, distribution or use of products, and internal quantitative regulations requiring the mixture, processing or use of products in specified amounts or proportions, should not be applied to imported or domestic products so as to afford protection to domestic production.

2. The products of the territory of any contracting party imported into the territory of any other contracting party shall not be subject, directly or indirectly, to internal taxes or other internal charges of any kind in excess of those applied, directly or indirectly, to like domestic products. Moreover, no contracting party shall otherwise apply internal taxes or other internal charges to imported or domestic products in a manner contrary to the principles set forth in paragraph 1.

3. With respect to any existing tax which is inconsistent with the provisions of paragraph 2, but which is specifically authorized under a trade agreement, in force on April 10, 1947, in which the import duty on the taxed product is bound against increase, the contracting party imposing the tax shall be free to postpone the application of the provisions of paragraph 2 to such tax until such time as it can obtain release from the obligations of such trade agreement in order to permit the increase of such duty to the extent necessary to compensate for the elimination of the protective element of the tax.

4. The products of the territory of any contracting party imported into the territory of any other contracting party shall be accorded treatment no less favourable than that accorded to like products of national origin in respect of

all laws, regulations and requirements affecting their internal sale, offering for sale, purchase, transportation, distribution or use. The provisions of this paragraph shall not prevent the application of differential internal transportation charges which are based exclusively on the economic operation of the means of transport and not on the nationality of the product.

5. No contracting party shall establish or maintain any internal quantitative regulation relating to the mixture, processing or use of products in specified amounts or proportions which requires, directly or indirectly, that any specified amount or proportion of any product which is the subject of the regulation must be supplied from domestic sources. Moreover, no contracting party shall otherwise apply internal quantitative regulations in a manner contrary to the principles set forth in paragraph 1.

6. The provisions of paragraph 5 shall not apply to any internal quantitative regulation in force in the territory of any contracting party on July 1, 1939, April 10, 1947, or March 24, 1948, at the option of that contracting party; *Provided* that any such regulation which is contrary to the provisions of paragraph 5 shall not be modified to the detriment of imports and shall be treated as a customs duty for the purpose of negotiation.

7. No internal quantitative regulation relating to the mixture, processing or use of products in specified amounts or proportions shall be applied in such a manner as to allocate any such amount or proportion among external sources of supply.

8. (a) The provisions of this Article shall not apply to laws, regulations or requirements governing the procurement by governmental agencies of products purchased for governmental purposes and not with a view to commercial resale or with a view to use in the production of goods for commercial sale.

(b) The provisions of this Article shall not prevent the payment of subsidies exclusively to domestic producers, including payments to domestic producers derived from the proceeds of internal taxes or charges applied consistently

with the provisions of this Article and subsidies effected through governmental purchases of domestic products.

9. The contracting parties recognize that internal maximum price control measures, even though conforming to the other provisions of this Article, can have effects prejudicial to the interests of contracting parties supplying imported products. Accordingly, contracting parties applying such measures shall take account of the interests of exporting contracting parties with a view to avoiding to the fullest practicable extent such prejudicial effects.

10. The provisions of this Article shall not prevent any contracting party from establishing or maintaining internal quantitative regulations relating to exposed cinematograph films and meeting the requirements of Article IV.

Article IV.—SPECIAL PROVISIONS RELATING TO CINEMATOGRAPH FILMS

If any contracting party establishes or maintains internal quantitative regulations relating to exposed cinematograph films, such regulations shall take the form of screen quotas which shall conform to the following requirements:

(a) Screen quotas may require the exhibition of cinematograph films of national origin during a specified minimum proportion of the total screen time actually utilized, over a specified period of not less than one year, in the commercial exhibition of all films of whatever origin, and shall be computed on the basis of screen time per theatre per year or the equivalent thereof;

(b) With the exception of screen time reserved for films of national origin under a screen quota, screen time including that released by administrative action from screen time reserved for films of national origin, shall not be allocated formally or in effect among sources of supply;

(c) Notwithstanding the provisions of sub-paragraph (b) of this Article, any contracting party may maintain screen quotas conforming to the requirements of sub-paragraph (a) of this Article which reserve a minimum proportion of screen time for films of a specified origin other than that of the contracting party imposing such screen quotas; *Provided* that no such minimum proportion of screen time shall be increased above the level in effect on April 10, 1947;

(d) Screen quotas shall be subject to negotiation for their limitation, liberalization or elimination.

Article V.—FREEDOM OF TRANSIT

1. Goods (including baggage), and also vessels and other means of transport, shall be deemed to be in transit across the territory of a contracting party when the passage across such territory, with or without trans-shipment, warehousing, breaking bulk, or change in the mode of transport, is only a portion of a complete journey beginning and terminating beyond the frontier of the contracting party across whose territory the traffic passes. Traffic of this nature is termed in this Article "traffic in transit".

2. There shall be freedom of transit through the territory of each contracting party, via the routes most convenient for international transit, for traffic in transit to or from the territory of other contracting parties. No distinction shall be made which is based on the flag of vessels, the place of origin, departure, entry, exist or destination, or on any circumstances relating to the ownership of goods, of vessels or of other means of transport.

3. Any contracting party may require that traffic in transit through its territory be entered at the proper custom house, but, except in cases of failure to comply with applicable customs laws and regulations, such traffic coming from or going to the territory of other contracting parties shall not be subject to any unnecessary delays or restrictions and shall be exempt from customs duties and from all transit duties or other charges imposed in respect of transit, except charges for transportation or those commensurate with administrative expenses entailed by transit or with the cost of services rendered.

4. All charges and regulations imposed by contracting parties on traffic in transit to or from the territories of other contracting parties shall be reasonable, having regard to the conditions of the traffic.

5. With respect to all charges, regulations and formalities in connection with transit, each contracting party shall accord to traffic in transit to or from the territory of any other contracting party treatment no less favourable than the treatment accorded to traffic in transit to or from any third country.

6. Each contracting party shall accord to products which have been in transit through the territory of any other contracting party treatment no less favourable than that which would have been accorded to such products had they been transported from their place of origin to their destination without going through the territory of such other contracting party. Any contracting party shall, however, be free to maintain its requirements of direct consignment existing on the date of this Agreement, in respect of any goods in regard to which such direct consignment is a requisite condition of eligibility for entry of the goods at preferential rates of duty or has relation to the contracting party's prescribed method of valuation for duty purposes.

7. The provisions of this Article shall not apply to the operation of aircraft in transit, but shall apply to air transit of goods (including baggage).

Article VI.—ANTI-DUMPING AND COUNTERVAILING DUTIES

1. The contracting parties recognize that dumping, by which products of one country are introduced into the commerce of another country at less than the normal value of the products, is to be condemned if it causes or threatens material injury to an established industry in the territory of a contracting party or materially retards the establishment of a domestic industry. For the purposes of this Article, a product is to be considered as being introduced into the commerce of an importing country at less than its normal value, if the price of the product exported from one country to another—

(a) is less than the comparable price, in the ordinary course of trade, for the like product when destined for consumption in the exporting country, or

(b) in the absence of such domestic price, is less than either (i) the highest comparable price for the like product for export to any third country in the ordinary course of trade, or (ii) the cost of production of the product in the country of origin plus a reasonable addition for selling cost and profit.

Due allowance shall be made in each case for differences in conditions and terms of sale, for differences in taxation, and for other differences affecting price comparability.

2. In order to offset or prevent dumping, a contracting party may levy on any dumped product an anti-dumping duty not greater in amount than the margin of dumping in respect of such product. For the purposes of this Article, the margin of dumping is the price difference determined in accordance with the provisions of paragraph 1.

3. No countervailing duty shall be levied on any product of the territory of any contracting party imported into the territory of another contracting party in excess of an amount equal to the estimated bounty or subsidy determined to have been granted, directly or indirectly, on the manufacture, production or export of such product in the country of origin or exportation, including any special subsidy to the transportation of a particular product. The term "countervailing duty" shall be understood to mean a special duty levied for the purpose of offsetting any bounty or subsidy bestowed, directly or indirectly, upon the manufacture, production or export of any merchandise.

4. No product of the territory of any contracting party imported into the territory of any other contracting party shall be subject to anti-dumping or countervailing duty by reason of the exemption of such product from duties or taxes borne by the like product when destined for consumption in the country of origin or exportation, or by reason of the refund of such duties or taxes.

5. No product of the territory of any contracting party imported into the territory of any other contracting party shall be subject to both anti-dumping and countervailing duties to compensate for the same situation of dumping or export subsidization.

6.(a) No contracting party shall levy any anti-dumping or countervailing duty on the importation of any product of the territory of another contracting party unless it determines that the effect of the dumping or subsidization, as the case may be, is such as to cause or threaten material injury to an established domestic industry, or is such as to retard materially the establishment of a domestic industry.

(b) The Contracting Parties may waive the requirement of subparagraph (a) of this paragraph so as to permit a contracting party to levy an anti-dumping or countervailing duty on the importation of any product for the purpose of offsetting dumping or subsidization which causes or threatens material injury to an industry in the territory of another contracting party exporting the product concerned to the territory of the importing contracting party. The Contracting Parties shall waive the requirements of sub-paragraph (a) of this paragraph, so as to permit the levying of a countervailing duty, in cases in which they find that a subsidy is causing or threatening material injury to an industry in the territory of another contracting party exporting the product concerned to the territory of the importing contracting party.

(c) In exceptional circumstances, however, where delay might cause damage which would be difficult to repair, a contracting party may levy a countervailing duty for the purpose referred to in sub-paragraph (b) of this paragraph without the prior approval of the Contracting Parties; *Provided* that such action shall be reported immediately to the Contracting Parties and that the countervailing duty shall be withdrawn promptly if the Contracting Parties disapprove.

7. A system for the stabilization of the domestic price or of the return to domestic producers of a primary commodity, independently of the movements of export prices, which results at times in the sale of the commodity for export at a price lower than the comparable price charged for the like commodity to buy-

ers in the domestic market, shall be presumed not to result in material injury within the meaning of paragraph 6 if it is determined by consultation among the contracting parties substantially interested in the commodity concerned that:

(a) the system has also resulted in the sale of the commodity for export at a price higher than the comparable price charged for the like commodity to buyers in the domestic market, and

(b) the system is so operated, either because of the effective regulation of production, or otherwise, as not to stimulate exports unduly or otherwise seriously prejudice the interests of other contracting parties.

Article VII.—VALUATION FOR CUSTOMS PURPOSES

1. The contracting parties recognize the validity of the general principles of valuation set forth in the following paragraphs of this Article, and they undertake to give effect to such principles, in respect of all products subject to duties or other charges or restrictions on importation and exportation based upon or regulated in any manner by value. Moreover, they shall, upon a request by another contracting party review the operation of any of their laws or regulations relating to value for customs purposes in the light of these principles. The Contracting Parties may request from contracting parties reports on steps taken by them in pursuance of the provisions of this Article.

2. (a) The value for customs purposes of imported merchandise should be based on the actual value of the imported merchandise on which duty is assessed, or of like merchandise, and should not be based on the value of merchandise of national origin or on arbitrary or fictitious values.

(b) "Actual value" should be the price at which, at a time and place determined by the legislation of the country of importation, such or like merchandise is sold or offered for sale in the ordinary course of trade under fully competitive conditions. To the extent to which the price of such or like merchandise is governed by the quantity in a particular transaction, the price to be considered should uniformly be related to either (i)

comparable quantities, or (ii) quantities not less favourable to importers than those in which the greater volume of the merchandise is sold in the trade between the countries of exportation and importation.

(c) When the actual value is not ascertainable in accordance with subparagraph (b) of this paragraph, the value for customs purposes should be based on the nearest ascertainable equivalent of such value.

3. The value for customs purposes of any imported product should not include the amount of any internal tax, applicable within the country of origin or export, from which the imported product has been exempted or has been or will be relieved by means of refund.

4. (a) Except as otherwise provided for in this paragraph, where it is necessary for the purposes of paragraph 2 of this Article for a contracting party to convert into its own currency a price expressed in the currency of another country, the conversion rate of exchange to be used shall be based, for each currency involved, on the par value as established pursuant to the Articles of Agreement of the International Monetary Fund or on the rate of exchange recognized by the Fund, or on the par value established in accordance with a special exchange agreement entered into pursuant to Article XV of this Agreement.

(b) Where no such established par value and no such recognized rate of exchange exist, the conversion rate shall reflect effectively the current value of such currency in commercial transactions.

(c) The Contracting Parties, in agreement with the International Monetary Fund, shall formulate rules governing the conversion by contracting parties of any foreign currency in respect of which multiple rates of exchange are maintained consistently with the Articles of Agreement of the International Monetary Fund. Any contracting party may apply such rules in respect of such foreign currencies for the purposes of paragraph 2 of this Article as an alternative to the use of par values. Until such rules are adopted by the Contracting

Parties, any contracting party may employ, in respect of any such foreign currency, rules of conversion for the purposes of paragraph 2 of this Article which are designed to reflect effectively the value of such foreign currency in commercial transactions.

(d) Nothing in this paragraph shall be construed to require any contracting party to alter the method of converting currencies for customs purposes which is applicable in its territory on the date of this Agreement, if such alteration would have the effect of increasing generally the amounts of duty payable.

5. The bases and methods for determining the value of products subject to duties or other charges or restrictions based upon or regulated in any manner by value should be stable and should be given sufficient publicity to enable traders to estimate, with a reasonable degree of certainty, the value for customs purposes.

Article VIII.—FEES AND FORMALITIES CONNECTED WITH IMPORTATION AND EXPORTATION

1. (a) All fees and charges of whatever character (other than import and export duties and other than taxes within the purview of Article III) imposed by contracting parties on or in connection with importation or exportation shall be limited in amount to the approximate cost of services rendered and shall not represent an indirect protection to domestic products or a taxation of imports or exports for fiscal purposes.

(b) The contracting parties recognize the need for reducing the number and diversity of fees and charges referred to in sub-paragraph (a).

(c) The contracting parties also recognize the need for minimizing the incidence and complexity of import and export formalities and for decreasing and simplifying import and export documentation requirements.

2. A contracting party shall, upon request by another contracting party or by the Contracting Parties, review the operation of its laws and regulations in the light of the provisions of this Article.

3. No contracting party shall impose substantial penalties for minor breaches of customs regulations or procedural requirements. In particular, no penalty in respect of any omission or mistake in customs documentation which is easily rectifiable and obviously made without fraudulent intent or gross negligence shall be greater than necessary to serve merely as a warning.

4. The provisions of this Article shall extend to fees, charges, formalities and requirements imposed by governmental authorities in connection with importation and exportation, including those relating to:

(a) consular transactions, such as consular invoices and certificates;

(b) quantitative restrictions;

(c) licensing;

(d) exchange control;

(e) statistical services;

(f) documents, documentation and certification;

(g) analysis and inspection; and

(h) quarantine, sanitation and fumigation.

Article IX.—MARKS OF ORIGIN

1. Each contracting party shall accord to the products of the territories of other contracting parties treatment with regard to marking requirements no less favourable than the treatment accorded to like products of any third country.

2. The contracting parties recognize that, in adopting and enforcing laws and regulations relating to marks of origin, the difficulties and inconveniences which such measures may cause to the commerce and industry of exporting countries should be reduced to a minimum, due regard being had to the necessity of protecting consumers against fraudulent or misleading indications.

3. Whenever it is administratively practicable to do so, contracting parties should permit required marks of origin to be affixed at the time of importation.

4. The laws and regulations of contracting parties relating to the marking of imported products shall be such as to permit compliance without seriously damaging the products, or materially reducing their value, or unreasonably increasing their cost.

5. As a general rule, no special duty or penalty should be imposed by any con-

tracting party for failure to comply with marking requirements prior to importation unless corrective marking is unreasonably delayed or deceptive marks have been affixed or the required marking has been intentionally omitted.

6. The contracting parties shall cooperate with each other with a view to preventing the use of trade names in such manner as to misrepresent the true origin of a product, to the detriment of such distinctive regional or geographical names of products of the territory of a contracting party as are protected by its legislation. Each contracting party shall accord full and sympathetic consideration to such requests or representations as may be made by any other contracting party regarding the application of the undertaking set forth in the preceding sentence to names of products which have been communicated to it by the other contracting party.

Article X.—PUBLICATION AND AD-MINISTRATION OF TRADE REG-ULATIONS

1. Laws, regulations, judicial decisions and administrative rulings of general application, made effective by any contracting party, pertaining to the classification or the valuation of products for customs purposes, or to rates of duty, taxes or other charges, or to requirements, restrictions or prohibitions on imports or exports or on the transfer of payments therefor, or affecting their sale, distribution, transportation, insurance, warehousing, inspection, exhibition, processing, mixing or other use, shall be published promptly in such a manner as to enable governments and traders to become acquainted with them. Agreements affecting international trade policy which are in force between the government or a governmental agency of any contracting party and the government or governmental agency of any other contracting party shall also be published. The provisions of this paragraph shall not require any contracting party to disclose confidential information which would impede law enforcement or otherwise be contrary to the public interest or would prejudice the legitimate commercial interests of particular enterprises, public or private.

2. No measure of general application taken by any contracting party effecting an advance in a rate of duty or other charge on imports under an established and uniform practice, or imposing a new or more burdensome requirement, restriction or prohibition on imports, or on the transfer of payments therefor, shall be enforced before such measure has been officially published.

3. (a) Each contracting party shall administer in a uniform, impartial and reasonable manner all its laws, regulations, decisions and rulings of the kind described in paragraph 1 of this Article.

(b) Each contracting party shall maintain, or institute as soon as practicable, judicial, arbitral or administrative tribunals or procedures for the purpose, *inter alia,* of the prompt review and correction of administrative action relating to customs matters. Such tribunals or procedures shall be independent of the agencies entrusted with administrative enforcement and their decisions shall be implemented by, and shall govern the practice of, such agencies unless an appeal is lodged with a court or tribunal of superior jurisdiction within the time prescribed for appeals to be lodged by importers; *Provided* that the central administration of such agency may take steps to obtain a review of the matter in another proceeding if there is good cause to believe that the decision is inconsistent with established principles of law or the actual facts.

(c) The provisions of sub-paragraph (b) of this paragraph shall not require the elimination or substitution of procedures in force in the territory of a contracting party on the date of this Agreement which in fact provide for an objective and impartial review of administrative action even though such procedures are not fully or formally independent of the agencies entrusted with administrative enforcement. Any contracting party employing such procedures shall, upon request, furnish the Contracting Parties with full information thereon in order that they may determine whether such procedures conform to the requirements of this sub-paragraph.

Article XI.—GENERAL ELIMINATION OF QUANTITATIVE RESTRICTIONS

1. No prohibitions or restrictions other than duties, taxes or other charges, whether made effective through quotas, import or export licenses or other measures, shall be instituted or maintained by any contracting party on the importation of any product of the territory of any other contracting party or on the exportation or sale for export of any product destined for the territory of any other contracting party.

2. The provisions of paragraph 1 of this Article shall not extend to the following:

(a) Export prohibitions or restrictions temporarily applied to prevent or relieve critical shortages of foodstuffs or other products essential to the exporting contracting party;

(b) Import and export prohibitions or restrictions necessary to the application of standards or regulations for the classification, grading or marketing of commodities in international trade;

(c) Import restrictions on any agricultural or fisheries product, imported in any form, necessary to the enforcement of governmental measures which operates:

(i) to restrict the quantities of the like domestic product permitted to be marketed or produced, or, if there is no substantial domestic production of the like product, of a domestic product for which the imported product can be directly substituted; or

(ii) to remove a temporary surplus of the like domestic product, or, if there is not substantial domestic production of the like product, of a domestic product for which the imported product can be directly substituted, by making the surplus available to certain groups of domestic consumers free of charge or at prices below the current market level; or

(iii) to restrict the quantities permitted to be produced of any animal product the production of which is directly dependent, wholly or mainly, on the imported commodity, if the domestic production of that commodity is relatively negligible.

Any contracting party applying restrictions on the importation of any product pursuant to sub-paragraph (c) of this paragraph shall give public notice of the total quantity or value of the product permitted to be imported during a specified future period and of any change in such quantity or value. Moreover, any restrictions applied under (i) above shall not be such as will reduce the total of imports relative to the total of domestic production, as compared with the proportion which might reasonably be expected to rule between the two in the absence of restrictions. In determining this proportion, the contracting party shall pay due regard to the proportion prevailing during a previous representative period and to any special factors which may have affected or may be affecting the trade in the product concerned.

Article XII.—RESTRICTIONS TO SAFEGUARD THE BALANCE OF PAYMENTS

1. Notwithstanding the provisions of paragraph 1 of Article XI, any contracting party, in order to safeguard its external financial position and its balance of payments, may restrict the quantity or value of merchandise permitted to be imported, subject to the provisions of the following paragraphs of this Article.

2. (a) Import restrictions instituted, maintained or intensified by a contracting party under this Article shall not exceed those necessary:

(i) to forestall the imminent threat of, or to stop, a serious decline in its monetary reserves, or

(ii) in the case of a contracting party with very low monetary reserves, to achieve a reasonable rate of increase in its reserves.

Due regard shall be paid in either case to any special factors which may be affecting the reserves of such contracting party or its need for reserves, including, where special external credits or other resources are available to it, the need to provide for the appropriate use of such credits or resources.

(b) Contracting parties applying restrictions under sub-paragraph (a) of this paragraph shall progressively relax them as such conditions improve, maintaining them only to the extent that the conditions specified in that sub-paragraph still justify their application. They shall eliminate the restrictions when conditions would no longer justify their institution or maintenance under that sub-paragraph.

3. (a) Contracting parties undertake, in carrying out their domestic policies, to pay due regard to the need for maintaining or restoring equilibrium in their balance of payments on a sound and lasting basis and to the desirability of avoiding an uneconomic employment of productive resources. They recognize that in order to achieve these ends, it is desirable so far as possible to adopt measures which expand rather than contract international trade.

(b) Contracting parties applying restrictions under this Article may determine the incidence of the restrictions on imports of different products or classes of products in such a way as to give priority to the importation of those products which are more essential.

(c) Contracting parties applying restrictions under this Article undertake:

(i) to avoid unnecessary damage to the commercial or economic interests of any other contracting party;

(ii) not to apply restrictions so as to prevent unreasonably the importation of any description of goods in minimum commercial quantities the exclusion of which would impair regular channels of trade; and

(iii) not to apply restrictions which would prevent the importation of commercial samples or prevent compliance with patent, trade mark, copyright, or similar procedures.

(d) The contracting parties recognize that, as a result of domestic policies directed towards the achievement and maintenance of full and productive employment or towards the development of economic resources, a contracting party may experience a high level of demand for imports involving a threat to its monetary reserves of the sort referred to in paragraph 2(a) of this Article. Accordingly, a contracting party otherwise

complying with the provisions of this Article shall not be required to withdraw or modify restrictions on the ground that a change in those policies would render unnecessary restrictions which it is applying under this Article.

4. (a) Any contracting party applying new restrictions or raising the general level of its existing restrictions by a substantial intensification of the measures applied under this Article shall immediately after instituting or intensifying such restrictions (or, in circumstances in which prior consultation is practicable, before doing so) consult with the contracting parties as to the nature of its balance of payments difficulties, alternative corrective measures which may be available, and the possible effect of the restrictions on the economies of other contracting parties.

(b) On a date to be determined by them, the Contracting Parties shall review all restrictions still applied under this Article on that date. Beginning one year after that date, contracting parties applying import restrictions under this Article shall enter into consultations of the type provided for in sub-paragraph (a) of this paragraph with the Contracting Parties annually.

(c)(i) If, in the course of consultations with a contracting party under sub-paragraph (a) or (b) above, the Contracting Parties find that the restrictions are not consistent with the provisions of this Article or with those of Article XIII (subject to the provisions of Article XIV), they shall indicate the nature of the inconsistency and may advise that the restrictions be suitably modified.

(ii) If, however, as a result of the consultations, the Contracting Parties determine that the restrictions are being applied in a manner involving an inconsistency of a serious nature with the provisions of this Article or with those of Article XIII (subject to the provisions of Article XIV) and that damage to the trade of any contracting party is caused or threatened thereby, they shall so inform the contracting party applying the restrictions and shall make appropriate recommendations for securing conformity with such provisions within a specified period of time. If such, contracting party does not comply with these recommendations within the specified period, the Contracting Parties may release any contracting party the trade of which is adversely affected by the restrictions from such obligations under this Agreement towards the contracting party applying the restrictions as they determine to be appropriate in the circumstances.

(d) The Contracting Parties shall invite any contracting party which is applying restrictions under this Article to enter into consultations with them at the request of any contracting party which can establish a *prima facie* case that the restrictions are inconsistent with the provisions of this Article or with those of Article XIII (subject to the provisions of Article XIV) and that its trade is adversely affected thereby. However, no such invitation shall be issued unless the contracting parties have ascertained that direct discussions between the Contracting Parties concerned have not been successful. If, as a result of the consultations with the Contracting Parties, no agreement is reached and they determine that the restrictions are being applied inconsistently with such provisions, and that damage to the trade of the contracting party initiating the procedure is caused or threatened thereby, they shall recommend the withdrawal or modification of the restrictions. If the restrictions are not withdrawn or modified within such time as the Contracting Parties may prescribe, they may release the contracting party initiating the procedure from such obligations under this Agreement towards the contracting party applying the restrictions as they determine to be appropriate in the circumstances.

(e) In proceeding under this paragraph, the Contracting Parties shall have due regard to any special external factors adversely affecting the export trade of the contracting party applying restrictions.

(f) Determinations under this paragraph shall be rendered expeditiously and, if possible, within sixty days of the initiation of the consultations.

5. If there is a persistent and widespread application of import restrictions under this Article, indicating the existence of a general disequilibrium which is restricting international trade, the Contracting Parties shall initiate discussions to consider whether other measures might be taken, either by those contracting parties the balances of payments of which are under pressure or by those the balances of payments of which are tending to be exceptionally favourable, or by any appropriate intergovernmental organization, to remove the underlying causes of the disequilibrium. On the invitation of the Contracting Parties, contracting parties shall participate in such discussions.

Article XIII.—NON-DISCRIMINATORY ADMINISTRATION OF QUANTITATIVE RESTRICTIONS

1. No prohibition or restriction shall be applied by any contracting party on the importation of any product of the territory of any other contracting party or on the exportation of any product destined for the territory of any other contracting party, unless the importation of the like product of all third countries or the exportation of the like product to all third countries is similarly prohibited or restricted.

2. In applying import restrictions to any product, contracting parties shall aim at a distribution of trade in such product approaching as closely as possible the shares which the various contracting parties might be expected to obtain in the absence of such restrictions, and to this end shall observe the following provisions:

(a) Whenever practicable, quotas representing the total amount of permitted imports (whether allocated among supplying countries or not) shall be fixed, and notice given of their amount in accordance with paragraph 3(b) of this Article;

(b) In cases in which quotas are not practicable, the restrictions may be applied by means of import licences or permits without a quota;

(c) Contracting parties shall not, except for purposes of operating quotas allocated in accordance with subparagraph (d) of this paragraph, require that import licenses or permits be utilized for the importation of the product concerned from a particular country or source;

(d) In cases in which a quota is allocated among supplying countries, the contracting party applying the restrictions may seek agreement with respect to the allocation of shares in the quota with all other contracting parties having a substantial interest in supplying the product concerned. In cases in which this method is not reasonably practicable, the contracting party concerned shall allot to contracting parties having a substantial interest in supplying the product shares based upon the proportions, supplied by such contracting parties during a previous representative period, of the total quantity or value of imports of the product, due account being taken of any special factors which may have affected or may be affecting the trade in the product. No conditions or formalities shall be imposed which would prevent any contracting party from utilizing fully the share of any such total quantity or value which has been allotted to it, subject to importation being made within any prescribed period to which the quota may relate.

3. (a) In cases in which import licences are issued in connection with import restrictions, the contracting party applying the restrictions shall provide, upon the request of any contracting party having an interest in the trade in the product concerned, all relevant information concerning the administration of the restrictions, the import licences granted over a recent period and the distribution of such licences among supplying countries; *Provided* that there shall be no obligation to supply information as to the names of importing or supplying enterprises.

(b) In the case of import restrictions involving the fixing of quotas, the contracting party applying the restrictions shall give public notice of the total quantity or value of the product or products which will be permitted to be imported during a specified future period and of any change in such quantity or value. Any supplies of the product in question which were *en route* at the time at which public notice was given shall not be excluded from entry; *Provided* that they may be counted so far as practicable, against the quantity permitted to be imported in the period in question, and also, where necessary, against the quanti-

ties permitted to be imported in the next following period or periods; and *Provided* further that if any contracing party customarily exempts from such restrictions products entered for consumption or withdrawn from warehouse for consumption during a period of thirty days after the day of such public notice, such practice shall be considered full compliance with this sub-paragraph.

(c) In the case of quotas allocated among supplying countries, the contracting party applying the restrictions shall promptly inform all other contracting parties having an interest in supplying the product concerned of the shares in the quota currently allocated, by quantity or value, to the various supplying countries and shall give public notice thereof.

4. With regard to restrictions applied in accordance with paragraph 2(d) of this Article or under paragraph 2(c) of Article XI, the selection of a representative period for any product and the appraisal of any special factors affecting the trade in the product shall be made initially by the contracting party applying the restriction; *Provided* that such contracting party shall, upon the request of any other contracting party having a substantial interest in supplying that product or upon the request of the Contracting Parties, consult promptly with the other contracting party or the Contracting Parties regarding the need for an adjustment of the proportion determined or of the base period selected, or for the reappraisal of the special factors involved, or for the elimination of conditions, formalities or any other provisions established unilaterally relating to the allocation of an adequate quota or its unrestricted utilization.

5. The provisions of this Article shall apply to any tariff quota instituted or maintained by any contracting party, and, in so far as applicable, the principles of this Article shall also extend to export restrictions.

Article XIV.—EXCEPTIONS TO THE RULE OF NON-DISCRIMINATION[1]

1. A contracting party which applies restrictions under Article XII or under

[1]Text as amended Feb. 15, 1961, on which date Annex J was deleted.

Section B of Article XVIII may, in the application of such restrictions, deviate from the provisions of Article XIII in a manner having equivalent effect to restrictions on payments and transfers for current international transactions which that contracting party may at that time apply under Article VIII or XIV of the Articles of Agreement of the International Monetary Fund, or under analogous provisions of a special exchange agreement entered into pursuant to paragraph 6 of Article XV.

2. A contracting party which is applying import restrictions under Article XII or under Section B of Article XVIII may, with the consent of the Contracting Parties, temporarily deviate from the provisions of Article XIII in respect of a small part of its external trade where the benefits to the contracting party or contracting parties concerned substantially outweigh any injury which may result to the trade or other contracting parties.

3. The provisions of Article XIII shall not preclude a group of territories having a common quota in the International Monetary Fund from applying against imports from other countries, but not among themselves, restrictions in accordance with the provisions of Article XII or of Section B of Article XVIII on condition that such restrictions are in all other respects consistent with the provisions of Article XIII.

4. A contracting party applying import restrictions under Article XII or under Section B of Article XVIII shall not be precluded by Articles XI to XV or Section B of Article XVIII of this Agreement from applying measures to direct its exports in such a manner as to increase its earnings of currencies which it can use without deviation from the provisions of Article XIII.

5. A contracting party shall not be precluded by Articles XI to XV, inclusive, or by Section B of Article XVIII, of this Agreement from applying quantitative restrictions:

(a) having equivalent effect to exchange restrictions authorized under Section 3(b) of Article VII of the Articles of Agreement of the International Monetary Fund, or

(b) under the preferential arrangements provided for in Annex A of this Agreement, pending the outcome of the negotiations referred to therein.

Article XV.—EXCHANGE ARRANGEMENTS

1. The Contracting Parties shall seek co-operation with the International Monetary Fund to the end that the Contracting Parties and the Fund may pursue a coordinated policy with regard to exchange questions within the jurisdiction of the Fund and questions of quantitative restrictions and other trade measures within the jurisdiction of the Contracting Parties.

2. In all cases in which the Contracting Parties are called upon to consider or deal with problems concerning monetary reserves, balances of payments or foreign exchange arrangement, they shall consult fully with the International Monetary Fund. In such consultations, the Contracting Parties shall accept all findings of statistical and other facts presented by the Fund relating to foreign exchange, monetary reserves and balances of payments, and shall accept the determination of the Fund as to whether action by a contracting party in exchange matters is in accordance with the Articles of Agreement of the International Monetary Fund, or with the terms of a special exchange agreement between that contracting party and the Contracting Parties. The Contracting Parties, in reaching their final decision in cases involving the criteria set forth in paragraph 2(a) of Article XII or in paragraph 9 of Article XVIII, shall accept the determination of the Fund as to what constitutes a serious decline in the contracting party's monetary reserves, a very low level of its monetary reserves or a reasonable rate of increase in its monetary reserves, and as to the financial aspects of other matters covered in consultation in such cases.

3. The Contracting Parties shall seek agreement with the Fund regarding procedures for consultation under paragraph 2 of this Article.

4. Contracting parties shall not, by exchange action, frustrate the intent of the provisions of this Agreement, nor, by trade action, the intent of the provisions of the Articles of Agreement of the International Monetary Fund.

5. If the Contracting Parties consider, at any time, that exchange restrictions on

payments and transfers in connection with imports are being applied by a contracting party in a manner inconsistent with the exceptions provided for in this Agreement for quantitative restrictions, they shall report thereon to the Fund.

6. Any contracting party which is not a member of the Fund shall, within a time to be determined by the Contracting Parties after consultation with the Fund, become a member of the Fund, or, failing that, enter into a special exchange agreement with the Contracting Parties. A contracting party which ceases to be a member of the Fund shall forthwith enter into a special exchange agreement with the Contracting Parties. Any special exchange agreement entered into by a contracting party under this paragraph shall thereupon become part of its obligations under this Agreement.

7. (a) A special exchange agreement between a contracting party and the Contracting Parties under paragraph 6 of this Article shall provide to the satisfaction of the Contracting Parties that the objectives of this Agreement will not be frustrated as a result of action in exchange matters by the contracting party in question.

(b) The terms of any such agreement shall not impose obligations on the contracting party in exchange matters generally more restrictive than those imposed by the Articles of Agreement of the International Monetary Fund on members of the Fund.

8. A contracting party which is not a member of the Fund shall furnish such information within the general scope of section 5 of Article VIII of the Articles of Agreement of the International Monetary Fund as the Contracting Parties may require in order to carry out their functions under this Agreement.

9. Nothing in this Agreement shall preclude:

(a) the use by a contracting party of exchange controls or exchange restrictions in accordance with the Articles of Agreement of the International Monetary Fund or with that contracting party's special exchange agreement with the Contracting Parties, or

(b) the use by a contracting party of restrictions or controls on imports or exports, the sole effect of which, additional to the effects permitted under Article XI, XII, XIII and XIV, is to make effective such exchange controls or exchange restrictions.

Article XVI.—SUBSIDIES
Section A—Subsidies in General

1. If any contracting party grants or maintains any subsidy, including any form of income or price support, which operates directly or indirectly to increase exports of any product from, or to reduce imports of any product into, its territory, it shall notify the Contracting Parties in writing of the extent and nature of the subsidization, of the estimated effect of the subsidization on the quantity of the affected product or products imported into or exported from its territory and of the circumstances making the subsidization necessary. In any case in which it is determined that serious prejudice to the interests of any other contracting party is caused or threatened by any such subsidization, the contracting party granting the subsidy shall, upon request, discuss with the other contracting party or parties concerned, or with the Contracting Parties, the possibility of limiting the subsidization.

Section B—Additional Provisions on Export Subsidies

2. The contracting parties recognize that the granting by a contracting party of a subsidy on the export of any product may have harmful effects for other contracting parties, both importing and exporting, may cause undue disturbance to their normal commercial interests, and may hinder the achievement of the objectives of this Agreement.

3. Accordingly, contracting parties should seek to avoid the use of subsidies on the export of primary products. If, however, a contracting party grants directly or indirectly any form of subsidy which operates to increase the export of any primary product from its territory, such subsidy shall not be applied in a manner which results in that contracting party having more than an equitable share of world export trade in that product, account being taken of the shares of the contracting parties in such

trade in the product during a previous representative period, and any special factors which may have affected or may be affecting such trade in the product.

4. Further, as from 1 January 1958 or the earliest practicable date thereafter, contracting parties shall cease to grant either directly or indirectly any form of subsidy on the export of any product other than a primary product which subsidy results in the sale of such product for export at a price lower than the comparable price charged for the like product to buyers in the domestic market. Until 31 December 1957 no contracting party shall extend the scope of any such subsidization beyond that existing on 1 January 1955 by the introduction of new, or the extension of existing, subsidies.

5. The Contracting Parties shall review the operation of the provisions of this Article from time to time with a view to examining its effectiveness, in the light of actual experience, in promoting the objectives of this Agreement and avoiding subsidization seriously prejudicial to the trade or interests of contracting parties.

Article XVII.—STATE TRADING ENTERPRISES

1. (a) Each contracting party undertakes that if it establishes or maintains a State enterprise, wherever located, or grants to any enterprise, formally or in effect, exclusive or special privileges, such enterprise shall, in its purchases or sales involving either imports or exports, act in a manner consistent with the general principles of nondiscriminatory treatment prescribed in this Agreement for governmental measures affecting imports or exports by private traders.

(b) The provisions of sub-paragraph (a) of this paragraph shall be understood to require that such enterprises shall, having due regard to the other provisions of this Agreement, make any such purchases or sales solely in accordance with commercial considerations, including price, quality, availability, marketability, transportation and other conditions of purchase or sale, and shall afford the enterprises of the other contracting parties adequate opportunity, in accordance with customary business practice, to complete for participation in such purchases or sales.

(c) No contracting party shall prevent any enterprise (whether or not an enterprise described in sub-paragraph (a) of this paragraph) under its jurisdiction from acting in accordance with the principles of sub-paragraphs (a) and (b) of this paragraph.

2. The provisions of paragraph 1 of this Article shall not apply to imports of products for immediate or ultimate consumption in governmental use and not otherwise for re-sale or use in the production of goods for sale. With respect to such imports, each contracting party shall accord to the trade of the other contracting parties fair and equitable treatment.

3. The contracting parties recognize that enterprises of the kind described in paragraph 1(a) of this Article might be operated so as to create serious obstacles to trade; thus negotiations on a reciprocal and mutually advantageous basis designed to limit or reduce such obstacles are of importance to the expansion of international trade.

4. (a) Contracting parties shall notify the Contracting Parties of the products which are imported into or exported from their territories by enterprises of the kind described in paragraph 1(a) of this Article.

(b) A contracting party establishing, maintaining or authorizing an import monopoly of a product, which is not the subject of a concession under Article II, shall, on the request of another contracting party having a substantial trade in the product concerned, inform the Contracting Parties of the import markup on the product during a recent representative period, or, when it is not possible to do so, of the price charged on the resale of the product.

(c) The Contracting Parties may, at the request of a contracting party which has reason to believe that its interests under this Agreement are being adversely affected by the operations of an enterprise of the kind described in paragraph 1(a), request the contracting party establishing, maintaining or authorizing such enterprise to supply information about its operations related to the carrying out of the provisions of this Agreement.

(d) The provisions of this paragraph shall not require any contracting party to disclose confidential information which would impede law enforcement or otherwise be contrary to the public interest or would prejudice the legitimate commercial interests of particular enterprises.

Article XVIII.—GOVERNMENTAL ASSISTANCE TO ECONOMIC DEVELOPMENT

1. The contracting parties recognize that the attainment of the objectives of this Agreement will be facilitated by the progressive development of their economies, particularly of those contracting parties the economies of which can only support low standards of living and are in the early stages of development.

2. The contracting parties recognize further that it may be necessary for those contracting parties, in order to implement programmes and policies of economic development designed to raise the general standard of living of their people, to take protective or other measures affecting imports, and that such measures are justified in so far as they facilitate the attainment of the objectives of this Agreement. They agree, therefore, that those contracting parties should enjoy additional facilities to enable them (a) to maintain sufficient flexibility in their tariff structure to be able to grant the tariff protection required for the establishment of a particular industry and (b) to apply quantitative restrictions for balance of payments purposes in a manner which takes full account of the continued high level of demand for imports likely to be generated by their programmes of economic development.

3. The contracting parties recognize finally that with those additional facilities which are provided for in Sections A and B of this Article, the provisions of this Agreement would normally be sufficient to enable contracting parties to meet the requirements of their economic development. They agree, however, that there may be circumstances where no measure consistent with those provisions is practicable to permit a contracting party in the process of economic development to grant the governmental assistance required to promote the establishment of particular industries with a view to raising the general standard of living of its people. Special procedures are laid down in Sections C and D of this Article to deal with those cases.

4. (a) Consequently, a contracting party the economy of which can only support low standards of living and is in the early stages of development shall be free to deviate temporarily from the provisions of the other Articles of this Agreement, as provided in Sections A, B, and C of this Article.

(b) A contracting party the economy of which is in the process of development but which does not come within the scope of sub-paragraph (a) above, may submit applications to the Contracting Parties under Section D of this Article.

5. The contracting parties recognize that the export earnings of contracting parties the economies of which are of the type described in paragraph 4 (a) and (b) above, and which depend on exports of a small number of primary commodities may be seriously reduced by a decline in the sale of such commodities. Accordingly, when the exports of primary commodities by such a contracting party are seriously affected by measures taken by another contracting party, it may have resort to the consultation provisions of Article XXII of this Agreement.

6. The Contracting Parties shall review annually all measures applied pursuant to the provisions of Sections C and D of this Article.

Section A

7. (a) If a contracting party coming within the scope of paragraph 4(a) of this Article considers it desirable, in order to promote the establishment of a particular industry with a view to raising the general standard of living of its people, to modify or withdraw a concession included in the appropriate Schedule annexed to this Agreement, it shall notify the Contracting Parties to this effect and enter into negotiations with any contracting party with which such concession was initially negotiated, and with any other contracting party determined by the Contracting Parties to

have a substantial interest therein. If agreement is reached between such contracting parties concerned, they shall be free to modify or withdraw concessions under the appropriate Schedules to this Agreement in order to give effect to such agreement, including any compensatory adjustments involved.

(b) If agreement is not reached within sixty days after the notification provided for in sub-paragraph (a) above, the contracting party which proposes to modify or withdraw the concession may refer the matter to the Contracting Parties, which shall promptly examine it. If they find that the contracting party which proposes to modify or withdraw the concession has made every effort to reach an agreement and that the compensatory adjustment offered by it is adequate, that contracting party shall be free to modify or withdraw the concession if at the same time, it gives effect to the compensatory adjustment. If the Contracting Parties do not find that the compensation offered by a contracting party proposing to modify or withdraw the concession is adequate, but find that it has made every reasonable effort to offer adequate compensation, that contracting party shall be free to proceed with such modification or withdrawal. If such action is taken, any other contracting party referred to in sub-paragraph (a) above shall be free to modify or withdraw substantially equivalent concessions initially negotiated with the contracting party which has taken the action.

Section B

8. The contracting parties recognize that contracting parties coming within the scope of paragraph 4(a) of this Article tend, when they are in rapid process of development, to experience balance of payments difficulties arising mainly from efforts to expand their internal markets as well as from the instability in their terms of trade.

9. In order to safeguard its external financial position and to ensure a level of reserves adequate for the implementation of its programme of economic development, a contracting party coming within the scope of paragraph 4(a) of this Article may, subject to the provi-

sions of paragraphs 10 to 12, control the general level of its imports by restricting the quantity or value of merchandise permitted to be imported; *Provided* that the import restrictions instituted, maintained or intensified shall not exceed those necessary:

(a) to forestall the threat of, or to stop, a serious decline in its monetary reserves, or

(b) in the case of a contracting party with inadequate monetary reserves, to achieve a reasonable rate of increase in its reserves.

Due regard shall be paid in either case to any special factors which may be affecting the reserves of the contracting party or its need for reserves, including, where special external credits or other resources are available to it, the need to provide for the appropriate use of such credits or resources.

10. In applying these restrictions, the contracting party may determine their incidence on imports of different products or classes of products in such a way as to give priority to the importation of those products which are more essential in the light of its policy of economic development; *Provided* that the restrictions are so applied as to avoid unnecessary damage to the commercial or economic interests of any other contracting party and not to prevent unreasonably the importation of any description of goods in minimum commercial quantities the exclusion of which would impair regular channels of trade; and *Provided* further that the restrictions are not so applied as to prevent the importation of commercial samples or to prevent compliance with patent, trademark, copyright or similar procedures.

11. In carrying out its domestic policies, the contracting party concerned shall pay due regard to the need for restoring equilibrium in its balance of payments on a sound and lasting basis and to the desirability of assuring an economic employment of productive resources. It shall progressively relax any restrictions applied under this Section as conditions improve, maintaining them only to the extent necessary under the terms of paragraph 9 of this Article and shall eliminate them when condi-

tions no longer justify such maintenance; *Provided* that no contracting party shall be required to withdraw or modify restrictions on the ground that a change in its development policy would render unnecessary the restrictions on the ground that a change in its development policy would render unnecessary the restrictions which it is applying under this Section.

12. (a) Any contracting party applying new restrictions or raising the general level of its existing restrictions by a substantial intensification of the measures applied under this Section, shall immediately after instituting or intensifying such restrictions (or, in circumstances in which prior consultation is practicable, before doing so) consult with the Contracting Parties as to the nature of its balance of payments difficulties, alternative corrective measures which may be available, and the possible effect of the restrictions on the economies of other contracting parties.

(b) On a date to be determined by them, the Contracting Parties shall review all restrictions still applied under this Section on that date. Beginning two years after that date, contracting parties applying restrictions under this Section shall enter into consultations of the type provided for in sub-paragraph (a) above with the Contracting Parties at intervals of approximately, but not less than, two years according to a programme to be drawn up each year by the Contracting Parties; *Provided* that no consultation under this sub-paragraph shall take place within two years after the conclusion of a consultation of a general nature any other provision of this paragraph.

(c)(i) If, in the course of consultations with a contracting party under sub-paragraph (a) or (b) of this paragraph, the Contracting Parties find that the restrictions are not consistent with the provisions of this Section or with those of Article XIII (subject to the provisions of Article XIV), they shall indicate the nature of the inconsistency and may advise that the restrictions be suitably modified.

(ii) If, however, as a result of the consultations, the Contracting Parties determine that the restrictions are being applied in a manner involving an inconsistency of a serious nature with the provisions of this Section or with those of Article XIII (subject to the provisions of Article XIV) and that damage to the trade of any contracting party is caused or threatened thereby, they shall so inform the contracting party applying the restrictions and shall make appropriate recommendations for securing conformity with such provisions within a specified period. If such contracting party does not comply with these recommendations within the specified period, the Contracting Parties may release any contracting party the trade of which is adversely affected by the restrictions from such obligations under this Agreement towards the contracting party applying the restrictions as they determine to be appropriate in the circumstances.

(d) The Contracting Parties shall invite any contracting party which is applying restrictions under this Section to enter into consultations with them at the request of any contracting party which can establish a *prima facie* case that the restrictions are inconsistent with the provisions of this Section or with those of Article XIII (subject to the provisions of Article XIV) and that its trade is adversely affected thereby. However, no such invitation shall be issued unless the Contracting Parties have ascertained that direct discussions between the contracting parties concerned have not been successful. If, as a result of the consultations with the Contracting Parties no agreement is reached and they determine that the restrictions are being applied inconsistently with such provisions, and that damage to the trade of the contracting party initiating the procedure is caused or threatened thereby, they shall recommend the withdrawal or modification of the restrictions. If the restrictions are not withdrawn or modified within such time as the Contracting Parties may prescribe, they may release the contracting party initiating the procedure from such obligations under this Agreement towards the contracting party applying the restrictions as they determine to be appropriate in the circumstances.

(e) If a contracting party against which action has been taken in accordance with the last sentence of subparagraph (c)(ii) or (d) of this paragraph, finds that the release of obligations authorized by the Contracting Parties adversely affects the operation of its programme and policy of economic development, it shall be free, not later than sixty days after such action is taken, to give written notice to the Executive Secretary to the Contracting Parties of its intention to withdraw from this Agreement and such withdrawal shall take effect on the sixtieth day following the day on which the notice is received by him.

(f) In proceeding under this paragraph, the Contracting Parties shall have due regard to the factors referred to in paragraph 2 of this Article. Determinations under this paragraph shall be rendered expeditiously and, if possible, within sixty days of the initiation of the consultations.

Section C

13. If a contracting party coming within the scope of paragraph 4(a) of this Article finds that governmental assistance is required to promote the establishment of a particular industry with a view to raising the general standard of living of its people, but that no measure consistent with the other provisions of this Agreement is practicable to achieve that objective, it may have recourse to the provisions and procedures set out in this Section.

14. The contracting party concerned shall notify the Contracting Parties of the special difficulties which it meets in the achievement of the objective outlined in paragraph 13 of this Article and shall indicate the specific measure affecting imports which it proposes to introduce in order to remedy these difficulties. It shall not introduce that measure before the expiration of the time-limit laid down in paragraph 15 or 17, as the case may be, or if the measure affects imports of a product which is the subject of a concession included in the appropriate Schedule annexed to this Agreement, unless it has secured the concurrence of the Contracting Parties in accordance with the provisions of paragraph 18; *Provided* that, if the industry receiving assistance has already started production, the contracting party may, after informing the Contracting Parties, take such measures as may be necessary to prevent, during that period, imports of the product or products concerned from increasing substantially above a normal level.

15. If, within thirty days of the notification of the measure, the Contracting Parties do not request the contracting party concerned to consult with them, that contracting party shall be free to deviate from the relevant provisions of the other Articles of this Agreement to the extent necessary to apply the proposed measure.

16. If it is requested by the Contracting Parties to do so, the contracting party concerned shall consult with them as to the purpose of the proposed measure, as to alternative measures which may be available under this Agreement, and as to the possible effect of the measure proposed on the commercial and economic interests of other contracting parties. If, as a result of such consultation, the Contracting Parties agree that there is no measure consistent with the other provisions of this Agreement which is practicable in order to achieve the objective outlined in paragraph 13 of this Article, and concur in the proposed measure, the contracting party concerned shall be released from its obligations under the relevant provisions of the other Articles of this Agreement to the extent necessary to apply that measure.

17. If, within ninety days after the date of the notification of the proposed measure under paragraph 14 of this Article, the Contracting Parties have not concurred in such measure, the contracting party concerned may introduce the measure proposed after informing the Contracting Parties.

18. If the proposed measure affects a product which is the subject of a concession included in the appropriate Schedule annexed to this Agreement, the contracting party concerned shall enter into consultations with any other contracting party with which the concession was initially negotiated, and with any other contracting party determined by

the Contracting Parties to have a substantial interest therein. The Contracting Parties shall concur in the measure if they agree that there is no measure consistent with the other provisions of this Agreement which is practicable in order to achieve the objective set forth in paragraph 13 of this Article, and if they are satisfied:

(a) that agreement has been reached with such other contracting parties as a result of the consultations referred to above, or

(b) if no such agreement has been reached within sixty days after the notification provided for in paragraph 14 has been received by the Contracting Parties, that the contracting party having recourse to this Section has made all reasonable efforts to reach an agreement and that the interests of other contracting parties are adequately safeguarded.

The contracting party having recourse to this Section shall thereupon be released from its obligations under the relevant provisions of the other Articles of this Agreement to the extent necessary to permit it to apply the measure.

19. If a proposed measure of the type described in paragraph 13 of this Article concerns an industry the establishment of which has in the initial period been facilitated by incidental protection afforded by restrictions imposed by the contracting party concerned for balance of payments purposes under the relevant provisions of this Agreement that contracting party may resort to the provisions and procedures of this Section; *Provided* that it shall not apply the proposed measure without the concurrence of the Contracting Parties.

20. Nothing in the preceeding paragraphs of this Section shall authorize any deviation from the provisions of Articles I, II and XIII of this Agreement. The provisos to paragraph 10 of this Article shall also be applicable to any restriction under this Section.

21. At any time while a measure is being applied under paragraph 17 of this Article any contracting party substantially affected by it may suspend the application to the trade of the contracting party having recourse to this Section

of such substantially equivalent concessions or other obligations under this Agreement the suspension of which the Contracting Parties do not disapprove; *Provided* that sixty days' notice of such suspension is given to the Contracting Parties not later than six months after the measure has been introduced or changed substantially to the detriment of the contracting party affected. Any such contracting party shall afford adequate opportunity for consultation in accordance with the provisions of Article XXII of this Agreement.

Section D

22. A contracting party coming within the scope of subparagraph 4(b) of this Article desiring, in the interest of the development of its economy, to introduce a measure of the type described in paragraph 13 of this Article in respect to the establishment of a particular industry may apply to the Contracting Parties for approval of such measure. The Contracting Parties shall promptly consult with such contracting party and shall, in making their decision, be guided by the considerations set out in paragraph 16. If the Contracting Parties concur in the proposed measure the contracting party concerned shall be released from its obligations under the relevant provisions of the other Articles of this Agreement to the extent necessary to permit it to apply the measure. If the proposed measure affects a product which is the subject of a concession included in the appropriate Schedule annexed to this Agreement, the provisions of paragraph 18 shall apply.

23. Any measure applied under this Section shall comply with the provisions of paragraph 20 of this Article.

Article XIX.—EMERGENCY ACTION ON IMPORTS OF PARTICULAR PRODUCTS

1. (a) If, as a result of unforeseen developments and of the effect of the obligations incurred by a contracting party under this Agreement, including tariff concessions, any product is being imported into the territory of that contracting party in such increased quantities and under such conditions as to cause or threaten serious injury to do-

mestic producers in that territory of like or directly competitive products, the contracting party shall be free, in respect of such product, and to the extent and for such time as may be necessary to prevent or remedy such injury, to suspend the obligation in whole or in part or to withdraw or modify the concession.

(b) If any product, which is the subject of a concession with respect to a preference, is being imported into the territory of a contracting party in the circumstances set forth in sub-paragraph (a) of this paragraph, so as to cause or threaten serious injury to domestic producers of like or directly competitive products in the territory of a contracting party which receives or received such preference, the importing contracting party shall be free, if that other contracting party so requests, to suspend the relevant obligation in whole or in part or to withdraw or modify the concession in respect of the product, to the extent and for such time as may be necessary to prevent or remedy such injury.

2. Before any contracting party shall take action pursuant to the provisions of paragraph 1 of this Article, it shall give notice in writing to the Contracting Parties as far in advance as may be practicable and shall afford the Contracting Parties and those contracting parties having a substantial interest as exporters of the product concerned an opportunity to consult with it in respect of the proposed action. When such notice is given in relation to a concession with respect to a preference, the notice shall name the contracting party which has requested the action. In critical circumstances, where delay would cause damage which it would be difficult to repair, action under paragraph 1 of this Article may be taken provisionally without prior consultation, on the condition that consultation shall be effected immediately after taking such action.

3. (a) If agreement among the interested contracting parties with respect to the action is not reached, the contracting party which proposes to take or continue the action shall, nevertheless, be free to do so, and if such action is taken

or continued, the affected contracting parties shall then be free, not later than ninety days after such action is taken, to suspend, upon the expiration of thirty days from the day on which written notice of such suspension is received by the Contracting Parties, the application to the trade of the contracting party taking such action, or, in the case envisaged in paragraph 1(b) of this Article, to the trade of the contracting party requesting such action, of such substantially equivalent concessions or other obligations under this Agreement the suspension of which the Contracting Parties do not disapprove.

(b) Notwithstanding the provisions of sub-paragraph (a) of this paragraph, where action is taken under paragraph 2 of this Article without prior consultation and causes or threatens serious injury in the territory of a contracting party to the domestic producers of products affected by the action, that contracting party shall, where delay would cause damage difficult to repair, be free to suspend, upon the taking of the action and throughout the period of consultation, such concessions or other obligations as may be necessary to prevent or remedy the injury.

Article XX.—GENERAL EXCEPTIONS

Subject to the requirement that such measures are not applied in a manner which would constitute a means of arbitrary or unjustifiable discrimination between countries where the same conditions prevail, or a disguised restriction on international trade, nothing in this Agreement shall be construed to prevent the adoption or enforcement by any contracting party of measures:

(a) necessary to protect public morals;

(b) necessary to protect human, animal or plant life or health;

(c) relating to the importation or exportation of gold or silver;

(d) necessary to secure compliance with laws or regulations which are not inconsistent with the provisions of this Agreement, including those relating to customs enforcement, the enforcement of monopolies operated under paragraph 4 of Article II and Article XVII, the protection of patents, trade marks and copyrights, and the prevention of deceptive practices;

(e) relating to the products of prison labour;

(f) imposed for the protection of national treasures of artistic, historic or archaeological value;

(g) relating to the conservation of exhaustible natural resources if such measures are made effective in conjunction with restrictions on domestic production or consumption;

(h) undertaken in pursuance of obligations under any intergovernmental commodity agreement which conforms to criteria submitted to the Contracting Parties and not disapproved by them or which is itself so submitted and not so disapproved;

(i) involving restrictions on exports of domestic materials necessary to assure essential quantities of such materials to a domestic processing industry during periods when the domestic price of such materials is held below the world price as part of a governmental stabilization plan; *Provided* that such restrictions shall not operate to increase the exports of or the protection afforded to such domestic industry, and shall not depart from the provisions of this Agreement relating to non-discrimination;

(j) essential to the acquisition or distribution of products in general or local short supply; *Provided* that any such measures shall be consistent with the principle that all contracting parties are entitled to an equitable share of the international supply of such products, and that any such measures, which are inconsistent with the other provisions of this Agreement shall be discontinued as soon as the conditions giving rise to them have ceased to exist. The Contracting Parties shall review the need for this subparagraph not later than 30 June 1960.

Article XXI.—SECURITY EXCEPTIONS

Nothing in this Agreement shall be construed;

(a) to require any contracting party to furnish any information the disclosure of which it considers contrary to its essential security interests; or

(b) to prevent any contracting party from taking any action which it considers necessary for the protection of its essential security interests—

(i) relating to fissionable materials or the materials from which they are derived;

(ii) relating to the traffic in arms, ammunition and implements of war and to such traffic in other goods and materials as is carried on directly or indirectly for the purpose of supplying a military establishment;

(iii) taken in time of war or other emergency in international relations; or

(c) to prevent any contracting party from taking any action in pursuance of its obligations under the United Nations Charter for the maintenance of international peace and security.

Article XXII.—CONSULTATION

1. Each contracting party shall accord sympathetic consideration to, and shall afford adequate opportunity for consultation regarding, such representations as may be made by another contracting party with respect to any matter affecting the operation of this Agreement.

2. The Contracting Parties may, at the request of a contracting party, consult with any contracting party or parties in respect of any matter for which it has not been possible to find a satisfactory solution through consultation under paragraph 1.

Article XXIII.—NULLIFICATION OR IMPAIRMENT

1. If any contracting party should consider that any benefit accruing to it directly or indirectly under this Agreement is being nullified or impaired or that the attainment of any objective of the Agreement is being impeded as the result of (a) the failure of another contracting party to carry out its obligations under this Agreement, or (b) the application by another contracting party of any measure, whether or not it conflicts with the provisions of this Agreement, or (c) the existence of any other situation, the

contracting party may, with a view to the satisfactory adjustment of the matter, make written representations or proposals to the other contracting party or parties which it considers to be concerned. Any contracting party thus approached shall give sympathetic consideration to the representations or proposals made to it.

2. If no satisfactory adjustment is effected between the contracting parties concerned within a reasonable time, or if the difficulty is of the type described in **paragraph 1(c) of this Article, the matter** may be referred to the Contracting Parties. The Contracting Parties shall promptly investigate any matter so referred to them and shall make appropriate recommendations to the contracting parties which they consider to be concerned, or give a ruling on the matter, as appropriate. The Contracting Parties may consult with contracting parties, with the Economic and Social Council of the United Nations and with any appropriate inter-governmental organization in cases where they consider such consultation necessary.

If the Contracting Parties consider that the circumstances are serious enough to justify such action, they may authorize a contracting party or parties to suspend the application to any other contracting party or parties of such concessions or other obligations under this Agreement as they determine to be appropriate in the circumstances. If the application to any contracting party of any concession or other obligation is in fact suspended, that contracting party shall then be free, not later than sixty days after such action is taken to give written notice to the Executive Secretary to the Contracting Parties of its intention to withdraw from this Agreement and such withdrawal shall take effect upon the sixtieth day following the day of which such notice is received by him.

Part III

Article XXIV.—TERRITORIAL APPLICATION—FRONTIER TRAFFIC—CUSTOMS UNIONS AND FREE-TRADE AREAS

1. The provisions of this Agreement shall apply to the metropolitan customs territories of the contracting parties and to any other customs territories in respect of which this Agreement has been accepted under Article XXVI or is being applied under Article XXXIII or pursuant to the Protocol of Provisional Application. Each such customs territory shall, exclusively for the purposes of the territorial application of this Agreement, be treated as though it were a contracting party; *Provided* that the provisions of this paragraph shall not be construed to create any rights or obligations as between two or more customs territories in respect of which this Agreement has been accepted under Article XXVI or being applied under Article XXXIII or pursuant to the Protocol of Provisional Application by a single contracting party.

2. For the purposes of this Agreement a customs territory shall be understood to mean any territory with respect to which separate tariffs or other regulations of commerce are maintained for a substantial part of the trade of such territory with other territories.

3. The provisions of this Agreement shall not be construed to prevent:

(a) advantages accorded by any contracting party to adjacent countries in order to facilitate frontier traffic;

(b) advantages accorded to the trade with the Free Territory of Trieste by countries contiguous to that territory, provided that such advantages are not in conflict with the Treaties of Peace arising out of the Second World War.

4. The contracting parties recognize the desirability of increasing freedom of trade by the development, through voluntary agreements, of closer integration between the economies of the countries parties to such agreements. They also recognize that the purpose of a customs union or of a free-trade area should be to facilitate trade between the constituent territories and not to raise barriers to the trade of other contracting parties with such territories.

5. Accordingly, the provisions of this Agreement shall not prevent, as between the territories of contracting parties, the formation of a customs union or of a free-trade area or the adoption of an interim agreement necessary for the formation

of a customs union or of a free-trade area; *Provided* that:

(a) with respect to a customs union, or an interim agreement leading to the formation of a customs union, the duties and other regulations of commerce imposed at the institution of any such union or interim agreement in respect of trade with contracting parties not parties to such union or agreement shall not on the whole be higher or more restrictive than the general incidence of the duties and regulations of commerce applicable in the constituent territories prior to the formation of such union or the adoption of such interim agreement, as the case may be;

(b) with respect to a free-trade area, or an interim agreement leading to the formation of a free-trade area, the duties and other regulations of commerce maintained in each of the constituent territories and applicable at the formation of such free-trade area or the adoption of such interim agreement to the trade of contracting parties not included in such area or not parties to such agreement shall not be higher or more restrictive than the corresponding duties and other regulations of commerce existing in the same constituent territories prior to the formation of the free-trade area, or interim agreement, as the case may be; and

(c) any interim agreement referred to in sub-paragraphs (a) and (b) shall include a plan and schedule for the formation of such a customs union or of such a free-trade area within a reasonable length of time.

6. If, in fulfilling the requirements of **sub-paragraph 5(a), a contracting party** proposes to increase any rate of duty inconsistently with the provisions of Article II, the procedure set forth in Article XXVIII shall apply. In providing for compensatory adjustment, due account shall be taken of the compensation already afforded by the reductions brought about in the corresponding duty of the other constituents of the union.

7. (a) Any contracting party deciding to enter into a customs union or free-trade area, or an interim agreement leading to the formation of such a union or area, shall promptly notify the Contracting Parties and shall make available to them such information regarding the proposed union or area as will enable them to make such reports and recommendations to contracting parties as they may deem appropriate.

(b) If, after having studied the plan and schedule included in an interim agreement referred to in paragraph 5 in consultation with the parties to that agreement and taking due account of the information made available in cccordance with the provisions of sub-paragraph (a), the Contracting Parties find that such agreement is not likely to result in the formation of a customs union or of a free-trade area within the period contemplated by the parties to the agreement or that such period is not a reasonable one, the Contracting Parties shall make recommendations to the parties to the agreement. The parties shall not maintain or put into force, as the case may be, such agreement if they are not prepared to modify it in accordance with these recommendations.

(c) Any substantial change in the plan or schedule referred to in paragraph 5(c) shall be communicated to the Contracting Parties, which may request the contracting parties concerned to consult with them if the change seems likely to jeopardize or delay unduly the formation of the customs union or of the free-trade area.

8. For the purposes of this Agreement:

(a) A customs union shall be understood to mean the substitution of a single customs territory for two or more customs territories, so that—

(i) duties and other restrictive regulations of commerce (except, where necessary, those permitted under Articles XI, XII, XIII, XIV, XV, and XX) are eliminated with respect to substantially all the trade between the constituent territories of the union or at least with respect to substantially all the trade in products originating in such territories, and,

(ii) subject to the provisions of paragraph 9, substantially the same duties and other regulations of commerce are applied by each of the members of the union to the trade of territories not included in the union;

(b) A free-trade area shall be understood to mean a group of two or more customs territories in which the duties and other restrictive regulations of commerce (except, where necessary, those permitted under Articles XI, XII, XIII, XIV, XV and XX) are eliminated on substantially all the trade between the constituent territories in products originating in such territories.

9. The preferences referred to in paragraph 2 of Article I shall not be affected by the formation of a customs union or of a free-trade area but may be eliminated or adjusted by means of negotiations with contracting parties affected. This procedure of negotiations with affected contracting parties shall, in particular, apply to the elimination of preferences required to conform with the provisions of paragraph 8 (a)(i) and paragraph 8(b).

10. The Contracting Parties may be a two-thirds majority approve proposals which do not fully comply with the requirements of paragraphs 5 to 9 inclusive, provided that such proposals lead to the formation of a customs union or a free-trade area in the sense of this Article.

11. Taking into account the exceptional circumstances arising out of the establishment of India and Pakistan as independent States and recognizing the fact that they have long constituted an economic unit, the contracting parties agree that the provisions of this Agreement shall not prevent the two countries from entering into special arrangements with respect to the trade between them, pending the establishment of their mutual trade relations on a definitive basis.

12. Each contracting party shall take such reasonable measures as may be available to it ensure observance of the provisions of this Agreement by the regional and local governments and authorities within its territory.

Article XXV.—JOINT ACTION BY THE CONTRACTING PARTIES

1. Representatives of the contracting parties shall meet from time to time for the purpose of giving effect to those provisions of this Agreement which involve joint action and, generally, with a view to facilitating the operation and furthering the objectives of this Agreement. wherever reference is made in this Agreement to the contracting parties acting jointly they are designated as the Contracting Parties.

2. The Secretary-General of the United Nations is requested to convene the first meeting of the Contracting Parties, which shall take place not later than March 1, 1948.

3. Each contracting party shall be entitled to have one vote at all meetings of the Contracting Parties.

4. Except as otherwise provided for in this Agreement, decisions of the Contracting Parties shall be taken by a majority of the votes cast.

5. In exceptional circumstances not elsewhere provided for in this Agreement, the Contracting Parties may waive an obligation imposed upon a contracting party by this Agreement; *Provided* that any such decision shall be approved by a two-thirds majority of the votes cast and that such majority shall comprise more than half of the contracting parties. The Contracting Parties may also by such a vote—

(i) define certain categories of exceptional circumstances to which other voting requirements shall apply for the waiver of obligations, and

(ii) prescribe such criteria as may be necessary for the application of this paragraph.[1]

Article XXVI.—ACCEPTANCE, ENTRY INTO FORCE AND REGISTRATION

1. The date of this Agreement shall be 30 October 1947.

2. This Agreement shall be open for acceptance by any contracting party which, on 1 March 1955, was a contracting party or was negotiating with a view to accession to this Agreement.

3. This Agreement, done in a single English orginal and in a single French original, both texts authentic, shall be deposited with the Secretary-General of the United Nations, who shall furnish certified copies thereof to all interested governments.

4. Each government accepting this Agreement shall deposit an instrument of acceptance with the Executive Secretary to the Contracting Parties, who will

---

[1]The word "paragraph" has been substituted for the word "sub-paragraph" since paragraph 5 is no longer divided into sub-paragraphs (a), (b), etc., as was formerly the case. The text of the present paragraph 5 was formerly sub-paragraph 5(a).

inform all interested governments of the date of deposit of each instrument of acceptance and of the day on which this Agreement enters into force under paragraph 6 of this Article.

5. (a) Each government accepting this Agreement does so in respect of its metropolitan territory and of the other territories for which it has international responsibility, except such separate customs territories as it shall notify to the Executive Secretary to the Contracting Parties at the time of its own acceptance.

(b) Any government, which has so notified the Executive Secretary under the exceptions in sub-paragraph (a) of this paragraph, may at any time give notice to the Executive Secretary that its acceptance shall be effective in respect of any separate customs territory or territories so excepted and such notice shall take effect on the thirtieth day following the day on which it is received by the Executive Secretary.

(c) If any of the customs territories, in respect of which a contracting party has accepted this Agreement, possesses or acquires full autonomy in the conduct of its external commercial relations and of the other matters provided for in this Agreement, such territory shall, upon sponsorship through a declaration by the responsible contracting party establishing the above-mentioned fact, be deemed to be a contracting party.

6. This Agreement shall enter into force, as among the governments which have accepted it, on the thirtieth day following the day on which instruments of acceptance have been deposited with the Executive Secretary to the Contracting Parties on behalf of governments named in Annex H, the territories of which account for 85 per centum of the total external trade of the territories of such governments, computed in accordance with the applicable column of percentages set forth therein. The instrument of acceptance of each other government shall take effect on the thirtieth day following the day on which such instrument has been deposited.

7. The United Nations is authorized to effect registration of this Agreement as soon as it enters into force.

Article XXVII.—WITHHOLDING OR WITHDRAWAL OF CONCESSIONS

Any contracting party shall at any time be free to withhold or to withdraw in whole or in part any concession, provided for in the appropriate Schedule annexed to this Agreement, in respect of which such contracting party determines that it was initially negotiated with a government which has not become, or has ceased to be, a contracting party. A contracting party taking such action shall notify the Contracting Parties and, upon request, consult with contracting parties which have a substantial interest in the product concerned.

Article XXVIII.—MODIFICATIONS OF SCHEDULES

1. On the first day of each three-year period, the first period beginning on 1 January 1958 (or on the first day of any other period that may be specified by the Contracting Parties by two-thirds of the votes cast) a contracting party (hereafter in this Article referred to as the "applicant contracting party") may, by negotiation and agreement with any contracting party with which such concession was initially negotiated and with any other contracting party determined by the Contracting Parties to have a principal supplying interest (which two preceding categories of contracting parties, together with the applicant contracting party, are in this Article hereinafter referred to as the "contracting parties primarily concerned"), and subject to consultation with any other contracting party determined by the Contracting Parties to have a substantial interest in such concession, modify or withdraw a concession included in the appropriate Schedule annexed to this Agreement.

2. In such negotiations and agreement, which may include provision for compensatory adjustment with respect to other products, the contracting parties concerned shall endeavour to maintain a general level of reciprocal and mutually advantageous concessions not less favourable to trade than that provided for in this Agreement prior to such negotiations.

3. (a) If agreement between the contracting parties primarily concerned

cannot be reached before 1 January 1958 or before the expiration of a period envisaged in paragraph 1 of this Article, the contracting party which proposes to modify or withdraw the concession shall, nevertheless, be free to do so and if such action is taken any contracting party with which such concession was initially negotiated, any contracting party determined under paragraph 1 to have a principal supplying interest and any contracting party determined under paragraph 1 to have a substantial interest shall then be free not later than six months after such action is taken, to withdraw, upon the expiration of thirty days from the day on which written notice of such withdrawal is received by the Contracting Parties, substantially equivalent concessions initially negotiated with the applicant contracting party.

(b) If agreement between the contracting parties primarily concerned is reached but any other contracting party determined under paragraph 1 of this Article to have a substantial interest is not satisfied, such other contracting party shall be free, not later than six months after action under such agreement is taken, to withdraw, upon the expiration of thirty days from the day on which written notice of such withdrawal is received by the Contracting Parties, substantially equivalent concessions initially negotiated with the applicant contracting party.

4. The Contracting Parties may, at any time, in special circumstances, authorize a contracting party to enter into negotiations for modification or withdrawal of a concession included in the appropriate Schedule annexed to this Agreement subject to the following procedures and conditions:

(a) Such negotiations and any related consultations shall be conducted in accordance with the provisions of paragraphs 1 and 2 of this Article.

(b) If agreement between the contracting parties primarily concerned is reached in the negotiations, the provisions of paragraph 3(b) of this Article shall apply.

(c) If agreement between the contracting parties primarily concerned is not reached within a period of sixty days after negotiations have been authorized,

or within such longer period as the Contracting Parties may have prescribed, the applicant contracting party may refer the matter to the Contracting Parties.

(d) Upon such reference, the Contracting Parties shall promptly examine the matter and submit their views to the contracting parties primarily concerned with the aim of achieving a settlement. If a settlement is reached, the provisions of paragraph 3(b) shall apply as if agreement between the contracting parties primarily concerned had been reached. If no settlement is reached between the contracting parties primarily concerned, the applicant contracting party shall be free to modify or withdraw the concession, unless the Contracting Parties determine that the applicant contracting party has unreasonably failed to offer adequate compensation. If such action is taken, any contracting party with which the concession was initially negotiated, any contracting party determined under paragraph 4(a) to have a principal supplying interest and any contracting party determined under paragraph 4(a) to have a substantial interest, shall be free, not later than six months after such action is taken, to modify or withdraw, upon the expiration of thirty days from the day on which written notice of such withdrawal is received by the Contracting Parties, substantially equivalent concessions initially negotiated with the applicant contracting party.

5. Before January 1958 and before the end of any period envisaged in paragraph 1 a contracting party may elect by notifying the Contracting Parties to reserve the right, for the duration of the next period, to modify the appropriate Schedule in accordance with the procedures of paragraphs 1 to 3. If a contracting party so elects, other contracting parties shall have the right, during the same period, to modify or withdraw in accordance with the same procedures, concessions initially negotiated with that contracting party.

Article XXVIII bis.—TARIFF NEGOTIATIONS

1. The contracting parties recognize that customs duties often constitute

serious obstacles to trade; thus negotiations on a reciprocal and mutually advantageous basis, directed to the substantial reduction of the general level of tariffs and other charges on imports and exports and in particular to the reduction of such high tariffs as discourage the importation even of minimum quantities, and conducted with due regard to the objectives of this Agreement and the varying needs of individual contracting parties, are of great importance to the expansion of international trade. The Contracting Parties may therefore sponsor such negotiations from time to time.

2. (a) Negotiations under this Article may be carried out on a selective product-by-product basis or by the application of such multilateral procedures as may be accepted by the contracting parties concerned. Such negotiations may be directed towards the reduction of duties, the binding of duties at then existing levels or undertakings that individual duties or the average duties on specified categories of products shall not exceed specified levels. The binding against increase of low duties or of duty-free treatment shall, in principle, be recognized as a concession equivalent in value to the reduction of high duties.

(b) The contracting parties recognize that in general the success of multilateral negotiations would depend on the participation of all contracting parties which conduct a substantial proportion of their external trade with one another.

3. Negotiations shall be conducted on a basis which affords adequate opportunity to take into account:

(a) the needs of individual contracting parties and individual industries;

(b) the needs of less-developed countries for a more flexible use of tariff protection to assist their economic development and the special needs of these countries to maintain tariffs for revenue purposes; and

(c) all other relevant circumstances, including the fiscal, developmental, strategic and other needs of the contracting parties concerned.

Article XXIX.—THE RELATION OF THIS AGREEMENT TO THE HAVANA CHARTER

1. The contracting parties undertake to observe to the fullest extent of their executive authority the general principles of Chapters I to VI inclusive and of Chapter IX of the Havana Charter pending their acceptance of it in accordance with their constitutional procedures.

2. Part II of this Agreement shall be suspended on the day on which the Havana Charter enters into force.

3. If by September 30, 1949, the Havana Charter has not entered into force, the contracting parties shall meet before December 31, 1949, to agree whether this Agreement shall be amended, supplemented or maintained.

4. If at any time the Havana Charter should cease to be in force, the Contracting Parties shall meet as soon as practicable thereafter to agree whether this Agreement shall be supplemented, amended or maintained. Pending such agreement, Part II of this Agreement shall again enter into force; *Provided* that the provisions of Part II other than Article XXIII shall be replaced, *mutatis mutandis,* in the form in which they then appeared in the Havana Charter; and *Provided* further that no contracting party shall be bound by any provisions which did not bind it at the time when the Havana Charter ceased to be in force.

5. If any contracting party has not accepted the Havana Charter by the date upon which it enters into force, the Contracting Parties shall confer to agree whether, and if so in what way, this Agreement in so far as it affects relations between such contracting party and other contracting parties, shall be supplemented or amended. Pending such agreement the provisions of Part II of this Agreement shall, notwithstanding the provisions of paragraph 2 of this Article, continue to apply as between such contracting party and other contracting parties.

6. Contracting parties which are Members of the International Trade Organization shall not invoke the provisions of this Agreement so as to prevent the operation of any provision of the Havana Charter. The application of the principle underlying this paragraph to any contracting party which is not a Member of the International Trade Organization shall be the subject of an agree-

ment pursuant to paragraph 5 of this Article.

Article XXX.—AMENDMENTS

1. Except where provision for modification is made elsewhere in this Agreement, amendments to the provisions of Part I of this Agreement or to the provisions of Article XXIX or of this Article shall become effective upon acceptance by all the contracting parties, and other amendments to this Agreement shall become effective, in respect of those contracting parties which accept them, upon acceptance by two-thirds of the contracting parties and thereafter for each other contracting party upon acceptance by it.

2. Any contracting party accepting an amendment to this Agreement shall deposit an instrument of acceptance with the Secretary-General of the United Nations within such period as the Contracting Parties may specify. The Contracting Parties may decide that any amendment made effective under this Article is of such a nature that any contracting party which has not accepted it within a period specified by the Contracting Parties shall be free to withdraw from this Agreement, or to remain a contracting party with the consent of the Contracting Parties.

Article XXXI.—WITHDRAWAL

Without prejudice to the provisions of paragraph 12 of Article XVIII or of Article XXIII or of paragraph 2 of Article XXX, any contracting party may withdraw from this Agreement, or may separately withdraw on behalf of any of the separate customs territories for which it has international responsibility and which at the time possesses full autonomy in the conduct of its external commercial relations and of the other matters provided for in this Agreement. The withdrawal shall take effect upon the expiration of six months from the day on which written notice of withdrawal is received by the Secretary-General of the United Nations.

Article XXXII.—CONTRACTING PARTIES

1. The contracting parties to this Agreement shall be understood to mean those governments which are applying the provisions of this Agreement under Article XXVI or XXXIII or pursuant to the Protocol of Provisional Application.

2. At any time after the entry into force of this Agreement pursuant to paragraph 6 of Article XXVI, those contracting parties which have accepted this Agreement pursuant to paragraph 4 of Article XXVI may decide that any contracting party which has not so accepted it shall cease to be a contracting party.

Article XXXIII.—ACCESSION

A government not party to this Agreement, or government acting on behalf of a separate customs territory possessing full autonomy in the conduct of its external commercial relations and of the other matters provided for in this Agreemtnt, may accede to this Agreement, on its own behalf or on behalf of that territory, on terms to be agreed between such government and the Contracting Parties. Decisions of the Contracting Parties under this paragraph shall be taken by a two-thirds majority.

Article XXXIV.—ANNEXES

The annexes to this Agreement are hereby made an integral part of this Agreement.

Article XXXV.—NON-APPLICATION OF THE AGREEMENT BETWEEN PARTICULAR CONTRACTING PARTIES

1. This Agreement, or alternatively Article II of this Agreement shall not apply as between any contracting party and any other contracting party if:

(a) the two contracting parties have not entered into tariff negotiations with each other, and

(b) either of the contracting parties, at the time either becomes a contracting party, does not consent to such application.

2. The Contracting Parties may review the operation of this Article in particular cases at the request of any contracting party and make appropriate recommendations.

PROTOCOL*

AMENDING THE GENERAL AGREEMENT ON TARIFFS AND TRADE TO INTRODUCE A PART IV ON TRADE AND DEVELOPMENT

(Done at Geneva February 8, 1965; Signed on Behalf of the United States of America February 8, 1965; Entered Into Force June 27, 1966)

The Governments which are contracting parties to the General Agreement on Tariffs and Trade (hereinafter referred to as "the contracting parties" and the "General Agreement" respectively),

DESIRING to effect amendments to the General Agreement pursuant to the provisions of Article XXX thereof,

HEREBY AGREE as follows:

* * *

The following heading and Articles shall be inserted after Article XXXV:

"Part IV
"TRADE AND DEVELOPMENT
"Article XXXVI. — PRINCIPLES AND OBJECTIVES

"1. The contracting parties,

(a) recalling that the basic objectives of this Agreement include the raising of standards of living and the progressive development of the economies of all contracting parties, and considering that the attainment of these objectives is particularly urgent for less-developed contracting parties;

(b) considering that export earnings of the less-developed contracting parties can play a vital part in their economic development and that the extent of this contribution depends on the prices paid by the less-developed contracting parties for essential imports, the volume of their exports, and the prices received for these exports;

(c) noting, that there is a wide gap between standards of living in less-developed countries and in other countries;

___
* TIAS 6139

(d) recognizing that individual and joint action is essential to further the development of the economies of less-developed contracting parties and to bring about a rapid advance in the standards of living in these countries;

(e) recognizing that international trade as a means of achieving economic and social advancement should be governed by such rules and procedures—and measures in conformity with such rules and procedures—as are consistent with the objectives set forth in this Article;

(f) noting that the Contracting Parties may enable less-developed contracting parties to use special measures to promote their trade and development;
agree as follows.

"2. There is need for a rapid and sustained expansion of the export earnings of the less-developed contracting parties.

"3. There is need for positive efforts designed to ensure that less-developed contracting parties secure a share in the growth in international trade commensurate with the needs of their economic development.

"4. Given the continued dependence of many less-developed contracting parties on the exportation of a limited range of primary products, there is need to provide in the largest possible measure more favourable and acceptable conditions of access to world markets for these products, and wherever appropriate to devise measures designed to stabilize and improve conditions of world markets in these products, including in particular measures designed to attain stable, equitable and remunerative prices, thus permitting an expansion of world trade and demand and a dynamic and steady growth of the real export earnings of these countries so as to provide them with expanding resources for their economic development.

"5. The rapid expansion of the economies of the less-developed contracting parties will be facilitated by a diversification of the structure of their economices and the avoidance of an excessive dependence on the export of primary products. There is, therefore, need for increased access in the largest possible measure to markets under favourable conditions for processed and manufactured products currently or potentially of particular export interest to less-developed contracting parties.

"6. Because of the chronic deficiency in the export proceeds and other foreign exchange earnings of less-developed contracting parties, there are important inter-relationships between trade and financial assistance to development. There is. therefore, need for close and continuing collaboration between the Contracting Parties and the international lending agencies so that they can contribute most effectively to alleviating the burdens these less-developed contracting parties assume in the interest of their economic development.

"7. There is need for appropriate collaboration between the Contract Parties, other intergovernmental bodies and the organs and agencies of the United Nations system, whose activities relate to the trade and economic development of less-developed countries.

"8. The developed contracting parties do not expect reciprocity for commitments made by them in trade negotiations to reduce or remove tariffs and other barriers to the trade of less-developed contracting parties.

"9. The adoption of measures to give effect to these principles and objectives shall be a matter of conscious and purposeful effort on the part of the contracting parties both individually and jointly.

"Article XXXVII.—COMMITMENTS

"1. The developed contracting parties shall to the fullest extent possible—that is, except when compelling reasons, which may include legal reasons, make it impossible—give effect to the following provisions:

(a) accord high priority to the reduction and elimination of barriers to products currently or potentially of particular export interest to less-developed contracting parties, including customs duties and other restrictions which differentiate unreasonably between such products in their primary and in their processed forms;

(b) refrain from introducing, or increasing the incidence of, customs duties or non-tariff import barriers on products currently or potentially of particular

export interest to less-developed contracting parties; and

(c) (i) refrain from imposing new fiscal measures, and (ii) in any adjustments of fiscal policy accord high priority to the reduction and elimination of fiscal measures,

which would hamper, or which hamper, significantly the growth of consumption of primary products, in raw or processed form, wholly or mainly produced in the territories of less-developed contracting parties, and which are applied specifically to those products.

"2. (a) Whenever it is considered that effect is not being given to any of the provisions of sub-paragraph (a), (b) or (c) of paragraph 1, the matter shall be reported to the Contracting Parties either by the contracting party not so giving effect to the relevant provisions or by any other interested contracting party.

"(b)(i) The Contracting Parties shall, if requested so to do by any interested contracting party, and without prejudice to any bilateral consultations that may be undertaken, consult with the contracting party concerned and all interested contracting parties with respect to the matter with a view to reaching solutions satisfactory to all contracting parties concerned in order to further the objectives set forth in Article XXXVI. In the course of these consultations, the reasons given in cases where effect was not being given to the provisions of sub-paragraph (a), (b) or (c) of paragraph 1 shall be examined.

"(ii) As the implementation of the provisions of sub-paragraph (a), (b) or (c) of paragraph 1 by individual contracting parties may in some cases be more readily achieved where action is taken jointly with other developed contracting parties, such consultation might, where appropriate, be directed towards this end.

"(iii) The consultations by the Contracting Parties might also, in appropriate cases, be directed towards agreement on joint action designed to further the objectives of this Agreement as envisaged in paragraph 1 of Article XXV.

"3. The developed contracting parties shall:

(a) make every effort, in cases where a government directly or indirectly determines the resale price of products wholly or mainly produced in the territories of less-developed contracting parties, to maintain trade margins at equitable levels;

(b) give active consideration to the adoption of other measures designed to provide greater scope for the development of imports from less-developed contracting parties and collaborate in appropriate international action to this end;

(c) have special regard to the trade interests of less-developed contracting parties when considering the application of other measures permitted under this Agreement to meet particular problems and explore all possibilities of constructive remedies before applying such measures where they would affect essential interests of those contracting parties.

"4. Less-developed contracting parties agree to take appropriate action in implementation of the provisions of Part IV for the benefit of the trade of other less-developed contracting parties, in so far as such action is consistent with their individual present and future development, financial and trade needs taking into account past trade developments as well as the trade interests of less-developed contracting parties as a whole.

"5. In the implementation of the commitments set forth in paragraphs 1 to 4 each contracting party shall afford to any other interested contracting party or contracting parties full and prompt opportunity for consultations under the normal procedures of this Agreement with respect to any matter or difficulty which may arise.

"Article XXXVIII.—JOINT ACTION

"1. The contracting parties shall collaborate jointly, within the framework of this Agreement and elsewhere, as appropriate to further the objectives set forth in Article XXXVI.

"2. In particular, the Contracting Parties shall:

(a) where appropriate, take action, including action through international arrangements, to provide improved and acceptable conditions of access to world markets for primary products of particular interest to less-developed contracting parties and to devise measures designed to stabilize and improve conditions of world markets in these products including measures designed to attain stable, equitable and remunerative prices for exports of such products;

(b) seek appropriate collaboration in matters of trade and development policy with the United Nations and its organs and agencies, including any institutions that may be created on the basis of recommendations by the United Nations Conference on Trade and Development;

(c) collaborate in analyzing the development plans and policies of individual less-developed contracting parties and in examining trade and aid relationships with a view to devising concrete measures to promote the development of export potential and to facilitate access to export markets for the products of the industries thus developed and, in this connexion seed appropriate collaboration with governments and international organizations, and in particular with organizations having competence in relation to financial assistance for economic development, in systematic studies of trade and aid relationships in individual less-developed contracting parties aimed at obtaining a clear analysis of export potential, market prospects and any further action that may be required;

(d) keep under continuous review the development of world trade with special reference to the rate of growth of the trade of less-developed contracting parties and make such recommendations to contracting parties as may, in the circumstances, be deemed appropriate;

(e) collaborate in seeking feasible methods to expand trade for the purpose of economic development, through international harmonization and adjustment of national policies and regulations, through technical and commercial standards affecting production, transportation and marketing, and through export promotion by the establishment of facilities for the increased flow of trade information and the development of market research; and

(f) establish such institutional arrangements as may be necessary to further the objectives set forth in Article XXXVI and to give effect to the provisions of this Part."

ANNEXES
ANNEX A
List of Territories Referred to in Paragraph 2(a) of Article I

United Kingdom of Great Britain and Northern Ireland.
Dependent territories of the United Kingdom of Great Britian and Northern Ireland.
Canada.
Commonwealth of Australia.
Dependent territories of the Commonwealth of Australia.
New Zealand.
Dependent territories of New Zealand.
Union of South Africa including South West Africa.
Ireland.
India (as on April 10, 1947).
Newfoundland.
Southern Rhodesia.
Burma.
Ceylon.

Certain of the territories listed above have two or more preferential rates in force for certain products. Any such territory may, by agreement with the other contracting parties which are principal suppliers of such products at the most-favoured-nation rate, substitute for such preferential rates a single preferential rate which shall not on the whole be less favourable to suppliers at the most-favored-nation rate than the preferences in force prior to such substitution.

The imposition of an equivalent margin of tariff preference to replace a margin of preference in an internal tax existing on April 10, 1947, exclusively between two or more of the territories listed in this Annex or to replace the preferential quantitative arrangements described in the following paragraph, shall not be deemed to constitute an increase in a margin of tariff preference.

The preferential arrangements referred to in paragraph 5(b) of Article XIV are those existing in the United Kingdom on April 10, 1947, under contractual agreements with the Governments of Canada, Australia and New Zealand, in respect of chilled and frozen beef and veal, frozen mutton and lamb, chilled and frozen pork, and bacon. It is the intention, without prejudice to any action taken under part I(h) of Article XX, that these arrangements shall be eliminated or replaced by tariff preferences, and that negotiations to this end shall take place as soon as practicable among the countries substantially concerned or involved.

The film hire tax in force in New Zealand or April 10, 1947, shall, for the purposes of this Agreement, be treated as a customs duty under Article I. The renters' film quota in force in New Zealand on April 10, 1947, shall, for the purposes of this Agreement, be treated as a screen quota under Article IV.

The Dominions of India and Pakistan have not been mentioned separately in the above list since they had not come into existence as such on the base date of April 10, 1947.

ANNEX B
List of Territories of the French Union Referred to in Paragraph 2(b) of Article I

France.
French Equatorial Africa (Treaty Basin of the Congo[1] and other territories).
French West Africa.
Cameroons under French Mandate.[1]
French Somali Coast and Dependencies.
French Establishments in India.[1]
French Establishments in Oceania.
French Establishments in the Condominim of the New Hebrides.[1]
Guadeloupe and Dependencies.
French Guiana.
Indo-China.
Madagascar and Dependencies.
Morocco (French zone).[1]
Martinique.
New Caledonia and Dependencies.
Réunion.
Saint-Pierre and Miquelon.
Togo under French Mandate.[1]
Tunisia.

---

[1]For imports into Metropolitan France and Territories of the French Union.

ANNEX C

List of Territories of the Customs Union of Belgium, Luxembourg and the Netherlands Referred to in Paragraph 2(b) of Article I

The Economic Union of Belgium and Luxembourg.

Belgian Congo.

Ruanda Urundi.

Netherlands.

New Guinea.

Surinam.

Netherlands Antilles.

Republic of Indonesia.

For imports into the metropolitan territories constituting the Customs Union.

ANNEX D

List of Territories Referred to in Paragraph 2(b) of Article I as Respects the United States of America

United States of America (customs territory).

Dependent territories of the United States of America.

Republic of the Philippines.

The imposition of an equivalent margin of tariff preference to replace a margin of preference in an internal tax existing on April 10, 1947, exclusively between two or more of the territories listed in this Annex shall not be deemed to constitute an increase in a margin of tariff preference.

ANNEX E

List of Territories Covered by Preferential Arrangements Between Chile and Neighbouring Countries Referred to in Paragraph 2(d) of Article I

Preferences in force exclusively between Chile on the one hand, and (1) Argentina, (2) Bolivia, and (3) Peru on the other hand.

ANNEX F

List of Territories Covered by Preferential Arrangements Between Lebanon and Syria and Neighbouring Countries Referred to in Paragraph 2(d) of Article I

Preferences in force exclusively between the Lebano-Syrian Customs Union, on the one hand, and (1) Palestine, (2) Transjordan on the other hand.

ANNEX G

Dates Establishing Maximum Margins of Preference Referred to in Paragraph 4[1] of Article I

Australia: October 15, 1946.

Canada: July 1, 1939.

France: January 1, 1939.

Lebano-Syrian Customs Union: November 30, 1938.

Union of South Africa: July 1, 1938.

Southern Rhodesia: May 1, 1941.

ANNEX H

Percentage Shares of Total External Trade To Be Used for the Purpose of Making the Determination Referred to in Article XXVI

(Based on the average of 1949-1953)

If, prior to the accession of the Government of Japan to the General Agreement, the present Agreement has been accepted by contracting parties the external trade of which under column I accounts for the percentage of such trade specified in paragraph 6 of Article XXVI, column I shall be applicable for the purposes of that paragraph. If the present Agreement has not been so accepted prior to the accession of the Government of Japan, column II shall be applicable for the purposes of that paragraph.

	Col. I (contracting parties on Mar. 1, 1955)	Col. II (contracting parties on Mar. 1, 1955, and Japan)
Australia	3.1	3.0
Austria	.9	.8
Belgium-Luxembourg	4.3	4.2
Brazil	2.5	2.4
Burma	.3	.3
Canada	6.7	6.5
Ceylon	.5	.5
Chile	.6	.6
Cuba	1.1	1.1
Czechoslovakia	1.4	1.4
Denmark	1.4	1.4
Dominican Republic	.1	.1
Finland	1.0	1.0
France	8.7	8.5
Germany, Federal Republic of	5.3	5.2
Greece	.4	.4
Haiti	.1	.1
India	2.4	2.4
Indonesia	1.3	1.3
Italy	2.9	2.8

[1]The number "4" has been substituted for the number "3" in the heading of Annex G. The reference to Article I was intended to be a reference to the last paragraph of Article I, which originally consisted of only three numbered paragraphs.

	Col. I (contracting parties on Mar. 1, 1955)	Col. II (contracting parties on Mar. 1, 1955, and Japan)
Netherlands, Kingdom of the	4.7	4.6
New Zealand	1.0	1.0
Nicaragua....................	.1	.1
Norway	1.1	1.1
Pakistan	.9	.8
Peru.........................	.4	.4
Rhodesia and Nyasland.....	.6	.6
Sweden......................	2.5	2.4
Turkey.......................	.6	.6
Union of South Africa	1.8	1.8
United Kingdom	20.3	19.8
United States of America...	20.6	20.1
Uruguay	.4	.4
Japan	....	2.3
Total	100.0	100.0

Note: These percentages have been computed taking into account the trade of all territories in respect of which the General Agreement on Tariffs and Trade is applied.

ANNEX I
Notes and Supplementary Provisions
Ad Article I

Paragraph 1

The obligations incorporated in paragraph 1 of Article I by reference to paragraphs 2 and 4 of Article III and those incorporated in paragraph 2(b) of Article II by reference to Article VI shall be considered as falling within Part II for the purposes of the Protocol of Provisional Application.

The cross-references, in the paragraph immediately above and in paragraph 1 of Article I, to paragraphs 2 and 4 of Article III shall only apply after Article III has been modified by the entry into force of the amendment provided for in the Protocol Modifying Part II and Article XXVI of the General Agreement on Tariffs and Trade, dated September 14, 1948.

Paragraph 4

The term "margin of preference" means the absolute difference between the most-favoured-nation rate of duty and the preferential rate of duty for the like product, and not the proportionate relation between those rates. As examples:

(1) If the most-favoured-nation rate were 36 percent *ad valorem* and the preferential rate were 24 percent *ad valorem*, the margin of preference would

be 12 percent *ad valorem*, and not one-third of the most-favoured-nation rate.

(2) If the most-favoured-nation rate were 36 percent *ad valorem* and the preferential rate were expressed as two-thirds of the most-favoured-nation rate, the margin of preference would be 12 percent *ad valorem*.

(3) If the most-favoured-nation rate were 2 francs per kilogramme and the preferential rate were 1.50 francs per kilogramme, the margin of preference would be 0.50 francs per kilogramme.

The following kinds of customs action, taken in accordance with established uniform procedures, would not be contrary to a general binding of margins of preference:

(i) The re-application to an imported product of a tariff classification or rate of duty, properly applicable to such product, in cases in which the application of such classification or rate to such product was temporarily suspended or inoperative on April 10, 1947; and

(ii) The classification of a particular product under a tariff item other than that under which importations of that product were classified on April 10, 1947, in cases in which the tariff law clearly contemplates that such product may be classified under more than one tariff item.

Ad Article II

Paragraph 2 (a)

The cross-reference, in paragraph 2(*a*) of Article II, to paragraph 2 of Article III shall only apply after Article III has been modified by the entry into force of the amendment provided for in the Protocol Modifying Part II and Article XXVI of the General Agreement on Tariffs and Trade, dated September 14, 1948.[1]

Paragraph 2 (b)

See the note relating to paragraph 1 of Article I.

Paragraph 4

Except where otherwise specifically agreed between the contracting parties which initially negotiated the concession, the provisions of this paragraph will be

---

[1] This Protocol entered into force on December 14, 1948.

applied in the light of the provisions of Article 31 of the Havana Charter.

Ad Article III

Any internal tax or other internal charge, or any law, regulation or requirement of the kind referred to in paragraph 1 which applies to an imported product and to the like domestic product and is collected or enforced in the case of the imported product at the time or point of importation, is nevertheless to be regarded as an internal tax or other internal charge, or a law, regulation or requirement of the kind referred to in paragraph 1, and is accordingly subject to the provisions of Article III.

Paragraph 1

The application of paragraph 1 to internal taxes imposed by local governments and authorities within the territory of a contracting party is subject to the provisions of the final paragraph of Article XXIV. The term "reasonable measures" in the last-mentioned paragraph would not require, for example, the repeal of existing national legislation authorizing local governments to impose internal taxes which, although technically inconsistent with the letter of Article III, are not in fact inconsistent with its spirit, if such repeal would result in a serious financial hardship for the local governments or authorities concerned. With regard to taxation by local governments or authorities which is inconsistent with both the letter and spirit of Article III, the term "reasonable measures" would permit a contracting party to eliminate the inconsistent taxation gradually over a transition period, if abrupt action would create serious administrative and financial difficulties.

Paragraph 2

A tax conforming to the requirements of the first sentence of paragraph 2 would be considered to be inconsistent with the provisions of the second sentence only in cases where competition was involved between, on the one hand, the taxed product and, on the other hand, a directly competitive or substitutable product which was not similarly taxed.

Paragraph 5

Regulations consistent with the provisions of the first sentence of paragraph 5 shall not be considered to be contrary to the provisions of the second sentence in any case in which all of the products subject to the regulations are produced domestically in substantial quantities. A regulation cannot be justified as being consistent with the provisions of the second sentence on the ground that the proportion or amount allocated to each of the products which are the subject of the regulation constitutes an equitable relationship between imported and domestic products.

Ad Article V

Paragraph 5

With regard to transportation charges, the principle laid down in paragraph 5 refers to like products being transported on the same route under like conditions.

Ad Article VI

Paragraph 1

1. Hidden dumping by associated houses (that is, the sale by an importer at a price below that corresponding to the price invoiced by an exporter with whom the importer is associated, and also below the price in the exporting country) constitutes a form of price dumping with respect to which the margin of dumping may be calculated on the basis of the price at which the goods are resold by the importer.

2. It is recognized that, in the case of imports from a country which has a complete or substantially complete monopoly of its trade and where all domestic prices are fixed by the State, special difficulties may exist in determining price comparability for the purposes of paragraph 1, and in such cases importing contracting parties may find it necessary to take into account the possibility that a strict comparison with domestic prices in such a country may not always be appropriate.

Paragraphs 2 and 3

Note 1.—As in many other cases in customs administration, a contracting party may require reasonable security (bond or cash deposit) for the payment of anti-dumping or countervailing duty pending final determination of the facts in any case of suspected dumping or subsidization.

Note 2.—Multiple currency practices can in certain circumstances constitute a subsidy to exports which may be met by countervailing duties under paragraph 3 or can constitute a form of dumping by means of a partial depreciation of a country's currency which may be met by action under paragraph 2. By "multiple currency practices" is meant practices by governments or sanctioned by governments.

Paragraph 6(b)

Waivers under the provisions of this sub-paragraph shall be granted only on application by the contracting party proposing to levy an anti-dumping or countervailing duty, as the case may be.

Ad Article VII

Paragraph 1

The expression "or other charges" is not to be regarded as including internal taxes or equivalent charges imposed on or in connection with imported products.

Paragraph 2

1. It would be in conformity with Article VII to presume that "actual value" may be represented by the invoice price, plus any non-included charges for legitimate costs which are proper elements of "actual value" and plus any abnormal discount or other reduction from the ordinary competitive price.

2. It would be in conformity with Article VII, paragraph 2(b), for a contracting party to construe the phrase "in the ordinary course of trade ... under fully competitive conditions", as excluding any transaction wherein the buyer and seller are not independent of each other and price is not the sole consideration.

3. The standard of "fully competitive conditions" permits a contracting party to exclude from consideration prices involving special discounts limited to exclusive agents.

4. The wording of sub-paragraphs (a) and (b) permits a contracting party to determine the value for customs purposes uniformly either (1) on the basis of a particular exporter's prices of the imported merchandise, or (2) on the

basis of the general price level of like merchandise.

Ad Article VIII

1. While Article VIII does not cover the use of multiple rates of exchange as such, paragraphs 1 and 4 condemn the use of exchange taxes or fees as a device for implementing multiple currency practices; if, however, a contracting party is using multiple currency exchange fees for balance of payments reasons with the approval of the International Monetary Fund, the provisions of paragraph 9(a) of Article XV fully safeguard its position.

2. It would be consistent with paragraph 1 if one the importation of products from the territory of a contracting party into the territory of another contracting party, the production of certificates of origin should only be required to the extent that is strictly indispensable.

Ad Articles XI, XII, XIII, XIV, And XVIII

Throughout Articles XI, XII, XIII, XIV and XVIII the terms "import restrictions" or "export restrictions" include restrictions made effective through state-trading operations.

Ad Article XI

Paragraph 2(c)

The term "in any form" in this paragraph covers the same products when in an early stage of processing and still perishable, which compete directly with the fresh product and if freely imported would tend to make the restriction on the fresh product ineffective.

Paragraph 2, last sub-paragraph

The term "special factors" includes changes in relative productive efficiency as between domestic and foreign producers, or as between different foreign producers, but not changes artificially brought about by means not permitted under the Agreement.

Ad Article XII

The Contracting Parties shall make provision for the utmost secrecy in the conduct of any consultation under the provisions of this Article.

Paragraph 3(c)(i)

Contracting parties applying restrictions shall endeavour to avoid causing serious prejudice to exports of a commodity on which the economy of a contracting party is largely dependent.

Paragraph 4(b)

It is agreed that the date shall be within ninety days after the entry into force of the amendments of this Article effected by the Protocol Amending the Preamble and Parts II and III of this Agreement. However, should the Contracting Parties find that conditions were not suitable for the application of the provisions of this sub-paragraph at the time envisaged, they may determine a later date: *Provided,* that such date is not more than thirty days after such time as the obligations of Article VIII, Sections 2, 3 and 4 of the Articles of Agreement of the International Monetary Fund become applicable to contracting parties, members of the Fund, the combined foreign trade of which constitutes at least fifty per centum of the aggregate foreign trade of all contracting parties.

Paragraph 4(e)

It is agreed that paragraph 4(e) does not add any new criteria for the imposition or maintenance of quantitative restrictions for balance of payments reasons. It is solely intended to ensure that all external factors such as changes in the terms of trade, quantitative restrictions, excessive tariffs and subsidies, which may be contributing to the balance of payments difficulties of the contracting party applying restrictions will be fully taken into account.

Ad Article XIII

Paragraph 2(d)

No mention was made of "commercial considerations" as a rule for the allocation of quotas because it was considered that its application by governmental authorities might not always be practicable. Moreover, in cases where it is practicable, a contracting party could apply these considerations in the process of seeking agreement, consistently with the general rule laid down in the opening sentence of paragraph 2.

Paragraph 4

See note relating to "special factors"

in connection with the last subparagraph of paragraph 2 of Article XI.

Ad Article XIV

Paragraph 1

The provisions of this paragraph shall not be so construed as to preclude full consideration by the Contracting Parties, in the consultations provided for in paragraph 4 of Article XII and in paragraph 12 of Article XVIII, of the nature, effects and reasons for discrimination in the field of import restrictions.[1]

Paragraph 2

One of the situations contemplated in paragraph 2 is that of a contracting party holding balances acquired as a result of current transactions which it finds itself unable to use without a measure of discrimination.

Ad Article XV

Paragraph 4

The word "frustrate" is intended to indicate, for example, that infringements of the letter of any Article of this Agreement by exchange action shall not be regarded as a violation of that Article if, in practice, there is no appreciable departure from the intent of the Article. Thus, a contracting party which, as part of its exchange control operated in accordance with the Articles of Agreement of the International Monetary Fund, requires payment to be received for its exports in its own currency or in the currency of one or more members of the International Monetary Fund will not thereby be deemed to contravene Article XI or Article XIII. Another example would be that of a contracting party which specifies on an import license the country from which the goods may be imported, for the purpose not of introducing any additional element of discrimination in its import licensing system but of enforcing permissible exchange controls.

Ad Article XVI

The exemption of an exported product from duties or taxes borne by the like product when destined for domestic consumption, or the remission of such

---

[1]Text as amended Feb 15, 1961.

duties or taxes in amounts not in excess of those which have accrued, shall not be deemed to be a subsidy.

Section B

1. Nothing in Section B shall preclude the use by a contracting party of multiple rates of exchange in accordance with the the Articles of Agreement of the International Monetary Fund.

2. For the purposes of Section B, a "primary product" is understood to be any product of farm, forest or fishery, or any mineral, in its natural form or which has undergone such processing as is customarily required to prepare it for marketing in substantial volume in international trade.

Paragraph 3

1. The fact that a contracting party has not exported the product in question during the previous representative period would not in itself preclude that contracting party from establishing its right to obtain a share of the trade in the product concerned.

2. A system for the stabilization of the domestic price or of the return to domestic producers of a primary product independently of the movements of export prices, which results at times in the sale of the product for export at a price lower than the comparable price charged for the like product to buyers in the domestic market, shall be considered not to involve a subsidy on exports within the meaning of paragraph 3 if the Contracting Parties determine that:

(a) the system has also resulted, or is so designed as to result, in the sale of the product for export at a price higher than the comparable price charged for the like product to buyers in the domestic market; and

(b) the system is so operated, or is designed so to operate, either because of the effective regulation of production or otherwise, as not to stimulate exports unduly or otherwise seriously to prejudice the interests of other contracting parties.

Notwithstanding such determination by the Contracting Parties, operations under such a system shall be subject to the provisions of paragraph 3 where they are wholly or partly financed out of government funds in addition to the funds collected from producers in respect of the product concerned.

Paragraph 4

The intention of paragraph 4 is that the contracting parties should seek before the end of 1957 to reach agreement to abolish all remaining subsidies as from 1 January 1958; or, failing this, to reach agreement to extend the application of the standstill until the earliest date thereafter by which they can expect to reach such agreement.

Ad Article XVII

Paragraph 1

The operations of Marketing Boards, which are established by contracting parties and are engaged in purchasing or selling, are subject to the provisions of sub-paragraphs (a) and (b).

The activities of Marketing Boards which are established by contracting parties and which do not purchase or sell but lay down regulations covering private trade are governed by the relevant Articles of this Agreement.

The charging by a state enterprise of different prices for its sales of a product in different markets is not precluded by the provisions of this Article, provided that such different prices are charged for commercial reasons, to meet conditions of supply and demand in export markets.

Paragraph 1(a)

Governmental measures imposed to ensure standards of quality and efficiency in the operation of external trade, or privileges granted for the exploitation of national natural resources but which do not empower the government to exercise control over the trading activities of the enterprise in question, do not constitute "exclusive or special privileges".

Paragraph 1(b)

A country receiving a "tied loan" is free to take this loan into account as a "commercial consideration" when purchasing requirements abroad.

Paragraph 2

The term "goods" is limited to products as understood in commercial practice, and is not intended to include the purchase or sale of services.

Paragraph 3

Negotiations which contracting parties agree to conduct under this paragraph may be directed towards the reduction of duties and other charges on imports and exports or towards the conclusion of any other mutually satisfactory arrangement consistent with the provisions of this Agreement. (See paragraph 4 of Article II and the note to that paragraph.)

Paragraph 4(b)

The term "import mark-up" in this paragraph shall represent the margin by which the price charged by the import monopoly for the imported product (exclusive of internal taxes within the purview of Article III, transportation, distribution, and other expenses incident to the purchase, sale or further processing, and a reasonable margin of profit) exceeds the landed cost.

Ad Article XVIII

The Contracting Parties and the contracting parties concerned shall preserve the utmost secrecy in respect of matters arising under this Article.

Paragraphs 1 and 4

1. When they consider whether the economy of a contracting party "can only support low standards of living," the Contracting Parties shall take into consideration the normal positions of that economy and shall not base their determination on exceptional circumstances such as those which may result from the temporary existence of exceptionally favorable conditions for the staple export product or products of such contracting party.

2. The phrase "in the early states of development" is not meant to apply only to contracting parties which have just started their econmic development, but also to contracting parties the economies of which are undergoing a process of industrialization to correct an excessive dependence on primary production.

Paragraphs 2, 3, 7, 13 and 22

The reference to the establishment of particular industries shall apply not only to the establishment of a new industry, but also to the establishment of a new branch of production in an existing industry and to the substantial transformation of an existing industry, and to the substantial expansion of an existing industry supplying a relatively small proportion of the domestic demand. It shall also cover the reconstruction of an industry destroyed or substantially damaged as a result of hostilities or natural disasters.

Paragraph 7(b)

A modification or withdrawal, pursuant to paragraph 7(b), by a contracting party, other than the applicant contracting party, referred to in paragraph 7(a), shall be made within six months of the day on which the action is taken by the applicant contracting party, and shall become effective on the thirtieth day following the day on which such modification or withdrawal has been notified to the Contracting Parties.

Paragraph 11

The second sentence in paragraph 11 shall not be interpreted to mean that a contracting party is required to relax or remove restrictions if such relaxation or removal would thereupon produce conditions justifying the intensification or institution, respectively, of restrictions under paragraph 9 of Article XVIII.

Paragraph 12(b)

The date referred to in paragraph 12(b) shall be the date determined by the Contracting Parties in accordance with the provisions of paragraph 4(b) of Article XII of this Agreement.

Paragraphs 13 and 14

It is recognized that, before deciding on the introduction of a measure and notifying the Contracting Parties in accordance with paragraph 14, a contracting party may need a reasonable period of time to assess the competitive position of the industry concerned.

Paragraphs 15 and 16

It is understood that the Contracting Parties shall invite a contracting party proposing to apply a measure under Section C to consult with them pursuant to paragraph 16 if they are requested to do so by a contracting party the trade of which would be appreciably affected by the measure in question.

Paragraphs 16, 18, 19, and 22

1. It is understood that the Contracting Parties may concur in a proposed measure subject to specific conditions or limitations. If the measure as applied

does not conform to the terms of the concurrence it will to that extent be deemed a measure in which the Contracting Parties have not concurred. In case in which the Contracting Parties have concurred in a measure for a specified period, the contracting party concerned, if it finds that the maintenance of the measure for a further period of time is required to achieve the objective for which the measure was originally taken, may apply to the Contracting Parties for an extension of that period in accordance with the provisions and procedures of Section C or D, as the case may be.

2. It is expected that the Contracting Parties will, as a rule, refrain from concurring in a measure which is likely to cause serious prejudice to exports of a commodity on which the economy of a contracting party is largely dependent.

Paragraphs 18 and 22

The phrase "that the interests of other contracting parties are adequately safeguarded" is meant to provide latitude sufficient to permit consideration in each case of the most appropriate method of safeguarding those interests. The appropriate method may, for instance, take the form of an additional concession to be applied by the contracting party having recourse to Section C or D during such time as the deviation from the other Articles of the Agreement would remain in force or of the temporary suspension by any other contracting party referred to in paragraph 18 of a concession substantially equivalent to the impairment due to the introduction of the measure in question. Such contracting party would have the right to safeguard its interests through such a temporary suspension of a concession; *Provided* that this right will not be exercised when, in the case of a measure imposed by a contracting party coming within the scope of paragraph 4(a), the Contracting Parties have to determine that the extent of the compensatory concession proposed was adequate.

Paragraph 19

The provisions of paragraph 19 are intended to cover the cases where an industry has been in existence beyond the "reasonable period of time" referred to in the note to paragraphs 13 and 14,

and should not be so construed as to deprive a contracting party coming within the scope of paragraph 4(a) of Article XVIII, of its right to resort to the other provisions of Section C, including paragraph 17, with regard to a newly established industry even though it has benefited from incidental protection afforded by balance of payments import restrictions.

Paragraph 21

Any measure taken pursuant to the provisions of paragraph 21 shall be withdrawn forthwith if the action taken in accordance with paragraph 17 is withdrawn or if the Contracting Parties concur in the measure proposed after the expiration of the ninety-day time limit specified in paragraph 17.

Ad Article XX

Sub-paragraph (h)

The exception provided for in this sub-paragraph extends to any commodity agreement which conforms to the principles approved by the Economic and Social Council in its Resolution 30 (IV) of 28 March 1947.

Ad Article XXIV

Paragraph 9

It is understood that the provisions of Article I would require that, when a product which has been imported into the territory of a member of a customs union or free-trade area at a preferential rate of duty is reexported to the territory of another member of such union or area, the latter member should collect a duty equal to the difference between the duty already paid and any higher duty that would be payable if the product were being imported directly into its territory.

Paragraph 11

Measures adopted by India and Pakistan in order to carry out definitive trade arrangements between them, once they have been agreed upon, might depart from particular provisions of this Agreement, but these measures would in general be consistent with the objectives of the Agreement.

Ad Article XXVIII

The Contracting Parties and each contracting party concerned should arrange to conduct the negotiations and consultations with the greatest possible secrecy in order to avoid premature disclosure of details of prospective tariff changes. The Contracting Parties shall be informed immediately of all changes in national tariffs resulting from recourse to this Article.

Paragraph 1

1. If the Contracting Parties specify a period other than a three-year period, a contracting party may act pursuant to paragraph 1 or paragraph 3 of Article XXVIII on the first day following the expiration of such other period and, unless the Contracting Parties have again specified another period, subsequent periods will be three-year periods following the expiration of such specified period.

2. The provision that on 1 January 1958, and on other days determined pursuant to paragraph 1, a contracting party "may *** modify or withdraw a concession" means that on such day, and on the first day after the end of each period, the legal obligation of such contracting party under Article II is altered; it does not mean that the changes in its customs tariff should necessarily be made effective on that day. If a tariff change resulting from negotiations undertaken pursuant to this Article is delayed, the entry into force of any compensatory concessions may be similarly delayed.

3. Not earlier than six months, nor later than three months, prior to 1 January 1958, or to the termination date of any subsequent period, a contracting party wishing to modify or withdraw any concession embodied in the appropriate Schedule, should notify the Contracting Parties to this effect. The Contracting Parties shall then determine the contracting party or contracting parties with which the negotiations or consultations referred to in paragraph 1 shall take place. Any contracting party so determined shall participate in such negotiations or consultations with the applicant contracting party with the aim of reaching agreement before the end of the period. Any extension of the assured life of the Schedules shall relate to the Schedules as modified after such negotiations, in accordance with paragraphs 1,

2, and 3 of Article XXVIII. If the Contracting Parties are arranging for multilateral tariff negotiations to take place within the period of six months before 1 January 1958, or before any other day determined pursuant to paragraph 1, they shall include in the arrangements for such negotiations suitable procedures for carrying out the negotiations referred to in this paragraph.

4. The object of providing for the participation in the negotiations of any contracting party with a principal supplying interest, in addition to any contracting party with which the concession was initially negotiated, is to ensure that a contracting party with a larger share in the trade affected by the concession than a contracting party with which the concession was initially negotiated shall have an effective opportunity to protect the contractual right which it enjoys under this Agreement. On the other hand, it is not intended that the scope of the negotiations should be such as to make negotiations and agreement under Article XXVIII unduly difficult nor to create complications in the application of this Article in the future to concessions which result from negotiations thereunder. Accordingly, the Contracting Parties should only determine that a contracting party has a principal supplying interest if that contracting party has had, over a reasonable period of time prior to the negotiations, a larger share in the market of the applicant contracting party than a contracting party with which the concession was initially negotiated or would, in the judgment of the Contracting Parties, have had such a share in the absence of discriminatory quantitative restrictions maintained by the applicant contracting party. It would therefore not be appropriate for the Contracting Parties to determine that more than one contracting party, or in those exceptional cases where there is near equality more than two contracting parties, had a principal supplying interest.

5. Notwithstanding the definition of a principal supplying interest in note 4 to paragraph 1, the Contracting Parties may exceptionally determine that a contracting party has a principal supplying

interest if the concession in question affects trade which constitutes a major part of the total exports of such contracting party.

6. It is not intended that provision for participation in the negotiations of any contracting party with a principal supplying interest, and for consultation with any contracting party having a substantial interest in the concession which the applicant contracting party is seeking to modify or withdraw, should have the effect that it should have to pay compensation or suffer retaliation greater than the withdrawal or modification sought, judged in the light of the conditions of trade at the time of the proposed withdrawal or modification, making allowance for any discriminatory quantitative restrictions maintained by the applicant contracting party.

7. The expression "substantial interest" is not capable of a precise definition and accordingly may present difficulties for the Contracting Parties. It is, however, intended to be construed to cover only those contracting parties which have, or in the absence of discriminatory quantitative restrictions affecting their exports could reasonably be expected to have, a significant share in the market of the contracting party seeking to modify or withdraw the concession.

Paragraph 4

1. Any request for authorization to enter into negotiations shall be accompanied by all relevant statistical and other data. A decision on such request shall be made within thirty days of its submission.

2. It is recognized that to permit certain contracting parties, depending in large measure on a relatively small number of primary commodities and relying on the tariff as an important aid for furthering diversification of their economies or as an important source of revenue, normally to negotiate for the modification or withdrawal of concessions only under paragraph 1 of Article XXVIII, might cause them at such a time to make modifications or withdrawals which in the long run would prove unnecessary. To avoid such a situation the Contracting Parties shall authorize any such contracting party, under paragraph 4, to enter into negoti-

ations unless they consider this would result in, or contribute substantially towards, such an increase in tariff levels as to threat the stability of the Schedules to this Agreement or lead to undue disturbance of international trade.

3. It is expected that negotiations authorized under paragraph 4 for modification or withdrawal of a single item, or a very small group of items, could normally be brought to a conclusion in sixty days. It is recognized, however, that such a period will be inadequate for cases involving negotiations for the modification or withdrawal of a larger number of items and in such cases, therefore, it would be appropriate for the Contracting Parties to prescribe a longer period.

4. The determination referred to in paragraph 4(d) shall be made by the Contracting Parties within thirty days of the submission of the matter to them, unless the applicant contracting party agrees to a longer period.

5. In determining under paragraph 4(d) whether an applicant contracting party has unreasonably failed to offer adequate compensation, it is understood that the Contracting Parties will take due account of the special position of a contracting party which has bound a high proportion of its tariffs at very low rates of duty and to this extent has less scope than other contracting parties to make compensatory adjustment.

Ad Article XXVIII Bis
Paragraph 3

It is understood that the reference to fiscal needs would include the revenue aspect of duties and particularly duties imposed primarily for revenue purposes or duties imposed on products which can be substituted for products subject to revenue duties to prevent the avoidance of such duties.

Ad Article XXIX
Paragraph 1

Chapters VII and VIII of the Havana Charter have been excluded from paragraph 1 because they generally deal with the organization, functions and procedures of the International Trade Organization.

Ad Part IV

The words "developed contracting

parties" and the words "less-developed contracting parties" as used in Part IV are to be understood to refer to developed and less-developed countries which are parties to the General Agreement on Tariffs and Trade.

Ad Article XXXVI

Paragraph 1

This Article is based upon the objectives set forth in Article I as it will be amended by Section A of paragraph 1 of the Protocol Amending Part I and Articles XXIX and XXX when that Protocol enters into force.

Paragraph 4

The term "primary products" includes agricultural products, *vide* paragraph 2 of the note ad Article XVI, Section B.

Paragraph 5

A diversification programme would generally include the intensification of activities for the processing of primary products and the development of manufacturing industries, taking into account the situation of the particular contracting party and the world outlook for production and consumption of different commodities.

Paragraph 8

It is understood that the phrase "do not expect reciprocity" means, in accordance with the objectives set forth in this Article, that the less-developed contracting parties should not be expected, in the course of trade negotiations, to make contributions which are inconsistent with their individual development, financial and trade needs, taking into consideration past trade developments.

This paragraph would apply in the event of action under Section A of Article XVIII, Article XXVIII, Article XXVIII bis (Article XXIX after the amendment set forth in Section A of paragraph 1 of the Protocol Amending Part I and Articles XXIX and XXX shall have become effective), Article XXXIII, or any other procedure under this Agreement.

Ad Article XXXVII

Paragraph 1(a)

This paragraph would apply in the event of negotiations for reduction or elimination of tariffs or other restrictive regulations of commerce under Articles XXVIII, XXVIII bis (XXIX after the amendment set forth in Section A of paragraph 1 of the Protocol Amending Part I and Articles XXIX and XXX shall have become effective[1]), and Article XXXIII, as well as in connexion with other action to effect such reduction or elimination which contracting parties may be able to undertake.

Paragraph 3(b)

The other measures referred to in this paragraph might include steps to promote domestic structural changes, to encourage the consumption of particular products, or to introduce measures of trade promotion.

2. This Protocol shall be deposited with the Executive Secretary to the Contracting Parties to the General Agreement. It shall be open for acceptance, by signature or otherwise, by the contracting parties to the General Agreement and by the governments which have acceded provisionally to the General Agreement, until 31 December 1965; *provided* that the period during which this Protocol may be accepted in respect of a contracting party or such government may, by a decision of the Contracting Parties, be extended beyond that date.*

3. Acceptance of this Protocol in accordance with the provisions of paragraph 2 shall be deemed to constitute an acceptance of the amendments set forth in paragraph 1 in accordance with the provisions of Article XXX of the General Agreement.

4. The amendments set forth in paragraph 1 shall become effective in accordance with the provisions of Article XXX of the General Agreement following acceptance of the Protocol by two thirds of the governments which are then contracting parties.* *

5. The amendments set forth in paragraph 1 shall become effective between a government which has acceded provisionally to the General Agreement and a government which is a contracting par-

---

[1] This Protocol was abandoned on January 1, 1968.

*Extended until the close of the twenty-fourth session of the contracting parties (Decision of Jan. 17, 1966; not printed).

* *Entered into force June 27, 1966.

ty, and between two governments which have acceded provisionally when such amendments shall have been accepted by both such governments; *provided* that the amendments shall not become so effective before an instrument of provisional accession shall have become effective between the two governments nor before the amendments shall have become effective in accordance with the provisions of paragraph 4.

6. Acceptance of this Protocol by a contracting party, to the extent that it shall not have already taken final action to become a party to the following instruments and except as it may otherwise notify the Executive Secretary in writing at the time of such acceptance, shall constitute final action to become a party to each of the following instruments:

PROTOCOL OF PROVISIONAL APPLICATION OF THE GENERAL AGREEMENT ON TARIFFS AND TRADE

1. The Governments of the Commonwealth of Australia, the Kingdom of Belgium (in respect of its metropolitan territory), Canada, the French Republic (in respect of its metropolitan territory), the Grand-Duchy of Luxemburg, the Kingdom of the Netherlands (in respect of its metropolitan territory), the United Kingdom of Great Britain and Northern Ireland (in respect of its metropolitan territory), and the United States of America, undertake, provided that this Protocol shall have been signed on behalf of all the foregoing Governments not later than November 15, 1947, to apply provisionally on and after January 1, 1948:

(a) Parts I and III of the General Agreement on Tariffs and Trade, and

(b) Part II of that Agreement to the fullest extent not inconsistent with existing legislation.

2. The foregoing Governments shall make effective such provisional application of the General Agreement, in respect of any of their territories other than their metropolitan territories, on or after January 1, 1948, upon the expiration of thirty days from the day on which notice of such application is received by the Secretary-General of the United Nations.

3. Any other Government signatory to this Protocol shall make effective such provisional application of the General Agreement, on or after January 1, 1948, upon the expiration of thirty days from the day of signature of this Protocol on behalf of such Government.

4. This Protocol shall remain open for signature at the Headquarters of the United Nations, (a) until November 15, 1947, on behalf of any Government named in paragraph 1 of this Protocol which has not signed it on this day, and (b) until June 30, 1948, on behalf of any other Government signatory to the Final Act adopted at the conclusion of the Second Session of the Preparatory Committee of the United Nations Conference on Trade and Employment which has not signed it on this day.

5. Any Government applying this Protocol shall be free to withdraw such application, and such withdrawal shall take effect upon the expiration of sixty days from the day on which written notice of such withdrawal is received by the Secretary-General of the United Nations.

6. The original of this Protocol shall be deposited with the Secretary-General of the United Nations, who will furnish certified copies thereof to all interested Governments.

In Witness Whereof the respective Representatives, after having communicated their full powers, found to be in good and due form, have signed this Protocol.

Done at Geneva, in a single copy, in the English and French languages, both texts authentic, this thirtieth day of October, one thousand nine hundred and forty-seven.

Appendix C

MTN Subsidies Agreement

Agreement on Interpretation and Application of Articles VI, XVI and XXIII of the General Agreement on Tariffs and Trade

TABLE OF CONTENTS

The signatories[1] to this Agreement,

Noting that Ministers on 12-14 September 1973 agreed that the Multilateral Trade Negotiations should, *inter alia,* reduce or eliminate the trade restricting or distorting effects of non-tariff measures, and bring such measures under more effective international discipline;

Recognizing that subsidies are used by governments to promote important objectives of national policy;

Recognizing also that subsidies may have harmful effects on trade and production;

Recognizing that the emphasis of this Agreement should be on the effects of subsidies and that these effects are to be assessed in giving due account to the internal economic situation of the signatories concerned as well as to the state of international economic and monetary relations;

Desiring to ensure that the use of subsidies does not adversely affect or prejudice the interests of any signatory to this Agreement, and that countervailing measures do not unjustifiably impede

[Ed. Note: Text published as TIAS 9619 by the U.S. Department of State.]

[1] The term "signatories" is hereinafter used to mean Parties to this Agreement.

international trade, and that relief is made available to producers adversely affected by the use of subsidies within an agreed international framework of rights and obligations;

Taking into account the particular trade, development and financial needs of developing countries;

Desiring to apply fully and to interpret the provisions of Articles VI, XVI and XXIII of the General Agreement on Tariffs and Trade[2] (hereinafter referred to as "the General Agreement" or "GATT") only with respect to subsidies and countervailing measures and to elaborate rules for their application in order to provide greater uniformity and certainty in their implementation;

Desiring to provide for the speedy, effective and equitable resolution of disputes arising under this Agreement,

Have agreed as follows:

PART I

Article 1—*Application of Article VI of the General Agreement*[3]

Signatories shall take all necessary steps to ensure that the imposition of a countervailing duty[4] on any product of the territory of any signatory imported into the territory of another signatory is in accordance with the provisions of Article VI of the General Agreement and the terms of this Agreement.

Article 2—*Domestic procedures and related matters*

1. Countervailing duties may only be imposed pursuant to investigations initiated[5] and conducted in accordance with the provisions of this Article. An investigation to determine the existence, degree and effect of any alleged subsidy shall

normally be initiated upon a written request by or on behalf of the industry affected. The request shall include sufficient evidence of the existence of (a) a subsidy and, if possible, its amount; (b) injury within the meaning of Article VI of the General Agreement as interpreted by this Agreement[6] and (c) a causal link between the subsidized imports and the alleged injury. If in special circumstances the authorities concerned decide to initiate an investigation without having received such a request, they shall proceed only if they have sufficient evidence on all points under (a) to (c) above.

2. Each signatory shall notify the Committee on Subsidies and Countervailing Measures[7] (a) which of its authorities are competent to initiate and conduct investigations referred to in this Article and (b) its domestic procedures governing the initiation and conduct of such investigations.

3. When the investigating authorities are satisfied that there is sufficient evidence to justify initiating an investigation, the signatory or signatories, the products of which are subject to such investigation and the exporters and importers known to the investigating authorities to have an interest therein and the complainants shall be notified and a public notice shall be given. In determining whether to initiate an investigation, the investigating authorities should take into account the position adopted by the affiliates of a complainant party[8] which are resident in the territory of another signatory.

4. Upon initiation of an investigation and thereafter, the evidence of both a subsidy and injury caused thereby should be considered simultaneously. In any event the evidence of both the existence of subsidy and injury shall be considered

---

[3]The provisions of both Part I and Part II of this Agreement may be invoked in parallel: however, with regard to the effects of a particular subsidy in the domestic market of the importing country, only one form of relief (either a countervailing duty or an authorized countermeasure) shall be available.

[4]The term "countervailing duty" shall be understood to mean a special duty levied for the purpose of off-setting any bounty or subsidy bestowed directly or indirectly upon the manufacture, production or export of any merchandise, as provided for in Article VI: 3 of the General Agreement.

[5]The term "initiated" as used hereinafter means procedural action by which a signatory formally commences an investigation as provided in paragraph 3 of this Article.

[6]Under this Agreement the term injury shall, unless otherwise specified, be taken to mean material injury to a domestic industry, threat of material injury to a domestic industry or material retardation of the establishment of such an industry and shall be interpreted in accordance with the provisions of Article 6.

[7]As established in Part V of this Agreement and hereinafter referred to as the "Committee."

[8]For the purpose of this Agreement 'party' means any natural or juridical person resident in the territory of any signatory.

simultaneously (a) in the decision whether or not to initiate an investigation and (b) thereafter during the course of the investigation, starting on a date not later than the earliest date on which in accordance with the provisions of this Agreement provisional measures may be applied.

5. The public notice referred to in paragraph 3 above shall describe the subsidy practice or practices to be investigated. Each signatory shall ensure that the investigating authorities afford all interested signatories and all interested parties[9] a reasonable opportunity, upon request, to see all relevant information that is not confidential (as indicated in paragraphs 6 and 7 below) and that is used by the investigating authorities in the investigation, and to present in writing, and upon justification orally, their views to the investigating authorities.

6. Any information which is by nature confidential or which is provided on a confidential basis by parties to an investigation shall, upon cause shown, be treated as such by the investigating authorities. Such information shall not be disclosed without specific permission of the party submitting it.[10] Parties providing confidential information may be requested to furnish non-confidential summaries thereof. In the event such parties indicate that such information is not susceptible of summary, a statement of reasons why summarization is not possible must be provided.

7. However, if the investigating authorities find that a request for confidentiality is not warranted and if the party requesting confidentiality is unwilling to disclose the information, such authorities may disregard such information unless it can otherwise be demonstrated to their satisfaction that the information is correct.[11]

8. The investigating authorities may carry out investigations in the territory of other signatories as required, provided they have notified in good time the signatory in question and unless the latter objects to the investigation. Further, the investigating authorities may carry out investigations on the premises of a firm and may examine the records of a firm if (a) the firm so agrees and (b) the signatory in question is notified and does not object.

9. In cases in which any interested party or signatory refuses access to, or otherwise does not provide, necessary information within a reasonable period or significantly impedes the investigation, preliminary and final findings[12], affirmative or negative, may be made on the basis of the facts available.

10. The procedures set out above are not intended to prevent the authorities of a signatory from preceeding expeditiously with regard to initiating an investigation, reaching preliminary or final findings, whether affirmative or negative, or from applying provisional or final measures, in accordance with relevant provisions of this Agreement.

11. In cases where products are not imported directly from the country of origin but are exported to the country of importation from an intermediate country, the provisions of this Agreement shall be fully applicable and the transaction or transactions shall, for the purposes of this Agreement, be regarded as having taken place between the country of origin and the country of importation.

12. An investigation shall be terminated when the investigating authorities are satisfied either that no subsidy exists or that the effect of the alleged subsidy on the industry is not such as to cause injury.

13. An investigation shall not hinder the procedures of customs clearance.

14. Investigations shall, except in special circumstances, be concluded within one year after their initiation.

15. Public notice shall be given of any preliminary or final finding whether affirmative or negative and of the revocation of a finding. In the case of a positive finding each such notice shall set forth

[9]Any "interested signatory" or "interested party" shall refer to a signatory or a party economically affected by the subsidy in question.

[10]Signatories are aware that in the territory of certain signatories disclosure pursuant to a narrowly-drawn protective order may be required.

[11]Signatories agree that requests for confidentiality should not be arbitrarily rejected.

[12]Because of different terms used under different systems in various countries the term "finding" is hereinafter used to mean a formal decision or determination.

the findings and conclusions reached on all issues of fact and law considered material by the investigating authorities, and the reasons and basis therefor. In the case of a negative finding each notice shall set forth at least the basic conclusions and a summary of the reasons therefor. All notices of finding shall be forwarded to the signatory or signatories the products of which are subject to such finding and to the exporters known to have an interest therein.

16. Signatories shall report without delay to the Committee all preliminary or final actions taken with respect to countervailing duties. Such reports will be available in the GATT secretariat for inspection by government representatives. The signatories shall also submit, on a semi-annual basis, reports on any countervailing duty actions taken within the preceding six months.

Article 3 — *Consultations*

1. As soon as possible after a request for initiation of an investigation is accepted, and in any event before the initiation of any investigation, signatories the products of which may be subject to such investigations shall be afforded a reasonable opportunity for consultations with the aim of clarifying the situation as to the matters referred to in Article 2, paragraph 1 above and arriving at a mutually agreed solution.

2. Furthermore, throughout the period of investigation, signatories the products of which are the subject of the investigation shall be afforded a reasonable opportunity to continue consultations, with a view to clarifying the factual situation and to arriving at a mutually agreed solution.[13]

3. Without prejudice to the obligation to afford reasonable opportunity for consultations, these provisions regarding consultations are not intended to prevent the authorities of a signatory from proceeding expeditiously with regard to initiating the investigation, reaching preliminary or final findings, affirmative or

negative, or from applying provisional or final measures, in accordance with relevant provisions to this Agreement.

4. The signatory which intends to initiate any investigation or is conducting such an investigation shall permit, upon request, the signatory or signatories the products of which are subject to such investigation access to non-confidential evidence including the non-confidential summary of confidential data being used for initiating or conducting the investigation.

Article 4 — *Imposition of countervailing duties*

1. The decision whether or not to impose a countervailing duty in cases where all requirements for the imposition have been fulfilled and the decision whether the amount of the countervailing duty to be imposed shall be the full amount of the subsidy or less are decisions to be made by the authorities of the importing signatory. It is desirable that the imposition be permissive in the territory of all signatories and that the duty be less than the total amount of the subsidy if such lesser duty would be adequate to remove the injury to the domestic industry.

2. No countervailing duty shall be levied[14] on any imported product in excess of the amount of the subsidy found to exist, calculated in terms of subsidization per unit of the subsidized and exported product.[15]

3. When a countervailing duty is imposed in respect of any product, such countervailing duty shall be levied, in the appropriate amounts, on a non-discriminatory basis on imports of such product from all sources found to be subsidized and to be causing injury, except as to imports from those sources which have renounced any subsidies in question or from which undertakings under the terms of this Agreement have been accepted.

4. If, after reasonable efforts have been made to complete consultations, a signa-

---

[13]It is particularly important, in accordance with the provisions of this paragraph, that no affirmative finding whether preliminary or final be made without reasonable opportunity for consultations having been given. Such consultations may establish the basis for proceeding under the provisions of Part VI of this Agreement.

[14]As used in this Agreement "levy" shall mean the definitive or final legal assessment or collection of a duty or tax.

[15]An understanding among signatories should be developed setting out the criteria for the calculation of the amount of the subsidy.

tory makes a final determination of the existence and amount of the subsidy and that, through the effects of the subsidy, the subsidized imports are causing injury, it may impose a countervailing duty in accordance with the provisions of this section unless the subsidy is withdrawn.

5(a) Proceedings may[16] be suspended or terminated without the imposition of provisional measures or countervailing duties, if undertakings are accepted under which:

(i) the government of the exporting country agrees to eliminate or limit the subsidy or take other measures concerning its effects; or

(ii) the exporter agrees to revise its prices so that the investigating authorities are satisfied that the injurious effect of the subsidy is eliminated. Price increases under undertakings shall not be higher than necessary to eliminate the amount of the subsidy. Price undertakings shall not be sought or accepted from exporters unless the importing signatory has first (1) initiated an investigation in accordance with the provisions of Article 2 of this Agreement and (2) obtained the consent of the exporting signatory. Undertakings offered need not be accepted if the authorities of the importing signatory consider their acceptance impractical, for example if the number of actual or potential exporters is too great, or for other reasons.

(b) If the undertakings are accepted, the investigation of injury shall nevertheless be completed if the exporting signatory so desires or the importing signatory so decides. In such a case, if a determination of no injury or threat thereof is made, the undertaking shall automatically lapse, except in cases where a determination of no threat of injury is due in large part to the existence of an undertaking; in such cases the authorities concerned may require that an undertaking be maintained for a reasonable period consistent with the provisions of this Agreement.

(c) Price undertakings may be suggested by the authorities of the importing signatory, but no exporter shall be forced

---

[16]The word "may" shall not be interpreted to allow the simultaneous continuation of proceedings with the implementation of price undertakings, except as provided in paragraph 5(b) of this Article.

to enter into such an undertaking. The fact that governments or exporters do not offer such undertakings or do not accept an invitation to do so, shall in no way prejudice the consideration of the case. However, the authorities are free to determine that a threat of injury is more likely to be realized if the subsidized imports continue.

6. Authorities of an importing signatory may require any government or exporter from whom undertakings have been accepted to provide periodically information relevant to the fulfilment of such undertakings, and to permit verification of pertinent data. In case of violation of undertakings, the authorities of the importing signatory may take expeditious actions under this Agreement in conformity with its provisions which may constitute immediate application of provisional measures using the best information available. In such cases definitive duties may be levied in accordance with this Agreement on goods entered for consumption not more than ninety days before the application of such provisional measures, except that any such retroactive assessment shall not apply to imports entered before the violation of the undertaking.

7. Undertakings shall not remain in force any longer than countervailing duties could remain in force under this Agreement. The authorities of an importing signatory shall review the need for the continuation of any undertaking, where warranted, on their own initiative, or if interested exporters or importers of the product in question so request and submit positive information substantiating the need for such review.

8. Whenever a countervailing duty investigation is suspended or terminated pursuant to the provisions of paragraph 5 above and whenever an undertaking is terminated, this fact shall be officially notified and must be published. Such notices shall set forth at least the basic conclusions and a summary of the reasons therefor.

9. A countervailing duty shall remain in force only as long as, and to the extent necessary to counteract the subsidization

which is causing injury. The investigating authorities shall review the need for continued imposition of the duty, where warranted, on their own initiative or if any interested party so requests and submits positive information substantiating the need for review.

Article 5 — *Provisional measures and retroactivity*

1. Provisional measures may be taken only after a preliminary positive finding has been made that a subsidy exists and that there is sufficient evidence of injury as provided for in Article 2, paragraph 1(a) to (c). Provisional measures shall not be applied unless the authorities concerned judge that they are necessary to prevent injury being caused during the period of investigation.

2. Provisional measures may take the form of provisional countervailing duties guaranteed by cash deposits or bonds equal to the amount of the provisionally calculated amount of subsidization.

3. The imposition of provisional measures shall be limited to as short a period as possible, not exceeding four months.

4. The relevant provisions of Article 4 shall be followed in the imposition of provisional measures.

5. Where a final finding of injury (but not of a threat thereof or of a material retardation of the establishment of an industry) is made or in the case of a final finding of threat of injury where the effect of the subsidized imports would, in the absence of the provisional measures, have led to a finding of injury, countervailing duties may be levied retroactively for the period for which provisional measures, if any, have been applied.

6. If the definitive countervailing duty is higher than the amount guaranteed by the cash deposit or bond, the difference shall not be collected. If the definitive duty is less than the amount guaranteed by the cash deposit or bond, the excess amount shall be reimbursed or the bond released in an expeditious manner.

7. Except as provided in paragraph 5 above, where a finding of threat of injury or material retardation is made (but no injury has yet occurred) a definitive countervailing duty may be imposed only from the date of the finding of threat of injury or material retardation and any

cash deposit made during the period of the application of provisional measures shall be refunded and any bonds released in an expeditious manner.

8. Where a final finding is negative any cash deposit made during the period of the application or provisional measures shall be refunded and any bonds released in an expeditious manner.

9. In critical circumstances where for the subsidized product in question the authorities find that injury which is difficult to repair is caused by massive imports in a relatively short period of a product benefiting from export subsidies paid or bestowed inconsistently with the provisions of the General Agreement and of this Agreement and where it is deemed necessary. in order to preclude the recurrence of such injury, to assess countervailing duties retroactively on those imports, the definitive countervailing duties may be assessed on imports which were entered for consumption not more than ninety days prior to the date of application of provisional measures.

Article 6 — *Determination of injury*

1. A determination of injury[17] for purposes of Article VI of the General Agreement shall involve an objective examination of both (a) the volume of subsidized imports and their effect on prices in the domestic market for like products[18] and (b) the consequent impact of these imports on domestic producers of such products.

2. With regard to volume of subsidized imports the investigating authorities shall consider whether there has been a significant increase in subsidized imports, either in absolute terms or relative to production or consumption in the importing signatory. With regard to the

---

[17]Determinations of injury under the criteria set forth in this Article shall be based on positive evidence. In determining threat of injury the investigating authorities, in examining the factors listed in this Article, may take into account the evidence on the nature of the subsidy in question and the trade effects likely to arise therefrom.

[18]Throughout this Agreement the term "like product" ("produit similaire") shall be interpreted to mean a product which is identical, i.e. alike in all respects to the product under consideration or in the absence of such a product, another product which, although not alike in all respects, has characteristics closely resembling those of the product under consideration.

effect of the subsidized imports on prices, the investigating authorities shall consider whether there has been a significant price undercutting by the subsidized imports as compared with the price of a like product of the importing signatory, or whether the effect of such imports is otherwise to depress prices to a significant degree or prevent price increases, which otherwise would have occurred, to a significant degree. No one or several of these factors can necessarily give decisive guidance.

3. The examination of the impact on the domestic industry concerned shall include an evaluation of all relevant economic factors and indices having a bearing on the state of the industry such as actual and potential decline in output. sales, market share, profits, productivity, return on investments, or utilization of capacity; factors affecting domestic prices; actual and potential negative effects on cash flow, inventories, employment, wages, growth, ability to raise capital or investment and, in the case of agriculture, whether there has been an increased burden on government support programmes. This list is not exhaustive, nor can one or several of these factors necessarily give decisive guidance.

4. It must be demonstrated that the subsidized imports are, through the effects[19] of the subsidy, causing injury within the meaning of this Agreement. There may be other factors[20] which at the same time are injuring the domestic industry, and the injuries caused by other factors must not be attributed to the subsidized imports.

5. In determining injury, the term "domestic industry" shall, except as provided in paragraph 7 below, be interpreted as referring to the domestic producers as a whole of the like products or to those of them whose collective output of the products constitutes a major proportion of the total domestic production of those products, except that when producers are related[21] to the exporters or importers or are themselves importers of the allegedly subsidized product the industry may be interpreted as referring to the rest of the producers.

6. The effect of the subsidized imports shall be assessed in relation to the domestic production of the like product when available data permit the separate identification of production in terms of such criteria as: the production process, the producers' realization, profits. When the domestic production of the like product has no separate identity in these terms the effects of subsidized imports shall be assessed by the examination of the production of the narrowest group or range of products, which includes the like product, for which the necessary information can be provided.

7. In exceptional circumstances the territory of a signatory may, for the production in question, be divided into two or more competitive markets and the producers within each market may be regarded as a separate industry if (a) the producers within such market sell all or almost all of their production of the product in question in that market, and (b) the demand in that market is not to any substantial degree supplied by producers of the product in question located elsewhere in the territory. In such circumstances, injury may be found to exist even where a major portion of the total domestic industry is not injured provided there is a concentration of subsidized imports into such an isolated market and provided further that the subsidized imports are causing injury to the producers of all or almost all of the production within such market.

8. When the industry has been interpreted as referring to the producers in a certain area, as defined in paragraph 7 above, countervailing duties shall be levied only on the products in question consigned for final consumption to that area. When the constitutional law of the importing signatory does not permit the levying of countervailing duties on such a basis, the importing signatory may levy the countervailing duties without limitation, only if (a) the exporters shall have been given an opportunity to cease ex-

---

[19] As set forth in paragraphs 2 and 3 of this Article.

[20] Such factors can include *inter alia,* the volume and prices of nonsubsidized imports of the product in question, contraction in demand or changes in the pattern of consumption, trade restrictive practices of and competition between the foreign and domestic producers, developments in technology and the export performance and productivity of the domestic industry.

[21] The Committee should develop a definition of the word "related" as used in this paragraph.

porting at subsidized prices to the area concerned or otherwise give assurances pursuant to Article 4, paragraph 5, of this Agreement, and adequate assurances in this regard have not been promptly given, and (b) such duties cannot be levied only on products of specific producers which supply the area in question.

9. Where two or more countries have reached under the provisions of Article XXIV:8(a) of the General Agreement such a level of integration that they have the characteristics of a single, unified market the industry in the entire area of integration shall be taken to be the industry referred to in paragraphs 5 to 7 above.

PART II

Article 7 — *Notification of subsidies*[22]

1. Having regard to the provisions of Article XVI:1 of the General Agreement, any signatory may make a written request for information on the nature and extent of any subsidy granted or maintained by another signatory (including any form of income or price support) which operates directly or indirectly to increase exports of any product from or reduce imports of any product into its territory.

2. Signatories so requested shall provide such information as quickly as possible and in a comprehensive manner, and shall be ready upon request to provide additional information to the requesting signatory. Any signatory which considers that such information has not been provided may bring the matter to the attention of the Committee.

3. Any interested signatory which considers that any practice of another signatory having the effects of a subsidy has not been notified in accordance with the provisions of Article XVI:1 of the General Agreement may bring the matter to the attention of such other signatory. If the subsidy practice is not thereafter notified promptly, such signatory may itself bring

the subsidy practice in question to the notice of the Committee.

Article 8 — *Subsidies* — *General Provisions*

1. Signatories recognize that subsidies are used by governments to promote important objectives of social and economic policy. Signatories also recognize that subsidies may cause adverse effects to the interests of other signatories.

2. Signatories agree not to use export subsidies in a manner inconsistent with the provisions of this Agreement.

3. Signatories further agree that they shall seek to avoid causing, through the use of any subsidy:

(a) injury to the domestic industry of another signatory;[23]

(b) nullification or impairment of the benefits accruing directly or indirectly to another signatory under the General Agreement;[24] or

(c) serious prejudice to the interests of another signatory.[25]

4. The adverse effects to the interests of another signatory required to demonstrate nullification or impairment[26] or serious prejudice may arise through:

(a) the effects of the subsidized imports in the domestic market of the importing signatory;

(b) the effects of the subsidy in displacing or impeding the imports of like products into the market of the subsidizing country; or

(c) the effects of the subsidized exports in displacing[27] the exports of like prod-

---

[22]In this Agreement, the term "subsidies" shall be deemed to include subsidies granted by any government or any public body within the territory of a signatory. However, it is recognized that for signatories with different federal systems of government, there are different divisions of powers. Such signatories accept nonetheless the international consequences that may arise under this Agreement as a result of the granting of subsidies within their territories.

[23]Injury to the domestic industry is used here in the same sense as it is used in Part I of this Agreement.

[24]Benefits accruing directly or indirectly under the General Agreement include the benefits of tariff concessions bound under Article II of the General Agreement.

[25]Serious prejudice to the interests of another signatory is used in this Agreement in the same sense as it is used in Article XVI:1 of the General Agreement and includes threat of serious prejudice.

[26]Signatories recognize that nullification or impairment of benefits may also arise through the failure of a signatory to carry out its obligations under the General Agreement or this Agreement. Where such failure concerning export subsidies is determined by the Committee to exist, adverse effects may, without prejudice to paragraph 9 of Article 18 below, be presumed to exist. The other signatory will be accorded a reasonable opportunity to rebut this presumption.

[27]The term "displacing" shall be interpreted in a manner which takes into account the trade and development needs of developing countries and in

ucts of another signatory from a third country market.[28]

Article 9 — *Export subsidies on products other than certain primary products*[29]

1. Signatories shall not grant export subsidies on products other than certain primary products.

2. The practices listed in points (a) to (1) in the Annex are illustrative of export subsidies.

Article 10 — *Export subsidies on certain primary products*

1. In accordance with the provisions of Article XVI:3 of the General Agreement, signatories agree not to grant directly or indirectly any export subsidy on certain primary products in a manner which results in the signatory granting such subsidy having more than an equitable share of world export trade in such product, account being taken of the shares of the signatories in trade in the product concerned during a previous representative period, and any special factors which may have affected or may be affecting trade in such product.

2. For purposes of Article XVI:3 of the General Agreement and paragraph 1 above:

(a) "more than an equitable share of world export trade" shall include any case in which the effect of an export subsidy granted by a signatory is to displace the exports of another signatory bearing in mind the developments on world markets;

(b) with regard to new markets traditional patterns of supply of the product concerned to the world market, region or country, in which the new market is situated shall be taken into account in determining "equitable share of world export trade";

(c) "a previous representative period" shall normally be the three most recent calendar years in which normal market conditions existed.

---

this connection is not intended to fix traditional market shares.

[28]The problem of third country markets so far as certain primary products are concerned are dealt with exclusively under Article 10 below.

[29]For purposes of this Agreement "certain primary products" means the products referred to Note Ad Article XVI of the General Agreement, Section B, paragraph 2, with the deletion of the words "or any mineral".

3. Signatories further agree not to grant export subsidies on exports of certain primary products to a particular market in a manner which results in prices materially below those of other suppliers to the same market.

Article 11 — *Subsidies other than export subsidies*

1. Signatories recognize that subsidies other than export subsidies are widely used as important instruments for the promotion of social and economic policy objectives and do not intend to restrict the right of signatories to use such subsidies to achieve these and other important policy objectives which they consider desirable. Signatories note that among such objectives are:

(a) the elimination of industrial, economic and social disadvantages of specific regions;

(b) to facilitate the restructuring, under socially acceptable conditions, of certain sectors, especially where this has become necessary by reason of changes in trade and economic policies, including international agreements resulting in lower barriers to trade;

(c) generally to sustain employment and to encourage re-training and change in employment;

(d) to encourage research and development programmes, especially in the field of high-technology industries;

(e) the implementation of economic programmes and policies to promote the economic and social development of developing countries;

(f) redeployment of industry in order to avoid congestion and environmental problems.

2. Signatories recognize, however, that subsidies other than export subsidies, certain objectives and possible forms of which are described, respectively, in paragraphs 1 and 3 of this Article, may cause or threaten to cause injury to a domestic industry of another signatory or serious prejudice to the interests of another signatory or may nullify or impair benefits accruing to another signatory under the General Agreement, in particular where such subsidies would adversely affect the conditions of normal competition. Signatories shall therefore seek to avoid causing such effects through the

use of subsidies. In particular, signatories, when drawing up their policies and practices in this field, in addition to evaluating the essential internal objectives to be achieved, shall also weigh, as far as practicable, taking account of the nature of the particular case, possible adverse effects on trade. They shall also consider the conditions of world trade, production (e.g. price, capacity utilization etc.) and supply in the product concerned.

3. Signatories recognize that the objectives mentioned in paragraph 1 above may be achieved, *inter alia,* by means of subsidies granted with the aim of giving an advantage to certain enterprises. Examples of possible forms of such subsidies are: government financing of commercial enterprises, including grants, loans or guarantees; government provision or government financed provision of utility, supply distribution and other operational or support services or facilities; government financing of research and development programmes; fiscal incentives; and government subscription to, or provision of, equity capital.

Signatories note that the above forms of subsidy are normally granted either regionally or by sector. The enumeration of forms of subsidies set out above is illustrative and non-exhaustive, and reflects these currently granted by a number of signatories to this Agreement.

Signatories recognize, nevertheless, that the enumeration of forms of subsidy set out above should be reviewed periodically and that this should be done, through consultations, in conformity with the spirit of Article XVI:5 of the General Agreement.

4. Signatories recognize further that, without prejudice to their rights under this Agreement, nothing in paragraphs 1-3 above and in particular the enumeration of forms of subsidies creates, in itself, any basis for action under the General Agreement, as interpreted by this Agreement.

Article 12 — *Consultations*

1. Whenever a signatory has reason to believe that an export subsidy is being granted or maintained by another signatory in a manner inconsistent with the provisions of this Agreement, such signa-

tory may request consultations with such other signatory.

2. A request for consultations under paragraph 1 above shall include a statement of available evidence with regard to the existence and nature of the subsidy in question.

3. Whenever a signatory has reason to believe that any subsidy is being granted or maintained by another signatory and that such subsidy either causes injury to its domestic industry, nullification or impairment of benefits accruing to it under the General Agreement, or serious prejudice to its interests, such signatory may request consultations with such other signatory.

4. A request for consultations under paragraph 3 above shall include a statement of available evidence with regard to (a) the existence and nature of the subsidy in question and (b) the injury caused to the domestic industry or, in the case of nullification or impairment, or serious prejudice, the adverse effects caused to the interests of the signatory requesting consultations.

5. Upon request for consultations under paragraph 1 or paragraph 3 above, the signatory believed to be granting or maintaining the subsidy practice in question shall enter into such consultations as quickly as possible. The purpose of the consultations shall be to clarify the facts of the situation and to arrive at a mutually acceptable solution.

Article 13 — *Conciliation, dispute settlement and authorized countermeasures*

1. If, in the case of consultations under paragraph 1 of Article 12, a mutually acceptable solution has not been reached within thirty days[30] of the request for consultations, any signatory party to such consultations may refer the matter to the Committee for conciliation in accordance with the provisions of Part VI.

2. If, in the case of consultations under paragraph 3 of Article 12, a mutually acceptable solution has not been reached within sixty days of the request for consultations, any signatory party to such consultations may refer the matter to the Committee for conciliation in

---

[30]Any time periods mentioned in this Article and in Article 18 may be extended by mutual agreement.

accordance with the provisions of Part VI.

3. If any dispute arising under this Agreement is not resolved as a result of consultations or conciliations, the Committee shall, upon request, review the matter in accordance with the dispute settlement precedures of Part VI.

4. If, as a result of its review, the Committee concludes that an export subsidy is being granted in a manner inconsistent with the provisions of this Agreement or that a subsidy is being granted or maintained in such a manner as to cause injury, nullification or impairment, or serious prejudice, it shall make such recommendations[31] to the parties as may be appropriate to resolve the issue and, in the event the recommendations are not followed, it may authorize such countermeasures as may be appropriate, taking into account the degree and nature of the adverse effects found to exist, in accordance with the relevant provisions of Part VI.

PART III

Article 14 — *Developing countries*

1. Signatories recognize that subsidies are an integral part of economic development programmes of developing countries.

2. Accordingly, this Agreement shall not prevent developing country signatories from adopting measures and policies to assist their industries, including those in the export sector. In particular the commitment of Article 9 shall not apply to developing country signatories, subject to the provisions of paragraphs 5 through 8 below.

3. Developing country signatories agree that export subsidies on their industrial products shall not be used in a manner which causes serious prejudice to the trade or production of another signatory.

4. There shall be no presumption that export subsidies granted by developing country signatories result in adverse effects, as defined in this Agreement, to the trade or production of another signatory. Such adverse effects shall be demonstrated by positive evidence, through an economic examination of the impact on trade or production of another signatory.

5. A developing country signatory should endeavour to enter into a commitment[32] to reduce or eliminate export subsidies when the use of such export subsidies is inconsistent with its competitive and development needs.

6. When a developing country has entered into a commitment to reduce or eliminate export subsidies, as provided in paragraph 5 above, countermeasures pursuant to the provisions of Parts II and VI of this Agreement against any export subsidies of such developing country shall not be authorized for other signatories of this Agreement, provided that the export subsidies in question are in accordance with the terms of the commitment referred to in paragraph 5 above.

7. With respect to any subsidy, other than an export subsidy, granted by a developing country signatory, action may not be authorized or taken under Parts II and VI of this Agreement, unless nullification or impairment of tariff concessions or other obligations under the General Agreement is found to exist as a result of such subsidy, in such a way as to displace or impede imports of like products into the market of the subsidizing country, or unless injury to domestic industry in the importing market of a signatory occurs in terms of Article VI of the General Agreement, as interpreted and applied by this Agreement. Signatories recognize that in developing countries, governments may play a large role in promoting economic growth and development. Intervention by such governments in their economy, for example through the practices enumerated in paragraph 3 of Article 11, shall not, *per se,* be considered subsidies.

8. The Committee shall, upon request by an interested signatory, undertake a review of a specific export subsidy practice of a developing country signatory to examine the extent to which the practice is in conformity with the objectives of this Agreement. If a developing country has entered into a commitment pursuant to paragraph 5 of this Article, it shall not

---

[31]In making such recommendations, the Committee shall take into account the trade, development and financial needs of developing country signatories.

[32]It is understood that after this Agreement has entered into force, any such proposed commitment shall be notified to the Committee in good time.

be subject to such review for the period of that commitment.

9. The Committee shall, upon request by an interested signatory, also undertake similar reviews of measures maintained or taken by developed country signatories under the provisions of this Agreement which affect interests of a developing country signatory.

10. Signatories recognize that the obligations of this Agreement with respect to export subsidies for certain primary products apply to all signatories.

PART IV

Article 15 — *Special situations*

1. In cases of alleged injury caused by imports from a country described in the NOTES AND SUPPLEMENTARY PROVISIONS to the General Agreement (Annex I, Article VI, paragraph 1, point 2) the importing signatory may base its procedures and measures either

(a) on this Agreement, or, alternatively

(b) on the Agreement on Implementation of Article VI of the General Agreement on Tariffs and Trade.

2. It is understood that in both cases (a) and (b) above the calculation of the margin of dumping or of the amount of the estimated subsidy can be made by comparison of the export price with:

(a) the price at which a like product of a country other than the importing signatory or those mentioned above is sold, or

(b) the constructed value[33] of a like product in a country other than the importing signatory or those mentioned above.

3. If neither prices nor constructed value as established under (a) or (b) of paragraph 2 above provide an adequate basis for determination of dumping or subsidization then the price in the importing signatory, if necessary duly adjusted to reflect reasonable profits, may be used.

4. All calculations under the provisions of paragraphs 2 and 3 above shall be based on prices or costs ruling at the same level of trade, normally at the ex

factory level, and in respect of operations made as nearly as possible at the same time. Due allowance shall be made in each case, on its merits, for the difference in conditions and terms of sales or in taxation and for the other differences affecting price comparability, so that the method of comparison applied is appropriate and not unreasonable.

PART V

Article 16 — *Committee on Subsidies and Countervailing Measures*

1. There shall be established under this Agreement a Committee on Subsidies and Countervailing Measures composed of representatives from each of the signatories to this Agreement. The Committee shall elect its own Chairman and shall meet not less than twice a year and otherwise as envisaged by relevant provisions of this Agreement at the request of any signatory. The Committee shall carry out responsibilities as assigned to it under this Agreement or by the signatories and it shall afford signatories the opportunity of consulting on any matters relating to the operation of the Agreement or the furtherance of its objectives. The GATT secretariat shall act as the secretariat to the Committee.

2. The Committee may set up subsidiary bodies as appropriate.

3. In carrying out their functions, the Committee and any subsidiary bodies may consult with and seek information from any source they deem appropriate. However, before the Committee or a subsidiary body seeks such information from a source within the jurisdiction of a signatory, it shall inform the signatory involved.

PART VI

Article 17 — *Conciliation*

1. In cases where matters are referred to the Committee for conciliation failing a mutually agreed solution in consultations under any provision of this Agreement, the Committee shall immediately review the facts involved and, through its good offices, shall encourage the signatories involved to develop a mutually acceptable solution.[34]

---

[33]Constructed value means cost of production plus a reasonable amount for administration, selling and any other costs and for profits.

[34]In this connexion, the Committee may draw signatories' attention to those cases in which, in its

2. Signatories shall make their best efforts to reach a mutually satisfactory solution throughout the period of conciliation.

3. Should the matter remain unresolved, notwithstanding efforts at conciliation made under paragraph 2 above, any signatory involved may, thirty days after the request for conciliation, request that a panel be established by the Committee in accordance with the provisions of Article 18 below.

Article 18 — *Dispute settlement*

1. The Committee shall establish a panel upon request pursuant to paragraph 3 of Article 17.[35] A panel so established shall review the facts of the matter and, in light of such facts, shall present to the Committee its findings concerning the rights and obligations of the signatories party to the dispute under the relevant provisions of the General Agreement as interpreted and applied by this Agreement.

2. A panel should be established within thirty days of a request therefor[36] and a panel so established should deliver its findings to the Committee within sixty days after its establishment.

3. When a panel is to be established, the Chairman of the Committee, after securing the agreement of the signatories concerned, should propose the composition of the panel. Panels shall be composed of three or five members, preferably governmental, and the composition of panels should not give rise to delays in their establishment. It is understood that citizens of countries whose governments[37] are parties to the dispute would not be members of the panel concerned with that dispute.

4. In order to facilitate the constitution of panels, the Chairman of the Commit-

tee should maintain an informal indicative list of governmental and non-governmental persons qualified in the fields of trade relations, economic development, and other matters covered by the General Agreement and this Agreement, who could be available for serving on panels. For this purpose, each signatory would be invited to indicate at the beginning of every year to the Chairman of the Committee the name of one or two persons who would be available for such work.

5. Panel members would serve in their individual capacities and not as government representatives, nor as representatives of any organization. Governments would therefore not give them instructions with regard to matters before a panel. Panel members should be selected with a view to ensuring the independence of the members, a sufficiently diverse background and a wide spectrum of experience.

6. To encourage development of mutually satisfactory solutions between the parties to a dispute and with a view to obtaining their comments, each panel should first submit the descriptive part of its report to the parties concerned, and should subsequently submit to the parties to the dispute its conclusions, or an outline thereof, a reasonable period of time before they are circulated to the Committee.

7. If a mutually satisfactory solution is developed by the parties to a dispute before a panel, any signatory with an interest in the matter has a right to enquire about and be given appropriate information about that solution and a notice outlining the solution that has been reached shall be presented by the panel to the Committee.

8. In cases where the parties to a dispute have failed to come to a satisfactory solution, the panels shall submit a written report to the Committee which should set forth the findings of the panel as to the questions of fact and the application of the relevant provisions of the General Agreement as interpreted and applied by this Agreement and the reasons and bases therefor.

9. The Committee shall consider the panel report as soon as possible and, taking into account the findings contained therein, may make recommenda-

---

view, there is no reasonable basis supporting the allegations made.

[35]This does not preclude, however, the more rapid establishment of a panel when the Committee so decides, taking into account the urgency of the situation.

[36]The parties to the dispute would respond within a short period of time, i.e., seven working days, to nominations of panel members by the Chairman of the Committee and would not oppose nominations except for compelling reasons.

[37]The term "governments" is understood to mean governments of all member countries in cases of customs unions.

tions to the parties with a view to resolving the dispute. If the Committee's recommendations are not followed within a reasonable period, the Committee may authorize appropriate countermeasures (including withdrawal of GATT concessions or obligations) taking into account the nature and degree of the adverse effect found to exist. Committee recommendations should be presented to the parties within thirty days of the receipt of the panel report.

PART VII

Article 19 — *Final provisions*

1. No specific action against a subsidy of another signatory can be taken except in accordance with the provisions of the General Agreement, as interpreted by this Agreement.[38]

Acceptance and accession

2. (a) This Agreement shall be open for acceptance by signature or otherwise, by governments contracting parties to the GATT and by the European Economic Community.

(b) This Agreement shall be open for acceptance by signature or otherwise by governments having provisionally acceded to the GATT, on terms related to the effective application of rights and obligations under this Agreement, which take into account rights and obligations in the instruments providing for their provisional accession.

(c) This Agreement shall be open to accession by any other government on terms, related to the effective application of rights and obligations under this Agreement, to be agreed between that government and the signatories, by the deposit with the Director-General to the CONTRACTING PARTIES to the GATT of an instrument of accession which states the terms so agreed.

(d) In regard to acceptance, the provisions of Article XXVI:5(a) and (b) of the General Agreement would be applicable.

Reservations

3. Reservations may not be entered in respect of any of the provisions of this

Agreement without the consent of the other signatories.

Entry into force

4. This Agreement shall enter into force on 1 January 1980 for the governments[39] which have accepted or acceded to it by that date. For each other government it shall enter into force on the thirtieth day following the date of its acceptance or accession to this Agreement.

National legislation

5. (a) Each government accepting or acceding to this Agreement shall take all necessary steps, of a general or particular character, to ensure, not later than the date of entry into force of this Agreement for it, the conformity of its laws, regulations and administrative procedures with the provisions of this Agreement as they may apply to the signatory in question.

(b) Each signatory shall inform the Committee of any changes in its laws and regulations relevant to this Agreement and in the administration of such laws and regulations.

Review

6. The Committee shall review annually the implementation and operation of this Agreement taking into account the objectives thereof. The Committee shall annually inform the CONTRACTING PARTIES to the GATT of developments during the period covered by such reviews.[40]

Amendments

7. The signatories may amend this Agreement having regard, *inter alia,* to the experience gained in its implementation. Such an amendment, once the signatories have concurred in accordance with procedures established by the Committee, shall not come into force for any signatory until it has been accepted by such signatory.

Withdrawal

8. Any signatory may withdraw from this Agreement. The withdrawal shall

---

[38]This paragraph is not intended to preclude action under other relevant provisions of the General Agreement, where appropriate.

[39]The term "governments" is deemed to include the competent authorities of the European Economic Community.

[40]At the first such review, the Committee shall, in addition to its general review of the operation of the Agreement, offer all interested signatories an opportunity to raise questions and discuss issues concerning specific subsidy practices and the impact on trade, if any, of certain direct tax practices.

take effect upon the expiration of sixty days from the day on which written notice of withdrawal is received by the Director-General to the CONTRACT-ING PARTIES to the GATT. Any signatory may upon such notification request an immediate meeting of the Committee.

Non-application of this Agreement between particular signatories

9. This Agreement shall not apply as between any two signatories if either of the signatories, at the time either accepts or accedes to this Agreement, does not consent to such application.

Annex

10. The annex to this Agreement constitutes an integral part thereof.

Secretariat

11. This Agreement shall be serviced by the GATT secretariat.

Deposit

12. This Agreement shall be deposited with the Director-General to the CON-TRACTING PARTIES to the GATT, who shall promptly furnish to each signatory and each contracting party to the GATT a certified copy thereof, of each amendment thereto pursuant to paragraph 7, and a notification of each acceptance thereof or accession thereto pursuant to paragraph 2, or each withdrawal therefrom pursuant to paragraph 8 above.

Registration

13. This Agreement shall be registered in accordance with the provisions of Article 102 of the Charter of the United Nations.

Done at Geneva this twelfth day of April nineteen hundred and seventy-nine in a single copy, in the English, French and Spanish languages, each text being authentic.

ANNEX
Illustrative List of Export Subsidies

(a) The provision by governments of direct subsidies to a firm or an industry contingent upon export performance.

(b) Currency retention schemes or any similar practices which involve a bonus on exports.

(c) Internal transport and freight charges on export shipments, provided or mandated by governments, on terms more favourable than for domestic shipments.

(d) The delivery by governments or their agencies of imported or domestic products or services for use in the production of exported goods, on terms or conditions more favourable than for delivery of like or directly competitive products or services for use on the production of goods for domestic consumption, if (in the case of products) such terms or conditions are more favourable than those commercially available on world markets to their exporters.

(e) The full or partial exemption, remission, or deferral specifically related to exports, of direct taxes[1] or social welfare charges paid or payable by industrial or commercial enterprises.[2]

(f) The allowance of special deductions directly related to exports or export performance, over and above those granted in respect to production for domestic consumption, in the calculation of the base on which direct taxes are charged.

(g) The exemption or remission in respect of the production and distribution of exported products, of indirect taxes[1] in excess of those levied in respect of the production and distribution of like products when sold for domestic consumption.

(h) The exemption, remission or deferral of prior stage cumulative indirect taxes[1] on goods or services used in the production of exported products in excess of the exemption, remission or deferral of like prior stage cumulative indirect taxes on goods or services used in the production of like products when sold for domestic consumption; provided, however, that prior stage cumulative indirect taxes may be exempted, remitted or deferred on exported products even when not exempted, remitted or deferred on like products when sold for domestic consumption, if the prior stage cumulative indirect taxes are levied on goods that are physically incorporated (making normal allowance for waste) in the exported product.[3]

(i) The remission or drawback of import charges[1] in excess of those leveled on imported goods that are physically incorporated (making normal allowance for waste) in the exported product; provided, however, that in particular cases a firm may use a quantity of home market goods equal to, and having the same quality and characteristics as, the imported goods as a substitute for them in order to benefit from this provision if the import and the corresponding export operations both occur within a reasonable time period, normally not to exceed two years.

(j) The provision by governments (or special institutions controlled by governments) of export credit guarantee or insurance programmes, of insurance or guarantee programmes against increases in the costs of exported products[4] or of exchange risk programmes, at premium rates, which are manifestly inadequate to cover the long-term operating costs and losses of the programmes.[5]

(k) The grant by governments (or special institutions controlled by and/or acting under the authority of governments) of export credits at rates below those which they actually have to pay for the funds so employed (or would have to pay if they borrowed on international capital markets in order to obtain funds of the same maturity and denominated in the same currency as the export credit), or the payment by them of all or part of the costs incurred by exporters or financial institutions in obtaining credits, in so far as they are used to secure a material advantage in the field of export credit terms. Provided, however, that if a signatory is a party to an international undertaking on official export credits to which at least twelve original signatories[6] to this Agreement are parties as of 1 January 1979 (or a successor undertaking which has been adopted by those original signatories), or if in practice a signatory applies the interest rates provisions of the relevant undertaking, an export credit practice which is in conformity with those provisions shall not be considered an export subsidy prohibited by this Agreement.

(1) Any other charge on the public account constituting an export subsidy in the sense of Article XVI of the General Agreement.

NOTES

[1]For the purpose of this Agreement:

The term "direct taxes" shall mean taxes on wages, profits, interest, rents, royalties, and all other forms of income, and taxes on the ownership of real property.

The term "import charges" shall mean tariffs, duties, and other fiscal charges not elsewhere enumerated in this note that are levied on imports.

The term "indirect taxes" shall mean sales, excise, turnover, value added, franchise, stamp, transfer, inventory and equipment taxes, border taxes and all taxes other than direct taxes and import charges.

"Prior stage" indirect taxes are those levied on goods or services used directly or indirectly in making the product.

"Cumulative" indirect taxes are multi-staged taxes levied where there is no mechanism for subsequent crediting of the tax if the goods or services subject to tax at one stage of production are used in a succeeding stage of production.

"Remission" of taxes includes the refund or rebate of taxes.

[2]The signatories recognize that deferral need not amount to an export subsidy where, for example, appropriate interest charges are collected. The signatories further recognize that nothing in this text prejudges the disposition by the Contracting Parties of the specific issues raised in GATT document L/4422.

The signatories reaffirm the principle that prices for goods in transactions between exporting enterprises and foreign buyers under their or under the same control should for tax purposes be the prices which would be charged between independent enterprises acting at arm's length. Any signatory may draw the attention of another signatory to administrative or other practices which may contravene this principle and which result in a significant saving of direct taxes in export transactions. In such circumstances the signatories shall normally attempt to resolve their differences using the facilities of existing bilateral tax treaties or other specific international mechanisms, without prejudice to the rights and obligations of signatories under the General Agreement, including the right of consultation created in the preceding sentence.

Paragraph (e) is not intended to limit a signatory from taking measures to avoid the double taxation of foreign source income earned by its enterprises or the enterprises of another signatory.

Where measures incompatible with the provisions of paragraph (e) exist, and where major practical difficulties stand in the way of the signatory concerned bringing such measures promptly into conformity with the Agreement, the signatory concerned shall, without prejudice to the rights of other signatories under the General Agreement or this Agreement, examine methods of bringing these measures into conformity within a reasonable period of time.

In this connection the European Economic Community has declared that Ireland intends to withdraw by 1 January 1981 its system of preferential tax measures related to exports, provided for under the Corporation Tax Act of 1976, whilst continuing nevertheless to honour legally binding commitments entered into during the lifetime of this system.

[3]Paragraph (h) does not apply to value-added tax systems and bordertax adjustment in lieu thereof; the problem of the excessive remission of value-added taxes is exclusively covered by paragraph (g).

'The signatories agree that nothing in this paragraph shall prejudge or influence the deliberations of the panel established by the GATT Council on 6 June 1978 (C/M/126).

'In evaluating the long-term adequacy of premium rates, costs and losses of insurance programmes, in principle only such contracts shall be taken into account that were concluded after the date of entry into force of this Agreement.

'An original signatory to this Agreement shall mean any signatory which adheres ad referendum to the Agreement on or before 30 June 1979.

Appendix D

MTN Antidumping Agreement

Agreement on Implementation of Article VI of the General Agreement on Tariffs and Trade

TABLE OF CONTENTS

The Parties to this Agreement (hereinafter referred to as "Parties")

[Ed. Note: Text published as TIAS 9650 by the U.S. Department of State.]

Recognizing that anti-dumping practices should not constitute an unjustifiable impediment to international trade and that anti-dumping duties may be applied against dumping only if such dumping causes or threatens material injury to an established industry or materially retards the establishment of an industry;

Considering that it is desirable to provide for equitable and open procedures as the basis for a full examination of dumping cases;

Taking into account the particular trade, development and financial needs of developing countries;

Desiring to interpret the provisions of Article VI of the General Agreement on Tariffs and Trade (hereinafter referred to as "General Agreement" or "GATT") and to elaborate rules for their application in order to provide greater uniformity and certainty in their implementation; and

Desiring to provide for the speedy, effective and equitable resolution of disputes arising under this Agreement;

Hereby agree as follows:

PART I — ANTI-DUMPING CODE

Article 1
Principles

The imposition of an anti-dumping duty is a measure to be taken only under the circumstances provided for in Article VI of the General Agreement and pursuant to investigations initiated[1] and conducted in accordance with the provisions of this Code. The following provisions govern the application of Article VI of the General Agreement in so far as action is taken under anti-dumping legislation or regulations.

Article 2
Determination of Dumping

1. For the purpose of this Code a product is to be considered as being dumped, i.e. introduced into the commerce of another country at less than its normal value, if the export price of the product exported from one country to another is less than the comparable price, in the ordinary course of trade, for the like product when destined for consumption in the exporting country.

2. Throughout this Code the term "like product" ("product similaire") shall be interpreted to mean a product which is identical, i.e. alike in all respects to the product under consideration, or in the absence of such a product, another product which, although not alike in all respects, has characteristics closely resembling those of the product under consideration.

3. In the case where products are not imported directly from the country of origin but are exported to the country of importation from an intermediate country, the price at which the products are sold from the country of export to the country of importation shall normally be compared with the comparable price in the country of export. However, comparison may be made with the price in the country of origin, if, for example, the products are merely trans-shipped through the country of export, or such products are not produced in the country of export, or there is no comparable price for them in the country of export.

4. When there are no sales of the like product in the ordinary course of trade in the domestic market of the exporting country or when, because of the particular market situation, such sales do not permit a proper comparison, the margin of dumping shall be determined by comparison with a comparable price of the like product when exported to any third country which may be the highest such export price but should be a representative price, or with the cost of production in the country of origin plus a reasonable amount for administrative, selling and any other costs and for profits. As a general rule, the addition for profit shall not exceed the profit normally realized on sales of products of the same general category in the domestic market of the country of origin.

5. In cases where there is no export price or where it appears to the authorities[2] concerned that the export price is unreliable because of association or a compensatory arrangement between the exporter and the importer or a third party, the export price may be constructed on the basis of the price at which the imported products are first resold to an independent buyer, or if the products are not resold to an independent buyer, or not resold in the condition as imported, on such reasonable basis as the authorities may determine.

6. In order to effect a fair comparison between the export price and the domestic price in the exporting country (or the country of origin) or, if applicable, the price established pursuant to the provisions of Article VI:1(b) of the General Agreement, the two prices shall be compared at the same level of trade, normally at the ex-factory level, and in respect of sales made at as nearly as possible the same time. Due allowance shall be made in each case, on its merits, for the differences in conditions and terms of sale, for the differences in taxation, and for the other differences affecting price comparability. In the cases referred to in paragraph 5 of Article 2 allowance for costs, including duties and taxes, incurred between importation and resale, and for profits accruing, should also be made.

7. This Article is without prejudice to the second Supplementary Provision to

---

[1] The term "initiated" as used hereinafter means the procedural action by which a Party formally commences an investigation as provided in paragraph 6 of Article 6.

[2] When in this Code the term "authorities" is used, it shall be interpreted as meaning authorities at an appropriate, senior level.

paragraph 1 of Article VI in Annex I of the General Agreement.

Article 3
Determination of Injury[3]

1. A determination of injury for purposes of Article VI of the General Agreement shall be based on positive evidence and involve an objective examination of both (a) the volume of the dumped imports and their effect on prices in the domestic market for like products, and (b) the consequent impact of these imports on domestic producers of such products.

2. With regard to volume of the dumped imports the investigating authorities shall consider whether there has been a significant increase in dumped imports, either in absolute terms or relative to production or consumption in the importing country. With regard to the effect of the dumped imports on prices, the investigating authorities shall consider whether there has been a significant price undercutting by the dumped imports as compared with the price of a like product of the importing country, or whether the effect of such imports is otherwise to depress prices to a significant degree or prevent price increases, which otherwise would have occurred, to a significant degree. No one or several of these factors can necessarily give decisive guidance.

3. The examination of the impact on the industry concerned shall include an evaluation of all relevant economic factors and indices having a bearing on the state of the industry such as actual and potential decline in output, sales, market share, profits, productivity, return on investments, or utilization of capacity; factors affecting domestic prices; actual and potential negative effects on cash flow, inventories, employment, wages, growth, ability to raise capital or investments. This list is not exhaustive, nor can one or several of these factors necessarily give decisive guidance.

4. It must be demonstrated that the dumped imports are, through the effects[4] of dumping, causing injury within the meaning of this Code. There may be other factors[5] which at the same time are injuring the industry, and the injuries caused by other factors must not be attributed to the dumped imports.

5. The effect of the dumped imports shall be assessed in relation to the domestic production of the like product when available data permit the separate identification of production in terms of such criteria as: the production process, the producers' realizations, profits. When the domestic production of the like product has no separate identity in these terms the effects of the dumped imports shall be assessed by the examination of the production of the narrowest group or range of products, which includes the like product, for which the necessary information can be provided.

6. A determination of threat of injury shall be based on facts and not merely on allegation, conjecture or remote possibility. The change in circumstances which would create a situation in which the dumping would cause injury must be clearly foreseen and imminent.[6]

7. With respect to cases where injury is threatened by dumped imports, the application of anti-dumping measures shall be studied and decided with special care.

Article 4
Definition of Industry

1. In determining injury the term "domestic industry" shall be interpreted as referring to the domestic producers as a whole of the like products or to those of them whose collective output of the products constitutes a major proportion of the total domestic production of those products, except that

---

[3]Under this Code the term "injury" shall, unless otherwise specified, be taken to mean material injury to a domestic industry, threat of material injury to a domestic industry or material retardation of the establishment of such an industry and shall be interpreted in accordance with the provisions of this Article.

[4]As set forth in paragraphs 2 and 3 of this Article.
[5]Such factors include, *inter alia,* the volume and prices of imports not sold at dumping prices, contraction in demand or changes in the patterns of consumption, trade restrictive practices of and competition between the foreign and domestic producers, developments in technology and the export performance and productivity of the domestic industry.
[6]One example, though not an exclusive one, is that there is convincing reason to believe that there will be, in the immediate future, substantially increased importations of the product at dumped prices.

(i) when producers are related[7] to the exporters or importers or are themselves importers of the allegedly dumped product, the industry may be interpreted as referring to the rest of the producers;

(ii) in exceptional circumstances the territory of a Party may, for the production in question, be divided into two or more competitive markets and the producers within each market may be regarded as a separate industry if (a) the producers within such market sell all or almost all of their production of the product in question in that market, and (b) the demand in that market is not to any substantial degree supplied by producers of the product in question located elsewhere in the territory. In such circumstances, injury may be found to exist even where a major portion of the total domestic industry is not injured provided there is a concentration of dumped imports into such an isolated market and provided further that the dumped imports are causing injury to the producers of all or almost all of the production within such market.

2. When the industry has been interpreted as referring to the producers in a certain area, i.e. a market as defined in paragraph 1(ii), anti-dumping duties shall be levied[8] only on the products in question consigned for final consumption to that area. When the constitutional law of the importing country does not permit the levying of anti-dumping duties on such a basis, the importing Party may levy the anti-dumping duties without limitation only if (1) the exporters shall have been given an opportunity to cease exporting at dumped prices to the area concerned or otherwise give assurances pursuant to Article 7 of this Code, and adequate assurances in this regard have not been promptly given, and (2) such duties cannot be levied on specific producers which supply the area in question.

3. Where two or more countries have reached under the provisions of Article XXIV:8(a) of the General Agreement such a level of integration that they have the characteristics of a single, unified market, the industry in the entire area of integration shall be taken to be the industry referred to in paragraph 1 above.

4. The provisions of paragraph 5 of Article 3 shall be applicable to this Article.

Article 5
Initiation and Subsequent Investigation

1. An investigation to determine the existence, degree and effect of any alleged dumping shall normally be initiated upon a written request by or on behalf of the industry[9] affected. The request shall include sufficient evidence of the existence of (a) dumping; (b) injury within the meaning of Article VI of the General Agreement as interpreted by this Code and (c) a causal link between the dumped imports and the alleged injury. If in special circumstances the authorities concerned decide to initiate an investigation without having received such a request, they shall proceed only if they have sufficient evidence on all points under (a) to (c) above.

2. Upon initiation of an investigation and thereafter, the evidence of both dumping and injury caused thereby should be considered simultaneously. In any event the evidence of both dumping and injury shall be considered simultaneously (a) in the decision whether or not to initiate an investigation, and (b) thereafter, during the course of the investigation, starting on a date not later than the earliest date on which in accordance with the provisions of this Code provisional measures may be applied, except in the cases provided for in paragraph 3 of Article 10 in which the authorities accept the request of the exporters.

3. An application shall be rejected and an investigation shall be terminated promptly as soon as the authorities concerned are satisfied that there is not sufficient evidence of either dumping or of injury to justify proceeding with the case. There should be immediate termination in cases where the margin of dumping or the volume of dumped im-

---

[7]An understanding among Parties should be developed defining the word "related" as used in this Code.

[8]As used in this Code "levy" shall mean the definitive or final legal assessment or collection of a duty or tax.

[9]As defined in Article 4.

ports, actual or potential, or the injury is negligible.

4. An anti-dumping proceeding shall not hinder the procedures of customs clearance.

5. Investigations shall, except in special circumstances, be concluded within one year after their initiation.

Article 6
Evidence

1. The foreign suppliers and all other interested parties shall be given ample opportunity to present in writing all evidence that they consider useful in respect to the anti-dumping investigation in question. They shall also have the right, on justification, to present evidence orally.

2. The authorities concerned shall provide opportunities for the complainant and the importers and exporters known to be concerned and the governments of the exporting countries, to see all information that is relevant to the presentation of their cases, that is not confidential as defined in paragraph 3 below, and that is used by the authorities in an anti-dumping investigation, and to prepare presentations on the basis of this information.

3. Any information which is by nature confidential (for example, because its disclosure would be of significant competitive advantage to a competitor or because its disclosure would have a significantly adverse effect upon a person supplying the information or upon a person from whom he acquired the information) or which is provided on a confidential basis by parties to an anti-dumping investigation shall, upon cause shown, be treated as such by the investigating authorities. Such information shall not be disclosed without specific permission of the party submitting it.[10] Parties providing confidential information may be requested to furnish non-confidential summaries thereof. In the event that such parties indicate that such information is not susceptible of summary, a statement of the reasons why summarization is not possible must be provided.

4. However, if the authorities concerned find that a request for confidentiality is not warranted and if the supplier is either unwilling to make the information public or to authorize its disclosure in generalized or summary form, the authorities would be free to disregard such information unless it can be demonstrated to their satisfaction from appropriate sources that the information is correct.[11]

5. In order to verify information provided or to obtain further details the authorities may carry out investigations in other countries as required, provided they obtain the agreement of the agreement of the firms concerned and provided they notify the representatives of the government of the country in question and unless the latter object to the investigation.

6. When the competent authorities are satisfied that there is sufficient evidence to justify initiating an anti-dumping investigation pursuant to Article 5, the Party or Parties the products of which are subject to such investigation and the exporters and importers known to the investigating authorities to have an interest therein and the complainants shall be notified and a public notice shall be given. In determining whether to initiate an investigation, the investigating authority should take into account the position adopted by the affiliates of a complainant party which are resident in the territory of another Party.

7. Throughout the anti-dumping investigation all parties shall have a full opportunity for the defence of their interests. To this end, the authorities concerned shall, on request, provide opportunities for all directly interested parties to meet those parties with adverse interests, so that opposing views may be presented and rebuttal arguments offered. Provision of such opportunities must take account of the need to preserve confidentiality and of the convenience to the parties. There shall be no obligation on any party to attend a meeting and failure to do so shall not be prejudicial to that party's case.

8. In cases in which any interested party refuses access to, or otherwise does

---

[10]Parties are aware that in the territory of certain Parties disclosure pursuant to a narrowly drawn protective order may be required.

[11]Parties agree that requests for confidentiality should not be arbitrarily rejected.

not provide, necessary information within a reasonable period or significantly impedes the investigation, preliminary and final findings,[12] affirmative or negative, may be made on the basis of the facts available.

9. The provisions of this Article are not intended to prevent the authorities of a Party from proceeding expeditiously with regard to initiating an investigation, reaching preliminary or final findings, whether affirmative or negative, or from applying provisional or final measures, in accordance with the relevant provisions of this Code.

Article 7
Price Undertakings

1. Proceedings may[13] be suspended or terminated without the imposition of provisional measures or anti-dumping duties upon receipt of satisfactory voluntary undertakings from any exporter to revise its prices or to cease exports to the area in question at dumped prices so that the authorities are satisfied that the injurious effect of the dumping is eliminated. Price increases under such undertakings shall not be higher than necessary to eliminate the margin of dumping.

2. Price undertakings shall not be sought or accepted from exporters unless the authorities of the importing country have initiated an investigation in accordance with the provisions of Article 5 of this Code. Undertakings offered need not be accepted if the authorities consider their acceptance impractical, for example, if the number of actual or potential exporters is too great, or for other reasons.

3. If the undertakings are accepted, the investigation of injury shall nevertheless be completed if the exporter so desires or the authorities so decide. In such a case, if a determination of no injury or threat thereof is made, the undertaking shall automatically lapse except in cases where a determination of no threat of injury is

due in large part to the existence of a price undertaking. In such cases the authorities concerned may require that an undertaking be maintained for a reasonable period consistent with the provisions of this Code.

4. Price undertakings may be suggested by the authorities of the importing country, but no exporter shall be forced to enter into such an undertaking. The fact that exporters do not offer such undertakings, or do not accept an invitation to do so, shall in no way prejudice the consideration of the case. However, the authorities are free to determine that a threat of injury is more likely to be realized if the dumped imports continue.

5. Authorities in an importing country may require any exporter from whom undertakings have been accepted to provide periodically information relevant to the fulfilment of such undertakings, and to permit verification of pertinent data.

In case of violation of undertakings, the authorities of the importing country may take, under this Code in conformity with its provisions, expeditious actions which may constitute immediate application of provisional measures using the best information available. In such cases definitive duties may be levied in accordance with this Code on goods entered for consumption not more than ninety days before the application of such provisional measures, except that any such retroactive assessment shall not apply to imports entered before the violation of the undertaking.

6. Undertakings shall not remain in force any longer than anti-dumping duties could remain in force under this Code. The authorities of an importing country shall review the need for the continuation of any price undertaking, where warranted, on their own initiative or if interested exporters or importers of the product in question so request and submit positive information substantiating the need for such review.

7. Whenever an anti-dumping investigation is suspended or terminated pursuant to the provisions of paragraph 1 above and whenever an undertaking is terminated, this fact shall be officially notified and must be published. Such notices shall set forth at least the basic conclusions and a summary of the reasons therefor.

---

[12]Because of different terms used under different systems in various countries the term "finding" is used hereinafter to mean a formal decision or determination.

[13]The word "may" shall not be interpreted to allow the simultaneous continuation of proceedings with the implementation of price undertakings except as provided in paragraph 3.

Article 8
Imposition and Collection of Anti-Dumping Duties

1. The decision whether or not to impose an anti-dumping duty in cases where all requirements for the imposition have been fulfilled and the decision whether the amount of the anti-dumping duty to be imposed shall be the full margin of dumping or less, are decisions to be made by the authorities of the importing country or customs territory. It is desirable that the imposition be permissive in all countries or customs territories Parties to this Agreement, and that the duty be less than the margin, if such lesser duty would be adequate to remove the injury to the domestic industry.

2. When an anti-dumping duty is imposed in respect of any product, such anti-dumping duty shall be collected in the appropriate amounts in each case, on a non-discriminatory basis on imports of such product from all sources found to be dumped and causing injury, except as to imports from those sources, from which price undertakings under the terms of this Code have been accepted. The authorities shall name the supplier or suppliers of the product concerned. If, however, several suppliers from the same country are involved, and it is impracticable to name all these suppliers, the authorities may name the supplying country concerned. If several suppliers from more than one country are involved, the authorities may name either all the suppliers involved, or, if this is impracticable, all the supplying countries involved.

3. The amount of the anti-dumping duty must not exceed the margin of dumping as established under Article 2. Therefore, if subsequent to the application of the anti-dumping duty it is found that the duty so collected exceeds the actual dumping margin, the amount in excess of the margin shall be reimbursed as quickly as possible.

4. Within a basic price system the following rules shall apply, provided that their application is consistent with the other provisions of this Code:

If several suppliers from one or more countries are involved, anti-dumping duties may be imposed on imports of the product in question found to have been dumped and to be causing injury from the country or countries concerned, the duty being equivalent to the amount by which the export price is less than the basic price established for this purpose, not exceeding the lowest normal price in the supplying country or countries where normal conditions of competition are prevailing. It is understood that, for products which are sold below this already established basic price, a new anti-dumping investigation shall be carried out in each particular case, when so demanded by the interested parties and the demand is supported by relevant evidence. In cases where no dumping is found, anti-dumping duties collected shall be reimbursed as quickly as possible. Furthermore, if it can be found that the duty so collected exceeds the actual dumping margin, the amount in excess of the margin shall be reimbursed as quickly as possible.

5. Public notice shall be given of any preliminary or final finding whether affirmative or negative and of the revocation of a finding. In the case of affirmative finding each such notice shall set forth the findings and conclusions reached on all issues of fact and law considered material by the investigating authorities, and the reasons and basis therefor. In the case of a negative finding, each notice shall set forth at least the basic conclusions and a summary of the reasons therefor. All notices of finding shall be forwarded to the Party or Parties the products of which are subject to such finding and to the exporters known to have an interest therein.

Article 9
Duration of Anti-Dumping Duties

1. An anti-dumping duty shall remain in force only as long as, and to the extent necessary to counteract dumping which is causing injury.

2. The investigating authorities shall review the need for the continued imposition of the duty, where warranted, on their own initiative or if any interested party so requests and submits positive information substantiating the need for review.

Article 10
Provisional Measures

1. Provisional measures may be taken only after a preliminary affirmative finding has been made that there is dumping and that there is sufficient evidence of injury, as provided for in (a) to (c) of paragraph 1 of Article 5. Provisional measures shall not be applied unless the authorities concerned judge that they are necessary to prevent injury being caused during the period of investigation.

2. Provisional measures may take the form of a provisional duty or, preferably, a security — by cash deposit or bond — equal to the amount of the anti-dumping duty provisionally estimated, being not greater than the provisionally estimated margin of dumping. Withholding of appraisement is an appropriate provisional measure, provided that the normal duty and the estimated amount of the anti-dumping duty be indicated and as long as the withholding of appraisement is subject to the same conditions as other provisional measures.

3. The imposition of provisional measures shall be limited to as short a period as possible, not exceeding four months or, on decision of the authorities concerned, upon request by exporters representing a significant percentage of the trade involved to a period not exceeding six months.

4. The relevant provisions of Article 8 shall be followed in the application of provisional measures.

Article 11
Retroactivity

1. Anti-dumping duties and provisional measures shall only be applied to products which enter for consumption after the time when the decision taken under paragraph 1 of Article 8 and paragraph 1 of Article 10, respectively, enters into force, except that in cases:

(i) Where a final finding of injury (but not of a threat thereof or of a material retardation of the establishment of an industry) is made or, in the case of a final finding of threat of injury, where the effect of the dumped imports would, in the absence of the provisional measures, have led to a finding of injury, anti-dumping duties may be levied retroactively for the period for which provisional measures, if any, have been applied.

If the anti-dumping duty fixed in the final decision is higher than the provisionally paid duty, the difference shall not be collected. If the duty fixed in the final decision is lower than the provisionally paid duty or the amount estimated for the purpose of the security, the difference shall be reimbursed or the duty recalculated, as the case may be.

(ii) Where for the dumped product in question the authorities determine

(a) either that there is a history of dumping which caused injury or that the importer was, or should have been, aware that the exporter practices dumping and that such dumping would cause injury, and

(b) that the injury is caused by sporadic dumping (massive dumped imports of a product in a relatively short period) to such an extent that, in order to preclude it recurring, it appears necessary to levy an anti-dumping duty retroactively on those imports,

the duty may be levied on products which were entered for consumption not more than 90 days prior to the date of application of provisional measures.

2. Except as provided in paragraph 1 above where a finding of threat of injury or material retardation is made (but no injury has yet occurred) a definitive anti-dumping duty may be imposed only from the date of the finding of threat of injury or material retardation and any cash deposit made during the period of the application of provisional measures shall be refunded and any bonds released in an expeditious manner.

3. Where a final finding is negative any cash deposit made during the period of the application of provisional measures shall be refunded and any bonds released in an expeditious manner.

Article 12
Anti-Dumping Action on behalf of a Third Country

1. An application for anti-dumping action on behalf of a third country shall

be made by the authorities of the third country requesting action.

2. Such an application shall be supported by price information to show that the imports are being dumped and by detailed information to show that the alleged dumping is causing injury to the domestic industry concerned in the third country. The government of the third country shall afford all assistance to the authorities of the importing country to obtain any further information which the latter may require.

(c) The authorities of the importing country in considering such an application shall consider the effects of the alleged dumping on the industry concerned as a whole in the third country; that is to say the injury shall not be assessed in relation only to the effect of the alleged dumping on the industry's exports to the importing country or even on the industry's total exports.

(d) The decision whether or not to proceed with a case shall rest with the importing country. If the importing country decides that it is prepared to take action, the initiation of the approach to the CONTRACTING PARTIES seeking their approval for such action shall rest with the importing country.

Article 13
Developing Countries

It is recognized that special regard must be given by developed countries to the special situation of developing countries when considering the application of anti-dumping measures under this Code. Possibilities of constructive remedies provided for by this Code shall be explored before applying anti-dumping duties where they would affect the essential interests of developing countries.

PART II

Article 14
Committee on Anti-Dumping Practices

1. There shall be established under this Agreement a Committee on Anti-Dumping Practices (hereinafter referred to as the "Committee") composed of representatives from each of the Parties to this Agreement. The Committee shall elect its own Chairman and shall meet not less than twice a year and otherwise as

envisaged by relevant provisions of this Agreement at the request of any Party. The Committee shall carry out responsibilities as assigned to it under this Agreement or by the Parties and it shall afford Parties the opportunity of consulting on any matters relating to the operation of the Agreement or the furtherance of its objectives. The GATT secretariat shall act as the secretariat to the Committee.

2. The Committee may set up subsidiary bodies as appropriate.

3. In carrying out their functions, the Committee and any subsidiary bodies may consult with and seek information from any source they deem appropriate. However, before the Committee or a subsidiary body seeks such information from a source within the jurisdiction of a Party, it shall inform the Party involved. It shall obtain the consent of the Party and any firm to be consulted.

Article 15[14]
Consultation, Conciliation and Dispute Settlement

1. Each Party shall afford sympathetic consideration to, and shall afford adequate opportunity for consultation regarding representations made by another Party with respect to any matter affecting the operation of this Agreement.

2. If any Party considers that any benefit accruing to it, directly or indirectly, under this Agreement is being nullified or impaired, or that the achievement of any objective of the Agreement is being impeded by another Party or Parties, it may, with a view to reaching a mutually satisfactory resolution of the matter, request in writing consultations with the Party or Parties in question. Each Party shall afford sympathetic consideration to any request from another Party for consultation. The Parties concerned shall initiate consultation promptly.

3. If any Party considers that the consultation pursuant to paragraph 2 has failed to achieve a mutually agreed solution and final action has been taken by the administering authorities of the im-

---

[14] If disputes arise between Parties relating to rights and obligations under this Agreement, Parties should complete the dispute settlement procedures under this Agreement before availing themselves of any rights which they have under the GATT.

porting country to levy definitive anti-dumping duties or to accept price undertakings it may refer the matter to the Committee for conciliation. When a provisional measure has a significant impact and the Party considers the measure was taken contrary to the provisions of paragraph 1 of Article 10 of this Agreement, a Party may also refer such matter to the Committee for conciliation. In cases where matters are referred to the Committee for conciliation the Committee shall meet within thirty days to review the matter, and, through its good offices, shall encourage the Parties involved to develop a mutually acceptable solution.[15]

4. Parties shall make their best efforts to reach a mutually satisfactory solution throughout the period of conciliation.

5. If no mutually agreed solution has been reached after detailed examination by the Committee under paragraph 3 within three months, the Committee shall, at the request of any party to the dispute, establish a panel to examine the matter, based upon

(a) a written statement of the Party making the request indicating how a benefit accruing to it, directly or indirectly, under this Agreement has been nullified or impaired, or that the achieving of the objectives of the Agreement is being impeded, and

(b) the facts made available in conformity with appropriate domestic procedures to the authorities of the importing country.

6. Confidential information provided to the panel shall not be revealed without formal authorization from the person or authority providing the information. Where such information is requested from the panel but release of such information by the panel is not authorized, a non-confidential summary of the information, authorized by the authority or person providing the information, will be provided.

7. Further to paragraphs 1-6 the settlement of disputes shall *mutatis mutandis* be governed by the provisions of the Understanding regarding Notification, Consultation, Dispute Settlement and Surveillance (MTN/FR/W/20/Rev.2). Panel members shall have relevant experience and be selected from the Parties not parties to the dispute.

PART III
Article 16
Final Provisions

1. No specific action against dumping of exports from another Party can be taken except in accordance with the provisions of the General Agreement, as interpreted by this Agreement.[16]

Acceptance and accession

2. (a) This Agreement shall be open for acceptance by signature or otherwise, by governments contracting parties to the GATT and by the European Economic Community.

(b) This Agreement shall be open for acceptance by signature or otherwise by governments having provisionally acceded to the GATT on terms related to the effective application of rights and obligations under this Agreement, which take into account rights and obligations in the instruments providing for their provisional accession.

(c) This Agreement shall be open to accession by any other government on terms, related to the effective application of rights and obligations under this Agreement, to be agreed between that government and the Parties, by the deposit with the Director-General to the CONTRACTING PARTIES to the GATT of an instrument of accession which states the terms so agreed.

(d) In regard to acceptance, the provisions of Article XXVI:5(a) and (b) of the General Agreement would be applicable.

Reservations

3. Reservations may not be entered in respect of any of the provisions of this Agreement without the consent of the other Parties.

Entry into force

4. This Agreement shall enter into force on 1 January 1980 for the governments[17] which have accepted or acceded

---

[15] In this connection the Committee may draw Parties' attention to those cases in which, in its view, there are no reasonable bases supporting the allegations made.

[16] This is not intended to preclude action under other relevant provisions of the General Agreement, as appropriate.

[17] The term "government" is deemed to include the competent authorities of the European Economic Community.

to it by that date. For each other government it shall enter into force on the thirtieth day following the date of its acceptance or accession to this Agreement.

Denunciation of the 1967 Agreement

5. Acceptance of this Agreement shall carry denunciation of the Agreement on Implementation of Article VI of the General Agreement on Tariffs and Trade, done at Geneva on 30 June 1967, which entered into force on 1 July 1968, for Parties to the 1967 Agreement. Such denunciation shall take effect for each Party to this Agreement on the date of entry into force of this Agreement for each such Party.

National legislation

6. (a) Each government accepting or acceding to this Agreement shall take all necessary steps, of a general or particular character, to ensure, not later than the date of entry into force of this Agreement for it, the conformity of its laws, regulations and administrative procedures with the provisions of this Agreement as they may apply for the Party in question.

(b) Each Party shall inform the Committee of any changes in its laws and regulations relevant to this Agreement and in the administration of such laws and regulations.

Review

7. The Committee shall review annually the implementation and operation of this Agreement taking into account the objectives thereof. The Committee shall annually inform the CONTRACTING PARTIES to the GATT of developments during the period covered by such reviews.

Amendments

8. The Parties may amend this Agreement having regard, *inter alia,* to the experience gained in its implementation. Such an amendment, once the Parties have concurred in accordance with pro-

cedures established by the Committee, shall not come into force for any Party until it has been accepted by such Party.

Withdrawal

9. Any Party may withdraw from this Agreement. The withdrawal shall take effect upon the expiration of sixty days from the day on which written notice of withdrawal is received by the Director-General to the Contracting PARTIES to the GATT. Any Party may upon such notification request an immediate meeting of the Committee.

Non-application of this Agreement between particular Parties

10. This Agreement shall not apply as between any two Parties if either of the Parties, at the time either accepts or accedes to this Agreement, does not consent to such application.

Secretariat

11. This Agreement shall be serviced by the GATT secretariat.

Deposit

12. This Agreement shall be deposited with the Director-General to the contracting party to the GATT, who shall promptly furnish to each Party and each contracting party to the GATT a certified copy thereof and of each amendment thereto pursuant to paragraph 8, and a notification of each acceptance thereof or accession thereto pursuant to paragraph 2, and of each withdrawal therefrom pursuant to paragraph 9 of this Article.

Registration

13. This Agreement shall be registered in accordance with the provisions of Article 102 of the Charter of the United Nations.

Done at Geneva this twelfth day of April nineteen hundred and seventy-nine in a single copy, in the English, French and Spanish languages, each text being authentic.

Appendix E

ITA Protection of Proprietary Information in Import Investigations

U.S. Department of Commerce
Import Administration
September, 1982

PROPRIETARY INFORMATION

PROTECTION OF PROPRIETARY INFORMATION

The U.S. Department of Commerce's Import Administration is required by law to protect proprietary information submitted for a proceeding or investigation. Information considered "protected" is used only by U.S. government employees directly involved in the case or by persons specifically authorized by the submitter. Information ordinarily will be protected if its disclosure would:

● cause substantial harm to the competitive position of the submitter; or

● have a substantial adverse effect upon the submitter or person from whom the information was obtained; or

● impair the ability of the Import Administration to obtain necessary information in the future.

WHAT IS PROPRIETARY INFORMATION

Types of information usually protected include:

● business or trade secrets;

● production costs;

● distribution costs;

● prices of actual transactions or offers;

● names of particular customers or suppliers;

● exact amounts of the gross subsidies received and used; and

● names of persons from whom protected information was obtained.

WHAT IS NOT USUALLY PROTECTED

Types of information usually not protected include:

● prices, market conditions, terms of sale or similar information that is published or otherwise available to the public;

● laws, regulations, executive orders, and other official documents, which are published or otherwise available to the public (and translations of these); or

● information submitted by a domestic interested party about a foreign interested party, except when disclosing the information might reveal a protected source.

PROCEDURES FOR PROTECTING PROPRIETARY INFORMATION

If you want to protect information that you are submitting to the Import Administration for a proceeding or investigation:

1. Request protection of the information for proprietary reasons in a cover letter, giving the reasons why each type of information should be protected.

649

2. Submit one of the following:

— A full and descriptive summary of all the proprietary information submitted, which includes an approximated presentation of the protected information. Generally, prices and costs should be presented within a range of 10% of the actual figure or as indices. This summary will be public information. (If possible, please submit three copies of a complete public version of the entire document. This will minimize the possibility of our putting the wrong material in the public file. Mark these copies "Public Version").

— A statement that the information cannot be summarized and a full statement of the reasons why not.

— An agreement to permit disclosure of the information under an administrative protective order and a brief statement for the public describing the protected information.

3. Mark the top and bottom of the cover page and each page that includes proprietary information:

"PROPRIETARY INFORMATION protection from disclosure requested."

GRANTING OF PROTECTION

The Import Administration normally will notify you within ten business days from receipt of materials if the information you have submitted is not granted protection.

If protection is not granted, you may:

● agree to make the material available to the public; or

● withdraw the material.

FOR FURTHER INFORMATION

See the Import Administration Regulations, 19 CFR 353.29 and 355.19.

ADMINISTRATIVE PROTECTIVE ORDER

Proprietary information that is being considered in a proceeding before the U.S. Department of Commerce's Import Administration may be provided under an administrative protective order to an attorney or other representative of another party to that proceeding. The purpose of supplying information under a protective order procedure is to allow to all parties in a proceeding maximum access to the facts being considered in the case without thereby supplying proprietary information to competitors.

Parties that submit proprietary information are protected: 1) by the strict rules governing use of the information released under administrative protective order; 2) by the strict limitation on handling of the materials; and 3) by the severe sanctions for breach of the protective order.

Protective orders are issued only for specific stages of the proceeding and for very limited periods of time.

APPLICATION

An administrative protective order can be obtained by application to the Import Administration.

The application must:

● describe exactly the information requested and the reason for the request;

● indicate how the information will be protected in order to avoid unauthorized access; and

● demonstrate good cause for the release of such information.

The requester also must submit a sworn personal statement promising:

● not to divulge the information to unauthorized persons;

● to use the information only for the proceeding for which it was provided;

● not to consult about the information with unauthorized persons;

● to take adequate precautions to ensure the security of the information; and

● promptly to report any violation of the order.

RELEASE BY SUBMITTER

When a request for release of information under protective order is received, the Import Administration will first inform the party who submitted the information and provide them an opportunity to comment on the request.

The Import Administration will then decide whether release of the requested information will facilitate the proceeding in the case, and whether the need of the requester for the information outweighs the need of the submitter for protection of the information in this particular situation. This decision will include consideration of the probable effectiveness of sanctions for breach of the order.

If the Import Administration decides that the information should be released, but the submitter does not consent, then the Import Administration will not consider that particular information in the proceeding. The materials including that information will be returned to the submitter.

The Import Administration will identify the documents to be provided under the order, verify the accuracy of the copies, and provide them to the requester through the Central Files office.

At the expiration of the order, or when the information is no longer needed, or whenever required by the Import Administration, the materials released under protective order must be returned to the Import Administration along with any notes or materials that were prepared using the protected information. The return of the materials must be accompanied by a certificate attesting to the recipient's good faith effort to determine that no other copies have been made and no protected information was revealed to unauthorized persons.

SANCTIONS FOR BREACH OF PROTECTIVE ORDER

Anyone who has violated a protective order, and the entire firm the violator is associated with, may be barred from practice before any agency of the U.S. Department of Commerce for up to seven years; and, in the case of violation by an attorney, the ethics panels of the appropriate bar associations will be notified for possible consideration of disbarment. All materials submitted by the violator or by the party represented by the violator may be excluded from the record of the proceeding.

FOR FURTHER INFORMATION

See the Import Administration Regulations 19 CFR 353.27-31 and 355.17-21.

Appendix F

MTN Customs Valuation Agreement

Agreement on Implementation of Article VII of the General Agreement on Tariffs and Trade

Having regard to the Multilateral Trade Negotiations, the Parties to this Agreement (hereinafter referred to as "Parties");

Desiring to further the objectives of the General Agreement on Tariffs and Trade (hereinafter referred to as "General Agreement" or "GATT") and to secure additional benefits for the international trade of developing countries;

Recognizing the importance of the provisions of Article VII of the General Agreement on Tariffs and Trade and desiring to elaborate rules for their application in order to provide greater uniformity and certainty in their implementation;

Recognizing the need for a fair, uniform and neutral system for the valuation of goods for customs purposes that precludes the use of arbitrary or fictitious customs values;

Recognizing that the basis for valuation of goods for customs purposes should, to the greatest extent possible, be the transaction value of the goods being valued;

Recognizing that customs value should be based on simple and equitable criteria consistent with commercial practices and that valuation procedures should be of general application without distinction between sources of supply;

[Ed. Note: Text to be published as TIAS 10402 by the U.S. Department of State.]

Recognizing that valuation procedures should not be used to combat dumping;

Hereby agree as follows:

Part I
RULES ON CUSTOMS VALUATION
Article 1

1. The customs value of imported goods shall be the transaction value, that is the price actually paid or payable for the goods when sold for export to the country of importation adjusted in accordance with the provisions of Article 8, provided:

(a) that there are no restrictions as to the disposition or use of the goods by the buyer other than restrictions which:

(i) are imposed or required by law or by the public authorities in the country of importation;

(ii) limit the geographical area in which the goods may be resold; or

(iii) do not substantially affect the value of the goods;

(b) that the sale or price is not subject to some condition or consideration for which a value cannot be determined with respect to the goods being valued;

(c) that no part of the proceeds of any subsequent resale, disposal or use of the goods by the buyer will accrue directly or indirectly to the seller, unless an appropriate adjustment can be made in accordance with the provisions of Article 8; and

(d) that the buyer and seller are not related, or where the buyer and seller are related, that the transaction value is acceptable for customs purposes under the provisions of paragraph 2 of this Article.

2. (a) In determining whether the transaction value is acceptable for the purposes of paragraph 1, the fact that the buyer and the seller are related within the meaning of Article 15 shall not in itself be grounds for regarding the transaction value as unacceptable. In such case the circumstances surrounding the sale shall be examined and the transaction value shall be accepted provided that the relationship did not influence the price. If, in the light of information provided by the importer or otherwise, the customs administration has grounds for considering that the relationship influenced the price, it shall communicate its grounds to the importer and he shall be given a reasonable opportunity to respond. If the importer so requests, the communication of the grounds shall be in writing.

(b) In a sale between related persons, the transaction value shall be accepted and the goods valued in accordance with the provisions of paragraph 1 whenever the importer demonstrates that such value closely approximates to one of the following occurring at or about the same time:

(i) the transaction value in sales to unrelated buyers of identical or similar goods for export to the same country of importation;

(ii) the customs value of identical or similar goods as determined under the provisions of Article 5;

(iii) the customs value of identical or similar goods as determined under the provisions of Article 6;

(iv) the transaction value in sales to unrelated buyers for export to the same country of importation of goods which would be identical to the imported goods except for having a different country of production provided that the sellers in any two transaction being compared are not related.

In applying the foregoing tests, due account shall be taken of demonstrated differences in commercial levels, quantity levels, the elements enumerated in Article 8 and costs incurrrd by the seller in sales in which he and the buyer are not related that are not incurred by the seller in sales in which he and the buyer are related.

(c) The tests set forth in paragraph 2(b) are to be used at the initiative of the importer and only for comparison purposes. Substitute values may not be established under the provisions of paragraph 2(b).

Article 2

1. (a) If the customs value of the imported goods cannot be determined under the provisions of Article 1, the customs value shall be the transaction value of identical goods sold for export to the same country of importation and exported at or about the same time as the goods being valued.

(b) In applying this Article, the transaction value of identical goods in a sale at the same commercial level and in substantially the same quantity as the goods being valued shall be used to determine the customs value. Where no such sale is found, the transaction value of identical goods sold at a different commercial level and/or in different quantities, adjusted to take account of differences attributable to commercial level and/or to quantity, shall be used, provided that such adjustments can be made on the basis of demonstrated evidence which clearly establishes the reasonableness and accuracy of the adjustment, whether the adjustment leads to an increase or a decrease in the value.

2. Where the costs and charges referred to in Article 8.2 are included in the transaction value, an adjustment shall be made to take account of significant differences in such costs and charges between the imported goods and the identical goods in question arising from differences in distances and modes of transport.

3. If, in applying this Article, more than one transaction value of identical goods is found, the lowest such value shall be used to determine the customs value of the imported goods.

Article 3

1. (a) If the customs value of the imported goods cannot be determined under the provisions of Articles 1 and 2, the customs value shall be the transaction value of similar goods sold for export to the same country of importation and exported at or about the same time as the goods being valued.

(b) In applying this Article, the transaction value of similar goods in a sale at the same commercial level and in substantially the same quantity as the goods being valued shall be used to determine the customs value. Where no such sale is found, the transaction value of similar goods sold at a different commercial level and/or in different quantities, adjusted to take account of differences attributable to commercial level and/or to quantity, shall be used, provided that such adjustments can be made on the basis of demonstrated evidence which clearly establishes the reasonableness and accuracy of the adjustment, whether the adjustment leads to an increase or a decrease in the value.

2. Where the costs and charges referred to in Article 8.2 are included in the transaction value, an adjustment shall be made to take account of significant differences in such costs and charges between the imported goods and the similar goods in question arising from differences in distances and modes of transport.

3. If, in applying this Article, more than one transaction value of similar goods is found, the lowest such value shall be used to determine the customs value of the imported goods.

Article 4

If the customs value of the imported goods cannot be determined under the provisions of Articles 1, 2 and 3 the customs value shall be determined under the provisions of Article 5 or, when the customs value cannot be determined under that Article, under the provisions of Article 6 except that, at the request of the importer, the order of application of Articles 5 and 6 shall be reversed.

Article 5

1. (a) If the imported goods or identical or similar imported goods are sold in the country of importation in the condition as imported, the customs value of the imported goods under the provisions of this Article shall be based on the unit price at which the imported goods or identical or similar imported goods are so sold in the greatest aggregate quantity, at or about the time of the importation of the goods being valued, to persons who are not related to the persons from whom they buy such goods, subject to deductions for the following:

(i) either the commissions usually paid or agreed to be paid or the additions usually made for profit and general expenses in connexion with sales in such country of imported goods of the same class or kind;

(ii) the usual costs of transport and insurance and associated costs incurred within the country of importation;

(iii) where appropriate, the costs and charges referred to in Article 8.2; and

(iv) the customs duties and other national taxes payable in the country of importation by reason of the importation or sale of the goods.

(b) If neither the imported goods nor identical nor similar imported goods are sold at or about the time of importation of the goods being valued, the customs value shall, subject otherwise to the provisions of paragraph 1(a) of this Article, be based on the unit price at which the imported goods or identical or similar imported goods are sold in the country of importation in the condition as imported at the earliest date after the importation of the goods being valued but before the expiration of ninety days after such importation.

2. If neither the imported goods nor identical nor similar imported goods are sold in the country of importation in the condition as imported, then, if the importer so requests, the customs value shall be based on the unit price at which the imported goods, after further processing, are sold in the greatest aggregate quantity to persons in the country of importation who are not related to the persons from whom they buy such goods, due allowance being made for the value added by such processing and the deductions provided for in paragraph 1(a) of this Article.

Article 6

1. The customs value of imported goods under the provisions of this Article shall be based on a computed value. Computed value shall consist of the sum of:

(a) the cost or value of materials and fabrication or other processing employed in producing the imported goods;

(b) an amount for profit and general expenses equal to that usually reflected in sales of goods of the same class or kind as the goods being valued which are made by producers in the country of exportation for export to the country of importation;

(c) the cost or value of all other expenses necessary to reflect the valuation option chosen by the Party under Article 8.2.

2. No party may require or compel any person not resident in its own territory to produce for examination, or to allow access to, any account or other record for the purposes of determining a computed value. However, information supplied by the producer of the goods for the purposes of determining the customs value under the provisions of this Article may be verified in another country by the authorities of the country of importation with the agreement of the producer and provided they give sufficient advance notice to the government of the country in question and the latter does not object to the investigation.

Article 7

1. If the customs value of the imported goods cannot be determined under the provisions of Articles 1 to 6, inclusive, the value shall be determined using reasonable means consistent with the principles and general provisions of this Agreement and of Article VII of the General Agreement and on the basis of data available in the country of importation.

2. No customs value shall be determined under the provisions of this Article on the basis of:

(a) the selling price in the country of importation of goods produced in such country;

(b) a system which provides for the acceptance for customs purposes of the higher of two alternative values;

(c) the price of goods on the domestic market of the country of exportation;

(d) the cost of production other than computed values which have been determined for identical or similar goods in accordance with the provisions of Article 6;

(e) the price of the goods for export to a country other than the country of importation;

(f) minimum customs values; or

(g) arbitrary or fictitious values.

3. If he so requests, the importer shall be informed in writing of the customs value determined under the provisions of this Article and the method used to determine such value.

Article 8

1. In determining the customs value under the provisions of Article 1, there shall be added to the price actually paid or payable for the imported goods:

(a) the following, to the extent that they are incurred by the buyer but are not included in the price actually paid or payable for the goods:

(i) commissions and brokerage, except buying commissions;

(ii) the cost of containers which are treated as being one for customs purposes with the goods in question;

(iii) the cost of packing whether for labour or materials;

(b) the value, apportioned as appropriate, of the following goods and services where supplied directly or indirectly by the buyer free of charge or at reduced cost for use in connexion with the production and sale for export of the imported goods, to the extent that such value has not been included in the price actually paid or payable:

(i) materials, components, parts and similar items incorporated in the imported goods;

(ii) tools, dies, moulds and similar items used in the production of the imported goods;

(iii) materials consumed in the production of the imported goods;

(iv) engineering, development, artwork, design work, and plans and sketches undertaken elsewhere than in the country of importation and necessary for the production of the imported goods;

(c) royalties and licence fees related to the goods being valued that the buyer must pay, either directly or indirectly, as a condition of sale of the goods being valued, to the extent that such royalties and fees are not included in the price actually paid or payable;

(d) the value of any part of the proceeds of any subsequent resale, disposal or use of the imported goods that accrues directly or indirectly to the seller

2. In framing its legislation, each Party shall provide for the inclusion in or the exclusion from the customs value, in whole or in part, of the following:

(a) the cost of transport of the imported goods to the port or place of importation;

(b) loading, unloading and handling charges associated with the transport of the imported goods to the port or place of importation; and

(c) the cost of insurance.

3. Additions to the price actually paid or payable shall be made under this Article only on the basis of objective and quantifiable data.

4. No additions shall be made to the price actually paid or payable in determining the customs value except as provided in this Article.

Article 9

1. Where the conversion of currency is necessary for the determination of the customs value, the rate of exchange to be used shall be that duly published by the competent authorities of the country of importation concerned and shall reflect as effectively as possible, in respect of the period covered by each such document of publication, the current value of such currency in commercial transactions in terms of the currency of the country of importation.

2. The conversion rate to be used shall be that in effect at the time of exportation or the time of importation, as provided by each party.

Article 10

All information which is by nature confidential or which is provided on a confidential basis for the purposes of customs valuation shall be treated as strictly confidential by the authorities concerned who shall not disclose it without the specific permission of the person or government providing such information, except to the extent that it may be required to be disclosed in the context of judicial proceedings.

Article 11

1. The legislation of each Party shall provide in regard to a determination of customs value for the right of appeal, without penalty, by the importer or any other person liable for the payment of the duty.

2. An initial right of appeal without penalty may be to an authority within the customs administration or to an independent body, but the legislation of each Party shall provide for the right of appeal without penalty to a judicial authority.

3. Notice of the decision on appeal shall be given to the appellant and the reasons for such decision shall be provided in writing. He shall also be informed of his rights of any further appeal.

Article 12

Laws, regulations, judicial decisions and administrative rulings of general application giving effect to this Agreement shall be published in conformity with Article X of the General Agreement by the country of importation concerned.

Article 13

If, in the course of determining the customs value of imported goods, it becomes necessary to delay the final determination of such customs value, the importer shall nevertheless be able to withdraw his goods from customs if, where so required, he provides sufficient guarantee in the form of a surety, a deposit or some other appropriate instrument, covering the ultimate payment of customs duties for which the goods may be liable. The legislation of each Party shall make provisions for such circumstances.

Article 14

The notes at Annex I to this Agreement form an integral part of this Agreement and the Articles of this Agreement are to be read and applied in conjunction with their respective notes. Annexes II and III also form an integral part of this Agreement.

Article 15

1. In this Agreement:

(a) "customs value of imported goods" means the value of goods for the purposes of levying ad valorem duties of customs on imported goods;

(b) "country of importation" means country or customs territory of importation; and

(c) "produced" includes grown, manufactured and mined.

2. (a) In this Agreement "identical goods" means goods which are the same in all respects, including physical characteristics, quality and reputation. Minor differences in appearance would not preclude goods otherwise conforming to the definition from being regarded as identical.

(b) In this Agreement "similar goods" means goods which, although not alike in all respects, have like characteristics and like component materials which enable them to perform the same functions and to be commercially interchangeable. The quality of the goods, their reputation and the existence of a trademark are among the factors to be considered in determining whether goods are similar.

(c) The terms "identical goods" and "similar goods" do not include, as the case may be, goods which incorporate or reflect engineering, development, artwork, design work, and plans and sketches for which no adjustment has been made under Article 8.1(b)(iv) because such elements were undertaken in the country of importation.

(d) Goods shall not be regarded as "identical goods" or "similar goods" unless they were produced in the same country as the goods being valued.

(e) Goods produced by a different person shall be taken into account only when there are no identical goods or similar goods, as the case may be, produced by the same person as the goods being valued.

3. In this Agreement "goods of the same class or kind" means goods which fall within a group or range of goods produced by a particular industry or industry sector, and includes identical or similar goods.

4. For the purposes of this Agreement, persons shall be deemed to be related only if:

(a) they are officers or directors of one another's business;

(b) they are legally recognized partners in business;

(c) they are employer and employee;

(d) any person directly or indirectly owns, controls, or holds 5 per cent or more of the outstanding voting stock or shares of both of them;

(e) one of them directly or indirectly controls the other;

(f) both of them are directly or indirectly controlled by a third person;

(g) together they directly or indirectly control a third person; or

(h) they are members of the same family.

5. Persons who are associated with one another in that one is the sole agent, sole distributor or sole concessionaire, however described, of the other shall be deemed to be related for the purposes of this Agreement if they fall within the criteria of paragraph 4 of this Article.

Article 16

Upon written request, the importer shall have the right to an explanation in writing from the customs administration of the country of importation as to how the customs value of his imported goods was determined.

Article 17

Nothing in this Agreement shall be construed as restricting or calling into question the rights of customs administrations to satisfy themselves as to the truth or accuracy of any statement, document or declaration presented for customs valuation purposes.

Part II
ADMINISTRATION,
CONSULTATION AND DISPUTE
SETTLEMENT
Institutions
Article 18

There shall be established under this Agreement:

1. A Committee on Customs Valuation (hereinafter referred to as the Commit-

tee) composed of representatives from each of the Parties to this Agreement. The Committee shall elect its own Chairman and shall normally meet once a year, or as is otherwise envisaged by the relevant provisions of this Agreement, for the purpose of affording parties to this Agreement the opportunity to consult on matters relating to the administration of the customs valuation system by any Party to this Agreement as it might affect the operation of this Agreement or the furtherance of its objectives and carrying out such other responsibilities as may be assigned to it by the Parties. The GATT secretariat shall act as the secretariat to the Committee.

2. A Technical Committee on Customs Valuation (hereinafter referred to as the Technical Committee) under the auspices of the Customs Cooperation Council, which shall carry out the responsibilities described in Annex II to this Agreement and shall operate in accordance with the rules of procedure contained therein.

Consultation
Article 19

1. If any Party considers that any benefit accruing to it, directly or indirectly, under this Agreement is being nullified or impaired, or that the achievement of any objective of this Agreement is being impeded, as a result of the actions of another Party or of other Parties, it may, with a view to reaching a mutually satisfactory solution of the matter, request consultations with the Party or Parties in question. Each Party shall afford sympathetic consideration to any request from another Party for consultations.

2. The Parties concerned shall initiate requested consultations promptly.

3. Parties engaged in consultations on a particular matter affecting the operation of this Agreement shall attempt to conclude such consultations within a reasonably short period of time. The Technical Committee shall provide, upon request, advice and assistance to Parties engaged in consultations.

Dispute Settlement
Article 20

1. If no mutually satisfactory solution has been reached between the Parties concerned in consultations under Article 19 above, the Committee shall meet at the request of any Party to the dispute, within thirty days of receipt of such a request, to investigate the matter, with a view to facilitating a mutually satisfactory solution.

2. In investigating the matter and in selecting its procedures, the Committee shall take into account whether the issues in dispute related to commercial policy considerations or to questions requiring detailed technical consideration. The Committee may request on its own initiative that the Technical Committee carry out an examination, as provided in paragraph 4 below, of any question requiring technical consideration. Upon the request of any Party to the dispute that considers the issues to relate to questions of a technical nature, the Committee shall request the Technical Committee to carry out such an examination.

3. During any phase of a dispute settlement procedure, competent bodies and experts in matters under consideration may be consulted; appropriate information and assistance may be requested from such bodies and experts. The Committee shall take into consideration the results of any work of the Technical Committee that pertain to the matter in dispute.

Technical issues

4. When the Technical Committee is requested under the provisions of paragraph 2 above, it shall examine the matter and report to the Committee no later than three months from the date the technical issue was referred to it, unless the period is extended by mutual agreement between the parties to the dispute.

Panel proceedings

5. In cases where the matter is not referred to the Technical Committee, the Committee shall establish a panel upon the request of any party to the dispute if no mutually satisfactory solution has been reached within three months from the date of the request to the Committee to investigate the matter. Where the matter is referred to the Technical Committee, the Committee shall establish a panel upon the request of any party to the dispute if no mutually satisfactory

solution has been reached within one month from the date when the Technical Committee presents its report to the Committee.

6. (a) When a panel is established, it shall be governed by the procedures as set forth in Annex III.

(b) If the Technical Committee has made a report on the technical aspects of the matter in dispute, the panel shall use this report as the basis for its consideration of the technical aspects of the matter in dispute.

Enforcement

7. After the investigation is completed or after the report of the Technical Committee or panel is presented to the Committee, the Committee shall give the matter prompt consideration. With respect to panel reports, the Committee shall take appropriate action normally within thirty days of receipt of the report. Such action shall include:

(i) a statement concerning the facts of the matter; and

(ii) recommendations to one or more Parties or any other ruling which it deems appropriate.

8. If a Party to which recommendations are addressed considers itself unable to implement them, it should promptly furnish reasons in writing to the Committee. In that event, the Committee shall consider what further action may be appropriate.

9. If the Committee considers that the circumstances are serious enough to justify such action, it may authorize one or more Parties to suspend the application to any other Party or Parties of such obligations under this Agreement as it determines to be appropriate in the circumstances.

10. The Committee shall keep under surveillance any matter on which it has made recommendations or given rulings.

11. If a dispute arises between Parties relating to rights and obligations under this Agreement, Parties should complete the dispute settlement procedures under this Agreement before availing themselves of any rights which they have under the GATT, including invoking Article XXIII thereof.

Part III
SPECIAL AND DIFFERENTIAL TREATMENT
Article 21

1. Developing country Parties may delay application of its provisions for a period not exceeding five years from the date of entry into force of this Agreement for such countries. Developing country Parties who choose to delay application of this Agreement shall notify the Director-General to the CONTRACTING PARTIES to the GATT accordingly.

2. In addition to paragraph 1 above, developing country Parties may delay application of Article 1.2(b)(iii) and Article 6 for a period not exceeding three years following their application of all other provisions of this Agreement. Developing country Parties that choose to delay application of the provisions specified in this paragraph shall notify the Director-General to the CONTRACTING PARTIES to the GATT accordingly.

3. Developed country Parties shall furnish, on mutually agreed terms, technical assistance to developing country Parties that so request. On this basis developed country Parties shall draw up programmes of technical assistance which may include, *inter alia,* training of personnel, assistance in preparing implementation measures, access to sources of information regarding customs valuation methodology, and advice on the application of the provisions of this Agreement.

Part IV
FINAL PROVISIONS
Acceptance and accession
Article 22

1. This Agreement shall be open for acceptance by signature or otherwise by governments contracting parties to the GATT and by the European Economic Community.

2. This Agreement shall be open for acceptance by signature or otherwise by governments having provisionally acceded to the GATT, on terms related to the effective application of rights and obligations under this Agreement, which take into account rights and obligations in the instruments providing for their provisional accession.

3. This Agreement shall be open to accession by any other government on terms, related to the effective application of rights and obligations under this Agreement, to be agreed between that government and the Parties by the deposit with the Director-General to the CONTRACTING PARTIES to the GATT of an instrument of accession which states the terms as agreed.

4. In regard to acceptance, the provisions of Article XXVI: 5(a) and (b) of the General Agreement would be applicable.

Reservations
Article 23

Reservations may not be entered in respect of any of the provisions of this Agreement without the consent of the other Parties.

Entry into force
Article 24

This Agreement shall enter into force on 1 January 1981 for the governments* which have accepted or acceded to it by that date. For each other government it shall enter into force on the thirtieth day following the date of its acceptance or accession to this Agreement.

National legislation
Article 25

1. Each government accepting or acceding to this Agreement shall ensure, not later than the date of entry into force of this Agreement for it, the conformity of its laws, regulations and administrative procedures with the provisions of this Agreement.

2. Each Party shall inform the Committee of any changes in its laws and regulations relevant to this Agreement and in the administration of such laws and regulations.

Review
Article 26

The Committee shall review annually the implementation and operation of this Agreement taking into account the objectives thereof. The Committee shall annually inform the CONTRACTING PAR-

---

* The term "governments" is deemed to include the competent authorities of the European Economic Community.

TIES to the GATT of developments during the period covered by such reviews.

Amendments
Article 27

The Parties may amend this Agreement, having regard, *inter alia,* to the experience gained in its implementation. Such an amendment, once the Parties have concurred in accordance with procedures established by the Committee, shall not come into force for any Party until it has been accepted by such Party.

Withdrawal
Article 28

Any Party may withdraw from this Agreement. The withdrawal shall take effect upon the expiration of sixty days from the date on which written notice of withdrawal is received by the Director-General to the CONTRACTING PARTIES to the GATT. Any Party may, upon the receipt of such notice, request an immediate meeting of the Committee.

Secretariat
Article 29

This Agreement shall be serviced by the GATT secretariat except in regard to those responsibilities specifically assigned to the Technical Committee, which will be serviced by the secretariat of the Customs Co-operation Council.

Deposit
Article 30

This Agreement shall be deposited with the Director-General to the CONTRACTING PARTIES to the GATT, who shall promptly furnish to each Party and each contracting Party to the GATT a certified copy thereof and of each amendment thereto pursuant to Article 27, and a notification of each acceptance thereof or instrument of accession thereto pursuant to Article 22 and of each withdrawal therefrom pursuant to Article 28.

Registration
Article 31

This Agreement shall be registered in accordance with the provisions of Article 102 of the Charter of the United Nations.

Done at Geneva this twelfth day of April nineteen hundred and seventy-nine

in a single copy, in the English, French and Spanish languages, each text being authentic.

ANNEX I
INTERPRETATIVE NOTES
General Note

Sequential application of valuation methods

1. Articles 1 to 7, inclusive, define how the customs value of imported goods is to be determined under the provisions of this Agreement. The methods of valuation are set out in a sequential order of application. The primary method for customs valuation is defined in Article 1 and imported goods are to be valued in accordance with the provisions of this Article whenever the conditions prescribed therein are fulfilled.

2. Where the customs value cannot be determined under the provisions of Article 1, it is to be determined by proceeding sequentially through the succeeding Articles to the first such Article under which the customs value can be determined. Except as provided in Article 4, it is only when the customs value cannot be determined under the provisions of a particular Article that the provisions of the next Article in the sequence can be used.

3. If the importer does not request that the order of Articles 5 and 6 be reversed, the normal order of the sequence is to be followed. If the importer does so request but it then proves impossible to determine the customs value under the provisions of Article 6, the customs value is to be determined under the provisions of Article 5, if it can be so determined.

4. Where the customs value cannot be determined under the provisions of Articles 1 to 6, inclusive, it is to be determined under the provisions of Article 7.

Use of generally accepted accounting principles

1. "Generally accepted accounting principles" refers to the recognized consensus or substantial authoritative support within a country at a particular time as to which economic resources and obligations should be recorded as assets and liabilities, which changes in assets and liabilities should be recorded, how the assets and liabilities and changes in them sould be measured, what informa-

tion should be disclosed and how it should be disclosed, and which financial statements should be prepared. These standards may be broad guidelines of general application as well detailed practices and procedures.

2. For the purposes of this Agreement, the customs administration of each party shall utilize information prepared in a manner consistent with generally accepted accounting principles in the country which is appropriate for the Article in question. For example, the determination of usual profit and general expenses under the provisions of Article 5 would be carried out utilizing information prepared in a manner consistent with generally accepted accounting principles of the country of importation. On the other hand, the determination of usual profit and general expenses under the provisions of Article 6 would be carried out utilizing information prepared in a manner consistent with generally accepted accounting principles of the country of production. As a further example, the determination of an element provided for in Article 8.1(b)(ii) undertaken in the country of importation would be carried out utilizing information in a manner consistent with the generally accepted accounting prinicples of that country.

Note to Article 1
Price actually paid or payable

The price actually paid or payable is the total payment made or to be made by the buyer to or for the benefit of the seller for the imported goods. The payment need not necessarily take the form of a transfer of money. Payment may be made by way of letters of credit or negotiable instruments. Payment may be made directly or indirectly. An example of an indirect payment would be the settlement by the buyer, whether in whole or in part, of a debt owed by the seller.

Activities undertaken by the buyer on his own account, other than those for which an adjustment is provided in Article 8, are not considered to be an indirect payment to the seller, even though they might be regarded as of benefit to the seller. The costs of such activities shall not, therefore, be added to the price actually paid or payable in determining the customs value.

The customs value shall not include the following charges or costs, provided that they are distinguished from the price actually paid or payable for the imported goods:

(a) charges for construction, erection, assembly, maintenance or technical assistance, undertaken after importation on imported goods such as industrial plant, machinery or equipment;

(a) the cost of transport after importation;

(c) duties and taxes of the country of importation.

The price actually paid or payable refers to the price for the imported goods. Thus the flow of dividends or other payments from the buyer to the seller that do not relate to the imported goods are not part of the customs value.

Paragraph 1 (a) (iii)

Among restrictions which would not render a price actually paid or payable unacceptable are restrictions which do not substantially affect the value of the goods. An example of such restrictions would be the case where a seller requires a buyer of automobiles not to sell or exhibit them prior to a fixed date which represents the beginning of a model year.

Paragraph 1 (b)

If the sale or price is subject to some condition or consideration for which a value cannot be determined with respect to the goods being valued, the transaction value shall not be acceptable for customs purposes. Some examples of this include:

(a) the seller establishes the price of the imported goods on condition that the buyer will also buy other goods in specified quantities;

(b) the price of the imported goods is dependent upon the price or prices at which the buyer of the imported goods sells other goods to the seller of the imported goods;

(c) the price is established on the basis of a form of payment extraneous to the imported goods, such as where the imported goods are semi-finished goods which have been provided by the seller on condition that he will receive a specified quantity of the finished goods.

However, conditions or considerations relating to the production or marketing of the imported goods shall not result in rejection of the transaction value. For example, the fact that the buyer furnishes the seller with engineering and plans undertaken in the country of importation shall not result in rejection of the transaction value for the purposes of Article 1. Likewise, if the buyer underakes on his own account, even though by agreement with the seller, activities relating to the marketing of the imported goods, the value of these activities is not part of the customs value nor shall such activities result in rejection of the transaction value.

Paragraph 2

1. Paragraphs 2(a) and 2(b) provide different means of establishing the acceptability of a transaction value.

2. Paragraph 2(a) provides that where the buyer and the seller are related, the circumstances surrounding the sale shall be examined and the transaction value shall be accepted as the customs value provided that the relationship did not influence the price. It is not intended that there should be an examination of the circumstances in all cases where the buyer and the seller are related. Such examination will only be required where there are doubts about the acceptability of the price. Where the customs administration have no doubts about the acceptability of the price, it should be accepted without requesting further information from the importer. For example, the customs administration may have previously examined the relationship, or it may already have detailed information concerning the buyer and the seller, and may already be satisfied from such examination or information that the relationship did not influence the price.

3. Where the customs administration is unable to accept the transaction value without further inquiry, it should give the importer an opportunity to supply such further detailed information as may be necessary to enable it to examine the circumstances surrounding the sale. In this context, the customs administration should be prepared to examine relevant aspects of the transaction, including the way in which the buyer and seller orga-

nize their commercial relations and the way in which the price in question was arrived at, in order to determine whether the relationship influenced the price. Where it can be shown that the buyer and seller, although related under the provisions of Article 15, buy from and sell to each other as if they were not related, this would demonstrate that the price had not been influenced by the relationship. As an example of this, if the price had been settled in a manner consistent with the normal pricing practices of the industry in question or with the way the seller settles prices for sales to buyers who are not related to him, this would demonstrate that the price had not been influenced by the relationship. As a further example, where it is shown that the price is adequate to ensure recovery of all costs plus a profit which is representative of the firm's overall profit realized over a representative period of time (e.g. on an annual basis) in sales of goods of the same class or kind, this would demonstrate that the price had not been influenced.

4. Paragraph 2(b) provides an opportunity for the importer to demonstrate that the transaction value closely approximates to a "test" value previously accepted by the customs administration and is therefore acceptable under the provisions of Article 1. Where a test under paragraph 2(b) is met, it is not necessary to examine the question of influence under paragraph 2(a). If the customs administration has already sufficient information to be satisfied, without further detailed inquiries, that one of the tests provided in paragraph 2(b) has been met, there is no reason for it to require the importer to demonstrate that the test can be met. In paragraph 2(b) the term "unrelated buyers" means buyers who are not related to the seller in any particular case.

Paragraph 2 (b)

A number of factors must be taken into consideration in determining whether one value "closely approximates" to another value. These factors include the nature of the imported goods, the nature of the industry itself, the season in which the goods are imported, and, whether the difference in values is commercially significant. Since these factors may vary

from case to case, it would be impossible to apply a uniform standard such as a fixed percentage, in each case. For example, a small difference in value in a case involving one type of goods could be unacceptable while a large difference in a case involving another type of goods might be acceptable in determining whether the transaction value closely approximates to the "test" values set forth in Article 1.2(b).

Note to Article 2

1. In applying Article 2, the customs administration shall, wherever possible, use a sale of identical goods at the same commercial level and in substantially the same quantities as the goods being valued. Where no such sale is found, a sale of identical goods that takes place under any one of the following three conditions may be used:

(a) a sale at the same commercial level but in different quantities;

(b) a sale at a different commercial level but in substantially the same quantities; or

(c) a sale at a different commercial level and in different quantities.

2. Having found a sale under any one of these three conditions adjustments will then be made, as the case may be, for:

(a) quantity factors only;

(b) commercial level factors only; or

(c) both commercial level and quantity factors.

3. The expression "and/or" allows the flexibility to use the sales and make the necessary adjustments in any one of the three conditions described above.

4. For the purposes of Article 2, the transaction value of identical imported goods means a customs value, adjusted as provided for in paragraphs 1(b) and 2 of this Article, which has already been accepted under Article 1.

5. A condition for adjustment because of different commercial levels or different quantities is that such adjustment, whether it leads to an increase or a decrease in the value, be made only on the basis of demonstrated evidence that clearly establishes the reasonableness and accuracy of the adjustments, e.g. valid price lists containing prices referring to different levels or different quantities. As

an example of this, if the imported goods being valued consist of a shipment of 10 units and the only identical imported goods for which a transaction value exists involved a sale of 500 units, and it is recognized that the seller grants quantity discounts, the required adjustment may be accomplished by resorting to the sellers' price list and using that price applicable to a sale of 10 units. This does not require that a sale had to have been made in quantities of 10 as long as the price list has been established as being *bona fide* through sales at other quantities. In the absence of such an objective measure, however, the determination of a customs value under the provisions of Article 2 is not appropriate.

Note to Article 3

1. In applying Article 3, the customs administration shall, wherever possible, use a sale of similar goods at the same commercial level and in substantially the same quantities as the goods being valued. Where no such sale is found, a sale of similar goods that takes place under any one of the following three conditions may be used:

(a) a sale at the same commercial level but in different quantities;

(b) a sale at a different commercial level but in substantially the same quantities; or

(c) a sale at a different commercial level and in different quantities.

2. Having found a sale under any one of these three conditions adjustments will then be made, as the case may be, for:

(a) quantity factors only;

(b) commercial level factors only; or

(c) both commercial level and quantity factors.

3. The expression "and/or" allows the flexibility to use the sales and make the necessary adjustments in any one of the three conditions described above.

4. For the purpose of Article 3, the transaction value of similar imported goods means a customs value, adjusted as provided for in paragraphs 1(b) and 2 of this Article, which has already been accepted under Article 1.

5. A condition for adjustment because of different commercial levels or different quantities is that such adjustment, whether it leads to an increase or a decrease in the value, be made only on the basis of demonstrated evidence that clearly establishes the reasonableness and accuracy of the adjustment, e.g. valid price lists containing prices referring to different levels or different quantities. As an example of this, if the imported goods being valued consist of a shipment of 10 units and the only similar imported goods for which a transaction value exists involved a sale of 500 units, and it is recognized that the seller grants quantity discounts, the required adjustment may be accomplished by resorting to the seller's price list and using that price applicable to a sale of 10 units. This does not require that a sale had to have been made in quantities of 10 as long as the price list has been established as being *bona fide* through sales at other quantities. In the absence of such an objective measure, however, the determination of a customs value under the provisions of Article 3 is not appropriate.

Note to Article 5

1. The term "unit price at which ... goods are sold in the greatest aggregate quantity "means the price at which the greatest number of units is sold in sales to persons who are not related to the persons from whom they buy such goods at the first commercial level after importation at which such sales take place.

2. As an example of this, goods are sold from a price list which grants favourable unit prices for purchases made in larger quantities.

Sale quantity	Unit price	Number of sales	Total quantity sold at each price
1-10 units	100	10 sales of 5 units 5 sales of 3 units	65
11-25 units	95	5 sales of 11 units	55
over 25 units	90	1 sale of 30 units 1 sale of 50 units	80

The greatest number of units sold at a price is 80; therefore, the unit price in the greatest aggregate quantity is 90.

3. As another example of this, two sales occur. In the first sale 500 units are sold at a price of 95 currency units each. In the second sale 400 units are sold at a price of 90 currency units each. In this example, the greatest number of units sold at a particular price is 500; therefore, the unit price in the greatest aggregate quantity is 95.

4. A third example would be the following situation where various quantities are sold at various prices.

(a) Sales	
Sale quantity	Unit price
40 units	100
30 units	90
15 units	100
50 units	95
25 units	105
35 units	90
5 units	100

(b) Totals	
Total quantity sold	Unit price
65	90
50	95
60	100
25	105

In this example, the greatest number of units sold at a particular price is 65; therefore, the unit price in the greatest aggregate quantity is 90.

5. Any sale in the importing country, as described in paragraph 1 above, to a person who supplies directly or indirectly free of charge or at reduced cost for use in connection with the production and sale for export of the imported goods any of the elements specified in Article 8.1(b), should not be taken into account in establishing the unit price for the purposes of Article 5.

6. It should be noted that "profit and general expenses" referred to in Article 5.1 should be taken as a whole. The figure for the purposes of this deduction should be determined on the basis of information supplied by or on behalf of the importer unless his figures are inconsistent with those obtaining in sales in the country of importation of imported goods of the same class or kind. Where the importer's figures are inconsistent

with such figures, the amount for profit and general expenses may be based upon relevant information other than that supplied by or on behalf of the importer.

7. The "general expenses" include the direct and indirect costs of marketing the goods in question.

8. Local taxes payable by reason of the sale of the goods for which a deduction is not made under the provisions of Article 5.1(a)(iv) shall be deducted under the provisions of Article 5.1(a)(i).

9. In determining either the commissions or the usual profits and general expenses under the provisions of Article 5.1, the question whether certain goods are "of the same class or kind" as other goods must be determined on a case-by-case basis by reference to the circumstances involved. Sales in the country of importation of the narrowest group or range of imported goods of the same class or kind, which includes the goods being valued, for which the necessary information can be provided, should be examined. For the purposes of Article 5, "goods of the same class or kind" include goods imported from the same country as the goods being valued as well as goods imported from other countries.

10. For the purposes of Article 5.1(b), the "earliest date" shall be the date by which sales of the imported goods or of identical or similar imported goods are made in sufficient quantity to establish the unit price.

11. Where the method in Article 5.2 is used, deductions made for the value added by further processing shall be based on objective and quantifiable data relating to the cost of such work. Accepted industry formulas, recipes, methods of construction, and other industry practices would form the basis of the calculations.

12. It is recognized that the method of valuation provided for in Article 5.2 would normally not be applicable when, as a result of the further processing, the imported goods lose their identity. However, there can be instances where, although the identity of the imported goods is lost, the value added by the processing can be determined accurately without unreasonable difficulty. On the other hand, there can also be instances

where the imported goods maintain their identity but form such a minor element in the goods sold in the country of importation that the use of this valuation method would be unjustified. In view of the above, each situation of this type must be considered on a case-by-case basis.

Note to Article 6

1. As a general rule, customs value is determined under this Agreement on the basis of information readily available in the country of importation. In order to determine a computed value, however, it may be necessary to examine the costs of producing the goods being valued and other information which has to be obtained from outside the country of importation. Furthermore, in most cases the producer of the goods will be outside the jurisdiction of the authorities of the country of importation. The use of the computed value method will generally be limited to those cases where the buyer and seller are related, and the producer is prepared to supply to the authorities of the country of importation the necessary costings and to provide facilities for any subsequent verification which may be necessary.

2. The "cost or value" referred to in Article 6.1(a) is to be determined on the basis of information relating to the production of the goods being valued supplied by or on behalf of the producer. It is to be based upon the commercial accounts of the producer, provided that such accounts are consistent with the generally accepted accounting principles applied in the country where the goods are produced.

3. The "cost or value" shall include the cost of elements specified in Article 8.1(a)(ii) and (iii). It shall also include the value, apportioned as appropriate under the provisions of the relevant note to Article 8, of any element specified in Article 8.1(b) which has been supplied directly or indirectly by the buyer for use in connexion with the production of the imported goods. The value of the elements specified in Article 8.1(b)(iv) which are undertaken in the country of importation shall be included only to the extent that such elements are charged to the producer. It is to be understood that no cost or value of the elements referred

to in this paragraph shall be counted twice in determining the computed value.

4. The "amount for profit and general expenses" referred to in Article 6.1(b) is to be determined on the basis of information supplied by or on behalf of the producer unless his figures are inconsistent with those usually reflected in sales of goods of the same class or kind as the goods being valued which are made by producers in the country of exportation for export to the country of importation.

5. It should be noted in this context that the "amount for profit and general expenses" has to be taken as a whole. It follows that if, in any particular case, the producer's profit figure is low and his general expenses are high, his profit and general expenses taken together may nevertheless be consistent with that usually reflected in sales of goods of the same class or kind. Such a situation might occur, for example, if a product were being launched in the country of importation and the producer accepted a nil or low profit to offset high general expenses associated with the launch. Where the producer can demonstrate that he is taking a low profit on his sales of the imported goods because of particular commercial circumstances, his actual profit figures should be taken into account provided that he has valid commercial reasons to justify them and his pricing policy reflects usual pricing policies in the branch of industry concerned. Such a situation might occur, for example, where producers have been forced to lower prices temporarily because of an unforeseeable drop in demand, or where they sell goods to complement a range of goods being produced in the country of importation and accept a low profit to maintain competitivity. Where the producer's own figures for profit and general expenses are not consistent with those usually reflected in sales of goods of the same class or kind as the goods being valued which are made by producers in the country of exportation for export to the country of importation, the amount for profit and general expenses may be based upon relevant information other than that supplied by or on behalf of the producer of the goods.

6. Where information other than that supplied by or on behalf of the producer

is used for the purposes of determining a computed value, the authorities of the importing country shall inform the importer, if the latter so requests, of the source of such information, the data used and the calculations based upon such data, subject to the provisions of Article 10.

7. The "general expenses" referred to in Article 6.1(b) covers the direct and indirect costs of producing and selling the goods for export which are not included under Article 6.1(a).

8. Whether certain goods are "of the same class or kind" as other goods must be determined on a case-by-case basis with reference to the circumstances involved. In determining the usual profits and general expenses under the provisions of Article 6, sales for export to the country of importation of the narrowest group or range of goods, which includes the goods being valued, for which the necessary information can be provided, should be examined. For the purposes of Article 6, "goods of the same class or kind" must be from the same country as the goods being valued.

Note to Article 7

1. Customs values determined under the provisions of Article 7 should, to the greatest extent possible, be based on previously determined customs values.

2. The methods of valuation to be employed under Article 7 should be those laid down in Articles 1 to 6, inclusive, but a reasonable flexibility in the application of such methods would be in conformity with the aims and provisions of Article 7.

3. Some examples of reasonable flexibility are as follows:

(a) Identical goods—the requirement that the identical goods should be exported at or about the same time as the goods being valued could be flexibly interpreted; identical imported goods produced in a country other than the country of exportation of the goods being valued could be the basis for customs valuation; customs values of identical imported goods already determined under the provisions of Article 5 and 6 could be used.

(b) Similar goods—the requirement that the similar goods should be exported at or about the same time as the goods being valued could be flexibly interpreted; similar imported goods produced in a country other than the country of exportation of the goods being valued could be the basis for customs valuation; customs values of similar imported goods already determined under the provisions of Articles 5 and 6 could be used.

(c) Deductive method—the requirement that the goods shall have been sold in the "condition as imported" in Article 5.1(a) could be flexibly interpreted; the "ninety days" requirement could be administered flexibly.

Note to Article 8

Paragraph 1(a)(i)

The term "buying commissions" means fees paid by an importer to his agent for the service of representing him abroad in the purchase of the goods being valued.

Paragraph 1(b)(ii)

1. There are two factors involved in the apportionment of the elements specified in Article 8.1(b)(ii) to the imported goods—the value of the element itself and the way in which that value is to be apportioned to the imported goods. The apportionment of these elements should be made in a reasonable manner appropriate to the circumstances and in accordance with generally accepted accounting principles.

2. Concerning the value of the element, if the importer acquires the element from a seller not related to him at a given cost, the value of the element is that cost. If the element was produced by the importer or by a person related to him, its value would be the cost of producing it. If the element had been previously used by the importer, regardless of whether it had been acquired or produced by such importer, the original cost of acquisition or production would have to be adjusted downward to reflect its use in order to arrive at the value of the element.

3. Once a value has been determined for the element, it is necessary to apportion that value to the imported goods. Various possibilities exist. For example, the value might be apportioned to the first shipment if the importer wishes to pay duty on the entire value at one time.

As another example, the importer may request that the value be apportioned over the number of units produced up to the time of the first shipment. As a further example, he may request that the value be apportioned over the entire anticipated production where contracts or firm commitments exist for theat production. The method of apportionment used will depend upon the documentation provided by the importer.

4. As an illustration of the above, an importer provides the producer with a mould to be used in the production of the imported goods and contracts with him to buy 10,000 units. By the time of arrival of the first shipment of 1,000 units, the producer has already produced 4,000 units. The importer may request the customs administration to apportion the value of the mould over 1,000 units, 4,000 units or 10,000 units.

Paragraph 1(b)(iv)

1. Additions for the elements specified in Article 8.1(b)(iv) should be based on objective and quantifiable data. In order to minimize the burden for both the importer and customs administration in determining the values to be added, data readily available in the buyer's commerical record system should be used in so far as possible.

2. For those elements supplied by the buyer which were purchased or leased by the buyer, the addition would be the cost of the purchase or the lease. No addition shall be made for those elements available in the public domain, other than the cost of obtaining copies of them.

3. The ease with which it may be possible to calculate the values to be added will depend on a particular firm's structure and management practice, as well as its accounting methods.

4. For example, it is possible that a firm which imports a variety of products from several countires maintains the records of its design centre outside the country of importation in such a way as to show accurately the costs attributable to a given product. In such cases, a direct adjustment may appropriately be made under the provisions of Article 8.

5. In another case, a firm may carry the cost of the design centre outside the country of importation as a general over-head expense without allocation to specific products. In this instance, an appropriate adjustment could be made under the provisions of Article 8 with respect to the imported goods by apportioning total design centre costs over total production benefiting from the design centre and adding such apportioned cost on a unit basis to imports.

6. Variations in the above circumstances will, of course, require different factors to be considered in determining the proper method of allocation.

7. In cases where the production of the element in question involves a number of countries and over a period of time, the adjustment should be limited to the value actually added to that element outside the country of importaion.

Paragraph 1 (c)

1. The royalties and licence fees referred to in Article 8.1 (c) may include, among other things, payments in respect to patents, trademarks and copyrights. However, the charges for the right to reproduce the imported goods in the country of importation shall not be added to the price actually paid or payable for the imported goods in determining the customs value.

2. Payments made by the buyer for the right to distribute or resell the imported goods shall not be added to the price actually paid or payable for the imported goods if such payments are not a condition of the sale for export to the country of importation of the imported goods.

Paragraph 3

Where objective and quantifiable data do not exist with regard to the additions required to be made under the provisions of Article 8, the transaction value cannot be determined under the provisions of Article 1. As an illustration of this, a royalty is paid on the basis of the price in a sale in the importing country of a litre of a particular product that was imported by the kilogram and made up into a solution after importation. If the royalty is based partially on the imported goods and partially on other factors which have nothing to do with the imported goods (such as when the imported goods are mixed with domestic ingredients and are no longer separately identifiable, or when the royalty cannot be distinguished from special financial arrangements between the buyer and the seller), it would be inappropriate to attempt to make an addition for the royalty. However, if the amount of this royalty is based only on the imported goods and can be readily quantified, an addition to the price actually paid or payable can be made.

Note to Article 9

For the purposes of Article 9, "time of importation" may include the time of entry for customs purposes.

Note to Article 11

1. Article 11 provides the importer with the right to appeal against a valuation determination made by the customs administration for the goods being valued. Appeal may first be to a higher level in the customs administration, but the importer shall have the right in the final instance to appeal to the judiciary.

2. "Without penalty" means that the importer shall not be subject to a fine or threat of fine merely because he chose to exercise his right of appeal. Payment of normal court costs and lawyers' fees shall not be considered to be a fine.

3. However, nothing in Article 11 shall prevent a Party from requiring full payment of assessed customs duties prior to an appeal.

Note to Article 15

Paragraph 4

For the purposes of this Article, the term "persons" includes legal persons, where appropriate.

Paragraph 4 (e)

For the purposes of this Agreement, one person shall be deemed to control another when the former is legally or operationally in a position to exercise restraint or direction over the latter.

ANNEX II

Technical Committee on Customs Valuation

1. In accordance with Article 18 of this Agreement, the Technical Committee shall be established under the auspices of the Customs Co-operation Council with a view, at the technical level, towards uniformity in interpretation and application of this Agreement.

2. The responsibilities of the Technical Committee shall include the following:

(a) to examine specific technical problems arising in the day-to-day administration of the customs valuation system of parties to this Agreement and to give advisory opinions on appropriate solutions based upon the facts presented;

(b) to study, as requested, valuation laws, procedures and practices as they relate to this Agreement and to prepare reports on the results of such studies;

(c) to prepare and circulate annual reports on the technical aspects of the operation and status of this Agreement;

(d) to furnish such information and advice on any matters concerning the valuation of imported goods for customs purposes as may be requested by any Party or the Committee. Such information and advice may take the form of advisory opinions, commentaries or explanatory notes;

(e) to facilitate, as requested, technical assistance to Parties with a view to furthering the international acceptance of this Agreement; and

(f) to exercise such other responsibilities as the Committee may assign to it.

General

3. The Technical Committee shall attempt to conclude its work on specific matters, especially those referred to it by Parties or the Committee, in a reasonably short period of time.

4. The Technical Committee shall be assisted as appropriate in its activities by the Secretariat of the Customs Co-operation Council.

Representation

5. Each Party shall have the right to be represented on the Technical Committee. Each Party may nominate one delegate and one or more alternates to be its representatives on the Technical Committee. Such a Party so represented on the Technical Committee is hereinafter referred to as a member of the Technical Committee. Representatives of members of the Technical Committee may be assisted by advisers. The GATT secretar-

1at may also attend such meetings with observer status.

6. Members of the Customs Co-operation Council who are not Parties may be represented at meetings of the Technical Committee by one delegate and one or more alternates. Such representatives shall attend meetings of the Technical Committee as observers.

7. Subject to the approval of the Chairman of the Technical Committee, the Secretary-General of the Customs Co-operation Council (hereinafter referred to as "the Secretary-General") may invite representatives of governments which are neither Parties nor members of the Customs Co-operation Council and representatives of international governmental and trade organizations to attend meetings of the Technical Committee as observers.

8. Nominations of delegates, alternates and advisers to meetings of the Technical Committee shall be made to the Secretary-General.

Technical Committee meetings

9. The Technical Committee shall meet as necessary but at least two times a year. The date of each meeting shall be fixed by the Technical Committee at its preceding session. The date of the meeting may be varied either at the request of any member of the Technical Committee concurred in by a simple majority of the members of the Technical Committee or, in cases requiring urgent attention, at the request of the Chairman.

10. The meeting of the Technical Committee shall be held at the headquarters of the Customs Co-operation Council unless otherwise decided.

11. The Secretary-General shall inform all members of the Technical Committee and those included under paragraphs 6 and 7 at least thirty days in advance, except in urgent cases, of the opening date of each session of the Technical Committee.

Agenda

12. A provisional agenda for each session shall be drawn up by the Secretary-General and circulated to the members of the Technical Committee and to those included under paragraphs 6 and 7 at least thirty days in advance of the session, except in urgent cases. This agenda shall comprise all items whose inclusion has been approved by the Technical Committee during its preceding session, all items included by the Chairman on his own initiative, and all items whose inclusion has been requested by the Secretary-General, by the Committee or by any member of the Technical Committee.

13. The Technical Committee shall determine its agenda at the opening of each session. During the session the agenda may be altered at any time by the Technical Committee.

Officers and conduct of business

14. The Technical Committee shall elect from among the delegates of its members a Chairman and one or more Vice-Chairmen. The Chairman and Vice-Chairmen shall each hold office for a period of one year. The retiring Chairman and Vice-Chairmen are eligible for re-election. A Chairman or Vice-Chairman who ceases to represent a member of the Technical Committee shall automatically lose his mandate.

15. If the Chairman is absent from any meeting or part thereof, a Vice-Chairman shall preside. In that event, the latter shall have the same powers and duties as the Chairman.

16. The Chairman of the meeting shall participate in the proceedings of the Technical Committee as such and not as the representative of a member of the Technical Committee.

17. In addition to exercising the powers conferred upon him elsewhere by these rules, the Chairman shall declare the opening and closing of each meeting, direct the discussion, accord the right to speak, and, pursuant to these rules, have control of the proceedings. The Chairman may also call a speaker to order if his remarks are not relevant.

18. During discussion of any matter a delegation may raise a point of order. In this event, the Chairman shall immediately state his ruling. If this ruling is challenged, the Chairman shall submit it to the meeting for decisions and it shall stand unless overruled.

19. The Secretary-General, or officers of the Secretariat designated by him, shall perform the secretarial work of meetings of the Technical Committee.

Quorum and voting

20. Representatives of a simple majority of the members of the Technical Committee shall constitute a quorum.

21. Each member of the Technical Committee shall have one vote. A decision of the Technical Committee shall be taken by a majority comprising at least two thirds of the members present. Regardless of the outcome of the vote on a particular matter, the Technical Committee shall be free to make a full report to the Committee and to the Customs Co-operation Council on that matter indicating the different views expressed in the relevant discussions.

Languages and records

22. The official languages of the Technical Committee shall be English, French and Spanish. Speeches or statements made in any of these three languages shall be immediately translated into the other official languages unless all delegations agree to dispense with translation. Speeches or statements made in any other language shall be translated into English, French and Spanish, subject to the same conditions, but in that event the delegation concerned shall provide the translation into English, French or Spanish. Only English, French and Spanish shall be used for the official documents of the Technical Committee. Memoranda and correspondence for the consideration of the Technical Committee must be presented in one of the official languages.

23. The Technical Committee shall draw up a report of all its sessions and, if the Chairman considers it necessary, minutes or summary records of its meetings. The Chairman or his designee shall report on the work of the Technical Committee at each meeting of the Committee and at each meeting of the Customs Co-operation Council.

ANNEX III
Ad Hoc Panels

1. *Ad hoc* panels established by the Committee under this Agreement shall have the following responsibilities:

(a) to examine the matter referred to it by the Committee;

(b) to consult with the parties to the dispute and give full opportunity for them to develop a mutually satisfactory solution; and

(c) to make a statement concerning the facts of the matter as they relate to the application of the provisions of this Agreement and, make such findings as will assist the Committee in making recommendations or giving rulings on the matter.

2. In order to facilitate the constitution of panels, the Chairman of the Committee shall maintain an informa¹ indicative list of government officials knowledgeable in the area of customs valuation and experienced in the field of trade relations and economic development. This list may also include persons other than government officials. In this connexion, each Party shall be invited to indicate at the beginning of every year to the Chairman of the Committee the name(s) of the one or two governmental experts whom the Parties would be willing to make available for such work. When a panel is established, the Chairman, after consultation with the Parties concerned, shall, within seven days of such establishment propose the composition of the panel consisting of three or five members and preferably government officials. The Parties directly concerned shall react within seven working days to nominations of panel members by the Chairman and shall not oppose nominations except for compelling reasons.

Citizens of countries whose governments are parties to a dispute shall not be eligible for membership of the panel concerned with that dispute. Panel members shall serve in their individual capacities and not as government representatives, nor as representatives of any organization. Governments or organizations shall therefore not give them instructions with regard to matters before a panel.

3. Each panel shall develop its own working procedures. All parties having a substantial interest in the matter and having notified this to the Committee shall have an opportunity to be heard. Each panel may consult and seek information and technical advice from any source it deems appropriate. Before a panel seeks such information or technical advice from a source within the jurisdiction of a Party, it shall inform the government of that Party. Any Party to this Agreement shall respond promptly and fully to any request by a panel for

such information as the panel considers necessary and appropriate. Confidential information provided to the panel shall not be disclosed without the specific permission of the person or government providing such information. Where such information is requested from the panel but release of such information by the panel is not authorized, a non-confidential summary of the information, authorized by the person or government providing the information, will be provided.

4. Where the parties to the dispute have failed to reach a satisfactory solution the panel shall submit its findings in writing. The report of a panel should normally set out the rationale behind its findings. Where a settlement of the matter is reached between the parties, the report of the panel may be confined to a brief description of the dispute and to a statement that a solution has been reached.

5. Panels shall use such report of the Technical Committee as may have been issued under Article 20.4 of this Agreement as the basis for their consideration of issues that involve questions of a technical nature.

6. The time required by panels will vary with the particular case. They should aim to deliver their findings, and where appropriate, recommendations, to the Committee without undue delay, normally within a period of three months from the date that the panel was established.

7. To encourage development of mutually satisfactory solutions between the parties to a dispute and with a view to obtaining their comments, each panel should first submit the descriptive part of its report to the Parties concerned, and should subsequently submit to the parties to the dispute its conclusions, or an outline thereof, a reasonable period of time before they are circulated to the Parties.

Chart of Federal Import Standards

Federal Standards for Imported Merchandise

Class of Merchandise	Statutes	Regulations	Regulatory Agency	Import Regulations
Animals and Animal Products and Feeds				
Domestic	21 U.S.C. 102-105	9 C.F.R. parts 92, 94, 95, 96	Veterinary Services unit, Animal and Plant Health Inspection Service, Agriculture Dept.	Quarantine and inspection by Veterinary Services of all animals, poultry, birds, and products covered by the regulations; entry only at named ports.
		19 C.F.R. 12.24	Customs Service	Importations of domestic animals, products, and feeds subject to Agriculture inspection and quarantine.
Wild				
Wildlife generally	18 U.S.C. 42-44	50 C.F.R. parts 10-14	U.S. Fish and Wildlife Service, Interior Dept.	Importations only at designated ports except by permit. Documentation in conformity with applicable foreign laws required. Declaration required from importer. Container to be mailed with name and address of consignee and shipper and with conspicuous accurate statement of contents by species and number.
	16 U.S.C. chs. 9, 24, 31, 35 19 U.S.C. 1527	19 C.F.R. 12.26-12.32 19 C.F.R. 12.28	Customs Service	

Federal Standards for Imported Merchandise—Contd.

Class of Merchandise	Statutes	Regulations	Regulatory Agency	Import Regulations
Feathers or skins of birds	19 U.S.C. 1202; Schedule 1, part 15D, TSUS	50 C.F.R. part 15	U.S. Fish and Wildlife Service, Interior Dept.	Imports prohibited except for skins bearing feathers under quota and permit from Fish and Wildlife Service.
Injurious wildlife	18 U.S.C. 42-44	50 C.F.R. part 16	U.S. Fish and Wildlife Service, Interior Dept.	Imports prohibited except by permit.
Endangered and threatened	16 U.S.C. 1531-1543	50 C.F.R. part 17	U.S. Fish and Wildlife Service, Interior Dept.	Imports prohibited except by permit for scientific purposes or enhancement of survival or economic hardship.
Endangered species-antique articles made before 1830	16 U.S.C. 1539	19 C.F.R. 10.53(g) and 12.26(g)(2)	Customs Service	Importations at designated ports, and entry filing of Declaration for Importation or Exportation of Fish and Wildlife, USFWS Form 3-177
Marine mammals and parts (polar bears, otters, walrus)	16 U.S.C. 1361-1407	50 C.F.R. part 18	U.S. Fish and Wildlife Service, Interior Dept.	Importation prohibited except as permitted under international convention or for scientific research or public display.
Marine mammals, including fur, skin, and other parts (whales, sea lions, seals, porpoises, etc.).	16 U.S.C. 1361-1407	50 C.F.R. part 216	National Marine Fisheries Service, National Oceanic and Atmospheric Admin., Commerce Dept.	Importation unlawful except as permitted under international convention or by permit for scientific or public display purposes.
Fur products	15 U.S.C. 69	16 C.F.R. part 301	Federal Trade Commission	Labeling required in compliance with the Fur Products Labeling Act and regulations.
		19 C.F.R. 11.12a	Customs Service	
Wool products	15 U.S.C. 68	16 C.F.R. part 300	Federal Trade Commission	Labeling required in compliance with the Wool Products Labeling Act and regulations.
		19 C.F.R. 11.12	Customs Service	

Subject	U.S.C.	C.F.R.	Administering agency	Certification of compliance
Chemical substances	15 U.S.C. 2601			
Distilled Spirits (including wines and beers, and perfumes containing distilled spirits)	26 U.S.C. ch. 51	19 C.F.R. 12.118–.127	Customs Service	Taxes imposed on importations; payment evidenced by stamps affixed to container, as rules require.
		27 C.F.R. part 251	Bureau of Alcohol, Tobacco and Firearms, Treasury Dept.	
	27 U.S.C. 203	27 C.F.R. part 1.20	Bureau of Alcohol, Tobacco and Firearms, Treasury Dept.	Basic permit and occupation tax required for business of importing spirits, wine, and malt beverages.
		19 C.F.R. 12.37	Customs Service	
	27 U.S.C. 205; 18 U.S.C. 1263	27 C.F.R. parts 4, 5, 7, 251	Bureau of Alcohol, Tobacco and Firearms, Treasury Dept.	Requirements for bottling and labeling under approved certificates.
		19 C.F.R. 12.38	Customs Service	
	19 U.S.C. 467	19 C.F.R. 11.6	Customs Service	Inspection, marking, gauging, and stamp affixation on importations in pipes, barrels, casks, or similar bulk containers, as rules require.
Food, Drugs, and Cosmetics	21 U.S.C. 381	19 C.F.R. 12.1(a)	Customs Service	Submission of samples on request of FDA for examination by FDA for compliance with manufacturing and labeling and other requirements of Federal Food, Drug and Cosmetics Act.
		21 C.F.R. 1.83–1.99	Food and Drug Administration, Health and Human Services Dept.	
Economic poisons, insecticides, etc.	7 U.S.C. 1360	19 C.F.R. 12.1(b)	Customs Service	Detention of imports and submission of samples to EPA for examination for compliance with manufacturing, labeling, and other requirements of Federal Insecticide, Fungicide and Rodenticide Act.
		40 C.F.R. part 162	Environmental Protection Agency	
Narcotics	21 U.S.C. 951 et seq.	21 C.F.R. parts 1311, 1312	Drug Enforcement Administration, Justice Dept.	Registration by importer and permit from DEA obtained for each consignment imported.

Federal Standards for Imported Merchandise—Contd.

Class of Merchandise	Statutes	Regulations	Regulatory Agency	Import Regulations
Food Meats and meat products	21 U.S.C. 620	9 C.F.R. part 327	Food Safety and Inspection Service, Agriculture Dept.	Foreign meat-inspection certificate required for fresh meat and meat by-products. Inspection by meat and poultry
		19 C.F.R. 12.8	Customs Service	Inspection branch for adulteration and misbranding.
Milk and cream	21 U.S.C. 141-149	21 C.F.R. part 1210	Food and Drug Administration, Health and Human Services Dept.	Inspection of exporting dairy farms and plants; permits required for imports; tagging of containers with required information.
		19 C.F.R. 12.7	Customs Service	
Electronic Products	42 U.S.C. 216, 263d	19 C.F.R. 12.90, 12.91	Customs Service	Certification required by tag or label of compliance with the Radiation Control for Health and Safety Act and declaration by importer of compliance or intended compliance. Samples may be taken for testing.
		21 C.F.R. part 1005	Food and Drug Administration, Health and Human Services Dept.	
Hazardous Substances	15 U.S.C. 1261-1274	16 C.F.R. part 1500	Consumer Product Safety Commission	Samples to be delivered to commission on its request; importer to hold until notice of results of examination.
		19 C.F.R. 12.1(c)	Customs Service	
Matches	Schedule 7, Part 9A Hdnte 1, TSUS	19 C.F.R. 12.34	Customs Service	Certification by government of country of manufacture that matches are not white phosphorous matches prohibited entry by TSUS or evidence from importer and declaration by importer of absence of any white phosphorous in imported matches.

Product	U.S.C.	Agency	C.F.R.	Requirements
Plants and Plant Products	7 U.S.C. 151-167	Customs Service	19 C.F.R. 12.10-12.15	Permit required from Plant Protection and Quarantine Programs of the Animal and Plant Health Inspection Service. Imports to be marked, inspected, and treated as required by Agriculture Dept. regulations.
		Animal and Plant Health Inspection Service, Agriculture Dept.	7 C.F.R. parts 319,321,352	
Seeds—agricultural and vegetable	7 U.S.C. 1551-1610	Customs Service	19 C.F.R. 12.16	Importations held subject to examination of samples; if containers sufficiently marked, release possible under bond pending examination of samples.
		Agricultural Marketing Service, Agriculture Dept.	7 C.F.R. part 201	
Tea	21 U.S.C. 41-50	Customs Service	19 C.F.R. 12.33	Importations held subject to sampling to determine whether standards set under the act are met. Released by permit.
		Food and Drug Administration, Health and Human Services Dept.	21 C.F.R. part 1220	
Textile Fiber Products	15 U.S.C. 70-70k	Customs Service	19 C.F.R. 11.12b	Importations to be stamped, tagged, and labeled in accordance with statute and regulations, including English name of country of manufacture or processing.
		Federal Trade Commission	16 C.F.R. part 303	
Tobacco (cigars and cigarettes, cigarette papers, and tubes)	26 U.S.C. ch. 52	Customs Service	19 C.F.R. 11.1-11.3	Internal revenue taxes to be paid before removal from customs custody, with few exceptions, principally to a manufacturer, under a bond. Packaging and marking, labeling, and stamping requirements to be met before release.
		Bureau of Alcohol, Tobacco and Firearms, Treasury Dept.	27 C.F.R. part 275	

Federal Standards for Imported Merchandise—Contd.

Class of Merchandise	Statutes	Regulations	Regulatory Agency	Import Regulations
Vehicles Motor vehicles and engines—models 1968 and later	42 U.S.C. 7522	19 C.F.R. 12.73	Customs Service	Declaration showing conformity with emission standards of Clean Air Act and regulations; conditional temporary admission possible; tagging and labeling required.
		40 C.F.R. part 85,subpart P	Environmental Protection Agency	
Motor vehicles and engines—models 1968 and later	15 U.S.C. 1392, 1397	19 C.F.R. 12.80.	Customs Service	Certification label by manufacturer of conformity to federal motor vehicle safety standards by label permanently affixed or declaration by importer of conformity obtained or being obtained or not required.
		49 C.F.R. part 571	National Highway Traffic Safety Administration, Transportation Dept.	
Pleasure boats and equipment	46 U.S.C. 1454, 1461	19 C.F.R. 12.85	Customs Service	Certification label showing compliance with the Federal Boat Safety Act and regulations; hull identification affixed; or declaration by importer of conformity being obtained or not required by exemption.
		33 C.F.R. parts 181,183	U.S. Coast Guard, Transportation Dept.	
Viruses, Serums, Toxins, and Analogous Biological Products— for Animals	21 U.S.C. 151-158	9 C.F.R. parts 101-123	Veterinary Services unit of Animal and Plant Health Inspection Service, Agriculture Dept.	Permit required for each importation of a biological product. Plant and labeling requirements. Sampling, testing, and inspections.
		19 C.F.R. 12.17-12.20	Customs Service	

for Treatment of Man	42 U.S.C. 262	21 C.F.R. parts 600-680	Food and Drug Administration, Health and Human Services Dept.	Importations allowed only if manufactured in a foreign establishment licensed under FDA regulations. Samples to be submitted.
		19 C.F.R. 12.21-12.23	Customs Service	Package and container label requirements.
Watches, Clocks, and Timing Apparatus (including movements and parts)	19 U.S.C. 1202 Schedule 7, part 2E, headnotes 4 and 5, TSUS	19 C.F.R. 11.9	Customs Service	Special marking requirements, including the country of manufacture for all items, the name of the manufacturer or purchaser for watch and clock movements and watch cases, the number of jewels for watch and clock movements, and the adjustments, if any, for watch movements.
Works-Ancient Pre-Columbian Monumental or Architectural Sculpture or Murals	19 U.S.C. 2091-2095	19 C.F.R. 12.105-12.109	Customs Service	Certificate required from government of country of origin certifying that exportation not in violation of its laws, unless export prior to May 2, 1973, or not covered by regulations.
Archeological or Ethnological Articles over 250 years old	19 U.S.C. 2601-2613 (1983)	19 CFR 12.104-12.104i	Customs Service	Certificate required from State of origin, a Party to Cultural Convention, of compliance with its law.

ITC Report: Conversion to the Harmonized System

Conversion of the Tariff Schedules of the United States Annotated Into the Nomenclature Structure of the Harmonized System

USITC Publication 1400
June 1983

EXECUTIVE SUMMARY*

On August 24, 1981, the President of the United States requested the U.S. International Trade Commission to initiate an investigation under section 332(g) of the Tariff Act of 1930 for the purpose of preparing a conversion of the Tariff Schedules of the United States into the structure of the Harmonized Commodity Description and Coding System (Harmonized System). In preparing the converted tariff, the Commission was directed to avoid tariff-rate changes to the extent practicable and to simplify the tariff where possible without rate changes significant for U.S. industry, workers, or trade. It was to include in its report a statement of the probable economic effect of adoption of the converted tariff. The Commission report was to be submitted no later than June 30, 1983. Accordingly, on September 16, 1981, the Commission initiated investigation No. 332-131 in order to prepare a converted tariff schedule in accordance with the guidelines included with the President's request.

* [Ed. Note: Pages v–vii of original.]

The Harmonized System

The Harmonized System is intended to serve as a single modern product nomenclature for use in classifying products for customs tariff, statistical, and transport documentation purposes. Based on the Customs Cooperation Council Nomenclature, the Harmonized System is a detailed classification containing approximately 5,000 headings and subheadings describing articles in trade. These provisions are organized in 96 chapters arranged in 20 sections which, along with the interpretative rules and the legal notes to the chapters and sections, form the legal text of the system. Countries adopting the Harmonized System may add provisions for national tariff or statistical purposes indented below the level of the six-digit Harmonized System categories and may also make use of chapters 98 and 99 for similar purposes.

The Converted Tariff Schedule

In accordance with the President's guidelines, the Commission prepared drafts of each chapter, including suggested rates of duty, and cross-reference tables showing the relationship of current tariff and statistical subdivisions to those of the converted schedule. Three public hearings were held in connection with the investigation, and approximately 270 written comments were received from interested parties and Government agencies.

The converted tariff set forth in this report takes into account the public comments received by the Commission on the draft converted chapters. Although some changes in rates of duty have been proposed, the Commission has attempted to avoid changes which would have a significant impact on U.S. industry and trade and has indicated the amount of each change.

Economic Impact

* * * * *

Implementation of the Converted Schedule

In order to implement the converted schedule, legislative action must be taken to replace the existing tariff schedules with the new one, address the issues involved in adhering to the Harmonized System convention and conforming our international obligations to the new schedule, provide for the implementation of amendments to the system, and make conforming changes in related laws and programs. Similarly, previous Presidential proclamations and Executive orders and existing administrative regulations must be reviewed and revised.

Impact on Statistical Programs

To achieve the objective of using the Harmonized System as the basis for statistical programs, the Statistical Classification of Domestic and Foreign Commodities Exported From the United States (Schedule B) should be converted into the format of the Harmonized System, and the classifications for domestic production and the commodity control program should be made compatible with the system. In addition, changes to the statistical programs should be implemented at the same time as the converted tariff sched-

ule to assure comparability and minimize the impact on the international trade community.

* * * * *

III. THE HARMONIZED COMMODITY DESCRIPTION AND CODING SYSTEM*

Background

For decades, the international trading community has confronted difficulties caused by the number of diverse classification systems covering goods moving in international trade. Shippers, importers, and brokers must understand and apply a number of different systems, each of which employs different product categories, numbering, and organizational formats. This situation has complicated the preparation of customs and transport documents, impeded a wider use of electronic data processing in international transactions, hampered the analysis of trade data, and created uncertainty in the negotiation and interpretation of trade agreements.

The Harmonized System is the result of a 10-year effort by the Customs Cooperation Council to develop a single modern structure for product classification which would be used for customs tariff, statistical, and transport documentation purposes.[1]

Based on the Customs Cooperation Council Nomenclature, the Harmonized System is a more detailed classification scheme, containing many new subdivisions to reflect changes in technology, trade patterns, and user requirements. The Harmonized System was designed as a "core" system, permitting individual countries adopting it to make further product subdivisions according to their particular tariff or statistical needs.

---

* [Ed. Note: Pages 15-20 of original.]

[1] For a more detailed description of the Harmonized System, see *Interim Report on the Harmonized Commodity Description and Coding System,* USITC Publication 1106, November 1980. [Ed. Note: Footnote, p. 15 of original.]

Description of the Harmonized System

As structured by the Council, the Harmonized System comprises approximately 5,000 article descriptions, which appear as headings and subheadings. These descriptions are arranged into 96 chapters (some of which are divided into subchapters for organizational purposes) grouped in 20 sections.[1] As a legal document, the system consists of—

(1) The Rules for the Interpretation of the Harmonized System;

(2) The section and chapter legal notes; and

(3) The headings and subheadings.

Under interpretative rule 1, the chapter and section titles are not legally binding but are provided for ease of reference only. In addition, the nonlegal Explanatory Notes and Classification Opinions assist in the interpretation of the legal text.

The Numbering System

In the Harmonized System, each heading is assigned a four-digit number, and each associated subheading, if any, is identified by a six-digit number. The first two digits represent the chapter in which the category appears, the second two indicate its position in that chapter, and the third two denote its status as a subdivision of the heading. Further subordinate subdivisions may be created by countries adopting the system to meet national tariff or statistical needs.

Rules for the Interpretation of the Harmonized System

Since the Harmonized System is intended for use by customs officials in the assessment of duties, it is essential

that each product be classified in only one provision. Thus, the Harmonized System begins with basic rules of classification to insure correct and consistent legal interpretation at all times.

Interpretative rule 1, which takes precedence over the remaining rules, provides that classification shall be based on the terms of the headings, on the provisions of any relevant section or chapter legal notes, and, when the headings and legal notes do not otherwise require, also on the terms of interpretative rules 2 through 6.

Rule 2 provides procedures for classifying products which are (a) incomplete or unfinished, (b) unassembled or disassembled, or (c) composed of mixtures or combinations of materials or substances.

Rule 3 controls the classification of products which are prima facie classifiable under two or more headings. Rule 3 requires that these articles be classified—

(1) In the heading which provides the most specific description; or

(2) In the heading applicable to the material or component which gives the articles their essential character; or

(3) Under the heading which occurs last in the system.

These classification criteria must be applied in the order in which they are set out.

Rule 4, which is likely to be infrequently used, provides that articles which cannot be classified in accordance with the above rules shall be classified in the heading appropriate to the products to which they are most akin.

Rule 5 prescribes the classification of cases and similar containers specially shaped or fitted to contain specific articles and of packing materials and containers entered with the articles for which they are intended. Such cases or packing materials and containers are classifiable with such articles if they are

---

[1] The Harmonized System as formulated by the Council consists of 96 chapters numbered 1 through 97. Chapter 77 is not used; the space has been reserved for future expansion. Two other possible chapters, 98 and 99, have been reserved for individual nations' uses and will not be part of the international system. [Ed. Note: Footnote, p. 16 of original.]

normally sold with them. The rule does not apply to containers which give the whole its essential character, or to packing materials and containers suitable for repetitive use.

Finally, rule 6 provides that the classification of articles described in the subheadings of a given heading shall be based on the terms of the subheadings and of any relevant legal notes, and that general interpretative rules 1 through 5 shall apply to subheadings as well as the headings. Rule 6 further states that only subheadings at the same level are comparable.

Section and Chapter Legal Notes

Many of the sections and chapters of the Harmonized System commence with legal notes applicable to headings within them. Like the interpretative rules, the legal notes form an integral part of the system and have the same legal force as the headings and subheadings. Unlike the nonbinding Explanatory Notes, these legal notes can determine the scope of headings or subheadings or direct the classification of products in particular sections, chapters, headings, or subheadings.

Examples of the types of legal notes are—

(1) General definitions delimiting the coverage of a heading or subheading or fixing the meaning of particular terms;

(2) Exhaustive lists of the articles covered by a subheading, heading, or group of headings; and

(3) Lists of excluded articles.

It would have been possible in many cases to incorporate the substance of some notes in the texts of the pertinent headings or subheadings. However, this would have greatly lengthened the texts, making them difficult to understand and involving a great deal of repetition. Using legal notes has made it possible both to draft the headings and subheadings in concise form and to assure the precision of interpretation which is essential to avoid problems in classification.

Headings and Subheadings

As previously mentioned, the headings and subheadings are arranged in chapters, which are themselves grouped in sections. For the most part, the Harmonized System has been organized according to levels of processing, so that so-called primary products are classified in early chapters and more complex products, in later chapters. Within a chapter, headings containing articles requiring higher levels of processing are generally placed later in the chapter. For example, chapter 7 covers edible vegetables first in fresh or chilled form, then in frozen form, and, finally in dried form. Similarly, sections I to IV are devoted to agricultural products, while machinery and most manufactured goods are classified in the later sections.

Each heading and subheading of the Harmonized System will be aligned to a provision of the United Nations' Standard International Trade Classification (SITC). Although there will not be a one-to-one correlation between Harmonized System headings or subheadings and SITC provisions, the product descriptions of the two systems are generally compatible and can be aligned by aggregating certain provisions.

Explanatory Notes

Although the Explanatory Notes are not part of the Harmonized System convention, they constitute the official interpretation of the Harmonized System by the Customs Cooperation Council. Following the order of the system, they provide a commentary on the scope of each heading by listing included and excluded products; appropriate technical descriptions of the articles concerned; their appearance, properties, methods of production, and uses; and practical guidance for their identification. The Explanatory Notes are thus a complement to the Harmonized System and are useful in ascertaining the classification of merchandise under the system.

Appendix I

Antidumping Duty Findings and Orders

Antidumping Duty Findings and Orders in Effect October 1, 1985

	Date	Commodity	Country
1.	01/03/85	Cell-Site Transceivers	Japan
2.	01/07/81	Anhydrous Sodium Metasilicate (ASM)	France
3.	01/16/74	Expanded Metal	Japan
4.	01/17/74	Calcium Pantothenate	Japan
5.	01/17/84	Potassium Permanganate	Spain
6.	01/31/84	Potassium Permanganate	China (PRC)
7.	02/02/77	Melamine	Japan
8.	02/17/78	Railway Track Equipment	Austria
9.	02/18/76	Birch 3-Ply Doorskins	Japan
10.	02/27/74	Racing Plates	Canada
11.	03/01/85	Brass Fire Protection Equipment	Italy
12.	03/02/83	Pipe and Tubing	Japan
13.	03/10/71	Television Receiving Sets	Japan
14.	03/13/71	Ferrite Cores	Japan
15.	03/21/79	Rayon Staple Fiber	Finland
16.	03/21/79	Rayon Staple Fiber	France
17.	03/22/84	Chloropicrin	China (PRC)
18.	03/23/73	Canned Bartlett Pears	Australia
19.	03/25/83	Sodium Nitrate	Chile
20.	04/01/72	Diamond Tips	United Kingdom
21.	04/08/80	Spun Acrylic Yarn	Italy
22.	04/08/80	Spun Acrylic Yarn	Japan
23.	04/09/80	Sugar and Syrups	Canada
24.	04/09/82	Sorbitol	France
25.	04/12/73	Roller Chain	Japan
26.	04/13/79	Bicycle Tires and Tubes	South Korea
27.	04/18/85	Calcium Hypochlorite	Japan
28.	04/21/64	Steel Reinforcing Bars	Canada
29.	04/27/84	Cyanuric Acid	Japan
30.	04/27/84	Dichloroisocyanurates	Japan
31.	04/27/84	Trichloroisocyanuric Acid	Japan
32.	04/30/84	Color Television Receivers	South Korea
33.	04/30/84	Color Television Receivers	Taiwan
34.	05/04/63	Portland Cement	Dominican Republic
35.	05/07/84	Circular Pipes and Tubes	South Korea
36.	05/07/84	Circular Pipes and Tubes	Taiwan
37.	05/07/84	Rectangular Pipes and Tubes	South Korea
38.	05/09/80	Portable Electric Typewriters (PETs)	Japan
39.	05/25/78	Impression Fabric	Japan
40.	05/30/78	Carbon Steel Plate	Japan
41.	06/07/82	Fireplace Mesh Panels	Taiwan
42.	06/08/73	Stainless Steel Plate	Sweden
43.	06/09/72	Fishnetting	Japan
44.	06/12/84	Bicycle Tires & Tubes	Taiwan
45.	06/13/79	Carbon Steel Plate	Taiwan
46.	06/13/79	Rayon Staple Fiber	Italy

Antidumping Duty Findings and Orders in Effect October 1, 1985—Contd.

	Date	Commodity	Country
47.	06/13/79	Sugar	Belgium
48.	06/13/79	Sugar	France
49.	06/13/79	Sugar	West Germany
50.	06/14/72	Large Power Transformers	France
51.	06/14/72	Large Power Transformers	Italy
52.	06/14/72	Large Power Transformers	Japan
53.	06/22/83	Stainless Steel Sheet and Strip	France
54.	06/23/83	Stainless Steel Sheet and Strip	West Germany
55.	06/24/85	Raspberries	Canada
56.	06/25/81	Strontium Nitrate	Italy
57.	06/25/81	Barium Carbonate	West Germany
58.	06/28/72	Elemental Sulphur	Mexico
59.	06/30/78	Polyvinyl Chloride (PVC) Sheet and Film	Taiwan
60.	07/08/85	Salted Codfish	Canada
61.	07/10/73	Synthetic Methionine	Japan
62.	07/19/85	Neoprene Laminate	Japan
63.	07/20/82	Amplifier Assemblies and Parts	Japan
64.	07/24/71	Pig Iron	Canada
65.	07/25/83	Tool Steel	West Germany
66.	08/04/72	Cadmium	Japan
67.	08/10/83	Nitrocellulose	France
68.	08/16/83	High Capacity Paging Devices	Japan
69.	08/17/76	Tapered Roller Bearings (TRBs)	Japan
70.	08/21/71	Clear Sheet Glass	Taiwan
71.	08/22/84	Carbon Steel Plate	South Korea
72.	08/24/73	Printed Vinyl Film	Brazil
73.	08/28/68	Titanium Sponge	USSR
74.	08/28/73	Stainless Steel Wire Rods	France
75.	08/30/76	Acrylic Sheet	Japan
76.	09/07/77	Paving Equipment	Canada
77.	09/07/77	Swimming Pools	Japan
78.	09/10/81	Montan Wax	East Germany
79.	09/13/66	Steel Jacks	Canada
80.	09/16/83	Printcloth	China (PRC)
81.	09/21/84	Woodwind Pads	Italy
82.	09/21/79	Condenser Paper	Finland
83.	09/25/64	Steel Bars and Shapes	Canada
84.	09/27/72	Potato Granules	Canada
85.	10/04/83	Shop Towels	China (PRC)
86.	10/15/73	Steel Wire Rope	Japan
87.	10/17/84	Barium Chloride	China (PRC)
88.	10/21/77	Pressure Sensitive Plastic Tape	Italy
89.	11/02/72	Drycleaning Machinery	West Germany
90.	11/16/83	Wire Rods	Trinidad/Tobago
91.	11/19/84	Choline Chloride	Canada
92.	11/22/72	Bicycle Speedometers	Japan
93.	11/23/84	Carbon Steel Wire Rods	Spain
94.	11/23/84	Carbon Steel Wire Rods	Argentina
95.	11/30/84	Titanium Sponge	Japan
96.	12/06/73	Polyrubber	Japan
97.	12/09/71	Clear Sheet Glass	Italy
98.	12/12/70	Tuners	Japan

Antidumping Duty Findings and Orders in Effect October 1, 1985—Contd.

	Date	Commodity	Country
99.	12/17/73	Elemental Sulphur	Canada
100.	12/18/78	Steel Wire Strand	Japan
101.	12/20/83	Staples	Sweden
102.	12/20/83	Staplers	Sweden
103.	12/22/77	Animal Glue	Netherlands
104.	12/22/77	Animal Glue	Sweden
105.	12/22/77	Animal Glue	West Germany
106.	12/22/77	Animal Glue	Yugoslavia
107.	12/24/80	Large Electric Motors	Japan

Suspensions

	Date	Commodity	Country
108.	09/14/82	Sheet Piling	Canada
109.	11/06/80	Small Motors	Japan

Source: International Trade Administration, U.S. Department of Commerce.

Appendix J

Countervailing Duty Orders

Countervailing Duty Orders in Effect October 1, 1985

	Date	Commodity	Country
1.	01/03/83	Stainless Steel Wire Rod	Spain
2.	01/03/83	Certain Steel Products	Spain
3.	01/04/83	Forged Undercarriages	Italy
4.	01/04/84	Wire Rod	Trinidad/Tobago
5.	01/14/85	Auto Glass	Mexico
6.	01/17/79	Footwear	Argentina
7.	02/01/83	Cotton Yarn	Peru
8.	02/01/83	Cotton Sheeting and Sateen	Peru
9.	02/07/85	Oil Country Tubular Goods	Brazil
10.	02/07/85	Oil Country Tubular Goods	Spain
11.	02/11/77	Scissors and Shears	Brazil
12.	02/11/85	Flat Rolled Steel Products	South Korea
13.	02/18/83	Pipe	South Korea
14.	02/18/83	Certain Steel Products	South Korea
15.	03/02/83	Castings	Mexico
16.	03/09/84	Shop Towels	Pakistan
17.	03/11/81	Ferrochrome	South Africa
18.	03/12/85	Textiles and Apparel	Argentina
19.	03/12/85	Textiles and Apparel	Sri Lanka
20.	03/12/85	Textiles and Apparel	Peru
21.	03/15/77	Cotton Yarn	Brazil
22.	03/15/85	Certain Apparel	Thailand
23.	03/16/76	Castor Oil	Brazil
24.	03/18/83	Leather Wearing Apparel	Argentina
25.	03/18/85	Textiles and Apparel	Mexico
26.	03/24/23	Sugar Content	Australia
27.	04/04/80	Pig Iron	Brazil
28.	04/04/83	Wool	Argentina
29.	04/10/81	Leather Wearing Apparel	Mexico
30.	04/26/84	Cold Rolled Steel Sheet	Argentina
31.	05/06/77	Fasteners	Japan
32.	05/08/84	Bricks	Mexico
33.	05/10/82	Ceramic Tile	Mexico
34.	05/15/79	Rayon Staple Fiber	Sweden
35.	06/20/83	Carbon Black	Mexico
36.	06/22/83	Nitrocellulose	France
37.	06/23/83	Stainless Steel Plate	United Kingdom
38.	06/24/83	Certain Steel Products	Brazil
39.	07/10/84	Wire Rod	Spain
40.	07/17/82	Leather Wearing Apparel	Uruguay
41.	07/21/80	Fasteners	India
42.	07/31/78	Sugar	European Community
43.	08/05/85	Copper Rod and Wire	New Zealand
44.	08/14/85	Pipes and Tubes	Thailand
45.	08/15/85	Live Swine	Canada
46.	08/16/84	Bars, Rebars and Shapes	Mexico
47.	09/04/80	Roses	Israel

688

Countervailing Duty Orders in Effect October 1, 1985—Contd.

	Date	Commodity	Country
48.	09/08/82	Certain Steel Products	South Africa
49.	09/11/84	Lime	Mexico
50.	09/12/74	Footwear	Brazil
51.	09/17/85	Lamb Meat	New Zealand
52.	09/21/83	Cement	Mexico
53.	09/27/82	Wire Rod	South Africa
54.	10/06/83	Bicycle Tires and Tubes	South Korea
55.	10/16/80	Castings	India
56.	10/28/82	Rebars	South Africa
57.	10/31/83	Tuna	Philippines
58.	11/16/78	Woolen Garments	Argentina
59.	11/22/84	Oil Country Tubular Goods	Argentina
60.	11/30/84	Oil Country Tubular Goods	Mexico
61.	12/06/82	Litharge	Mexico
62.	12/27/82	Float Glass	United Kingdom
63.	12/27/82	Float Glass	West Germany
64.	12/27/82	Toy Balloons	Mexico

Suspensions

	Date	Commodity	Country
1.	01/04/82	Axles	Hungary
2.	01/12/83	Cut Flowers	Colombia
3.	02/02/83	Stainless Steel Products	Brazil
4.	02/07/83	Polypropylene Yarn	Mexico
5.	03/01/84	Float Glass	Mexico
6.	03/04/83	Orange Juice	Brazil
7.	03/12/85	Textiles and Apparel	Thailand
8.	03/12/85	Textiles and Apparel	Colombia
9.	03/21/83	Tool Steel Products	Brazil
10.	04/02/81	Leather and Apparel	Colombia
11.	04/29/83	Galvanized Steel	South Africa
12.	05/21/82	PC Strand	South Africa
13.	05/29/85	Iron Ore Pellets	Brazil
14.	06/01/84	Pipe & Tube	South Africa
15.	09/12/84	Shop Towels	Peru
16.	09/27/82	Wire Rod	Argentina
17.	11/07/83	Compressors	Singapore
18.	11/30/81	Sodium Gluconate	European Community
19.	12/01/82	Wire Rope	South Africa
20.	12/03/84	Cement	Costa Rica
21.	12/07/82	Polypropylene Film	Mexico
22.	12/07/82	Pectin	Mexico

Source: International Trade Administration; U.S. Department of Commerce.

MTN Code Signatures and Acceptances

**OFFICE OF THE
UNITED STATES TRADE REPRESENTATIVE**
EXECUTIVE OFFICE OF THE PRESIDENT
WASHINGTON, D.C. 20506

October 1, 1985

INTERNATIONAL AGREEMENTS AND ARRANGEMENTS
CONCLUDED DURING THE TOKYO ROUND

Status of Acceptances

The attached computer print-out provides the current status of acceptances of the nontariff measure codes and international arrangements negotiated during the Tokyo Round of Multilateral Trade Negotiations (MTN).

The terms utilized signify the following:

Accepted: formal agreement by the signatory to be bound by the provisions of the particular agreement or arrangement.

Accepted With Reservation: formal agreement by the signatory to be bound by the provisions of the particular agreement or arrangement, except with respect to those provisions specified in the reservation.

Subject to Ratification: acceptance of the agreement by the signatory pending the completion of domestic ratification procedures and the deposit of an appropriate instrument of ratification with the GATT Secretariat.

Notes:

Acceptances by the European Community: Under international law, the acceptance by the Community of the Tokyo Round agreements and arrangements is legally binding on the ten Member States (each identified with an asterisk) without their individual signatures. However, with regard to the Standards and Aircraft

690

Agreements, the Member States have chosen to sign individually in order to reflect the view of certain member states that their national governments have legal authority over some aspects of these agreements, and, therefore, jointly share jurisdiction with the Community.

<u>Acceptances by the United Kingdom</u>: Acceptances by the United Kingdom of the respective agreements and arrangements may apply as well to U.K. territories. In those instances in which the United Kingdom's acceptance covers only certain territories, it is listed in the "Accepted with Reservation" column. Hong Kong is listed separately in those instances in which it is covered by the United Kingdom's acceptance.

For further information contact:

Office of GATT Affairs
395-3063

STATUS OF TOKYO ROUND MTN AGREEMENT SIGNATURES AND ACCEPTANCES
(GATT AND NON-GATT MEMBERS)
(BY CODE)
AS OF OCTOBER 1, 1985

CODE	ACCEPTED	ACCEPTED WITH RESERVATION	SIGNED SUBJECT TO RATIFICATION
A. TARIFF PROTOCOL	ARGENTINA, AUSTRIA, BELGIUM*, CANADA, CZECHOSLOVAKIA, EUROPEAN ECONOMIC COMMUNITY, FINLAND, FRANCE*, HUNGARY, ICELAND, IRELAND*, ITALY*, JAMAICA, LUXEMBORG*, NETHERLANDS*, NEW ZEALAND, NORWAY, POLAND, ROMANIA, SOUTH AFRICA, SPAIN, SWEDEN, SWITZERLAND, UNITED KINGDOM*, UNITED STATES, WEST GERMANY*, YUGOSLAVIA	DENMARK*, JAPAN	ISRAEL
B. SUPPLEMENT TO THE TARIFF PROTOCOL	AUSTRALIA, BELGIUM*, BRAZIL, CANADA, CHILE, DOMINICAN REPUBLIC, EGYPT, EUROPEAN ECONOMIC COMMUNITY, HAITI, INDIA, INDONESIA, ISRAEL, IVORY COAST, KOREA, MALAYSIA, PAKISTAN, PERU, SINGAPORE, SPAIN, URUGUAY, ZAIRE		
C. STANDARDS	AUSTRIA, BELGIUM*, BRAZIL, CANADA, CHILE, CZECHOSLOVAKIA, EGYPT, EUROPEAN ECONOMIC COMMUNITY, FINLAND, FRANCE*, HONG KONG, HUNGARY, INDIA, IRELAND*, ITALY*, JAPAN, KOREA, LUXEMBORG*, NETHERLANDS*, NEW ZEALAND, NORWAY, PAKISTAN, PHILIPPINES, ROMANIA, SINGAPORE, SPAIN, SWEDEN, SWITZERLAND, TUNISIA, UNITED STATES, WEST GERMANY*, YUGOSLAVIA	DENMARK*, UNITED KINGDOM*	ARGENTINA, GREECE*, RWANDA
D. PROCUREMENT	AUSTRIA, CANADA, EUROPEAN ECONOMIC COMMUNITY (FOR MEMBER STATES), FINLAND, HONG KONG, ISRAEL, JAPAN, NORWAY, SINGAPORE, SWEDEN, SWITZERLAND, UNITED STATES	UNITED KINGDOM*	
E. SUBSIDIES	AUSTRIA, BRAZIL, CANADA, CHILE, EGYPT, EUROPEAN ECONOMIC COMMUNITY (FOR MEMBER STATES), FINLAND, HONG KONG, INDIA, INDONESIA, ISRAEL, JAPAN, KOREA, NEW ZEALAND, NORWAY, PAKISTAN, PHILIPPINES, SPAIN, SWEDEN, SWITZERLAND, TURKEY, UNITED STATES, URUGUAY	AUSTRALIA, PORTUGAL, UNITED KINGDOM*	YUGOSLAVIA
F. MEAT	ARGENTINA, AUSTRALIA, AUSTRIA, BRAZIL, BULGARIA, CANADA, COLOMBIA, EGYPT, EUROPEAN ECONOMIC COMMUNITY (FOR MEMBER STATES), FINLAND, GUATEMALA, HUNGARY, JAPAN, NEW ZEALAND, NORWAY, POLAND, ROMANIA, SOUTH AFRICA, SWEDEN, SWITZERLAND, TUNISIA, UNITED STATES, URUGUAY, YUGOSLAVIA	PARAGUAY	
G. DAIRY	ARGENTINA, AUSTRALIA, BULGARIA, EUROPEAN ECONOMIC COMMUNITY (FOR MEMBER STATES), FINLAND, HUNGARY, JAPAN, NEW ZEALAND, NORWAY, POLAND, ROMANIA, SOUTH AFRICA, SWEDEN, SWITZERLAND, URUGUAY		EGYPT
H. CUSTOMS	AUSTRALIA, AUSTRIA, BOTSWANA, CZECHOSLOVAKIA, EUROPEAN ECONOMIC COMMUNITY (FOR MEMBER STATES), FINLAND, HONG KONG, HUNGARY, JAPAN, NORWAY, ROMANIA, SOUTH AFRICA, SWEDEN, SWITZERLAND, UNITED STATES, YUGOSLAVIA	BRAZIL, CANADA, INDIA, KOREA, MALAWI, NEW ZEALAND, SPAIN, UNITED KINGDOM*	ARGENTINA
I. CUSTOMS VALUATION PROTOCOL	AUSTRALIA, AUSTRIA, BRAZIL, CANADA, EUROPEAN ECONOMIC COMMUNITY (FOR MEMBER STATES), FINLAND, HONG KONG, HUNGARY, JAPAN, NORWAY, ROMANIA, SOUTH AFRICA, SPAIN, SWEDEN, SWITZERLAND, UNITED STATES, YUGOSLAVIA	INDIA, KOREA, MALAWI, NEW ZEALAND, UNITED KINGDOM*	ARGENTINA
J. LICENSING	AUSTRALIA, AUSTRIA, CANADA, CHILE, CZECHOSLOVAKIA, EGYPT, EUROPEAN ECONOMIC COMMUNITY (FOR MEMBER STATES), FINLAND, HONG KONG, HUNGARY, INDIA, JAPAN, NEW ZEALAND, NORWAY, PAKISTAN, ROMANIA, SINGAPORE, SOUTH AFRICA, SWEDEN, SWITZERLAND, UNITED STATES, YUGOSLAVIA	PHILIPPINES, UNITED KINGDOM*	ARGENTINA
K. AIRCRAFT	AUSTRIA, BELGIUM*, CANADA, EUROPEAN ECONOMIC COMMUNITY, FRANCE*, IRELAND*, ITALY*, JAPAN, LUXEMBORG*, NETHERLANDS*, NORWAY, ROMANIA, SWEDEN, SWITZERLAND, UNITED STATES, WEST GERMANY*	DENMARK*, UNITED KINGDOM*	EGYPT, GREECE*
L. ANTIDUMPING	AUSTRALIA, AUSTRIA, BRAZIL, CANADA, CZECHOSLOVAKIA, EGYPT, EUROPEAN ECONOMIC COMMUNITY (FOR MEMBER STATES), FINLAND, HONG KONG, HUNGARY, INDIA, JAPAN, NORWAY, PAKISTAN, POLAND, ROMANIA, SINGAPORE, SPAIN, SWEDEN, SWITZERLAND, UNITED STATES, YUGOSLAVIA	UNITED KINGDOM*	

EC MEMBER STATES SIGN INDIVIDUALLY DUE TO JURISDICTION DIVISIONS
BETWEEN THE EUROPEAN COMMISSION AND THE MEMBER STATES

USTR COMPUTER GROUP

STATUS OF TOKYO ROUND MTN AGREEMENT SIGNATURES AND ACCEPTANCES
(GATT AND NON-GATT MEMBERS)
(BY COUNTRY)
AS OF OCTOBER 1, 1985

GATT MEMBER	TARIFF PROTOCOL	SUPPLEMENT	STANDARDS	PROCUREMENT	SUBSIDIES	MEAT	DAIRY	CUSTOMS VALUATION	CUSTOMS VALUATION PROTOCOL	LICENSING	AIRCRAFT	ANTIDUMPING
ARGENTINA	ACCPTD		SUBJECT TO RATIFICATION			ACCPTD	ACCPTD	SUBJECT TO RATIFICATION	SUBJECT TO RATIFICATION	SUBJECT TO RATIFICATION		
AUSTRALIA		ACCPTD			ACCPTD WITH RESERVATION	ACCPTD	ACCPTD	ACCPTD	ACCPTD	ACCPTD		ACCPTD
AUSTRIA	ACCPTD		ACCPTD	ACCPTD	ACCPTD	ACCPTD		ACCPTD	ACCPTD	ACCPTD	ACCPTD	ACCPTD
BRAZIL		ACCTPD	ACCPTD		ACCPTD	ACCPTD		ACCPTD WITH RESERVATION	ACCPTD			ACCPTD
CANADA	ACCPTD	ACCPTD	ACCPTD	ACCPTD	ACCPTD	ACCPTD		ACCPTD WITH RESERVATION	ACCPTD	ACCPTD	ACCPTD	ACCPTD
CHILE		ACCPTD	ACCPTD		ACCTPD					ACCPTD		
COLOMBIA						ACCPTD						
CZECHOSLOVAKIA	ACCPTD		ACCPTD					ACCPTD		ACCTPD		ACCPTD
DOMINICAN REPUBLIC		ACCPTD										
EGYPT		ACCPTD	ACCPTD		ACCPTD	ACCPTD		SUBJECT TO RATIFICATION		ACCPTD	SUBJECT TO RATIFICATION	ACCPTD
EUROPEAN ECONOMIC COMMUNITIES:	ACCPTD	ACCPTD	ACCPTD	ACCTPD (FOR MEMBER STATES)	ACCPTD (FOR MEMBER STATES)	ACCPTD (FOR MEMBER STATES)	ACCPTD (FOR MEMBER STATES)	ACCPTD (FOR MEMBER STATES)	ACCPTD (FOR MEMBER STATES)	ACCPTD (FOR MEMBER STATES)	ACCPTD	ACCPTD (FOR MEMBER STATES)
A. BELGIUM	ACCPTD	ACCPTD	ACCPTD								ACCPTD	
B. DENMARK	ACCPTD, WITH RESERVATION		ACCPTD, WITH RESERVATION						↑		ACCPTD, WITH RESERVATION	
C. FRANCE	ACCPTD		ACCPTD								ACCPTD	
D. GREECE			SUBJECT TO RATIFICATION								SUBJECT TO RATIFICATION	
E. IRELAND	ACCPTD		ACCPTD								ACCPTD	
F. ITALY	ACCPTD		ACCPTD								ACCPTD	
G. LUXEMBOURG	ACCPTD		ACCPTD								ACCPTD	
H. NETHERLANDS	ACCPTD		ACCPTD								ACCPTD	
I. UNITED KINGDOM	ACCPTD		ACCPTD WITH RESERVATION	ACCPTD WITH RESERVATION	ACCPTD WITH RESERVATION			ACCPTD WITH RESERVATION	ACCPTD WITH RESERVATION	ACCPTD WITH RESERVATION	ACCPTD WITH RESERVATION	ACCPTD WITH RESERVATION
J. WEST GERMANY	ACCPTD		ACCPTD								ACCPTD	
FINLAND	ACCPTD		ACCPTD	ACCPTD	ACCPTD	ACCPTD	ACCPTD	ACCPTD	ACCPTD	ACCPTD		ACCPTD
HAITI		ACCPTD										
HONG KONG			ACCPTD	ACCPTD	ACCPTD			ACCPTD	ACCPTD	ACCPTD		ACCPTD
HUNGARY	ACCPTD		ACCPTD			ACCPTD	ACCPTD	ACCPTD	ACCPTD	ACCPTD		ACCPTD
ICELAND	ACCPTD											

USTR COMPUTER GROUP

STATUS OF TOKYO ROUND MTN AGREEMENT SIGNATURES AND ACCEPTANCES
(GATT AND NON-GATT MEMBERS)
(BY COUNTRY)
AS OF OCTOBER 1, 1985

GATT MEMBER	TARIFF PROTOCOL	SUPPLEMENT	STANDARDS	PROCUREMENT	SUBSIDIES	MEAT	DAIRY	CUSTOMS VALUATION	CUSTOMS VALUATION PROTOCOL	LICENSING	AIRCRAFT	ANTIDUMPING
INDIA		ACCPTD	ACCPTD		ACCPTD			ACCPTD WITH RESERVATION	ACCPTD WITH RESERVATION	ACCPTD		ACCPTD
INDONESIA		ACCPTD			ACCPTD							
ISRAEL	SUBJECT TO RATIFICATION	ACCPTD		ACCPTD	ACCPTD							
IVORY COAST		ACCPTD										
JAMAICA	ACCPTD											
JAPAN	ACCPTD WITH RESERVATION		ACCPTD	ACCPTD	ACCPTD	ACCPTD	ACCPTD	ACCPTD	ACCPTD	ACCPTD	ACCPTD	ACCPTD
KOREA		ACCPTD	ACCPTD		ACCPTD			ACCPTD WITH RESERVATION	ACCPTD WITH RESERVATION			
MALAWI								ACCPTD WITH RESERVATION	ACCPTD WITH RESERVATION			
MALAYSIA		ACCPTD										
NEW ZEALAND	ACCPTD		ACCPTD		ACCPTD	ACCPTD	ACCPTD	ACCPTD WITH RESERVATION	ACCPTD WITH RESERVATION	ACCPTD		
NORWAY	ACCPTD		ACCPTD	ACCPTD	ACCPTD	ACCPTD	ACCPTD	ACCPTD	ACCPTD	ACCPTD	ACCPTD	ACCPTD
PAKISTAN		ACCPTD	ACCPTD		ACCPTD					ACCPTD		ACCPTD
PERU		ACCPTD										
PHILIPPINES			ACCPTD		ACCPTD					ACCPTD WITH RESERVATION		
POLAND	ACCPTD					ACCPTD	ACCPTD					ACCPTD
PORTUGAL					ACCPTD WITH RESERVATION							
ROMANIA	ACCPTD		ACCPTD			ACCPTD	ACCPTD	ACCPTD	ACCPTD	ACCPTD	ACCPTD	ACCPTD
RWANDA			SUBJECT TO RATIFICATION									
SINGAPORE		ACCPTD	ACCPTD	ACCPTD						ACCPTD		ACCPTD
SOUTH AFRICA	ACCPTD					ACCPTD	ACCPTD	ACCPTD	ACCPTD	ACCPTD		
SPAIN	ACCPTD	ACCPTD	ACCPTD		ACCPTD			ACCPTD WITH RESERVATION	ACCPTD			ACCPTD
SWEDEN	ACCPTD		ACCPTD	ACCPTD	ACCPTD	ACCPTD	ACCPTD	ACCPTD	ACCPTD	ACCPTD	ACCPTD	ACCPTD
SWITZERLAND	ACCPTD		ACCPTD	ACCPTD	ACCPTD	ACCPTD	ACCPTD	ACCPTD	ACCPTD	ACCPTD	ACCPTD	ACCPTD
TURKEY					ACCPTD							
UNITED STATES	ACCPTD		ACCPTD	ACCPTD	ACCPTD	ACCPTD		ACCPTD	ACCPTD	ACCPTD	ACCPTD	ACCPTD
URUGUAY		ACCPTD			ACCPTD	ACCPTD	ACCPTD					
YUGOSLAVIA	ACCPTD		ACCPTD		SUBJECT TO RATIFICATION	ACCPTD		ACCPTD	ACCPTD	ACCPTD		ACCPTD
ZAIRE		ACCPTD										

STATUS OF TOKYO ROUND MTN AGREEMENT SIGNATURES AND ACCEPTANCES
(GATT AND NON-GATT MEMBERS)
(BY COUNTRY)
AS OF OCTOBER 1, 1985

GATT MEMBER	TARIFF PROTOCOL	SUPPLEMENT	STANDARDS	PROCUREMENT	SUBSIDIES	MEAT	DAIRY	CUSTOMS VALUATION	CUSTOMS VALUATION PROTOCOL	LICENSING	AIRCRAFT	ANTIDUMPING
OTHER COUNTRIES												
BOTSWANA								ACCPTD				
BULGARIA						ACCPTD	ACCPTD					
GUATEMALA						ACCPTD						
PARAGUAY						ACCPTD WITH RESERVATION						
TUNISIA			ACCPTD			ACCPTD						

USTR COMPUTER GROUP

Table of Cases

Case citations appear on pages indicated. Individual citations are provided below for different cases carrying the same name.

Index